Treat this book with care and respect.

It should become part of your personal and professional library. It will serve you well at any number of points during your professional career.

D1622253

MANAGEMENT & ORGANIZATION

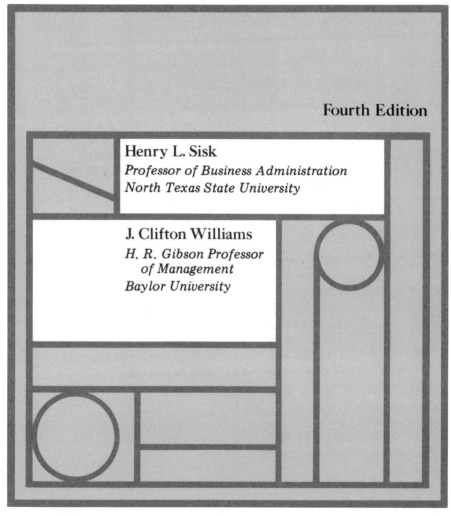

Fourth Edition

Henry L. Sisk
Professor of Business Administration
North Texas State University

J. Clifton Williams
H. R. Gibson Professor
of Management
Baylor University

Published by

G43 SOUTH-WESTERN PUBLISHING CO.

CINCINNATI   WEST CHICAGO, ILL.   DALLAS   PELHAM MANOR, N.Y.   PALO ALTO, CALIF.

Copyright © 1981

by

SOUTH-WESTERN PUBLISHING CO.

Cincinnati, Ohio

All Rights Reserved

The text of this publication, or any part thereof, may not be reproduced or transmitted in any form or by any means, electronic or mechanical, including photocopying, recording, storage in an information retrieval system, or otherwise, without the prior written permission of the publisher.

ISBN: 0–538–07430–2
Library of Congress Catalog Card Number: 79–65192

1 2 3 4 5 6 7 D 7 6 5 4 3 2 1

Printed in the United States of America

Preface

Several assumptions are involved in writing a management textbook. First, we assume that there are aspects of the practice of management that can be taught to others. This assumption runs counter to the belief that managers are born or that experience is the only teacher; yet the belief that managers can be taught minimizes in no way the value of experience and practice in the development of managerial skills and insights. We believe, however, that those who enter managerial positions with knowledge and concepts gained from a formal study of management require less time to develop an acceptable level of managerial performance than those who have not studied management as a discipline. Second, we assume that *management* is best defined as a process of coordinating all the resources of an organization in order to achieve organizational objectives. Defining management as a process permits the description and analysis of that process, thus making it possible to develop the concepts and techniques of management in a systematic way. Third, we assume that the management process is present in and necessary to all formal organizations—business, governmental, educational, social, religious, and charitable—if they are to achieve their respective organizational objectives effectively. Because of the universality of management and the consequent demand for managers, the study of management fulfills an important educational need.

This book is intended for use in the introductory management course in four-year colleges and universities and in those community colleges offering either a midmanagement curriculum or the introductory management course. The book may also be used in management development programs offered by companies and by governmental agencies.

As a result of extensive planning and updating, the fourth edition constitutes a major revision. Chapter 7, "Production Management," and Chapter 13, "Personnel Management," do not appear in previous editions. We consider these to be important additions in light of the recent emphasis on production management by accrediting agencies and the improved status of personnel management because of increasing government controls. Since an entry level textbook is expected to introduce students to all major aspects of management, we believe that these topics merit greater attention than they receive in most texts.

Several chapters have been rewritten to incorporate the changing emphases and the latest research in the field of management. Notable among these are Chapter 8, "Organization and Management Theory"; Chapter 9, "The Structural Design of Organizations"; Chapter 14, "Personal and Social Dimensions of Organizational Behavior"; Chapter 15, "Motivation in Organizations"; and Chapter 17, "Leadership Patterns." Chapter 3 of the third edition, "Objectives and Ethics," has been reorganized and rewritten to give more attention to ethics. In this text, ethical and social responsibilities of management are discussed in Chapter 3 and organizational objectives are discussed in Chapter 4. The organization of chapters is roughly the same as in the third edition, even though most of the chapter numbers have changed. The positions of the chapters on leadership and motivation have been reversed to permit the early presentation of motivational concepts as a basis for understanding certain leadership theories.

As in the third edition, we have included what we believe are important concepts of behavioral science research methods (Chapter 13 of the third edition and Chapter 14 of the fourth edition). Although our treatment of this subject is presented in nontechnical terms and does not purport to give sufficient depth for understanding many of the research articles published in management journals, it does provide a global introduction to the subject. Students who appreciate the empirical foundations on which management theory is based tend to have more respect for the discipline and are less likely to perceive what they are taught as mere opinion.

We have continued the practice of beginning and ending each chapter with a short case problem. These cases serve to illustrate and make practical some of the important concepts presented in the chapters. Since the response to the cases from both students and professors has been favorable, we have retained those cases that have proved most useful while replacing some of the less effective ones.

Many persons contribute to the writing of a book. However, in writing the fourth edition we owe a special debt of gratitude to the professors and students who provided us with direct feedback on the third edition. Their suggestions were given serious consideration, and many are incorporated in this edition. We continue to encourage this valuable input. We are also indebted to the administrators of North Texas State University and Baylor University for providing us with the release time that has made this revision possible.

Henry L. Sisk
J. Clifton Williams

Contents

Planning for Productivity

Part

3

The Organizing Function

Part 4

Leadership in Organizations

1 Management in Perspective

What do you think of when you hear or read the word *management?* Do you think of management as a group, as a profession, as a science, or as an art? How widespread is management and when is it needed? What does a manager do? These are the questions that form the framework of a discussion on the nature of management. From our discussion, a definition of management as a telic, or purposeful, process is developed. One of the approaches, the modern or systems approach, to the study of management is introduced briefly. Though systems theory is introduced in the first chapter and referred to throughout the text, the approach used in this book is best described as eclectic; that is, information is drawn from a broad range of sources so that the different needs and interests of students may be met.

When introducing a field of study a brief statement of the historical development of that field is helpful. From time to time different aspects of management have been emphasized. In Chapter 2 the development of management concepts is traced. First, there is an emphasis on production, not surprising when one considers the industrial revolution and the need to know how to best utilize mass-production facilities. Then the emphasis shifts to the administration of the entire enterprise. Some refer to an emphasis on one aspect of management in preference to another as a school of management. The emphasis on production and administration is often referred to as the classical school. Another area of emphasis is human relations. There are so many schools or approaches to the study of management that they are referred to as a jungle and their proponents are accused of engaging in inky warfare. Some of the brush in this jungle is cut away, however, and an integrative view is presented.

Part 1 closes with a discussion of the ethical and social responsibilities of management. First, the value judgments of managers are discussed; next, the major determinants of ethical standards and practices are reviewed; and finally, the section closes with a discussion of the value systems of managers.

Chapter 1

The Nature and Scope of Management

WHO IS "MANAGEMENT"?

As he entered the conference room, Mr. Martin, division manager of a gas utility company serving 200 communities, noted that all the members of his staff were present for the special meeting called for the purpose of organizing a management club. Seated at the table were the division accounting supervisor, the supervisor of engineering, the construction superintendent, the sales manager, the employee relations manager, and the division home economist.

Mr. Martin opened the meeting with a brief review of some previous discussions that had taken place regarding the formation of a management club. He continued, "As you may remember, four suggestions have been made as criteria for membership in the club. These are: first, all people whose names appear on the division organization chart, including district office supervisory personnel; second, all employees with supervisory responsibility; third, all persons exempt from the overtime provisions of the Wage and Hour Law; or, finally, everyone whose earnings are over $175 a week."

Mr. Harmon, engineering supervisor, immediately voiced his doubts concerning the value of such a club. "I'm not sure that the people working under me have either the time or the inclination to participate in a management club. It seems to me that it is important to first determine the purpose for having this sort of organization and the possible benefits that may be gained from it."

"John, let's get to that in just a minute," Mr. Martin replied. "First, I'd like to hear what some of you think about the criteria that have been suggested for membership."

The employee relations manager, Mrs. Ross, said, "Well, I can foresee some difficulties arising if we use earnings of $175 a week as a criterion. All of us know that we have people in some departments who earn that much money each week simply because of their length of service. For instance, two of the clerks in our customer service department who have been with us for 20 years are earning more than $175 a week. Yet they have no managerial responsibilities. What do we do about them?"

Ms. Walker, sales manager for the division, agreed with both Mr. Harmon and Mrs. Ross. "Frankly my district sales supervisors have more than they can do now, without getting involved in a management club. And, as Mrs. Ross pointed out, even though they would most certainly qualify for membership if the criterion is earnings of $175 a week,

3

many of them don't supervise any other employees. In addition, the situation is further complicated because some of these people are on commission and their total earnings vary from month to month."

"I was going to suggest that we say *salary* rather than *earnings*," Mr. Fowler, the accounting supervisor, said. "However, the budget director falls in that category and he doesn't supervise other people."

Miss Carter, the home economist, commented, "Yes, I would qualify for membership under those conditions, too, though my responsibilities are professional rather than managerial."

"And in the engineering department the situation is just the reverse," remarked Mr. Harmon. "Some of the engineers, who are also professionals, do have people working for them."

Mr. Perez, the construction superintendent, asked, "Who would qualify if we follow the suggestion of having as members all whose names appear on the organization chart?"

Mr. Martin replied, "That would include any person who is exempt from overtime pay. Some of you may remember that that was the qualifying factor considered when we made up the organization chart last year."

Noting that few positive suggestions were being offered, Mr. Martin said, "At any rate, possibly the best way to decide this matter will be to have Mrs. Ross prepare a summary recommendation for our regular staff meeting next week, taking into consideration the questions mentioned today. Mrs. Ross, I suggest that you begin with a statement of the purpose or objectives of such an organization, that is, whether we will be getting together to solve some of the problems that we share as managers, or to improve the flow of information through the division, or even for purely social reasons. And include recommendations for a name for the club and who will be eligible for membership."

PROBLEMS

1. Assume that you are in the position of Mrs. Ross, employee relations supervisor. Write a brief memo to Mr. Martin as requested.

2. Of the possible objectives stated for the management club, which do you believe are important? Justify your selection of the important objectives.

3. *Research Assignment.* Mr. Martin indicated that if an employee did not receive overtime pay for extra hours worked, he or she was eligible for inclusion on the company organization chart. Such employees are normally termed *exempt*, since they are exempt from the overtime provisions of the Fair Labor Standards Act, commonly called the Wage and Hour Law. Consult your nearest wage and hour office, either in person or by letter, and review those publications which discuss the basis for exemption. Discuss briefly whether exemption from overtime payment serves as a valid criterion for membership in a management club.

Seemingly each person has different ideas concerning the meaning of the term *management*. Some use the word *management* as a collective noun that refers to a certain group within an organization. Others define management as a process calling for the performance of specific functions, and there are those who view management as a profession, a science, or an art. Management may also be regarded as an academic discipline and a field of study. Each of these concepts of management reflects a different aspect of the nature of management. Serious study of management requires a relatively precise definition, and as a means of developing such a definition, we must examine more closely the nature of management.

THE NATURE OF MANAGEMENT

The lead sentence of any news story should answer the questions Who? What? When? Where? Why? How? These questions must also be answered in order to arrive at a precise definition of management. In Case Problem 1-A, one question to be resolved is the *who* of management: Who is considered a member of management? However, before the *who* of management can be determined, it is necessary to know *what* management does, *how* it is done, *when* management becomes necessary, *where* management is found, and *why* management is necessary. These key questions form the broad organizational outline of the first part of this chapter.

The Need for Management

Our discussion of the need for management answers the question: *Why* is management necessary? Management is needed *to run the business.* Management is responsible for the success or failure of the business.

The statement that management is needed to direct the affairs of a business tells *why* management is needed, but does not indicate *when* and *where.* Whenever and wherever a group is formed having stated objectives, management is needed to direct and coordinate those efforts. Group action often requires that the members of a group subordinate their individual desires to attain the group goal. Effective group action requires management to provide leadership in order to attain stated objectives.

The Functions of Management

An analysis of the primary functions of the management process tells us what management does. Also, an analysis of the functions of management provides the first step in the development of a precise definition of the word *management.*

When studying management as an academic discipline, it is necessary to consider management as a *process.* When management is regarded as a process, it can be analyzed and described in terms of several major functions. When discussing the process of management, it is convenient, and even necessary, to describe and study each function of the process separately. As a result, it may seem that the management process is a series of discrete functions. However, nothing could be further from the truth. In practice, a manager may, and often does, perform simultaneously, or at least as a part of a continuum, all of the following four functions: planning, organizing, leading, and controlling.

Planning. Planning is generally accorded a position of primacy among the management functions since logically it is the first function that is performed. Also, planning is considered pervasive in nature, since planning is required to form the organization, to determine the patterns of leadership, and to design the control system. The results of planning are plans that serve as guides for the actions of the members of the organization in the achievement of stated objectives. In addition to those plans that are developed to serve a given project, such as locating and building a new plant, some plans become relatively permanent in nature and are sometimes called standing plans. These standing plans, depending on their breadth or scope, are classified as policies, procedures, or methods.

In its simplest form planning is an activity that can be executed by any member of an organization as illustrated by the planning of one's activities for a day, several days, or a week. As the nature of a problem under consideration becomes more complex, so do the methods of planning. In medium and large organizations the volume of data gathered to be analyzed and evaluated prior to making a final choice has increased significantly with the utilization of electronic data processing in the planning process. Part of this increase in the amount of data evaluated in the planning process is the result of a desire to improve the quality of the final plan by developing and examining many alternative courses of action, and part is due to the capabilities of information processing equipment. Because of virtually unlimited capabilities for storage, retrieval, and processing of data, there is a tendency to examine more data than needed simply because it is available.

Organizing. The classical approach to the study of organization reveals two major themes. The first is concerned with the structuring of work and results in the creation of roles that guide and limit the behavior of people. Closely associated with and a part of the process of structuring is the subsequent arrangement of work into manageable units. The structuring and arranging of work into units is known as departmentation. The arrangement of these units of work under the jurisdiction of a single manager creates a span of management. The second theme that appears in the classical discussions of the organizing function is the concept of authority. There are two major opinions concerning the source of authority—the institutional source which states that authority is derived from society and the subordinate acceptance view which holds that authority is granted by subordinates.

Another facet of authority is its transfer within the organization. Superior-subordinate relationships are referred to as the chain of command, and the process of transferring authority from superior to subordinate is known as the delegation of authority. When the subordinate is a manager of a lower level organizational unit, the process of delegating authority to that manager is known as the decentralization of authority. Although the phrase, decentralization of authority, is used frequently to describe the authority relationships between a plant manager and a vice-president of manufacturing or between a district sales manager and a vice-president of marketing, it is best to reserve the term *decentral-*

ization for those instances where the decentralized unit is of sufficient scope to have a clear responsibility for profits. Such a limitation requires the unit manager to have responsibility for both the production function and the marketing function.

It is apparent that there is an obvious need for an organization—defining an organization as people with assigned and interrelated roles—to execute the planning function. Of equal significance are the benefits obtained for the well-defined organization in executing the control function. A clearly defined organization aids in the flow of information necessary for the measurement of performance. The corrective action of the control function is accomplished by the managers responsible for the variance from expected standards. It is difficult to designate which managers are responsible without a clearly defined organization.

Leading. The leadership function is termed variously as leading, directing, actuating, or motivating. Despite the variation in terminology used to designate the function, it is agreed that the purpose of the function is to elicit desired forms of behavior on the part of the members of the organization. Within the context of independent, intervening, and dependent variables, leadership is best regarded as an independent variable—an input into the organization intended to influence behavior. The results of effective leadership are expressed in many ways. The statement of objectives may be an expression of the goals of one person, or it may represent a consensus of the top echelon of the organization. The quality of leadership is reflected in the development and execution of plans, in the clarity and appropriateness of the organizational structure, and in the design and administration of control systems.

Leadership in formal organizations includes not only those characteristics of interpersonal relationships known as leadership style; but also includes all the actions of a manager necessary for the performance of the managerial functions of planning, organizing, and controlling, as well as the selection of an appropriate style of leadership. Consequently, the concept of managing is broader in scope than the concept of leading. Similarly, the managerial function known as leading is broader than the interpersonal relationships between manager and subordinate. Among the managerial functions associated with the function of leadership are the design and administration of motivational systems, planning and executing formal communication programs, and the staffing and development of the organization on a continuing basis. The performance of these managerial functions is a major contribution to the formation of organizational climate, which in turn becomes a significant determinant of behavior of the members of the organization.

Control. The purpose of the control function is to insure the proper execution of plans. Control is accomplished through a three-step process—determining expected standards of performance, measuring current performance in relation to expected standards, and, when necessary, taking corrective action to insure that standards are met. The sequence of events, the date each event is to be completed, and the organization responsible for the completion of a given event are quite evident when plans are developed in detail and are highly structured. The budget, the instrument most frequently associated with the control function, is a plan for profit that has been converted into dollars to be received, spent, and earned during a specified period of time. Similarly, the time-event-network analysis used as a means of control is a statement of the sequence and timing of activities to be accomplished in order to complete a given project.

The planning and control functions of management are best described as a planning-control-planning cycle, since each of these functions is a different aspect of the same continuous management information system. Information for planning is drawn from external environmental sources such as socioeconomic data. Financial and other internal resources available in the form of physical plant and personnel are also utilized in planning. Control relies heavily on internal data developed as the result of the execution of plans; yet changes in the external environment, for example the actions of competitors and customers, are also significant. More often than not, when corrective action is required the modification of plans is a part of that action. However, the planning-control-planning cycle is but one phase of the management process. Organizations are required to develop and execute plans, and organizations must be actuated in order to achieve the desired level of effectiveness.

The analysis of the functions of management as a process not only answers the question concerning what management does, it also tells us how stated goals are achieved.

Management as a Group

One of the questions asked at the beginning of this chapter is whether management may be regarded as a group of people—the *who* of management. To some it is unfortunate that the word *management* is used as a collective noun to designate a group of managers instead of limiting the use of the word to describe the specific processes of planning, organizing, leading, and controlling. Nonetheless, reference to management as a group is deeply imbedded in our everyday language, and the clarification of who is normally considered a member of management is needed.

Managers are those persons in an organization who accomplish their work primarily by directing the work of others. Some of the managers in Case Problem 1-A are seeking an answer to the question: Who is eligible to join the management club? Stated another way, who are the persons performing all or any of the functions of planning, organizing, leading, and controlling?

In a typical corporation there are a board of directors, a president, a group of vice-presidents or major executives, managers of divisions or departments, and supervisors of specific areas or functions who report to the manager of that department. Reporting to a departmental supervisor are workers who perform specific duties assigned by the supervisor. There is general agreement that those who direct the work of others are a part of management. However, there are some who do not direct the work of others, yet participate in planning, organizing, or controlling. These people are usually referred to as *staff specialists*, rather than managers, and are also considered a part of management. Those who perform relatively specific and routine duties under the direction of a manager or a staff specialist are called *operative personnel* and are not considered a part of management.

As a rule, the distribution of a manager's time spent in planning, organizing, leading, or controlling is a function of the level of that person's position in the organization. The major executives of a company devote much of their time to planning and organizing. They are charged with policy making, a form of planning, and they must also determine the organization necessary to execute these policies. On the other hand, a departmental supervisor directs the operative personnel in one department and is responsible for the amount and quality of work produced. Consequently, a large portion of the supervisor's time is spent in leading and controlling the efforts of subordinates.

Is Management a Profession?

The question is often asked: Is management a profession? If a profession is defined as an occupation that serves others, it is possible to consider management a profession. However, if a profession is defined as a vocation requiring licensing and graduate study, such as medicine and law, then management is not a profession. There are certain characteristics implied when considering management a profession that are worth discussing.

There is a body of knowledge that is peculiar to the study of management. Over the years certain concepts of management have been developed, and there is a vast amount of technical information related to the management of specialized areas such as production, marketing, finance, and personnel. Thus, in respect to specialized knowledge, management is a technical field that requires mastery. One of the reasons for studying an introductory course in management is to become acquainted with some of this information. However, neither a license nor a degree is required in order to be a manager. The absence of formal licensing and educational requirements is essentially sound because it places the emphasis where it belongs: on performance rather than on academic training. Although academic training is to be highly regarded, access to the field of management should not be limited only to those who have completed a prescribed course of study. Nonetheless, a trained manager usually performs better than an untrained one, particularly in today's complex industrial society.

Is Management a Science or an Art?

A discussion of management as a science or an art seldom resolves the question to anyone's satisfaction. However, since the question is raised frequently in management literature, it is well to establish a point of reference so that students may answer the question to their own satisfaction.

Historically scientific management is defined as management that uses the methods of science in making decisions and evaluating subsequent courses of action. Every effort is made to obtain complete, valid, reliable information pertinent to the problem under consideration before a decision is made. Under these conditions the decision is consistent with and derived from the obtained information, and subsequent courses of action are subject to rigorous control procedure as a further check on the correctness of the original decision. The antithesis of the scientific approach is management that operates "by the seat of its pants." It is an approach to management that places emphasis on sources of information such as personal experiences, intuition, and hunches, all of which have unknown validity.

The art of management refers specifically to the practice of management. There are many phases of business operations that are not readily amenable to rigorous examination and control. Consequently, information developed in these fields is less precise than information obtained by means of the scientific method. As a result, greater emphasis is placed on the individual manager's past experience and judgment than on knowledge resulting from a technical course of study, such as engineering or accounting. The solutions to problems involving human relations require skills developed primarily through experience as opposed to technical knowledge acquired through formal study. When those skills are practiced smoothly and successfully by a manager, they are often regarded as an art; yet in their development and acquisition, they differ only in degree, not in kind, from skills and knowledge acquired through the more critical methods of science.[1]

A Definition of Management

A precise definition of management is needed as a basis for the study of management. There are three aspects to a definition of management as a process. First, there is the coordination of resources; second, consideration must be given to performance of the managerial functions; and, third, since management is purposeful in nature, the purpose of the management process must be included.

The manager of an enterprise coordinates the resources of an organization— specifically financial resources, physical resources, and personnel. In a business enterprise, and for that matter in all formally organized groups, a prime requisite is money. There is seldom an organization without some measure of capital, a requisite for fraternal, social, and nonprofit groups as well as for business organizations. Physical resources include such properties of an organization as production equipment, plant facilities and offices, and, in the case of manufacturing, inventories. The people who are members of the organization are the human resources needed to perform the functions of the organization. These resources, coordinated through the primary functions of the management process, enable the organization to reach its stated goals or objectives.

---

[1] For a discussion concerning the views as to whether management is a science or an art, the following are recommended: Henry M. Boettinger, "Is Management Really an Art?" *Harvard Business Review*, Vol. 53, No. 1 (January–February, 1975), p. 54, and Ronald E. Gribbins and Shelby D. Hunt, "Is Management a Science?" *Academy of Management Review*, Vol. 3, No. 1 (January, 1978), p. 139.

From the latter discussion a definition of management may then be stated: *Management* is the coordination of all resources through the processes of planning, organizing, leading, and controlling in order to attain stated objectives.

The Universality of Management

The definition of management as a purposive, coordinative process is universal in its application to all forms of group endeavor. It is not confined to business enterprises alone, but is applicable whenever people attempt to reach a stated goal through group efforts. The concept of universality of management is also applicable to all levels of managers within an organization and is not confined to the top echelon. Every manager and every staff specialist of an organization participates in the coordination of resources and the exercise of one or all of the managerial functions. All work to achieve the stated objectives.

ABOUT THIS BOOK

An introductory course to any field of study introduces and discusses a broad range of topics. As can be expected neither all students nor all instructors are in complete agreement about the amount of space assigned to each topic by the authors. In the field of management the problem of selecting content is compounded by the various approaches (sometimes called schools) to the study of management. The texts of 15 or 20 years ago are representative of the classical approach to management. Presently there are texts with titles that indicate a behavioral approach, a systems approach, or a quantitative approach. One way of lending some order to the diversity of opinion concerning the content and emphasis of the introductory course is to examine the introductory course within the context of the sequence of courses normally taught in the business administration curriculum.

Most authors of management textbooks define management as a process. As a result their books have, in addition to an introductory section, four major sections—planning, organizing, leading or directing, and controlling. The execution of the planning function and the control function rely more heavily on mathematical techniques than the other two functions of the management process. The application of quantitative techniques to the problems of management, primarily related to the functions of planning and controlling, has emerged as an academic field of study known as management science. It is questionable whether it is either desirable or possible for the introductory course to do more than indicate the problems that may be resolved by mathematical techniques. The interested student may explore the quantitative aspects of managerial problem solving and decision making in subsequent management science courses.

The origin of that body of knowledge discussed in the organizing function is lost in antiquity; however, much of it does come from the writings of military leaders. Most introductory courses confine the discussion of the organizing function to the level of description. The chapter titles of the section concerned with organizing in this text are typical of the material presented in most texts. Beyond the introductory course there are advanced courses in organization theory and detailed studies of specific organizational forms such as the bureaucratic model.

The behavioral sciences—especially psychology, sociology, and anthropology—are the academic disciplines that provide the subject matter content applicable to the leadership function. Most business schools offer additional courses in organizational behavior, industrial and organizational psychology, and industrial sociology so that the interested student may explore the behavioral sciences in depth.

The student who is studying the discipline of management is at the same time specializing in one of the functional areas of business management in order to perform one of the specialized jobs in the business organization. The student may complete a major in accounting, personnel, finance, marketing, or production, or may receive special training for positions in quality control, industrial engineering, or purchasing. Since these are the traditional majors within schools of business administration, they are not explored in depth in the introductory course to management.

When the introductory course to management is viewed as the beginning course within the emerging academic discipline known as management and when it is recognized that the student is acquiring necessary skills and knowledge for performing a specific function within the modern industrial organization, it seems best to adopt an eclectic approach to the study of management. Consequently, the concepts of planning and control that draw heavily on management science in their more complex applications are introduced in their simpler forms. Systems theory, organization theory, and the major findings of the behavioral sciences are presented in the discussions of the functions of organizing and leading. The breadth of an eclectic approach best meets the needs of those students who will have no additional courses in management and at the same time best prepares students who have the opportunity for further study in the field of management.

Case Problem 1-B describes some of the problems that must be resolved by the managers of Kmart. At one point in the history of the company it was necessary for Kmart to change directions completely. If Kmart is to continue its present rate of growth new objectives must be set and new plans must be developed.

Case Problem 1-B
KMART

Seldom are the same managers of a company required to make a decision that can change the course of that company twice during their careers as managers. Yet that is precisely what the managers of Kmart have been asked to do.[2] In the early 1960's the first decision was necessary in order for the corporation to survive. It is perhaps ironic that the second vital decision confronting the same management resulted from the extremely successful execution of the 1960 decision.

In 1960 S. S. Kresge Co., now known as Kmart, was a variety chain in an industry that had completed its life cycle. The president of Kresge knew that a change in direction was needed in order for the company to survive. He picked a general vice-president, Harry Blair Cunningham, to find an alternative. Mr. Cunningham was told to travel extensively and see what he could find.

What he found was the discount store— a form of merchandising in its infancy. He discovered E. J. Korvette's discount department stores. These stores were separate buildings with ample parking space and were usually located in the suburbs. National brands were discounted and sold at bargain prices. Mass media advertising was a major factor, and, because of the low markup, sales volume and inventory turnover were a must. Cunningham kept to himself his thoughts about entering the discount field; and, when he became president, S. S. Kresge became a discount chain.

Oddly enough, Mr. Cunningham is best described as a planner and an organizer, one who can persuade his co-workers to enthusiastically change directions. He is not a merchandising innovator. He borrowed the discount store idea from Korvette, and the initial stock selected by Kmart came from an analysis of the sales made at Sears. From this analysis, fast-moving items with good

---

[2] For a more detailed account, read Eleanore Carruth, "Kmart Has to Open Some New Doors on the Future," *Fortune*, Vol. XCVI, No. 1 (July, 1977), p. 144. The account in *Fortune* presents a complete analysis of the alternatives and problems to be resolved by Kmart's top management.

profit margins formed the initial Kmart inventory. The result has been outstanding—so outstanding that it is difficult to conceive of Kmart developing an encore that can match its first performance.

How Successful Has Kmart Been?

Kmart started with zero sales in the discount field in the early 1960's. By 1976 Kmart's sales were approximately $8.5 billion—a sales volume that placed it ahead of J. C. Penney and third after Sears and Safeway. At first discount stores held 10 percent of the general merchandise market, which consisted of apparel, furniture, and home products, and which amounted to approximately $100 billion. Since 1970, however, the rate of growth for the industry has slowed. Yet in 1976 discount stores accounted for 20 percent of the $100 billion market. Kmart's share was 25 percent of that 1976 market. In addition to this, Kmart has accounted for at least one half of the growth of the discount market during the past 15 years. Some of the discount stores, such as W. T. Grant, have dropped by the wayside. Financial analysts predict that 10 discount chains will replace the more than 50 chains now in the field. The competition is strong; for example, there are Federated Department Store's Gold Circle chain, May Department Store's Venture stores, Dayton-Hudson's Target stores, and Woolco. Nevertheless Kmart has projected 1981 sales of $16 billion.

Even so, doubling sales volume between 1976 and 1981 represents a decline in sales growth. If Kmart sales reach the $16 billion mark by 1981, the rate of growth for the five-year period, 1976–1981, will be 14 percent and a projected 15 percent return on investment. These figures represent a 7 percent decline from the 22 percent rate of growth in sales and profit from 1960 until the mid-1970's. Forecasts beyond 1981 project a 10 percent growth in sales and an 11 percent growth in profit annually.

Kmart's problem is not money. Between 1976 and 1981 Kmart expects to have $500 million a year for new investments, and by 1985 that number should stabilize at approximately $400 million a year. The current dividend rate is approximately 25 percent of net income and the return on investment is 18.5 percent. None of these forecasts include any new fields of business; instead they are based solely on the sales from Kmart's current operations and contemplated expansion in the discount field. Thus, Kmart has two problems: first, maintaining its position in the discount industry; second, discovering new businesses that will hopefully be as profitable as the discount industry has been.

Some Alternatives

Kmart has explored several possibilities: Kmart entered the fast-food business, but that proved to be unsuccessful. Following the lead of Sears, Kmart tried to enter the credit card business, but discovered that it did not have the big-ticket items necessary for credit card purchases. Furthermore, it appears that Kmart customers want to pay cash and believe that by so doing they save money. Kmart has entered the insurance field and has a subsidiary corresponding to Sears' Allstate. The insurance venture is not proving to be as profitable as desired, since the volume needed to make insurance profitable has not been obtained. The possibility of manufacturing has also been examined. One of the difficulties in manufacturing is that Kmart is selling name-brand merchandise. To distribute similar merchandise under a private label may antagonize some name-brand manufacturers. It is also questionable whether the profit in manufacturing is as great as that shown by Kmart's merchandising operations. All these possibilities take capital—currently not a problem—and people. In order to obtain the necessary personnel Kmart is actively recruiting on college campuses.

PROBLEMS

1. Is growth at Kmart the name of the game? Why or why not?
2. What internal problems do you foresee in maintaining present growth in the discount field and at the same time growing in other business fields?
3. Is there a possibility that the discount store merchandising techniques will follow the same cycle of growth and decline shown by the variety stores? Discuss.

CHAPTER QUESTIONS FOR STUDY AND DISCUSSION

1. Briefly answer the questions who, what, when, where, why, and how as they relate to the study of management.
2. Is it possible for a manager to be at the same time highly skilled in scientific management and also an excellent practitioner in the art of management? Give an example.
3. Describe in your own words the interrelationships that exist between the four functions of the management process. Is it possible to rank these functions in order of significance within the management process? Discuss.
4. Is management still responsible for the success or failure of a business when economic fluctuations or changes in the political environment affect an entire industry? Why or why not?

5. Do you agree with the statement made in the text that it would be undesirable to require a prescribed course of study as a requisite for a management position? Why?

6. What is meant by *universality of management*?

7. What is the definition of management given in the text? What are the three major aspects included in the definition of management? Develop a series of definitions using only two aspects for each definition. Evaluate each definition thus developed in respect to its completeness.

Chapter 2

Development of Management Concepts

Case Problem 2-A

SYMPTOMS OR CAUSES?

It was six o'clock in the evening on the last Friday in April as Marsh Saunders sat at his desk organizing the impressions he had gained during his first month as plant manager for Excellent Foods, Inc. Though he had been a plant manager for Excellent Foods for more than five years, this was the first time he had managed a can manufacturing plant for the company; his previous experience had been in food processing plants. He jotted down a list of his major observations on a sheet of paper. Following each "symptom" he listed possible causes. The following is a copy of his notes with the causes in italics.

1. Production—all operating departments (assembly, shipping, lithography, and press room) operating in the red as measured by engineered standards. Losses range from −20% to −5%; average monthly loss for plant is −15%.
   Machines not properly maintained. Personnel not capable, need more training. Applies to all four departments.
2. Labor relations—poor.
   Every effort to increase efficiency called for a speedup. Too many grievances; 150 last year. (Is this the cause of symptom No. 1, or is it the result of poor performance?)

3. Quality—very poor, many complaints.
   Operating personnel and supervisors don't seem to care. Improperly maintained and poorly adjusted equipment.
4. Housekeeping—lousy.
   Entire plant dirty with nothing ever in its right place. Machine shop has no idea of spare parts inventory.
5. Quality of supervision—probably technically competent as they all came up from the ranks. Seem to be beat down, no spirit, poor human relations in all departments.
   Do not consider themselves a part of the management team. Afraid to do anything, seem fearful of losing job. Would a guarantee of no personnel changes for six months be a good move?
6. Manager's staff—all heads of staff departments (industrial, engineering, personnel, purchasing, quality control, production control, and accounting) have been in their respective jobs for at least three years. No one willing to exercise authority or take responsibility—all seem mediocre in ability.
   Is poor performance of this group due to lack of native ability or would additional training help? Should training be in respective technical fields or general

management? Though mediocre, these people know the organization.

7. Low morale at all levels from the hourly production workers, through the clerical help, to supervision and staff.
The plant seems to lack a common purpose or goal. An esprit de corps *is completely lacking.*

As he looked at this list, Mr. Saunders wondered if symptom No. 7, poor morale, should not be listed as the number one problem in place of low production. He knew that the list was incomplete and that another 10 to 15 items could be added without much difficulty. He also knew that before he could start the much needed management training program he envisioned he would have to group his problems, or symptoms, into several major areas.

PROBLEMS

1. Assume that you are Mr. Saunders. How would you group the seven symptoms so that a training program could be directed toward three major subject matter areas?
2. Do you think that the words *symptoms* and *causes* are better choices than *problems* and *solutions*? Why?
3. In his notes on the probable causes for symptoms No. 2 and No. 5, Mr. Saunders raised several questions. How would you answer these questions?
4. Which of the approaches to management offers the greatest value to the solution of the problems faced by Mr. Saunders?

As you read this chapter, you will discover that the problems confronting Mr. Saunders are neither new nor unique to his plant; they are as old as management itself.

There is considerable evidence that effective management of complex social groups has existed for well over 6,000 years. The early civilizations of the Egyptians, the Greeks, and the Roman Empire could not have existed for centuries had there not been well-developed administrative organizations and procedures. Even before these civilizations, there is reason to believe that considerable thought and effort had been expended on studying and formulating the management process.

One of the earliest analytical statements of management concepts appears in the Bible, Exodus 18:13–26. This passage tells how Jethro, Moses' father-in-law, observed Moses spending an entire day listening to the complaints and problems of his people. Following this observation, Jethro told Moses that what he was doing was too much for one man and suggested specific steps that should be taken to relieve him of his burden. His first recommendation was that "ordinances and laws" should be taught to the people. The modern counterpart of this advice is an organization's statement of policies and procedures. Secondly, he recommended that leaders be selected and assigned "to be rulers of thousands, and rulers of hundreds, and rulers of fifties, and rulers of ten." The process of appointing leaders, each of whom is responsible for a given number of subordinates, is referred to as delegation of authority. Jethro's third point, that these rulers should administer all routine matters and should bring to Moses only the important questions, forms the basis for a well-known control procedure. The procedure of attending to the exception that does not conform to expected results is known as the *principle of the exception* and is discussed in Chapter 19.

The recounting of Jethro's advice to Moses illustrates that interest in management as a process existed in antiquity. However, the systematic study and development of the formal literature of management appears much later. Most students of management recognize three phases in the development of management thought. First there is the classical approach, which includes an emphasis on the production and administrative processes within organizations. Second, there are those who emphasize the importance of establishing sound practices of human relations as a means of improving the management process. Those who stress the importance of human relations are concerned with the human element in management. It is a convincing point of view for there are many instances where improved relationships between management and the workers and among the workers themselves have solved the problems of a particular company. Finally, there are several contemporary approaches to the study of management that emphasize either the social system, the decision-making process, the application of quantitative methods, or the systems approach to the study of management. These may be grouped together as modern approaches to the study of management.

Since the classical approach to the study of management emphasizes both production and administration each topic is treated separately. These discussions are followed by a review of some of the major findings in the human relations approach. Finally, an analysis of the modern approaches to the study of management is presented.

THE EMPHASIS ON PRODUCTION

The industrial revolution, with its development and utilization of semiautomatic and automatic machinery, made possible the mass production of goods and also created the modern industrial organization. These new organizations with their vast potential for production were little understood and, as a result, the need for knowledge about the management of such organizations soon became apparent. It is not surprising that the first approach to the study of management emphasized the dominant characteristic of these new industrial organizations—production. The contributions of Charles Babbage and Frederick Winslow Taylor, two pioneers in the study of the production function, are examined.

Charles Babbage

Charles Babbage laid the groundwork for much of the work that later became known as *scientific management.* A project which he worked on throughout his life and unfortunately was never successful in fully developing was the "Difference Engine," an invention considered to be the forerunner of our modern data processing equipment. His interest in production problems resulted in two contributions that remain as valid today as when they were first presented. The first contribution stressed the importance of dividing and assigning labor on the basis of skill. The second provided a means for determining the feasibility of replacing manual operations with automatic machinery.

Division of Labor. In 1832, in his *On the Economy of Machinery and Manufactures,*[1] Babbage presented a keen analysis of the alternative methods then available in making pins. In his analysis of making pins by hand, he offered convincing and complete data showing that a division of labor on the basis of skill is an economic necessity. He cited as advantages of dividing labor by its level of skill the fact that learning time is reduced, since any one worker has to learn only one skill rather than all. Secondly, in the actual process of manufacturing, there is a saving because less time is lost as the result of changing from one set of skills to another. Babbage also pointed out that a high degree of precision can be acquired by each worker, for the worker is learning only one task and repeating it many times. In addition, since the job is broken down into its component parts on a basis of the skills required, there is the obvious possibility of developing specialized tools and equipment to further aid the process. All these observations resulted in the conclusion that dividing a job into its component levels of skill enables the manufacturer to acquire and pay for only the exact amount of skill required for each operation.

Manual versus Automatic Operations. Following his discussion on the art of making pins by hand, Babbage mentioned briefly a new (remember, 1832) American process of making pins by machine. He suggested several questions, the answers to which determined whether or not the introduction of machine methods was desirable:

1. To what defects pins so made (i.e., by machine) are liable?
2. What advantages they possess over those made in the usual way?
3. What is the prime cost of a machine for making them?
4. What is the expense of keeping it in repair?
5. What is the expense of moving it and attending to it? [2]

These questions are as important today as they were when originally asked by Babbage (almost 150 years ago) in that they raise questions concerning quality, the original cost of the machine, and the cost of operation including labor and maintenance. Much of management's effort is directed toward obtaining answers to these questions.

Frederick Winslow Taylor

By far the ablest exponent of the probing, analytical attitude expressed by Babbage was Frederick Winslow Taylor, commonly regarded as the father of scientific management. A strike at a navy arsenal against the Taylor System led to a Congressional investigation of "the Taylor and Other Systems of Shop Management" in 1912. The hearings afforded Taylor the opportunity to present his views regarding the concept of scientific management—the term he and his associates adopted before the hearings began to refer to the Taylor System.

---

[1] Charles Babbage, *On the Economy of Machinery and Manufactures* (Philadelphia: Carey and Lea, 1832), Chap. 17, p. 121, "On the Division of Labour," reprinted in *Classics in Management*, edited by Harwood F. Merrill (New York City: American Management Association, 1960), pp. 29–44.

[2] *Ibid.*, p. 43.

Taylor opened his testimony with a statement that eliminated many misconceptions concerning scientific management.[3] In part he said that scientific management is not merely cost-keeping systems, time studies, functional foremanship, new schemes for paying workers, or efficiency systems. He emphasized that while these devices in whole or in part are not scientific management they are useful adjuncts to scientific management as well as to other systems of management.

Scientific Management—A Mental Revolution. Taylor, after stating what scientific management was not, went on to state clearly the main characteristic of scientific management. To him, "a complete mental revolution" was necessary for scientific management to come into being. Furthermore—and this is important because it points up the fact that Taylor was far more than a capable technician—he stated that the mental revolution must occur in the *worker's* mind as well as in the minds of management. Taylor's analysis of industrial problems existing between management and labor concluded that, to a large extent, it was an argument over the division of the surplus created by industry. Indeed, this still remains one of the major issues in current collective bargaining. The first part of the mental revolution, according to Taylor, was that both parties stop quarreling about how the surplus should be divided and instead unite to increase the size of the surplus so that the need for hairsplitting over the division of earnings becomes less acute.

The second phase of the mental revolution was that the scientific method must be the sole basis for obtaining information to determine the proper procedure to be used in the performance of each job and to establish the proper level of output per work-hour. It was the second phase of scientific management that caused most of the criticism of the Taylor System. The reason is that the application of the scientific method requires so much detailed work and time that the original goal of increasing the surplus is never realized. An example of the extensive work necessary in some areas to determine the scientific basis for the performance of an operation is found in the series of experiments conducted by Taylor extending over a 26-year period to determine the best methods of machining or cutting metals. In the process, high-speed tool steels were developed, and the science of cutting metals was broken down into 12 interrelated variables. These interrelationships were expressed mathematically by formulas, and slide rules were developed so that the optimum conditions for any given task could be computed. It is no wonder that a person becoming immersed in the mathematical analysis of production problems loses sight of the first great mental revolution required; namely, a change in attitude.

---

[3] Merrill, *op. cit.*, p. 77. The statement concerning scientific management is based upon testimony of Frederick W. Taylor at hearings before the Special Committee of the House of Representatives to Investigate the Taylor and Other Systems of Shop Management, January 25, 1912, p. 1387. For a review of Taylor's work, which is highly critical in nature, the following is recommended: Charles D. Wrege and Amedeo G. Perroni, "Taylor's Pig-Tale: A Historical Analysis of Frederick W. Taylor's Pig-Iron Experiments," *Academy of Management Journal*, Vol. 17, No. 1 (March, 1974), p. 6.

The Need for Scientific Mangement. Scientific management was developed to solve two major problems: (1) to increase the output of the average worker and (2) to improve the efficiency of management. To a degree, increasing the productivity of the average worker is the same problem that challenged Elton Mayo, an able exponent of the human relations approach. But the approaches used by each of these men were different. Mayo sought the answer in terms of the social forces that affect the worker as a member of a group while Taylor considered each worker as a separate economic individual motivated by financial needs.

Taylor believed that the basis of a worker's tendency to restrict output was fear of displacement—a fear similar to the fear expressed in some quarters today in regard to automation. He suggested two methods of minimizing the fear of displacement expressed by the workers. One method was to educate the workers to understand that their economic salvation lay in producing more at a lower cost. The other method was to prove to the workers the effectiveness of producing more by placing them on a piecework, or incentive, system, and thereby permitting them to earn more.

Taylor's Principles of Management. The second major problem—improving the efficiency of management—was to be solved through the application of Taylor's four principles of management. The first of these principles urged a gathering, analysis, and codification of all rule-of-thumb data existing in the business. The second principle urged careful selection and a thorough study of workers so that they may be developed to their maximum capabilities. Third, was the persuasive principle of educating or, more properly, inspiring people to use the scientific principles derived from the careful analysis of all data and methods used in each job. Lastly, Taylor urged that management organize in such a manner as to properly manage and carry out its duties.[4] (See Table 2-1.)

THE EMPHASIS ON ADMINISTRATION

The second of the classical approaches to the study of management emphasizes the administrative aspects of management. The emphasis is on an overall approach to the problems of management.

The task of management has been summarized in a single word, *coordination*, by Mary Parker Follett. However, in order to understand this concept it is

---

[4] Although Frederick W. Taylor is the author of *The Principles of Scientific Management*, a recent analysis of the manuscript of an unpublished book, written by Morris L. Cooke, indicates that Taylor used a great deal of Cooke's manuscript in his preparation of *The Principles of Scientific Management*. Charles D. Wrege and Anne Marie Stotka, "Cooke Creates a Classic: The Story behind F. W. Taylor's Principles of Scientific Management," *The Academy of Management Review*, Vol. 3, No. 4 (October, 1978), p. 736.

For a defense of Taylor, Louis W. Fry, "The Maligned F. W. Taylor: A Reply to His Many Critics," *The Academy of Management Review*, Vol. 1, No. 3 (July, 1976), p. 124.

necessary to know what is being coordinated and to review suggestions as to how coordination can be best accomplished.[5]

Fayol's Principles of Management

Henri Fayol, a French engineer and geologist, was the first to state a series of principles of management that provide guideposts for successful management coordination. Concurrent with Taylor's study of management through a detailed analysis of the individual worker, Fayol, manager of a large French mining and metallurgical company, analyzed the problems of top management. He modestly believed that his success was not due to any personal characteristics of leadership, but was the result of applying a set of general administrative principles that could be isolated and taught to others. In *General and Industrial Management*, Fayol presented 14 principles of management.[6]

Five of Fayol's 14 principles were concerned primarily with the improvement of human relations. One of his principles emphasized production efficiency, and the remaining eight were directed toward administration of the organization. (See Table 2-1, page 25.)

Principles Emphasizing Human Relations

The five principles applicable to problems in the field of human relations are *subordination of individual interest to the general interest, equity, stability of tenure of personnel, initiative, and esprit de corps.* In discussing subordination of individual interest to the general interest, Fayol stated that individuals and small groups within the overall organization should make their needs secondary to those of the firm. He also emphasized that it is necessary for the firm to place its interests second to those of the society in which it operates. Recognition of the fact that the administrator of an organization is dealing with a number of groups, in contrast to a number of individuals, is fundamentally the same group concept of Elton Mayo. Fayol suggested that subordination of interest could be achieved by close supervision, good examples of subordination of personal interest by supervisors, and making agreements with various employees and groups of employees as fair as possible.

In discussing equity, he defined what is meant by fair agreements. Equity is composed of two ingredients—kindliness and justice. The equal application of policies and practices to all groups and individuals within an organization is certainly a concept difficult to quarrel with, yet also difficult to apply at all times. Fayol applied the concept of desirability of stability of tenure to all levels of the organization. Production workers must have a sense of tenurial security in order to learn their jobs so that they may perform them well, and they must also have a sense of psychological security.

---

[5] Mary Parker Follett, *Freedom and Coordination* (London: Management Publications Trust, 1949), reprinted in Merrill, *op. cit.*, p. 337.

[6] Henri Fayol, *General and Industrial Management* (London: Sir Isaac Pitman and Sons, 1949), p. 19, reprinted in Merrill, *op. cit.*, p. 217. The copyright date, 1949, is the date of the English translation. Fayol's "General Principles of Management" first appeared in 1916 in an industrial association bulletin published in France.

Stability of tenure for top management is necessary; for it takes time to know the organization, its problems, and its personnel. Fayol even suggested that it may be better for a concern to have a mediocre manager with long tenure than a succession of brilliant managers. In this connection the following interesting question was raised: Is the poor performance of a company experiencing a high turnover of managerial personnel the result of the turnover; or, is the poor performance of managerial personnel the cause of the turnover? It is a question that plagues many companies today, and they are no closer to the answer than Fayol was.

To Fayol, participation in the solution of problems was represented by the principle of initiative. This principle is still with us today and is illustrated, for example, by companies that establish suggestion systems at all levels of the organizations so that the ideas and energies of all workers may be tapped in the solution of common problems. Effective employee suggestion programs utilize the principle of initiative, which enables employees to see their ideas carried through to a successful conclusion.

In his last principle concerning human relations, *esprit de corps*, Fayol stated his belief that in union there is strength and warned against a system of divide and conquer in an organization. For though dividing and conquering may be a good way of eliminating the opposition, it does not work within a single group such as a business organization. Thus, the manager's task is not to eliminate the opposition; instead, it is to unify all divergent groups and individuals.

Production Efficiency

Fayol's principle concerning production efficiency, *division of work*, is similar to the thesis that Charles Babbage presented in "On the Division of Labour." [7] Fayol offered the same reasons for dividing work and creating groups of specialists. He mentioned the resulting increased skill, the reduction in learning time, and the increased efficiency resulting from not having to change from one task to another. But he went further than Babbage and applied the principle of the division of work to all levels of management, as well as to the hourly worker. Also, the principle of division of work is an expression of the same interest shown by Babbage and Taylor; namely, an emphasis on the production process with a desire to increase efficiency. Division of work is the only one of Fayol's 14 principles that can be classed as solely emphasizing production. However, there are two principles of such breadth that production processes are included in their application: *remuneration* and *order*. These will be discussed later.

Principles Emphasizing Administration

The remaining principles are new in concept, for they deal with the problems of top management—*administration*, the direction of day-to-day operations, and

---

[7] Babbage, *loc. cit.*

organization. Fayol's principle of authority is the first of this group. *Authority* is defined as the right to give orders and is discussed with its corollary, *responsibility*, the obligation to complete assigned duties. The granting of authority to a manager implies that by accepting that authority the manager has also accepted responsibility. Fayol recognized that authority might be misused and suggested that preventing the abuse of authority depended on the integrity of the individual exercising that authority.[8]

Discipline is the respect shown by all members of the organization toward the written agreements or policies governing their conduct in the firm. Fayol proposed that good discipline could be achieved by having all agreements between the company and the employees presented as clearly and as fairly as possible, that all supervisors throughout the organization should be thoroughly capable, and that, if the need for penalties or discipline arose, such penalties should be as fair as possible.

The principles of *unity of command* and *unity of direction* are similar and closely related. Yet there is sufficient difference in their purposes so that two separate principles are warranted. The first, unity of command, states that orders should originate from one source only. Thus, subordinates are assured that only one superior in the organization can give them orders. Unity of direction is not directed toward the individual, but refers to the plan or work activities of the group and emphasizes that for one plan there should be one head or director. Thus, these two principles complement each other; unity of command assures the employee that there will be only one superior, and unity of direction assures organizational effectiveness, since for every group of workers carrying out a plan, there shall be only one director.

These principles of organization—authority, discipline, unity of command, and unity of direction—leave little room for deviation or individual choice. Because of their nature they appear to be an all-or-none proposition. However, not all of Fayol's principles that concern organization are as rigid, as illustrated by his principles concerning *centralization* and the scalar chain (*line of authority*). In the *scalar chain* principle, Fayol urged that definite lines of authority be established from the bottom of an organization to its very top in such a manner that the exact lines of authority relationships between the successive levels of management are unmistakably clear. When it becomes necessary for individuals in different sections of the organization to work directly with each other in order to attain speed of action, the formal chain of command should be short-circuited, provided all people concerned are properly informed.

The same type of flexibility is evident in determining the optimum degree of *centralization* of authority in an organization. In general, those actions that tend to reduce the authority and responsibility of subordinates by placing more authority in the hands of a superior may be considered as actions which lead to a greater degree of centralization of authority to make decisions. Those acts that increase responsibility and authority at lower levels result in what is termed

---

[8] The problem of integrity is discussed in Chapter 3, "Ethical and Social Responsibilities of Management."

a greater degree of *decentralization* of authority to make decisions. With the concept of varying degrees of centralization of authority, there is no recommended absolute level of centralization or decentralization. The desired level or degree depends on the situation and includes such factors as the nature of the organization, the problem of the department at hand, and the capabilities of the subordinates in question.

Table 2–1
SUMMARY OF
THE PRINCIPLES
OF THE
CLASSICAL
APPROACH

TAYLOR'S PRINCIPLES OF SCIENTIFIC MANAGEMENT

1. Management must gather, analyze, and codify all existing rule-of-thumb data pertaining to the business in order to develop a science.
2. Workers must be carefully selected and thoroughly studied so that each one may be developed to maximum capabilities.
3. Workers must be inspired or trained to use the scientific methods developed as the result of analyzing and codifying rule-of-thumb data.
4. Management must organize in such a manner that it can properly manage and carry out its duties

FAYOL'S PRINCIPLES OF MANAGEMENT

Human Relations

Subordination of individual interest to the general interest	Stability of tenure of personnel
	Initiative
Equity	*Esprit de corps*

Production Efficiency

Division of work

Administration

Authority	Centralization
Discipline	Scalar chain (line of authority)
Unity of command	Remuneration
Unity of direction	Order

The remaining two principles describe operating procedures of such breadth that they are difficult to classify within the framework of either human relations, production, or administration. These principles, *remuneration* and *order,* encompass all three areas. Since they are expressed as problems of top management rather than problems in human relations or the improvement of production, the principles of remuneration and order are considered among those principles contributing to the administrative efforts of management. The principle of remuneration rests on the assumption that the wages paid to personnel should be based on concepts of equity and should be satisfactory to both the employee and the company. In discussing the various methods of paying hourly employees, Fayol demonstrated that he was thoroughly familiar with the piecework system advocated by Taylor. He also mentioned the problems involved in profit-sharing plans and bonuses, not only for hourly workers, but for all members of the organization. Again, Fayol developed a flexible conclusion: the method of payment selected should be the one that works best for the particular situation. Furthermore, the definition of *best* should include the views of all interested parties.

The other principle, also broad in scope, is that of order. At first glance, the meaning of order may seem to be the same as Taylor's admonition that the placement of materials and tools should be the result of a methods study to assure efficient production. Fayol's principle does include the concept of a place for everything and everything in its place. However, it means much more than the neat arrangement of physical materials. Fayol's idea of order also applies to the human element of the organization. An application of the principle of order is the organization chart, a device which literally shows the place of every person in the organization and the relationships of each to the other. In addition to knowing personnel as they appear on the organization chart, Fayol recommended they be considered human resources with different capabilities and desires.

THE EMPHASIS ON HUMAN RELATIONS

The works of two proponents of the human relations school are examined briefly. The first statement, expressed by Robert Owen, appeared in 1828 and is regarded as one of the first formal writings in the field of management. Although he is considered a proponent of the human relations approach to management, Owen's views are now regarded as highly paternalistic in nature. Secondly, a brief review of the work of Elton Mayo, who is considered the founder of the human relations approach to management, is presented.

Robert Owen

Robert Owen, a successful textile mill manager in Scotland from 1800 to 1828, made some remarkable observations concerning the factors that influenced the productivity of the personnel in his plants. He referred to his employees as "vital machines," and, in describing how they should be regarded and treated, he compared the importance and nature of "vital machines" with the "inanimate machines" of the factory. A summary of his position was presented in "An Address: To the Superintendents of Manufactures, and to those Individuals generally, who, by giving Employment to an aggregated Population, may easily adopt the means to form the Sentiments and Manners of such a Population." The date of publication of this address was 1813, and in some ways it foreshadowed the conclusions of the famous Hawthorne Studies of Mayo which were not undertaken until more than a century later.[9]

Owen stated that it was generally accepted that mechanical equipment kept in good repair more than paid for itself by its increased productivity and longer life. Reasoning by analogy, he concluded that if this were true for the "inanimate

---

[9] Robert Owen, *A New View of Society* (1st American ed. from the 3d London ed.; New York City: E. Bliss & F. White, 1825), p. 57, reprinted in Merrill, *op. cit.*, p. 21.

machines," it should also be true for the "vital machines." He applied this conclusion to his own plants in New Lanark, Scotland, and claimed that as a result of attention to his personnel, he was receiving more than a 50 percent return on any money so spent.

George Elton Mayo

Closely related to the work of Owen, though separated by slightly more than 100 years, were the efforts of George Elton Mayo and his team of Harvard researchers. Mayo was born and educated in Australia, came to the United States in 1922, and was first associated with the University of Pennsylvania. In 1926, he joined the faculty of Harvard University, where he remained until his retirement in 1947. One of his early studies, completed while he was at Pennsylvania, clearly illustrated the results that may have been expected by following Owen's admonition "to treat it (the vital machine) with kindness, that its mental movements might not experience too much irritating friction." Appropriately, the title given to Mayo's first work was "The First Inquiry." [10]

"The First Inquiry." Mayo and his group were asked to solve an industrial problem, the symptoms of which were an excessive turnover of employees in a certain department of a Philadelphia textile mill. The department in question was that of the mule-spinners, whose annual turnover rate was nearly 250 percent while that of other departments in the mill was between 5 and 6 percent. Several consulting firms, then called efficiency engineers, had previously worked on the problem and, among other things, had established a financial incentive plan. The reasoning behind this approach assumed that people are economic animals, and, as such, will respond to financial incentives or rewards. However, this was not the case, for not once did the workers in the department produce enough to earn the rewards of the financial incentive plan. The morale of the department was low. There were many complaints of foot trouble, neuritis, and other miscellaneous aches and pains. The employees were working five 10-hour days each week, and the day was broken only by a 45-minute lunch period at the end of the first five hours. There were no rest periods during the day, and since the workers were continually on their feet, it was assumed that fatigue was creating their general feelings of depression.

The experiment began with the introduction of rest periods for some of the workers in the mule-spinner's department. But rest alone was not the only changed condition in the experiment. The problem was discussed with all employees in the department, and, as a result, they felt they were a part of the whole program. In addition, these workers were fondly attached to the manager of the plant, a colonel with whom many had served in World War I. They were confident that if the rest periods worked for the experimental group, about one third of the workers, then soon all would have rest periods because of the essential fairness of "the Colonel."

---

[10] Elton Mayo, *The Social Problems of an Industrial Civilization* (Boston: Division of Research, Graduate School of Business Administration, Harvard University, 1945). Portions of this work and the Hawthorne Studies are reprinted in Merrill, *op. cit.*, p. 407.

The results of the experiment were almost immediate, not only for the third who received the rest periods, but also for the two thirds who served as the control group and did not receive rest periods, although they had taken part in discussing the problem. For the first time since the installation of the incentive bonus plan by the efficiency engineers, the mule-spinners earned incentive pay, which continued for a period of four and one-half months. Then, within a period of seven days, the entire department returned to their initial pessimism and production dropped to its former low level.

What happened? Nothing that has not happened thousands of times in industrial plants prior to this experiment and thousands of times since. There was a sudden demand for the product of the textile mill, and, as a result, the supervisor in the department simply ordered the abandonment of all rest periods. The results were immediate and nearly disastrous.

However, the Colonel, the one person in whom the workers had complete personal confidence, took immediate charge. He reinstated the rest periods and guaranteed every employee two 10-minute rest periods in the morning and two in the afternoon. Practically everyone, except the Colonel himself, doubted that the loss of 40 minutes a day per employee could be made up since the machines could not be speeded up. However, the Colonel was right. During the month that followed the workers made a bonus, and the rate of production continued to climb until the efficiency figures were well above 85 percent, a considerable change from the low of 70 percent. In addition to reestablishing the rest periods in a manner that left no doubt in anyone's mind as to what management believed, the Colonel did something else of great significance. He delegated responsibility to the workers themselves. Each group of three employees was to determine the exact time when the group would take its individual rest periods, but each knew that, without fail, the group would receive four such periods a day. Thus, a guaranteed policy of management and the fact that the workers themselves participated to some extent in the decisions turned the tide.

The Hawthorne Studies. Shortly after completing "The First Inquiry," Mayo joined the faculty of Harvard University where, as head of the Industrial Research Department, he led a series of pioneering studies at the Hawthorne plant of the Western Electric Company.[11] Initially, the purpose of the study was to determine the effect of illumination on the output of workers; however, at a later date, the studies sought to determine methods of establishing teamwork and continuing cooperation in industrial groups.

---

[11] There have been several major books published by Mayo and his co-workers describing the extensive work completed at Western Electric. Among them are:

Elton Mayo, *The Human Problems of an Industrial Civilization* (Boston: Division of Research, Harvard Business School, 2d ed.; New York City: Macmillan, Inc., 1946).

F. J. Roethlisberger and W. J. Dickson, *Management and the Worker* (Cambridge: Harvard University Press, 1939, 10h printing, 1950).

F. J. Roethlisberger, *Management and Morale* (Cambridge: Harvard University Press, 1942).

F. J. Roethlisberger, *Man-in-Organization* (Cambridge: Belknap Press of Harvard University Press, 1968). This book is a series of essays by F. J. Roethlisberger, several of which are concerned with Elton Mayo and the Hawthorne studies.

In the illumination study, workers were divided into two groups—an experimental group and a control group. Lighting conditions for the experimental group were varied from 24 to 46 to 70 footcandles in intensity while the lighting of the control group remained constant. As expected, the output of the experimental group increased with each increase in light intensity. However, the performance of the control group did not remain constant as expected. Their production increased at about the same rate as the production of the experimental group. Later the light of the experimental group was reduced from ten to three footcandles. Again, the output of the experimental group continued to increase, and so did the output of the control group. Finally, a decline in productivity of the experimental group did occur, but only when the intensity of light was low enough to approach the level of moonlight. Clearly something other than illumination was the cause of changes in productivity.

Similar results were obtained in the relay assembly test room experiment, only this time the variable was the amount of rest, rather than lighting, to determine the effects of fatigue on productivity. First, normal production was established, then rest periods of varying lengths and frequency were introduced. Production increased with the increase in frequency and length of rest periods. Finally, in Period XII of the experiments, it was decided to return to the original conditions: no formal rest periods, no lunches, and a full 48-hour week. The return to the original conditions did not result in the expected drop in production; instead, production stayed at its usual high level.

The Hawthorne Effect. The Hawthorne Studies show quite clearly that factors other than working conditions and the physiological state of the worker have a marked influence on productivity. These factors are recognized as social and psychological in nature. The workers of these studies were the subjects of experiments of interest to the managers of the plant and to their immediate supervisors. Further, the workers knew that they were participating in experiments that were of interest to management. They responded to this interest, a social force, rather than to the experimentally induced changes in the external physical environment. The phenomenon of responding to the social and psychological aspects of the situation on the part of individuals participating as subjects of the experiment has come to be known as the *Hawthorne Effect.* Because of this phenomenon it is sometimes very difficult to determine whether the subjects of an experimental study are responding to the environmental factor that is being varied by the experimenter or whether they are responding to the knowledge that they are the subjects and participants of an experiment.

Conclusions

Several conclusions from Owen and Mayo can be drawn at this time. First, people are essentially social beings, not economic, and should be regarded as such. Second, as social beings they are members of a group; therefore, it is the group that should be approached to participate in discussing problems and in determining the solution. There is a third conclusion to be drawn from a study of these two works. Mayo touched on this point only lightly and Owen not at all, although in the case of the latter it might have been considered immodest if he had. In both instances, the men running the company (Owen in New Lanark, Scotland, the Colonel in Philadelphia) were leaders and were perceived as such by the employees. Both were men who knew when they were right, and both were sincere in their desire to do the best that they could for the physical well-being of their employees. However, these attributes on their part were not sufficient without a reciprocal feeling on the part of the employees. In each instance, the employees had strong feelings of confidence regarding the ability and sincerity of their leader. Therefore, it is clear that for any successful program in human relations there must be a leader with ability and sincerity, and these traits must be recognized by the employees.

MODERN APPROACHES TO THE STUDY OF MANAGEMENT

In addition to the approaches to the study of management that emphasize production, administration, and human relations, there are other areas that have been stressed in the development of management concepts. Indeed, there have been so many ideas concerning the central problems of management that one writer has referred to "The Management Theory Jungle" [12] and another writer has called the sometimes vituperative statements of the proponents of the various management schools a form of "inky warfare." [13] Let us examine this "jungle" so that we may obtain a broader view of management concepts. Also, though not fully developed, there is the beginning of an integrative point of view in management theory. The diverse theories or schools of management thought are presented as the jungle, which is followed by an integrative point of view.

The Jungle

Professor Harold Koontz in his article, "The Management Theory Jungle," described briefly six major schools of management. He grouped Taylor and Fayol together and referred to their approach as the "management process" school. The work of those who emphasize human relations was recognized separately as the "human behavior school." In addition he recognized four other schools or theories of management: the empirical school, the social systems school, the decision theory school, and the mathematical school. [14]

The Empirical School. The empirical school studies management through an analysis of the experience of successful managers. The purpose is to permit

---

[12] Harold Koontz, "The Management Theory Jungle," *Academy of Management Journal*, Vol. 4, No. 4 (December, 1961), p. 174.
[13] Lyndall F. Urwick, "The Tactics of Jungle Warfare," *Academy of Management Journal*, Vol. 6, No. 4 (December, 1963), p. 316.
[14] The discussion that follows is based on Koontz, *op. cit.*

the formation of generalizations concerning the nature of management. An example of this approach is found in Ernest Dale's *The Great Organizers*, a review of the operations of such companies as DuPont, General Motors, National Steel, and Westinghouse Electric Corporation as seen through the eyes of the chief executive of each of these organizations.[15]

In a sense this approach to management is saying, "Let us look at several successful operations, their chief executives, and how they did it, and as a result we will be able to transfer this information to another situation." To a degree the empirical school of management is closely related to the management process school of Taylor and Fayol. Each was a highly successful manager in his own right and much of the writings of each was a distillation and reporting of his own experience as a manager, while Dale's work was a reporting of the experience of others. Thus the two approaches were closely related, the difference lying in who was doing the reporting, with both schools hoping to derive a set of concepts or principles to serve as the basis for managing organizations.

The Social Systems School. Closely related to but distinct from the behavioral school is the social systems school. The behavioral school had its origin in the work of academicians, such as Mayo, but the social systems school is attributed to Chester Barnard, a former president of the New Jersey Bell Telephone Company. It has been said that Barnard wrote "with authority about authority" and perhaps he should, having been president of a major corporation. Yet Barnard viewed the organization primarily as a social system.[16]

One of the major contributions of this point of view is recognition of the importance of the informal organization and its impact upon the formal organization as portrayed by the organization chart. Another contribution concerns the nature of authority. The management process school views authority as being derived from ownership and flowing downward throughout the organization; however, Barnard saw authority as depending upon the extent to which it was accepted by members of the organization. This view concerning the origin of authority, known as *subordinate acceptance*, is discussed and reconciled with the institutional view of authority of the management process school in Chapter 10.

The Decision Theory School. The decision theory school is concerned with the making of a choice, or decision, between two or more alternatives and considers decision making as one of the primary activities of management. Decision theory is not as narrow as it may seem at first glance; instead, it can and does study not only the decision but also the decision-making process and the behavioral aspects of the decision maker.

---

[15] Ernest Dale, *The Great Organizers* (New York City: McGraw-Hill Inc., 1960). In addition to the experiences of the organizers of each of these four companies, Professor Dale examined concepts of organizational theory in the first chapter and in the concluding chapter discussed the accountability of management.

[16] Chester Barnard, *The Functions of the Executive* (Cambridge: Harvard University Press, 1938).

The Mathematical School. Intertwined with the decision theory school is that group referred to as the mathematical school. The relationship between these two schools is very close because many of the decisions made by managers may be expressed as mathematical models and subsequently solved by mathematical processes. In early years, the mathematical approach was called operations research or operations analysis, but presently the term *management science* seems to predominate. Significantly the emergence of mathematics to a dominant position among the approaches to the study of management has coincided with the development of the high-speed electronic computer, thereby permitting the management scientist to construct mathematical models containing as many as one thousand simultaneous equations.[17]

An Integrative View

The divergence of opinion concerning the central issue of management is reminiscent of the three blind men, each of whom described in turn an elephant as a rope (the one who touched the tail), a snake (the one who touched the trunk), and a tree stump (the one who touched a leg). Similarly, the question arises whether there is a sighted one among us who can describe management in its entirety rather than describing a single aspect of the process. There are those who believe that there is such a theoretical framework available at the present time; however, there are discrepancies concerning the details of this framework. Professor Scott supplied us with a fine summary of an integrative approach to the study of management that is generally referred to as *modern* organization theory.[18] Scott noted that modern approaches to the study of management have one thing in common—the utilization of the systems concept as a means of describing the total organization rather than emphasizing a specific function such as decision making (the decision theory school) or an elaboration of a method (the mathematical school) to solve organizational problems. The following questions are asked in the systems approach to understanding the management of organizations:

---

[17] A discussion of management science for the student interested in learning more about this field may be found in Harvey M. Wagner, *Principles of Operations Research with Applications to Managerial Decisions* (2d ed.; Englewood Cliffs, N. J.: Prentice-Hall, Inc., 1975). Note that the title shows the close relationship between the mathematical and the decision theory approach to the study of management.

[18] William G. Scott, "Organization Theory: Overview and an Appraisal," *Academy of Management Journal*, Vol. 4, No. 1 (April, 1961), p. 7. Professor Scott reviewed briefly earlier theories of management and classified them as the classical doctrine. The human relations movement was classified as a neoclassical theory of organization. However, the major portion of the article was devoted to modern organization theory. The discussion that follows is based on this article.

The following additional references concerning systems theories are also significant:

Kenneth E. Boulding, "General Systems Theory—The Skeleton of Science," *Management Science*, Vol. 2, No. 3 (April, 1956), p. 197.

Ludwig von Bertalanffy, "The History and Status of General Systems Theory," *Academy of Management Journal*, Vol. 15, No. 4 (December, 1972). p. 407.

Newman S. Peery, Jr., "General Systems Theory: An Inquiry into Its Social Philosophy," *Academy of Management Journal*, Vol. 15, No. 4 (December, 1972), p. 495.

Frederick Thayer, "General System(s) Theory: The Promise That Could Not Be Kept," *Academy of Management Journal*, Vol. 15, No. 4 (December, 1972), p. 481.

1. What are the strategic parts of the system?
2. What is the nature of their mutual dependency?
3. What are the main processes in the system which link the parts together and facilitate their adjustments to each other?
4. What are the goals sought by systems? [19]

The Parts of the System. The individual is the fundamental unit of the organizational system. The individual is considered in terms of personality, defining personality as the sum total of one's experiences and abilities. One of the significant aspects of the individual's personality is that it sets forth one's expectations as an individual and as a member of the organization.

The second part of an organization is the arrangement of the individuals and the functions they perform into what is termed the *formal organization*, often portrayed—albeit inadequately—by the formal organization chart. A fundamental question arises at this point: to what extent do these two parts of the organization conflict? Some students of management believe that the extent of the conflict is considerable; that is, the demands of the formal organization are contrary to the nature of its individual members.[20]

The third part of the organizational system is known as the *informal organization*. The informal organization, not shown on the official organization charts, is composed of informal groups that arise out of the work situations. Sometimes the informal groups develop as a means of completing the assigned work of the formal organization; when this happens the goals of the two groups are frequently in accord. However, there are instances where the expectations of the formal organization are in conflict with the desires of the informal organization, and when this happens the individual is frequently torn between the conflicting demands of the formal and informal organization.

The fourth part of the organization derives from the study of social processes and consequent recognition of the demands of both the formal and informal organization. One of the demands of the organization, formal or informal, is that individuals assume a *role*—a prescribed and expected pattern of behavior—that is a result of their position and function in the organization.[21] A specific concept of role that has developed is that of the role at the interface, the demands that are made of the person who is figuratively in the middle and must bring together two segments, or interfaces, of the organization.

Finally, the last part of the system is the *physical setting* within which the individual or the group performs its respective duties. It is not limited, however, to the physical factors and working conditions such as those investigated by the Hawthorne illumination studies. Instead, it is a concept that seeks the optimum relationship between employees and their environments and at-

---

[19] *Ibid.*, p. 16. In a more recent article, Dr. Scott indicates the forces that are from outside the organization rather than those forces from within the organization. It complements his 1961 article. William G. Scott, "Organization Theory: A Reassessment," *Academy of Management Journal*, Vol. 17, No. 2 (June, 1974), p. 242.

[20] Chris Argyris, *Personality and Organization* (New York City: Harper & Brothers, 1957). Of a special interest in regard to the question raised above are Chapters 2, 3, and 7.

[21] For a full discussion of the concept of roles in organizations, see Daniel Katz and Robert L. Kahn, *The Social Psychology of Organizations* (New York City: John Wiley & Sons, Inc., 1966).

tempts to allocate the resources and capabilities of employees so that they mesh effectively with those of the physical settings of their environment. The study of this method of viewing employees in relation to their environment is known as *human factors engineering*, a concept that strives to optimize the capabilities and performance of every employee in relation to his or her physical environment.

In summary, the individual, the fundamental building block of the organization, is a member of and is influenced by the formal organization. The requirements of the formal organization determine the composition and nature of work groups. The work groups in turn may form the basis for the informal organization, which is composed of individuals who are simultaneously members of the formal and the informal organization. Both the formal and the informal organization have goals that do not necessarily coincide. In addition, the goals of the formal and the informal organization are related to the expectations and goals of the individual. Also, there is the role that is demanded of the individual as a member of the formal organization and the role demanded as a member of the informal organization. As a result, there is the realization that all organizational functions occur within a physical setting that evolves beyond the concept of the relationship between the individual and the physical environment to the concept of the relationship between the individual and the organizational system.

The Linking Processes. It is easy to state that the parts of the organization are interrelated, simply because they appear to be so. However, the student of organizational theory must do more than make the statement; the ways in which the processes link the various parts of the organization must be designated and described. One of the linking processes is the *role*, or actions, performed by the individual member of the organization which serves as a means of relating to other people and to other groups in the organization. *Communication* is another means of linking the parts of the organization. The term *communication* includes not only verbal expressions, both written and oral, but also all information needed for effective operation of the organization. When communication is used in this sense, the organization is viewed as a total information system. Thus, there is concern for the flow of information from one subsystem to another subsystem so that the parts are linked together. Closely related to the concept of an organization as an information system is the concept of *balance* or homeostasis. This concept, sometimes referred to as a steady state, is one of the fundamental aspects of systems theory; that is, there is a normal state for the system and when the system is out of balance there is a tendency for it to return to its normal homeostatic state. Another linking process is *decision making*. The process of making decisions may be used to change the direction or goal of the organization, or the decision may be designed so that it restores balance to the system.

Organizational Goals. Scott has stated that the "organization has three goals which may be intermeshed or may be independent ends in themselves. They are growth, stability, and interaction." [22] He points out that the last goal,

---

[22] Scott, "Organization Theory: Overview and an Appraisal," p. 20.

interaction, refers to those organizations which exist primarily as vehicles that permit their members to interact with other members—for example, professional societies and certain social organizations. In setting the goals of organizations, it is necessary not only to seek a balance between potentially conflicting organizational goals, but also to relate these goals to those of the individual and to the goals of the informal organization. Thus the problem of establishing congruent goals for all components of an organization is highly critical.

The Next Development

It has been suggested by several people, among them Professor William C. Frederick, that the next step in the study of management is the development of a general systems theory.[23] His reason for making this statement is that a review of the development of management concepts indicates that five components of a potential general theory of management have been developed. In discussing these components, Frederick points out that the classical management of Fayol and Taylor resulted in the establishment of management principles, including a delineation of the functions and processes of management. The human relations school, a second component, stresses that the formal organization is at the same time a human and social organization and as such should serve these purposes as well as fulfilling purely economic ends. The third component is the contribution made by the decision theory school, including mathematical approaches to management processes, and recognition that decision making performs a linking function in the organization. The fourth factor is the behavioral sciences. Though quite similar to the human relations school and in the opinion of some an extension of the work of Mayo, this group stresses that individuals may be regarded as systems and function within larger social systems. Finally, the fifth component is value theory, a means of establishing the social responsibility of organizations and managements and placing in perspective the diverse contributions of the classical, human relations, decision theory, and behavioral approaches to the study of management.[24]

The conclusion is inescapable. Modern approaches to the study of management or organizations are pointing toward the development of what will someday be a general systems theory of organizations. Such a theory is often referred to as a contingency theory. A contingency theory is presented in Chapter 8, "Organization and Management Theory."[25]

---

[23] William C. Frederick, "The Next Development in Management Science: A General Theory," *Academy of Management Journal*, Vol. 6, No. 3 (September, 1963), p. 212. The discussion that follows is based on the five major components of a general theory of management as described by Professor Frederick.

[24] A similar point of view has been expressed by Professor William T. Greenwood who notes that there are eleven existing management theory concepts that can be reduced to four concurrently and sequentially developing ones. He also states that the evolutionary developments in management theory indicate that a future "general theory" probably can result from an analysis and synthesis within the present decade by utilizing the management process theory as a comparative base. William T. Greenwood, "Future Management Theory: A 'Comparative' Evolution to a General Theory," *Academy of Management Journal*, Vol. 17, No. 3 (September, 1974), p. 503.

[25] In Chapter 8 a contingency theory developed by Luthans and Stewart is discussed. Fred Luthans and Todd Stewart, "A General Contingency Theory of Management," *The Academy of Management Review*, Vol. 2, No. 2 (April, 1977).

In Case Problem 2-B, a modern counterpart of making pins by hand is described. The solution of the decision to be made by this management relies not only on the work of Charles Babbage but on the fundamental concepts developed by Taylor, Fayol, and Mayo.

Case Problem 2-B
ELIMINATING AN ASSEMBLY LINE

Plasco, Inc., is a company that molds and manufactures plastic products. Some of the molded parts are sold to other firms for use in their finished products; however, the company also manufactures and distributes several completed products that require the assembly of molded parts as well as the molding process itself. One such product is a hand-actuated lever-type pump spray used with window cleaners, detergents, and similar products normally packaged in a plastic bottle that is also produced by Plasco.

The lever-type pump consists of 15 plastic parts, a steel pin to hold the lever in place, and a plastic hose which extends into the container holding the liquid to be sprayed. Present production methods utilize an assembly line operating two shifts to assemble the product. There are five workers (semiskilled) engaged in the assembly of subassemblies. The final assembly line consists of 20 to 25 workers, depending on attendance, who are seated on either side of a moving assembly conveyor belt. One inspector is assigned to each shift. There is also a supervisor who oversees the assembly operation and performs coordinative functions with the molding department to assure that the necessary parts for the product are available for the assembly area. The total annual cost of the assembly operation for direct wages and fringe benefits for both shifts is approximately $300,000 a year.

Recently the president of Plasco has had several discussions with a designer and builder of special machinery. The engineering design company has built several similar products and has presented a firm offer to Plasco to build a machine that will perform all subassemblies and final assemblies. The price of the machine installed is $300,000. Plasco estimates that the payback period for the machine will be approximately one year since it equals the annual amount spent for total wages for the manual assembly operation.

The manufacturer of the proposed machine has indicated that there is need for at least two highly skilled mechanics, one for each shift, to be trained by the manufacturer in order to maintain the equipment. Further, a high degree of uniformity of component parts is required since nonstandard parts are automatically rejected. However, such parts are not necessarily scrapped since a rework department of four or five employees may be established to salvage an estimated 75 percent of the rejections by means of hand assembly. It is expected that the two inspectors and approximately 60 subassemblers and final assembly employees will be eliminated. For each shift, two operators, in all probability former assembly-line employees, are required to fill the hoppers at each station so that continuous production may be maintained. Maintenance costs on the new equipment are expected to be minimal though slightly higher than the maintenance costs of the present assembly line; however, these costs should be offset in part because of the reduced number of defective assemblies. No significant change in total units assembled per shift is anticipated.

It is expected that approximately six to eight months' production experience may be required before all minor difficulties normally encountered with complex automatic equipment that performs humanlike motions are eliminated. Even so, it is estimated that the payback period, based on savings in wages, will range between the 12 months suggested by the manufacturer of the automatic assembler and a maximum of 18 months assuming the greatest number of problems.

PROBLEMS

1. Which of the questions raised by Charles Babbage are applicable to the situation described above?
2. Answer each of Babbage's five questions.
3. What are the social implications of displacing approximately 55 to 60 workers? Is your answer dependent on the level of unemployment in the area?
4. To what extent do the principles of Taylor and Fayol and the observations of Mayo contribute to the decision to be made by the Plasco management?

CHAPTER QUESTIONS FOR STUDY AND DISCUSSION

1. What basic management concepts are illustrated in the biblical passage concerning Moses and Jethro?
2. What advantages did Babbage see in the division of labor on the basis of skill?
3. Scientific management principles were developed to solve what two major problems? In what way or ways did Elton Mayo's approach to solving these problems differ from that of Frederick Taylor?
4. What was the initial purpose of Mayo's Hawthorne Studies? What areas or problems did the studies later consider? Briefly discuss the phenomenon known as the Hawthorne Effect.
5. What major conclusions can be drawn from the work of Owen and Mayo?
6. In what respect does Fayol's concept of the division of work differ from Babbage's concept in "On the Division of Labour"?
7. Why is it unsound for a manager to approach an organization with a divide-and-conquer philosophy?
8. Differentiate between Fayol's principles of unity of command and unity of direction.
9. Is there *one best way* in the application of the management process in view of modern organization theory? Explain.
10. What is the meaning of the term *centralization* according to Fayol?
11. What six major schools of management are described by Professor Koontz in his article, "The Management Theory Jungle"?

Chapter 3

Ethical and Social Responsibilities of Management

Case Problem 3-A
THE OIL ENTERPRISES AUDIT

Nancy Sherman was an outstanding student. During her senior year in college she had several opportunities to go to work for one of the big eight accounting firms. She finally accepted a generous offer from a smaller firm, Seemore, Brown, Leonard, and Fisk, whose main offices are located in Houston. She was particularly impressed with the friendliness of the firm's top management and the climate of warmth and mutual support within the organization.

During her first year of employment, Sherman passed the CPA exams and worked on a number of small company audits as a junior member of an audit team. She enjoyed her work and respected her colleagues. At no time did she have occasion to question the ethics or technical judgment of the firm's partners or the auditors with whom she worked. The ethical code of the American Institute of Certified Public Accountants seemed adequate as a guide to conduct, and no business situation arose that presented problems of conscience for Sherman.

About the middle of her second year, Sherman was assigned to a team that audited the books of Oil Enterprises Equipment Company, a firm whose primary business was renovation and sale of oil field equipment (mostly for drilling, well servicing, and pumping). Oil Enterprises, one of the accounting firm's first clients, had been with the firm since 1950. Oil Enterprises was virtually a backyard operation at that time, but it grew rapidly. In 1967 it went public in order to raise capital for expansion; and, after the Arab oil embargo, it made a secondary stock issue. In 1979 company sales, many overseas, were in excess of $200 million. Profits were high. Continued prosperity seemed inevitable.

The president and founder of Oil Enterprises, William O. Hasketts, was an engineer whose primary interest was in the equipment renovation end of the business. Soon after the company was founded, responsibility for sales was assigned to Charles Arnold, who later became vice-president for sales. Because of the nature and magnitude of some of the sales, Arnold was intimately involved in daily sales activities. He therefore took frequent trips overseas, especially to the Middle East where large sales often took place.

Because much overseas travel was necessary, high sales expenses were expected. One particular expense item, however, attracted Sherman's attention. That was payment to a Pierre LeBlanc, a French consultant. Sherman's immediate superior and manager of the audit, Helene Shipley, explained that LeBlanc had, for a number of years, been employed by Oil Enterprises because of his contacts in the Middle East. He had been able to locate used equipment and find markets for new and renovated equipment when everyone else within the company failed. He was a personal acquaintance of members of the royal Arabian families, and he knew the languages and customs of the people in the Middle East oil-exporting countries.

Sherman was concerned about the lack of records relating to LeBlanc's activities and about his unusually high fees. He was neither an executive nor a commissioned sales representative and was not considered a full-time consultant with the company, yet for the fiscal year he had been paid $600,000.

Shipley was not concerned about the matter. "LeBlanc is a consultant," Shipley explained. "He makes contacts, introduces company sales representatives to the right people, and provides information. He bills the company, and they pay without asking questions because they believe he's worth it. So what's the problem?"

Nancy Sherman was not satisfied. All the publicity about bribes to foreign business and government leaders and kickbacks to company executives suggested too many possibilities about how the money may have been used. Against Shipley's advice, Sherman brought the matter to the attention of the sales vice-president, Charles Arnold. Arnold was evasive and noticeably irritated. He definitely did not want to discuss the matter. His only comments were, "LeBlanc is a high-priced consultant, but he gets results. He's worth what we pay him and more. I had a consultant in the office last week who charged only $2,500 for five days, and he wasted our time. It is not what a consultant charges that's important. It's results that count, and LeBlanc gets results. Anyway, expenses are high in that part of the world, and this is big business."

As the audit continued, Sherman became more frustrated about the $600,000 consulting fee. She believed that it was an extraordinarily large sum to be treated so lightly and thought that LeBlanc should account for his expenses and that the stockholders should be aware of the large expenditure. Her refusal to drop the matter deeply irritated Shipley; and when she casually mentioned it to one of the partners in the auditing firm, Shipley became so enraged that she threatened to transfer Sherman to another audit team. "Why can't you just accept my judgment on this?" she growled. "I wouldn't be in charge of this audit if I didn't know my business. You're not the only one around here with a conscience. Don't get the idea that you have to be the guardian of our ethics. If you can't be a little flexible, you can't make it in the real world." Shipley had discussed the LeBlanc expenses with the major auditing partners, and they agreed with her.

Sherman wondered how often she would be expected to keep quiet when she really believed she should speak out. Was her own firm accepting Oil Enterprises' view of the situation just to keep peace with a client? Was she being foolishly suspicious, overly conscientious, and naive? Under what conditions should she take a strong stand—one that might cost her her job or require that she blow the whistle on her own employer to a government agency or to the American Institute of Certified Public Accountants?

PROBLEMS

1. What ethical issues are involved?
2. To what extent should Sherman heed her own conscience in the matter rather than go along with the behavior of those around her?
3. If Nancy Sherman is not absolutely certain that something unethical or irresponsible is going on, does she have a responsibility to Oil Enterprises not to do

or say anything that may hurt its relations with shareholders, customers, and the public?

4. What do you think of employees who expose what they believe to be an unethical practice? What are the ethical implications of damaging an employer by blow-ing the whistle when it is ultimately found that the employer was in the right and the employee's conscience was a faulty guide to ethical behavior?

5. Arnold said, "It's results that count." Some people who say this mean that the ends justify the means. Evaluate.

The human relations movement that began in the 1930's introduced a humanizing element into management theory and practice. It was a turn away from regarding employees solely as articles of commerce and a turn toward acknowledging their intrinsic value. During the 1950's, the national conscience was further sensitized by a growing awareness of social problems, especially concerning discrimination and the effects of poverty. This led in the 1960's and 1970's to a spate of legislation expressing concern for individual rights and the public good. This legislation and the public sentiment that inspired it destroyed the notion that private business is free to pursue selfish objectives without concern for their impact on society.

THE VALUE JUDGMENTS OF MANAGERS

The value judgments of managers are no longer considered peripheral to organizational purpose and effectiveness. There was a time, not long ago, when the ethical concerns of managers for employee safety were something of an academic matter. This, however, is no longer the case, as is shown by such legislation as the Occupational Safety and Health Act (1970), which made employee safety and health a critical issue to companies and to their managers as individuals. Whether employees have rights to privacy or rights to information is no longer a matter of speculation. These rights and many others are expressed in statutory law and numerous court decisions. Making false claims in advertising and lending, selling products that are dangerous, paying women less than men who do the same work, dumping plant refuse into streams, and discrimination in the employment of minorities are not only ethical issues but are also serious legal issues.

Virtually every aspect of management and organizational life involves values—questions concerning right and wrong, or decisions to which there are no unequivocal answers because people are committed to greatly differing value systems. As a result, the subject of business ethics and social responsibility has become important to all managers and has become a critical aspect of managerial education. Obviously, however, managers make many decisions that are not directly related to ethical judgments, such as whether to increase inventory levels or which machine to use in order to make a certain product. Nevertheless, no manager can for long avoid ethical decisions.

The Current Emphasis on Ethics

A number of interrelated events contributed to the current emphasis on ethics in business, government, and other organizations. For example, the Civil Rights Act of 1964, a landmark legislation for business ethics, reflected a growing sentiment that discrimination against minority groups is morally wrong and dangerous to society. Moreover, the Kennedy and Johnson administrations created high expectations of a new era of social justice, equality of opportunity, removal of urban blight, and even the elimination of poverty. Whatever progress may have been made, these aspirations proved to be highly idealistic. They could not be achieved overnight. Thus, people who had been given hope became disillusioned; they reacted with political activism and overt expressions of frustration and resentment, such as riots and aggressive demonstrations.

The general unrest of the 1960's, some of which was associated with attitudes toward the Vietnam War, served to rush the passage of social legislation and to focus public attention on a diversity of nationwide problems such as crime, inflation, environmental pollution, and corruption in business and government. Since society has increasingly looked to government for solutions to its problems, it was predictable that laws would proliferate in response to every social evil. According to pollsters, public trust in business had reached an all-time low by the mid-1970's. The Watergate scandal set the mood for investigative news reporting, and business managers provided excellent grist for that mill. Illegal campaign contributions were admitted by many of the nation's most respected corporations. Bribes to foreign companies and government officials were exposed; and when these events were seen alongside such glaringly unethical practices as Korean payoffs to members of the United States Congress, many people concluded that business managers in general were corrupt. Most were not and are not, but the message is nevertheless clear: Business must put its house in order or increasingly lose control of its own destiny.

The Meaning of Ethics and Social Responsibility

The terms *ethics* and *social responsibility* refer to value-oriented decisions and behavior. The word *ethics* comes from the Greek root, *ēthos*, meaning character; guiding beliefs, standards, or ideals that pervade a group, a community, a people. . . . Today *ethics* is the study of moral behavior—the study of how the standards of moral conduct among individuals are established and expressed behaviorally. Terms such as *business ethics, corporate ethics, medical ethics,* or *legal ethics* are used to indicate the particular area of application. But to have meaning, the ethics involved in each area must still refer to the value-oriented decisions and behavior of individuals.

Social responsibility is a relatively new term. It is the moral conduct that relates to such broad issues as environmental pollution, discrimination, poverty, unemployment, and inflation. Accordingly, an organization whose practices contribute to inflation, unemployment, increased poverty of minority groups, and the like would be viewed as socially irresponsible—as not fulfilling its responsibility to society. An automobile manufacturer who produces cars with faulty brakes, a pharmaceutical house that makes false claims about its cold remedies, or the food company whose TV ads mesmerize young children into compulsively eating its nutritionally deficient cereals are socially irresponsible.

There is a tendency to think of social responsibility in terms of organizations and to think of ethics in terms of individuals, but this is not a useful distinction. In the final analysis, decisions are made by people and, therefore, individual managers at some level must assume responsibility for every corporate decision. The executive who lies about a competitor's product, the manufacturer who markets a highly flammable article of clothing, the industrialist who dumps pollutants into a stream—all behave in an ethically irresponsible way. The most meaningful way to distinguish business ethics from social responsibility is in terms of a decision's implications for society as a whole. Within this frame of reference, business ethics are concerned with *microethics* (relating to daily operating decisions with limited social impact); social responsibility is concerned with *macroethics* (relating to decisions with broad implications for a large segment of society).[1] Even this distinction is hard to maintain consistently. For convenience in communication, the term *business ethics* is sometimes used in the broad sense to include both microethics and macroethics as expressed in profit-making organizations.

VIEWS OF SOCIAL RESPONSIBILITY

The differing views of social responsibility that influence managerial behavior reflect a vast array of values, perceptions, attitudes, needs, and experiences. Since they reflect the social, religious, and political philosophies of their authors, it would be realistic—but totally impracticable—to describe many viewpoints which differ from one another by small degrees. For practical purposes, however, scholars typically describe three views of social responsibility: (1) the classical view, (2) the accountability view, and (3) the public view.

The Classical View

The classical view of corporate social responsibility prevailed during the nineteenth and early twentieth centuries. Although it is far from dead today, it has fewer advocates, and virtually everyone recognizes that in its original form it had serious flaws. At the heart of the classical view is Adam Smith's belief that in a capitalistic, free-enterprise economy an "invisible hand" is continually at work for the good of the public.[2] From this perspective, to form concepts of social responsibility in terms of an objective set of ethical standards or intensity of commitment to the welfare of others makes no sense. It is the invisible hand—the competitive system itself—that protects society.

---

[1] Donald G. Jones, *A Bibliography of Business Ethics, 1971–1975* (Charlottesville, Va.: The University Press of Virginia, 1977), p. xii.

[2] Adam Smith, *An Inquiry into the Nature and Causes of the Wealth of Nations* (New York City: Modern Library, 1937), p. 423.

The Values of Capitalism. The values of capitalism originate in the belief that, when a business selfishly pursues its profit objective while competing with other businesses, the system forces it to be efficient and to produce the best possible product at the lowest possible price. Competition further demands that businesses produce what people need and that they deal fairly and honestly with the public. To do otherwise results in a loss of customers to competing companies. Competition for labor and the need for a good public image require companies to be fair in dealing with their employees, and free competition for jobs encourages employees to be efficient and productive.

An example of the positive effects of competition appears in the automobile industry, where foreign and domestic companies compete for a larger share of the market through innovative design, improved quality, and lower pricing. Competition forces manufacturers to introduce computerized ignition, fuel injection, front-wheel drive, and dozens of other improvements at prices that are acceptable to the public. The profit motive and competition compel companies to pay attention to the public's needs where presumably unselfish concern for the public good does not. These movements of the invisible hand result in economic growth, more jobs, better products—more wealth for everybody.

The classical position concerning business investments in social programs is well expressed by economist Milton Friedman, its most prominent spokesman of this decade.

> In a free-enterprise, private-property system, a corporate executive is an employee of the owners of the business. He has direct responsibility to his employers. That responsibility is to conduct the business in accord with their desires, which generally will be to make as much money as possible while conforming to the basic rules of society. . . . Insofar as his actions in accord with his social responsibility reduce returns to stockholders, he is spending their money. Insofar as his actions raise the price to customers, he is spending the customer's money. Insofar as his actions lower the wages of some employees, he is spending their money.[3]

This position reflects Friedman's deep commitment to a philosophy with far-reaching implications. One important implication is the belief that society is best served when it interferes least with the complex operations of a free, competitive economy. This is not a valueless viewpoint.

Problems with the Classical View. Critics of the classical view believe that for all its benefits, the system is basically amoral—that its impersonality leaves no place for the expression of values such as love, mercy, compassion, concern for the individual, and deep commitment to codes of personal ethics. Even if the invisible hand serves the public well in the long run, in the short run many people are hurt.

If allowed to operate without constraints, free competition will destroy itself and result in monopoly. As early as the nineteenth century, beginning with

---

[3] Milton Friedman, "Does Business Have a Social Responsibility?" *Bank Administration*, April, 1971, p. 13. Also see Milton Friedman, *Capitalism and Freedom* (Chicago: University of Chicago Press, 1962).

the Interstate Commerce Act in 1887, it was obvious that unrestrained trade was not in the public interest. Since that time the public has realized the need to exercise an ever-increasing amount of control over business. Antitrust laws encourage competition and other laws protect various segments of society from the ravages of unrestrained competition. These laws are intended to protect society from the freedom of business to pursue immediate self-interest without concern for its immediate and long-term effect on the physical environment, consumers, labor, the general economy, and other aspects of the business environment.

Critics of the classical view believe that the question of whether or not free competition works for the public good is really immaterial since it exists only in theory. The influences of power blocks, such as labor unions and suppliers of capital, raw materials, and energy, severely disrupt the functioning of a free-market system. It is probably hampered most, however, by eight decades of restrictive legislation and bureaucratic regulations.

Modern advocates of the classical view recognize that the clock cannot be turned back. Consequently, they concern themselves primarily with preventing a total collapse of the private enterprise system—a system for which they see no substitute as protector of the public interest. The following statement by Mayo J. Thompson, Commissioner of the Federal Trade Commission, reflects this sentiment:

> I don't claim that our economic system is letter perfect. We do have some monopolies in America. We do have false advertising and other unethical business practices. But these things are cancers on a free-market economy, not an inherent part of it. There is a moral case against a free market as such. Any economics student in a good university can demonstrate that, under free and open competition, product quality will be maximized, price will be minimized, and the personal freedom of every member of society—business, labor, and consumers—will be as high as is attainable in any imaginable social arrangement.[4]

Joseph McGuire points out that capitalism is an open system that rewards individuals on the basis of merit and thereby encourages initiative and productivity.[5] To refuse to employ members of a minority group, to allow bias to influence promotion decisions, to provide an unsafe workplace, or to deceive consumers is inconsistent with capitalistic ideology. Such actions are not in the self-interest of business. Progress, however, toward perfecting capitalism has been and will be made in such areas. Thus, the delicate task of the master planners is to continue to perfect the system without destroying it.

The Accountability View

A small step removed from the contemporary version of the classical view is the accountability view of social responsibility. The accountability view recog-

---

[4] Mayo J. Thompson, "Free Enterprise and Free Men," *Financial Executive,* Vol. 42, No. 6 (July, 1974), p. 29.

[5] Joseph W. McGuire, "Perfecting Capitalism—An Economic Dilemma," *Business Horizons,* Vol. 19, No. 1 (February, 1976), p. 10.

nizes the virtues of a free market and seeks to preserve them. On the other hand, it accepts the fact that business is chartered by society and should therefore be accountable to it. Business should not only fulfill its responsibility to its stockholders but should also deal equitably with others upon whom its success is dependent. These include employees, customers, suppliers, creditors, and the community and larger economy in which the business functions.

The accountability view encourages employers to spend whatever money is required to prevent such evils as water and air pollution. This is one cost of doing business and is an obligation to society. A business should not create social problems by discriminating against minorities, by setting inflationary prices, or by paying low wages. It should not offend the aesthetic values of society by defacing the landscape nor be unfair to present and future generations by wasting fuel. Simply put, the accountability view of social responsibility is that each business should pay its own way and treat each of its publics with fairness and consideration.

Corporate investments that compensate for past abuses and elevate business to a fully responsible position have been substantial. Dow Chemical, for example, invested $20 million in pollution control equipment during a single year, $6 million of which was offset through reduced corrosion of cooling towers and through the recovery of chemicals that would have been wasted.

The Public View

The *public view* of social responsibility, also called the *quality of life view*,[6] goes beyond mere accountability and portrays business as a partner with government, education, and other institutions in solving society's problems and thereby improving the quality of life for everyone. One goal of business is to make a profit, but business is not free to pursue only selfish goals. A business which is committed to the public view sets genuinely altruistic as well as selfish goals. It actively works at solving public problems, such as poverty, unemployment, pollution, inflation, and crime.

The public view differs from the accountability view in that the obligation of business goes beyond paying its own way. Because society has given business the right to function and has provided an environment favorable to profit making, business is a servant of the public and is not private in the classical sense. Therefore, the public has a right and an obligation to control business for the public good. "Where the public interest . . . is at issue, there is no natural right to be left alone." [7]

Investment in Social Programs. Putting into practice the public view of social responsibility, many businesses contribute to United Fund drives and to

---

[6] Robert D. Hay, Edmond R. Gray, and Jessie E. Gates (eds.), *Business and Society* (Cincinnati: South-Western Publishing Co., 1976), p. 9.

[7] John K. Galbraith, "On the Economic Image of Corporate Enterprise," *Corporate Power in America*, edited by Ralph Nader and Mark Green (New York City: Grossman Publishers, 1973), p. 7.

specific charitable causes with which organizational members are identified. Tenneco, for example, matches the gifts of its personnel to nonprofit organizations. Other large corporations with records of generous giving and direct contributions to social programs are Eli Lilly & Co., Coca-Cola, Xerox, Chase Manhattan Bank, and IBM.

The types of social programs in which corporations engage vary greatly. One contributes to an educational institution, finances research, or sponsors a minority business; while another provides scholarships for needy students or supports athletic programs in high-crime areas. In 1968 IBM located a new plant in the Bedford-Stuyvesant neighborhood of Brooklyn, a decision that was influenced by a desire to provide jobs in an economically depressed area with one of the highest unemployment rates in the United States. Although the results were financially disastrous at first, the plant became profitable in 1970. The typical amount contributed to such programs is small when compared with the total profits of the corporation. In one notable exception, the Boise Cascade Corporation's promotion of a minority enterprise in the heavy construction industry resulted in a pretax loss of about $40 million and a significant drop in the price of its stock.[8] When this happens, one has to question whether management is fulfilling its responsibility to the stockholders.

Arguments for the Public View. The primary argument for the public view is that private business is sanctioned and promoted by society for the good of society and, therefore, it has a moral obligation to society. Galbraith goes one step further with his contention that business is no longer private, that corporations are essentially public entities.[9] Other arguments for the public view are more pragmatic. Supporting the public view may be one way for business to avoid ever-increasing government controls; and, to the extent that the public view provides a solution to society's ills, the long-term interests of business will be served.

Arguments against the Public View. In opposition to the public view is the belief that the efficiency of business and the subsequent benefit to all members of society lie in a limited business objective—in a commitment to profit. The introduction of social goals clashes with the traditional orientation of managers toward efficiency, competitiveness, and profit. One may argue that the traditional contributions of business are sufficient in themselves to justify the place of business in society—assuming that it pays its way as advocated by the accountability view.

Managers differ greatly in their reaction to the public view. In one survey of over 180 executives, more than half expressed the belief that business should help solve social problems, regardless of who or what created them.[10] Although current research data are unavailable to support or negate such a contention,

---

[8] Robert D. Hay, Edmund R. Gray, and Jessie E. Gates (eds.), *Business and Society* (Cincinnati: South-Western Publishing Co., 1976), p. 14.

[9] *Ibid.*, p. 7.

[10] Sandra L. Holmes, "Executive Perceptions of Corporate Social Responsibility," *Business Horizons*, Vol. 19, No. 3 (June, 1976), p. 36.

it is reasonable to suspect that managers of companies that have few problems at the accountability level (e.g., IBM and Coca-Cola) will be more favorably inclined toward an altruistic viewpoint than will managers of companies that have difficulty meeting minimum requirements (e.g., Exxon, Dow Chemical, and U. S. Steel).

The Costs of Social Responsibility

The costs to society of irresponsible managerial actions are often unacceptably high. Not so obvious, however, is the fact that society also pays when business begins to set its house in order. The expenditure of billions of dollars for pollution control, whether for plant filter systems, auto emission controls, or no-lead gasoline, must be absorbed by the consumer. The same applies to auto safety devices, such as airbags and impact-absorbing bumpers. These outlays result in less cash for other essentials and luxuries to which people have become accustomed. As companies assume additional responsibility for the welfare of their employees by providing full coverage health insurance or guaranteed annual wages to an already massive employee benefit program, the costs must be passed on.

Society in general must bear the brunt of business expenditures associated with the social responsibility issue. Everyone pays when wage increases become inflationary and investment in pollution abatement is substituted for plant expansion which would produce new jobs. The social costs are enormous when the investments companies make, in order to be socially responsible, reduce their ability to compete internationally, thereby causing unemployment and a balance-of-payments problem. The closing of steel plants in the 1970's is a good example of how efforts to solve one problem may cause another. Because of foreign competition, these companies simply could not afford to modernize in order to meet the government's antipollution requirements.

Since coal companies that do strip mining cannot totally restore the land to its original form, severe restrictions have been placed on this practice. This calls for a trade-off between preserving the beauty of the landscape and paying higher prices for fuel. A similar price is paid for restrictions on the development of offshore oil reserves and on the building of dams where the backwater interferes with wildlife.

Primarily through the actions of government, society reflects its values and priorities. Legislators and government officials make judgments, strongly influenced by their personal values and political considerations, about whether the price society must pay is offset by the benefits received. Since individual values and needs differ, there are no universally acceptable solutions to society's ills, and managers often disagree with the conclusions that legislators draw.

DETERMINANTS OF ETHICAL STANDARDS AND PRACTICES

The microethics that influence daily decisions have received less attention in the news media than macroethics issues. However, it is in the small, day-to-day decisions that managers most often express their ethical values. Seemingly insignificant decisions that are routinely made by individual managers affect all members of society who interact with business. Collectively these decisions comprise the conscience and moral behavior of the enterprise. The major social responsibility decisions a company makes are usually consistent with the values expressed in its management's daily operating decisions.

Since the values of managers differ greatly, it is understandable that managers disagree about whether a particular course of action is ethical. When questioned, they often mention actions intended to buy loyalty for the company and its products as one practice that should be eliminated. These actions include giving gifts, providing lavish entertainment, and offering outright bribes. Managers also consider certain forms of price discrimination as unethical. Other practices with unethical implications include misleading advertising, cheating customers, unfair credit practices, overselling, failure to live up to contracts, and prejudice in hiring and promoting. Specific practices are, of course, viewed differently by different people. Is it dishonest, for example, to have a celebrity talk about "my soap" or "my beer" in a TV commercial? Some people think it is. How many Wheaties must Bruce Jenner have eaten to be able ethically to promote them on TV? Must Wheaties really have contributed to his winning the Olympics decathlon gold medal? Does a customer have the right to expect that a new automobile will have zero defects, or is it enough that the defects be corrected under the warranty? Many different criteria are used to make ethical judgments. We look now at some of the more common ones.

Common Practice

Everybody does it is a common justification for questionable business practices. This justification usually rests on a belief that failure to engage in a certain practice—be it bribery, espionage, or paying slave wages—is to place oneself at a competitive disadvantage and thereby to court financial disaster. Reliance upon common practice as a behavior guide is a pragmatic or instrumental, essentially amoral basis for ethical behavior. Since it has no foundation in an absolute system of values, it often leads to unacceptable behavior and to external controls.

Legality

When managers behave in ways that society considers detrimental, laws are passed to reflect the values of society and to define correct or ethical behavior. At present there are innumerable statutory laws, far-reaching court decisions, and countless government regulations defining right and wrong in virtually every area of business life.

The seemingly endless catalog of laws and regulations has led some managers to accept the logic that if it's legal it's right. Laws do change behavior, and at times the higher standards are internalized (accepted as part of the managers' value system). But laws also provoke hostility, especially when managers do not really believe in the law and, therefore, feel no moral compunction about breaking it.

Although the law does influence behavior in significant ways, it is no substitute for moral character and personal integrity. One problem with reliance upon the law as a basis for ethics is that

> . . . a good part of the laws passed are not meant to be implemented, at least not systematically and effectively. Passing laws is part of the make-believe or theatre of politics, in which politicians try to placate two (or more) opposing camps. They give one faction the law (saying, in effect, "You see, I took care of it") while the other faction more or less retains the freedom to pursue activities which violate the law.[11]

This purposeful ambiguity of the law leads in many cases to deliberate lawbreaking on the assumptions that (1) one may not get caught, (2) one may not be convicted, and (3) if one is caught and convicted, the financial gains will more than offset the losses.

There are, of course, many laws that are not ambiguous. The Occupational Safety and Health Act of 1970 is a law that is clear in its intent and harsh in dealing with offenders. It has definitely changed behavior even though it has elicited resentment and charges of unfairness to business. There is a current trend toward surer and stiffer penalties for corporate officials who fail to comply with federal regulations or who otherwise do wrong. The increasing risk of criminal prosecution expresses a determination on the part of the public and the government to make business more accountable through its officers.[12]

Enlightened Self-Interest

Questionnaire responses from 144 major corporation executives showed enlightened self-interest to be the most important motive for social performance in the areas of urban, consumer, and environmental affairs.[13] Such motivation undoubtedly influences ethical decisions of every variety. There is a distinction, however, between the belief that it pays to be ethical in relating to others and the belief that the payoff provides a basis for ethical standards. It is helpful for managers to recognize that unethical behaviors are detrimental to business— that in the long run, at least, they lose customers, provoke costly lawsuits, and result in government penalties. It is amoral, however, to behave ethically only because it pays.

Enlightened self-interest, also called *intelligent selfishness*, is sometimes used as the public justification for ethical behavior that is motivated, in part at least, by a manager's personal system of religious or social values. Justifying a decision

---

[11] Amitai Etzioni, "There Oughta Be a Law—or Should There Be?" *Business and Society Review/Innovation*, No. 8 (Winter, 1973–74), p. 10.

[12] Tony McAdams and Robert C. Miljus, "Growing Criminal Liability of Executives," *Harvard Business Review*, Vol. 55, No. 2 (March–April, 1977), p. 35.

[13] Vernon M. Buehler and Y. K. Shetty, "Motivations for Corporate Social Action," *Academy of Management Journal*, Vol. 17, No. 1 (December, 1974), p. 769.

in terms of enlightened self-interest sounds more businesslike to persons who do not share a manager's personal value system. It takes little moral sensitivity to recognize that *unselfish* behavior is often in one's own *self-interest*. The need of highly moral people for self-respect often results in unselfish behavior—in behavior that is not calculated to bring an external return or payoff. Their payoff is internal; it is expressed in the satisfaction of being a good person as judged by one's own values. These considerations show how complex the motivation of enlightened self-interest can be. Enlightened self-interest does not, however, provide a basis for deciding between right and wrong. It is only a motivation for behavior perceived to be right or expedient.

Codes of Ethics

There is a need for objective standards, other than laws and government regulations, to help managers make ethical decisions.[14] When dependent solely on the subjective standards of individual managers, ethical decisions are unpredictable and subject to all forms of perceptual, defensive, and self-serving bias.

Most professions have dealt with the need for objective standards by developing codes of ethics by which their members are expected to live. Notable among these are the ethical codes of physicians, psychologists, lawyers, and certified public accountants. A number of private corporations have also developed such codes for use by their own personnel. IBM, for example, publishes its code in an 84-page booklet, *Business Conduct Guidelines*. All managers must review this code annually and then certify in writing that they understand it.

Ethical codes may exert significant influence over the persons to whom they apply, whether or not those persons agree fully with them, because of the penalties involved in noncompliance. An IBM executive knows that failure to comply can lead to dismissal, and professionals are aware of the seriousness of losing their license to practice. Nevertheless, ethical codes are relatively ineffective with persons of questionable moral character. The most publicized example of the failure of professionals to live by their own code is the Watergate scandal, which resulted in more than 100 lawyers being cited for disciplinary action by their state bar associations.[15]

In recent years Certified Public Accountants (CPAs) have received heavy criticism for their alleged failure to disclose the illegal or unethical practices of their clients. A number of lawsuits have been filed involving members of the nation's most respected accounting firms.[16] The major ethical problem appears to revolve around the fact that CPAs are expected to protect the interests of investors but are being paid by corporate executives whose activities they are expected to audit. With every new disclosure of corporate misdeeds, the

---

[14] Paul L. Wilkins, "The Case for Ethical Absolutes in Business," *Business and Society Review*, No. 13 (Spring, 1975), p. 61.

[15] Thomas B. Mechling, "The Mythical Ethics of Law, PR, and Accounting," *Business and Society Review*, No. 20 (Winter, 1976–77), p. 6.

[16] "Accountants Cleaning up America's Mystery Profession," *U. S. News & World Report*, December 19, 1977, p. 39.

importance of CPAs to the public is underscored, and their ethics are called into question. Although the hundreds of lawsuits brought against accountants by stockholders and government agencies reflect an eroding public image, there is no conclusive evidence at this time that most CPAs have been unfaithful to their public trust.

Personal Morality

There are many determinants of the ethical standards and practices of managers, but no single determinant is sufficient to protect individuals and society from the consequences of unethical behavior. The one determinant most likely to lead to ethical behavior is high personal standards of conduct—individual commitment to values that respect human rights and dignity. Managers with personal integrity and moral sensitivity are capable of the understanding and motivation required to benefit from codes of ethics and legal statements of socially responsible conduct. Managers who are deficient in these qualities can be expected to behave unethically in spite of external constraints.

Managers comprise just one segment of a larger society that may be suffering from an erosion of moral convictions.[17] In recent years a breakdown in the ethics of government officials (or an increase in public awareness of this breakdown) has focused attention on the ethical behavior of leadership in all organizations. This coincides with what is often labeled a *new morality* in society in general—a rejection of traditional Judeo-Christian values with nothing substantial taking their place.

VALUE SYSTEMS OF MANAGERS

Authors of articles and books dealing with values are not consistent in the way they define the term.[18] As used here, *personal values* refer to the relatively stable beliefs and ideals which determine how an individual perceives and judges the worth of the people, behaviors, objects, ideas, and other aspects of his or her environment. Values are of practical significance because of their influence on decisions and behavior. They serve as subjective criteria for judging right and wrong conduct, success and failure in life, worthwhile and useless goals, and for making other uniquely personal decisions.

The Concept of Value Systems

A person's values tend to form more or less homogeneous clusters referred to as *value systems*. For example, the individual who holds specific interlocking beliefs and their accompanying feelings—together referred to as *attitudes*—

---

[17] Mary S. Miller and A. Edward Miller, "It's Too Late for Ethics Courses in Business Schools," *Business and Society Review*, No. 17 (Spring, 1976), p. 39.

[18] Several definitions and extensive references may be found in Patrick Ed Connor and Boris W. Becker, "Values and the Organization: Suggestions for Research," *Academy of Management Journal*, Vol. 18, No. 3 (September, 1975), p. 550.

against unbalanced budgets, deficit spending, and artificial market controls is said to have a value system of economic conservatism. That same person may also hold a complex system of religious values that could either be relatively independent of or closely integrated with the economic system. Although most people experience a compulsion to integrate their various value systems or clusters into one general system, some have a remarkable capacity to keep them separated. In such cases one's religious beliefs, for example, may have very little influence on work-related behavior.

The Value Profile

Although research on the values of managers continues, the landmark study was published by George W. England in 1967.[19] This study was duplicated by Lusk and Oliver in 1972 with similar results, showing that the values of managers are relatively stable over time.[20] Subsequent studies, using different experimental designs, do not negate England's general findings.[21] There are, of course, many individual differences among managers. Yet, as a group, there is a striking similarity among managers with respect to family origins, sex, race, religion, politics, educational background, and age.[22] This suggests that their values may also be relatively homogeneous.

Figure 3–1 shows the values of managers according to England's research. The 29 *operative values* of high importance are perceived as being related to success and should, therefore, have maximum influence on managerial behavior. It is noteworthy that high productivity and profit are among the most valued aspects of the work environment. In light of the purpose for which managers are employed, this should be expected. These are closely followed by employees, customers, and co-workers, thereby reflecting the fact that people, as well as task-oriented variables, are highly valued.

The nine values in the *Adopted Values—Situationally Induced* category are recognized as an essential part of organizational life, but managers find it difficult to internalize these and see them as having little intrinsic worth. Labor unions, for example, must be dealt with; but managers do not value them as they do employees and customers.

The ten factors in the *Intended Values—Socio-culturally Induced* category are considered highly important throughout the managers' lives but are not viewed as directly related to managerial success. To illustrate, religion and employee welfare (as contrasted with employees) are important values to managers but are not primary determinants of organizational success.

---

[19] George W. England, "Personal Value Systems of American Managers," *Academy of Management Journal*, Vol. 10, No. 1 (March, 1967), p. 53.

[20] Edward J. Lusk and Bruce L. Oliver, "American Managers' Personal Value Systems—Revisited," *Academy of Management Journal*, Vol. 17, No. 3 (September, 1974), p. 549.

[21] Avery Comarow, "When Conscience and Career Collide," *Money*, September, 1976, p. 48; John C. Watson and Sam Barone, "The Self-Concept, Personal Values, and Motivational Orientations of Black and White Managers," *Academy of Management Journal*, Vol. 19, No. 1 (March, 1976), p. 36.

[22] Frederick D. Sturdivant and Roy D. Adler, "Executive Origins: Still a Gray Flannel World?" *Harvard Business Review*, Vol. 54, No. 6 (November–December, 1976), p. 125.

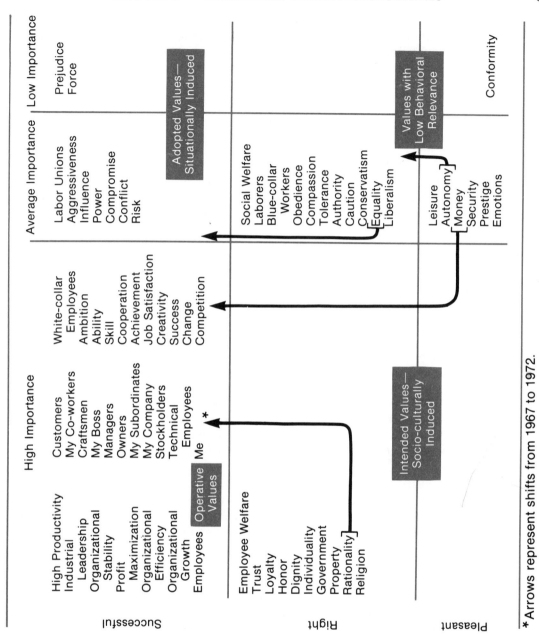

Figure 3–1
MANAGERIAL
VALUE PROFILE

* Arrows represent shifts from 1967 to 1972.

The *Values with Low Behavioral Relevance* should not be expected to influence managerial behavior, since they are perceived as lacking practical value in the work environment. Apparently persons who place high value on leisure, security, prestige, emotions, and conformity are not attracted to management or do not progress within management ranks. The few shifts in values from 1967 to the 1972 repeated study are interesting. Money shifted from the *Average—Pleasant* category to *High—Successful,* a more realistic position in a competitive economy where money is the primary medium of exchange. Rationality and Equality shifted from *Right* to *Successful.* Trends toward more objectivity and rationality in decision making (as opposed to reliance on authority) and an increasing emphasis on egalitarian relationships may have influenced this shift. A shifting of Autonomy from *Pleasant* to *Right* may reflect a growing expectation that managers should be given increased autonomy rather than be overcontrolled by superiors or bureaucratic rules.

The meaning of these shifts in managerial values is mostly a matter of speculation. They may, in fact, be an artifact of the surveys themselves rather than actual shifts. It is doubtful, for example, that the value managers place on money changed from 1967 to 1972. Perhaps, for some reason, managers felt more freedom by 1972 to give it a place of high importance. For many years, researchers proclaimed that achievement was the dominant motive of managers; then it changed to power and upward mobility. It is probable that only the researchers' conclusions changed—not the dominant motives of managers. Both the profit motives of business and the power and upward-mobility motives of managers suggest that the 1967 survey failed to correctly register the value managers place on money.

A 1975 study confirmed previous findings that a majority of managers sometimes feel pressure to compromise their personal standards in order to succeed. It is worth noting that top managers were about equally divided on this issue; while 65 percent of the middle managers and 84 percent of the lower managers agreed with the statement that "managers today feel under pressure to compromise personal standards to achieve company goals."[23] Although the facts do not detract from the undesirable effects of this pressure, it is noteworthy that (1) interaction with people in all areas of life involves pressures to compromise personal standards and (2) since personal value judgments differ greatly, some compromise is likely to be required, even in businesses that are highly ethical.

Values, Perception, and Behavior

Although many different variables influence ethical behavior, values inevitably influence both perception and behavior as shown in Table 3–1. In spite of the great strides made since the 1930's in placing a high value on the intrinsic

[23] Archie B. Carroll, "Managerial Ethics: A Post-Watergate View," *Business Horizons,* Vol. 18, No. 2 (April, 1975), p. 77. Also see "The Pressure to Compromise Personal Ethics," *Business Week,* January 31, 1977, p. 107.

worth of employees as human beings, it should be expected that managers will perceive employees more in terms of their productivity than their social welfare. Business is a place where employees satisfy their economic needs, and their employment agreement calls for productivity. It is doubtful that persons who value leisure, liberalism, and compassion (to use three of England's categories) more than productivity, profit, and employees will attempt to become managers or will perform satisfactorily if they do.

PERSONAL DETERMINANTS OF ETHICAL BEHAVIOR

A manager's early home and community influence
Commitment to religious and/or other value systems
Explicitness of a personal code of business ethics
Extent of financial and other personal needs
Maturity and resistance to an unhealthy need to conform

ORGANIZATIONAL DETERMINANTS OF ETHICAL BEHAVIOR

Behavior of superiors within the company
Behavior of organizational peers
Nature and extent of company policy
Availability of a company code of ethics
Consequences of unethical behavior
Pressures to conform to organizational norms
Excessive pressure to be productive

DETERMINANTS FROM THE EXTERNAL ENVIRONMENT

Ethical climate in the industry
Ethical climate in government
Values and ethical expectation of society
Extent of relevant laws and other constraints
Extent of prosecution and penalties for lawbreaking
Emphasis of news media on unethical behavior

Table 3–1 DETERMINANTS OF ETHICAL BEHAVIOR

Some critics of business, impressed by numerous exposures of management misdeeds, conclude that managers by and large are corrupt and untrustworthy. The truth is that lack of personal integrity or character is one quality that will usually ensure the demise of a would-be mobile manager. Most managers of America's corporations are graduates of its best universities and are typically included among their community's most civic-minded citizens and lay religious leaders. Although managers often believe that they must compromise their values to be successful, this does not mean that they are expected to lie, steal, or cheat for their employers.

Most managers are seldom, if ever, required to perform acts that are blatantly unethical. More often the conviction that they must compromise their values stems from guilt feelings associated with actions about which there are serious grounds for questioning what in reality is ethical. It is also noteworthy that managers sometimes describe actions as guilt-provoking when, in actuality, their emotions are better described as anxiety, apprehensiveness, or fear. For example, managers sometimes feel guilt when they have to fire a subordinate, when an inefficient competitor is forced out of business, and when they must take bold action that evokes rejection and hostility. These guilt feelings are often misplaced and misunderstood. Some managers are just too sensitive and self-critical to make business decisions—even highly ethical ones if someone must be hurt—without believing that they are compromising their own values.

Most companies go to great lengths to hire managers with character and demand ethical conduct thereafter. Some companies, such as IBM, not only demand compliance with an ethical code but go far beyond legal requirements and the recommendations of most writers and legislators by requiring an ethical practice such as protecting employee privacy—an area of rights to which the national conscience has only recently been sensitized.[24] Contrary to the stereotype of business managers as repressive, conservative, and resistant to issues of rights, most corporate leaders express strong support for an expanded concept of employee rights, including the freedom to blow the whistle on their employer when they witness unethical behavior.[25] The current pressures for increased concern for people come from within management as well as from business critics.

The following three industrial situations describe an employee-employer relationship. In each instance the employer used a form of surveillance, either closed-circuit television or wiretapping, to secure information that may not otherwise be available.

Case Problem 3-B

ELECTRONIC SURVEILLANCE

Since formal organizations are made up of individuals who are members of management or of the work force, it is not surprising that there are occasionally charges from the members of the work force that management is not acting in an ethical manner. When the employees of a company are members of a union, the process of arbitration provides a means of settling such disputes between management and its employees through the selection of a third party, an arbitrator. The decision of the arbitrator is usually final and binding. The following incidents concerning the use of electronic surveillance have been ruled on by arbitrators. You are asked to decide for each

---

[24] "IBM's Guidelines to Employee Privacy—An Interview with Frank T. Cary," *Harvard Business Review*, Vol. 54, No. 5 (September–October, 1976), p. 82.

[25] David W. Ewing, "What Business Thinks about Employee Rights," *Harvard Business Review*, Vol. 55, No. 5 (September–October, 1977), p. 81. Also Kenneth D. Walters, "Your Employees' Right to Blow the Whistle," Vol. 53, No. 4 (July–August, 1975), p. 26.

incident whether the management of the company was justified in using electronic surveillance.[26]

Incident 1

The company installed a closed-circuit television network in one of its plants. The employees contend that the use of closed-circuit TV is a violation of their privacy, that it amounts to employer spying, and that it violates a provision of the agreement between the employees and management which provides that present conditions of employment beneficial to employees shall not be changed unilaterally by the management of the company. There was no evidence presented during the arbitration hearing by the company indicating any need for the closed-circuit TV as a means of improving production in respect to either quantity or quality.

Incident 2

Again closed-circuit television was installed by management, and again the employees filed a grievance contending that it violated their right to privacy. However, there are some differences between this incident and Incident 1. In this case management had reason to suspect that there was pilferage in the receiving room. One of the monitors from the television camera was located in an office where a salaried employee controlled the flow of materials through the plant by radio contact with forklift truck drivers. Thus, the device aided the company in

maintaining a more even flow of materials to the production departments. The union contended that the dignity of the workers was being violated by the use of this device. The company, on the other hand, contended that the use of television in the receiving room was in effect another supervisor and afforded another pair of eyes, allowing observations which would normally be made had another supervisor been employed.

Incident 3

In this instance a large drug company had reason to believe that one of its employees was "writing numbers" on a large scale. The management of the company also believed that this activity was disruptive in addition to being illegal, and decided to obtain evidence against the employee. The evidence was obtained by tapping a telephone located in the warehouse. Conversations between the employee who was writing numbers and the person for whom he was writing numbers were recorded on a tape recorder. Based on the information obtained, the company discharged the employee. The union protested the discharge claiming, among other things, that it was an invasion of privacy and that such evidence should not be admitted that was obtained by means of wiretapping.

PROBLEMS

1. How would you rule as an arbitrator in each of the above cases.
2. Are the three incidents described properly considered problems of ethical relationships between employer and employee?
3. The last two incidents described are concerned with illegal activities on the part of employees; Incident 2 is concerned with possible theft, and Incident 3 is concerned with illegal gambling. If the company is denied the right to use electronic surveillance, how can it stop such practices?

---

[26] The Bureau of National Affairs, Washington, D. C., publishes a complete Labor Reporting Service. Among the reports published are current labor arbitration cases selected by BNA for publication in its Labor Arbitration series. The following are the references for each of the incidents:

    Incident 1—44 LA 563
    Incident 2—46 LA 335
    Incident 3—31 LA 191

CHAPTER QUESTIONS FOR
STUDY AND DISCUSSION

1. To what do you attribute the recent emphasis on business ethics? Do you believe it is justified?

2. What is the classical view of social responsibility?

3. What are the most serious problems with the classical view?

4. Which of the three views of social responsibility do you believe is best? Why?

5. Assume the role of the chief executive of a large corporation whose profits are unimpressive and whose dividends represent a low return on investment. How would you defend your investments in social programs to a small investor who has been buying company stock for years as part of a retirement income program?

6. What is wrong with basing one's ethical decisions on what others in similar situations are doing?

7. The statement has often been made that you cannot legislate morality. What does this mean? How valid is the statement?

8. Differentiate between enlightened self-interest as a motivation for personal ethics and as a basis for deciding what is and is not ethical.

9. What is the difference between self-interest and selfishness? What kinds of payoff is a person most likely to receive from unselfish behavior?

10. Why do more low-level than high-level managers feel pressure to compromise their standards in order to succeed? Why, in the most ethically managed companies, should one expect to find managers who feel pressure to compromise their standards?

2 Planning for Productivity

The planning function of management occupies a special position of importance since it logically precedes the other three management functions and significantly influences their nature. The formation of an organization implies purpose on the part of its founders; and if the organization is to succeed, that purpose must be expressed in the strategies, goals, policies, and other plans that guide the behavior of its members. In the final analysis, the original purpose or mission of an organization's founders must find expression in the way managers and employees utilize their time each day. Accordingly, Part 2 is concerned with the process through which plans are developed, through which plans influence managerial decisions, and through which they result in the production of goods and services in order to fulfill the organization's ultimate mission.

Chapter 4 describes six kinds of plans and explains the process through which effective planning occurs in organizations. In addition, Chapter 4 elaborates on one particular type of planning and approach to managing: management by objectives. Finally, criteria for evaluating the probable success of a plan are presented. Building on this foundation, Chapter 5 discusses planning applications in the selected functional areas of finance, marketing, and personnel.

Chapter 6 is concerned with decision making. Discussed are typical approaches to managerial decision making, the major personal and organizational influences on managerial decisions, and the means by which managerial decisions can be improved. The last chapter in Part 2 discusses production management, the major functional area in which planning and decision making are expressed. In this chapter, full recognition is given to the fact that more often than not an organization exists to produce services rather than goods—to produce health services, education, and machine repair, for example, rather than to produce fuel, automobiles, or buildings. Given this broad perspective, Chapter 7 discusses what production managers do, the technological aspects of production, efficiency methods in job design, and a few of the quantitative methods that are used by managers as aids in decision making.

Chapter 4

Setting Objectives and Planning for Results

Case Problem 4-A
SELECTING A PLANT SITE

The Bojo Corporation is an established manufacturer located in a small town in southwestern New York State. The company was founded about 90 years ago and initially served both the railroad industry and the oil fields of northern Pennsylvania. At present a large part of its business is still associated with the oil industry. In recent years, however, it has branched into other fields and has been able to develop applications of products originally used in the oil fields to other areas. The Bojo Corporation is a subsidiary company of a large national firm with headquarters in St. Louis. The national headquarters controls all capital expenditures, reviews operating budgets developed by its subsidiary corporations, follows up to ensure that budgetary goals are met, and also exerts strong influence in the labor relations area. All labor contracts and labor policies are determined by the headquarters' staff.

In recent years the Bojo Corporation developed a new type of pipe coupling that joins two pieces of pipe without having to thread the ends of the pipes being joined or having to cut them to an exact length. The coupling saves time and money and has experienced a remarkable sales volume from

municipalities since it is used primarily to replace existing water and gas lines. There is every reason to believe that the market will expand and that the Bojo Corporation will receive a large share of the increase. Since the coupling is particularly useful in the replacement market with the oldest water and gas systems on the eastern seaboard, the greatest potential market for the immediate future is in this area.

Present manufacturing facilities, a department in the main plant, are now running at capacity; and, in order to meet the anticipated increase in demand, new facilities are needed. Since the present plant location does not permit expansion, it has been decided that a new plant should be built to house the present coupling department and to provide for future increases in volume. A member of the St. Louis controller's staff, Ms. Minelli, has been assigned the task of conducting a plant location survey and submitting subsequent recommendations to the president of the Bojo Corporation and officials of the parent company.

In preparing for her assignment, Ms. Minelli contacted several executives, among them the executive vice-president responsi-

61

ble for the Bojo Corporation and other subsidiaries in Pennsylvania, New York, and Massachusetts. It was the executive vice-president's wish that the plant be located on a direct route between Pittsburgh, Pennsylvania, and the present location, or between Buffalo, New York, and the present location. His reason for desiring the plant in these areas was that it would be convenient for him as a company executive to fly into either the Buffalo or Pittsburgh airport, rent a car, and drive directly to the plant.

A conversation with the home office vice-president for industrial relations revealed that the company, as a matter of policy, wished to have a different international union in the new plant rather than have the employees represented by the same union that organized Bojo's New York plant. The reason for the policy was that having a different union in each plant would lessen the possibility of all plants closing as the result of a strike, since no one international union would represent more than one plant. The vice-president indicated that it would be necessary to locate at least 100 miles from the present plant in order to be assured of a different union. He also recommended analyzing the labor rates of any community proposed as a location for the new plant so that maximum savings might be realized from low initial labor costs. He stated further that by starting operations with labor rates as low as possible, the company would be in a better position to increase rates in the future.

When Ms. Minelli contacted the president of the Bojo Corporation and reviewed the wishes of the two central office executives, she learned that the president had a few ideas of his own to add to the picture. The president indicated that it was mandatory that the new location have complete rail

facilities, since raw materials were received most economically by rail and many of the finished product shipments could be made by rail. He wanted the plant located east of the present facility to minimize transportation costs by establishing a direct flow of materials from Pittsburgh to the East Coast markets. He was also insistent, as operating head of the company, that the new plant be located in an area where there is a well-defined, stable tax structure. He believed that tax stability was necessary in order to predict long-range profits with some degree of accuracy. Another requirement was that the site be large enough to permit future expansion of the proposed plant to twice its initial size. The president of Bojo placed no exact limitations on construction costs provided such costs were in line with typical costs for the area selected.

PROBLEMS

1. Assume you are Ms. Minelli. Prepare an initial statement of the relative significance of the factors considered important by
   a. The executive vice-president of the home office
   b. The vice-president for industrial relations, home office
   c. The president of the subsidiary Bojo Corporation
2. Indicate in detail the steps that you would follow in conducting a study to evaluate alternative sites for the new plant.
3. Before Ms. Minelli received her assignment, certain decisions had been made by the Bojo management. What were these decisions? What additional decisions must be made after a satisfactory location for the new plant has been found?

Effective management begins with planning; no organization can succeed without it. There are, of course, many approaches to planning. Some are so informal and subjective that even organizational insiders see little evidence of them, while others are highly structured, involving virtually every member of the organization. The planning requirements of General Motors or ITT are necessarily different from the requirements of Joe's Delicatessen or the Dutton Street Garage. Even in companies with similar planning needs—for example, competing automobile manufacturers—the planning function may be performed in different ways. There is no one best way to plan.

This chapter explains some of the major aspects of planning as practiced in a wide range of companies. The importance of planning is stressed, especially the importance of systematic goal setting and of anticipating, as much as possible, future changes in the environment that will influence the success of an enterprise.

FUNDAMENTAL CONCEPTS OF PLANNING

Planning is the process through which decisions are made about the results an organization expects to achieve and about the courses of action most likely to lead to their achievement. A *plan* is a statement—ideally and typically a written statement—of those results and the means to be used in achieving them. Plans are blueprints for action. They are guidelines that enable members of an organization to work purposefully together to achieve a worthwhile end.

Benefits of Planning

Deliberate and systematic planning is beneficial to an organization in many ways. Perhaps its greatest benefit is that it clearly defines the organization's purpose and goals, thereby providing a basis for coordinated, unified action by all its members. This is especially important in large organizations.

Another major benefit of planning is the reduction of risk—decreasing the statistical probability of failure. In the process of planning, management gathers and analyzes information about the firm's resources—its personnel, money, markets, technologies, raw materials, and energy sources—thereby reducing risk by increasing predictability. Management also attempts to predict the actions of competitors, changes in the economy, and even the possible actions of foreign groups, such as the leaders of the oil-exporting nations and other controllers of scarce materials. The more accurately a firm predicts the events that are likely to occur in its external environment, the better it is able to select courses of action that minimize risk. Risks may be minimized, for example, through buffering actions such as stockpiling raw materials, or through aggressive strategies such as initiating an advertising campaign and rushing a new product to the market to offset the moves of a competitor. Planning will not eliminate risks, but it can greatly reduce them; at least it can enable managers to be aware of the risks they are taking.

Planning increases individual motivation by providing a sense of direction and by reducing the inner frustrations and interpersonal conflicts that accompany poorly defined goals, ambiguous policies, and inadequate methods. Planning also enables a manager to be more effective as a leader; the sense of direction provided by goals and the coordination and information required for effective planning are all contributors to leadership effectiveness.

Finally, planning contributes significantly to management's ability to maintain control of the organization. The sequence of steps, the timetables and completion dates, the goals, the performance standards, and the evaluation checkpoints established in the planning process are all essential aspects of the organizational control function.

It is noteworthy that planning requires a great deal of decision making. Setting priorities, formulating policy, establishing rules, selecting one strategy over another—all these and the other dimensions of planning involve decision making, the foundation of all management behavior. The decision making involved underscores the importance of planning and suggests why formal approaches to planning are increasing.[1] Planning is an exciting, dynamic process and not just a "getting ready for action," as the word tends to imply.

Types of Plans

The effective operation of organizations requires several different types of plans. Types of plans included here are purpose or mission, strategies, objectives or goals, policies, procedures, methods, and rules. Budgets are also plans that make a unique contribution to organizational planning; they are particularly important in evaluating the feasibility of goals and in maintaining the control needed to reach them. Budgets will be discussed at length in later chapters.

Purpose or Mission. The most general plan of an organization is its purpose or mission. As determined by its founders, owners, or board of directors, a *mission* is a firm's reason for existence. A distinction is ordinarily made between the primary motivation of investors—in most companies a desire for profit—and the company's mission, which may be to provide rail transportation, design and build airplanes, construct bridges, or provide a retail sales outlet for certain merchandise.

A firm's mission should be clearly formulated because it provides a broad sense of direction which is sometimes critical to the firm's survival and success. The mission of the Ford Motor Company is not simply to make automobiles. In fact, its mission is not restricted to manufacturing transportation vehicles, including trucks. It also makes farm tractors and implements, industrial construction equipment, and a variety of other products believed by its board of directors to be compatible with its original mission. Had Ford decided that its sole mission was to build automobiles, its stability, profitability, and competitive position certainly would not be what it is today. And, if the mission of some other automobile manufacturers, such as Hudson and Packard, had been defined differently, perhaps their automobiles would still be on the market. When the mission of the J. I. Case Company was changed by adding industrial equipment to its existing line of farm machinery, it was transformed from a losing company to a profitable one.

---

[1] Leslie W. Rue, "The How and Who of Long-Range Planning," *Business Horizons,* Vol. 16, No. 6 (December, 1973), p. 28.

Strategies. A firm's mission can be accomplished in a variety of ways. Its planners may, for example, decide to launch an aggressive program of diversification by moving out into related businesses through the acquisition of companies. Or a manufacturer may decide to restrict its business activities to a relatively narrow product line and to develop its own retail outlets rather than sell through distributors (see Figure 4–1). These general plans, or *strategies*, are commitments to emphasize specific programs of action and to commit to those programs the resources needed to fulfill the organization's mission.[2]

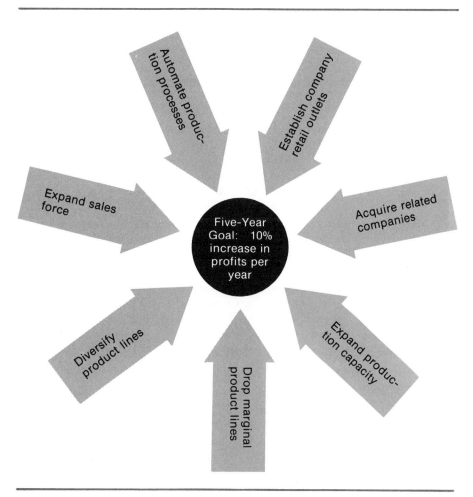

**Figure 4–1
POSSIBLE
STRATEGIES
FOR ACHIEVING
A PROFIT
GOAL**

Strategy is a term that military planners have long used to refer to master plans for overcoming an adversary under different assumptions about the enemy's

[2] Harold Koontz, "Making Strategic Planning Work," *Business Horizons*, Vol. 19, No. 2 (April, 1976), p. 37.

tactics and strength. Similarly, the idea of meeting the challenge of a competitor is involved in a business strategy.[3] Like military strategies, business strategies do not attempt to provide the details of how the mission is to be accomplished.

Goals. The implementation of strategies occurs through the achievement of goals or objectives.[4] Goals are more specific and concrete than strategies. Suppose top management decides that the company has been investing too heavily in growth to the detriment of profits, and consequently commits the firm to the strategy of increasing profits each year over the next five years. The goals required to implement this strategy will specify, among other things, exactly how much profit the company will attempt to make each year of the planning period and the means by which the increase in profits will be achieved. Goals are, therefore, an elaboration or extension of strategies.

Goal setting in support of organizational strategies occurs at successively lower levels of the organization in what is typically described as an *ends-means chain*. This means that a goal (an end) at one organizational level is a means toward achieving a higher level or broader goal at higher organizational levels. Success in carrying out a plan requires continuity of the ends-means chain throughout the organization.

The Time Factor. Goals are set for greatly varying lengths of time. In most organizations, a one-year goal is considered *short-range*, a one- to five-year goal is *intermediate-range*, and a five-year and beyond goal is *long-range*. However, there are many exceptions, depending on the nature of the business and the predictability of the environment. In the rapidly changing business of designing high-style clothes, one or two years may be considered long-range. In contrast, the long-range goals of a tree grower may encompass more than fifty years. As a rule, the further these goals extend into the future, the more unpredictable the environment is. Consequently, it becomes increasingly difficult to make such long-range goals realistic, concrete, and specific. For that reason, few companies set goals beyond five years.

The Maximization Concept. In their attempts to understand and forecast events in the national economy, economists employ a number of complex mathematical models based on the questionable assumption that businesses maximize profits: that they make as much profit as possible. Granted that from an investor's viewpoint the primary objective of a business is profit, the evidence is overwhelming that businesses actually seek to *satisfice*: to make a satisfactory profit rather than the maximum possible profit.[5] This concept is crucial to understanding the nature of business objectives.

---

[3] Michael E. Porter, "How Competitive Forces Shape Strategy," *Harvard Business Review*, Vol. 57, No. 2 (March–April, 1979), p. 137.

[4] Some writers make a distinction between goals and objectives. To avoid confusion, this text does not.

[5] This term, popularized by March and Simon, has become commonplace in management literature. See James G. March and Herbert A. Simon, *Organizations* (New York City: John Wiley & Sons, Inc., 1958), p. 140.

Obviously business firms that do not make a profit cannot survive; and managers of businesses that do not make a satisfactory profit, as defined by the shareholders, will have difficulty keeping their jobs. But businesses have many objectives besides profit, such as proper treatment of employees, meeting the demands of government, making a quality product, growing, providing acceptable management compensation, and serving the best interests of society.[6] Theoretically managers may seek to maximize profits, but in practice they seek satisfactory achievement of many goals which are not only important to the organization's success but to their success as individuals. If there were no other barriers to profit maximization, just the concerns of managers for their own careers—their self-interests as individuals—would prevent it, since personal and company goals are often in conflict. This conflict is most obvious when a manager decides to subordinate all the company's goals to his or her own and accept a better job offer.

Policies. *Policies* are general statements (preferably written statements) that mirror an organization's objectives and provide guidelines for administrative action. They are *standing plans*, since they are relatively stable and change slowly. *Policymaking* is decision making that limits the discretion of managers and provides limits within which acceptable decisions must fall. Examples of policies at different organizational levels and functional areas are selecting personnel in order to achieve a specific racial, ethnic, and sex balance; filling vacant positions from within the company; making decisions at the lowest possible organizational level; and giving essentially the same price considerations to large and small customers.

Procedures and Methods. More limited to departments or other operating divisions of a company than policies are *procedures*, which are specific guides to action. The term *standard operating procedure* reflects the concrete and confining nature of procedures. The how-to details of a procedure define the standard way to complete a task or sequence of tasks. Thus, a procedure may be the steps that an organization specifies to its employees for filling an order, paying a bill, or maintaining the proper inventory level. Procedures often cut across departmental lines. Filling an order, for example, may involve the sales, credit, accounting, production, and shipping departments.

Procedures are closely related to, and sometimes indistinguishable from, *methods*. A work method may specify the exact nature and sequence of each arm and hand movement; it may even specify a standard time span allowed for the sequence. The planning of methods is particularly common in assembly-line and other manufacturing operations.

Rules. Some plans are expressed in the form of rules, and, like procedures and methods, they are specific guides to action. Rules either forbid or require certain behavior. Unlike policies, which guide but do not eliminate discretion, rules are meant to replace thinking and deciding. A rule is an unequivocal

---

[6] Charles P. Edmonds III and John H. Hand, "What Are the Real Long-Run Objectives of Business?" *Business Horizons,* Vol. 19, No. 6 (December, 1976), p. 79.

statement: Always wear goggles while grinding, No smoking in this area, All units must be approved by quality control before storing or shipping. The notion that rules are made to be broken is generally misleading; although an inflexible, slavish obedience to rules may become an organizational sickness. If a rule cannot ordinarily be followed, if frequent exceptions must be made, the rule should be modified to specify the conditions under which it does or does not apply.

DIMENSIONS OF EFFECTIVE PLANNING

If, as stated earlier, there is no single best way to plan, and if each situation has its unique characteristics that must be considered in planning, it is foolish to attempt the formulation of an ideal or model sequence of planning steps. We can, however, describe some of the features typically found in effective planning programs.

Preparation

Effective planning begins with an executive decision concerning the nature and extent of the planning. This necessarily includes a decision about who will do the planning and how much time and money will be allocated for it. Because planning involves extensive decision making, ultimate responsibility for it must rest with line management, with the managers who have authority to direct the activities of subordinates in achieving the firm's primary objectives. Committees and staffs of professional planners are, however, increasingly involved in planning because of its technical and time-consuming nature; and they assume a great deal of responsibility for its effectiveness.[7]

In some situations virtually everyone in an organization, at least every manager, is involved in the goal setting aspect of planning. In such cases, a lengthy period of preparation may be necessary to ensure that participants recognize the value of planning and are motivated to plan. Even high-ranking executives, who are sometimes preoccupied with the complexities of their daily work, neglect the planning function, failing to give it either the time or the concentration and emotional involvement it deserves.

Statement of Purpose and Objectives

Before rational planning can occur, all planners must have a clear understanding of the firm's mission and strategies. This demands that at least some planning take place at the board of directors and executive levels before middle

---

[7] Thomas H. Naylor, "The Future of Corporate Planning Models," *Managerial Planning* (March–April, 1976), p. 1. Also Leslie W. Rue, *op. cit.*, p. 30. For further insight into how firms organize the work of planning, see G. A. Steiner and J. B. Miner, *Management Policy and Strategy* (New York City: Macmillan, Inc., 1977).

and supervisory management can plan effectively. This high-level planning has a coordinating and unifying effect on all subsequent planning. In the initial stage of planning, top management should express its objectives tentatively— as aspirations that may or may not prove to be realistic. They must, of course, be firmly stated before lower levels of management begin serious planning.

Forecasting

Planning that is based on inadequate information usually does more harm than good. It creates false security and consequently a boldness that may lead to foolish risk taking. Effective planning, in contrast, is based on the best possible forecasts of what will occur within the internal and external environments of the company. Such forecasts involve the following factors: availability of money, personnel, raw materials, and energy; actions of competitors; nature of markets; changes in technology; expectations of changes in society and government; and economic outlook. All these and other difficult-to-predict factors may affect the company's success.

Skeptics about planning cite examples of unpredictable events—an Arab oil embargo, an unexpected recession, an outbreak of war—to support their contention that long-range planning is an exercise in futility. But most executives, especially executives of large companies, know that risks can be reduced and opportunities increased through forecasting.

Large companies employ the services of economists and other technical experts (e.g., physical and behavioral scientists, specialists on population trends, foreign affairs specialists) to improve their predictions about the external environment. Such predictions often appear in government documents, trade publications, business magazines, and university research bureau journals. In addition, panels of experts may be asked for opinions, and opinion survey data may be used to obtain insights into future trends. Consultants are available in most areas that require forecasts.

A variety of mathematical models aid in the prediction of economic and other trends.[8] A time-series analysis, for example, shows the interaction between long-term growth trends, cyclical business fluctuations, and past seasonal fluctuations; and from this knowledge managers are able to make projections into the future.[9] Other models use correlation techniques and computer simulations designed to take as many variables as possible into consideration. Often simple extrapolation techniques, as shown in Figure 4–2, are also of value.

---

[8] Don Lebell and O. J. Krasner, "Selecting Environmental Forecasting Techniques from Business Planning Requirements," *Academy of Management Review*, Vol. 2, No. 3 (July, 1977), p. 173. Also see Robert S. Sobek, "A Manager's Primer on Forecasting," *Harvard Business Review*, Vol. 51, No. 3 (May–June, 1973), p. 6.

[9] For a discussion of a framework to deal with the possible effects of changes in a firm's products or production processes, see Robert H. Hayes and Steven G. Wheelwright, "The Dynamics of Process-Product Life Cycles," *Harvard Business Review*, Vol. 57, No. 2 (March–April, 1979), p. 127.

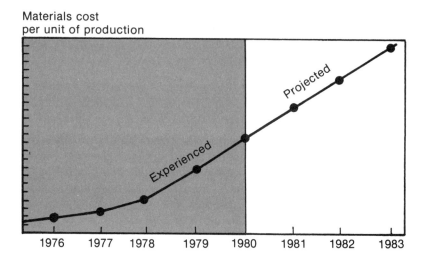

Figure 4-2
THE CONCEPT
OF EXTRAP-
OLATION

There is evidence that forecasting can be effective and that it is increasingly used as a planning tool.[10] Still, many remain skeptical of its value. Some of the most sophisticated forecasts have been abysmal failures. They are like weather forecasts—based on probabilities and subject to unpredictable influences. When the forecaster says the chance of rain is 20 percent, it seems to be a good day for a picnic. However, many picnics held on days with a 20 percent chance of rain are rained out. When business forecasts are unsuccessful, the results can mean disaster, not just discomfort. It takes only a few disasters to produce a skeptic about forecasting. On the other hand, forecasting is infinitely more rational than basing decisions on the muddle of hunches and hopes we call intuition.

Premising

A *premise* is an assumption from which conclusions are drawn and upon which action is based; and, regardless of whether planners are consciously aware of them, premises always play an important role in planning. Premises are made even when they are unstated and exist primarily as fuzzy hunches and vague hopes or fears in the thinking of the company's major powerholders and planners. Stating clearly the major premises on which planning is based is a critical aspect of effective planning. When different planners begin with different premises, conflict between the planners is inevitable, and the planning itself is frustrating and fatiguing; furthermore, the resulting plan is likely to be disjointed and unworkable.

---

[10] D. J. Dalrymple, "Sales Forecasting Methods and Accuracy," *Business Horizons*, Vol. 18, No. 6 (December, 1975), p. 69.

The point cannot be overemphasized that planners always begin with certain premises, although they are often hidden from consciousness. Imagine how much more effectively planning will proceed, however, when everyone begins with the same premises. It helps to know, for example, that all planners in the organization are assuming that for the planning period:

1. Inflation will continue at an average 8 percent rate.
2. Markets will remain strong, permitting increased sales.
3. No major technological advances are expected within the industry.
4. Competition from imports will level off or decline slightly.
5. Neither cash flow nor long-term financing will present serious problems.

Exactly how many premises should be stated depends on the number of premises that are likely to have a significant influence on the organization during the planning period. Obviously they cannot all be stated, but the premises that will most influence plans and about which there is most likely to be disagreement should be discussed until there is consensus or until an executive decision is made concerning each.

Developing Scenarios and Strategies

After establishing premises, management is in a position to formulate alternative strategies and tentative objectives for achieving the firm's mission. In the process, the initially stated strategies and objectives may be modified to increase their realism. Eventually they are solidified and different means for reaching them are developed.

The formulation of strategies is complicated by the fact that a given set of premises may not be valid. Often only one set of premises is accepted, although another set is almost as valid. What if markets do not continue to be strong during the planning period? What if there is another oil embargo? Perhaps one strategy is best if our premises are correct, while another runs a close second but is less hazardous if our best predictions prove to be wrong. It may be best to select a fail-safe strategy—one that is compatible with the premises that are most likely to be right but which will result in the least damage if they prove wrong.

The many unpredictable aspects of the future suggest the value of developing several *scenarios*, or descriptions of possible future operating environments.[11] Linneman and Kennell[12] recommend the formulation of three or four plausible scenarios, plausible meaning that the conditions described are likely to occur together. For example, double-digit inflation, rapid economic growth, and a prolonged embargo on foreign oil may each be a possibility, but it is unlikely that they will occur simultaneously. They should not, therefore, be part of

---

[11] In its common usage, a scenario is the outline of a motion picture, play, opera, etc., giving the main facts about the scenes, persons, and actions.

[12] Robert E. Linneman and John D. Kennell, "Shirt-Sleeve Approach to Long-Range Plans," *Harvard Business Review*, Vol. 55, No. 2 (March–April, 1977), p. 141.

the same scenario. Each scenario is brief, just one or two paragraphs such as the following:

> For the next three years, all the company's markets will remain strong, permitting present sales trends to continue. Government pressures will reduce foreign competition only slightly. Inflation will continue at an average rate of 10 percent. Labor pressure for raises that exceed inflation cannot be successfully resisted, and costs of materials will increase at a 10 percent rate. Because of rapid technological progress, the major threat from competitors will come from product innovation rather than from price-cutting or advertising. Interest rates will increase as a government effort to control inflation, but money will remain plentiful.

The strategy most likely to achieve the firm's mission is developed for each scenario.

Selecting a Strategy

Once alternative strategies are developed, the grand strategy most likely to achieve the organization's mission is selected, along with supportive substrategies and objectives. Since planning decisions are based on assumptions, and since the future is always filled with uncertainties, risk taking cannot be avoided. But formal planning does permit calculated risk taking. At least the risks are made explicit, and decisions are made only after a number of different alternatives have been considered.

Making Plans Operational

Grand strategies, however sound and eloquently written, are worthless unless concrete plans are developed for their implementation. These *action plans, tactical plans,* or *operational plans* may be developed at each organizational level or handed down from a master planning group.[13] They are often linked to the goals of operational units and individual managers. Management-by-objectives programs are compatible with programs of strategic planning, although some authors discuss the two as though they were totally unrelated.

Both strategic and tactical plans should be evaluated regularly. As premises prove to be right or wrong, strategies and tactics must be modified. Management must constantly navigate the uneasy course between a strong commitment to a plan and the flexibility required to adapt to changing circumstances.

MANAGEMENT BY OBJECTIVES

Management by objectives (MBO) is both a philosophy and a technique of management. It is based on a belief that the focal point of managerial decisions should be ends rather than means—results rather than organizational rules,

---

[13] For a discussion of how to maintain continuity between strategic and operational plans, read John M. Hobbs and Donald F. Heany, "Coupling Strategy to Operating Plans," *Harvard Business Review,* Vol. 55, No. 3 (May–June, 1977), p. 119.

policies, and controls that too often obscure the organization's goals and become ends in themselves. Closely identified in its early stages of development with Peter F. Drucker,[14] management by objectives has in recent years become the object of an increasing number of studies designed to evaluate its effectiveness. Although no universally accepted MBO technique has emerged, a consistent philosophy runs through all MBO programs: an emphasis on results and a belief that organizational behavior should be guided by consciously set goals. This philosophy implies that organizational behavior should be motivated by a pull toward the future rather than a push from the past.

MBO Process

The heart of the MBO technique is the practice of goal setting at every level of management, and sometimes throughout the ranks of nonmanagerial employees.[15] The technique can be applied in such a way that it is compatible with either an authoritarian or a participative leadership style. In some programs, each individual's goals are assigned; in others, each individual is able to set his or her own goals, subject to approval by supervisors. The effectiveness of an MBO program will be determined, in part, by the extent to which it has been tailored to take into consideration the characteristics of an organization and its leaders.[16]

Most MBO programs provide some means for superiors and subordinates on every level to review the subordinates' goals, making sure they meet certain criteria. The goals should be as follows:

1. Realistic (achievable but hard enough to be challenging)
2. Specific and concrete (e.g., to increase production by 10 percent rather than to increase production as much as possible)
3. Measurable [17] (preferably quantifiable, but at least definite enough that one can know whether or not the goals have been reached)
4. Compatible with the goals of one's organizational superiors
5. Flexible (capable of being altered as conditions change)

Typical MBO programs call for a regular performance evaluation on the basis of accomplished results. Actual achievements are evaluated against previously set goals; and, by allowing for any unpredictable and uncontrollable influences on productivity, the more effectively the goals are achieved, the higher a person's performance evaluation. This is better than evaluating an individual on the basis of personality characteristics and other equally irrelevant standards.

---

[14] Peter F. Drucker, *The Practice of Management* (New York City: Harper and Row, Publishers, Inc., 1954).

[15] G. Robert Lea, "An MBO Program for All Levels: One Company's Success Story," *Advanced Management Journal*, Vol. 42, No. 2 (Spring, 1977), p. 24.

[16] Heinz Weihrich, "MBO in Four Management Systems," *MSU Business Topics*, Vol. 24, No. 3 (Autumn, 1976), p. 51.

[17] Measuring results is easier for persons holding simple, nonmanagerial jobs than for those in managerial positions. This often leads to neglect of aspects of managerial jobs that are difficult to measure. For a discussion of this, read Harry Levinson, "Management by Whose Objectives?" *Harvard Business Review*, Vol. 48, No. 4 (July–August, 1970), p. 125.

However, the results criterion leaves much to be desired since how results are achieved can be vitally important. The manager whose lack of cooperation interferes with another manager's achievement or the one whose surly disposition gives the workplace a distasteful atmosphere should be appraised on these behaviors as well as on results. Increased attention has been justifiably placed on managerial ethics as an important consideration in comparatively evaluating the results of different managers.

Ivancevich describes an MBO program in which positive reinforcement (rewards for goal achievement and other desirable behaviors) was combined with goal setting to increase motivation.[18] The following were among the reinforcement techniques used: company executives sent letters to supervisors thanking them for their contributions, executives expressed similar sentiments to the supervisors in meetings, and the president sent letters to participants endorsing the program. The use of carefully planned reinforcement for motivational purposes has proved, in a number of situations, to be effective in modifying behavior. Its use with MBO is a logical application of *behavior modification*, a popular technique for bringing about specific behavioral change.

Evaluating MBO

After more than three decades of experience and research with MBO the results are mixed. Many companies that have tried some form of MBO have discarded it—enough to create a great deal of skepticism about it.[19] On the other hand, there is some evidence that a conclusion drawn by Locke in 1968 is valid: that conscious goals or intentions regulate action.[20] Furthermore, it is evident that some—certainly not all—MBO programs increase both productivity and job satisfaction.[21]

Unfortunately studies evaluating MBO programs have often covered relatively short time spans (six weeks to six months). In 1975 Latham and Baldes conducted a 12-month study of the effects of goal setting in the logging industry, where the judgment of truck drivers was a factor in determining the load weight of logs hauled to the mill. Since the logs varied in length and diameter, considerable discretion was involved in loading to approximate the legal weight limit. The results were encouraging. Corporate records revealed that the increase in efficiency due to goal setting would have otherwise cost the company a quarter of a million dollars just for the purchase of additional trucks needed to deliver

---

[18] John M. Ivancevich, "Changes in Performance by a Management by Objectives Program," *Administrative Science Quarterly*, Vol. 19, No. 4 (December, 1974), p. 563.

[19] Fred Schuster and Alva F. Kindall, "Management by Objectives, Where We Stand—A Survey of the Fortune 500," *Human Resources Management*, Vol. 13, No. 1 (Spring, 1974), p. 8.

[20] Edwin A. Locke, "Toward a Theory of Task Motivation and Incentive," *Organizational Behavior and Human Performance*, Vol. 3, No. 2 (1968), p. 157.

[21] Gary P. Latham and Gary A. Yukl, "A Review of Research on the Application of Goal Setting in Organizations," *Academy of Management Journal*, Vol. 1, No. 4 (December, 1975), p. 824. Also John M. Ivancevich, "Different Goal Setting Treatments and Their Effects on Performance and Job Satisfaction," *Academy of Management Journal*, Vol. 20, No. 3 (September, 1977), p. 406.

the same quantity of logs to the mill.[22] Performance improved immediately upon the assignment of specific hard goals. But whether goal setting will continue to yield these results indefinitely has not been demonstrated.

Two studies by Ivancevich suggest that the positive effects of MBO—of some MBO programs at least—may not be permanent. In a 1972 study of two medium-size companies, he concluded that "the findings in both organizations show that the effects of MBO training are short lived." [23] In a 1977 study his results were similar. Both in participating and assigned groups, performance and satisfaction increased more under formal goal setting than under do-your-best instructions. "However, the improvements began to dissipate six to nine months after training." [24]

A final evaluation of MBO cannot be accomplished until a number of long-term studies are made under clearly defined conditions. It is somewhat misleading to make sweeping statements about MBO in general, since no two programs are exactly alike—and probably never should be. A more fruitful view of MBO is the *contingency approach* in which if-then relationships are established between various aspects of the environment (the type of organization, the psychological climate, leadership styles, education of participants, etc.) and specific techniques of MBO (participative or assigned goals, use of positive reinforcement, involvement of upper management, etc.).[25] The fact that some programs fail and others succeed suggests the value of studying the conditions under which success and failure occur rather than making general evaluations about several nebulously defined techniques that we collectively call MBO.

As evaluations of MBO programs continue, the research designs need to become more rigorous—not an easy task in this type of applied research. Such designs are necessary, for example, to determine how often the positive effects of MBO diminish over time, and why. Research is needed to determine whether the amount of managerial attention that MBO gives to a group would increase productivity and satisfaction even if no goal setting were involved (the so-called Hawthorne Effect).[26] Difficult problems also exist concerning how an MBO program should be conducted when one person's performance is in part dependent upon the performance of others.[27] Many questions remain unanswered. We do know, however, that under certain conditions MBO is successful even though most of those conditions have yet to be defined.

---

[22] Gary P. Latham and James J. Baldes, "The Practical Significance of Locke's Theory of Goal Setting," *Journal of Applied Psychology*, Vol. 60, No. 1 (February, 1975), p. 122.

[23] John M. Ivancevich, "A Longitudinal Assessment of Management by Objectives," *Administrative Science Quarterly*, Vol. 17, No. 1 (March, 1972), p. 126.

[24] Ivancevich, *op. cit.* (1977), p. 406.

[25] Fred Luthans, "How to Apply MBO," *Public Personnel Management*, Vol. 5, No. 2 (March–April, 1976), p. 85.

[26] Named after the famous 1930's experiments at Western Electric's Hawthorne plant near Chicago. There, productivity increases that were first thought to be due to changing the environment (i.e., lighting changes) were actually due to the recognition given to the employees and to their desire to be cooperative. (See Chapter 2.)

[27] Wendell L. French and Robert W. Hollmann, "Management by Objectives: The Team Approach," *California Management Review*, Vol. 17, No. 3 (Spring, 1975), p. 13.

Guidelines for MBO Programs

What we do not know about MBO should not obscure what we do know, or at least what research and experience seem to indicate. Certainly it is unnecessary for persons instituting MBO programs to make all the mistakes that others have made. Granted that the unique features of each organization must be taken into consideration, Table 4–1 contains 12 statements that will serve as guidelines for making an MBO program effective.

1. Start MBO at the top of the organization; be sure to have the full support and cooperation of top management.
2. Before starting the program, make sure that participants understand the system and know how they can benefit from it.
3. Tailor the program to the organization. Avoid the canned programs of self-styled MBO experts.
4. Avoid excessive paperwork. Keep it simple.
5. Be extremely cautious when evaluating performance solely on results. MBO can easily be viewed as just another gimmick used by task-oriented managers to get something for nothing.
6. Where the firm's overall leadership style permits, allow individuals to set their own goals. Avoid authoritatively assigning goals to persons who value personal autonomy and responsibility.
7. Make sure that a person who is held responsible for results has access to the resources needed to achieve them (e.g., authority, money, materials, personnel, technology).
8. Provide for team effort where the success of one individual is dependent on the productivity of others over whom he or she has no authority.
9. Do not place too heavy an emphasis on results. Otherwise, people may be considered only as a means to an end.
10. Insofar as possible, allow participants the freedom to determine the means for achieving their goals.
11. Establish good controls and feedback systems to track the progress of subordinates, but avoid excessively close supervision.
12. Provide for changing goals as conditions change. Be adaptable enough to change any aspect of the MBO program that proves to be unworkable.

Table 4–1
GUIDELINES FOR
AN EFFECTIVE
MBO PROGRAM

EVALUATING PLANS

The most obvious way to evaluate a plan is in terms of its effectiveness in achieving the organization's mission or some lower level end toward which it is directed in the ends-means chain. Unfortunately, by the time the results of an inadequate plan are known, often the damage is already done. It is therefore important that we evaluate the probable effectiveness of a plan before it is implemented.

Three approaches to the evaluation of plans are discussed here. The first, *procedural analysis*, evaluates the methodology used in developing a plan against a checklist of characteristics that typically differentiate successful and unsuccessful plans. The second, *economic effectiveness*, evaluates a plan in terms of how well it utilizes available resources. The third approach, *cost-benefit analysis*, is similar to the economic effectiveness method but offers unique advantages where it is difficult to quantify inputs and outputs.

Procedural Analysis

In view of the wide range of plans discussed in this chapter (from missions to rules), it is obvious that a given list of evaluation criteria will not apply equally to all plans. The criteria discussed below are least applicable to standing plans such as policies, procedures, methods, and rules. They apply directly to strategies and objectives.

The criteria recommended for analyzing planning procedures are directed primarily toward making a procedure objective and explicit. In small, privately held firms, in particular, a plan is often subjectively conceived and justified solely on the basis of the authority of the executive responsible for planning— often the president-owner. In complex organizations, where many persons are involved in planning and a high degree of cooperation and coordination are required for implementation, successful planning requires objectivity and explicitness. Plans that meet the following criteria possess these qualities.

Statement of Purpose. Planners must have a clear concept of the mission of the firm and the specific purpose of a given plan.

Statement of Problems. The need for planning implies that a problem exists—that certain organizational needs are not being met or will not be met in the future without planning. The problem, the discrepancy between present performance and desired performance, should be clearly stated.

Designation of Planning Authority. Once a decision is made to engage in a formal program of planning, an individual or group should be assigned the responsibility for carrying out the planning function and should be given the authority needed to accomplish it.

Collection and Interpretation of Data. Planners throughout the firm must have free access to all relevant information, both from within the firm and without, including input from outside economic and technical experts if necessary. Collection and interpretation of data involve both forecasting and making explicit the premises on which plans are based.

Development of Alternative Plans. Because different premises can be defended in most situations, because plans which are appropriate under one set of premises may be inappropriate under another, and because under a given set of premises different plans may achieve essentially the same results, alternative plans should be developed.

Flexibility. Paradoxical as it may seem, the characteristic that contributes most to the stability and probable success of the plan is its flexibility. Rigid plans may appear to offer stability and firmness, but rigidity inevitably interferes with management's ability to meet the requirements of changing conditions.

Although flexibility requires certain attitudes on the part of planners and implementers, a plan achieves flexibility primarily through the development of alternatives and through alerting management to the conditions under which a change of plans will be appropriate. The availability of standby plans permits management to meet challenging external conditions without costly delay. It is also noteworthy that gaining approval of a plan is easier if alternatives are available for use under specified contingencies; building flexibility into a plan requires thoroughness in planning and consequently inspires confidence.

Comprehensiveness. The comprehensiveness of a plan—the extent to which it provides solutions to the original problem—is not necessarily expressed by its breadth. Simple plans that are well stated are often quite comprehensive. A production plan for a departmental supervisor may span a period of one day and affect the work of only two people, yet answer a particular need. Similarly, a plan requiring 100 people for its execution and a time span of one year may lack comprehensiveness.

Designated Time Span. A well-structured plan includes a definite statement of the time required for its completion. The starting and completion dates of a plan should be specific; in addition, complex plans specify the time spans of intermediate goals.

Assignment of Duties. To implement a plan effectively, duties must be assigned to designated personnel. The mere listing of activities to be performed is not sufficient. Activities must be expressed as job duties and assigned as responsibilities to individual members of the organization.

Control Features. An effective plan provides for controls during implementation. Provision may be made for periodic reviews by designated personnel who review progress at specific control points and recommend necessary action. To aid in such reviews, it is desirable to indicate the amount of variance from the original plan that can be tolerated.

Decision Making. After alternatives are developed, a choice must be made from among them. This is an action step involving commitment of the firm's resources. It also involves calculated risks to decision makers and to the firm.

Testing Tentative Plans. Although not always feasible, it is desirable to test a plan before its grand-scale application. The value of a training program, an advertising campaign, or a production process may be trial tested before a major commitment is made. In some situations, where plans can be expressed mathematically, testing may be carried out through *simulations*, through models of real life that can be computer tested rather than tested through more costly pilot studies or full-scale applications.

Statement of Final Plan. The last step in planning is the statement of the final plan. It should contain provisions for implementation throughout the organization. The ultimate test of a plan is whether it is used and gets results.

Economic Effectiveness

Over a period of years it has been observed that good plans have the afore-mentioned procedural characteristics. However, a procedurally correct plan carried through to its successful completion may not have been the most appropriate plan for a specific situation. The concept of *economic effectiveness*, widely used in economics, may determine whether a plan makes the maximum contribution to company objectives. The application of this concept as a management tool rests on two basic assumptions:

1. Management of a business enterprise is primarily an economic activity, and the principles and techniques of economics should be applicable and transferable as principles and techniques of management. The word *economic* means the effective utilization of all resources.
2. The primary objective of any organization is to maximize the return (units of output) in relation to the effort (units of input) expended. This premise is stated in broad terms because the concept of maximization of return applies not only to the management of a business, but also to the management of a charitable foundation seeking the best (most economic) distribution of its funds; to a religious organization seeking converts; or to a labor union demanding increased benefits for its members.

The Law of Diminishing Returns.[28] The second assumption implies that the units of return are compatible with organizational objectives. If so, the problem is one of determining the amount contributed by the last unit of input in relation to the amount contributed by the next to last unit of input. The method for making this determination can be accomplished in several ways, but all methods have one common characteristic—they represent a certain way of looking at input-output relationships. An example illustrating input-output relationships assumes a unit of land (say 640 acres), a worker, and corn, the product. The one worker farms the 640 acres and is able to produce 50 bushels of corn per acre with certain given tools (tractor, farm implements, etc.). It is reasonable to expect that by increasing the number of workers there will be an increase in the yield of corn. Eventually, however, adding workers does not result in additional product. This phenomenon has been stated variously as the *law of diminishing returns* or the *law of variable returns*.

Now to translate the classic economic example into a problem in production; Columns A, B, and C of Table 4–2 indicate the three elements of our first example. Assume that the tools (that is, the plant and the facilities), the product, and the methods remain the same. One unit of input is the work of one person for an eight-hour day. This one unit of input produces 10 units of output, the total produced. In this instance the average produced is also 10. Average production is obtained by dividing total units produced by the units of input. When another worker is added, the economic effectiveness of each worker increases and the total produced reaches 24; the average goes up to 12. The addition of

---

[28] For a more detailed discussion of the law of diminishing returns, see James R. McGuigan and R. Charles Moyer, *Managerial Economics* (2d ed.; St. Paul, Minn.: West Publishing Company, Inc., 1979), p. 216.

Table 4–2
RELATIONSHIP
BETWEEN
UNITS
OF INPUT,
TOTAL
PRODUCED,
AVERAGE
PRODUCED,
AND
MARGINAL
PRODUCT

A Units of Input	B Total Produced	C Average Produced	D Marginal Product
1	10	10	—
2	24	12	14
3	39	13	15
4	48	12	9
5	55	11	7
6	60	10	5
7	63	9	3
8	64	8	1
9	63	7	−1

the third worker results in total production of 39, with an average of 13. So far everything is increasing. When the fourth worker is added, total production continues to rise; but the average drops to 12. With the addition of a fifth worker, the production goes up and the average slips to 11; and with the addition of the sixth worker, the average is down to 10 again; however, the total number of units produced is 60, or six times as much as that produced by one worker. After the seventh, eighth, and ninth workers, the average production per worker is reduced to seven; and, by adding the ninth worker, the phenomenon of diminishing returns appears and the total production declines from 64 to 63.

This relatively simple example poses a problem that recurs as the central theme of many managerial decisions. Managers, in making their decisions, must answer the following question: What combination of resources results in the greatest economic return consistent with the objectives of the organization? If it can be said of a plan that it represents the best (most economic) combination of resources resulting in the achievement of desired objectives, the plan is appropriate. Obviously both aspects of the test must be met. If the plan does not result in the achievement of desired objectives, it is not appropriate; nor is it appropriate if in achieving the desired objectives there is anything less than the most economic use of resources.

The Concept of Marginal Product. How can it be determined when there is the most efficient use of available resources? The information in the first three columns of Table 4–2 does not provide sufficient data, but it does indicate some difficulty as reflected in the average units produced per worker. Note that the average starts falling when the fourth worker is added. A second indication that all is not well is revealed by the amount of total production. This measure drops when the ninth worker is added. Since our concern is with input-output relationships, does it not seem logical to study these relationships more carefully and find out what happens each time an additional person is added? It is necessary to determine exactly how much *additional* output results from each *additional* unit of input. Economists refer to this incremental relationship between additional units of input and resultant additional units of output as *marginal product*. The terms *marginal productivity*, *marginal revenue*, or *marginal profit*, may be interpreted as *additional* productivity, *additional* revenue, or *additional* profit in relation to an *additional* unit of input.

In Table 4–2, Column D shows the marginal (additional) product resulting from each additional unit of input. The first person working for eight hours (one unit of input) forms the base of the problem. The marginal productivity of this worker cannot be computed because there was no previous production. With the addition of the second worker, 24 units were produced, a gain of 14 units over that produced by the first worker alone (24–10). The addition of the third worker results in the production of 39 units, 15 units more than the amount produced by the previous two-worker team. The addition of the fourth worker yields only nine additional units, compared to the 14 added by the second worker and the 15 added by the third worker. The average production also drops by one unit from 13 to 12. The incremental increase in production resulting from additional units of input continues to drop and at a more rapid rate than the decline in average production. With the addition of the ninth worker, the results are negative, a marginal (additional) increase of −1; and the total number of units produced also declines by one. Column D shows that production increases until the fourth worker is added; thus, it seems that the maximum utilization of available resources occurs when the third worker is added.[29]

Management must continually ask if its action or plan maximizes the efficient utilization of resources in achieving its objectives. When a choice must be made between two plans, each of which is procedurally sound, the concept of marginal product may provide a useful decision criterion.

Cost-Benefit Analysis

When the two assumptions upon which the economic effectiveness criteria are based (see page 79) are not valid and data cannot be expressed in numerical form, a cost-benefit analysis provides an alternative framework for evaluating a plan. Such conditions often exist in nonprofit organizations—government units, educational institutions, and religious organizations—as well as in some businesses.[30]

Difficulties in quantifying the benefits of a course of action become obvious when managers begin to work with such output variables as improving employee morale, fulfilling social responsibility objectives, minimizing problems with government agencies, and reducing labor-management conflict. Although these variables can, to a degree, be expressed in numerical form, they are basically qualitative in nature and must be treated as such.

---

[29] Evan J. Douglas, *Managerial Economics* (Englewood Cliffs, N. J.: Prentice-Hall, Inc., 1979), p. 195; Also Milton H. Spencer, K. K. Seo, and Mark G. Simpkin, *Managerial Economics,* Text, Problems, and Short Cases (4h ed.; Homewood, Ill.: Richard D. Irwin, Inc., 1975), Chapter 7.

[30] A thorough discussion of cost-benefit analysis may be found in McGuigan and Moyer, *op. cit.*, p. 464.

Even if it were possible to express numerically all costs and benefits, thereby meeting the requirement of the economic effectiveness criterion that inputs and outputs be quantified, there would still remain a problem caused by the maximization assumption. As indicated previously in this chapter, managers often seek the satisfactory achievement of several objectives—they satisfice rather than maximize profits or some other organizational objective. In employment, for example, maximizing productive efficiency would demand that the organization's plans call for employing in every instance the person most likely to be productive; but a goal to offset past acts of unfair discrimination may result in plans to hire increased numbers of female and minority employees (an affirmative action plan) while upholding only less than ideal standards relating to productivity.

When conducting a cost-benefit analysis, planners make judgments about the comparative merits of different plans in achieving the organization's mission or specific objectives. What, for example, are the relative benefits of investing several million dollars in an antipollution device versus investing in additional machines, increased employee compensation, or increased dividends? Such judgments involve quantifiable financial considerations, but they also involve the values of the decision makers and judgments which cannot be expressed numerically. Since most organizations have objectives which are not completely quantifiable and since the maximization assumption often cannot be met, cost-benefit analysis is a practical tool for evaluating plans.

We have reviewed the methods of evaluating the potential effectiveness of plans. The first approach describes and evaluates the observable characteristics of the planning process itself. The second evaluates a plan in terms of its economic effectiveness. The third approach is cost-benefit analysis, a method used when the assumptions underlying the economic effectiveness method are not met and when it is difficult to quantify either the costs or the benefits.

Case Problem 4-B offers an opportunity to utilize cost-benefit analysis techniques in the area of the social responsibilities of a business organization.

Case Problem 4-B
COST-BENEFIT ANALYSIS OF SOCIAL RESPONSIBILITY[31]

A company manufacturing fabricated metal products employs approximately 400 hourly rated employees, most of whom are highly skilled machinists. The annual sales of the company are approximately $12 million with an annual payroll of approximately $4 million. The company is located in a city of about 200,000 and is one of the larger manufacturers in the city. Within the city there are approximately 15,000 low-income, socially disadvantaged people who have moved into the area during the past 25 years. About 25 of this category are employed in the plant in unskilled jobs.

[31] Case Problem 4-B is based on David Novick, "Cost-Benefit Analysis and Social Responsibility," *Business Horizons*, Vol. 16, No. 5 (October, 1973), p. 63.

The president of the company is extremely active in community affairs and believes that the company has a social responsibility to help alleviate unemployment and improve housing, schooling, and other problems confronting this disadvantaged social group. As a result of these beliefs the president of the company has requested that $100,000 be budgeted during the coming year to aid the company in meeting its social responsibilities to the community. Once the decision to budget the $100,000 was made, a planning committee was established to recommend how the $100,000 should be spent to gain the greatest benefits in aiding the company to meet its social responsibilities. The following are the alternatives presented by the committee. Anticipated benefits are stated for each of the five options.

1. Establish a training program for unskilled workers so that they may progress to the skilled positions in the organization. There have been sporadic efforts in this direction in the past, and the records thus far indicate that out of five workers placed in a formal apprenticeship program only one or two ever develop the skills necessary to become qualified machinists. The other three or four, though they remain with the company, are below average in output and quality of product produced. In addition, some employees resent the special treatment offered the socially deprived group and frictions develop between present employees and newly hired and trained disadvantaged employees.

2. Invest the $100,000 allocated for social responsibility in another industry, located in the town, that utilizes primarily unskilled and semiskilled workers. It is estimated that such an investment would create approximately 200 jobs. This option would possibly result in the other company receiving the credit for creating the additional job opportunities rather than the company making the investment.

In addition, there is potential criticism that, by creating 200 relatively low-paying unskilled jobs, one is simply perpetuating the plight of the disadvantaged social group and that the jobs would be labeled dead-end jobs.

3. Invest the $100,000 in research and development with the intent of developing a product line that would result in the creation of at least 50 semiskilled machine operator jobs. Such a move would result in the establishment of a product line of perhaps a lower quality than the present high-quality product and could conceivably result in damaging the company's image within the industry as a quality manufacturer. The number of jobs created would be relatively insignificant in relation to the number of jobs needed in the community.

4. Since the company is located on a piece of property much larger than is needed in terms of future expansion, spend part of the $100,000 to improve the landscaping and general appearance of the plant and offices and spend the remainder in building a community recreation center. Such a center could be used by many community organizations throughout the entire city. This option would have an immediate and long-range impact, hopefully favorable, on residents throughout the community and especially on those living in the neighborhood of the plant. It is also believed that such a move would enhance the image of the company.

5. Establish a public relations campaign including a well-organized institutional advertising program to inform the community of the current activities in which the company is involved. Any donations to such fine arts groups as civic opera, symphony, or other cultural activities would become a part of the institutional advertising program. Current donations to civic and charitable groups should be made public. Such a campaign might have positive effects on middle- and high-income groups, but there are questions

as to its favorable reception by low-income or disadvantaged groups. Also, it would not directly benefit such groups, since normally they do not participate in this type of community activity.

PROBLEMS

1. Prepare a cost-benefit analysis for each of the five options stated above. In one column present anticipated social benefits and in the other column the costs, or potential liabilities, involved with each option. Rank each cost and each benefit on a scale from 1 to 10 in terms of its potential liability (cost) or its potential benefit. Then rank each option in terms of its desirability.

2. State the reasons for your ranking of each of the options.

3. Discuss the basic value systems underlying the decision of a company to enter into the area of social responsibility as well as continuing its objective of making a profit.

4. Is there any basic conflict between maximizing profit and simultaneously establishing and fulfilling social objectives?

CHAPTER QUESTIONS FOR STUDY AND DISCUSSION

1. Visualize two managers, one of whom does an outstanding job of planning while the other neglects this function. Why will the good planner be a better manager?

2. How do goals differ from strategies? How do the qualities that distinguish goals from strategies motivate performance?

3. Briefly develop a concrete example of a company that satisfices rather than maximizes with reference to its main objectives.

4. In light of the definition of planning presented in this chapter, how can one justify classifying a rule as a plan?

5. As a recently employed executive in a rapidly expanding company, you want to convince your superiors that forecasting is beneficial. What arguments will you use?

6. What is the logic for developing multiple scenarios before deciding on a specific strategy?

7. What conceivable reasons could employees and managers have for objecting to being evaluated solely on the basis of results?

8. The long-range effectiveness of MBO programs has yet to be demonstrated. Why could an MBO program significantly improve performance in the early stages of its application and then level off?

9. Under what conditions and to reap what benefits will you want to test a plan through simulations before making a full-scale implementation of it?

10. What are the benefits of making a planning procedure explicit?

11. To what degree are the assumptions required to evaluate the economic effectiveness of a plan likely to be correct?

12. Why are value judgments of great importance in establishing the worth of a plan to reach a specific profit goal?

Chapter 5

Planning for Functional Areas

CHANNEL OF DISTRIBUTION

In 1920 Electroware began manufacturing electrical household appliances in Toledo, Ohio. For the next ten years its product line was limited to small appliances such as electric irons, toasters, waffle irons, portable ovens, and percolators. These items were sold directly to retail stores and were in turn sold to the consumer. Now there are approximately 1,000 retail outlets located in the midwestern and eastern states that are customers of Electroware. In 1930 the company introduced a line of electric hot water heaters designed for residential use; and, without giving the matter much thought, the existing channel of distribution from manufacturer to retail outlet to consumer was continued. Several years ago, however, the company discontinued the manufacturing of small appliances and devoted its full attention to manufacturing and selling electric hot water units.

Recently John Miller was promoted from the position of vice-president—manufacturing, to president. While in charge of the manufacturing function, he served as chairman of a product diversification committee. The committee recommended that Electroware manufacture electric stoves in order to supplement its existing line of hot water heaters.

This recommendation was adopted. As a result, Miller, during his first year as president, directed his attention toward the completion of a new addition to the plant and the installation of necessary equipment so that electric stoves could be produced. Reliable estimates from the production planning department indicated that the stove line could be in operation by the end of the year and that a total of 26,500 units could be assembled during the next calendar year. Furthermore, the production of electric hot water heaters was expected to remain constant at 40,000 units a year, or slightly more than 150 a day.

Tom Andrews, vice-president—marketing, had opposed the expansion of facilities in order to manufacture electric stoves. He pointed out that the present annual production of heaters amounted to less than four heaters a month for each of the 1,000 retail outlets, and that the store owners and managers were becoming dissatisfied, since they were not receiving a quantity of heaters sufficient to meet customer demand. One store owner described the situation as follows: "People don't come in here just to buy hot water heaters; usually they want something else for their home. Therefore, if they can't buy all the things they want in one place, they go to a store that will sell them everything they want at the same time. By not having enough heaters, I am losing sales in those items that I do have in stock."

Andrews also argued that the projected volume of electric stoves would be adding insult to injury because each dealer would receive an average of only two stoves a month. Mr. Miller then suggested that the stoves be sold through a different channel of distribution, such as directly to the builders of apartments and large housing projects. Andrews objected to this approach, insisting that the company must be loyal to its present dealers, since these dealers had stood by Electroware during the lean years. Furthermore, he feared that many dealers would refuse to handle the hot water heaters unless they received a commission on all Electroware products sold in their community.

Mr. Miller discussed the problem of selecting a channel of distribution with Ted Donham, the controller. Donham recommended that a distributor, or wholesaler, be appointed for each of the following cities: Chicago, Detroit, Cleveland, and Cincinnati. He did not like the idea of selling directly to the building contractors because he believed that many of them would be poor credit risks and that the cost of contacting each individual contractor would be exces-

sive. He was against extending the present method of distribution to electric stoves because it would require the shipment of one or two items a month to each of the 1,000 retailers, thereby creating a great deal of paperwork. He believed that the selection of four distributors would permit the company to ship in carload lots and reduce freight costs. He also emphasized that the production rate of electric stoves would be sufficient to satisfy the needs of four carefully selected distributors.

PROBLEMS

1. Define the problem that Electroware is attempting to solve.
2. State the policy that you believe Electroware should adopt in order to solve its current problem.
3. Do you recommend that both products be sold through the same channel of distribution? Why?
4. Do you subscribe to Mr. Andrews' point of view that the company should be loyal to its present dealers?
5. When Mr. Miller was vice-president—manufacturing, he served as chairman of a product diversification committee. Would Mr. Andrews, vice-president—marketing, be a more logical candidate for the chairmanship of such a committee?

In Chapter 4, "Setting Objectives and Planning for Results," the planning function is discussed. In Chapter 7, "Production Management," planning and goal setting for the production function are examined. This chapter will more closely examine the planning function as applied to the other major functions—finance, marketing, and personnel. Therefore, the emphasis will be on planning for policy statements concerning each of these three functional areas.

Table 5–1 summarizes the scope of policies for each of the four major functional areas. Although the production function is treated separately in Chapter 7, it is included in this table so that the student may see the high degree of interrelationship between each of the functional areas. The availability of capital and the manner in which capital is employed have their effect on the production process. There is also a close relationship between the policies govern-

FINANCE	MARKETING	PRODUCTION	PERSONNEL
Acquisition of Capital	*Product Selection*	*Product Policies*	*Staffing*
Long-term capital	Product diversification	Diversification	Selection
	Product obsolescence		Promotion
Stock	Product style	New products	Termination
Bonds	Product quality	Integration	
Mortgages	Product standardization	Make or buy	*Development*
Long-term notes			
	Pricing the Product	Quality	Training
Short-term capital		Standardization	Management development
	Product costs		
Commercial credits	Competition	Inventory	*Compensation*
Bank loans	Pricing new products		
Commercial factors	Terms of sale	*Facility Policies*	Amount of compensation
			Method of payment
Utilization of Capital	*Channel of Distribution*	Location	Employee benefit plans
		Capacity	
Fixed assets	*Promotion*	Maintenance	*Labor-Management Relations*
Working capital			
Inventory	Direct selling	*Selection of Vendors*	Organizational climate
Credit and collections	Advertising		Relation with nonunion
	Special promotional	Number of vendors	employees
Distribution of Profit	devices	Reciprocity	
Dividends			
Reinvestment			

Table 5–1
SUMMARY OF
THE SCOPE OF
POLICIES FOR
EACH
FUNCTIONAL
AREA

ing the production function and the marketing function. The quantity and quality of the product or service produced sets the upper limits of the level of achievement of the marketing function. Well-formulated and properly executed personnel policies have their effect on all the other functional areas.

THE FINANCE FUNCTION

As shown in Table 5–1, the finance function encompasses the acquisition of capital, the utilization of capital, and the distribution of profit. Since profit is necessary for the survival of a business, it is necessary to have an understanding of the various meanings of the term *profit*.[1]

The Meaning of Profit

Profit has been viewed as a form of compensation to the individual owner or to the stockholders of a publicly held corporation. It has also been defined within the framework of an economic process, a concept that states that profit is the result of a firm's operating in an economic environment that is not perfect. Differences in the desirability of location or holding a patent on a manufactured product are examples of these imperfections which are known as *frictions*. Profit can be considered the result of innovations, either with respect to the product or to the method in which the business is operated. Profit may be defined as the amount remaining after all expenses associated with conducting a business have been met. However, this definition leaves much to be desired since it is passive in nature and leads one to believe that profit is something left over. Profit must be regarded as an integral portion of the sales dollar and a management goal that can be realized through proper planning. Profit creates new capital to provide for expansion. Consequently, the continuance and growth of any industrial enterprise depend upon its ability to produce profit.

Profit may be measured as total dollars earned or may be expressed as a ratio. The most common method of expressing a company's profit is total dollars earned during a specified period of time. However, additional information is required to make this measure meaningful. Knowledge of past performance provides a basis for comparing a company's present performance with its past record. Profit for a given firm must be considered in light of the performance of its industry so that profitability in relation to other companies may be ascertained. The meaning of the statement that a company has increased its profits 10 percent over its profits for the preceding year changes significantly when it is known that the average profit for other companies in the same industry also increased 10 percent. Similarly, the meaning changes if the industry average decreased 10 percent or remained constant during the same period.

[1] Carl A. Dauten and Merle Welshans, *Principles of Finance* (4h ed.; Cincinnati: South-Western Publishing Co., 1975).

J. Fred Weston and Eugene F. Brigham, *Managerial Finance* (5h ed.; Hinsdale: Dryden Press, 1975).

The two most frequently used ratios, or percentages, to express profitability are (1) percentage return on capital invested and (2) percentage return on sales. In the opinion of many analysts, return on invested capital is by far the most important measure because it indicates the effectiveness of management's stewardship and has a marked effect on the company's ability to attract new investment capital. Consequently, a company's rate of growth is directly influenced by its return on invested capital. Percentage return on sales is a measure closely associated with the operating statement of a company and is affected directly by changes in operating costs. When expressed as a percentage of sales, profit decreases by the same amount that sales volume decreases unless costs are reduced correspondingly. Conversely, when sales volume increases profits should show the same percentage increase, provided that operating costs remain constant.

Acquisition of Capital

The sources of capital for an individual starting a business are savings, borrowed capital, or both. The same sources used by the individual—savings, or prior earnings, and borrowed capital—are available to a corporation. Capital acquired from outside sources is usually classified according to the length of time for which the financing is desired. Financing required for periods greater than one year is referred to as *long-term capital*, and capital required for a period of less than one year is referred to as *short-term capital*.

Long-Term Capital. The sources of long-term capital are stocks, bonds, mortgages, and long-term notes, each of which has distinct advantages and disadvantages.

The sale of *stock*, representing a share of ownership, is one of the most widely used means of raising capital for a corporation and may be designated as either *preferred stock* or *common stock*. When formulating policies concerning the issuance of preferred stock, a company must recognize that there may be occasions, especially when earnings are less than anticipated, that may result in the elimination of dividends on common stock in order to pay dividends on preferred stock. There is no such obligation with respect to common stock. Also, the concept of equity must be considered. Without a corresponding increase in fixed assets, the issuance of additional stock results in dilution of stockholder equity. Consideration must be given to determining whether the payment of a dividend on common stock is necessary to make the purchase of such equities an attractive investment.

When a company issues *bonds*, another means of long-term financing, it agrees that it will repay the face value of the bond on a specified date and that a fixed rate of interest will be paid until that date. One advantage of bonds is that management's control of the company is not jeopardized as it may be when additional stock with voting rights is issued. Second, the fixed rate that a company pays for a bond issue is an expense item and is not taxed as income; however, dividends paid to stockholders come from profits after the payment of income taxes. A disadvantage resulting from the issuance of bonds is the obligation to pay interest, thus resulting in an additional fixed charge to the issuing company.

Another means of obtaining capital is through *mortgages* secured by part or all of the company's real property. Most modern mortgages enable a company to retain its present management and control as long as payments on principal and interest are met as agreed. *Long-term notes* are also used as a means of raising capital. Again, interest payments are considered an expense item. However, there may be distinct disadvantages if the lender places restrictions on the payment of dividends or the purchase of additional assets, or requires representation on the board of directors.

Short-Term Capital. Short-term capital supplements the company's existing cash and may be used for such things as the purchase of additional inventory or taking advantage of cash or quantity discounts. The most frequently used source of short-term capital is bank loans; however, the degree to which banks are used as a source of credit depends on the company's reputation and the relationship it has established with the banking community. *Commercial credits* are another source of short-term capital. Commercial credits, which are similar to an individual's charge account, are extended by vendors to customers with good credit ratings. Such credits imply a deferral of payments for 30, 60, or even 90 days, thus establishing a source of short-term capital. A third source is *commercial factors.* These firms specialize in short-term financing usually through the purchase of a company's accounts receivable. In some instances factors prepare the required invoices and perform all the paperwork necessary to collect the accounts. To firms without an adequate clerical staff, the use of commercial factors may offer an attractive means of acquiring short-term capital.

Utilization of Capital

Once capital has been acquired, financial policies must be developed for its proper utilization. Elements to be considered in determining the most effective utilization of capital are the amount of capital to be placed into fixed assets, the ratio between fixed assets and working capital, the amount of inventory, and policies concerning credit and collections. Each of these elements demands cash; and unless there are policies that specify the amount to be allocated for each use, a serious imbalance may result, thereby impairing the firm's position.[2]

Fixed Assets. In its simplest form, the policy decision concerning the amount of capital to be allocated to fixed assets is a question of leasing or buying. The latter choice results in increasing fixed assets. The problems of obsolescence, maintenance, replacement, and the rate of return on specific assets arise. Tax liability must be considered since money paid for rentals or leases is usually

---

[2] Glenn H. Petry, "Effective Use of Capital Budgeting Tools," *Business Horizons*, Vol. XIX, No. 5 (October, 1975), p. 57.

Louis V. Gerstner, Jr., and M. Helen Anderson, "The Chief Financial Officer as Activist," *Harvard Business Review*, Vol. 54, No. 5 (September–October, 1976), p. 100.

considered an expense and tax deductible. Such tax advantages may be offset by a depreciation allowance on fixed assets. Fixed assets may also be converted into cash, should the need arise.

Working Capital. Closely related to the amount of capital to be placed in fixed assets is the capital to be retained and utilized for the operation of the business. Such capital is referred to as *working capital* and is used for the purchase of materials and services, for payment of payrolls, and for contingencies. Balance should be maintained between fixed assets, most of which require money to operate, and the working capital available for their operation. Policies define the proper ratio for a given company.

Inventory. Policy statements with regard to inventory should include a determination of the size of inventory of both in-process and finished goods, expressed as a unit portion of annual sales. A determination of the rate of inventory buildup and turnover is necessary in order to take advantage of price fluctuations of raw materials and to minimize the risk of obsolescence.

Credit and Collection. Virtually every business is forced to extend some credit to its customers. The extent to which credit is granted may be determined by general industry practices, or it may be the result of attempting to secure a better competitive position. In either event, clear-cut policies are needed to determine the amount of credit to be extended. Closely allied to credit policies are policies governing the collection of accounts receivable and the granting of discounts from list price for prompt payment. Accounts receivable, unless closely watched, may become abnormally large and reduce cash flow.

Distribution of Profit

The third area of financial policy determination concerns the distribution of profit. Policies must be developed to determine the amount to be retained for operating expenses and for expansion. Consideration must also be given to the allocation of funds for dividends.

Dividends. It is necessary to formulate policy statements concerning the payment of dividends in order to assure a fair return on investment to those who have invested in the firm and to make the continuing purchase of equities in the firm an attractive investment. Such policies may express the amount to be paid out in dividends as a percentage of profit earned. When profits increase so does the amount returned to investors; however, when profits decrease, dividends do also. The alternative is one of stating a fixed rate of return modified periodically based on long-term trends in earnings.

Reinvestment. The establishment of adequate cash reserves and the payment of dividends must also relate to policies concerning *reinvestment.* Questions to be answered are what portion of the profit is to be reinvested in the firm and how this money is to be reinvested. It may be placed in fixed assets, as a means of increasing sales volume. A method of increasing sales not ordinarily classified as reinvestment is to direct capital into an expanded advertising program or to establish sales territories not currently served by the company. Another major area for the utilization of capital is research and development.

THE MARKETING FUNCTION

The *marketing function* of a business organization encompasses those activities necessary to move goods and services from the producer to customers or consumers in a manner that satisfies both the needs of the organization and the needs of the customers or consumers. The business activities included in the above definition are the determination of (1) the product or service to be offered, (2) the price of the product or service, (3) the method of distribution so that the product or service is made available to consumers, and (4) the method of promotion to be used in order to enhance the volume of the product or service being offered. Each of these aspects of the marketing function is discussed in turn.[3]

Product Selection

The determination of policies concerning the product or service involves not only the marketing function but also the other functional areas. The contribution of the marketing department in forming product policies is its estimate of the potential market and its responsibility for the distribution of the product to the customer. There are four policy determinations that influence product selection. They are (1) product diversification, (2) product obsolescence, (3) product quality, and (4) product standardization.

Product Diversification. The term, *product diversification,* refers to the number of products produced and distributed and the extent to which they differ from each other in terms of physical characteristics, manufacturing processes, and selling methods. Product diversification implicitly refers to the acquisition of additional products. However, diversification policies should serve not only as guides for the acquisition of additional products but also should show the need for reducing the number of items in an existing product line. Factors to be considered in the acquisition of new products are available financing, the production facilities required, and the method of distribution. The qualifications of available personnel, particularly their ability to perform continuing research and development work, are a necessary consideration if a position of leadership is desired. Anticipated market size, the level of sales volume, and profitability serve as effective guides in determining whether an existing product should be retained or dropped from the product line.

Product Obsolescence. *Obsolescence* of durable goods occurs when a product is no longer usable for any one of several reasons. Durable goods, both consumer

[3] Roy T. Shaw, Richard J. Semenik, and Robert H. Williams, *Marketing, An Integrated Analytical Approach* (4h ed.; Cincinnati: South-Western Publishing Co., 1980). E. Jerome McCarthy, *Basic Marketing, A Managerial Approach* (6h ed.; Homewood, Ill.: Richard D. Irwin, Inc., 1978).

and capital, become obsolete when worn out, thereby having served their useful life. There is also the concept of *forced obsolescence* which is the direct result of a policy decision. Continued product improvement or change may be used to create consumer dissatisfaction with the product in its present form. Changes in style, for example in wearing apparel, are another means of inducing forced obsolescence. Policy statements concerning product obsolescence determine the extent and frequency of changes in design and style in order to create a desire for a product that is either new in appearance or better in performance.

Product Quality. *Quality* refers to those characteristics that are relevant in measuring the degree to which a product meets predetermined standards of performance. Quality is not an absolute value; yet there is an implied relationship between quality and excellence of design, workmanship, materials, and price. One policy question that must be resolved is the determination of how many levels of quality are to be produced or sold. Any given firm must determine whether or not it is going to carry multiple-quality product lines. Another policy consideration concerning quality is determining whether or not truly outstanding quality can be used as the primary basis for promotion.

Product Standardization. *Standardization* is closely related to the number of levels of quality in the product line. A reduction in the number of levels of quality or the number of models produced and distributed is a move toward product standardization, usually resulting in a lowering of production and distribution costs. Hence, policy statements setting forth the optimum degree of standardization of a given product line, with respect to either quality or the number of models, is a choice between potentially lower costs in production and distribution or the possibility of increased market share potential.

Pricing

It is recognized that the costs of production and distribution have a direct bearing on price. However, cost is only one of several factors that must be considered in establishing pricing policies. The actions of competitors often influence price. When pricing a new product, it is necessary to consider the proposed price in relation to the price structure of the current product line and whether or not the product should be introduced at a relatively low price then raised when it has gained market acceptance. The alternative is to price the product relative to actual cost and hope that as the result of increased volume to ultimately lower the price due to reduced production and distribution costs. Finally, the terms of sale, including the availability of credit and discount privileges, modify the significance of the stated price.[4]

---

[4] One of the best discussions concerning pricing policies for new products appeared in 1950 and was republished as a *Harvard Business Review* classic. Joel Dean, "Pricing Policies for New Products," *Harvard Business Review*, Vol. 54, No. 6 (November–December, 1976), p. 141.

Channel of Distribution

One of the underlying assumptions in selecting the channel of distribution is that certain functions are inherent in the process of distribution and must be performed. The decision to sell either directly to the consumer or through a series of intermediaries to the consumer is the selection of a channel of distribution. Orders are received, the product is drawn from stock, shipments are sent to the customer, a statement of the amount due is prepared, and provisions for collection are provided. Any of these functions may be combined or transferred to another position in the distribution cycle, but the function itself is not eliminated. A company selling directly to the consumer performs all these functions. However, if one or more intermediaries, variously called jobbers, distributors, wholesalers, or retailers, are introduced into the cycle some of these functions may be transferred to the intermediary. Sometimes the selection of the channel of distribution is determined by industry practices. Even so, the selection of a market channel offers an opportunity for innovation. Avon Products, Inc., for example, sells directly to the consumer through its own field sales force, while competitors distribute similar products through wholesalers, to retail stores, and ultimately to the consumer. The factors to be considered in selecting one channel of distribution in preference to another, assuming that such choice is possible, are (1) the costs incurred as the result of performing the functions of the distribution cycle and (2) the advantages gained by controlling the selling effort with the company's own sales force and direct contact with the customer. There is also the possibility that more than one channel of distribution may be utilized.

Promotion Policies

The final policy question to be considered is determining an effective means of persuading the customer to buy the product—the selection of the methods of *promotion*. Personal selling, advertising, and sales promotion are the most frequently used forms of promotion.

The process of a salesperson persuading a customer to buy a product is referred to as *personal selling*. Two aspects of personal selling are particularly significant in formulating promotion policies. The first is establishing the importance of the role of sales personnel in persuading the customer to buy a given product. At one extreme are those people—such as those employed by variety chains and supermarkets—who function as sales clerks and whose only contribution to the selling process is to respond to requests of customers. At the other extreme of the selling process are the agents of life insurance companies who locate a prospect, create a felt need for the product, and finally persuade the prospect to buy an intangible item that may never offer a tangible reward to the buyer personally.

The second aspect of personal selling is determining the optimum degree of control necessary to realize the greatest benefit from sales personnel. A close degree of control is usually possible when those who sell the product are employees of the company making the product. Many industrial products, such as machine tools, are sold in this manner; however, relatively few consumer products are sold by a sales force employed by the manufacturer. Instead they are sold through the efforts of employees of the retailer. If the efforts of sales personnel are incidental to the selling process, such personnel are usually not employed by the producer of the product. As a result, emphasis is placed on *advertising* or *sales promotional devices,* such as point-of-sale demonstrations used in department stores and other retail outlets. However, when sales personnel are the decisive factor in persuading the customer to buy, the producer of the product usually employs and exercises close control over the sales force. Consequently, advertising and other promotional devices are of lesser importance.

THE PERSONNEL FUNCTION

The functions of finance, marketing, and production are usually managed by an executive who is assigned sole responsibility for the performance of that particular function. If the organization is large enough, there is also an executive assigned responsibility for the performance of the personnel function; but, unlike other executives, the personnel manager shares the performance of the personnel function. The reason for the shared responsibility is inherent in the nature of the personnel function itself.[5]

The Nature of the Personnel Function

The personnel function includes all the activities associated with the management of personnel. Since organizations are composed of people and the work of organizations is accomplished by and through people, managers of operating units by necessity manage personnel. In addition, historically managers have performed, and still do in small organizations, all the duties normally associated with the management of personnel—including selecting, training, compensating, and administering any additional benefits associated with employment. Only recently has personnel management emerged as a separate function with a manager charged with the responsibility of administering the personnel function for the entire organization. Even so, many of the functions of personnel are still performed by other managers. For example, in most companies unit managers still retain the final decisions as to whom they will employ, make recommendations concerning promotions and level of pay, and are responsible for much of the training.

Several factors have contributed to the emergence of personnel as a separate function. First, as organizations grew in size and complexity it became increasingly difficult for the unit manager to continue successfully the performance of the personnel function. Second, knowledge developed from divergent sources

---

[5] Herbert J. Chruden and Arthur W. Sherman, Jr., *Personnel Management* (6h ed.; Cincinnati: South-Western Publishing Co., 1980).

George Strauss and Leonard R. Sayles, *Personnel,* The Human Problems of Management (3d ed.; Englewood Cliffs, N. J.: Prentice-Hall, Inc., 1972).

has had a direct bearing on the management of personnel. One source stressed the importance of measuring work, another the need for selection and training, and a third the need for determining the amount of compensation to be received for performing a job. Knowledge was also gained from the human relations approach to management, for it was this philosophy that emphasized that the worker was motivated by sociological and psychological factors as well as by economic interests. The development of labor unions and their bargaining for wages, hours, and other terms and conditions of employment forced companies to set up a counterpart to bargain with the unions. Indeed, the mere threat of unionization has forced many organizations to develop a competitive personnel program. Finally, the Civil Rights Act of 1964, as amended, has had a profound influence on personnel administration.

Perhaps the most obvious area of policy formulation is the process that creates employees—recruitment and selection. However, the problem is broader than recruitment of new employees. It also includes the placement of present employees in positions that are new for them. Therefore, the broader term, *staffing*, is used to designate the first area of personnel policies. After a person becomes an employee or is assigned to a new position, there is need for *training* or development, the second area of policy determination. Third, employees must be *compensated* for the work performed. For those organizations whose employees are represented by unions, it is necessary to develop policy statements concerning *labor-management relations.*

Staffing

Staffing policies affect an organization in two ways. First, effective staffing increases the general level of competence of employees in the performance of their assigned duties. Secondly, staffing policies have a direct bearing on the mobility of employees from one position to another within the organization, a factor that can contribute significantly to the motivation of employees. Three facets of the staffing process are significant in determining its effectiveness. Selection refers to the hiring of new employees who will best fit the needs of the organization. Also, since present employees are often selected to fill vacancies, policies concerning promotion become significant. Finally, provisions for the termination of employees must be considered.

Selection. An organization must know the training, education, and prior experience needed for the successful performance of its jobs. Without this information the selection process is little more than a game of chance. If those selected are underqualified, excessive turnover may result from terminations due to poor performance and dissatisfaction. Those who do remain are rarely capable of being promoted. Organizations that select candidates overqualified for the entry-level job may also experience excessive turnover if these people become restless because they do not receive promotions. Also, it may be necessary to pay more than the entry-level job is actually worth in order to attract highly qualified people. The recruitment of college graduates is an example of hiring overqualified candidates for entering positions in order to have personnel with potential for growth.

Promotion. Strictly defined, *promotion* is the vertical movement upward in the organizational hierarchy and usually is associated with an increase in pay. In practice the concept of promotion includes lateral transfers to other positions at the same organizational level since such transfers may be part of a long-range training plan. Also included in the concept of promotion are increased responsibilities in a current position with or without an increase in compensation. In any event, whether the new job is called a promotion, a transfer, or simply results in increased responsibilities, all movements represent a form of employee mobility. Consequently, all are potential motivators since they may satisfy the needs for growth, achievement, increased responsibility, and recognition. Policy statements encouraging promotion from within are effective only if there is a sufficient number of employees with the potential for promotion.

Termination. Policies governing the termination of employment have a marked effect on the mobility of employees. When the phrase *termination of employment* is mentioned, one usually thinks of discharge for cause or resignation. Yet there are other and increasingly more frequent reasons for the termination of employment: to name one, retirement. Policies requiring retirement at a stated age provide opportunities for mobility since positions in the organization become available as incumbents reach the stated age limit.[6] However, a mandatory retirement age may result in some employees, particularly executives, being forced to retire despite their potential contribution to the company. Ideally retirement policies should be flexible with provisions for extended service on a part-time or consulting basis and with provisions for early retirement.

Development

Policies concerning the development of personnel are related to the policies established for promotion. For organizations committed to promotion from within, the development of personnel is viewed as a vital function since it provides the means for continued organizational development and performance. However, for those organizations that elect to fill vacancies with outside personnel, development may be regarded as a chore that should make minimal demands with respect to time and expense.

Either term, training or development, refers to the process of learning. However, the term *training* is used with greater frequency when the development of hourly employees is discussed, while the term *development* is used more often when referring to the development of managers. This distinction in terminology is observed in the discussion that follows.

---

[6] It is uncertain as to the effect the statute on retirement will have on companies with a mandatory retirement at a fixed age.

Training. Training begins with first impressions. Orientation programs are designed to control first impressions. The extent of employee orientation may range from no formal program whatsoever, with the employees being directed to their work places and not even knowing their supervisors' names, to a carefully structured introduction to the organization. A well-planned orientation not only familiarizes employees with all aspects of their immediate work situation, but also acquaints them with the nature of the organization, its objectives, and their roles in the attainment of those objectives. Orientation affords the organization an opportunity to create a favorable first impression.

The area of greatest concern in the training of hourly employees, both clerical and operative, is the development of job skills. The methods used in developing these skills vary considerably and include on-the-job training and a combination of on-the-job experience and formal classroom training. By far the most widely used method is on-the-job training which may be informal instruction by the supervisor or a carefully planned sequence of activities with a formal assessment of achievement. However, on-the-job training, as a means of developing skills, requires that supervisors be prepared as trainers if the method is to be most effective.

Management Development. Three terms are used, often interchangeably, to designate programs classified as development. These terms are: *executive development, management development,* and *organization development.* However, each term carries a slightly different connotation. Executive development emphasizes the development of the individual executive; management development indicates a plan for the development of all members of management; and organization development implies that the entire management structure is involved, not as individuals, but as members of the organization, so that the organization can function in a different or improved manner. Regardless of the program undertaken there is a twofold responsibility for its success: that of the organization and that of individuals.

Compensation

Compensation is defined as money paid for work performed. In establishing compensation policies, there are three major considerations. First is the selection of criteria to determine the level or amount of compensation, and second is a determination concerning the method of payment. In addition to payment for work performed, referred to as a wage or salary, employees also receive other benefits—vacations, holidays, insurance, sick leave—that are economic in nature and are a part of the total compensation plan. These are referred to as *employee benefit plans.*

Amount of Compensation. Determining the amount of compensation to be paid for a given job is not an easy task since there is no single criterion applicable to all companies or even to the same company over a period of time. At least three criteria are used by most companies in determining the level of compensation; however, the significance assigned to each criterion varies considerably. The three criteria are area rates, industry rates, and internal rate structure equity.

For many businesses the rates paid in a given geographic area are the controlling factor in determining wage levels. The geographic area encompasses the labor market that a company draws upon; thus, it may consist of a single, small community or a vast metropolitan complex. When rates higher than those paid in the area are established, it may be possible to secure better employees. When rates lower than those of the area are adopted, increased turnover, absenteeism, and poor performance may result. Area rates are the chief determinant in setting the level of payment of many clerical workers and employees of local retail establishments.

For large industrial firms the prevailing rates of the specific industry may be the factor given the most weight. Industry patterns are prevalent in the manufacture of steel, autos, chemicals, and aircraft. To a large extent, industry rates are the result of collective bargaining agreements between the member firms of an industry and the unions representing that industry.

In addition to the determination of wage levels by either area or industry rates (external factors), internal criteria must also be satisfied. Within each organizational unit, such as a plant or headquarters office, there should be an equitable relationship between the amount paid for jobs requiring different levels of skill, responsibility, and training. Equitable pay structures are developed through the use of *job evaluation* procedures, a technique of weighting the various factors necessary for the performance of each job.

Method of Payment. Once the amount of compensation has been determined as the result of a judicious weighting of internal and external criteria, a method of payment must be selected. Fundamentally there are two methods of payment. One method is to pay for time spent on the job; the other is to pay for the amount of work produced. There is, of course, the possibility of a combined payment for both time and amount produced. However, such combinations are usually regarded as payment for work and are classed as incentive plans.

Payment for time is applicable to all levels of the organization even though the unit of time varies considerably. Production workers are paid for the actual number of hours worked, and the amount earned is usually computed and paid on a weekly basis. Time for nonexempt clerical employees—those who must be paid for overtime—is computed on a weekly basis and payment may be received weekly, semimonthly, or monthly. Although clerical workers are expected to work a predetermined number of hours each week, policy decisions determine whether or not pay is received for time not worked due to absence or tardiness. Those employees who are exempt from the provisions of the law requiring payment of overtime are called salaried employees, and their time is computed on a monthly basis with payment either monthly or semimonthly.

Payment for work performed, whether it be the piece rate of the garment industry with no hourly guarantee for time spent on the job or an hourly rate with additional pay for work produced in excess of a stated standard, rests on two assumptions. First, it is assumed that the worker has control over the amount of work that can be produced; and second, that the worker will respond to the monetary incentive and earn more money by increasing output. The second assumption leads to the designation of compensation based on the work produced as incentive compensation plans, or more simply, *incentive plans*.[7]

Employee Benefit Plans. Unlike compensation which is directly related to the job performed, employee benefits are not directly related to the job itself; instead, they are peripheral to the job and are aptly called *fringe benefits*. Included among the many fringe benefits are retirement plans, educational plans, tuition rebates, various forms of insurance, sick leave, recreation programs, supplemental unemployment compensation, and other items intended to improve the welfare of the employee. Employee benefits must be at competitive levels in order to attract and retain employees.[8]

Labor-Management Relations

The above discussion of staffing, development, and compensation is presented in a manner which implies that these are policies to be determined solely by the management of an organization. Such is not usually the case, particularly when employees are represented by a labor union, since unions are entitled to bargain for "wages, hours, and other terms and conditions of employment."[9] In addition, unions can and do use the strike as an economic weapon to obtain concessions from management. Though not participating formally in the development of personnel policies, labor unions have a marked impact on policy statements. The impact is not limited to those organizations whose employees are union members but extends to nonunion employers competing in the same labor market or industry. The threat of unionization has forced many employers to meet or exceed union gains in wages and benefits in an effort to avoid unionization.

Organizational Climate. The major policy consideration is that of determining the organizational climate within which a given set of labor-management relations are to occur. Frequently the nature of these relationships is described as ranging from open hostility to one of cooperative effort between management and labor. Open hostility most likely occurs during union organization and the negotiation of the initial labor agreement. A more mature relationship between labor and management is often described as a business relationship and is similar in many respects to the relationship that exists between a company and its suppliers and customers. The open hostility disappears and each side recognizes the responsibilities and rights of the other. The ultimate in labor-management relations is evidenced by complete cooperation and understanding on the part of both the union and the company. It is recognized that a mature

---

[7] This subject is discussed in Chapter 13, pp. 285–286.

[8] See Chapter 15 for a discussion concerning the motivational values of employee benefit plans.

[9] Labor Management Relations Act of 1947 as amended, Sec. 8(d).

cooperative relationship between a company and a union depends on factors other than the establishment of a conducive organizational climate; for example, the goals and strength of the union and the economic condition of the company. However, organizational climate sets the upper limits of the extent to which cooperative efforts may be realized not only in the negotiation of successive labor agreements but also in the manner of their administration.

Nonunion Employees. There is also a decision to be made concerning the treatment of *nonunion employees.* It is seldom that all hourly employees, both clerical and production, belong to a union. Often the production workers are unionized while the hourly clerical employees are not, and in those instances in which clerical employees are unionized they rarely belong to the same bargaining unit as the production employees. When clerical employees are not unionized and hourly production workers are, it should be decided beforehand whether any improvement in wages or benefits extended to production workers should be granted to clerical employees. Or a company may decide to extend to its nonunion employees those increases in wages and benefits that it believes can honestly be made for all employees, union and nonunion alike. Further, the extent to which increases in hourly benefits should be extended to supervisory personnel must be decided. Decisions in these areas may modify or even determine the bargaining tactics of a company.

INTEGRATING POLICY STATEMENTS

The scope of policy statements for each of the four functional areas—finance, marketing, production, and personnel—are summarized in Table 5–1 and serve as the basis for this chapter. Another means of integrating the functional areas is examining them within the context of a servo system as shown in the schematic diagram of Figure 5–1. A *servo system* is a system capable of reacting to changes occurring in any of the subsystems or to changes in the external environment so that a state of balance, or equilibrium, is maintained. Financial inputs to the production process supply the raw materials and the physical facilities necessary to produce the product. Personnel inputs furnish the required skills, knowledge, and judgment.

The marketing function is charged with the responsibility of selling the product to the customer. At this point, a feedback of information occurs which is interpreted and then relayed to production. If the customer buys the product in sufficient quantity the cycle continues, and production signals for a continuation of financial and personnel inputs. If the demand is greater than the quantity produced, production requests additional inputs. When customers do not buy, the signal from marketing calls for a reduction of inputs.

Note that there are both internal and external feedback loops. The loop between marketing and the customer provides information relating the efforts of the company to its external environment, specifically the customer. Information provided by this loop enables the firm to modify its product or service so that customer demand may continue. If these efforts are not successful, the

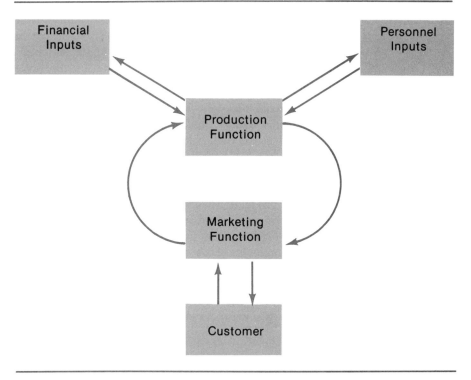

Figure 5–1
INTEGRATING
FUNCTIONAL
AREAS—A
SERVO SYSTEM

level of production can be modified to prevent excessive inventory buildup. The other feedback loops are internal to the organization and relate financial and personnel inputs with the functions of production and marketing. Should either of these inputs be inadequate in any respect, the initial impact is felt in the production function, usually by a diminution of that function. The extent and nature of the needs for financial and personnel inputs are the result of information obtained from the combined production-marketing cycle.

Case Problem 5-B provides an opportunity to develop a set of consistent policies for a specific organization.

Case Problem 5-B

FORMULATING PERSONNEL POLICIES

Joe Beck, vice-president of industrial relations for Diversified Manufacturing, completed some notes that he had been preparing for his conference with Diana Santos, the personnel director who reports to him.

"Diana," he began, "we have been asked to prepare a draft of proposed personnel policies to be submitted to the board of directors when they have their annual meeting here in Chicago next month. It seems that we are being criticized because of what appears to be a lack of consistency in some of the decisions made concerning the personnel function."

"Is that criticism true?" Diana asked.

"I believe there is a good basis for it. Here are some of the incidents that have been brought to my attention." Joe handed Diana the notes he had been preparing. The following is a copy of Joe's notes:

1. In the western division's Los Angeles plant, there was a 45-day strike because the company insisted that an incentive plan be installed as a way to raise average earnings of employees. The union had proposed a general wage increase to bring the rates up to the average of the area. As the strike progressed, it became clear that the real issue was one of permitting union participation in setting time standards. The company stated that determining standards was a company prerogative and no concern of the union. Yet in a New York plant a job evaluation plan had been installed with joint union-management participation.

2. The general manager of the eastern division responsible for both manufacturing and marketing had attended several management development seminars at the request of the president. These seminars emphasized the need for the establishment of a cooperative organizational climate as the backdrop for labor-management relations. Later other eastern division managers attended similar programs. Some of these managers were then transferred to the western division and have reported that they feel as though they were working for a different company. One even said that if he could not return to the eastern division he would resign.

3. The basis for determining wage levels is not clear. In the eastern division the company's position is that the area wage should be the basis for determining the wage level; yet, in the western division the company argues that the average of the industry, rather than the geographic area average, should determine the wage level. The union says the company is inconsistent.

4. Employee benefit programs are uniform throughout all plants in both divisions. As a result, there are locations where hospitalization benefits adequately cover the cost of hospitalization, and there are locations where the benefits received are inadequate. Uniform practices are also followed with respect to vacations, holidays, and leaves of absence; and, as in the case of the hospitalization benefits, there are instances where company practices are more liberal than those of other companies in the area and there are situations where company practices fall short of area standards.

5. The eastern division reimburses all employees for expenses for tuition and books after the completion of any course in an accredited school or college. This includes trade courses, secretarial courses, and degree courses. In addition, employees with five or more years' seniority are granted leaves of absence with one-half pay for periods of one year in order to complete their college work. The manager of the eastern division contends that such programs contribute to the division's ability to promote from within. The western division has no subsidies for self-improvement.

6. In the eastern division the plant supervisors, along with other members of management, attend a regularly scheduled monthly dinner meeting to discuss production schedules and methods for the coming month and to review performance of the past month. No supervisory meetings are held in the western division.

After reading these six incidents, Diana returned the list to Joe and said, "It almost seems as though we are talking about two different companies."

"It certainly does, and our job is to develop some policies that will bring these two divisions together. Try and get a draft of such policies within the next couple of days."

PROBLEMS

1. What key determination must be made before any policies can be developed for this company?
2. Is it necessary, or even desirable, for a company to have consistent personnel policies within separate operating divisions? Give reasons to support each point of view.
3. Develop a proposed set of personnel policies for this company.

CHAPTER QUESTIONS FOR STUDY AND DISCUSSION

1. What methods are commonly used to measure profit? What are the advantages and limitations of each of the methods?
2. For what purposes does a company generally seek to secure long-term capital? Short-term capital? What factors should be considered when choosing among the various means of obtaining long-term capital; i.e., stocks, bonds, mortgages, or long-term notes?
3. What policy decisions must be made regarding the utilization of capital? Discuss the effects of various types of imbalances in the allocation of capital.
4. Cite examples of the marketing policy questions that must be resolved when considering product diversification, obsolescence, quality, and standardization.
5. Refer to Table 5–1. Compare the meanings of the term *product diversification* when used in reference to marketing policies and when used in reference to production policies. Which meaning is broader?
6. What is the hoped for effect of national advertising upon the performance of a salesperson selling that product?
7. Discuss the significance of each of the areas of personnel policy. Which is the most important in your opinion? Why?
8. Discuss the relationship between policies concerning promotion and policies established for the development and training of personnel. What effect do policies in the area of labor-management relations have on promotion and training?
9. Discuss the factors to be considered in the development of compensation plans. Are these factors necessarily of the same weight for companies in different industries? Give an example.
10. Figure 5–1 shows a feedback loop between the marketing function and the external environment, the customer. What constitutes the external environment of the personnel function? Of the finance function?

Chapter 6

Managerial Decision Making

Case Problem 6-A

PERSONAL VALUES AND DECISION MAKING

Peggy Gleeson has been employed for the past 11 years as a pharmacist in a large chain of drugstores in a growing metropolitan area. She presently earns $17,000 a year. The organization for which she works is expanding at the rate of three to five new stores each year. This expansion is creating additional managerial positions in the organization, some paying as much as $30,000 a year including the company's rather generous profit-sharing plan. Pharmacists are sometimes promoted to the position of store manager and, while such managerial positions have not been open to women in the past, Miss Gleeson believes that such opportunities will become available in the near future.

Recently Peggy's father, who owns a pharmacy, was forced to retire because of poor health. Mr. Gleeson hired a recent graduate pharmacist on a temporary basis to operate the pharmacy, and Peggy's mother continues to manage the other departments of the drugstore. Peggy's father would like her to return home to manage the store which she will ultimately inherit. The small town in which the store is located is experiencing a growth in population because of

the completion of a large lake resort development near the city. As a result, the possibility for growth and expansion of the drugstore is better than it has been for a number of years.

In discussions with her parents, Peggy has found that the present volume of sales of the drugstore is about $100,000 a year and the gross margin on sales is roughly $39,000. Before Mr. Gleeson's retirement, he and Mrs. Gleeson were drawing salaries of $22,000, and had additional operating expenses of about $16,000 annually, which left a net profit before taxes of $1,000 a year. Since Mr. Gleeson's retirement, the level of profit from the drugstore has remained basically the same. Mr. Gleeson is presently paying the pharmacist he hired a salary of $15,000, and Mrs. Gleeson receives a salary of $13,000 a year. Mr. Gleeson no longer draws a salary from the business.

Should Peggy decide to assume the management of the drugstore, Mr. Gleeson has proposed that she draw a salary of $17,000, her present earnings. He has further proposed that Peggy's share of the profits from the store's operation be 25 percent initially, increasing to 50 percent after two years. Since Mrs. Gleeson will no longer work in the store, it will be necessary to hire a part-time clerk to assist Peggy. Mr. Gleeson estimates that such expense will be approximately $5,000.

Mr. Gleeson has received a tentative offer of $150,000 for the purchase of the store, a major portion of which Peggy will inherit. The Gleesons' financial position is such that it will not be necessary for them to tap this source of capital to a significant extent to see them through their retirement years.

PROBLEMS

1. What courses of action are available to Peggy?
2. Which alternative do you recommend?
3. What are the implications of her system of personal values on the decision she makes?
4. If Miss Gleeson were a man, would your recommendations be the same?

Managers constantly make decisions, and in a sense all their decisions are important. Some, however, are relatively limited in scope: a supervisor decides which project to complete first and to whom it should be assigned. In contrast, some decisions involve the entire organization: after extensive research and consultation, the president recommends that the firm accept the merger offer of a large competitor. Collectively the firm's decisions determine its direction, its effectiveness, its efficiency, and its life span. It is, therefore, imperative that managerial decisions, often made under adverse, high-risk conditions, be made as objectively as possible. In this chapter we discuss the nature and personal dimensions of managerial decisions, and show how research and experience have provided managers with a basis for refining the decision process.

PROFILE OF A MANAGERIAL DECISION

A *decision* is the selection of a course of action from two or more alternatives; the *decision-making process* is a sequence of steps leading to that selection.[1] Since there are many kinds of decisions that are made under vastly different circumstances by people with various styles of decision making, it is not possible to outline a fixed sequence of steps that is universally best. On the other hand, certain processes of decision making tend to produce better results than others, and it is these processes that comprise the content of a relatively new field of study called *decision theory*. We begin our study of decision theory by surveying some traditional approaches to decision making.

---

[1] Since judgments that do not involve overt action are also called decisions, this definition, commonly found in management literature, requires some clarification. A manager may decide that Plan A is best in terms of the firm's profits (a judgment without overt action) but may later decide to implement Plan B (an overt action) in order to avoid conflict with other executives. We sometimes refer to decisions that do not involve overt action as *covert* or concealed decisions. Contradictory though it may seem, a decision not to act (a covert decision) may itself be a very powerful form of action.

Types of Managerial Decisions

Classification is essential to clear thinking about decisions, since what applies to one kind of decision may not apply to another. Most managerial decisions fall into one or more of the following categories:

1. *Personal versus Organizational Decisions.* Chester I. Barnard, an early contributor to decision theory, recommended that decisions be categorized as personal or organizational.[2] As the name implies, organizational decisions are those that managers make in their official capacities, normally within the limits set by their formal authority. Such decisions may be, and often are, delegated to subordinates.

Personal decisions pertain to the manager as an individual rather than to the organization. They cannot be delegated, nor should they be subject to the influence of higher managers. Unfortunately, personal and organizational decisions cannot always be separated. An event that occurred in the life of an administrative aide to a President of the United States illustrates this point. When an altercation between the aide to the President and a woman in a Washington, D. C. bar attracted national attention, the aide's personal life immediately became an organizational issue. Similarly, when a manager's personal ambition leads to behavior that is calculated to impress superiors rather than to serve the company, personal and organizational decisions become intertwined.

Why make the distinction between personal and organizational decisions? Because confusing the two introduces bias into corporate decision making which is detrimental to the organization and often to the individual decision maker.

2. *Strategic versus Operational Decisions.* Strategic decisions normally fall within the purview of top management. They are often characterized by novelty, complexity, and openendedness,[3] and frequently involve uncontrollable variables such as the actions of competitors or the state of the economy. Typically strategic decisions involve the organization as a whole rather than a single department or division (e.g., a decision to increase dividends, expand product lines, change employee benefits, or strongly resist the contract demands of organized labor). Thus, strategic decisions tend to influence long-range plans.

Operational decisions (also called administrative decisions) are concerned with the day-to-day operation of the enterprise. Thus, operational decisions parallel short-range plans (see Figure 6–1). The middle manager who carries out company policy by promoting minority managers over others is making operational decisions. At the first level of management, a supervisor meticulously follows company policies and rules for handling disciplinary problems, grievances, and work assignments. At the supervisory level, in particular, operational decision making may involve only minor discretion and extremely limited opportunity for the exercise of creativity and independent judgment.

3. *Structured versus Unstructured Decisions.* One of the major differences between strategic and operational decisions is lack of structure. Because of the novelty and lack of precedent which characterize strategic decisions, they are typically

---

[2] Chester I. Barnard, *The Functions of the Executive* (Cambridge: Harvard University Press, 1938), p. 188. This book, written at a time when relatively unenlightened classical theories of management were dominant, represents a major turning point in management thought.

[3] Henry Mintzberg, Duru Raisinghani, and André Théorêt, "The Structure of Unstructured Decision Processes," *Administrative Science Quarterly*, Vol. 21, No. 2 (June, 1976), p. 250.

described as unstructured—relatively free from limitations imposed by prior decisions. In contrast, a supervisor's decisions may be highly structured by tradition, union contract provisions, policies, procedures, methods, and rules. Following the language of computer science, structured and unstructured decisions are also referred to as *programmed* and *nonprogrammed* decisions.[4]

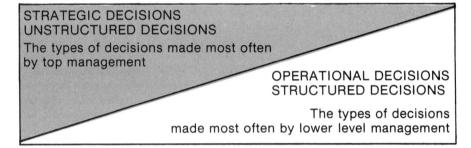

Figure 6-1
TYPES OF
DECISIONS AND
MANAGEMENT
LEVELS

STRATEGIC DECISIONS
UNSTRUCTURED DECISIONS
The types of decisions made most often
by top management

OPERATIONAL DECISIONS
STRUCTURED DECISIONS

The types of decisions
made most often by lower level management

4. *Crisis and Intuitive versus Research Decisions.* Decisions are sometimes classified on the basis of their urgency. A crisis decision at either the strategic or the operational level must be made under pressure. The crisis situation is characterized by stress, surprise, limited time for response, and threat to high-priority goals.[5] The time factor either precludes extensive data gathering and analysis or requires that they be done on a crash basis. A research decision, on the other hand, can be made with a minimum of time pressure. Usually because of inadequate planning, operating managers often work under intense time pressures and may even come to regard crisis decisions as commonplace rather than the exception. Strategic decisions, in particular, suffer when made under crisis conditions.

Crisis decisions are often intuitive; that is, they are based on experience, instantaneous analysis, and an emotional element that collectively give the manager a feeling that the chosen course of action is the right one. Most of the rapid-fire operational decisions that managers constantly make are of this type. Although these decisions often lack objectivity and are difficult to justify on a logical basis, they can be quite accurate and effective.

5. *Initiative versus Referred Decisions.* Some managers avoid decisions until they are required to make them by the actions of a superior or until they are "delegated up" by a subordinate. These referred decisions contrast sharply with the initiative decisions of the aggressive manager who seeks out problems and opportunities and takes action that is not required. Ambitious and mobile managers with a high need for achievement make many initiative decisions, while timid shelf sitters with a need to play it safe usually prefer to remain inactive and inconspicuous until a decision is referred to them or can no longer be avoided because of a crisis.

[4] Herbert A. Simon, *The New Science of Management Decision*, rev. ed. (Englewood Cliffs, N. J.: Prentice Hall, Inc.; 1977), p. 45.

[5] Carolyn Smart and Ilan Vertinsky, "Designs for Crisis Decision Units," *Administrative Science Quarterly*, Vol. 22, No. 4 (December, 1977), p. 640.

6. *Problem versus Opportunity Decisions.* A problem decision is made to solve an existing or anticipated problem, while an opportunity decision is a positive action that takes advantage of a potential for growth, increased profits, or the achievement of some other valued objective. Opportunity decisions are often, but not always, initiative decisions. Whether a manager will take advantage of opportunities depends on a number of variables, such as the manager's motivation to take risks and his or her ability to recognize opportunities when they occur. The ranks of entrepreneurs and corporate executives are filled with persons who make initiative and opportunity decisions.

Bounded Rationality

No matter which types of decisions managers make, they would like to think that all their decisions are *rational*: that they are objective, logical, and designed to achieve concisely defined organizational goals with maximum efficiency. But managerial decisions are never completely rational. They are best characterized by what **March and Simon** called *bounded rationality*.[6] Their rationality is bounded or limited by such factors as (1) conflicting and continually changing goals; (2) vaguely defined problems: (3) limited resources for gathering data and generating alternative solutions; (4) human limitations of memory, reasoning, and objectivity; and (5) inadequate knowledge of the consequences of alternative courses of action.

As indicated in Chapter 4, managers attempt to find satisfactory solutions rather than the best possible solution. In other words, they *satisfice* with reference to a number of goals rather than *maximize* profits or any other single goal, though not necessarily as a matter of choice. Because of the physical, economic, social, and psychological limits within which managers must operate, they cannot do otherwise. Although managers must live with bounded rationality, they can continually strive for rationality in decision making. The primary thrust of applied decision theory helps managers to avoid irrationality and to use the processes of decision making that contribute most to rational decisions.

Decisions, Power, and Politics

To some degree decisions in organizations are always influenced by politics. Managers must often settle for a less-than-ideal decision because of the need to placate certain individuals or power groups whose private interests may not be consistent with the interests of the organization. The desires of financiers, unions, government agencies, energy cartels, and large suppliers or customers, for example, may require compromises or trade-offs that grossly interfere with rational decision making. Viewed another way, in order to behave as rationally as possible a manager must be responsive to a number of political considerations that relate indirectly to an organization's success but not directly to its goals and purpose.

---

[6] James G. March and Herbert A. Simon, *Organizations* (New York City: John Wiley & Sons, Inc., 1958), p. 140.

Politics, sometimes referred to as "the art of the possible," is as great an influence within an organization as without. Certain executives exercise informal control that extends far beyond their formal authority. By cultivating influential allies, controlling the flow of vital information, and intimidating through the power of personality, managers gain the power either to block a decision or to approve it. Sometimes a manager acquires inordinate power through the control of vital information, through expertise, or through an unusual ability to persuade. When such power is jealously guarded, as it usually is, rationality must often yield to political expediency. For example, in a large apparel manufacturing company, every major decision had to be made acceptable to the financial vice-president whose assertive personality, mastery of a complicated accounting system that she had repeatedly refused to simplify, and capacity to remember minute financial details gave her an awesome power that other executives dared not challenge.

Organizational decision making requires skill in bargaining, compromising, and in trading support for support and information for information. This is usually done with a subtlety and sophistication of which only insiders are aware. Organizational politics is intertwined with personal friendships, departmental loyalties, informal group pressures, and the complex psychological climate that results from the knowledge managers have of one another's needs, attitudes, personality characteristics, leadership styles, and lines of communication. Even in organizations whose managers are deeply committed to rationality and make a sincere effort to eliminate politics, it continues to flourish. It is an unavoidable aspect of organizational decision making, and effective managers are ever mindful of its importance.

Decision Styles

Following the classical tradition, decision making in some organizations is highly centralized, and decisions are defended more on the basis of one's legitimate authority to decide than on the process used to decide. In other organizations, an attempt is made to push decision making downward so that each decision is made at the lowest level possible. The latter is more effective in developing managerial talent and is generally preferable because it requires that a maximum number of people assume responsibility. Centralized decision making is just one of many approaches to decision making that collectively describe the decision style of a particular individual or organization. A few of the many others are described in the following sections.

Participation. In recent years increasing numbers of managers have learned to use the resources of subordinates, regardless of their organizational level, in decision making. Delegation is probably the most common means of achieving subordinate participation. In effect, the manager says to a subordinate, "In the future when problems of this type occur, you have the authority to decide rather than refer the problem to me." The subordinate is then held accountable for results and is expected to assume the additional responsibility.

Effective managers often rely heavily on subordinates and a variety of staff specialists for the information and insights needed in decision making. Their participation may be elicited by simply asking such questions as, "How do you think the problem should be solved?" or "Do you see any difficulty with this approach?" Standing committees (for example, grievance, compensation, and job evaluation committees) and special problem-solving task forces are common means of getting participation. Some companies have experimented with *junior boards of directors*—standing committees of lower and middle managers—that parallel the functions of the corporate board and, in addition, work on special problems.

The use of participating groups in most organizations is not synonymous with democratic decision making (usually defined in terms of one person-one vote and majority rule). Since groups are often dominated by one or more individuals and cannot easily be held accountable, most managers do not delegate important decisions to groups. This does not, of course, prevent managers from using a number of group participation techniques, including conferences on specific problems prior to decision making. It is generally accepted that subordinates are more likely to be enthusiastic about implementing a decision to which they make a contribution, even though their superior is actually the decision maker. Thus, group members are typically expected to assume responsibility for contributing to the decision process but not for the final decision.

The Mintzberg Model. Henry Mintzberg and others describe a common approach to making strategic decisions which involves three distinct phases but does not postulate a sequential relationship between them.[7] First is the *identification phase* in which opportunities, problems, and crises are recognized and diagnosed. The diagnosis involves understanding, as much as possible, the symptoms of the problem and its causes.

Development, the second phase, is the heart of this decision model. Here one or more solutions are developed through one of two techniques—search or design. *Search* activity, intended to find ready-made solutions, involves, first, a memory search for existing solutions; second, a degree of passive waiting for unsolicited solutions to appear; third, the activation of "search generators" to produce alternative solutions (for example, a supplier is asked to search for certain needed equipment); and, fourth, an active search, initiated to seek a ready-made solution from any possible source. If these efforts fail, the decision maker may revert to a *design routine* in which a custom-made solution is devised or a ready-made solution is modified for special application. Because of the expense of the design routine, organizations are usually unwilling to generate more than one design alternative.

In the third phase of Mintzberg's model (that is, the model Mintzberg based on the way managers in his study actually made decisions), the best alternative is selected. This *selection phase* does not, however, necessarily follow the development of alternative solutions as decision theorists advocate. In prac-

---

[7] Mintzberg *et al., op. cit.*, p. 252.

tice, a number of selections of choice steps are involved, and these are intricately bound up with the development phase. Creative thinking, critical analysis, and choice among alternatives are not separate and sequential steps; instead they are entangled in a morass of subdecisions and repetitions that continue until a final decision is reached. These steps are linked to *authorization routines* in which the approval of superiors is sought before continuing to further steps or cycles of decision making.

Mintzberg's model is intended to describe how managers actually make decisions rather than how they should make them. Nevertheless, in many cases such a model may be highly successful and, therefore, must have merit.[8]

Heuristics. Decision theorists have observed that a major problem of decision makers is holding in consciousness all the different bits of information and evaluation criteria that are needed to make a rational decision.[9] This same problem is encountered by managers who attempt to program computers to simulate human thought processes. So many variables are involved and the time factor is often so critical that neither the human nor the electronic system can encompass all the relevant information.

To deal with this information problem, real-world decision makers rely heavily on *heuristics,* or rules of thumb, in order to reduce the elements of a decision into manageable, bite-size pieces. For example, an operating manager's decision not to authorize overtime may be controlled by only two of several important criteria: employees do not want overtime and the company prefers to minimize overtime work. Thus, the use of these rules of thumb leads to a quick decision even though overtime work on a given day may be economically feasible and easily justified.

Decision heuristics are often uniquely personal. The decisions of one manager, a thoroughgoing pessimist, are usually influenced by the belief: If anything can go wrong, it will (the so-called Murphy's Law). Another manager who is unusually skilled in the use of power applies the belief: If you are not sure that you have the authority to make a decision, assume that you have and act accordingly—if you are wrong, apologize. Because of the overwhelming number of variables that can be considered, managers cannot avoid using heuristics in most decision-making processes. However, it is worth noting that essential to effective decision making is the need for managers to clearly define (at least to themselves) exactly which heuristics they are using. Therefore, the heuristics should be objectively defensible, and not just intuitively satisfying and convenient.

---

[8] This and other decision models, with comments about when their use is appropriate, are discussed in Paul C. Nutt, "Models for Decision Making in Organizations and Some Contextual Variables Which Stipulate Optimal Use," *Academy of Management Review*, Vol. 1, No. 2 (April, 1976), pp. 84–98.

[9] In Payne's research, subjects confronted with a complex decision employed decision strategies designed to eliminate some of the available alternatives as quickly as possible. See John W. Payne, "Task Complexity and Contingent Processing in Decision Making: An Information Search and Protocol Analysis," *Organizational Behavior and Human Performance*, Vol. 16, No. 2 (February, 1976), p. 366.

PERSONAL DIMENSIONS OF MANAGERIAL DECISIONS

As Virginia Hall, financial vice-president of Mason Plastics, prepared to leave for the day she was detained by a visit from the president, Richard Mason. She was not too surprised when he presented her with a final check and asked for her keys. She was being fired, just as the last two officers in her position had been. Mason stated his reasons and expressed his regrets. According to Mason, Hall had made a series of decisions with which he was dissatisfied. He could no longer trust her judgment, and he needed someone in that position who could make certain decisions without having to consult him. Hall was not too upset, although she would have preferred having the opportunity to resign. She had, in fact, intended to resign, but Mason moved first.

This was a regrettable incident, and not one that any person in Hall's position could easily avoid, regardless of his or her competence and political skill. Making good decisions would be virtually impossible for any vice-president of Mason Plastics, since *good* was always defined in terms of satisfying Mason, who was obviously hard to satisfy. The company's goals were locked in Mason's brain, and there were no firm policies or other objective criteria to serve as guidelines for decision making. This is an example of a bad situation in which the organizational environment has more influence on decision quality than the decision maker. Fortunately most organizations, especially those staffed by professional managers, are structured so that competent managers can make decisions that will achieve positive and acceptable results.

Nevertheless, even in the most favorable environment, great differences in the abilities of managers to make decisions are likely to exist, simply because of the differences in their personal characteristics. Thus, two managers evaluating identical data in terms of identical criteria may reach opposite conclusions. Some of the personal qualities that most often produce different conclusions and decisions are discussed here.

Intellectual Differences

Because of the formal education generally required of persons entering management, persons with average or below-average intelligence seldom have the opportunity to test their abilities. In fact, most middle- and top-level managers have intellectual standings in the upper 10 percent of the general population (an IQ of 119 and above on the Wechsler Adult Intelligence Scale). Undoubtedly the relatively high intelligence of managers contributes to their ability to make decisions. However, within the 10 percent range, the qualitative aspects of a manager's intelligence may have more influence on decisions than does the overall IQ. For example, a manager with an IQ of 120 and high commonsense judgment (one component of intelligence) may make better decisions than a manager with an IQ of 130 whose practical judgment is unusually low. Furthermore, the likelihood of better decisions increases greatly if the manager with an IQ of 120 is mature and highly knowledgeable in the decision-making area.

Thus, up to a point, intelligence is positively correlated with managerial performance, but the relationship is extremely complex.

Education and Experience

The more complex and technical the decision, the more important it is that the decision maker have a broad reservoir of information from which to draw. Education and experience are, therefore, significant contributors to the quality of managerial decisions. It should be noted, however, that the level of relevant knowledge is not directly correlated with years of education or experience. The nature and quality of a manager's learning opportunities and the individual's intellectual ambition (motivation to learn and remember) are important determinants of the impact of education and experience on managerial decisions. In some cases the effect of extensive experience on decisions is negative, especially where managers become "experience-bound," making decisions on the basis of past successes when current circumstances call for creativity and a break with tradition. The effect is also negative when a manager's experience leads to the development of undesirable managerial practices.

Perception, Values, and Attitudes

Reality is in the eye of the beholder. One manager sees a group of workers as a despicable collection of rabble who, in order to be productive, must be closely controlled and frequently threatened. To another manager they are valuable human beings who are waiting for someone with leadership skills to stimulate their potential for self-motivation and high productivity. To both managers the group is the same, but their interpretations differ. Because of differences in perception, some managers are able to recognize problems, opportunities, and resources while others are unaware of them. These more perceptive managers are, therefore, able to make better decisions.

Attitudes (predispositions to evaluate in a favorable or unfavorable way) always influence perception and consequently influence decisions. For example, racial or ethnic prejudice, one type of attitude, may so distort a manager's thinking that he or she views with contempt a large part of the population. Such attitudes necessarily affect the manager's personnel decisions. Attitudes toward oneself affect decisions, too. Managers who view themselves favorably are more likely to be considerate of others and to be optimistic about their ability to solve problems.

Attitudes contain both a belief and an emotional component. Thus, if a manager's attitudes toward profits are favorable and are based on a belief that profits are good, the manager is pleased when profits are high. The belief component of attitudes is often an expression of a person's *values*—expressions of what a person considers to have worth and potential for need satisfaction. The differences in the economic, social, and religious values of managers often serve as standards or criteria for decision making and account for many differences in managerial decisions. (Relate this to Case 6-A, Question 3.)

Motivational-Emotional Factors

Searching for solutions and analyzing data require creativity and analytical ability but do not often require courage. Making a decision to act on the results of those processes is another matter entirely. Taking action, the essence of decision making, often requires that a manager risk reputation, position, and even career; thus, a manager must be highly motivated and more confident than most people to be willing to take such risks.

Managers who are highly motivated by a need for affiliation (a need for the approval of others; a need to belong) often have difficulty making good decisions. Their unhealthy dependency detracts from the decision task, distorts perception, and lowers resolve to take unpopular action. An excessive need for security or safety usually has the same effect, since decision making involves risk taking. Conversely, managers with a high need for power—managers who enjoy the acquisition and use of power—usually feel comfortable making tough decisions. They may even find decision making pleasurable and self-affirming. Making decisions is an expression of their power and, consequently, a symbol of their worth and importance.

In some managers—even those who are decisive and enjoy making decisions—ego-defensive motivation distorts perception, disrupts logical thinking, and causes conflict with other managers and employees. Managers who are offended by a superior's constructive criticism, who are threatened when subordinates offer suggestions, and who feel insecure because of progress and change will too often make decisions that satisfy emotional needs but do not solve organizational problems.

Personality Structure

Many personal characteristics influence decisions; among them are a number of traits that comprise the basic structure of personality. One of the traits that most obviously affects decisions is impulsiveness. An _impulsive_ person becomes anxious and irritable over delays and consequently takes action without adequate fact-finding and analysis. The extreme opposite is the _compulsive_ person, a detail-minded and cautious individual who procrastinates, thereby losing opportunities and letting problem situations deteriorate because of an emotional need to minimize risks.

The personality characteristic most likely to influence _decisiveness_ (the ability to decide with a minimum of wavering and unnecessary procrastination) is _self-structure_. Persons with a strong self-structure have made decisions about themselves. They are basically inner-directed rather than controlled by others. They know who they are, where they are going, and how they are going to get there. In a sense, a strong self-structure is to an individual what plans, such as strategies, goals, and policies, are to an organization. Each provides standards or guidelines for decision making and contributes to the security and courage needed for risk taking. The elements of both self-structure and organizational plans are a result of decision making and provide a basis for further decisions. Managers who have made decisions about their own values can be decisive in issues that involve ethical behavior (for instance, whether to steal from the company or cheat a customer); and they can be even more decisive if their employer has established ethical policies relating to these issues.

Several aspects of a manager's self-concept influence decisiveness and decision quality. Managers who regard themselves as problem solvers, for example, are less likely to avoid or to unduly postpone decisions. A favorable perception of one's own decision-making ability inevitably makes a person more willing to make initiative decisions and less fearful that these decisions will lead to failure and personal loss.

Virtually any personality trait can influence managerial decisions. Such traits as sociability, shyness, and social ascendancy may affect decisions about whether a manager spends more time interacting with people or doing desk work; compulsive perfectionism may cause a manager to emphasize details excessively. Managers who understand themselves can, to some extent, control the negative influences of their personal traits on their decisions. Managers who understand their subordinates can predict and partially control any negative impact of their subordinates' characteristics. Thus, understanding the role of personality in making decisions has practical value in improving the quality of managerial decisions.

REFINING THE DECISION PROCESS

Although most decision makers, including some with excellent decision records, have their own unique decision styles, which are not likely to change dramatically, they can become better decision makers by following a few guidelines that have been formulated by decision theorists. At the heart of the decision theory is the belief that the steps in decision making should be explicit; that is, expressed directly, with precision and clarity. Complex decisions should be rationally divided into a series of small decisions that are simple enough to be held in one's consciousness and logically manipulated. Such decision components as assumptions, evaluation criteria, and estimates of risk should be rescued from the subjective, half-conscious, and intuitive morass into which they are usually submerged. According to decision theory, a manager should be held accountable for using good decision processes. Decision theorists assume that managers who use these decision processes will, on the average, achieve better results. It must be noted, however, that good results do not always follow. We look now at some of the principles and steps that will most likely produce good decisions.

Problem Awareness

As a prerequisite to effective decision making, managers must be aware of the problems and opportunities in their organizations. Problem awareness greatly depends on a manager's motivation to be aware, but the application of certain techniques can also help.

A *problem* is a deviation from a standard or expectation.[10] For example, the contractor who agrees to complete a new office building by August 15 has a problem if that expectation cannot be met. If the agreement calls for a one-thousand-dollar-a-day penalty for noncompletion after that date, the contractor has a serious problem; and, if that penalty could lead to bankruptcy, the problem becomes a crisis. Perhaps the most serious situation occurs when dire consequences can result and the decision maker is unaware that a problem exists. For example, because of rapid technological change a company's products are becoming obsolete, but its executives do not see what is taking place. The constant specter that management may be unaware of serious problems makes early detection of problems extremely important.

Thus, if a manager wants to be aware of problems rather than avoid them, the following two elements are involved: (1) a clear awareness of standards and expectations and (2) an effective feedback system so that deviations can be detected. The minimum requirement for the first element is effective planning: clearly stated goals, strategies, policies, procedures, methods, and rules. But expectations extend far beyond formal plans. For example, a problem-conscious manager is sensitive to the expectations of superiors in handling human relations problems, taking advantage of opportunities, exhibiting loyalty to the firm, and leading an exemplary personal life.

Defining the Problem

When feedback suggests that a problem exists, good decision makers begin to question and probe rather than jump to conclusions or place blame. They may ask, for example, when the problem was first detected and what changes in the environment were associated with it (a preliminary exploration of causes). Finally, the problem is clearly defined in terms of expectations. For example, "Product returns for the correction of defects are running 5 percent of sales rather than the 3 percent allowed." It is not advisable to imply a cause in the definition since to do so may restrict the search for alternative solutions. Thus, it would not be good to state, "Because of excessive labor turnover, product returns for correction are running 5 percent of sales rather than the 3 percent allowed."

Establishing Decision Criteria

Which of two or more alternative decisions is best? This depends on the criteria used in evaluation. In selecting a means of refinancing a company, for example, if the owner-manager's primary concern is growth, the best method may be a public stock offering. But, if maintaining control of the company is more important, a bank loan may be better. In the typical situation, both of these and several other criteria should be used in selecting the best alternative.

---

[10] Charles H. Kepner and Benjamin B. Tregoe, *The Rational Manager* (New York City: McGraw-Hill, Inc., 1965), p. 20.

These decision criteria should be explicit; ideally they should be written out in order of their priority, and all this should be done before the alternative strategies (solutions) are developed. If the criteria are decided upon afterward, or if the criteria are never made explicit, the alternatives themselves may influence the criteria used for their own evaluation. In the refinancing problem, the relative ease of obtaining a bank loan (relative, at least, to making a public stock offering) may be so attractive to management that no other alternatives will be seriously considered.

A second aspect of establishing decision criteria concerns decision processes and calls for decisions about who will make the final decision, when the final decision will be made, and how much time and money, if any, will be allocated for finding a solution. Managers who neglect this phase of problem solving may spend excessive time or money on decisions that offer only a small return on investment while avoiding others that involve the survival of the firm. They may spend $50,000 to solve a $10,000 problem, they may postpone a decision until an opportunity is lost, or they may fail to involve in the decision managers whose cooperation is necessary to ensure its successful implementation.

Notice how many decisions are made in establishing decision criteria and how much influence they have on the final solution. The cumulative impact of these small decisions demands that they be taken seriously.

Developing Alternative Solutions

Poor decision makers often settle for the most available solution. They ask, "Will it solve the problem?" rather than, "Is it the best solution obtainable within the limits of search we have set for ourselves?" The former results in an accept-reject decision, often preferred for its simplicity, while the latter demands a more complex comparison of alternatives. Some managers are driven to the accept-reject approach because of their inability to handle the information overload. Others routinely use the accept-reject method out of habit or because they see no reason to do otherwise. The creation of alternatives is a better method, however, especially when important and complex decisions are involved.

The search for alternatives may be made from the memory of how the decision maker has solved such problems in the past, or from learning how others have solved the problem. Consultants can be especially helpful in producing ready-made solutions. Input from suppliers, customers, or technical publications may also be helpful. As mentioned earlier, because custom-made solutions are expensive and time-consuming, managers are more likely to generate several alternative solutions of the ready-made type than of the custom-made type.

There are two main barriers to the creative thinking required to develop alternative solutions. The first is motivational. People who believe they are uncreative lack the motivation to attempt creativity. The second barrier is much more complex but is definitely manageable. It relates to the fact that everyone has cognitive, emotional, and perceptual predispositions or *sets* that interfere with the free association of ideas, thereby preventing new and useful combinations of ideas from emerging. Breaking these sets, caused by experience, education, prejudices, emotional conflicts, and the like, is the primary task of the person who aspires to think creatively.

Group Participation in Creative Thinking. Many human needs are satisfied by interaction with others; for example, the need for love, for acceptance or belonging, for status and power, and for cooperation to achieve common goals. As a result, most people have a capacity to be stimulated by a group and at the same time to contribute to shaping the group's behavior, a process known as *social facilitation*. Because of social facilitation, groups are occasionally established to engage in creative thinking; that is, to come up with a new idea or a new application.

Several group techniques aid creativity; their success is dependent upon the following two basic psychological phenomena:

1. Free association of ideas—a process of producing ideas in rapid succession with a minimum of inhibiting or restraining action. The original stimulus word is presented by the group leader and immediately the free associations thus produced function as additional stimuli for the group.
2. Social facilitation—a process that increases the productivity of each individual. Increased individual productivity further stimulates other members of the group.

One of the oldest and best known techniques that uses social facilitation to stimulate creative thinking is *brainstorming*. The technique, developed by Alex F. Osborn, was used as an aid in producing ideas for an advertising agency; however, since that time the technique has been applied in many other situations where there is a need to produce a large number of new solutions to a specific problem. In order to develop the desired quantity of ideas, an atmosphere conducive to the free flow of ideas is created. The group leader informs the participating members of the desired objective and cautions them against being critical of their ideas. The leader encourages freewheeling and usually bars all criticism. Occasionally checklists and suggestions for developing new ideas are distributed to the group. One such list, developed by Osborn, is as follows: [11]

1. Put to other uses
2. Adapt
3. Modify
4. Magnify
5. Minify
6. Substitute
7. Rearrange
8. Reverse
9. Combine

One of the major criticisms of brainstorming is that, by its very nature, it may produce superficial ideas, since the problem is worded in specific terms and thus limits the development of broad free association. Also, the technique may be very time-consuming; for, in addition to the hours spent in the session itself, time is required to evaluate the ideas produced. Nonetheless, it is a valuable group aid to encourage creative thinking, particularly in those situations in which a specific answer is desired such as a name for a new product or an advertising slogan.

---

[11] Alex F. Osborn, *Applied Imagination* (New York City: Charles Scribner's Sons, 1953), p. 284.

Although brainstorming has made valuable contributions, its popularity has declined since 1958, when a research study at Yale University showed that a group of individuals working alone (such noninteraction groups are called *nominal* groups) could collectively produce more unique ideas than they could produce working together.[12] This finding does not, however, mean that group creativity exercises have no value. In fact, where each member of a group has information that is not readily available to others (as managers from different departments often have), the group process may prove invaluable. Fortunately group creativity sessions may follow individual creativity efforts, thereby combining the advantages of both methods.

Another well-known creativity technique, *synectics*,[13] utilizes a carefully selected creativity team and an experienced leader whose task it is to structure situations that force participants to deviate from their usual modes of thinking. Various role-playing and fantasy exercises are used to invert, transpose, distort, and otherwise modify existing thought patterns in order to arrive at creative solutions. Although it is not widely used, the technique has merit. A variety of other techniques is also available to increase the creativity of groups, some of which make use of nominal rather than interacting groups.[14] Nevertheless, there is no one best technique for group creativity since situations and decision makers differ greatly.

Improving Individual Creativity. Individual creativity can be improved by several devices that help break perceptual sets. For example, a person may imagine how other people, say, an artist, engineer, lawyer, or accountant will view the problem. Direct input from others is even better. Learning how others have solved the problem, reading about the subject even if no solutions are offered, and combining elements of different solutions are further means of breaking the rigid thought patterns that prevent creativity.

Since creativity flourishes only if time is available for ideas to incubate, it is best to allow time lapses between periods of work on a problem. It is sometimes helpful to think about the problem just before going to bed and immediately after awakening. To break predispositions caused by negative thinking (where, for example, possible solutions are rejected because they appear to be unrealistic), solutions should be sought under widely differing assumptions, even under such idealistic assumptions as having no financial or other limitations. A single idea gained from such an exercise may provide the missing link for a workable solution under realistic assumptions.

---

[12] Thomas, J. Bouchard, "Whatever Happened to Brainstorming?" *Industry Week* (August 2, 1971), p. 26.

[13] W. J. Gordon, *Synectics* (New York City: Harper & Row, Publishers, Inc., 1961) and G. M. Prince, "The Operational Mechanism of Synectics," *The Journal of Creative Behavior,* Vol. 2 (1968), p. 1.

[14] Irving Summers and David E. White, "Creativity Techniques: Toward Improvement of the Decision Process," *Academy of Management Review,* Vol. 12, No. 2 (April, 1976), p. 103 and Andre L. Delbecq and Andrew H. Van de Ven, "A Group Process Model for Problem Identification and Program Planning," *The Journal of Applied Behavioral Science,* Vol. 7, No. 4 (April, 1971).

Managers should try to avoid critical analysis of alternative solutions during the creativity phase of problem solving; admittedly, this is difficult to do.[15] Analytical thinking interferes with the divergent thinking required in creativity, and the early rejection of a solution sometimes blocks the combining of a portion of the rejected solution with other ideas to produce an ideal solution.

Data Analysis

In the data analysis phase of problem solving (also called *critical analysis*), the alternative solutions developed earlier are evaluated. In one sense this is the least difficult part of problem solving because a wide choice of mathematical models is available, some of which can be followed like recipes. Some of these models are highly technical, but competent specialists in quantitative analysis are available as consultants (if specialists are not employed by the firm) to give managers whatever support they need. When solving major problems, the typical manager, even one with a good background in mathematics, should ordinarily make use of these specialists rather than rely solely on his or her own analytical skills.

The following techniques, named and briefly discussed, are most often used by decision analysts.

Payoff Matrix. One of the most useful analytical techniques is the payoff matrix. As shown in Table 6–1, it requires quantitative data, an awareness of

STRATEGIES	STATES OF NATURE			EXPECTED PAYOFF
	N_1 Recession	N_2 Stability	N_3 Upturn	
S_1 Build New Warehouse in Another City	($100,000)[1]	$10,000	$230,000	$92,500[2]
S_2 Rent Local Warehouse	($20,000)	$20,000	$150,000	$75,000
S_3 Expand Present Warehouse	($10,000)	$30,000	$160,000	$85,000
Probability	.25	.25	.50	

[1] Expected effect on net profit under specific assumptions.
[2] EP = −$100,000 (.25) + $10,000 (.25) + $230,000 (.50)

Table 6–1
PAYOFF MATRIX

---

[15] Mintzberg believes it is impossible to generate alternative solutions without evaluating them immediately (Mintzberg, *op. cit.*, p. 252), and he is probably right. There are, however, degrees of evaluation. There is definite value in setting aside a time for creativity when critical analysis is held to a minimum.

some of the most favorable *strategies* (possible solutions), judgments concerning important *states of nature* (uncontrollable influences on decision outcomes), and estimates of the probable occurrence of each state of nature (.25, .25, and .50 in Table 6–1).

After the expected payoffs are calculated, managers must judge whether the differences in payoff are large enough to be of practical significance. In addition, qualitative criteria must be integrated with the results of the analysis. For example, in Table 6–1, the new warehouse strategy is best if no factor except net profit is considered. But, since its profit advantage over expanding the present warehouse is only $7,500, management may prefer the warehouse expansion (Strategy 3) in order to avoid a cash flow problem that could occur if a recession were to cause a $100,000 loss. (There is a 25 percent chance of this.)[16]

Decision Tree. Decision trees may be used to express graphically the kinds of data presented in a payoff matrix and, in addition, to chart a sequence of possible actions that may be taken depending on the states of nature that actually occur and on the results of prior actions.[17]

Figure 6–2 shows the general structure of a decision tree. A fully developed decision tree may show several decision points and chance events as they may occur over a specific time period. The expected payoff for each course of action is computed just as in the payoff matrix (Table 6–1).

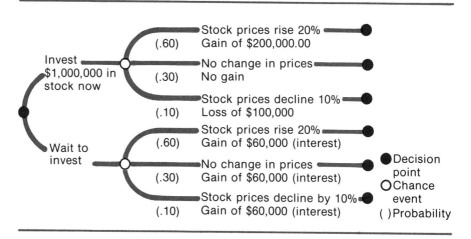

**Figure 6–2
DECISION TREE**

[16] See the following references for information on the use of payoff matrices under a variety of circumstances: K. J. Radford, *Managerial Decision Making* (Reston, Va.: Reston Publishing Company, Inc., 1975) and David W. Miller and Martin K. Starr, *The Structure of Human Decisions* (Englewood Cliffs, N. J.: Prentice-Hall, Inc., 1967).

[17] E. Frank Harrison, *The Managerial Decision-Making Process* (Boston: Houghton Mifflin Company, 1975), p. 136.

Decision Choice

Discovering the solution that will most likely yield good results often requires that numerous conclusions be drawn and places heavy demands on a manager's analytical abilities (or the analytical abilities of subordinates to whom the analysis has been delegated). But finding the best alternative is not synonymous with taking action. Techniques of analyzing data can be learned in school, but actually deciding, in the sense of committing oneself to a course of action, involves risk taking and can only be developed through actual experience.[18] The person who has not already acquired many of the qualities needed for decision making (discussed earlier in this chapter) is unlikely to be successful in doing so after becoming a manager.

Post-Choice Decisions

The quality of a decision is often determined by how well a manager implements it and follows up to make midcourse corrections as environmental conditions change and the unknowable future becomes the experience of the present. For example, a decision that appeared to be bad and irreversible, the purchase of a stock that immediately lost value, was salvaged somewhat when the decision maker rapidly sold, took a tax loss, and bought another stock that proved to be on its way up. In another case, a manufacturer's decision to reduce production capacity by selling off some unneeded machines appeared to have been a blunder when an upturn in the market increased product demand. Although the decision to sell the machines was based on an invalid market forecast, the decision turned out favorably because the alert owner quickly bought more modern machines in order to handle the new business.

Improving Managerial Decisions

Managers can improve the quality of their decisions by applying some of the guidelines that decision theorists have formulated. Because decision makers use different styles and have different needs, however, it is impossible to give advice for improving decisions that are applicable to everyone. The following recommendations have been selected because they relate to some common faults of managerial decision makers and summarize some major points presented in this chapter:

1. In order to increase objectivity, learn to distinguish personal and organizational decisions and keep them separate.
2. Through careful planning, minimize the number of decisions that must be made under crisis conditions.

---

[18] A variety of early experiences may contribute to a person's ability to decide and to take calculated risks. For example, some children manage their own money from an early age: they buy their own clothes, decide how to spend their entertainment budget, and either save money or don't at their own discretion. Leadership experiences at school, in sports, and during summer or part-time work may also develop this courage to take action and live with the consequences.

3. Reduce the number of decisions that are referred by subordinates. Insist that subordinates make all decisions that they are capable of making.
4. Seek out opportunities and make initiative decisions; do not procrastinate until action is forced.
5. Make an effort to be continually aware of political influences on decisions. This will not eliminate them, but it may help control them.
6. Learn ways of involving subordinates and staff specialists in decision making.
7. Insofar as possible, make each step explicit during the process of major decision making. It is especially important to state clearly the problem to be solved, the criteria to be used in evaluating the alternatives, and the assumptions on which the decisions are based.
8. Become aware of personal biases, perceptual sets, attitudes, and other personal qualities that influence your decisions. This awareness can lead to a degree of control and increased objectivity.
9. As a means of becoming more aware of problems, learn to view yourself as a problem solver and to view problems as opportunities to demonstrate your competence.
10. Make sure that the problem to which you seek a solution is the one that should receive first priority and that it is worthy of the attention you are giving it.
11. Do not settle for the most available solution. Develop alternatives before deciding on a course of action.
12. Demand creativity of yourself when generating alternative solutions, and use specific techniques to break perceptual sets and habitual thought patterns.
13. Do not attempt to be creative and analytical at the same time. While generating alternative solutions, withhold critical thinking as much as possible.
14. Make optimal use of quantitative models when critically analyzing alternatives. Delegate these alternatives to a staff specialist or to a consultant, if necessary.
15. Do not assume that problem solving ends when a decision is made. Effective follow-up and adaptation can often turn a mediocre decision into a good one or prevent a bad decision from becoming a disaster.
16. Maintain a log or decision bank in which you record your decisions (or the decisions you would have made if you had been in a position to do so). Occasionally review your success record and search for systematic flaws in your decision process.

There is no way to become a superior decision maker except through the sometimes painful experience of deciding and then living with the consequences. Because decisions about the future necessarily involve unknowns, good decisions will sometimes yield undesirable results, but the manager who recognizes this should have no need for regret when following a good process leads to bad results. The manager who never makes a wrong decision is too cautious and takes too few risks to reap the full advantage of his or her opportunities.

In Case Problem 6-B you are asked to make a series of decisions, a decision task known as the NASA Moon Survival Problem.[19] First, the project provides

---

[19] Jay Hall and W. H. Watson, "The Effects of a Normative Intervention on Group Decision-Making Performance," *Human Relations*, Vol. 23, No. 4 (Plenum Publishing Corporation, August, 1970), p. 299. The directions and the items to be ranked in importance are presented in the Appendix of the article, p. 316. The NASA Moon Survival Problem was developed by Jay Hall in 1963.

a measure of your ability to make decisions as an individual; second, since the subject matter is relatively new, a measure of creativity in decision making is required.

Case Problem 6-B

THE NASA MOON SURVIVAL PROBLEM

Directions: You are a member of a space crew originally scheduled to rendezvous with a mother ship on the lighted surface of the moon. Because of mechanical difficulties, however, your ship was forced to land at a spot some 200 miles from the rendezvous point. During reentry and landing, much of the equipment aboard was damaged and, since survival depends on reaching the mother ship, the most critical items available must be chosen for the 200-mile trip. Below are listed the 15 items left intact and undamaged after landing. Your task is to rank them in terms of their importance for your crew in allowing them to reach the rendezvous point. Place the number 1 by the most important item, the number 2 by the second most important and so on through number 15, the least important.

_____ Life raft

_____ Magnetic compass

_____ Five gallons of water

_____ Box of matches

_____ Food concentrate

_____ 50 feet of nylon rope

_____ Parachute silk

_____ Portable heating unit

_____ Two .45-caliber pistols

_____ One case dehydrated Pet milk

_____ Two 100-lb. tanks of oxygen

_____ Stellar map (of the moon's constellation)

_____ Signal flares

_____ First-aid kit containing injection needles

_____ Solar-powered FM receiver-transmitter

CHAPTER QUESTIONS FOR STUDY AND DISCUSSION

1. Select the five types of decisions which would most likely be made by a high-level executive concerned primarily with determining the direction of the firm, anticipating and solving major problems, and taking advantage of growth opportunities.

2. Which factors are most likely to introduce irrationality into managerial decision making?

3. What argument can you provide for the practical value of understanding Mintzberg's decision model?

4. Granting that intelligence is positively correlated with decision-making ability, why may a manager with an IQ of 120 make better decisions than another with an IQ of 130?

5. How does a manager's self-structure relate to decision making?

6. What is meant by making the decision process explicit? Why is it important?

7. What is a problem? Give five examples of different kinds of problems.

8. What is the barrier to creative thinking to which creativity exercises such as brainstorming are addressed?

9. Describe the main difference between the way a decision tree and payoff matrix function?

10. Which three distinct types of thinking or personal attributes are most likely to be at a premium in the search, critical-analysis, and decision-choice phases of problem solving?

Chapter 7

Production Management

Case Problem 7-A

PRODUCTIVITY IN THE AUTO SERVICE CENTER

In recent years most full-service department stores, such as Sears, Roebuck and Co. and Montgomery Ward & Co., several tire manufacturers, and numerous independent firms have invested heavily in auto service centers. Initially developed to install a retailer's batteries, tires, shock absorbers, mufflers, brakes, and other standard size auto parts and accessories, the functions of service centers have continued to expand. They now rival the service departments of major automobile dealers, draining much of the latter's most profitable business. In addition to supporting company sales, auto service centers perform selected maintenance and repair functions such as engine tune-ups, wheel balancing, and front-end alignments— all of which are frequently needed services that are suitable for standard pricing and mass advertising.

Auto service centers typically avoid engine overhauls and other work that requires the skills of a master mechanic. Their work is performed by specialists in balancing and installing tires, aligning wheels, and tuning engines, for example; but it does not require the services of employees who can perform all these functions with equal skill. Each specialist has access to tools and support systems needed to do a good job with a minimum of physical effort. Employees who mount tires, for example, elevate the car so that a minimum of stooping is required. They remove and install the wheel lugs with a power wrench that contributes to high productivity and quality (exactly the proper torque in tightening the lugs) while reducing human effort. Employees are taught to follow a definite sequence of steps in performing each job in order to eliminate unnecessary movements.

Expensive, specialized equipment is provided for tire balancing and front-end alignment, making both operations relatively easy to learn and easy to perform rapidly without sacrificing quality. The electronic equipment needed for engine tune-ups is probably the most sophisticated of all; and, although more skill is required for this work than for most other jobs in the shop, the required level of skill is far from that of a master mechanic who has served a full apprenticeship. As emission-control systems have increased the complexity of engine tuning, new tests have been added (such as carbon monoxide exhaust tests); but the requirements of such tests are detailed in a manufacturer's service manual and may be learned by the specialists without the need for formal training.

Manufacturer service manuals, updated regularly, provide performance guidelines so that even an amateur with the proper equipment can perform many repair operations. The manual shows, for example, how to adjust intake and exhaust valve clearances, and it specifies exactly what valve clearance should be used under hot and cold motor conditions. The several-hundred-page manual contains pictures of each repair operation, with notations concerning part numbers. It gives step-by-step descriptions of how to make each repair or adjustment for the entire automobile. The operations may differ somewhat from one make or model to another, but a specialist soon learns that for a given system (brakes, for example) the similarities far outweigh the differences, and adaptations are rapidly made from one automobile to another. For each functional unit of the automobile, a good service manual describes common problems, indicates possible causes, and recommends corrective actions.

Although auto service centers make excellent use of specialized labor, their employees often learn more than one job and are able to perform another employee's job in case of absenteeism. Since jobs require different degrees of skill, opportunities for promotion exist in many shops. An employee who has mastered several different jobs and has the flexibility to fill in for an absent employee may therefore earn more.

In some shops, compensation is based on the *standard hour*—the amount of work expected of a trained employee using approved methods in a period of one hour. Under this method of payment, a specific amount of time is allowed for performing a given job, and employees who complete their jobs in less than the standard time may accumulate extra time for which they are paid their regular hourly rate. In one shop, for example, tune-up specialists sometimes accumulate as many as eleven hours of work in an eight-hour period. Since the company charges its customers a flat rate for each job, employees are encouraged to accumulate as many hours as possible. Customers do not pay when a job must be redone; employees are required to stand behind their work and are paid only when the company can bill a customer.

PROBLEMS

1. List as many methods as you can which are used in auto service centers to increase productive efficiency.
2. What inefficiencies exist in auto service centers that may not be present in assembly-line production?
3. How do auto service centers motivate employees to be productive? Are there elements in the environment that may work against high motivation to be productive? Explain.
4. What other services may be compensated on a standard hour basis?

All organizations have a production function. That function is most recognizable in companies that produce tangibles such as automobiles, books, medical equipment, or appliances. Productivity in auto service centers, universities, hospitals, and restaurants, however, is quite a different matter—often more difficult to define and harder to measure. In this chapter, we take a broad view of productivity, including its role in providing an acceptable quality of life. A nation's ability to cope with problems of poverty, unemployment, and environmental pollution is closely linked to the productive efficiency of all its institutions.

PRODUCTION: ITS MEANING AND IMPORTANCE

Productivity is a measure of the output of a production unit—a business, a hospital, a government agency, or the entire nation—during a specific period of time. The productivity of a factory is defined as its total output divided by the hours of work required to produce it, assuming that the quality of output is constant. If, for example, with a given number of employee work hours, a plant produces 1,000 units one year and 1,100 units of like quality the next year, productivity increases by 10 percent. Productivity also increases if in the second year the plant produces 1,000 units of improved quality in 10 percent fewer employee hours, but measurement of the increase is more difficult in the latter case.

In manufacturing industries, measuring productivity may simply be a matter of counting the number of units produced in a given period, but in service industries measurement is complex and often subjective. Only recently have productivity studies in the service industries (education, medicine, government, entertainment, maintenance and repair, transportation, communication, etc.) been attempted, in spite of the fact that about seven out of every ten persons are now employed in some sort of service job. As technology has become increasingly sophisticated, machines have replaced employees, increasing productivity per employee hour and decreasing the role of individual effort in overall productive efficiency. Since factory systems have from their beginnings been committed to efficiency, they have, relative to service industries, been highly efficient; service industries have often been indifferent to efficiency methods.

The Production System

In recent years an increasingly useful framework for thinking about organizations and managerial functions has been the *systems model.* For our purposes, a *system* is defined as a set of relationships, interdependencies, and interacting functions which comprise a purposeful means for achieving an objective. A spring-wound alarm clock exemplifies a simple and relatively *closed*, or self-contained system—a system requiring minimal interaction with the external environment to function effectively.

An organization is considered an *open* system. It has certain boundaries that differentiate it from other systems, but it must constantly receive a multitude of inputs from its external environment—people, energy, raw materials, information, and the like—in order to achieve its objectives. To survive and prosper, a business organization must be productive. It must return to its external environment certain outputs in order to justify its existence and get the support it needs. It must create or generate something of value.

Figure 7–1 depicts organizations as production systems with various forms of input, transformation processes, and output. Depending on the nature and objectives of the organizations, their essential inputs may include patients (in hospitals), parts and sub-assemblies (in factories), or students (in schools). The transformation processes in these organizations perform the necessary operations

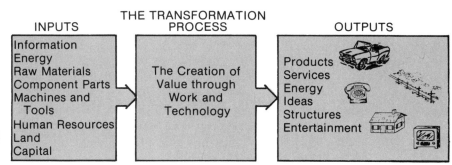

Figure 7–1
ORGANIZATIONS AS PRODUCTION SYSTEMS

to achieve the objectives of the systems; in the situations just listed, the transformations typically involve diagnosis and treatment, assembly into major subassemblies or completed products, and teaching and research. The expected output of these production units can be expressed in terms of diagnosed, treated, or healed patients; products such as bicycles or battleships; and educated students, creative ideas, and scientific discoveries.

The overall organizational system—which itself is part of a larger social, economic, and political system—is made up of a number of subsystems on which the success of the whole unit depends. Though interdependent, the boundaries of many subsystems are so clear that they function as distinct management units; for example, product research and development, production planning, personnel services, purchasing, payroll, production control, quality control, and machine maintenance. Thinking of these functional areas as subsystems within increasingly larger systems has been particularly helpful in communicating to managers the importance of coordination and the inevitability of significant changes in one part of the system affecting the total system.

Productivity in Service Industries

Fast-food businesses, such as McDonald's, Wendy's Old Fashioned Hamburgers, and Long John Silver's Sea Food Shoppes, have been among the most effective of the service industries in increasing productivity.[1] Small efforts have been exerted toward measuring the productivity of federal civil service employees,[2] and some progress has been made in increasing productivity in education and medicine.[3] Increasing productivity in education and medicine is difficult for several reasons. Both are dominated by professionals who place heavy emphasis on quality and for that reason resist efforts to increase quantity. Both profes-

---

[1] Theodore Levitt, "Production Line Approach to Service," *Harvard Business Review*, Vol. 50, No. 5 (September–October, 1972), p. 41.

[2] "Measuring and Enhancing Productivity in the Federal Government," Phase III: Summary Report, Office of Management and the Budget and Other Agencies, June, 1973.

[3] John F. Rockart, "An Approach to Productivity in Two Knowledge-Based Industries," *Sloan Management Review*, Vol. 15, No. 1 (Fall, 1973), p. 23.

sions emphasize the importance of rapport with the client (patient or student) and resist mass-production methods that threaten to depersonalize their work. Many physicians have noted that attitude and the will to live play an important role in patient recovery. And professors are typically concerned with inspiring students to want to learn and with teaching them to think rather than rely on memorized facts. Such variables are extremely difficult to control and measure.

Rockart notes, however, that productivity is not incompatible with considerations of quality or professional satisfaction and cites several examples to support his point.[4] Among the efficiency methods in medicine is one which has long been used in business and industry: substituting the labor of lower paid paraprofessionals for that of professionals. Many duties once thought to require a medical doctor are now performed with equal competence by paramedics, nurses, medical technicians, and clerks, permitting the physician to perform at the highest level of which he or she is capable.

Efficiency methods can also be used in educational settings. Rather than devote all their time to a few graduate students, full professors with outstanding credentials sometimes lecture to large numbers of undergraduates, leaving discussions and question-and-answer sessions to teaching assistants who meet with students in small groups. In other learning situations, audio and videotape presentations are used to communicate ideas normally presented in lectures, permitting the professor to allocate more time for personal contact with students. In some situations, computers, capable of providing an opportunity for both rote learning and high-level problem solving, perform certain functions which otherwise would be performed by professors.

The Importance of Productivity

Government agencies and other organizations, such as educational institutions, need not be very productive in order to survive, but productive efficiency is demanded of most business enterprises. In a competitive system, the very inefficient firm simply ceases to exist. In some service industries, where virtually everyone is inefficient (in the repair of home appliances, for example), survival and success depend more on other factors, such as marketing techniques, public relations, and effective information systems, than on production as such. It is understandable, however, why manufacturing industries must emphasize productivity and why they have at times emphasized it so heavily that human relations and the natural environment have been neglected. The drive for productive efficiency is intensified because a firm's competitors may extend far beyond national borders. In the apparel industry, for example, American firms must compete with producers in the Far East that operate under entirely different constraints, especially with regard to wages. The same is true to a large degree in the automotive industry.

Nations and individuals, as well as companies, have a high stake in efficient production. Increases in productivity on a national basis enable everyone to

---

[4] *Ibid*., p. 24.

enjoy a higher standard of living. They permit people to deal with critical social problems such as environmental pollution, poverty, and the decay of cities. Increases in productivity make it possible for Americans to maintain a high standard of living while investing in research which will benefit all nations. One of the most remarkable increases in productivity occurred in American agriculture from 1950 to 1970. In 1950 one agricultural worker produced enough to feed 15 people; by 1978 one worker fed 65 people, excluding exports. This increase in productivity was due to several factors, the most important of which were the use of larger and more efficient machines, improved seeds and agricultural technology, increased use of commercial fertilizer, and more and better irrigation. The productivity increase was measured in terms of employee hours, but, as so often is the case, the employees involved had relatively little influence on that increase.

INFLUENCES ON PRODUCTIVITY

The most significant gains in productivity have resulted from the substitution of machines for people. A single bulldozer can literally do the work of hundreds of workers using picks and shovels. Power shovels in open-pit mines and machines used for underground mining eliminate the need for thousands of coal miners to do dangerous, back-breaking work, and allow those who remain in mining to earn relatively high wages. Automatic typewriters, copiers, electronic communication systems, and computers significantly increase the productivity of clerical and managerial personnel. Although many manufacturing systems still require large numbers of assembly-line workers, the assembly-line technology itself has greatly increased productivity per employee hour. In the production of certain goods, such as petroleum and chemicals, mechanization and automation have almost eliminated the need for production workers, except to monitor and control operations and handle repair problems.

In spite of extensive mechanization and automation, individual effort is still a major contributor to productivity in many industries. In much assembly-line work, employee motivation is a major determinant of output, and in more highly automated industries, product quality is affected by the care with which the monitoring operations are performed. In all industries, the effectiveness of technicians, such as maintenance personnel, influences machine downtime and thereby influences productivity. In many kinds of work—in the work of the clerk, secretary, or accountant, for example—individual skills and motivation exert a critical influence on productivity, although the office machines and computers with which they work are also important.

Figure 7–2 shows a number of variables that influence productivity. Union-management relations, for example, can be such that all productivity ceases for a period of time, and union power may restrict production by various means. Examples of this are union demands for productivity quotas (a brick mason lays only a certain number of bricks in a day—often far below capability); the requirement of unnecessary personnel (a train crew must sometimes include an unneeded brakeman); restrictive work rules (in some situations an idle worker on one job cannot be temporarily transferred to another job, where extra help is needed). The rationale for such practices is not important at this point; the fact is that these practices significantly affect productivity in some firms.

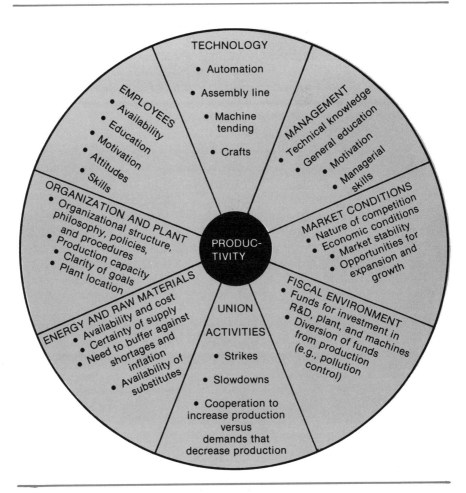

Figure 7–2 INFLUENCES ON PRODUCTIVITY

Among the many influences on productive efficiency is the availability of markets, which will permit a firm to produce in large quantities, to produce continuously, and to invest in modern machines and plants. The availability of money at reasonable interest rates and economic and political factors that affect risks are other important factors in determining production efficiency. After World War II, the United States government helped Germany and Japan rebuild their steel industries, using modern and efficient technology, while our own steel industry languished because of the understandable cautiousness of private investors. Unable to predict the strength of the postwar market and wary of their government-backed foreign competitors, steel companies in the United States were slow to modernize, and because of that slowness lost their competitive advantage. Thus, when the opportunity arose to produce the pipe needed for the trans-Alaskan oil pipeline, American steel companies were unable to compete with the Japanese. In addition to their high production capacity, the Japanese were aided by industry-goverment cooperation which helped absorb the enormous financial risks involved.

WHAT PRODUCTION MANAGERS DO

Production managers come to their jobs from a variety of backgrounds. Different types of education, training, and experience are required to achieve high productivity goals in a fast-food restaurant, a chemicals plant, an automobile plant, a diamond-cutting operation, a hospital, and a university. Within a single production unit—a factory, for example—managers with different knowledge and skills are needed to ensure that such production functions as planning, scheduling, routing, product design, and methods engineering are successfully carried out. Specialists in any one of these areas may eventually become head of the production unit, usually after occupying several specialist positions.

Depending on the nature of the industry, production managers with specialized engineering degrees (e.g., mechanical, industrial, chemical, or electrical) may be uniquely qualified to perform well. Industrial engineers are particularly well suited for factory management because of the broad curriculum required by that degree and because of its special emphasis on job design, time and motion studies, and other production-oriented subjects. Nevertheless, production managers, even those who manage large production units, have widely varying backgrounds. This variety is appropriate in view of the greatly differing production environments and the large number of job specialties within production management.

We look briefly at four of the many work areas in which production managers are often engaged: facilities location, process design, scheduling, and supervision.

Facilities Location

As indicated in Chapter 5, the location of facilities is one aspect of production planning. Because businesses grow, add new products, change markets, and require various environments for energy and raw materials, properly locating facilities is a constant challenge.

Depending on the nature of the enterprise, managers learn to seek specific location characteristics that will contribute to the firm's success. For instance, if there is a choice of many locations, should a McDonald's restaurant be opened in a small town of 30,000? What is the effect of entering a cluster of established fast-food restaurants? How profitable will a McDonald's restaurant be that is near a large university campus or on a particular interstate freeway? These are questions that must be answered by research and experience, taking into account a number of interacting variables.

One common problem faced by manufacturers is plant location. The following variables should be seriously considered when solving such a problem:

1. *Availability of personnel.* Plants seldom locate in areas where labor shortages are known to exist. In some instances, it is important that specific kinds of skilled workers be available.
2. *Proximity to markets and materials.* Beverage bottles are produced close to where they are used because of breakage; grocery stores locate near residential centers; lumber mills locate near forests; and aluminum plants locate where fuel to generate electricity is abundant.
3. *Legal restrictions.* Zoning and environmental protection laws are an ever-increasing consideration in plant location. Some areas are off limits to industrial expansion because of pollution problems.
4. *Transportation.* Almost every manufacturer must consider transportation facilities: the accessibility of airlines, interstate highways, railroad spurs, and docking facilities. These may be critical factors in the profitability of an enterprise.
5. *Living conditions.* Locations with inadequate housing, schools, churches, shopping centers, and entertainment contribute to manager and worker dissatisfaction, especially among employees transferred from other company facilities. Inadequate living conditions may contribute directly to employee turnover.

Process Design

Production managers make frequent decisions about *process design*; that is, decisions about how the firm's inputs will be converted into outputs. A particularly troublesome process-design problem concerns the replacement of machines when changes are occurring so rapidly that a new model can become obsolete almost immediately. This problem is especially acute when rapid advances in computer technology are increasing the pace of automation.

A special problem in process design occurs in hospitals where administrators are not completely free to choose a course of action that will best achieve the organization's objectives. Decisions to purchase major pieces of equipment, complicated by a need for state control board approval, may be made prematurely in order to get the purchase permit before a local competitor does. If, in order to control medical costs, the control board allows only one computerized X-ray scanner in a specific locality, a hospital administrator may rush to make the purchase before the equipment is adequately tested.

The importance of capital investments in process design varies greatly among industries. Many firms that make a product are *capital intensive*: they require large capital investments in machines, tools, equipment, computers, and plants. A steel mill or a highly automated candy plant is capital intensive. Other firms are *labor intensive*: they require large investments in people rather than large investments in machines. Consulting firms and a number of factory assembly operations fall into the labor-intensive category. Because of the high cost of labor and the relative unpredictability of employees, most manufacturers prefer to move toward capital-intensive processes.

Scheduling

One of the complex duties of production managers is scheduling the many production resources in order to reduce costs and to assure that commitments to customers are met on time. In a small printing shop, scheduling may involve little more than deciding which customer's needs will be met first. Even this can be a frustrating task, however, when production facilities are strained and it is important to expand production as far as possible before investing in new equipment. The scheduling problems of developing a new missile system or even of producing an automobile or television set are much more complex, placing high demands on a staff of professional production schedulers.

The problems of scheduling are simply illustrated in the construction of a house where a certain sequence of operations is critical. The owner, who has already gone through a lengthy process of purchasing a lot, developing plans, negotiating a loan, and taking bids, is frustrated because construction does not begin immediately after the contract is awarded. But the contractor, who had no assurance of getting the job, is building other homes and must schedule the firm's employees as well as establish agreements with subcontractors and suppliers. After permits are obtained and work is begun, scheduling is complicated by unpredictable weather and by delays due to subcontractor miscalculations. Scheduling may be further complicated by shortages of materials, incorrect shipments, and labor problems. Delays are sometimes caused by public inspectors who must, at specific stages in construction, approve the plumbing, wiring, and other aspects of the structure. If the work is not approved, still further delays are likely, and each delay upsets subsequent steps. If, for example, a delay forces the masonry contractor to move on to another job, it becomes necessary for the general contractor to locate another subcontractor or wait until the original subcontractor is available.

To reduce scheduling problems, schedules may include *lead time*—a period between the officially scheduled and anticipated beginning of the project—between the phases of construction; but allowing too much lead time may excessively extend the completion date, resulting in a failure to win the contract. Furthermore, failure to build in lead time may result in heavy penalties for not performing according to the agreement. To cope with some of the unpredictable and uncontrollable variables such as those described in building a house, manufacturers resort to various *buffering devices* such as stockpiling fuel, raw materials, and finished products. If shortages are expected, they may even hire additional personnel who are not needed at the time. Thus, production scheduling is closely interlocked with other functions—in this case inventory control and personnel management—that greatly complicate scheduling problems and often require complex scheduling processes. In Chapter 20, "Nonbudgetary Control," we will discuss two techniques, PERT and CPM, which are uniquely suited for scheduling and controlling complex projects.

Supervision

One of the important functions of production managers is the supervision of personnel. Although supervision occurs throughout all levels of management, the first-line production manager is the one person for whom supervision (in contrast to planning or scheduling, for example) is a primary responsibility. In automated industries, the actual volume of productivity may not depend greatly on employee effort, but few production units can function for long without production employees. In some service industries—in telephone companies, for example—management personnel can for a time keep service going when the rank and file are on strike; but in all industries effective supervision is an important aspect of production management to which much attention is given. Even in automated industries the quality of supervision will ordinarily influence employee turnover, absenteeism, and job satisfaction. Thus, production managers, educated in technical specialties such as engineering, must receive additional training in the supervisory methods.

TECHNOLOGICAL ASPECTS OF PRODUCTION

Reference has already been made to the effects of technology on production. Although the term itself has been defined many ways, the concept of technology is relatively simple.[5] *Technology*, according to Galbraith, is "the systematic application of scientific or other organized knowledge to practical tasks." [6] Simon's definition is similar, but places more emphasis on knowledge: "Technology is knowledge of how to do things, how to accomplish human goals." [7] Although Galbraith's definition may in some ways be less accurate, it is more useful to management since it places greater emphasis on application. Knowledge in the areas of science and the industrial arts is recognized as technology when it proves to be a practical method of solving practical problems at the management level.

The level of technology within a given organization can be described by one or more of several dimensions. Burack suggests the following five dimensions: (1) degree of mechanization, (2) degree of time dependence, (3) degree of control instrumentation and computerized process control, (4) degree of division of labor, and (5) degree of technical engineering intrinsic to the technological processes of the organization.[8] Four classifications of technology are described here; allowing for slight variations in terminology, they are the ones most often used by experts in the field of production technology. As shown in Figure 7–3, they are crafts, machine tending, assembly line, and automation (continuous-process technology).

---

[5] For a technical treatment of the definition problem see David F. Gillespie and Dennis S. Mileti, "Technology and the Study of Organizations: An Overview and Appraisal," *The Academy of Management Review*, Vol. 2, No. 1 (January, 1977), p. 7.

[6] John Kenneth Galbraith, *The New Industrial State* (Boston: Houghton Mifflin Company, 1967), p. 12.

[7] Herbert Simon, "Technology and Environment," *Emerging Concepts in Management*, edited by Max S. Wortman and Fred Luthans (2d ed.; New York City: Macmillan, Inc., 1975), p. 4.

[8] Elmer E. Burack, "Technology and Some Aspects of Industrial Supervision: A Model Building Approach," *Academy of Management Journal*, Vol. 45, No. 3 (March, 1966), p. 47.

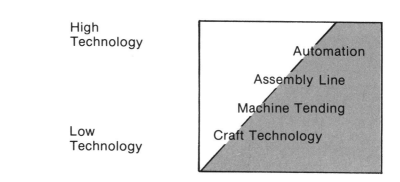

High
Technology

Automation

Assembly Line

Machine Tending

Low
Technology

Craft Technology

**Figure 7–3
LEVELS OF
TECHNOLOGY**

Craft Technology

The earliest records of human history depict the use of tools to provide the food, clothing, shelter, and other items necessary to satisfy human needs. Until the industrial revolution, little technological progress was made from the time of the early Babylonian, Egyptian, Greek, and Roman civilizations. A suit, a dress, or a pair of shoes was made by an artisan, a skilled craftsperson who took orders from customers and, with few exceptions, produced the goods one at a time.

Artisans were respected for their skill and took pride in their work. They were, however, typically poorer than even unskilled laborers are today because their technology was incapable of producing great wealth. Although modern artisans still exist (carpenters and tailors, for example) their technology is still inefficient compared with say, the assembly line; and, as a result, assembly-line methods are making rapid inroads into their trades. In home construction, much of the work of a carpenter, for example, is performed by semiskilled specialists who do nothing but shingle roofs, install wallboard, apply siding, or cut and nail with power hammers the subassemblies of which the house frames are made. Today even cabinets (once built by only the best of carpenters) are usually mass-produced by semiskilled or unskilled workers in a technology much like a factory assembly line. A few tailors and dressmakers survive today by catering to wealthy customers, but most clothing is now mass-produced. Shoemakers or cobblers, once among the most respected of all artisans, now exist primarily for shoe and boot repair. They are part of a small service industry rather than a producer-of-goods industry in the traditional sense.

Machine Tending

Machine tenders monitor and operate semiautomatic equipment. Machine tending takes advantage of specialized equipment; simple, efficient movements; the use of unskilled or semiskilled workers; and minimal human input in terms of thinking and decision making. Depending on the sophistication of the machine, machine tending may require considerable physical effort, or it may only require monitoring. Metal-stamping machines, which a few years ago required the worker to place a piece of sheet metal on the machine, position it, activate the machine, then remove the finished part, are now so internally automated that the worker is required to do little more than watch for possible malfunctions. This, of course, places no great mental demands on the machine tender—which has its advantages and disadvantages—but it does remove the burden of physical labor, and it greatly increases productivity.

Assembly Line

Sometimes called *mass production* and *Detroit automation* (because of its early applications in the automobile industry),[9] assembly-line technology represents a monumental advance over craft technology in productive efficiency. However, it makes less use of an organization's human resources because it minimizes the need for employees to think and make decisions. Assembly-line technology capitalizes on the advantages of job dilution—breaking down complex jobs into a large number of small, simple, efficient, and easy-to-learn operations. Instead of performing several different operations in the assembly of an automobile, for example, a semiskilled specialist, using scientifically engineered methods and the most advanced tools, does nothing but install overhead upholstery, headlights, brakes, or radiators. The work is routine and often boring. Since the worker is ordinarily expected to work at a fast pace, some assembly-line jobs are extremely tiring. Assembly-line workers are usually paced by a conveyor device, since the product is mechanically transported past fixed work stations.

Mass-production techniques are used in most factory systems and even in some services. McDonald's restaurants, for example, can make a profit on a relatively inexpensive meal because they use some very efficient and highly standardized mass-production methods. Houston's famous M.D. Anderson Hospital and Cancer Institute moves masses of outpatients through its blood-test, X-ray, and treatment facilities by using various mass-production techniques. Even the world-renowned heart surgeon, Dr. Michael E. DeBakey, uses a mass-production approach. Other specialists and less experienced physicians prepare the patient for surgery, and make and close incisions, leaving only the most delicate and demanding parts of the operation for Dr. DeBakey. Thus, by practicing this form of job dilution, more patients have the benefit of this outstanding surgeon's expertise; yet each part of the total operation is performed expertly.

In mass-production systems an increasing number of jobs, which in the past were performed by workers, are performed by machines. Complicated welding jobs on the curved surfaces of automobile bodies, for example, were once performed only by skilled technicians; now they are performed by computer-controlled machines. Many tasks, previously performed in the assembly of such

---

[9] The terminology used in this area is ambiguous and is particularly troublesome when applied to service industries. The ambiguity is inevitable because of (1) the great variety of production processes covered and (2) the rapid evolution of assembly-line methods toward mechanization and automation.

electronic equipment as computers, radios, and television sets, are no longer performed at all because of the advances recently made in the development of microprocessors—miniature computers on an integrated-circuit chip. Exemplified by the increasingly sophisticated pocket calculator, the number of circuits contained in one fingernail-sized silicon chip has for several years doubled every 14 months. Thus, microprocessors have dramatically changed the nature of the work in the computer industry, and the changes that computerization is bringing in automating other industries are equally spectacular.

Because of advances made in mechanization and control systems, Detroit-style automated plants vary from those in which most of the assembly-line work is performed by hand to others in which most manual work has been replaced by machines operating in series. At one extreme the word *automation* hardly applies at all, and at the other extreme the assembly line is automated in the full sense of the word. The Smith-Corona Marchant Company, for example, uses machines to assemble typewriters, thereby eliminating manual labor. One major United States clock manufacturing company assembles 6,000 clocks daily on a totally automated line; and, in still another industry, machines assemble spark plugs and inspect and pack them for shipping.[10] Thus, assembly-line or Detroit-style automation evolves into true (continuous-process) automation.

Automation (Continuous-Process Technology)

Until now we have used the term *automation* without discussing its meaning. John Diebold describes the essential qualities of automation in the following statement:

> I think this is perhaps the basic meaning of automation—we are beginning to look at our industrial processes as complete, integrated systems, from the introduction of raw material until the completion of the final product . . . . One way of defining automation is to say that it is a means of organizing or controlling production processes to achieve optimum use of all production resources—mechanical, material, and human.[11]

As Diebold's definition implies, automation is based on the concept of production as a continuous flow as opposed to intermittent batches of work. In some situations, automation links together already highly mechanized, internally automated operations through the use of computers and sophisticated machines. Thus, automation is an extension of mechanization—an extension of electronically and mechanically controlled machines rather than a new concept in technology. One advantage of automation is that it increases the speed and precision with which tasks are completed. It does so, however, only at a cost of increased rigidity.[12] Compared with lower level technologies, automated processes gener-

---

[10] Richard A. Johnson, William T. Newell, and Roger C. Vergin, *Production and Operations Management* (Boston: Houghton Mifflin Company, 1974), p. 185.

[11] Richard P. Hopeman, *Production: Concepts, Analysis, Control* (3d ed.; Columbus: Charles E. Merrill Publishing Company, 1976), p. 266.

[12] Mariann Jelinek, "Technology, Organizations, and Contingency," *The Academy of Management Review*, Vol. 2, No. 1 (January, 1977), p. 17.

ally have less tolerance for variations in raw materials and less potential for modifying the nature of the product as needs change. Fortunately in automated processes there is also less likelihood of variation in the quality of the final product.

The best examples of continuous-process technologies are found in the production of petroleum, chemicals, and electricity.[13] In these industries, there is literally a continuous flow of raw materials through the plants; and the major responsibility of employees is to monitor instruments and make adaptations as needed. For example, in a water-powered electrical generating plant, as long as the water power is available and the equipment is working successfully, electricity continuously flows to the consumer, and the amount produced is not dependent on human effort; that is, the operator cannot produce more electricity by working harder.

In industries with different levels of technology, employees exercise varying degrees of personal control. An _open-loop_ system requires the employee to perform certain operations when a deviation from standard is detected. In a semi-automated oil refinery, for example, an employee may be required to open a valve in order to bring the octane level of gasoline up to standard. In a more completely automated system, a _closed-loop_ system, the valve will be automatically activated if feedback from a sensing device detects any deviation from standard. Another example of a closed-loop system is the use of an automobile cruise control that maintains a constant driving speed (Figure 7–4). In this situation, feedback from the speedometer automatically activates an increase

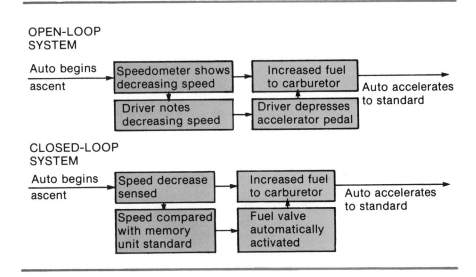

**Figure 7–4
OPEN- AND
CLOSED-LOOP
SYSTEMS IN
AUTOMOBILE
CRUISE
CONTROL**

OPEN-LOOP
SYSTEM

Auto begins ascent → Speedometer shows decreasing speed → Increased fuel to carburetor → Auto accelerates to standard

Driver notes decreasing speed → Driver depresses accelerator pedal

CLOSED-LOOP
SYSTEM

Auto begins ascent → Speed decrease sensed → Increased fuel to carburetor → Auto accelerates to standard

Speed compared with memory unit standard → Fuel valve automatically activated

---

[13] Process industries are those that modify bulk solids, liquids, or gases by physical or chemical means in order to produce a finished product. The term _continuous-process automation_ is used by some authors to refer only to such industries.

or decrease in the amount of fuel sent to the engine. The cruise-control unit illustrates both the effectiveness and the rigidity of an automated system: the automobile will cruise at a more consistent speed than if the typical driver were in control; however, driver control allows for much more flexibility when slowing and accelerating are required.

EFFICIENCY METHODS IN JOB DESIGN

In later chapters we will discuss recent developments in designing jobs that are intended to make them more interesting, to reduce boredom, and, in general, to increase employee satisfaction in the workplace. Traditionally, however, production managers have been concerned primarily with efficiency and have had minimal concern for job satisfaction. The practice of job dilution, on which mass production is based, is a case in point. Its one purpose is to increase efficiency. Thus, even in an organization that deliberately tries to make jobs more interesting, efficiency is essential to the firm's survival in a competitive environment.

Efficiency is concerned with how well a firm's input resources are utilized during the production process. Thus, it compares actual output achieved with the expected output that should have resulted from the utilization of given resources.[14]

$$\text{Efficiency} = \frac{\text{Actual output}}{\text{Normal or expected output}}$$

In such a formula, output is usually expressed in terms of productivity per employee hour, but it is sometimes more rational to express it in terms of other variables such as materials or capital. Of the many efficiency methods available to production managers, three are discussed here. They are process charts, motion studies, and time studies.

Process Charts

The American Society of Mechanical Engineers defines a *process chart* as

. . . a graphic presentation of the sequence of all operations, transportations, inspections, delays, and storages occurring during a process or procedure, and includes information considered desirable for analysis, such as time required and distance moved.[15]

Many different kinds of process charts can be developed to help the job analyst visualize a job. Process charts show the details of some action—the routine work of an assembler, the flow of a purchase or shipping order through the firm, the product flow through the plant—and thereby help the analyst to identify

---

[14] Leonard Garrett and Milton Silver, *Production Management Analysis* (3d ed.; New York City: Harcourt Brace Jovanovich, Inc., 1973), p. 251.

[15] Raymond R. Mayer, *Production and Operations Management* (3d ed.; New York City: McGraw-Hill, Inc., 1975), p. 455.

and correct any inefficiencies. Depending on the situation, the analyst may recommend that actions be reversed, eliminated, combined, or changed in other ways. Figure 7–5 shows one of the many approaches to developing a process chart; notice that it provides a basis for both a time study and a method study.

TIME:	Per page				
		Present		Proposed	
		LH	RH	LH	RH
O	Operations				
→	Transport				
▽	Holds				
D	Delays				
	Total Time				

OPERATION: Copying loose pages
METHOD: ____ Present ____ Proposed
DATE: 2/9/82
OPERATOR: R. Smith
ANALYST: J.C.W.

Left Hand	OPER.	TRANS.	HOLD	DELAY	OPER.	TRANS.	HOLD	DELAY	Right Hand
Lift Cover	O	→	▽	D	O	→	▽	D	Reach for new page
Hold Cover	O	→	▽	D	O	→	▽	D	Grasp page
	O	→	▽	D	O	→	▽	D	Move page to machine window
	O	→	▽	D	O	→	▽	D	Position page
	O	→	▽	D	O	→	▽	D	Release page
Close Cover	O	→	▽	D	O	→	▽	D	Move hand to print button
	O	→	▽	D	O	→	▽	D	Push print button
	O	→	▽	D	O	→	▽	D	Wait for print light
Open Cover	O	→	▽	D	O	→	▽	D	Move hand to machine window
	O	→	▽	D	O	→	▽	D	Grasp page
	O	→	▽	D	O	→	▽	D	Move page to completed stack

Figure 7–5
PROCESS
CHART

Motion Studies

Several techniques are available for increasing efficiency through motion studies. One technique applies a set of motion study principles to the work situation. The following is a representative sample from a list of such techniques:[16]

I. Rules for minimizing human movements
1. Whenever possible, perform tasks by machine rather than by hand.
2. Reduce materials handling (say, by using gravity, where possible, and by handling several units at once).
3. Use the fewest motions possible (for example, do not use arm motions if hand or finger motions alone will do).
4. Use fixed positions for all materials and tools.
II. Rules for making the best use of personnel
1. Use two hands for productive work rather than one for holding when holding can be done better mechanically.
2. Use the feet as well as the hands when feet can be useful.
3. Eliminate all possible hesitations and short delays between operations.

[16] Franklin G. Moore, *Production Management* (6h ed.; Homewood, Ill.: Richard D. Irwin, Inc., 1973), p. 313.

III. Rules for saving energy
1. Use mechanical lifting devices for all heavy lifting.
2. Give preference to continuous, curved motions over more tiring motions involving sharp changes in direction.
3. Position work in such a way that body size and strength can best be utilized.
4. Eliminate fatiguing work conditions that are unnecessary (poor lighting, poor ventilation, fumes, dusty conditions, etc.).
5. Provide occasional breaks so as to reduce monotony and fatigue.
IV. Rules for placing personnel
1. Break jobs down into small tasks so that each worker can specialize and acquire greater proficiency (job dilution).
2. Assign work so that highly paid employees do only work that requires a high level of expertise.
3. Assign workers to jobs that match their unique personal qualities (such as strength, finger dexterity, or height).

The systematic use of motion principles such as these will result in the elimination of inefficiencies which could never be detected by undisciplined observation. Occasionally, on jobs involving large numbers of workers, a more detailed method of analysis called *micromotion study* is appropriate. With this technique motion pictures of a job are studied in great detail—one frame at a time—to detect any unnecessary or awkward movements.

One other method similar to micromotion studies is valuable but not frequently used. It is the *therblig analysis*.[17] A *therblig*, a basic element of motion, is an extremely small part of one aspect of a job (move hand toward hammer, grasp hammer, raise hammer, etc.). The motion study analyst first records the major activities within a job, then breaks each activity into therbligs with the expectation that some therbligs can be eliminated. By examining each therblig in detail, wasted motions can sometimes be observed that would have otherwise been imperceptible when looking at a large job segment.

Time Studies

Although time studies often provide insights that are of value in job redesign, their primary purpose is work measurement. They provide time standards (the time an average worker needs to do a particular job) which in turn are used as follows: (1) to estimate personnel needs and thereby to calculate the direct labor costs, (2) to provide a basis for a piece-rate incentive system, and (3) to facilitate scheduling. Since these are critical elements in such important functions as establishing costs for contract bidding, developing employee motivational systems, and meeting production deadlines, it is important that time studies be performed with great accuracy.

---

[17] The word *therblig* is Gilbreth spelled backwards (except for the *th*)—after Frank and Lillian Gilbreth who developed the concept of elemental units of motion and needed a word to represent it.

One method of studying a job is to measure output over a period of time, and, on the basis of employee hours worked, to calculate how long it should take an average worker to produce a unit under average conditions. Such a method, however, is not as scientific as the stopwatch method in which workers are observed and the actual times required to perform each job element are recorded through several work cycles. The standard time for each job includes, in addition to the combined times of the job elements, adjustments for unavoidable delays. Since speed increases with practice, the analyst may also make adjustments for worker inefficiency, especially where new jobs are being studied. Stopwatch methods are relatively objective, but judgments are involved; and workers often suspect management of using time studies to increase production at the workers' expense (demanding more work for the same pay or requiring excessively high production however satisfactory the pay may be).

OPERATIONS RESEARCH TECHNIQUES

Although the human aspects of production have received increasing attention during the past four decades, greatly influencing management decisions, that emphasis has not diminished advances in the development of quantitative techniques to assist in decision making. A group of such techniques, referred to as *scientific management* or *operations research* (OR), is broadly applicable in production management.[18] In the following discussion we briefly describe a few of the most useful OR applications.

Linear Programming—Allocation Problems

Linear programming techniques, which employ algebraic methods to analyze relationships that are capable of being expressed as linear functions, are most often used to solve allocation problems. Linear programming may, for example, be used to assign production capacity to numerous product lines or to help decide the best location for plant or warehouse facilities. When a location decision includes several quantifiable variables such as manufacturing cost, location of markets, and transportation costs, linear programming can greatly simplify the decisions of the production manager.

Queuing Theory—Intermittent Servicing Problems

Queuing theory, sometimes called *waiting-line theory*, is of value in determining the correct balance of factors necessary for the most efficient handling of intermittent service. There are costs involved in having a waiting line, whether it be customers waiting for service in a restaurant or machines waiting to be repaired and returned to production. Time lost in waiting, particularly the down-

---

[18] Arthur C. Laufer, *Operations Management* (Cincinnati: South-Western Publishing Co., 1975), p. 7.

time of machines needing repair, is also a factor of cost; and if the line is one of impatient customers sales volume is reduced. In order to eliminate the line or decrease its length, thereby reducing waiting-line costs, it is necessary to increase servicing capacity. In turn, there is an increase in the cost of physical facilities and labor necessary to perform the desired service. The restaurant has to enlarge its seating capacity and hire more employees to reduce its line of waiting customers; the industrial plant needs more maintenance workers and a large stock of repair parts to minimize production losses resulting from idle machines waiting for repair.

Game Theory—Simulation of System Operation

War games have been used for many years as a means of training personnel and testing plans and equipment under field conditions. The process of obtaining the essential qualities of reality without the reality itself is known as *simulation*. Management games have been developed to provide training in decision making by providing laboratory situations that simulate as nearly as possible real-life operations. The development of a management game is incredibly complex, particularly if it is a game involving a situation in which there is a competitor aware of changing conditions—an increase in price or volume of goods produced—who responds with countermoves. At the moment, the application of game theory to business problems has been used primarily for training purposes rather than for solving competitive problems because of the complexities in analyzing and programming the many variables as they exist in real life.

Probability Theory—Determining Degree of Risk

Predictions concerning the probable outcome of future events are inferences based on careful statistical analysis of existing data. Life expectancy tables used by insurance companies in setting their rates are statements of the probable death rate expected for each age group of the entire population during the present year. Statistical quality control is another application of the theory of probability. The volume of goods produced in high-speed manufacturing is so great that the cost of inspecting each item produced would be prohibitive. But a detailed inspection of a small sample, say one of every thousand, and periodic checking of the production equipment make it possible for a quality control supervisor to predict with high accuracy the number of defective products that may be expected in every thousand produced.

Limitations of OR

Operations research may contribute significantly to the decisions of production managers where quantitative data are available and when there is time to use a mathematical or statistical model. Unfortunately production decisions often involve highly subjective judgments and must be made under extreme time pressures. C. Jackson Grayson gives additional reasons why he, a person well educated in management science, has been limited in the use of OR techniques. He became convinced that OR techniques oversimplify real-life situations since it is unrealistic to omit nonquantifiable variables. Grayson also found that the strictly impersonal OR methods provoked resistance from other managers that he did not have the time to overcome.[19]

Case Problem 7-B describes a production problem which, like many problems in both service and manufacturing industries, does not readily lend itself to quantitative methods of analysis. The case demonstrates that what some persons may consider a relatively minor subsystem plays a critical role in the productivity of the total system.

Case Problem 7-B

LINEN CONTROL AT CITY HOSPITAL

City Hospital, founded in 1903 by the Presbyterian Church, became a tax-supported municipal hospital in 1943 and thereafter experienced phenomenal growth. By 1980 it occupied six city blocks, had 1,400 beds, admitted approximately 40,000 patients annually, and in 1979 registered 4,582 births. City Hospital is affiliated with an outstanding medical school and enjoys a reputation as a progressive institution with some of the nation's most qualified physicians and the very best medical equipment.

The national trend toward employing nonmedical, professional hospital administrators has made little impact on the management of City Hospital. As a result, every aspect of the hospital's operation has been dominated by physicians. Some of its systems have not received the kind of attention given to them in hospitals that are strongly influenced by professionally educated managers. The laundering, distribution, and control of linens (bed linens, towels, washcloths, gowns, and scrub suits) have been definitely neglected systems at City Hospital.

The problem appears to be a simple one, subject to a simple solution. Since linen shortages often occur in the wards or in operating rooms, the obvious solution—obvious to Dr. Ann Maxwell, the chief administrator—is to increase the inventories in the various linen closets and to check them more frequently. But that solution is not altogether adequate. In recent months the cost of linens has skyrocketed, and increasing inventories will require even greater financial outlays. There is also a problem of quality. When, for example, should a towel be taken out of use, and to what extent should a hospital gown be sewed or patched before being discarded? No one seems to have the answers to such mundane questions. On several occasions Dr. Maxwell has discussed the linen problem with her assistant, Richard Helms, to whom the laundry supervisor, Raymond Perry, reports. Helms believes that at least one problem is potentially more serious than the linen quality problem or the temporary linen shortages: namely, that dirty linens, often severely contaminated, are sometimes collected in the same carts used to distribute the clean linens. Although obviously soiled linens are always placed in disposable plastic bags for odor and infection control, sheets and pillow cases that do not appear to be soiled are thrown into dirty linen bins and are later collected and taken to the laundry in carts. The carts consist of metal frames

[19] C. Jackson Grayson, Jr., "Management Science and Business Practice," *Harvard Business Review*, Vol. 51, No. 4 (July–August, 1973), p. 41.

mounted on five-inch wheels from which a large, detachable canvass bag is suspended. Helms believes that staph and other serious infections can be transmitted to the new linens through these carts.

Both Perry and Helms have expressed concern over the fact that hundreds of patients and employees have opportunities every day to steal linens from hospital rooms and linen closets. Since a decision had been made years before to avoid the expense of an inventory control system that would provide records on each linen closet there is no way to determine whether certain wards are losing an excessive number of linens. Although Helms has no evidence, he believes strongly that large numbers of linens have been stolen: "I am certain that we don't discard or just lose anything like the number of linens that we buy every year."

Maxwell is inclined to place full responsibility for solving the problem on Perry, but it is obvious that Perry has minimal control over the linens beyond their pickup and delivery. Nurses, orderlies, physicians—virtually everybody—seem to have more control over the linens than Perry has. Maxwell, tiring of the laundry problem, has assigned it to Helms, saying, "Do whatever is necessary to solve the problem. I read somewhere that the hospital laundry business in the United States is a $400 million industry. In view of our recent laundry expenses, I can believe it."

PROBLEMS

1. In what sense is the City Hospital linen problem a production problem? Why is it an important problem? Relate the subsystem problem to the total production system.
2. How can Helms solve the linen problem?
3. In light of the information presented in this chapter, which techniques can Helms use for increasing efficiency?

CHAPTER QUESTIONS FOR STUDY AND DISCUSSION

1. Why is it valuable to think of all organizations as production systems?
2. How does a nation benefit from continually increasing its productivity?
3. What factors tend to diminish the importance of worker motivation?
4. List some factors that may be used in selecting a site for (1) a new hospital, (2) a fast-food restaurant, and (3) a steel mill. Show factors that are common to the three and those that differ.
5. In view of the high costs involved, why do most manufacturers prefer process designs that are capital intensive?
6. An important function of production managers is supervision. In what significant way does this differ from their other duties? For which functions are factory and plant managers best qualified? Discuss.
7. Compare the relative levels of machine tending and assembly-line technologies. Cite arguments for viewing one as higher than another.
8. Cite the major differences between machine tending and automation?
9. What is the main purpose of time studies? Cite three other benefits.
10. Describe the personnel problems most often associated with time studies.
11. Which OR technique will most likely be used for (1) determining the ideal number of automobiles waiting to be repaired and (2) training managers to solve some complex business problems?
12. Evaluate OR techniques as a management tool.

3

The Organizing Function

Underlying organization theory are assumptions, often implicit, concerning the structure and functions of organizations. One set of assumptions concerning work and the people performing that work is known as the work-centered, or classical, theory of organization. Another approach, with different assumptions concerning work and people, is people centered and sometimes called neoclassical theory. The third approach to understanding organizations is within the context of a system and is termed a contingency approach. The concepts of the work-centered and people-centered approaches to organization theory and resultant organizational characteristics are compared. Chapter 8 concludes with a contingency approach to organization theory; and specific parameters, all appearing with significant frequency in the literature, are also stated.

Although the contingency approach to organization theory is recognized as current in the study of organizations, there is much to be learned from the past. For this reason the classical concepts of organization structure, organizational relationships, and organizational processes are examined carefully. Departmentation, the prime determinant of organization structure, and recommendations for the subsequent arrangement of departments into effective spans of management are discussed in Chapter 9. Since committees are found in most organizations, they are considered within the framework of organization structure. There are two widely divergent views concerning source of authority. One holds that authority is derived from an institutional, or societal, source; the other states that authority is derived from acceptance by subordinates. Both views concerning source of authority and authority relationships between line and staff personnel are discussed. The analysis of the processes of transferring authority within organizations, delegation and decentralization, also considers the behavioral aspects of delegation and offers guides to determine the optimum degree of decentralization.

Since social organizations are not static, it is necessary to prepare for the inevitable change that is certain to occur. One form of change may be rather sudden in nature and stems from an organizational analysis, which sets forth specific recommendations for change; the other form of change is evolutionary in nature and is the result of planned organization development.

The section closes with a discussion of personnel management. It examines the role of the personnel manager, personnel selection, and the development and compensation of managers.

Chapter 8

Organization and Management Theory

Case Problem 8-A

AN EXPERIMENT IN PARTICIPATIVE MANAGEMENT

PART 1 The Experiment

Non-Linear Systems, Inc. (NLS) was founded in 1952 in Del Mar, California, by Andrew F. Kay, the sole owner. The company manufactures a line of digital electrical measuring instruments that range in price from $500 to over $20,000 per unit. By 1960 the company was a leader in its field. For many years it was one of seven companies that held 95 percent of the available market with approximately 50 other companies sharing the remaining 5 percent. The number of employees grew from 5 to 340 in the 1960's.

The experiment began in 1960 as the result of Mr. Kay's belief that the human rela-

---

Erwin L. Malone, "The Non-Linear Systems Experiment in Participative Management," *The Journal of Business of the University of Chicago*, Vol. 48, No. 1 (January, 1975), p. 52. Case Problem 8-A and its sequel, Case Problem 8-B, are based on the authoritative report of the Non-Linear Systems experiment as reported by Erwin L. Malone. Dr. Malone spent two weeks at Non-Linear Systems shortly after the termination of the experiment. He interviewed all levels of management and hourly employees and had free access to all records.

tions approach would work in an organization. Prior to the beginning of the experiment there was much consultation with experts in human relations. Also, there was continuing discussion and consultation with the employees of the company. When the experiment was put into effect, all personnel were thoroughly familiar with the goals of the experiment. It was begun as the result of a decision made solely by Andrew Kay.

In brief, the human relations approach to organization theory is as follows:

1. Work is a natural phenomenon and if satisfying it will be performed voluntarily.
2. If the employee is committed to the objectives of the organization, there is little need for external control.
3. The degree of commitment to objectives is primarily a function of the rewards associated with these objectives.
4. Many people are not only willing to accept responsibility, they actually seek such responsibility.
5. Powers of imagination, creativity, and ingenuity are widely distributed throughout the general population and the organization and are not limited to a few people at the top of the organization.

6. Modern industrial organizations only partially utilize a person's intellectual abilities. (For a complete discussion of these assumptions, see pages 158–159).

The experiment translated these assumptions concerning people into action by changing the organizational characteristics of NLS. The following changes were made.

Wages. At the time the experiment began, hourly workers were receiving $1.90 an hour ($76 a week). They received a 60 cents an hour increase and were classified as salaried workers receiving $100 a week. No records were kept of tardiness or absenteeism. Coffee and fatigue breaks were taken at the employee's convenience. Shortly after the experiment began, at the request of some of the senior employees, new employees were started at $85 a week rather than at $100. They were then advanced to the $100 a week salary at the end of a variable probationary period.

Organization. The classic organization structure is discussed on page 154 and is essentially pyramidal in nature as shown in Figure 8–1. At NLS a quite different approach was taken. Three zones of management were established. Zone I was the level of trustee management and consisted of the board of directors of the company including Andrew F. Kay, chairman of the board. Zone I had the responsibility of determining the basic policies and direction of the organization. Zone II was one of general management. It was an executive council consisting of seven members in addition to Mr. Kay. Essentially Zone II consisted of the vice-presidential level covering the functions of innovation (product development), productivity, physical and financial resources, profitability, manager performance and development, marketing, legal counsel and public responsibility. It should be noted that the office of president was eliminated; however, Kay did function as a member of the trustee management, Zone I, and general management, Zone II. Zone III corresponded to departmental managers. There were 30 department units, also referred to as project teams. Each unit consisted of 3 to 12 employees including the departmental manager. Departmental managers were responsible for the day-to-day operations of their respective units. The functions of the 30 departments included product development, the assembling of instruments, shipping and receiving, personnel services, and marketing functions including both sales promotion and distribution within specific geographic regions.

Production Set-up. Prior to the experiment the product was assembled by two assembly lines, each of which produced one of the two basic models of digital voltmeters. Minor changes in either of the basic models resulted in adaptations for the special needs of customers. These assembly lines were discontinued at the beginning of the experiment and were replaced by departmental units each consisting of a manager and 3 to 12 other people. Each unit was responsible for building the complete instrument. Each group worked at its own rate of speed and determined whether one person would make a complete instrument or whether it would be done by 3 to 12 people.

Indoctrination Programs. A thorough indoctrination program at all levels of the organization preceded the experiment. When new employees were hired subsequent to the beginning of the experiment they were thoroughly indoctrinated in the basic aims and goals of the company and the reasons for its operations.

Training Procedures. The indoctrination for new employees was followed by considerable on-the-job training. Training facilities both inside and outside the company were widely used. Employees who received training outside the company were reimbursed by the company upon completion of each course.

Time Clocks. Since punching a time clock is viewed by many as degrading and implies mistrust, all time clocks were removed.

Record Keeping. Records are a form of external control; therefore, they were literally abolished. NLS became a company that maintained very little in the way of formal records of productivity or product costs.

Accounting. The accounting department as a formal unit was dismantled. The personnel of that department worked in each of the Zone III departments. Individual records were kept for each of these departments, with summary statements being sent periodically to the treasurer.

Inspection. The formal inspection department was eliminated. Each of the production units performed its own inspection. Thus, there was no external control in this area.

PROBLEMS

1. Does the organization described in this case more closely parallel a Theory X organization or a Theory Y organization? Explain.
2. Based on your own experience and the materials presented in the chapter, what is your prediction concerning the outcome of the experiment?

Organizations are a major force in determining the course of our lives; yet few of us recognize the extent to which organizations shape our behavior. We are born in hospitals and immediately the process of adapting to formal organizations begins; for the hospital, an organization, imposes a schedule of eating, sleeping, and bathing. There is a brief respite from formal organizations during the next five years; then, at the age of five, we begin school and become members of a succession of formal organizations—grade school and high school, college, and the places where we work. Retirement from active employment does not mean retirement from all organizations, for usually memberships in social clubs, civic organizations, and churches continue.

The word *organization* has two distinct meanings: one refers to organization as an *entity*, and the other refers to organization as a *process*. Some of the more common organizations, as entities, are mentioned above—schools, places of employment (including industrial organizations, governmental agencies, or private institutions), social clubs, service organizations, and churches. There are three characteristics common to each of these organizations: first, each is composed of people; second, each has a distinct purpose or goal to achieve; third, each has a degree of formality in the structure of the organization that results in a definition and limitation of the behavior of its members. Thus, as an *entity*, an organization is a group of people bound together in a formal relationship to achieve organizational goals.

The second meaning of organization is that it is a *process* of structuring, or arranging, the parts of which the organization, as an entity, is composed. This meaning is exemplified by the expression, "What this place needs is more organization." The question arises, what is being organized? There are three possible answers to this question: first, *work* is being organized; second, *people* are being organized; and, third, *systems* are being organized. The answer you choose as being most descriptive of the process of organization is dependent upon certain fundamental assumptions with regard to the nature of work and the behavior of human beings in a work situation. These assumptions, known as *theories of organization*, are important for they determine the structure of an organization and the methods used in administering the organization. The theoretical framework leading to the conclusion that organization is a process of organizing *work* is known as *Theory X*; those assumptions concluding in the belief that people are the central theme of organization form *Theory Y*; and an approach that emphasizes the organization of *systems* is a *contingency approach* to organization.

THEORY X—A WORK-CENTERED APPROACH

Underlying every management action is a set of implicit assumptions concerning the nature of work and the nature of human beings. Theory X is a group of assumptions that results in what is known as the traditional, or classical, approach to organization.[1] In discussing Theory X, let us first examine the basic assumptions concerning work and the nature of human beings in a work situation.

Assumptions of Theory X

Theory X is based on four implicit assumptions. The first of these assumptions is concerned with the nature of work, and the remaining three describe the behavior of human beings in a work situation.

1. Work, if not downright distasteful, is an onerous chore that must be performed in order to survive.
2. The average human being has an inherent dislike of work and will avoid it if he or she can.
3. Because of this human characteristic of dislike of work, most people must be coerced, controlled, directed, or threatened with punishment to get them to put forth an adequate effort toward the achievement of organizational objectives.
4. The average human being prefers to be directed, wishes to avoid responsibility, has relatively little ambition, wants security above all.[2]

Briefly, Theory X states that there is no intrinsic satisfaction in work, that humans avoid it as much as possible, that positive direction is needed to achieve organizational goals, and that workers possess little ambition or originality. Let us assume that Theory X is an accurate statement of conditions as they exist today. How do these assumptions affect the structure and processes of an organization?

---

[1] Douglas McGregor, *The Human Side of Enterprise* (New York City: McGraw-Hill, Inc., 1960). Professor McGregor summarized the assumptions of traditional management under the heading of Theory X, and presented those assumptions which resulted in a human relations approach to management under the heading of Theory Y.

[2] *Ibid.*, p. 33. Assumptions 2, 3, and 4 are quoted directly from McGregor. Assumption 1 has been added as an explicit statement of the nature of the work to which humans are reacting. For a good treatment of work theory, see Dale Yoder, *Personnel Management and Industrial Relations* (6h ed.; Englewood Cliffs, N. J.: Prentice Hall, Inc., 1970), Chapter 4.

Effect on Organization

Adherence to Theory X results in a *work-centered* organization. As noted earlier, one of the characteristics of an organization is that it has a goal—a *raison d'être*. It is normal to be concerned about the work of an organization, and when work is distasteful, firm steps must be taken to assure its accomplishment. Thus, an external force is needed to accomplish organizational objectives. This force relies on the traditional concept of authority; indeed, it is so dependent on authority that organizations which subscribe to Theory X are frequently referred to as *authoritarian organizations.* Once the foundation of an organization has been laid upon the cornerstone of authority, the location of the decision-making process is determined, the organizational structure acquires certain characteristics, and the roles of the supervisor and the individual members of the organization are sharply defined.

Authority. Within the context of Theory X, *authority* is viewed as the institutionalized right to command—the right to employ power to exact obedience.[3] This definition raises questions concerning the source of the right and the method of power. One source of authority, used by the early European monarchies, is expressed by the phrase, the divine right of kings. A corresponding point of view applied to the management of industrial enterprises regards authority as emanating from the right to own property and the attendant obligation to manage that property. The power of the monarch in enforcing obedience is absolute, because the monarch can exact the supreme penalty—death—if it is deemed necessary. In the industrial situation the supreme penalty for disobedience is discharge, a penalty that prohibits an employee from fulfilling economic needs. It is interesting to note that many arbitrators, when writing decisions concerning the discharge of an employee, equate the death penalty to discharge by an employer. When we discuss Theory Y we will see that there is another concept of authority. But Theory X maintains that complete authority is the motivating force that directs the course of the organization.

Location of Decision Making. The analogy of a political monarchy and a highly authoritarian industrial organization is also an effective means of describing the location of the decision-making process. In the monarchy, decision making is highly centralized and located at the apex of the organization—the king—since it is the king who has the divine right to command. For the authoritarian industrial organization, the nominal head of the organization is the locus of the decision-making process; again, this is a logical location when the right to manage is derived from ownership. Centralized decision making requires organizational structure if the decisions are to be carried out effectively.

---

[3] Power within this context, sometimes referred to as *position power*, is the ability to influence the behavior of others, or the ability to exact obedience despite resistance. Thus, power implies the ability to impose sanction. Theory X managers tend to assume that the ability to influence accompanies authority, but the assumption is not always valid. For a discussion of several definitions of power, read Amad N. Azim and F. Glenn Boseman, "An Empirical Assessment of Etzioni's Topolgy of Power and Involvement within a University Setting," *Academy of Management Journal*, Vol. 18, No. 4 (December, 1975), p. 681.

Organization Structure. When authority to make decisions is centralized at the top of the organization and its primary purpose is the accomplishment of work, a structure must be designed that permits the ready exercise of authority at all levels of the organization, and maximum effectiveness in the accomplishment of work.

Figure 8–1 shows the structure of the traditional work-centered, or authoritarian, organization. Note that authority to manage flows from the owners through the board of directors to the president who is appointed by the board. Reporting to the president are several vice-presidents, each of whom is in charge of a specific phase of the work of the organization. Figure 8–1 is an exploded diagram of the organization reporting to the vice-president of manufacturing; similar pyramidal structures could be developed for each of the other vice-presidents. Reporting to the manufacturing vice-president is the manager in charge of a specific manufacturing unit, a plant. The major operations of the plant—receiving, machining, assembly, and shipping—are assigned to four general supervisors who report to the plant manager. The general supervisors direct the efforts of other supervisors who are in charge of the operating departments within each of the four major functions. Four assistant supervisors, each of whom directs the work of a specific area, report to each operating supervisor; and, finally, production employees report to their respective assistant supervisors.

Figure 8–1 refers to production workers as rank-and-file employees, a term borrowed from the military that describes the rows and columns of the infantry platoon. Another military term, *chain of command*, describes the means of transmitting the president's authority so that ultimately production employees produce the desired work. Authority is transmitted through a chain of command: the successive levels of management between the president and the production worker. When Figure 8–1 is read from top to bottom, the chain of command, which permits the ready exercise of authority at all levels in the organization, is easily followed; and when viewed from left to right, the division of the organization into units of work is apparent.

Role of Supervisor. The pyramidal structure of the organization determines the role, or function, assumed by supervisors. First, supervisors are an integral part of the chain of command, and as such it is their function to transmit authority to the succeeding lower levels of the organization. Decision making is a minor, if not nonexistent, function; for the authority to make decisions is vested in the head of the organization. Thus, supervisors are agents of a higher authority. Second, as agents of higher authority, they have the function of optimizing the goals of the organization; therefore, they may be expected to emphasize production. If, in addition, a particular supervisor is an agent of an organization built on the premise that work is distasteful and that people tend to avoid work, is it any wonder that all the supervisor's efforts are oriented toward production?

Role of Individual. The role of the individual worker is that of a cog in a machine. Workers are to be directed, coerced if need be, and controlled so

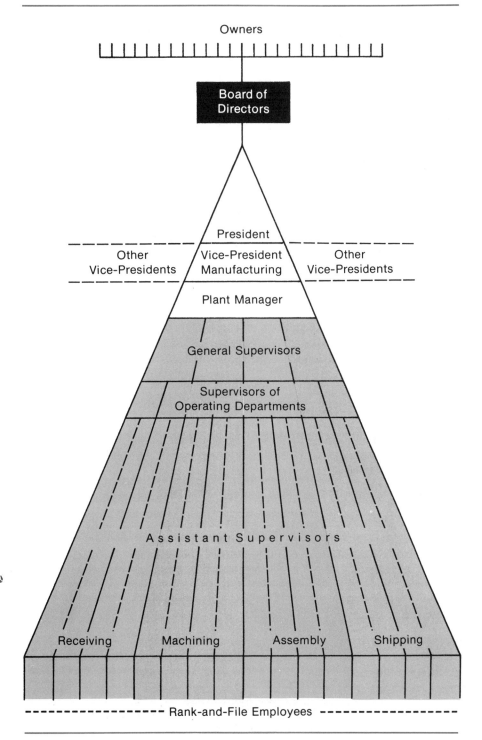

Figure 8–1
PYRAMIDAL STRUCTURE OF TRADITIONAL ORGANIZATION

that they will put forth the effort necessary for the achievement of organizational objectives. Their function is to perform their present jobs; there is little encouragement for self-development or advancement. The term, *rank and file*, is used to describe production workers in Figure 8–1; perhaps a more descriptive appellation is "hired hands," implying that only hands, not complete people, are hired. However described, production workers in a Theory X organization are regarded as individual units reporting only to their direct supervisor. They are not considered members of a group, nor for that matter members of several groups; instead, each stands isolated reporting to and influenced only by the supervisor.

The preceding discussion outlines the organizational effects implicit in the assumptions of Theory X and may seem exaggerated. However, there are many organizations that actually parallel the Theory X organization. The propositions of Theory X and the effectiveness of the authoritarian, work-centered organizations are evaluated following the presentation of Theory Y.

THEORY Y—A PEOPLE-CENTERED APPROACH

The assumptions of Theory Y concern the nature of human behavior based on an interpretation of modern behavioral sciences. The same format used in the presentation of Theory X is used in presenting Theory Y: first, the assumptions of the theory are stated and, second, the consequent effects of these assumptions on the organization are reviewed.

Assumptions of Theory Y

The assumptions of Theory Y are the antitheses of those of Theory X. The six assumptions of Theory Y are as follows:

1. *The expenditure of physical and mental effort in work is as normal as play or rest.* The average human being does not inherently dislike work. Depending on controllable conditions, work may be a source of satisfaction (and will be voluntarily performed) or a source of punishment (and will be avoided if possible).

2. *External control and the threat of punishment are not the only means for bringing about efforts directed toward organizational objectives. People will exercise self-direction and self-control in the service of objectives to which they are committed.*

3. *Commitment to objectives is a function of the rewards associated with their achievement.* The most significant of such rewards—e.g., the satisfaction of ego and self-actualization needs—can be direct products of efforts directed toward organizational objectives.

4. *The average human learns, under proper conditions, not only to accept but to seek responsibility.* Avoidance of responsibility, lack of ambition, and emphasis on security are general consequences of experience, not inherent human characteristics.

5. *The capacity to exercise a relatively high degree of imagination, ingenuity, and creativity in the solution of organizational problems is widely, not narrowly, distributed in the population.*

6. *Under the conditions of modern industrial life, the intellectual potentialities of the average human being are only partially utilized.*[4]

Effect on Organization

Adherence to Theory X results in work-centered, authoritative organizations. Theory Y is an approach to organizational problems that emphasizes human relations and results in an organization characterized as *participative.* The two forms of organization, authoritative and participative, are the extreme points of a continuum. Between these poles are many gradations of organizational behavior. One writer distinguishes the following steps: (1) exploitive authoritative, (2) benevolent authoritative, (3) consultative, and (4) participative group.[5] Thus, when discussing the effect of the propositions of Theory Y on organizational structure and processes, it is well to remember that we are dealing with the other end of the continuum in order to present in clear, sharp lines the differences that exist between the two approaches.

Authority. Authority, as presented in Theory X, is the institutionalized right to command—the right to use power to enforce obedience. However, there is more to authority than institutionalized rights and position power, as illustrated by the following story:

> An agent for the Textile Workers Union of America likes to tell the story of the occasion when a new manager appeared in the mill where he was working. The manger came into the weave room the day he arrived. He walked directly over to the agent and said, "Are you Belloc?" The agent acknowledged that he was. The manager said, "I am the new manager here. When I manage a mill, I run it. Do you understand?" The agent nodded, and then waved his hand. The workers, intently watched this encounter, shut down every loom in the room immediately. The agent turned to the manager and said, "All right, go ahead and run it." [6]

To the extent that ownership is the source of rights, the manager has the indisputable right to run a plant, and it is possible, under certain circumstances, for a manager to exercise the power needed to discharge all workers for engaging in an unauthorized work stoppage. Then the manager can start anew with a different group of workers—but this seems to be the hard way to manage a plant. Theory Y presents people as rational beings who are willing to work; in fact, they must work in order to satisfy deep-seated psychological needs (Propositions 1 and 3). Also, they have intelligence and are capable of making their own decisions. One of the decisions that an individual makes is that of deciding *which* leadership to accept. The foregoing incident does not portray

---

[4] Douglas McGregor, *The Human Side of Enterprise* (New York City: McGraw-Hill, Inc., 1960), p. 47. Another work by McGregor, published posthumously, *The Professional Manager*, edited by Warren G. Bennis and Caroline McGregor (New York City: McGraw Hill, Inc., 1967), discusses how a Theory Y organization may be developed.

[5] Rensis Likert, *New Patterns of Management* (New York City: McGraw-Hill, Inc., 1961), Chapter 14, "A Comparative View of Organizations," p. 222.

[6] McGregor, *The Human Side of Enterprise*, p. 23.

a situation in which there is no authority; on the contrary, there is a great deal of authority—in the hands of the agent for the union. The workers in the mill had decided to accept one source of authority and reject another source.

The notion that there is any basis for authority other than the rights associated with ownership is foreign to Theory X managers. Theory Y managers, in contrast, tend to support the position that *subordinate acceptance* of a superior's power is an essential aspect of the legitimate or rightful use of power. Following a line of reasoning proposed by Max Weber and others, the manager's institutionalized right to command depends on subordinates' willing compliance—a condition which does not exist when subordinates obey only because they fear punishment. According to Weber, employees who allow themselves to be influenced merely because they are afraid to do otherwise are submitting to coercion, not authority, in the same sense that a slave chooses to obey rather than be beaten or killed.[7]

If authority is contingent upon the willing acceptance of subordinates, managers are not free to rely solely on the position power which enables them to reward and punish in order to gain the compliance of subordinates. Instead, they use a variety of other power sources that are compatible with acceptance theory. They rely heavily on leadership, especially participative leadership, which involves subordinates in goal setting and decision making. Theory Y managers also rely heavily on their authority of competence—their right to influence because of their recognized skill, knowledge, or expertise.[8] Both leadership and competence contribute to the manager's *power of persuasion*, which combines with the manager's *authority of personality* and accompanying *personal power*, thereby making heavy reliance on formal authority unnecessary. Authority of personality results from a manager's charisma, assertiveness, and the inclination of some subordinates to develop strong bonds of identification with their superiors. Thus, managers with a high degree of power from sources other than their formal positions have an advantage in that they can often achieve their objectives by making suggestions rather than giving orders. They can more easily take a Theory Y approach to managing because they have an alternative to formal authority as a means of influencing subordinates. This should not, of course, be taken to mean that a direct use of formal authority can or should always be avoided.

Location of Decision Making. According to Theory X, decisions concerning organizational objectives, policies, and any other matters of significance, are made by the nominal head of the organization. Decisions made at lower levels—presumably involving only the implementation of executive decisions and the application of policy—are perceived to be qualitatively different from and inferior to executive decisions.

---

[7] A. M. Henderson and Talcott Parsons, eds. and trans., *Max Weber: The Theory of Social and Economic Organization* (New York City: Oxford University Press, Inc., 1947), p. 56.

[8] For a discussion of five important sources of power, (reward, coercive, legitimate, referent, and expert) read John R. P. French, Jr., and Bertram Raven, "The Bases of Social Power," *Studies in Social Power*, edited by D. Cartwright (Ann Arbor, Mich.: Research Center for Group Dynamics, University of Michigan, 1959) p. 150.

Contrary to the philosophy expressed in Theory X decision making, Proposition 5 of Theory Y states that "the capacity to exercise a relatively high degree of imagination, ingenuity, and creativity in the solution of organizational problems is widely, not narrowly, distributed in the population." Since, to the extent that this proposition is valid, it is unnecessary to retain decision making in the hands of a few, decision making in the Theory Y organization is widely dispersed throughout the organization. This practice expresses the essence of participation. Thus, at the heart of *participative management* is a commitment to maximum involvement of organizational members in decision making, including decision making about organizational objectives. This commitment is one of the cornerstones of Theory Y.

Organization Structure. Figure 8–1 shows the pyramidal structure of the typical traditional organization with successive layers of supervision and the development of work functions for each supervisor. The relationships between superior and subordinate at any level of the organization appear in the usual organization chart as shown in Figure 8–2.

Figure 8–2 emphasizes the work-centered aspects of the organization. Each subordinate is in charge of a specific function. It is an organization constructed primarily for the downward flow of authority in order to accomplish work. Communications between superior and subordinates are illustrated in Figure 8–3.

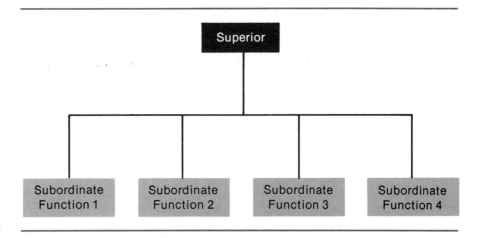

**Figure 8–2
THE TYPICAL
RELATIONSHIP
BETWEEN
SUPERIOR AND
SUBORDINATES**

Figure 8–3 implies that interpersonal face-to-face relationships occur only between a superior and each subordinate in succession. The individual is the basic unit of the organization and at best there can be no more than two-way communication between superior and subordinate. Earlier in this chapter, an organization was defined as a *group* of people bound together in a formal relationship to achieve organizational goals. Theory Y emphasizes that organization has to do with groups and that the individual who accepts organizational goals

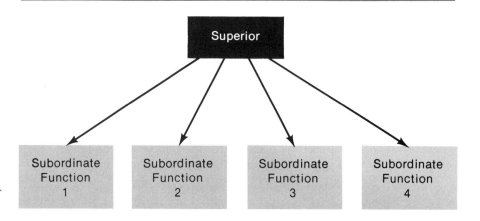

**Figure 8–3
INTERPERSONAL
RELATIONSHIPS
IN THEORY X
ORGANIZATION**

does so as a member of a group. Thus, the group, not the individual, becomes the basic unit of organization. The reasons for recognizing the group as the basic unit are found in Proposition 3 of Theory Y. Since the degree of commitment to organizational objectives is a function of the rewards derived from satisfying ego and self-actualization needs, which include participation in and recognition by a group, it is logical that superior and subordinates be considered a functional group. The large triangle of Figure 8–4, which encloses superior and subordinates, represents the group as the primary organizational unit. Figure 8–4 also illustrates free communication of ideas between every group member.

Role of Supervisor. Under the conditions of Theory X, the supervisor, a vital link in the chain of command, is an agent of higher authority. The supervisor's role is to optimize the goals of the organization by directing the efforts of *individuals*. But Theory Y replaces the traditional concept of authority with acceptance theory and substitutes position power with noncoercive forms of power that are consistent with the Theory Y view of human nature and with participative leadership. Furthermore, Theory Y acknowledges that the supervisor must relate to subordinates who, because of their interdependencies, lateral communications, social roles, behavioral expectations, and techniques of social control, have become members of highly organized informal groups. As a result, the supervisors themselves become group members with the specialized role of helping the group achieve its objectives.

Obviously the Theory Y supervisor, who has an *intragroup* function as the group's leader, is, at the same time, a member of a management group. Thus, being a member of two groups gives the supervisor a unique *intergroup* function to perform—coordinating the efforts of the two groups, mediating between the demands of each, and reducing conflict by improving communication. Likert refers to this coordinative function as the "linking pin" function.[9] Note the arrows in Figure 8–5; these are the linking pins which denote that the supervisor has an intergroup and an intragroup coordinative function.

---

[9] Likert, *op. cit.*, p. 113.

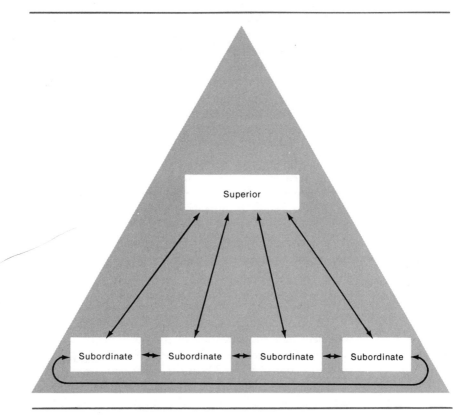

Figure 8–4
SUPERIOR-
SUBORDINATE
FUNCTIONING
AS A GROUP

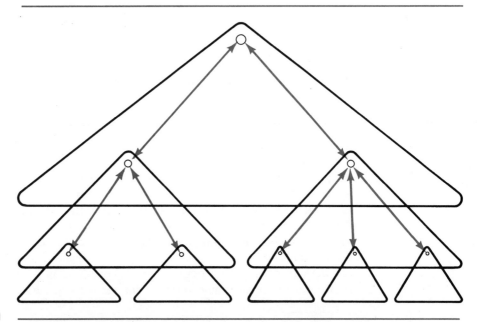

Figure 8–5
THE "LINKING
PIN" FUNCTION

SOURCE: Adapted from Rensis Likert, *New Patterns of Management* (New York City: McGraw Hill, Inc., 1961), p. 113.

Role of Individual. Theory X regards the individual as an isolated worker whose function is that of a cog in a machine. Personal responsibility is limited to quality and quantity of production, control of work is ever present and comes from external sources, and there is little opportunity or need for individual growth and development. The assumptions of Theory Y portray an intelligent, willing person functioning as an integral member of a group and contributing to the success of that group; thus, the need arises for maximizing the contribution of each member of the group by encouraging individual growth and development. External control and coercion are replaced by self-control and motivation derived from satisfying ego and self-actualization needs. The individual is creative and should participate in determining the objectives of the group, for it is through participation that the goals of the organization and the goals of the individual become congruent. It must be remembered that, although Theory Y encourages individual growth and development, the employee is not an isolated individual but a participating member of a group. The group is the smallest functioning unit of the organization.

Evaluation of Theories X and Y

Before presenting a contingency approach to organization theory, a summary statement and an evaluation of the positions of Theory X and Theory Y are in order. One such summary asserts that Theory X describes "organizations without people," while Theory Y describes "people without organizations." [10]

Describing a Theory X organization as an organization without people is admittedly an overstatement. Organizations using the Theory X approach also have been termed work-centered, traditional, classical, and authoritative. Such characterizations place these organizations at one extreme of a continuum of theoretical approaches to organizational theory. A Theory X organization often appears to ignore the psychological needs of its members. External controls and the accompanying overt resistance to these controls are very much in evidence. Further, the imposition of additional controls merely aggravates original problems which usually center around the quantity and quality of production.

The Theory Y organization—described as people without organizations—is the other extreme of the continuum and has been termed variously as the neoclassical, human relations, participative, or democratic approach to organization. Seemingly all that is needed is the freedom and opportunity for members of the organization to express their latent capabilities. Such an opportunity for self-expression would result in the achievement of organizational goals and at the same time fulfill the psychological needs of the individual member. Despite the limitations inherent in the extreme stance of each theory, acquaintance with the implicit assumptions of Theory X and Theory Y is of value for it defines the limits of the approaches to organizational theory.

Both theories suffer from too much generalization in that sweeping statements are made concerning work and human behavior. A study of the findings

---

[10] W. G. Bennis, "Leadership Theory and Administrative Behavior," *Administrative Science Quarterly*, Vol. 4 (December, 1959), p. 259.

of both sociology and psychology tells us that such generalizations do not accurately reflect conditions as they exist. There are marked variations in the demands placed on persons as the result of work, and what is considered as pleasant work by one individual is boredom and drudgery for another. Likewise, the behavioral characteristics suggested by each theory represent the extremes of the distribution of personality traits in the general population. Few people consistently demonstrate the characteristics postulated by either theory.

A second criticism that applies equally to each theory is that neither Theory X nor Theory Y is consistently in accord with research findings. The organization-without-people description of a Theory X organization is all too familiar to students of management, yet not all authoritarian, work-centered organizations fail to meet the needs of their members. Those that do fail, however, cannot consistently cure their illness by applying the prescriptions of Theory Y—by attempting to create jobs with intrinsic satisfaction, by becoming more democratic, and by permitting more participation in decision making (as shown by the NLS experiment in Case Problem 8-B).

A CONTINGENCY APPROACH

The classical approach to organization and management theory was based on the assumption that there are universal principles of management—principles that apply to all situations. As this assumption was increasingly called into question, the concept of *situational management* came into vogue—the idea that the situation must be taken into account in selecting the most appropriate course of action. But there is little value in knowing that what works in one situation may not work in another, unless we know where to use one approach rather than another. Contingency management is similar to situational management, but they differ in that the former attempts to state the conditions under which various methods are appropriate.[11] Contingency management establishes possible "if-then" relationships. For example, Fiedler's research on leadership style demonstrated that if very favorable or very unfavorable conditions exist within an organization, task-oriented leaders perform best; while people-oriented leaders perform best in situations of intermediate favorableness (as he defined these terms).[12] This will be further discussed in Chapter 17.

Contingency management lies somewhere between management principles and situational management. It attempts to establish principles, but not universal principles; thus, these principles apply only within limited situations and conditions. Although it is difficult to argue with such an approach, contingency theory can easily be viewed as no theory at all—it merely can be considered as a scientific method of establishing relationships based on independent studies that deal with an arbitrarily selected few of the infinite number of variables that

---

[11] Fred Luthans, *Introduction to Management: A Contingency Approach* (New York City: McGraw-Hill, Inc., 1976), p. 31.

[12] Fred E. Fiedler, "Predicting the Effects of Leadership Training and Experience from the Contingency Model: A Clarification," *Journal of Applied Psychology*, Vol. 57, No. 2 (1973), p. 110.

could be studied. One notable attempt has been made, however, to develop an integrated contingency theory. We look now at that attempt.

A General Contingency Theory

In 1977 Luthans and Stewart proposed what they call a *general contingency theory of management* (GCT), introduced as

> . . . an overall framework that integrates the diverse process, quantitative, and behavioral approaches to management; incorporates the environment; and begins to bridge the gap between management theory and practice.[13]

The GCT proposes that the following primary variables serve as the elemental building blocks for the organization:

1. *Environmental Variables.* These variables influence the organization but are beyond the direct control of management. They are the "givens" or independent variables. Federal legislation is an example of an *external* environmental variable. Top management policy is an *internal* environmental variable; it is a given for a specific manager but not for the entire organization.
2. *Resource Variables.* Management has control over these factors and uses them to achieve its objectives. Some resource variables are human (for example, the number, size, skills, race, age, and behavioral characteristics of personnel), while others are nonhuman (raw materials, equipment, capital, etc.).
3. *Management Variables.* These include the concepts and techniques expressed in policies and procedures, goals, plans, communication systems, and control techniques used by managers to operate on the resources in achieving the objectives of the system.[14]

Luthans and Stewart describe in detail not only these three primary variables but also an elaborate system of variables resulting from the interaction of these and other variables. They view the GCT as a framework for integrating research findings and arriving at conclusions that can be useful to practicing managers.

Although a contingency approach to management has had a high degree of acceptance, there is no consensus that Luthans and Stewart have succeeded in formulating an integrative, general contingency theory. Longenecker and Pringle, for example, note that theories cannot consist entirely of conceptual schemes, a simple listing of variables. Rather, theories must contain law-like propositions that interrelate concepts or variables.[15] In response, Luthans and Stewart concede that at present no viable body of contingency theory exists in "any significant state of generality." On the other hand, they are optimistic about prospects for "the systematic development and integration of specific functional relationships between operationally defined variables," and they believe that their GCT provides the conceptual framework for bringing into exis-

---

[13] Fred Luthans and Todd Stewart, "A General Contingency Theory of Management," *The Academy of Management Review*, Vol. 2, No. 2 (April, 1977), p. 181.

[14] *Ibid.*, p. 184.

[15] Justin G. Longenecker and Charles Pringle, "The Illusion of Contingency Theory as General Theory," *Academy of Management Review*, Vol. 3, No. 3 (July, 1978), p. 681.

tence a general contingency theory that will meet all the criteria for a good theory.[16] Everyone seems to agree on the following two points: (1) integrating the fragmented contingency research studies into a general theory is desirable and (2) the integration will be an extremely difficult and continuing task.

Parameters of a Contingency Approach

One complicating factor in the contingency approach is that there is potentially an infinite number of environmental, resource, and management variables (along with the various levels of interaction between these variables) that contribute to organizational effectiveness. Luthans and Stewart are not greatly concerned about this problem, however, for they believe that system performance can be measured by a few complementary dimensions—such as profit, sales, return on investment, growth, employee satisfaction, customer satisfaction, and social responsibility—which can be functionally and lawfully related to a few environmental, resource, and management variables. Although an infinite number of variables can be studied, they contend that from a practical point of view only a relatively limited and manageable number of system variables are relevant.[17]

Exactly how many variables are related to system performance is not known. Theories X and Y emphasize two global factors—work and the nature of people—as critical parameters of organizations. At the opposite extreme, March and Simon on one occasion suggested a staggering 206 variables,[18] an almost incomprehensible number when all possible interactions are taken into consideration. Though not attempting to suggest that these are the most important variables, we have selected the following six to help illustrate the contingency approach: (1) size of organization, (2) degree of interaction, (3) personality of members, (4) congruence of goals, (5) level of decision making, and (6) state of the system.

Although the research studies concerning these variables do not yield altogether consistent results, these are the kinds of conditional generalizations that the contingency theory seeks to make.

Size of Organization. As size (usually defined as number of people) increases, organizational structure tends to become increasingly formal and complex, with the result that the appropriate processes of motivating employees toward the achievement of organizational goals become more formal and directive, rather than informal and participative.[19]

[16] Fred Luthans and Todd Stewart, "The Reality or Illusion of a General Contingency Theory of Management: A Response to the Longenecker and Pringle Critique," *Academy of Management Review*, Vol. 3, No. 3 (July, 1978), p. 683.

[17] *Ibid.*, p. 686.

[18] James G. March and Herbert A. Simon, *Organizations* (New York City: John Wiley & Sons, Inc., 1958), p. 249.

[19] The following studies indicate the significance of size as a dimension of organization theory:
F. T. Evers, J. M. Bohlen, and R. D. Warren, "The Relationship of Selected Size and Structure Indicators in Economic Organizations," *Administrative Science Quarterly*, Vol. 21, No. 2 (June, 1976), p. 326. (Footnote 19 continued on page 168.)

Degree of Interaction. As the need for interaction between members of an organization increases in order to accomplish the prescribed work, the organizational structure should permit a free flow of information and exchange of ideas, and the accompanying processes of motivation should become more participative and informal.[20]

Personality of Members. Effective organizational structure and processes conform to the personalities and expectations of the organization's members (where personality is defined as the totality of an individual's skills, abilities, motivations, attitudes, self-perception, and other psychological attributes).[21] Although personality variables are complex and some researchers are pessimistic about the value of research that relates individual differences to organizational effectiveness,[22] there is evidence that members who do not expect to participate and who depend on others for motivation react best to formal patterns of structure and motivation, while those who expect to participate and are motivated largely from within react best to participative processes and informal organizational structure.[23]

Congruence of Goals. When the goals of the organization and those of its members are congruent, participative processes and a less formal structure are appropriate; but when organizational goals and members' goals are divergent, greater reliance must be placed on external controls and formal structure to assure adequate control.[24]

Jeffery D. Ford and John W. Slocum, Jr., "Size, Technology, Environment, and the Structure of Organizations," *Academy of Management Review*, Vol. 2, No. 4 (October, 1977) p. 561.

Marshall Meyer, "Size and Structure of Organizations: A Causal Analysis," *American Sociological Review*, Vol. 37, No. 4 (August, 1972), p. 434.

Daniel Robey, M. M. Bakr, and Thomas S. Miller, "Organizational Size and Management Autonomy: Some Structural Discontinuities," *Academy of Management Journal*, Vol. 20, No. 3 (September, 1977), p. 378.

[20] The following studies indicate the importance of interaction between members of an organization:

John J. Morse and Jay W. Lorsch, "Beyond Theory Y," *Harvard Business Review*, Vol. 48, No. 3 (May–June, 1970), p. 61.

Paul R. Lawrence and Jay W. Lorsch, "Differentiation and Integration in Complex Organizations," *Administrative Science Quarterly*, Vol. 12, No. 1 (June, 1967), p. 1.

[21] For a discussion of the role of personality in organizations read Marvin D. Dunnette (ed.), *Handbook of Industrial and Organizational Psychology* (Chicago: Rand McNally & Company, 1976), p. 81. Also Fred Fiedler and Martin Chemers, *Leadership and Effective Management* (Glenview, Ill.: Scott, Foresman & Company, 1974), p. 31.

[22] J. Kenneth White, "Individual Differences and the Job Quality—Worker Response Relationship: Review, Integration, and Comments," *Academy of Management Review*, Vol. 3, No. 2 (April, 1978), p. 267. Also Jon M. Shephard and James G. Hougland, Jr., "Contingency Theory: 'Complex Man' or 'Complex Organization?' " *Academy of Management Review*, Vol. 3, No. 3 (July, 1978), p. 413.

[23] Additional information on personality and organization may be found in the following:

Joseph Alluto and James Belasco, "A Typology for Participation in Organizational Decision Making," *Administrative Science Quarterly*, Vol. 17, No. 1 (March, 1972), p. 117.

Chris Argyris, "Personality and Organization Theory Revisited," *Administrative Science Quarterly*, Vol. 18, No. 2 (June, 1973) p. 141.

Jay Lorsch and John Morse, *Organizations and Their Members* (New York City: Harper & Row, Publishers, Inc., 1974).

[24] W. Keith Warner and A. Eugene Havens, "Goal Displacement and the Intangibility of Organizational Goals," *Administrative Science Quarterly*, Vol. 12, No. 4 (March, 1968), p. 539.

Level of Decision Making. The hierarchical level of decision making is greatly influenced by the technology of the organization. When technology permits and decision-making functions are retained within the primary work group of an organization, participative processes and informal structure are effective. As the decision-making processes move upward in the organizational hierarchy and away from the work group affected by those decisions, formal structure and directive processes are more appropriate.[25]

Other important influences on the decision strategies of organizations are the personal characteristics of the decision makers and the extent to which uncertainties exist in the decision environment.[26]

State of the System. When the performance of an organization is relatively poor with respect to the achievement of organizational goals (thereby creating a state of system imbalance), directive processes of motivation and formalized structure become necessary to initiate corrective action; however, as the organization achieves stated goals, participative processes and informal patterns of organization become more effective and are expected by the members of the organization.[27]

The Contingency Approach: A Summary Statement

The contingency approach does not make a sweeping, universally applicable generalization concerning the nature of work or the characteristics of human beings. Nor does it hold that there is one best way to organize and manage. Instead, it seeks, on the basis of empirical research, to establish contingent if-then relationships between major environmental, resource, and management variables and to draw generalizations that are likely to apply in specific situations. The research findings of the contingency approach are growing rapidly, but they have not yet resulted in an integrated, generally accepted theory of organization and management. The promise of the contingency approach lies primarily in its use of scientific methodology and in its commitment to the belief that there is no one best way to manage. In the chapters that follow concerning the organizing function, the contingency approach to the study of organizations is utilized.

Case Problem 8-B illustrates what happened after five years of the experiment in participative management described in Case Problem 8-A.

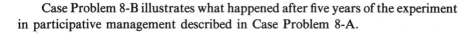

[25] L. Vaughn Blankenship and Raymond E. Miles, "Organizational Structure and Managerial Decision Behavior," *Administrative Science Quarterly*, Vol. 13, No. 1 (June, 1968), pp. 106–117.

William E. Reif, *Computer Technology and Organization* (Iowa City: Bureau of Business and Economic Research, University of Iowa, 1968). See discussion beginning on page 109.

Joan Woodward, *Industrial Organization: Behavior and Control* (New York City: Oxford University Press, Inc., 1970).

[26] Joseph Allutto and James Belasco, *op. cit.*

Lee Roy Beach and Terence R. Mitchell, "A Contingency Model for the Selection of Decision Strategies," *Academy of Management Review*, Vol. 3, No. 3 (July, 1978), p. 439.

[27] Gwen Andrew, "An Analytic System Model for Organization Theory," *Academy of Management Journal*, Vol. 8, No. 3 (September, 1965), p. 190.

AN EXPERIMENT IN PARTICIPATIVE MANAGEMENT

PART II The End of the Experiment

Between 1960 and 1965 there were many visitors to NLS. Most reported high praise for the experimental organization, and few were aware that there were any defects. Yet in 1965 there were a series of changes in the organization of NLS that clearly marked the end of the experiment in participative management. The following changes occurred:

1. Line organization procedures were reestablished at the top levels.
2. Direct supervision was provided.
3. Specific duties and responsibilities were assigned.
4. Standards of performance and quality were reestablished.
5. Authority was delegated commensurate with responsibility.
6. Records were reinstituted and maintained.
7. Remuneration was related to effort.
8. Factory department units were accorded a large measure of autonomy to schedule work within their units in the fashion they wished. In this respect the department units functioned reasonably closely to the manner in which they operated during the years of the experiment.[28]

It is difficult to evaluate why the experiment failed. Some of the reasons for ending the experiment were that sales volume was not at the level expected, and both administrative and sales costs were high in relation to sales volume. In addition, there was restlessness and dissatisfaction at the managerial levels of the organization. There were

layoffs in 1963, 1964, and 1965. Competition in the industry had increased. Significantly the sales force resisted all efforts to decrease sales cost, and finally the company was becoming progressively less profitable. Sales volume did increase during the time of the experiment; however, it was at a much lower rate with significant declines late in 1963 and 1965. The company was slow in carrying out its layoffs because it believed that such layoffs would be in conflict with the stated objectives of job and personal security. Thus, the company tended to keep more people than needed.

There was dissatisfaction at the upper levels of the organization. At the council level the vice-presidents had formerly been very active in their respective areas, but as part of the experiment they functioned only as sideline consultants. Their duties were not well defined and they were unable to function without clearly defined duties and the authority commensurate to fulfill these duties. At the Zone III level the departmental managers were also dissatisfied. They sought advice from the Executive Council as a whole rather than from individual members of the council who were formerly vice-presidents. The members of the council contacted at any given time may or may not have had the expertise in the area in which advice was sought. Some of the departmental managers, particularly those with minimal experience, needed the advice, counsel, and direction of someone with expertise in a specific functional area.

As mentioned in Part I, remuneration was increased from a wage of $76 a week to a salary of $100 a week, a 32 percent increase in direct labor costs. There is no evidence that there was a corresponding increase in productivity. The increased labor costs increased the sales costs of the product approximiately 5 percent. It is difficult

---

[28] Erwin L. Malone, "The Non-Linear Systems Experiment in Participative Management," *The Journal of Business of the University of Chicago*, Vol. 48, No. 1 (January, 1975), p. 57.

to evaluate productivity fully because of the absence of records, but it is known that in 1963 the production output was approximately 30 percent more than in 1960. However, the increase was not what it appeared to be on the surface. The total number of employees had risen from 240 to 340, an increase of 42 percent over the same period of time. Thus, there was an actual decrease in productivity. There is no evidence that production efficiency increased at any time during the experiment.

One of the most significant findings was related to the attitude and behavior of the sales force. At the beginning of the experiment NLS recognized the increasing competition by expanding its research and development efforts and enlarging its sales force to cover the entire country. Prior to the experiment the product had been distributed through sales representatives, but with the beginning of the experiment, salaried salespeople were employed and district sales offices were established with a stated annual sum to cover all sales expenses. Each office had its own bank account, paid its own bills, and sent receipts to the home office. Many salespeople considered servicing customers somewhat beneath their dignity, and there were no sales reports or expense books required of the sales force. In 1965 salaried salespeople were replaced by sales agents paid on a commission basis.

There appears to have been no significant difference in product quality with and without inspection.

The degree of job satisfaction was entirely a function of where one happened to be in the organization. The production workers, in general, reported that they were more satisfied with the experimental conditions than with the normal operations. There was no change in absenteeism or turnover rates between 1960 and 1965 as measured within NLS itself, nor was it significantly different from the Del Mar area in which the plant was located.

At the higher levels of the organization, job satisfaction was at a very low ebb. The following summary of what happened at Zone II, the vice-presidential level, indicates the severity of the problem:

> Initially three of the seven had favored the plan, two had cooperated even though unconvinced of its merit, and three had cooperated while privately believing that it could not succeed. During the five years of the experiment, one new member was added, and one was dismissed and then later rehired. After the end of the experiment in 1965 three were given long advance notice of employment termination, a fourth left of his own volition after refusing a salary reduction, and death overtook two.[29]

There is no evidence whatsoever that there was any increase in creativity or innovation on the part of employees.

Profits had increased yearly from 1953 to 1960. Though an increase in profitability was not one of the goals of the experiment, one would not have expected that profits would decline continually from 1961 until the losses incurred compelled the abandonment of the experiment in 1965.

PROBLEMS

1. Does the organization that was established at the close of the experiment more closely resemble the Theory X organization or the Theory Y organization? Explain.
2. State why you believe the experiment was a failure, or why you do not believe it was a failure.
3. Would a contingency approach to organization have been of help in this situation rather than the full application of Theory Y—the human relations approach? Discuss your answer.

---

[29] *Ibid.*, p. 62.

CHAPTER QUESTIONS FOR STUDY AND DISCUSSION

1. Give examples from your experience that illustrate the two meanings of the term *organization*. Are these meanings mutually exclusive, or is there a degree of overlap between the two meanings? Discuss your answer.

2. After reviewing the assumptions of Theory X, describe a work situation that reflects these assumptions as nearly as possible.

3. Describe a work situation that reflects the assumptions of Theory Y.

4. In your opinion, do most work situations in our industrial society conform more closely to the assumptions of Theory X or of Theory Y?

5. Compare a Theory X organization and a Theory Y organization with respect to the type of authority, the location of the decision-making process, the characteristics of the organizational structure, and the roles of the supervisor and the individual members of the organization.

6. Is it possible to have an organization that conforms to Theory X in some ways and to Theory Y in other ways? Give an example.

7. Describe what is meant by a systems approach to organization theory.

8. Contingency theory has sometimes been described as a middle ground between principles of management and situational management. What does this statement mean?

9. What problems do scholars encounter in developing a general contingency theory that describes the functional relationships among the major variables which influence organizational effectiveness?

Chapter 9

The Structural Design of Organizations

Case Problem 9–A

SPAN OF MANAGEMENT

Excelsior Products, originally a sales organization owned and operated by a manufacturer's representative, is now a wholly owned subsidiary of Triumph Chemical Company, a relatively large concern in its industry and engaged in the development, manufacture, and distribution of industrial maintenance chemicals. Excelsior, like the parent company, sells directly to the industrial consumer and counts among its best selling items degreasers, waxes, detergents, insecticides, weed killers, special paints, and liquid fertilizers. All told, there are 85 products currently in the line; new products are added at a rate of about ten a year and usually the five poorest selling items are dropped from the line.

The sales force is composed of commission sales representatives who are among the highest paid of any industry. Although the commission rate varies from a low of 20 percent on some items to a high of 35 percent on a very few items, the average rate paid—based on current sales analysis—is 25 percent of total sales volume. Representatives earn an average gross income of $21,000 a year, and out of this amount they pay their own expenses. However, many rep-

resentatives who have been with the company for more than a year earn as much as $37,000.

The sales expense of Excelsior Products includes the 25 percent direct selling cost paid to sales representatives as commissions and 8 percent allocated to advertising in trade journals, printed specification sheets carried by all representatives and distributed to customers, semiannual national sales meetings, and other miscellaneous sales expenses. Thus, from the $84,000 sales volume generated by each sales representative, the total sales expense is $27,720, or 33 percent.

During the first complete year of operations following the acquisition by Triumph, all five of the sales representatives employed by the former owner of Excelsior remained; true to expectation, they produced a total sales volume of $420,000. During this year no effort was made to expand the sales force by Thomas Jackson, a former district sales manager for Triumph and the new general manager of Excelsior. In the second year Jackson hired and trained ten new sales representatives, but by the year's end only five of the new representatives remained; however, sales for that year totaled $562,500. At the beginning of the third year, Jackson had ten good representatives, each capable of producing a sales volume of $84,000. The plans for the third year called for hiring and training two new representatives each month. Actually this goal was not realized, but he did hire 20 representatives, 12 of whom were still with the company at the end of the third year. Fortunately none of the ten representatives working at the beginning of the year quit, and as a group they produced $850,000. This amount, combined with the volume of the new representatives—none of whom sold for a full year—totaled $1,200,000. Jackson is convinced that the 22 representatives presently employed are capable of producing a sales volume of $1.5 million in a full calendar year. These 22 representatives are located in the following areas: Los Angeles, 2; San Francisco, 2; St. Louis, the home office, 5; Dallas, 2; Houston, 2; Florida, 1; New York City, 3; Chicago, 3; Detroit, 1; and Colorado, 1.

Now Jackson is planning for the coming year and realizes that the growth of Excelsior Products depends primarily on the number of sales representatives hired. Most of the representatives live in relatively large cities and sell not only to customers in that city but also to customers in the small towns in that section of the state. He recognizes that he has only one sales representative in the southeastern part of the United States and none in the Northwest or New England.

Jackson spends most of his time recruiting and training new sales representatives. Some of the new representatives are referred to the company by present sales representatives, but most are recruited through newspaper advertising. Usually a new representative is sent out on the road for a period of one week with an experienced representative; then Jackson spends a week with the new representative in the territory assigned to him. Jackson realizes that the training re-

ceived under these circumstances is probably inadequate, but it is all that time allows. In addition to recruiting and training new sales representatives, Jackson conducts two national sales meetings a year in order to introduce new products. These meetings afford an opportunity to brush up on sales techniques. Although the laboratories of the parent company develop new products, it is the general manager's responsibility to choose the product name, approve the package design, and prepare the layout and copy of the specification sheets that describe the product and are carried by all sales representatives. In the home office there are three clerical employees who process sales orders as they are received from the field. The billing of customers, the computation of commissions, and the payment of sales representatives are performed by personnel of the parent company. Jackson realizes that if Excelsior Products is to continue to grow, he needs more managerial help, but he feels obligated to stay within the 33 percent selling cost imposed by the parent corporation.

PROBLEMS

1. Develop an organizational structure for Excelsior Products that will permit the company to attain a sales volume of $7.5 million annually. Will this structure be effective when sales reach $22 million?
2. Of what significance are the findings of Graicunas in understanding Jackson's problems?
3. Is it possible to change the organizational structure of Excelsior Products and still remain within the 33 percent overall selling cost? Why or why not? How does the answer to this question affect the recommendations made concerning organizational structure in your answer to Problem 1?

The *structure of an organization* is the manner in which its components—its positions, departments, divisions, boards, committees, etc.—are designed and related to one another. Thus, structure includes degree of *formalization*—the extent to which the components of the organization are explicitly defined and its policies, procedures, and goals are clearly stated. It also includes such factors as technology, spans of management, and the number of levels within the management hierarchy. In a sense, these *structural variables* of an organization make up its inert anatomy; and that anatomy comes to life when its positions are filled with people—people whose behavior is guided by *management variables* such as objectives, policies, procedures, rules, standards, controls, and systems of motivation and communication. Thus, structural and management variables constantly interact and influence one another.

In this chapter we first approach the subject of the structural design of organizations in terms of their mechanistic and organic characteristics. The bureaucratic model is briefly described as an example of the mechanistic structure, while matrix organizations exemplify the organic. The contingency approach attempts to discover the conditions under which various aspects of structure will contribute most to organizational effectiveness. Finally, we focus on three specific components of organizational structure: departmentation, span of management, and committees. Additional components of organizational structure and process are discussed in Chapters 10, 11, and 12.

MECHANISTIC AND ORGANIC STRUCTURES

The differences among organizations are enormous, particularly when one considers the interactions between structural variables, management variables, and the personal characteristics of each organization's members. Nevertheless, there are many similarities in organizations that enable us to classify organizations and thereby understand more fully their structure and function. One useful classification is a twofold system developed by Burns and Stalker.[1] They described two contrasting forms of structural classification: mechanistic and organic.

The *mechanistic structure*—the most common form of organization and the most appropriate form when environmental conditions are relatively stable—is the traditional or classical design. The following are its most salient characteristics:

1. The work is broken down into precisely delineated jobs and responsibilities.
2. Middle- and low-level managers emphasize technically improving the means of achieving organizational objectives, sometimes losing sight of the objectives themselves. For example, production managers may become so committed to using the most modern machines that they lose sight of the fact that technological change should lead to increased profits.

---

[1] Tom Burns and G. M. Stalker, *The Management of Innovation* (London: Travistock Publications, 1961), p. 119.

3. Within the hierarchical structure, authority, control, and the flow of communication are centered at the top of a management pyramid. An authoritarian style of management is the rule.
4. The most significant interactions between members are presumed to be vertical in nature (i.e., between superior and subordinate).
5. Loyalty to one's superiors and to the organization is a condition of continuing employment. The loyalty theme contrasts with the idea that the employer-employee relationship is grounded in the contribution each makes to the other.
6. *Local expertise*—knowledge, skill, and experience obtained within the organization—is often more valued than *cosmopolitan expertise*—expertise which is generally accepted across organizations. Thus, long years of service and consequent knowledge of how matters are handled within the firm may be more highly valued than the professionalism of a manager with broad experience.
7. Decision making is more appropriate for persons in the upper reaches of the hierarchy than for those at successively lower levels. Middle- and low-level managers are expected to carry out decisions rather than make them.

The mechanistic organizational structure is obviously compatible with the Theory X view of human nature, but it is incorrect to label it a Theory X structure (as though Theory Y managers cannot function within it). Furthermore, it is worth noting that a given organization lacking some of these characteristics may be classified as mechanistic. The pure mechanistic structure is an abstraction, but many organizations do approximate it.

The *organic structure* is most appropriate for a changing environment—an environment in which problems are constantly arising because of radical changes in technology or market conditions, for example. The organic form is characterized as follows:

1. Specialization and narrowly defined jobs are deemphasized in favor of cooperative problem solving.
2. Continual focus on the overall mission and objectives at all levels of the firm keeps means and ends in proper perspective.
3. Responsibility, authority, and control rest in all members of the organization. Informal groups provide a valuable form of control.
4. Lateral interactions between peers and between persons of different ranks are encouraged; consultation often replaces command.
5. Commitment to organizational objectives is more valued than an individual's loyalty and compliance with rules and regulations.
6. Importance is placed on one's expertise and standing within the industry and on specialization (e.g., engineering or accounting).
7. Valued knowledge and the potential for making good decisions are presumed to exist at all organizational levels.

Generally speaking, enlightened managers and researchers express a preference for some variation of the organic model; but, as Gullett has noted, mechanistic structures still exist in most organizations and are more appropriate than organic forms in business units such as large automobile manufacturing plants and the clerical processing departments of large insurance companies.[2] Although

---

[2] C. Ray Gullett, "Mechanistic vs. Organic Organizations: What Does the Future Hold?" *The Personnel Administrator* (November, 1975), p. 17.

the rate of technological and social change has accelerated in recent years and employees have increasingly demanded autonomy (favoring a flexible model), mechanistic structures continue to be popular. However, many large organizations contain both mechanistic and organic substructures.

The Bureaucratic Model

Even though bureaucratic organizations are considered to be mechanistic, the characteristics attributed to mechanistic structures do not fully describe bureaucracies. As described by Max Weber, the German social scientist, bureaucracy was not, as we use it today, a derogatory term referring to organizations gone wrong—for example, a sick government agency that is characterized by inefficiency, low motivation, excessive red tape, oppressive rules, and unresponsiveness to the public and to its own objectives.[3] Rather, Weber's pure type of bureaucratic organization was conceived as a rational, goal-directed hierarchy. Weber attempted to abstract from his observations of organizations the one ideal organization, and any deviations from that ideal were regarded as aberrations or pathologies. Thus, actions of informal groups and modifications of organizational structure to meet the needs of individuals were considered pathological. Bureaucracy was, therefore, conceived as impersonal in the sense that decisions about people were to be objective, based on organizational needs and on individual merit and competence rather than on personal bias or social caste. As a result, the way to improve an organization was to make it more rational and less influenced by human emotion and personality.

The basic building blocks of the bureaucratic structure, above the worker level, are *organizational offices*. These *organizational offices*, as Weber called them, are now referred to as *managerial positions*, although we do on occasion make reference to *the office of the president* or some other high-level official within bureaucracies. These offices exist separately from the individuals who fill them and, therefore, give the organization stability. Since offices possess certain qualities that transcend the individuals who occupy them, their existence enables a manager to manage effectively long before his or her competence and leadership qualities are demonstrated to subordinates. Organizational offices require clearly defined areas of expertise and the performance of specific duties; they are also subject to specific controls that contribute to a high degree of orderliness and predictability, even in extremely large and complex organizations.[4]

Making organizations impersonal and relying heavily on formal controls to direct individual behavior suppresses initiative and decision making within the middle and low levels of management. Furthermore, impersonal controls

[3] For a description of the bureaucratic structure from Weber's perspective, see H. H. Gerth and C. Wright Mills, eds. and trans., *From Max Weber: Essays in Sociology* (New York City: Oxford University Press, Inc., 1946).

[4] Robert Dubin, "Technical Characteristics of a Bureaucracy," *Human Relations in Administration*, edited by Robert Dubin (4h ed.; Englewood Cliffs, N. J.: Prentice-Hall, Inc., 1974), p. 189.

often cause people to behave in ways that are demanded by the control system but in ways that actually interfere with the achievement of organizational objectives.[5] In one organization, for example, a study of the paper flow showed that three carbon copies of a much used form were filed when one would have sufficed. A blind commitment to following rules and the proliferation of useless rules can cause rapid and unnecessary organizational growth. Thus, in spite of their many admirable qualities, bureaucracies do tend to allocate excessive resources to their own self-preservation and maintenance.[6]

Matrix Organization

Traditional organizations, which are usually divided along functional lines—manufacturing, marketing, research, personnel, etc.—can often be adapted to solve problems and to take advantage of new opportunities simply by superimposing upon them a matrix structure (Figure 9–1). That is, instead of developing a new organization containing these functional departments, the original organization remains intact and makes available to the head of the matrix organization the resources of its departments. Thus, a *matrix organization* is a balanced compromise between a functional and a product organization; that is, between

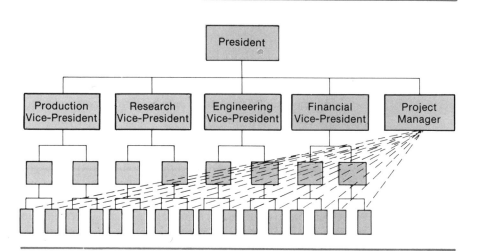

**Figure 9–1
MATRIX
ORGANIZATION**

SOURCE: J. Clifton Williams, *Human Behavior in Organizations* (Cincinnati: South-Western Publishing Co., 1978), p. 44.

---

[5] Edward E. Lawler III, "Control Systems in Organizations," *Handbook of Industrial and Organizational Psychology*, edited by Marvin D. Dunnette (Skokie, Ill.: Rand McNally & Company, 1976), p. 1247.

[6] For a broad view of bureaucracies in many settings, read Michael T. Dalby and Michael S. Wethman, *Bureaucracy in Historical Perspective* (Glenview, Ill.: Scott, Foresman & Company, 1971). Also read Victor A. Thompson, *Bureaucracy and the Modern World* (Morristown, N. J.: General Learning Press, 1976).

departmentation on the basis of functions and departmentation on the basis of specific products or projects to be completed.[7]

The matrix structure has often proved effective for coping with important projects that demand sustained, intensified attention for a limited time. It is used, for example, to develop a new product, to ensure the continuing success of a product to which several departments directly contribute, and to solve a difficult problem such as meeting Environmental Protection Agency antipollution standards. The one distinguishing feature of the matrix structure is that the manager in charge—a *project, program, systems,* or *product manager*—has the responsibility for getting results through employees who report directly to another manager or who have dual reporting responsibilities.[8]

Some project managers are assigned full responsibility for achieving the objectives of a project; while others are only responsible for integrating the related activities of a project or for monitoring it.[9] In either case, the authority of project managers is often less than their responsibility.[10] They must, therefore, rely heavily on human relations, politics, and persuasive skills to achieve their objectives. Persons with high prestige, recognized technical competence, and strong backing from high-level superiors often thrive as project managers; however, the role is usually a difficult one and involves many pitfalls.

Davis and Lawrence [11] discuss a number of problems inherent in matrix organizations, among which are the following:

1. A tendency toward anarchy—a confused situation in which employees have difficulty identifying their "boss"
2. Power struggles that are encouraged by the dual command
3. Excessive emphasis on group decision making; excessive democracy; not enough action
4. Uncontrolled layering—matrices lying within matrices
5. Too much time spent in self-analysis and conflict resolution, which at times detracts from the achievement of organizational objectives

In spite of these and other problems, however, Davis and Lawrence see matrix organizations as viable. They therefore offer explanations for why such pathologies arise and suggest ways of preventing such deficiencies.

Matrix organizations are similar to bureaucracies in their predisposition to develop certain pathologies, but, like bureaucracies, they offer some definite benefits. They often encourage the use of a firm's current personnel and facilities for the immediate achievement of an objective that would otherwise require

---

[7] Kenneth Knight, "Matrix Organization: A Review," *Journal of Management Studies*, Vol. 13, No. 2 (May, 1976), p. 111.

[8] Stanley Davis and Paul Lawrence, *Matrix* (Reading, Mass.: Addison-Wesley Publishing Co., Inc., 1978).

[9] Arthur G. Butler, Jr., "Project Management: A Study in Organizational Conflict," *Academy of Management Journal*, Vol. 16, No. 1 (January, 1973), p. 85.

[10] David McClelland and W. R. King, *Systems Analysis and Project Management* (New York City: McGraw-Hill, Inc., 1975).

[11] Stanley M. Davis and Paul R. Lawrence, "Problems of Matrix Organizations," *Harvard Business Review*, Vol. 56, No. 3 (May–June, 1978), p. 13.

the development of a completely new organization. Furthermore, matrix organizations can respond rapidly to external change and can facilitate change in situations that have high requirements for integrating vast amounts of data and reconciling conflicting demands. For example, to offset the actions of a competitor, a matrix form may be used in order to meet customer demands for an advanced technological computer without disrupting the marketing of existing computers. Thus, in this instance the ability of the matrix design to span marketing, research, and manufacturing departments obviously offers a unique advantage. In addition, the matrix structure provides an excellent training ground for well-rounded managers who, under traditional structures, may be constricted by undesirably narrow functional specialties.

Matrix organization is not a passing fad. It is complex and problem-prone because it violates the unity of command principle. But the opportunities and problems to which it is addressed are complex. It is now functioning within some of the nation's largest and most successful companies such as Bechtel, Dow Corning, Citibank, Dow Chemical, Texas Instruments, and General Electric, and its popularity is growing.

The Contingency Approach

If there is no one best organizational structure, and experts generally agree there is not, then we must look to contingency research for clues concerning when to use which structure. The following statements about structure are examples of limited generalizations of the sort a contingency approach produces. In each case the generalizations must be interpreted in light of the environments and types of organizations studied.

1. Formalization of structure (the use of standard procedures, job descriptions, policies, etc., to structure role expectations and to limit individual discretion) increases with organizational size. Degree of formalization is even more closely related, however, to complexity of organization (differentiation of functions and roles and degree of required specialization).[12]

2. Decentralized organizational structure[13] is more effective than centralized structure in dynamic, relatively unstable environments of industrialized countries, but decentralized structures are relatively ineffective in industrial enterprises in developing countries.[14]

3. The more volatile and uncertain the environment in which a firm operates, the more appropriate is an organic, liberal form of organization. Conversely, mechanistic structures are more appropriate for successful firms in stable environments.[15]

---

[12] John Child, "Predicting and Understanding Organization Structure," *Administrative Science Quarterly*, Vol. 18 (June, 1973), p. 168.

[13] Decentralization, to be discussed in Chapter 11, refers to a structure in which the authority to make decisions is delegated to the managers of lower echelon organizational units.

[14] Jack L. Simonetti and F. Glenn Boseman, "The Impact of Market Competition on Organizational Structure and Effectiveness: A Cross-Cultural Study," *Academy of Management Journal*, Vol. 18, No. 3 (September, 1975), p. 631.

[15] Paul Lawrence and Jay Lorsch, *Organization and Environment* (Cambridge, Mass.: Harvard Business School, Division of Research, 1967).

The research studies that produce such generalizations offer great promise for providing guidelines for the design of organizations. Such research can easily be misinterpreted, however, by persons who are not familiar with a broad spectrum of studies which have been conducted under a variety of conditions. When generalizing from contingency research projects, the following points should be considered:

1. The variables controlled in any given study represent only a few of the many variables that could be controlled and that may be important. Let us say that a principle of management can be established in certain situations—for example, in unionized apparel manufacturing firms in the southern United States that have less than 500 employees. However, does that situational principle hold equally when the industry is depressed and when it is prosperous? Does it hold equally for subsidiaries of large companies and for companies owned by one person? Does it matter whether the owner-manager is powerful and domineering or mild and easily intimidated?

2. Even when different researchers select the same variables for study, the companies involved may be so different in terms of size, type of industry, leadership, etc., that it is extremely difficult to compare them and to draw useful generalizations from them.

3. When two variables are found to be correlated—size and degree of formalization, for example—the correlation is often difficult to interpret. Does the correlation between size and formalization mean that increasing size made formalization imperative? Did the formalization contribute to the growth? Could growth have been faster and more solid within a more liberal, less formalized structure? Certainly correlation alone does not imply causation. Among children, for example, there is a high correlation between mental ability and shoe size, but not because one causes the other. Both are obviously influenced by a third variable, maturation. Extreme caution should be exercised in assuming causation in contingency research.

4. The variables studied may not be and often should not be defined the same way in different research projects. Size, for example, is typically expressed in terms of the number of employees in the organization. However, the number of employees can be a poor index of size. Evers, Bohlen, and Warren suggest other measurements of size, such as gross sales, fixed assets, or level of automation. In some situations, one or a combination of these measurements may be a more appropriate indicator of size than the number of employees.[16]

The reason for noting the problems associated with contingency studies is not to detract from the value of contingency research. Instead, it is to sound a note of cautiousness about drawing generalizations from research of all sorts. First, one must resist the temptation to generalize too much—in effect, to revert to the classical approach of developing universal principles. Second, when limited principles are established, caution must be exercised in applying them, since new variables that are introduced by rapidly changing environments may invali-

---

[16] Frederick T. Evers, Joe M. Bohlen, and Richard D. Warren, "The Relationships of Selected Size and Structure Indicators in Economic Organizations," *Administrative Science Quarterly*, Vol. 21 (June, 1976), p. 326.

date previous research findings. Finally, it is important to note that some research findings are merely *descriptive* (showing how organizations are now) and not necessarily *prescriptive* (demonstrating how organizations should be). Only persons who understand these and many other aspects of research design and application can adequately interpret contingency studies.

DEPARTMENTATION

Departmentation, usually the first step in designing an organization, is the grouping of work or individuals into manageable units. Some businesses begin with all functions performed by one person, the owner-manager, and only in that initial stage is departmentation unnecessary. For example, responding to the rising fuel costs of the late 1970's, John French started his own business selling storm doors and windows which he purchased from a manufacturer near his home in Dallas. He soon discovered that to be effective he had to hire installers. As the business prospered, French found it necessary to hire a secretary and then a bookkeeper. Within three years he was making his own products, and his fledgling company was organized into three departments: sales, manufacturing, and accounting. Thus, departmentation became necessary, as it virtually always does, by the specialization and organizational complexity that accompanied the company's growth.

Bases for Departmentation

As organizations grow they must constantly be reorganized in order to cope with increasing complexities. Over a period of years, certain well-recognized and accepted bases for departmentation have developed. The most common of these—function, product, customer, geography, process, and sequence—will be discussed. However, large organizations usually employ a variety of departmentation styles, selecting the most appropriate form for each subsystem.

Function. Departmentation by function is based on the nature of the work and the skills and technology that are required to perform it. The departments most often found in small manufacturing firms, where functional departmentation is especially appropriate, are production, finance, and marketing (or sales). Within a given department, the work may be further subdivided; finance, for example, may include subunits for accounts receivable, accounts payable, credit, and payroll.

The names of functional departments vary with the nature of the business. The production department of a manufacturing firm may be called buying, warehousing, and distribution in a wholesale company. Airlines use the word *operations* for their production function—the movement of passengers. Some organizations, such as hospitals and social service agencies, have no marketing function; instead, they have a public relations function. In companies such as pharmaceuticals, research is considered a primary function because of its importance to the success of the firm.

In addition to their primary functions, most organizations have auxiliary or staff functions, such as personnel and purchasing, that serve as a basis for departmentation. Delicate interpersonal relations, to be discussed in Chapter 10, often arise between those performing the primary and auxiliary functions.

Product. Companies with diversified product lines frequently create managerial units based on the product. Three forms of product departmentation are shown in Figure 9–2. Chart 1 shows the division of both the sales and the manufacturing functions into product departments, while Chart 2 shows product departmentation as applied to the sales function only. In Chart 3 the manufacturing function is departmentalized according to product, and sales remains as a single unit. Figure 9–2 also illustrates that the process of creating departments quite properly employs more than one basis. In this instance, the bases of function and product are used. (See page 184.)

Customer. Retail stores may organize their sales forces to meet the needs of a specific class of customer by forming special departments to cater to teenagers, career women and men, brides, homemakers, and so on. An industrial firm that manufactures valves may divide its sales force so that one part sells to original equipment manufacturers and another to the replacement market.

Geography. At one time, poor communications justified departmentation based on territorial or geographic units. While this reason may still have some validity for those companies with foreign operations, quality of communications is usually no longer a valid reason for geographic departmentation within the United States. When the number of people to be supervised is large and dispersed, territorial units afford a logical means of developing manageable units. The creation of regional units offers a possible solution to the organizational problem confronting Excelsior Products in Case Problem 9-A.

Process. The process or equipment used in producing a product may be the basis for determining departmental lines at the plant level. The grouping of all milling machines into one department and the placing of lathes in another department is illustrative of departmentation by equipment. In other industries the process serves as the basis for determining effective departmentation. Thus, in a chemical plant a process such as distillation becomes the operating unit.

Sequence. Departments sometimes conform to alphanumeric or time sequences. For those organizations not yet computerized the bookkeeping section may be subdivided into two units, one of which posts accounts for customers whose last names begin with the letters A through M; the other unit posts for those customers whose names begin with the letters N through Z. Numerical sequence is often the basis for dividing undifferentiated labor gangs into controllable units; i.e., every 30 employees are placed under the direction of a straw boss. Plants operating 16 or 24 hours a day establish separate shifts, and each shift is a distinct administrative unit.

CHART 1

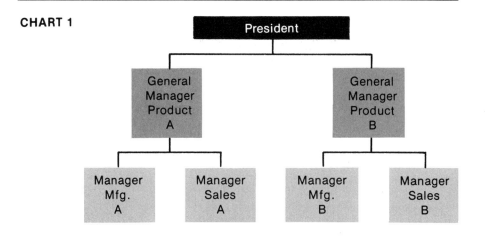

CHART 2

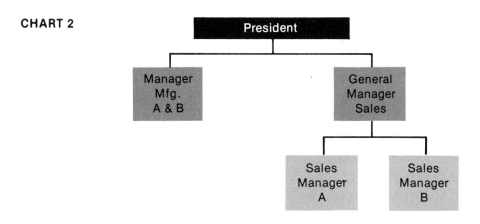

CHART 3

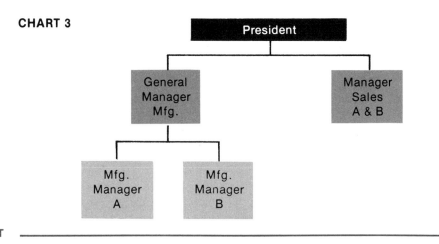

Figure 9–2
THREE POSSIBLE ARRANGE-MENTS OF DEPARTMEN-TATION BASED UPON PRODUCT

Creating Manageable Departments

The preceding bases of dividing work are an extension of the definition of departmentation and a description of the building blocks that make up the organizational structure. Creating manageable departments is not an end in itself; instead, it is a means of facilitating the achievement of organizational objectives. There is no set of rules that prescribes the one best pattern of organization structure; however, there are guides, discussed in Chapter 11, which are useful in selecting the most appropriate structure.

SPAN OF MANAGEMENT

Once the bases for departmentation are determined, another problem of structure immediately arises concerning how many departments or how many individual workers should be placed under the direction of one manager. Historically this has been referred to as the *span of control* problem; however, *span of management* may be a better term because, in addition to control, managers plan, organize, lead, and perform other functions. Although there are other definitions that may be more appropriate for certain types of research, span of management is here considered to be synonymous with span of control and is defined in terms of the total number of subordinates over whom a manager has authority and control.[17]

Long before the development of management as a formal discipline, leaders were formulating judgments concerning the span of management problem. Jethro advised Moses to establish "rulers of thousands, and rulers of hundreds, and rulers of fifties, and rulers of tens."[18] Napoleon believed that "no man can command more than five distinct bodies in the same theatre of war," and numerous statements about span of management were published during the nineteenth and early twentieth centuries.[19] Generally speaking, early writers focused on an upper limit to the number of subordinates a superior can effectively manage, while later writers tended to think in terms of an optimum number which may differ from that upper limit.[20]

Early Views

Of the many early writers on the span of management, two names stand out: V. A. Graicunas, a Lithuanian management consultant, and Lyndall Urwick, an Englishman, who at the time he and Graicunas began to collaborate (1929)

---

[17] There is some evidence that researchers give different meanings to *span of control, span of management,* and *span of supervision.* See William G. Ouchi and John B. Dowling, "Defining the Span of Control," *Administrative Science Quarterly*, Vol. 21, No. 3 (September, 1974), p. 357.

[18] See Chapter 2, page 17 for a more complete analysis of Jethro's recommendations (contained in Exodus 18:13–26).

[19] David Van Fleet and Arthur G. Bedeian, "A History of the Span of Management," *Academy of Management Review*, Vol. 2, No. 1 (July, 1977), p. 356. (This article contains 255 references.)

[20] *Ibid.*, p. 365.

was director of the International Management Institute at Geneva. Urwick recently restated the principle he and Graicunas originally formulated: "No executive should attempt to supervise directly the work of more than five, or at the most six, direct subordinates whose work interlocks." [21] This principle, expressed by Urwick on one occasion in terms of the "number of subordinates a supervisor can supervise," has often been misunderstood and criticized.[22] Urwick stresses that the principle was not meant to apply at the lowest level of supervision, particularly in situations where the work of subordinates clearly does not interlock.[23]

The major contribution of Graicunas was his quantification of the complex relationships that occur between superiors and subordinates and between the subordinates themselves. He clearly demonstrated the rapidity with which interactions increase as subordinates are added. As shown in Figure 9–3, when a supervisor has two subordinates who interact with one another, six relationships exist: (1) the supervisor relating to each subordinate as an individual, (2) the supervisor relating to each subordinate where each is a group member, and (3) the interactions between subordinates A and B as seen from the perspective of the two. (With reference to the last set of relationships, note that A may strongly identify with B without a reciprocal identification.) The addition of a third subordinate increases the total number to 18, and the addition of a fourth results in 44 relationships. A manager with eight subordinates operates from the center of a network of 1,080 potential relationships.[24] In fairness to Graicunas, he recognized the impossibility of laying down hard-and-fast universal rules, contrary to the apparent belief of many of his critics, and his emphasis on lateral as well as vertical interactions reflected a point of view more characteristic of the human relations movement than of classical writers.

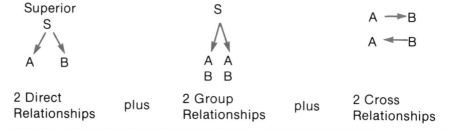

**Figure 9–3
POSSIBLE
RELATIONSHIPS
BETWEEN
SUPERIOR AND
SUBORDINATES**

[21] Lyndall Urwick, "V. A. Graicunas and the Span of Control," *Academy of Management Journal*, Vol. 17, No. 2 (June, 1974), p. 349.

[22] Lyndall Urwick, *Scientific Principles and Organization* (New York City: American Management Associates, 1938), p. 8.

[23] Urwick, *op. cit.*

[24] V. A. Graicunas, "Relationship in Organization," *Bulletin of the International Management Institute*, Vol. 7 (March, 1933), p. 39, reprinted in *Papers on the Science of Administration*, edited by Luther H. Gulick and Lyndall F. Urwick (New York City: Institute of Public Administration, Columbia University, 1937), p. 183. (Footnote 24 continued on page 187.)

Current Practice

Although most researchers recognize that there is an upper limit to the number of persons a manager can effectively supervise, most are reluctant to propose any rule as Graicunas did. Obviously a number of factors should be considered when deciding upon a span of management, among which are the following: [25]

1. The complexity of the subordinates' jobs and subsequent need for close interaction with a superior and others (for example, routine, rigidly structured machine tending versus the demanding, ever-changing work of the technical salesperson)
2. The complexity of the supervisors' jobs and how much nonsupervisory work they must perform
3. The time and attention given to the development and maintenance of control techniques other than direct supervision—for example, the effectiveness with which a supervisor clearly defines production expectations and devises means by which deviations are easily observed
4. The nature and number of a manager's interactions with persons other than subordinates—such as superiors, peers, engineers, quality control personnel, suppliers, financiers, government representatives, and customers
5. The extent to which staff assistants, quality control inspectors, and others provide support, thereby enabling a manager to effectively supervise more persons
6. Competence of the supervisor and subordinates

How many subordinates should actually report to a manager? The number varies greatly, depending on the situation. Certainly the recommendation of five, or, at the most, six is unrealistic. In a much quoted study of 100 medium-sized manufacturing firms in southern England, Woodward found spans of management of chief executives ranging from 2 to 18 with a median of 6. At the supervisory level, spans ranged from 10 to 90 with a median of 38.[26] Studies by Dale found the median number of executives reporting to the president to be from 8 to 9 in large American companies with a range from 1 to 17.[27] In a study of 221 middle insurance managers, Viola found spans ranging from 1

The number of relationships, r, may be determined by the following formula, in which n represents the number of subordinates:

$$r = n\left(2^{n-1} + n - 1\right)$$

As mentioned in the text, Graicunas does not take into account all possible relationships. Any one of the subordinates could conceivably initiate action, which in effect doubles the number of potential direct relationships; in addition, the supervisor could participate as a member of each group, with successive members of that group assuming the dominant role.

[25] The following articles deal with one or more of the factors that may influence span of management:

Gerald D. Bell, "Determinants of Span of Control," *American Journal of Sociology,* Vol. 73, No. 1 (July, 1967), p. 100.

Donald W. Domtra, "Is Your Span of Control Right for You?" *Supervisory Management,* Vol. 16, No. 8 (August, 1972), p. 16.

Jon G. Udell, "An Empirical Test of Hypotheses Relating to Span of Control," *Administrative Science Quarterly,* Vol. 10, No. 4 (December, 1967), p. 420.

[26] Joan Woodward, *Industrial Organization: Theory and Practice* (London: Oxford University Press, Inc., 1965).

[27] Ernest Dale, *Organization* (New York City: American Management Association, 1967), p. 94.

to 70 with a mean of 6.75 with 71 percent of all spans under 19.[28] A comprehensive survey of the span of management literature by Van Fleet and Bedeian describes several studies which support the notion that spans within effective companies vary greatly and are contingent upon a number of variables such as those listed earlier.[29]

COMMITTEES

Committees are a valuable but often maligned aspect of organizational structure. Time spent in committee meetings is often resented and criticized, even by persons who recognize their value. Thus, it has been said that the purpose of a committee is "to produce boredom, stimulate conflict, dilute responsibility, and prevent action." Unfortunately, some committees do just that. As for their effectiveness, everyone knows that a camel is a horse put together by a committee. Nevertheless, committees serve important functions within organizations. They cut across formal lines of authority and departmentation thereby making unique contributions, primarily in the areas of decision making, communication, and coordination.

Nature and Function of Committees

As a significant part of their structure, most organizations make use of *standing committees*. These permanent, ongoing committees virtually always present in large firms, are assigned responsibilities just as individual managers are, and may be routinely chaired by the incumbent of a specific position (president, production manager, etc.). In addition, most companies use *ad hoc* or temporary, special-purpose committees as the need arises. Such committees are appointed to deal with a specific problem with the understanding that they will automatically be dissolved when assignment is completed.

Based on their function, committees may be classified as *general management committees*, usually company-wide, policy-making bodies, or *restricted committees*, those that are limited to a single function (for example, production, marketing, or personnel) or a few related functions. Some of these committees are *authoritative*—they make and carry out decisions; others are *nonauthoritative*—they are limited to studying issues and making recommendations.[30] A typical corporate *executive committee* is an example of a standing, general management, authoritative committee. An *ad hoc committee*, say a committee to study the selection and promotion policy within a firm's marketing department, is classified as restricted and usually as nonauthoritative.

---

[28] Richard Viola, "The Span of Management in the Life Insurance Industry," *Economic and Business Bulletin*, No. 1 (1975), p. 18.

[29] Van Fleet and Bedeian, *op. cit.*

[30] M. R. Lohman, *Top Management Committees* (New York City: American Management Association, 1961), AMA Research Study 48, p. 5. This study covers 43 firms and 319 management committees.

General management committees tend to be primarily concerned with setting policy; thus, planning and making operating decisions are for them second and third in importance. Finance, control, research and development, and production committees are more often engaged primarily in planning. Labor and personnel committees usually become involved in making operating decisions, probably because they must interpret the effect of labor agreements on company operations. However, since the purpose and functions of a given committee vary substantially from one company to another, it is unwise to assume that the name of a committee reveals much about what its members actually do.

Contributions of Committees

Since there are many types of committees that operate with varying degrees of effectiveness, their actual contributions can only be assessed in specific situations. It is possible, however, to generalize concerning the potential contributions of committees. They are discussed here under the following headings: (1) group judgment, (2) improved motivation, (3) a check on authority, and (4) improved coordination.

Group Judgment. The consensus judgment of a committee is not always superior to the individual judgment of one or more of its members. However, group judgment is seldom less accurate than the judgment of the average group member, and it is often superior to that of any member working alone.[31] The potential superiority of committee decisions or contributions to the decisions of individuals stems from several factors. One factor is the wide range of knowledge contributed by the committee members. The knowledge factor is particularly important when technical specialists and managers of interdependent subsystems serve on the same committee. Consider, for example, the difficulty in making a decision about a major new product when there is no input from representatives of the research and development, marketing, production, and finance departments.

The potential benefits of group judgment are not limited, of course, to knowledge contributions. The interactions between members—the debating, the defending, the questioning, the brainstorming, even the competition and conflict that may be taken to unhealthy extremes—provide a potential group contribution that does not exist when an individual works alone. Such interaction introduces into the decision process a variety of personality, emotional, and attitudinal factors that may at times be frustrating, even destructive, but which often need to be part of an organizational decision.

Improved Motivation. Individuals who participate in developing a plan or making a decision are more likely to be enthusiastic about implementing it than are persons who are simply told what to do. Committees provide opportunities for participation and for the resulting pride of authorship that motivates

---

[31] Marvin E. Shaw, *Group Dynamics: The Psychology of Small Group Behavior* (New York City: McGraw-Hill, Inc., 1976), p. 63.

committee members to work for the success of a committee action. Employees, for example, who serve on a job evaluation committee may be motivated to persuade fellow employees of the fairness of the evaluations and resulting compensation program, even when those employee committee members have not been altogether successful in defending their position in the committee proceedings.

A Check on Authority. Committees often restrict the authority of individual managers, thereby reducing the likelihood that decisions will be made without taking into consideration their full implications. Such diverse groups as corporate boards of directors, municipal planning councils, university boards of regents, and standing faculty committees commonly serve this function. Committee members learn to anticipate the reactions of other members to proposed actions. Through this process they broaden their perspective and hopefully learn to think in terms of achieving broad organizational objectives rather than narrow, self-enhancing goals. The limitation that committees place on individual authority contributes to the commonly held belief that committee action makes an organization sluggish and inefficient, unable to act rapidly enough to take advantage of opportunities. But, as organizations grow in size and complexity, slowing down decisions is not always bad.

Improved Coordination. Since committee action necessarily requires the sharing of information and the expression of viewpoints and sentiments, most committees serve a coordinative function within an organization. A corporate executive committee, for example, consisting of heads of functional areas such as marketing, manufacturing, engineering, and finance, may schedule regular meetings primarily to coordinate departmental activities through person-to-person contact. Such interaction provides a form of communication and understanding not easily achieved through more formal, less personal means. Because of its unique potential for coordinated action, a committee may be granted authority that transcends that of any single member. A new products committee, for example, composed of the heads of marketing, manufacturing, finance, and research may have the authority to accept or reject a proposed product. It is primarily the need for coordination that leads to structuring organizations so that committees have decision-making power.

Problems of Committees

Although few companies of any size operate without committees, the potential advantages of committees are not always realized. Some problems that arise from the use of committees are not necessarily inherent weaknesses of the committee system itself. Many of the criticisms of committees apply equally to any type of problem-solving group. The criticisms most often made of the committee system are that (1) it is expensive, (2) it often produces poor decisions, and (3) its members are not fully accountable for their actions.

Expense. The cost of committee meetings, even when based only on the salaries of participants, can be enormous. Committee meetings often waste time.

They often involve too many people, and they may involve the wrong people. Furthermore, they may encourage too much inane, unproductive, and unnecessary talk.

Compromise Decisions. Committee decisions and recommendations that result from compromises and political trade-offs may be inferior to individual decisions and so watered down that nobody fully supports them. Committee pressures, often exerted to gain unanimity, suppress individuality and bold action while encouraging bland, inoffensive action at the lowest common denominator of the group. The potential advantages of the group process may be offset by inept leadership, the veto power of a vocal minority, or the dominance of one or more members whose potential contributions are less than their power and influence.

In spite of the recognized advantages of group judgment, much has been written about the potential dangers in group decision making. A major contribution to this thought was made by Irving Janis with his descriptions of how group dynamics may detract from, rather than facilitate, rational judgment. He originated the term *groupthink* to describe a type of thinking that leads to such foreign-policy decisions and fiascoes as the Bay of Pigs failure, and some poor decisions made prior to Pearl Harbor, during the Korean War, and during the Cuban missile crisis. Janis defines groupthink as:

> . . . a model of thinking that people engage in when they are deeply involved in a cohesive in-group, when the members' striving for unanimity override their motivation to realistically appraise alternative courses of action. . . . Groupthink refers to a deterioration of mental efficiency, reality testing, and moral judgment that results from in-group processes.[32]

Groupthink involves one or more of several thought patterns that undermine the effectiveness of committees and other groups. Group members may, for example, develop an illusion of invulnerability that leads to excessive optimism, engage in collective rationalization, exert pressure on any member who expresses strong disagreement with a group position, or share an illusion that a majority view is unanimously held. Because Janis emphasized groupthink within the federal government, it is easy to conclude that it is less likely to occur in business and industry. Evidence to the contrary is seen, however, in a number of major business decisions such as those leading to the production of Ford Motor Company's Edsel model and to DuPont's failure to market its Corfam shoe products.[33] An understanding of the groupthink concept has much to contribute to the effectiveness of committees and to other groups involved in decision making.

Lack of Accountability. Committee action is used too easily to avoid decisions and the personal risks decisions incur. Committees may be assigned respon-

---

[32] Irving L. Janis, *Victims of Groupthink* (Boston: Houghton Mifflin Company, 1972), p. 9.
[33] Richard C. Huseman and Russell W. Driver, "Groupthink: Implications for Small Group Decision Making in Business," in Richard C. Huseman and Archie B. Carroll, *Readings in Organizational Behavior: Dimensions of Management Actions* (Boston: Allyn & Bacon, Inc., 1979), p. 100.

sibilities and granted the authority to act, but it is extremely difficult to hold committee members accountable for results. When committee action gets poor results, individuals can blame the other members; and thus, the chairperson, who by definition does not have formal authority over committee members, is equally protected. Obviously such conditions do not provide the ideal motivation for each committee member to assume maximum responsibility.

Making Committees Effective

The effectiveness of committees, like the effectiveness of the firm, is contingent on a number of factors, many of which lie within the control of management. Generalizing from the limited research on committees and the extensive research on the behavior of groups, A.C. Filley makes the following suggestions for improving the effectiveness of committees: [34]

1. *Committees should be small.* Five members seem to be ideal (a) where this number allows for adequate representation of divergent interests and (b) where committee members possess the necessary skills and knowledge to achieve their objective.
2. *Leadership.* The chairperson should take charge and control group proceedings as needed to achieve its objectives (a task role). Effective leadership, however, requires group building, the development and support of certain social relationships among group members (a social role). Ideally the chairperson plays both roles, but if he or she cannot do so, dual leadership is necessary for optimal committee performance.
3. *Membership.* Groups in which members are committed to achieve common objectives and are, relatively speaking, cooperative rather than competitive will be most productive, and their members will find greatest satisfaction. For certain types of problem solving, however, individual differences that contribute to conflict, within the tolerance limits of the group, are preferred to homogeneity of group members. [35]

Chairpersons usually learn their skills by observing others and by trial and error. There is, however, some literature available concerning effective committee leadership. Anthony Jay makes some valuable suggestions about planning an agenda for a committee meeting, a matter to which an inexperienced leader would be likely to direct little attention. [36] He emphasizes, for example, that problems requiring the greatest mental energy should be dealt with first—before fatigue sets in and attention wanes. It is best to close a meeting with an item that unifies rather than divides the members into conflicting subgroubs; and meetings that should be short but that may easily drag on should begin at a time when a limited amount of time is available (for example, ten minutes before another meeting). As trivial as such techniques may seem, they often contribute significantly to differences in the effectiveness of chairpersons.

---

[34] A. C. Filley, "Committee Management: Guidelines from Social Science Research," *California Management Review*, Vol. 8, No. 1 (Fall, 1970), p. 13.

[35] Support for the belief that diversity of membership improves the ability of a committee to solve problems comes from Nicholas Dimarco, "Life Style, Work Group Structure, Compatibility, and Job Satisfaction," *Academy of Management Journal*, Vol. 18, No. 2 (June, 1975), p. 321.

[36] Anthony Jay, "How to Run a Meeting," *Harvard Business Review*, Vol. 54, No. 2 (March–April, 1976), p. 43.

Case Problem 9-B describes a company with problems that may be solved by the formation of a committee. Whether the committee should be advisory in nature or function as a plural executive is one of the choices that must be made.

Case Problem 9-B

A PROBLEM IN COORDINATION

Ray Talbert, the president and founder of Electric Manufacturing Corporation (Emcorp), is wondering how he can follow the advice of his doctor, who told him to take it easy after last year's coronary attack. Emcorp manufactures a full line of fractional horsepower electric motors sold to both original equipment manufacturers and distributors throughout the country. At the present time the company employs approximately 1,000 people.

Talbert, an engineer, has maintained tight control over all major functions throughout the years; and though each of the heads of the engineering, manufacturing, sales, finance, and personnel departments has the title of vice-president, they come to Talbert for approval before making any changes in procedure. Usually each of these executives sees Talbert several times a day. The personnel director once suggested a weekly meeting, but Talbert vetoed the idea as too time-consuming. Now, worried about his health as well as the problems of the company, Talbert is beginning to feel the need for some relief from the constant pressure.

The manufacturing department shows a picture of rising costs, consistent failure to meet delivery schedules, and an increasing number of quality complaints. John Stroud, vice-president of manufacturing, admits to poor performance, but says that the cost figures from accounting are pure history and of no use since they do not reach manufacturing until the 15th of the month following the month in which the work is completed. He states that his failure to meet delivery schedules is due almost entirely to the fact that the sales department makes unrealistic promises and does not bother to check manufacturing schedules. Stroud attributes most of the quality problems to the incessant flow of engineering changes that come without warning and with no time to work out the production problems present in all new products. Talbert admits to himself that he forgot to tell Stroud that he had approved the last set of engineering changes and that he had asked Frank Smyth, vice-president of engineering, to put all the approved changes into production immediately.

The vice-president and general manager of sales, Rita Linder, recognizes that she has no knowledge of the manufacturing schedules and realizes that she, too, is being criticized by Talbert for the many broken promises in regard to delivery dates. However, Linder's chief complaint at the present time is the result of having sold a large order of standard motors to a distributor having a supply of replacement parts in stock and then discovering that engineering had changed specifications—a change that made all replacement parts in the field obsolete. Another irritant for Linder is the tightened credit requirements instituted by the finance department without prior consultation with the sales department. Again Talbert admits privately that it is the same engineering change which caused so much trouble in manufacturing that is causing trouble for the sales department and making obsolete the existing stock of replacement parts. He also realizes that at his request, due to an unusually short cash position, the finance department tightened up on credit requirements.

PROBLEMS

1. Define the major problem facing Emcorp's management.

2. Will the formation of a committee be of any value in this situation? If a committee is needed, assign a title to the committee and indicate who should be members of the committee. Is there a need for an outside member on the committee?

3. Will an *ad hoc* committee be of any value?

4. In the event that Talbert decides to retire, will the presence of a committee make it easier or more difficult for Talbert's successor? Discuss.

CHAPTER QUESTIONS FOR STUDY AND DISCUSSION

1. Draw a distinction between organic and mechanistic structures in terms of (1) control, (2) decision making, and (3) communication.

2. What did Weber mean when he advocated that organizations should be impersonal? Do you agree with him?

3. In view of the unique demands placed on a project manager, what qualifications would you seek in such a person?

4. What is meant by formalization of structure? Why do you think that degree of formalization is positively related to size?

5. Which characteristics of a contingency study suggest that the research findings are descriptive but not prescriptive?

6. What conditions or circumstances make departmentation necessary?

7. Which type of departmentation would be most appropriate for a small manufacturing company? Why?

8. Describe an organization in which it would be proper to use more than one basis for departmentation.

9. Modern researchers tend to think more in terms of an optimum span of management than in terms of an upper limit. Why do you think this change has occurred?

10. Why do modern organization theorists avoid using a specific rule, as Graicunas did, for most appropriate spans of management?

11. Under what conditions may group judgment be superior to individual judgment?

12. If you were given the responsibility to appoint an *ad hoc* committee of managers in order to solve a specific business problem, which guidelines would you use?

Chapter 10

Authority and Power Relationships

Case Problem 10-A
A STRIKE VOTE

The Muskegon Machine Works is a Delaware corporation that operates two plants. One is located in Muskegon, Michigan, and employs 700 people; the other is located in Nashville, Tennessee, and employs 300 people. The Machine Works, as it is known locally, is proud of its relations with its stockholders and their active participation in annual meetings. At the last meeting the present board of directors was reelected and, in turn, the board reappointed the present officers of the company. A meeting of the board of directors of the Machine Works is now in progress.

"Gentlemen," John Johansen, president of the company and a member of the board, began, "I have asked for a meeting so that we may review our current labor negotiations. We have been negotiating with the local union for the past 60 days in an effort to reach an agreement satisfactory to both parties. Two months ago we met in this same room and authorized our negotiating team to hold the line with a 7-cent-an-hour increase, some slight improvement in the pension plan, and a modification of our group insurance to bring the benefits in line with the daily room charges of the local hospitals. Mr. Lasker, chairman of our negotiating com-

mittee, tells me that the union is adamant in its demands: a 12-cent-an-hour wage increase, one additional holiday which brings the total to 9, and 4 weeks' vacation for all employees with 10 years' service. The 7 cents an hour represents an increase in labor costs of $145,000 a year for the company since we give the same increase to the Nashville plant that we settle for here. The 12 cents that the union is demanding would add another $100,000 to the $145,000. You are well aware that our average hourly rate in Muskegon is 20 cents an hour above the average for the industry and 30 cents more than our average in the Nashville plant. Also, I am told that the union is meeting tonight to take a strike vote on our final offer presented to them this morning and in line with the instructions we gave our committee at the start of these negotiations. We have a meeting scheduled with the union tomorrow, the expiration date of our current labor agreement; if we don't reach an agreement then, the union is free to strike. Shall we stand firm in the face of what promises to be a long and costly strike?"

All issues are discussed thoroughly and the board votes unanimously in support of the company's final offer and instructs the negotiating team not to change its present position.

* * * *

In another part of town a special meeting of the local union is in progress. Norvell Slater, a 39-year old electrician with 20 years' seniority, is speaking to the membership. He has been an active member of the union since its certification as the bargaining agent of the employees of the Muskegon Machine Works by the National Labor Relations Board more than 15 years ago.

"I am reporting to you as president of the local and chairman of your bargaining committee. For the past two months we have been meeting with company representatives in an effort to reach agreement on a new contract. So far, not much has been accomplished. We have gained some slight improvement in our pension plan, and the daily room allowance of the hospitalization insurance has been increased so that it now covers the full cost of a hospital room. The real problem seems to be wages. When we started negotiations, we decided that we wouldn't take less than 12 cents an hour. The company says that they won't give more than 7 cents. They say that we are getting 20 cents an hour more than the rest of the industry and 30 cents more than Nashville. I don't know about that. All I know is that we are getting 10 cents an hour less than other workers here in Muskegon for the same kind of work and we live here, not in Nashville." At this point there is a roar of approval from the floor.

"The other things we can't get together on are holidays and vacations. Pat Toms, our international representative, tells us it would be a feather in our cap if we could lead the parade for once and get something first in this town. Getting that ninth holiday would put us out in front for a change. And about the four weeks' vacation for those of you with 10 years' service; you should get that now and not have to wait 20 years for it like I did. Anyway, that fourth week doesn't seem like much to me when you compare it to the three-month vacations that some companies are giving. Any questions?"

Again all issues are discussed thoroughly and the vote to strike is unanimous unless the company meets the union's demands for wages, vacations, and holidays.

At nine o'clock the next morning the negotiating teams meet in a downtown hotel. The meeting ends at 6 p.m. with no agreement. As the meeting closes, Norvell Slater makes this comment: "You know our contract expires at midnight. We have a strike vote backing us up, and since we can't get together we have no choice but to strike. Pickets will be placed around the plant in the morning."

The next morning pickets are at every gate and none of the hourly employees, all members of the union, make any effort to cross the picket line.

PROBLEMS

1. What is the source of authority granted to the board of directors of the Muskegon Machine Works? Did the board exceed that authority in authorizing the company negotiating committee to stand fast in the face of a certain strike?
2. What is the source of authority that permits the local union to enforce its contract demands by striking? Has the union exceeded its authority in the above case?
3. Does the action taken by the union, i.e., an economic strike, negate or cancel in any way the authority of management to operate the plant? If so, how?
4. What are the obligations of the employees of the Machine Works to (a) the company and (b) the union?

In the discussion of Theories X and Y in Chapter 8, brief statements were made concerning the *source* of authority. It was mentioned that Theory X assumes that the source of authority is related to the right to own property and the attendant obligation to manage property, while Theory Y states that in order for authority to exist, it must first be accepted by those who are being subjected to that authority. These two positions concerning the source of authority are diametrically opposed; one regards authority as being granted by a source external to the organization and the other views authority as being granted internally by the members of the organization through their acceptance of the exercise of authority. The first purpose of this chapter is to discuss the nature of authority and to reconcile these opposing points of view concerning the source of authority. In addition to understanding the sources of authority, it is necessary to appreciate the relationships between two types of authority that are exercised in most formal organizations. These different types of authority are usually called *line* authority and *staff* authority. The second part of the chapter discusses the important organizational relationship of line-and-staff authority.

AUTHORITY

One way of developing an understanding of the differences concerning the source of authority is to present statements representative of each point of view. However, before presenting and analyzing these statements, let us examine various familiar meanings of the word *authority*.

Meanings of Authority

There are many different meanings to authority. A board or a commission empowered to act in a specific area may be termed an authority; for example, the port authority. We recognize government as an authority in the term, the *authority of the state.* An individual may be recognized as competent in a given field of learning or possessing technical qualifications that enable that person to speak with authority. Technical writers and expert witnesses are examples of this kind of authority. When we refer to the authority of the president, we associate authority with an office or a position.

Authority is an abstract concept and, as shown by the above examples, it is a concept applicable to many situations. When used in management literature, the term *authority* has yet another meaning. *Managerial authority* may be defined as the right to act or to direct the action of others in the attainment of organizational goals. This definition states explicitly two characteristics of authority: (1) authority is a *right* and (2) as a result of possessing this right, one is entitled to *act,* either directly or indirectly through the actions of others. Implied, but not stated explicitly, is a third characteristic of authority—(3) the *power* to employ penalties or rewards so that the desired action is completed. Power remains implicit, for there is a great deal of variation in the amount of power associated with managerial authority; in fact, there is one form of authority, staff authority, that is primarily advisory in nature with the only power being that of persuasion. There are also situations in which two or more conflicting or overlapping authorities are entitled to act and the power assigned to one authority may outweigh the power of the others; yet the authority of those with lesser power remains.

Sources of Authority

Theory X, the work-centered approach, relates the source of authority to the right to own property. The right to own property and the association of authority with that right are dependent on the organization of the society in which we live. Relating the source of authority to the right to own property and the subsequent management of that property may be termed an *institutional* source of authority since it is dependent on the institution of organized society. Theory Y, the people-centered approach, regards authority as a situational phenomenon. Authority exists only when the subordinates of a situation accept another individual as having the authority to direct them. Therefore, this source of authority may be designated as *subordinate acceptance.*

Institutional Source. To state that authority is derived from the right to own private property is a narrow view of the source of authority and not entirely correct since there are instances of managerial authority not dependent on the ownership of property. To discover the source of authority one must first determine why it is possible to own private property. Our constitutional form of government in the United States rests on the concept that government represents the will of the people, a will expressed through the action of elected representatives in Congress and enforced by a judicial system. One aspect of our legal system is that it permits the ownership of private property and the management of that property in accordance with established law. Thus, the real source of managerial authority lies not in the right to own property, but rather in the laws that permit the ownership of property. Case Problem 10-A states that the Muskegon Machine Works is a Delaware Corporation, a statement which indicates that the company is created by law and, as such, possesses the authority necessary for its operation. Further evidence emphasizing that authority is derived from law and not the ownership of property is illustrated by the Tennessee Valley Authority. The managerial authority exercised by the managers of TVA, a publicly owned and operated utility, is derived from an action of Congress, which created the Tennessee Valley Authority. The authority of the management of TVA can come from no other source than law since the ownership of private property is not involved.[1]

Subordinate Acceptance. The following story, told by Douglas McGregor, illustrates the need for subordinates to accept authority if that authority is to be effective:

---

[1] Cyril J. O'Donnell, "The Source of Managerial Authority," *Political Science Quarterly,* Vol. 47 (December, 1952), p. 573. Professor O'Donnell's article is a skillful presentation of authority derived from institutional sources.

An agent for the Textile Workers Union of America likes to tell the story of the occasion when a new manager appeared in the mill where he was working. The manager came into a weave room the day he arrived. He walked directly over to the agent and said, "Are you Belloc?" The agent acknowledged that he was. The manager said, "I am the new manager here. When I manage a mill, I run it. Do you understand?" The agent nodded and then waved his hand. The workers, intently watching this maneuver, shut down every loom in the room immediately. The agent turned to the manager and said, "All right, go ahead and run it." [2]

This story illustrates, according to the subordinate-acceptance approach, that the manager has no authority because the subordinates—the workers in the mill room—refuse to accept the manager's authority.

Among the first to dissent from the institutional concept of authority was Chester I. Barnard, a successful business executive, who, in the words of Morton J. Mandeville, "writes with authority about authority." [3] The following quotations from Barnard present his definition of authority and the related concept that the source of authority is its acceptance by a subordinate.

> Authority is the character of a communication (order) in a formal organization by virtue of which it is accepted by a contributor to or "member" of the organization as governing the action he contributes, that is, as governing or determining what he does or is not to do so far as the organization is concerned. [4]

Barnard's statement concerning the source of authority follows:

> If a directive communication is accepted by one to whom it is addressed, its authority for him is confirmed or established. It is admitted as the basis of action. Disobedience of such a communication is a denial of its authority for him. Therefore, under this definition the decision as to whether an order has authority or not lies with the person to whom it is addressed, and does not reside in "persons of authority" or those who issue these orders. [5]

Before us are two conflicting views of authority. One, the institutional approach, says that authority is derived from the laws of the society in which we live. The other view of authority, the subordinate-acceptance approach, says that there is no authority unless the person who is the object of that authority accepts the order or directive as authoritative. One approach to reconciling these different views concerning the source of authority is to examine the factors contributing to the effectiveness of authority.

Effectiveness of Authority

Effective management requires a manager to have a clear understanding of the nature of authority. Managerial authority is not absolute; however, a

---

[2] Douglas McGregor, *The Human Side of Enterprise* (New York City: McGraw-Hill, Inc., 1960), p. 23.

[3] Morton J. Mandeville, "Organizational Authority," *Academy of Management Journal*, Vol. 3 (August, 1960), p. 107.

[4] Chester Barnard, *The Function of the Executive* (Cambridge: Harvard University Press, 1938), p. 163.

[5] *Ibid.*

manager cannot afford to be reduced to a state of indecision resulting from self-questioning concerning the right to manage. On the other hand, the manager cannot blithely assume that every action or directive will result in the fulfillment of organizational goals. There are three structural or organizational factors that limit the effectiveness of managerial authority: (1) superior authority, (2) overlapping authority, and (3) subordinate acceptance of authority. Note that subordinate acceptance does not negate or cancel managerial authority; *it merely limits the effectiveness of that authority.* Let us examine each of the three limitations on authority.

Superior Authority. The actions of the officers of a corporation are subject to review and limitations imposed by the board of directors. In Case Problem 10-A, the president of the company calls for a meeting of the board to review current labor negotiations. In so doing he is recognizing the higher authority of the board and seeking a course of action that meets with their approval. The board, in turn, is subject to the legal authority of the owners, the state, and the federal government. Companies impose limitations on the authority of managers by establishing policies and procedures; for example, a plant manager may be authorized to make capital expenditures up to $1,000 without prior approval, but required to submit for approval expenditures in excess of $1,000. These instances illustrate that authority is not absolute; rather, it is always subject to limitation by higher authority.

Overlapping Authority. Problem 3 of Case Problem 10-A asks whether or not the action of the union, i.e., the calling of a strike, negates or cancels the authority of management. If the source of authority lies in the acceptance of that authority by subordinates, then the answer to Problem 3 is affirmative. Now, analyze the situation carefully. The company, a corporation created by law, is exercising proper authority in determining what it believes to be best for its economic welfare. The union, too, is created by law and is certified by the National Labor Relations Board as the official bargaining agent for the employees of the Muskegon Machine Works. Also, the union is exercising properly the authority granted by law in enforcing its economic demands by striking. Thus, here is a situation in which both parties are exercising legally constituted authority to determine the wage rates of the employees of the company. Clearly there is overlapping and dual authority, with each authority having the same source, law, and each authority being properly exercised. The rejection of the company's offer by the union and the subsequent strike do not negate the authority of management; it simply means that at this time the power of the union is sufficient to prevent the management from exercising its authority to operate the plant. Later, as the strike progresses, the company may accede partially or fully to the union's demands, or the union may agree to the original offer made by the company. Authority is not cancelled by power conflicts, which arise frequently when authority overlaps; it is only held in abeyance until the forces of power are resolved.

Subordinate Acceptance. Some proponents of the subordinate-acceptance concept of authority leave the impression that disobedience and the rejection of authority are the normal behavior for members of an organization. Nothing could be further from the truth. The institutions of society, including authority, serve a purpose desired by the majority of that society; however, occasions do arise when subordinates refuse to accept authority. Most authority carries with it rewards and penalties that may be used to encourage compliance. Those who recognize authority as derived from the acceptance of subordinates also recognize that the weighing of rewards and penalties by subordinates is an important factor in their determining whether or not to accept authority. The weighing of rewards and penalties is in effect a recognition of authority. Disobedience does not cancel authority, but it does render it ineffective for that particular situation unless the reward or punishment is sufficient to exact compliance.

Authority and Power

Although there are many connotations associated with authority, the term *authority* has been defined as the *right* to act or to direct the actions of others in the attainment of organizational goals. *Power* is viewed as a force that results in a form of behavior that would not have occurred had that force not been used. Power is also defined as the ability or capacity to overcome resistance and to introduce change despite opposition. Power has also been referred to as the performance of an act that results in a change in another person. Sociologists have extended the concept of power from a relationship between individuals to the relationship between groups; that is, the ability of one group to influence another.[6] There is general consensus that power is the *ability* of a person or a group to change the behavior of another person or group; a definition which permits a differentiation between authority and power. Authority is the right to act, but that authority remains dormant unless the person or group having that authority has the ability (power) to exercise that authority in a manner that results in a change in the behavior of others.

Two major sources of authority were mentioned—an institutional or societal source, and the concept of subordinate acceptance. There are several sources of power and differing ways of exercising power so that change occurs in another person or group. The sources of a manager's power in formal organizations are related to that manager's position, the perceptions that subordinates have of the manager, and the extent of subordinate dependency on the organization. All these factors relate to the leader's or manager's position in the organization and are commonly referred to as *position power*. Position power as a source corresponds roughly to the institutional source of authority. Subordinates in formal organizations also have power. Paradoxically it is a power that stems

---

[6] For a brief review of the various definitions of power the following is recommended. Ahmad N. Azim and F. Glenn Boseman, "An Empirical Assessment of Etzioni's Topology of Power and Involvement within a University Setting," *Academy of Management Journal*, Vol. 18, No. 4 (December, 1975), p. 680.

from their subordinate position and gives subordinates the ability to control, within limits, the behavior of superiors. Each source of power—position power and subordinate power—is discussed in turn.

Position Power. There are many classifications of sources and types of power. Perhaps the best known and most widely accepted is that of French and Raven, which sets forth the following five sources of leader or managerial power in formal organizations: (1) position power or legitimate power, (2) coercive power, (3) reward power, (4) expertise power, and (5) referent or charismatic power.[7]

Position power, also known as *legitimate power*, is derived from the leader's or manager's position within the organizational hierarchy. Managers may enhance their power and consequent ability to exercise their authority through strategic planning, the design and control of information systems, and the formulation of policies and procedures. Also derived from the position is the power to delegate authority with its attendant power to subordinates. Associated with the power to delegate authority is the power to veto the actions of subordinates. Occasionally an overly ambitious manager seeking more power for his or her position disturbs the delicate balance of power between various positions within the organization. When other managers react to protect the powers of their respective positions, the well-known power struggle ensues.

Coercive power and reward power are commonly used as a means of controlling the actions of subordinates. *Coercive power* relies upon the use of sanctions, such as suspension, passing one over for a promotion or a salary increase, demotion, and the most severe industrial penalty of all—discharge. *Reward power* is the opposite side of the coin. It is the manager's ability to offer rewards to subordinates for appropriate behavior in the form of promotions, increased levels of responsibility and pay, and the granting of public recognition. However, the effectiveness of coercive power and reward power is dependent on the perceptions and needs of subordinates. For coercive power to be effective the subordinate must fear punishment and have a need to remain a member of the organization. Similarly, rewards are not effective unless there is an expectation and a need for reward as a form of recognition by a superior who represents the organization.

The effectiveness of expertise power and charismatic, or referent, power, is also dependent on the perceptions of subordinates. *Expertise*, in the form of specialized knowledge, skills, or abilities, is often a requisite in the selection of a manager and the granting of authority to that manager. Examples range from the specialized skills and knowledge of the conductor of a symphony orchestra to the engineering and technical knowledge required of the president of an electronics company. But subordinates must recognize such expertise and defer to that expertise if it is to be an effective source of power. In order for

---

[7] J. R. P. French and B. Raven, "The Basis of Social Power," *Studies in Social Power*, edited by D. Cartwright (Ann Arbor, MI.: Institute for Social Research, 1959), p. 150.

For a brief analysis of several models of power, the following is recommended: James A. Lee, "Leader Power for Managing Change," *The Academy of Management Review*, Vol. 2, No. 1 (January, 1977), p. 73.

a leader to be described as charismatic, outstanding personality traits must be completely acceptable to the subordinate. The source of *referent* or *charismatic power* is based upon subordinates' willingness and desire to identify with and accept certain personal characteristics as necessary for leadership. It is the belief that leaders must somehow stand apart from their followers in regard to personal characteristics.

Subordinate Power. The power associated with the manager's position is circumscribed to some extent by the countervailing power of subordinates. Although there is no agreed upon definitive list of sources of subordinate power, such as the one developed by French and Raven, David Mechanic has presented one of the most comprehensive analyses of subordinate power.[8]

Case Problem 10-A is an example of overlapping authority; that is, both the company and the union have legal rights to their respective positions. When subordinates, as members of a union, engage in collective bargaining it is known as *collective power*. In addition, as individuals subordinates have *legal powers* granted by federal and state statutes to guarantee fair treatment and to guard against discrimination in the work place because of race, sex, religion, national origin, age, or handicap.

In our discussion of coercive and reward power, it was stated that the effectiveness of those powers is dependent on the subordinates' perception of the organization and their need to remain members of the organization. As subordinates become economically more independent and their need to remain a member of a given organization diminishes, the coercive and reward powers of the manager become less effective. Such economic independence has been termed *affluence power*.

Seldom are managers able to perform all the tasks required to complete the various functions under their direction. Subordinates may develop an *expert power* of their own that is dependent on a long period of training and experience, responsibility, and the importance of their work to the attainment of the objectives of the organization. For example, several major paper companies and airlines have a vice-president in charge of maintenance as part of their top corporate structure. Subordinates with their expertise have the ability to influence the behavior of their superiors since they can make that superior appear either effective or ineffective.

LINE AND STAFF RELATIONSHIPS

The preceding discussion emphasizes superior-subordinate relationships—the relationships between the managers and the workers of an organization. There is another authority relationship that is equally important—the relationship between two different types of authority exercised by the managers of an

---

[8] David Mechanic, "Sources of Power of Lower Participants in Complex Organizations," *Administrative Science Quarterly*, Vol. 7, No. 1 (June, 1962), p. 349. See also Richard T. Mowday, "The Exercise of Upward Influence in Organizations," *Administrative Science Quarterly*, Vol. 23, No. 1 (March, 1978), p. 137.

organization. These two forms of authority are called *line authority* and *staff authority*, designations of authority that result in the corresponding expressions of *line organization* and *staff organization,* phrases which classify the entire organization according to the predominant type of authority exercised. In discussing line-and-staff authority relationships, we seek answers to the following four questions:

1. What is line authority and what are its functions?
2. What is staff authority and what are its functions?
3. What are the problems inherent in line and staff relationships?
4. Is the line-and-staff concept of authority obsolete?

Line Authority

The concept of line-and-staff authority recognizes that within an organization there are two types of managerial authority. There are also two aspects to the definition of line authority. First, line authority may be defined as a relatively simple authority relationship that exists between a superior and a subordinate. Second, line authority may be defined in terms of the organizational function supervised by a manager. When line authority is defined with respect to organizational function, the critical characteristic of the function that determines whether it is line or staff is the degree to which the function in question contributes to the direct achievement of organizational objectives. Let us examine each aspect of line authority.

An Authority Relationship. When defined as an authority relationship, line authority entitles a superior to direct the work of a subordinate—in essence a command relationship. It is a command relationship extending from the top of the organization to the lowest echelon and is aptly described as the *chain of command*, as shown in Figure 10–1. As a link in the chain of command, a manager has the authority to direct the work of subordinates, and, in turn, is subject to the direction of a superior.[9] Each manager reports "in line" to a superior and is a part of the line organization. Figure 10–1 shows the relationships that form the chain of command in an organization.

Contribution to Organizational Objectives. The second definition of line authority does not contradict the above view which holds that line authority is a command relationship between superior and subordinate. It does, however, shift the emphasis of the definition from one of relationship between superior and subordinate to organizational function. The shift in emphasis results in the following definition: The line functions of an organization are those functions that contribute directly to the creation and distribution of the goods or services of the organization.

---

[9] For a discussion of the point of view that every manager is a subordinate, the following is suggested: Andre Laurent, "Managerial Subordinacy: A Neglected Aspect of Organizational Hierarchies," *The Academy of Management Review,* Vol. 3, No. 2 (April, 1978), p. 220.

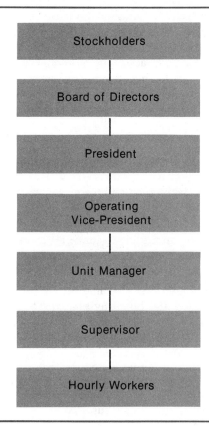

**Figure 10–1
LINE
AUTHORITY
RELATIONSHIP
AS A CHAIN OF
COMMAND**

The key to distinguishing between line and staff is not the function itself; rather, it is the degree to which the function contributes directly to the achievement of organizational objectives. In an army, the infantry, the artillery, and armored units are known as "line" since they contribute directly to organizational objectives—engaging the enemy in battle; the supporting services—ordnance, medical, engineering, and supply—are regarded as auxiliary in nature and referred to as "staff." In manufacturing organizations, production and sales are regarded as line functions, while purchasing (supplies) is usually classified as staff. Yet in a department store, the purchasing function, called buying, and sales make up the line organization. Most firms regard finance as a staff function, but for a loan company the acquisition and management of capital is part of the line organization. In each of these examples, the basis for designating a function as line is the contribution of that function to the direct achievement of organizational objectives.

Staff Authority

Staff authority is advisory or service in nature. A member of management possessing staff authority advises or provides a service for line managers. An organization may function quite effectively without any designated staff managers, and in small organizations such is the case.

In Case Problem 9-A, Thomas Jackson, the general manager of Excelsior Products, is effectively managing an organization of 22 sales representatives and 3 clerks. Assume that, as a first step in developing an organization structure capable of extended growth, Jackson appoints five regional sales managers, each of whom is responsible for the sales in one geographic area. These managers are line managers since they report directly to Jackson. They have the authority to direct the work of the sales representatives and are fully responsible for and contribute directly to the achievement of the organization's primary goal of selling its product. The first step in the development of staff might occur when Jackson employs Tom Richards as a *personal* assistant. At first the duties of Tom Richards are not specified, but in a letter to the sales managers, Jackson states that Richards is to function as his personal assistant. Perhaps Richards' first assignment is to make all arrangements for the next sales meeting. Then he completes a statistical analysis of the dollar volume of sales for each of the many products that Excelsior sells. Eventually Jackson may assign Richards to the specific job of training new sales representatives and discover that training demands the full time of a specialist. As a next step, he may hire someone whose sole function is the training of new sales representatives. Thus, the undifferentiated work of the personal assistant may develop into a specialized staff role.

This example illustrates that the need for staff services arises partially as the result of increasing size in an organization with an attendant increase in the work load of the chief executive.[10] Consequently, one of the functions of staff is to ease the load of top management. The personal assistant is frequently engaged as a means of easing the work load. As size increases, operations usually become more complex and the need for specialized services arises and results in the creation of a specialized staff. These two forms of staff, which are termed *personal staff* and *specialized staff,* are discussed briefly.

Personal Staff. There is need to define clearly the difference between an *assistant-to* a manager and an *assistant* manager. The assistant-to is a personal assistant to the manager. Duties vary widely from one organization to another and they also vary considerably from time to time within the same company. The assistant-to receives the necessary authority to perform duties from the manager and usually the authority is granted on a limited basis; that is, it is extended for a specific job and for a relatively short period of time. The duties of an assistant-to may range from the routine task of opening the chief executive's mail to negotiating a purchase agreement for a new plant site as a personal representative of the chief. Note that the assistant-to usually has no specific function to perform; duties vary with the assignment at hand. Second, there

---

[10] For a discussion of the relationship between size and complexity in the staff function the following is recommended: S. R. Klatzky, "Relationship of Organizational Size to Complexity and Coordination," *Administrative Science Quarterly*, Vol. 15, No. 4 (December, 1970), p. 428.

is no authority associated specifically with the position; it is authority granted only for each individual assignment. Third, the assistant-to acts only as a personal representative of the superior.

The assistant manager is not regarded as staff, but rather as part of the line. As shown in Figure 10–2 (A), the operating executive reports through the assistant general manager to the general manager. In the absence of the general manager, the assistant manager acts in his or her stead. The assistant-to, Figure 10–2 (B), usually does not have the authority to act as general manager when the latter is absent. The general manager may assign certain specific functions to the assistant manager. For example, all activities related to manufacturing may be reported to the assistant manager, while the general manager supervises those activities associated with sales. Another possible arrangement is for the general manager to oversee the line functions of the organization, while all staff services report to the assistant manager. In each of these possibilities we note that (1) subordinates report directly to the assistant manager, (2) the assistant manager is assigned fairly constant, well-defined responsibilities, and (3) in the absence of the general manager, the assistant manager assumes the full authority of the general manager's position.

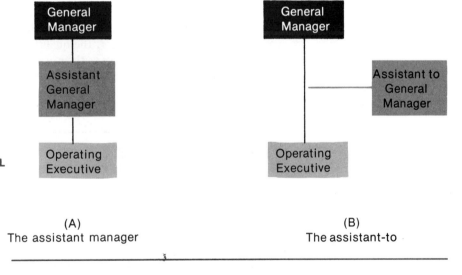

Figure 10–2
ORGANIZATIONAL
POSITION OF
THE ASSISTANT
GENERAL
MANAGER AND
THE ASSISTANT-
TO THE
GENERAL
MANAGER

(A)
The assistant manager

(B)
The assistant-to

Specialized Staff. As an organization grows in size and complexity, the undifferentiated role of the personal assistant develops into specialized staff assignments. There is no unanimity concerning the functions that may be performed by specialized staff personnel, nor is there complete agreement concerning the type of authority that may be exercised by staff managers. Nonetheless, the following three types of specialized staff authority appear in formal organizations with great frequency:

1. A staff specialist may have the authority to provide a specific *service* for the line organization and thus exercise *service authority*.
2. Not all staff positions are created for the purpose of providing service; some have as their sole function the offering of advice concerning a special group of problems. Staff personnel in these positions exercise *advisory authority*.
3. Another type of specialized staff authority is *functional authority*, an authority that provides the staff specialist with considerable latitude and freedom to make decisions in a given functional area.

It must be understood that these three forms of staff authority are not clear cut; there is considerable overlap, and many positions utilize all three forms of staff authority.

Figure 10–3 shows a typical staff organization at the plant level of a manufacturing firm. The production planning and control supervisor is responsible for planning and controlling the flow of production; the purchasing supervisor serves by making necessary purchases; and the plant engineer is responsible for maintaining physical facilities. The supervision of each of these functions exercises *service authority* in providing a service for the line organization. The authority of the personnel supervisor may be either service authority or advisory authority. When performing the employment function of recruiting and screening applicants, the personnel supervisor is clearly rendering a service for the line. Other duties may include the administration and analysis of morale surveys with the purpose of advising the line regarding actions necessary to improve employee morale. The staff supervisor, when offering advice to the line, is drawing upon advisory authority. The industrial engineer, the quality control supervisor, and the head of the accounting department have as their primary function the offering of advice in specialized areas; and though there is a strong element of service in the work that each performs, it is best to regard their authority as *advisory* in nature.

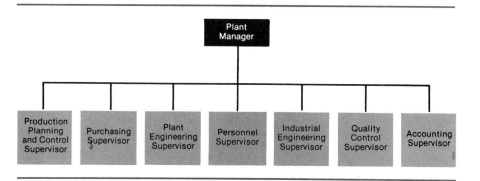

Figure 10–3 TYPICAL STAFF ORGANIZATION AT THE PLANT LEVEL

Functional authority broadens the concept of service and advisory authority so that a staff manager may exercise effective direction and control of a functional specialty. There are two ways of exercising functional authority. First, staff managers may be granted functional authority over their counterparts who are in lower levels of the organization; and second, the particular functional specialty in question may be separated from the line manager's job and assigned to the appropriate staff specialist.[11] Figure 10–4 shows both forms of functional authority. Note that the supervisor of each staff function reports functionally (usually indicated by a dotted line) to the staff counterpart at the next higher level. In large organizations this next higher level may be a geographic division, and the managers at the divisional level report to their counterparts on the corporate staff. In addition, the plant staff supervisor performs that portion of the production foreman's job which falls within a specialty. Thus, there are cost clerks in the production department who report to the supervisor of cost accounting and prepare all production costs. The plant industrial engineer supervises time studies and institutes changes in methods, and the quality control supervisor directs the work of inspectors who accept or reject the finished product. Although functional staff authority is limited to a specific function, it may sometimes be quite absolute within that particular function, with the result that the authority of the line manager may be severely restricted.[12]

Problems in Line-Staff (L/S) Relationships

The duality of the line-staff (L/S) concept inherently creates problems of interpersonal relationships. Two authorities exist within an organization—line authority with its right to command, and staff authority with its right to advise. There is a duality of function—the line function is associated with the achievement of primary company objectives and the staff function supports the line. It is a duality that results in referring to an organization as though it were two separate units—the line organization and the staff organization. The concepts of dual authorities, functions, and organizations set the stage for some rather serious misunderstandings between those who are designated as line and those designated as staff. The reasons for L/S misunderstandings and friction may be traced to the way in which the individuals involved define their respective roles within an organization with respect to responsibility and importance of function.[13]

---

[11] Frederick W. Taylor referred to the assignment of the specialized portions of the production foreman's job to the appropriate staff specialist as "functional foremanship." Further, he recommended that all the "brain work" be eliminated from the foreman's job and that the worker come in contact with many members of management for directions rather than just one member—the foreman.

Frederick W. Taylor, *Scientific Management* (New York City: Harper & Row, Publishers, Inc., 1947), p. 98.

[12] For a discussion of the functional authority of a specific staff specialist, the controller, the following is recommended: Dale A. Henning and Robert L. Moseley, "Authority Role of a Functional Manager: The Controller," *Administrative Science Quarterly*, Vol. 15, No. 4 (December, 1970), p. 482.

[13] For a discussion of line-staff relationships within the context of a systems framework, see Charles Coleman and Joseph Rich, "Line, Staff, and the Systems Perspective," *Human Resource Management*, Vol. 12, No. 3 (Fall, 1973), p. 20.

For a study of how individuals perceive themselves as either line or staff, the following is of value: Philip J. Browne and Robert T. Golembiewski, "The Line-Staff Concept Revisited: An Empirical Study of Organizational Images," *Academy of Management Journal*, Vol. 17, No. 3 (September, 1974), p. 406.

Another approach to the resolution of line-staff problems is the following: Vivian Nossiter, "A New Approach Toward Resolving the Line and Staff Dilemma," *Academy of Management Review*, Vol. 4, No. 1 (January, 1979), p. 103.

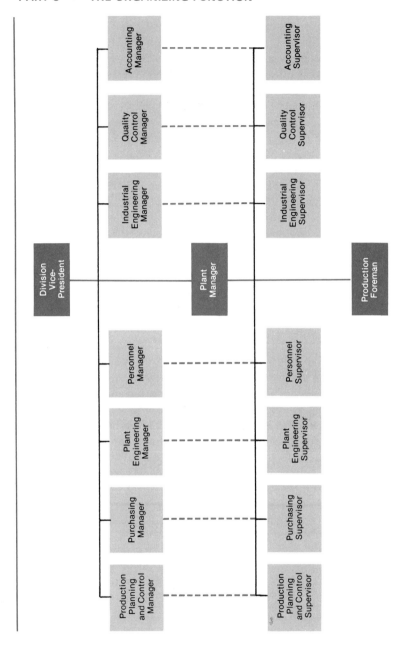

Figure 10–4
THE EXERCISE OF FUNCTIONAL AUTHORITY

Staff department supervisors report functionally to the next higher level, and the specialized portions of the production foreman's job are assigned to the appropriate staff specialist.

Responsibility. It is generally agreed that the line manager is responsible for achieving the primary objectives of the organization. When the organization is small and there is no staff, there are no restraints other than superior line authority on the line manager's freedom to make decisions and initiate action necessary to achieve the stated goals. When staff is introduced, restraints appear, for it is implied that the line manager should consult with staff. Frequently line managers view consultation with staff as an infringement upon their authority to manage, and the resulting resentment toward staff is expressed through such statements as "staff is impractical," "staff does not appreciate the technical problems," and "consultation means delay." Line may accuse staff of trying to take all the credit when things go well and at the same time be unwilling to accept any responsibility for failure.

However, it is the presence of functional staff with its authority to administer its own particular function that presents the severest test of interpersonal L/S relationships. For example, the president of a company that is one of several subsidiaries of a large corporation is responsible for the profits of that subsidiary; and, as a means of emphasizing this responsibility, part of the president's incentive pay is based on the profitability of the company. At the same time the corporate industrial relations staff, empowered by functional authority, is expected to negotiate the labor agreements for all subsidiary companies to prevent the various unions from playing one company against another. Thus, the president is responsible for profits, but one of the major cost factors—wages and work rules—is determined to a large extent by staff personnel who do not report to the responsible executive. Is it any wonder that resentment toward staff arises? It is only normal that friction builds up in a situation in which one believes that a significant part of the decision making and control necessary to operate effectively is lost, and the resulting tensions are expressed as a specific resentment toward staff. The same situation holds for the line managers in lower levels of the organization. The production foreman may be responsible for the costs of a department, yet the requirements of staff may force the hiring of additional clerks. To summarize, one of the main sources of friction between line and staff is the manner in which the line manager defines responsibilities. When the line manager defines responsibility, or when it is defined for the manager, as *total* responsibility, it is only normal to resent any intrusion of authority that tends to weaken the manager's control of the situation.

Importance of Function. Staff's infringement on the line manager's authority to manage is the major cause of L/S conflict from the point of view of line, but the idea that staff functions are supportive, with the attendant implication that they are secondary and somehow less important, is the main source of L/S conflict as viewed by staff managers. To understand staff's position, it is necessary to state briefly the personal characteristics of staff personnel. As a rule, staff personnel are highly ambitious and eager to advance, and they are somewhat younger and have a higher level of formal education than their line counterparts. Staff managers are also aware that the reason for their employment is their specialized knowledge, and, since they are ambitious and desire to advance, it is only natural that they advance by the avenue which seems most logical to them—advancing their ideas. When their ideas are restricted by line, they are told that it is the function of line to decide and that their role is supportive in nature. To the staff employee the statement that line makes the decision is a distortion of what happens in practice, if not pure fiction. The following example supports staff's contention that it is staff, not line, who makes critical decisions or, at the very least, makes it possible for the line manager to decide.[14]

In a typical manufacturing organization, the manager of manufacturing is responsible for producing the product and the sales manager is responsible for distributing the product. Both are line managers whose activities are coordinated by a higher line authority, a president or a general manager. Who determines how much of each product is to be manufactured and the sequence in which these items are to be produced and sold? As a result of analyzing market trends and customer needs, the staff manager of the market research department recommends the optimum product mix. The manager of production planning and inventory control, another staff department, interprets and translates the findings of market research into production schedules that specify quantity and sequence for manufacture of each product. Though the sales manager approves the recommendations of market research and the production manager approves schedules developed by production planning and inventory control, it is understandable why staff managers of market research and production planning consider that they in effect make the decisions. It is difficult to relegate either staff function to a supportive role when the very nature of these functions influences so greatly the success of the company in fulfilling its primary objectives—the manufacture and the distribution of a product.

Is Line-Staff Obsolete?

Conflict between line and staff has long been recognized as a major deterrent to organizational effectiveness, with the result that many students of management have offered suggestions to minimize such conflict. Such recommendations state that line has the final responsibility for the successful operation of the company and consequently should have the authority to make operating decisions. Staff functions are carefully defined as providing either service or advice to the line; an advice or service that should be presented when requested by line and also when, in the opinion of staff, it is considered necessary. It is suggested that whether or not staff's advice or service is accepted depends entirely on the judgment of line, and line is urged to seriously consider staff recommendations. The last recommendation suggests that both line and staff have the right of appeal to higher authority.

The recommendations presented above are helpful in some cases; however, such recommendations are of limited value primarily because they rest on assumptions that are of questionable validity. These assumptions are (1) that

---

[14] For a discussion of what staff personnel seek, the following is recommended: Neil B. Holbert, "The Life of Staff," *Business Horizons*, Vol. 21, No. 3 (June, 1978), p. 79.

line managers will accept the advice and recommendations of staff and (2) that staff is able and willing to accept a supportive role in the organization and continue to put forth its best effort when in fact its recommendations may be ignored. Also, recommendations for improving line-staff relationships implicitly assume that the line-staff concept is necessary for organizational effectiveness. There are two alternatives to the line-staff concept that deserve careful consideration.

Functional Teamwork. Functional teamwork is an organizational concept presented by Gerald Fisch, a management consultant, as an alternate to the line-staff concept.[15] It is suggested that three functional areas be defined and each area represent a function significant to the well-being of the organization. In addition to defining functional areas that are grouped under *time, resources,* and *human interrelations,* the task of top management is carefully defined. Let us see how the many activities of a business organization that are classed as either line or staff are treated under the functional teamwork concept.

Process Functions. All functions within the business that must be controlled with *time* as a major element are classed as *process functions*. Included as process functions are product design, purchasing, manufacturing, advertising, physical distribution (sales), and billing. Note that in this arrangement the usual line functions of sales and manufacturing are grouped with functions normally regarded as staff to form a functional unit concerned with the movement of the product from its inception in product design, through manufacturing, the distribution system, and the final billing—all related activities accomplished under the pressure of time; hence, they are process functions.

Resources Function. All resources—physical, monetary, and human—are considered part of the resources of a company, and it is the function of the resources manager to acquire, maintain, and utilize these resources in the most efficient manner possible. Physical facilities, capital invested in the business, the skills of employees, and patents on products or processes are all considered as resources that should be carefully controlled and utilized.

Relations Function. The relations function can be summed up in one word, communications, and it includes both internal and external communications. Business in our society has an acute communications problem; and, in most companies, little is being done to present a consistent, coherent picture of the company and its problems to employee groups, shareholders, the community, various government agencies, and customers. These are the relations that would be supervised by the director of the relations function.

General Management. Though not a function in the same sense as the above three functions, general management deserves particular attention under the

---

[15] Gerald G. Fisch, "Line-Staff Is Obsolete," *Harvard Business Review*, Vol. 39 (September–October, 1961), p. 67. This section is based on Fisch's article which states the author's belief that the line-staff concept is obsolete. In place of the line-staff (L/S) concept, Fisch suggests *functional teamwork* (F/T). The first part of the article presents a careful analysis of the line-staff concept and the second part presents in detail the functional-teamwork concept.

functional teamwork concept. With the day-to-day work allocated to the three functional managers, the top management of the organization is free to establish corporate goals and objectives, to offer leadership when needed, to coordinate and realign the functions when necessary, and to control the entire operation.

There are several characteristics of the functional teamwork concept that differentiate it from the line-staff concept of organization. First, there is only one authority, managerial authority, that is exercised by each of the managers of the process, resources, or relations function within each functional area. Second, once the goals of the organization are established and the resources determined to be adequate for the project at hand, the decisions concerning the production of the company's product or services fall within a logical framework. Third, a structure encouraging teamwork is stressed so that, when the actions of one function touch on those of another function, the problem is one of resolving the question on a teamwork basis rather than determining which party has the superior authority. Also, top management is free to encourage a teamwork solution to problems as they arise.

Task Force Organization. The functional teamwork concept implies a fundamental redesign of the organization structure. An approach similar to functional teamwork, though generally much more limited in its scope, is often called *task force organization* or *task force management.* Like functional teamwork, a task force is essentially a team effort. There are several distinctive characteristics of a task force. First, it is a tightly organized unit under the direction of a manager who usually has broad powers of authority. Second, a task force is organized to accomplish a specific task or goal such as the introduction of a new product or building and placing in operation a new physical facility. A task force is working against a time deadline since its objectives must be accomplished by a certain date. Third, the personnel who make up the task force possess a diverse range of skills and abilities, thus making it possible for each member of the group to make a unique contribution to the solution of the problem.[16]

A good example of the application of the task force concept of organization to the solution of a specific problem is Minneapolis-Honeywell's Polaris Missile task force headed by a manager of the team with a production manager, an account manager, a subcontract manager, and a procurement manager reporting to the manager. The task force organization is also successfully used in such diverse activities as construction, advertising, military fighting units, and motion picture film production. Whenever there is a need for concerted team effort to

---

[16] The following two papers discuss some of the problems that may arise in either functional teamwork or task force organization: Hans J. Thamhain and Gary R. Gemmill, "Influence Styles of Project Managers: Some Project Performance Correlates," *Academy of Management Journal,* Vol. 17, No. 2 (June, 1974), p. 216; David L. Wilemon and John P. Cicero, "The Project Manager— Anomalies and Ambiguities," *Academy of Management Journal,* Vol. 13, No. 3 (September, 1970), p. 269.

For a discussion of the concept of the application of task force organization to new product development see James D. Hlavacek and Victor A. Thompson, "Bureaucracy and New Product Innovation," *Academy of Management Journal,* Vol. 16, No. 3 (September, 1973), p. 361.

accomplish a specific goal within a relatively short period of time, the creation of a task force may offer a means of creating an organization capable of accomplishing the desired goals.[17]

There is no universal answer to the question raised at the beginning of this section—is line-staff obsolete? The line-staff concept serves many companies very well, particularly those companies operating in an environment of minimal change. However, when stress situations appear with the accompanying need for prompt action in order to survive, many companies turn to the functional teamwork concept of organization by creating a task force to solve the immediate problem. Since the application of the concept of functional teamwork is effective in a crisis situation, it is only logical to consider the possibility of applying the functional teamwork approach to organization as a continuing form of organizational structure to insure the maximum utilization of resources in meeting the daily challenges of competition. In addition to stress situations with their accompanying need for prompt action, the introduction of integrated information-decision-making systems also calls for a reexamination of the line-staff concept. Such systems cut across traditional departmental lines and functions with a resultant change in the locus of the decision-making function. Modern information systems also result in the creation of large functional units composed of several traditional line-staff departments. Further, when the need for interaction between the members of an organization is high, the functional teamwork concept offers a structure that makes possible highly effective communications.

Case Problem 10-B offers you an opportunity, as a chief executive, to resolve a typical conflict taking place between a line manager and a staff specialist.

Case Problem 10-B
LINE-STAFF RELATIONSHIPS

The Glass Container Company, with headquarters in Chicago, is a large manufacturer of glass containers that operates 18 plants located throughout the United States. The company has three geographic divisions—Eastern, Central, and Pacific—each of which is headed by a vice-president and general manager who is responsible for the sales and manufacturing functions within that division. The Central Division's general manager is a young, aggressive executive who seems destined to become the president of the company. Under his direction the profits and sales volume of the division have grown each day, a growth due in large part to the successful operations of the Minneapolis plant. The manager of the Minneapolis plant, a graduate engineer, was brought into the

---

[17] A. K. Wicksberg and T. C. Cronin, "Management by Task Force," *Harvard Business Review*, Vol. 40 (November–December, 1962), p. 111. In this article the authors stress team effort in task force management and offer practical suggestions for the reassignment of personnel after the completion of a specific project.

company as a plant manager as part of a planned program to strengthen the management of the company. Plans are now being made to transfer the Minneapolis manager to the corporate headquarters in Chicago, thus making it necessary to select a new manager for Minneapolis.

In Chicago, there is a director of organizational planning who is a member of the corporate staff and reports directly to the president of the company. At the suggestion of the director of organizational planning, the Minneapolis plant manager was recruited from outside the company, since a survey of key personnel indicated a need for technically trained managers. Normally the director of organizational planning works directly with the division vice-presidents in an advisory capacity; and when she and the vice-president agree on a proposed move of key personnel, the move is made without consulting the president of the company. However, when there is disagreement, the matter is usually referred to the president who makes the final decision.

There is still a need for graduate engineers capable of filling top managerial positions that are presently available and those expected to develop within the next five years as the result of expansion and the retirement of present personnel. It is believed by all concerned that sound preparation for top management should include two or three years of experience as a plant manager as a means of learning the technical aspects of the glass container industry.

In regard to the Minneapolis position, there are three possible choices. First, another manager can be recruited from outside the company and be assigned to the Minneapolis plant as manager, thus providing a period of training with subsequent assignment to a more responsible position in the corporation. Second, there are several young assistant plant managers who would profit from experience as manager of a large plant; and, although it would probably take longer for any of them to develop, they too could

be promoted to more responsible positions. The third possibility is to promote the present assistant plant manager, a man who is 50 years old with 25 years' service with the company. The assistant plant manager is responsible to a large extent for the success of the plant since he directly supervises the operating departments and is thoroughly familiar with the technical aspects of glass making. However, he has indicated an unwillingness to move from the Minneapolis area and has expressed a desire to retire upon the completion of 30 years' service at age 55, which is permissible under the terms of the company's pension plan.

In discussing these three possibilities with the vice-president of the Central Division, the director of organizational planning recommended either of the first two choices and pointed out that if the third choice were adopted, it would mean the blocking of a valuable training position for at least a five-year period. She also stated that should the assistant plant manager elect to work until normal retirement at age 65 it would mean an even longer period of time before the plant could be used as a training position. However, the division vice-president insists upon promoting the present assistant plant manager. He readily admits that the promotion of the assistant plant manager will effectively block the use of that position as a training position; but he does not want to see any of the young assistant plant managers in the Minneapolis position, nor will he approve the recruitment of a manager from outside the company. To him, either of the first two choices means putting an unknown quantity into an important operating position that markedly affects the profitability of his division. In summing up his position, he tells the director of organizational planning:

"I'm charged with the responsibility of maintaining profitable operations in the plants under my direction, and the extent to which I meet this responsibility determines to a large extent my future in this company. For me to accept either a new manager from outside or a young manager from within the company whom I don't know personally is to run the risk of being responsible for a less profitable plant. I realize that you are responsible for planning for corporate organizational needs, but I'm responsible for the operating success of this division."

Since the matter could not be resolved with the vice-president of the division, the director of organizational planning decided to refer the question to the company president.

PROBLEMS

1. As president of the company, how would you decide the matter?
2. Should the director of organizational planning be given the authority to overrule the division vice-president in the functional area of organizational planning?
3. Is the concept of functional teamwork applicable in this situation? If so, how?

CHAPTER QUESTIONS FOR STUDY AND DISCUSSION

1. What concept of authority is reflected in the following statement: Authority emanates from the office or the position that a person holds and not from the person? Cite examples of such authority.
2. Do you believe that the use of power—that is, the use of rewards or punishment to enforce direction—is prevalent in most industrial organizations? What alternative is available to executives in accomplishing the work for which they are responsible?
3. What is meant by the statement that managerial authority has its source in law rather than as the result of a right to own property?
4. Has the plant manager in the story quoted on page 199 lost the authority to manage the plant since it is no longer in operation? Why or why not?
5. What conditions limit the effectiveness of managerial authority? Can you give examples of such conditions other than those cited in the text?
6. Differentiate between authority and power.
7. Is charismatic power more important to a political leader or to a leader of a formal organization such as a university, hospital, or a business?
8. The designation of a function as either line or staff depends on the directness of the contribution of the function to a particular organization. Under such circumstances does a differentiation between line-and-staff authority have any usefulness? Explain.
9. Under what conditions can one find a chain of command within a staff department?
10. What is the nature of staff authority? Under what conditions may the line responsibilities of a given manager become staff functions?
11. What advantages result from utilizing the L/S concept in industrial groups?
12. Can the functional teamwork or the task force type of organization be utilized in all organizations? Discuss.
13. Under what conditions is the traditional L/S organization most effective? What circumstances within the organization call for a reorganization along the lines of the functional teamwork or task force type of organization?

Chapter 11

Delegation and Decentralization of Authority

A NEED FOR DELEGATION

Thomas Dayton, now 41 years old, is one of several candidates who are being considered for the position of general manager of manufacturing for Engineering Products, a firm with seven manufacturing plants. A review of Tom's personnel file indicates that he joined the firm as a design engineer immediately after receiving his degree in mechanical engineering from the state university. His first assignment was on the board as a draftsman, and a notation by the supervisor of the drafting department indicates that Tom did this job willingly and well. The notation reads in part:

"Mr. Dayton is now in his sixth month as a member of the design department. There have been several occasions when he has come in voluntarily on weekends to rework drawings so that they meet the most exacting specifications. It is unheard of for Mr. Dayton to turn in work that is smudged or messy in any way."

At the end of 18 months Tom was promoted to section chief and placed in charge of ten draftsmen. As might be expected, the work from his section was almost perfect. One reason for the high level of accuracy was that Tom actually performed the work of the section checker and personally reviewed all drawings thoroughly and carefully

before passing them on to the head of the department. On more than one occasion Tom reworked the drawings of his subordinates in order to meet specified deadlines.

Following these early years in the design section, Tom's rise was steady and sure. During the time that he served as assistant manager of the research laboratory, there were several important product modifications, primarily the result of his own work and effort. After several years in research, he was transferred to one of the larger plants as assistant manager in charge of all production departments so that he could supervise the introduction to manufacturing of one of the products which he had developed. He remained in this position for over five years and during most of this time the production costs for the manufacturing departments under Tom's supervision were the lowest in the company. Upon the retirement of the plant manager, Tom was moved up to manager with the honest congratulations of all concerned. There were no reservations concerning his ability to work long and hard in order to get the job done; nor was his loyalty to the company ever questioned.

It did not take long to realize the success predicted for Tom as plant manager, that is, success measured by the operating statement. Operating efficiency increased slightly, and when combined with the substantial reduction in administrative expenses, the result was a marked increase in the profitability of the plant. However, all was not well with Tom's administration. The chief industrial engineer of the plant resigned and told Tom his reason for resigning was that he had been offered a similar position in another company at considerably more money. Yet in a conversation with the corporate general manager of industrial engineering, the following remarks were made:

"We no longer have any weekly staff meetings at the plant. These were stopped about a month after Tom became plant manager. He told us then that they were a waste of time and that if we had any special ideas about improving operations we should see him personally. Also, he now approves all changes in pay. As a department manager, I used to be able to approve pay changes for the engineers in my department as long as they were within the provisions of the corporate salary plan; but not now, because he approves all changes in pay, regardless of the amount or whether they are within the terms of the salary plan. As for overtime, he approves all overtime in advance, not only in the general administrative departments but also within the production departments, a responsibility that normally lies within the control of the assistant plant manager. And the cost control program results in his actually running all departments. We are supposed to run our departments within the limitations set by the annual budgets, but not any more. Tom wants all expense accounts sent directly to him; as department managers, we no longer see them. The switchboard operator sends him a daily tally of all long-distance telephone calls with the name of the party called, the name of the person making the call, and the amount of the call. But what really irritates me is that he plans the work of my department and calls my people into his office to check on the accuracy of their work. If he wants to run the industrial engineering department, he is welcome to do so, but he doesn't need a department manager for the job—he needs a chief clerk."

Mr. Thompson, the present general manager of manufacturing, is slated to move to the presidency of the corporation. He is a staunch supporter of Tom Dayton and points to Tom's outstanding record of success in the company. The general manager of manufacturing coordinates the production of all seven plants and is accountable to the president of the company for the performance of the plants. Traditionally there is a substantial degree of delegation of authority to the individual plant managers for day-to-day operations. Such a policy of delegation results, on occasion, in some rather expensive mistakes on the part of plant managers and the attendant temptation to step in and correct things immediately; but the net result is the development of strong plant managers and a highly efficient manufacturing organization. Mr. Thompson realizes that Tom Dayton is not a good delegator, but he believes that as president of the company, he can develop Tom into a good manufacturing manager and teach him how to delegate.

PROBLEMS

1. What are the underlying causes of Tom's failure to delegate?
2. Do you agree with Mr. Thompson that Tom can be taught how to delegate?
3. Why should a manager be criticized for his or her failure to delegate?

Chapter 10 examines the sources of authority and the interpersonal relationships that exist between those people performing line functions and those engaged in staff work. Fundamental to the exercise of managerial authority, either as line authority or staff authority, is an organizational process that permits the transmission of authority from superior to subordinate—a process called the *delegation of authority*. It is the process of delegating authority from superior to subordinate that makes it possible for organizations to grow. The extent to which organizations consistently delegate authority downward to lower level organizational units is called the *process of decentralization of authority*. In this chapter we discuss the nature of the process of delegation of authority and the behavioral aspects of delegation. Decentralization of authority is discussed with emphasis on the relative nature of decentralization. The last part of the chapter applies the contingency approach to organization theory, presented in Chapter 8, to problems of organization structure, line/staff relationships, and the processes of delegation and decentralization of authority.

DELEGATION OF AUTHORITY

Delegation of authority is an organizational process that permits the transfer of authority from superior to subordinate. There is general agreement that the process of delegation consists of three distinct steps. Although there is considerable variation in the terminology used to describe each of the three steps, those listed below are the most widely accepted.

The Process of Delegation

This text uses the following terms to describe the three aspects of the process of delegation:

1. The assignment of responsibility
2. The delegation of authority
3. The creation of accountability

Assignment of Responsibility. The term, *responsibility*, refers to the work assigned. There are several reasons for limiting the meaning of responsibility to duties, or work, to be performed in fulfilling an assignment. In our everyday speech we frequently equate responsibility and duties by referring to the responsibilities of a parent or the responsibilities of a student. Also, many companies in their descriptions of managerial positions state the responsibilities of a position as duties to be performed. Another reason for limiting the meaning of the word *responsibility* to assigned duties is that there is a specific term, *accountability*, which is used to describe the obligation created by the assignment of responsibilities.

Thus, *responsibility* is defined as all duties that must be performed in order to complete a given task.

Delegation of Authority. *Delegation* has a precise meaning. One who delegates to another person empowers that person to act for the delegator. Two facets of this definition deserve careful attention. First, the delegator *empowers* the delegatee. In Chapter 10, authority is defined as the right to act or to direct others to act. Since responsibilities—or duties—are assigned as the first step in the process of delegation, it is necessary that the person to whom responsibility is assigned either act or direct others to act in the performance of those duties. Authority empowers such action—hence, the expression, the delegation of authority, with the result that the delegatee is empowered to act or to direct others to act.

The second facet of the definition deserving careful attention is the phrase, *for the delegator.* A person possessing delegated authority is acting for, or representing, the person who delegated the authority. The implications of acting for another are significant as an organizational process because it means that even though authority is delegated to subordinates so that they may successfully fulfill their assigned duties, the delegator still retains full control over the delegated authority and may recall that authority as the occasion demands. Delegation in no way implies abdication. When a king abdicates, he divests himself of all responsibility and authority; however, an executive who delegates remains responsible for the accomplishment of assigned duties and retains full control over delegated authority.

Creation of Accountability. The moment one accepts a loan from a bank, an obligation is incurred to repay the money borrowed. Likewise, when a subordinate accepts responsibility and the authority necessary to carry out those responsibilities, an obligation is incurred—a duty to perform the assigned work and to properly utilize the delegated authority. The creation of such an obligation on the part of a subordinate, when viewed as an organizational process, is defined as the creation of *accountability.* Subordinates are *accountable* to their superiors for the proper exercise of authority and performance of assigned responsibilities. An easy way to differentiate between the concepts of responsibility and accountability is to remember that a subordinate is *responsible for* the completion of assigned work and is *accountable* to a superior for the satisfactory performance of that work.

Conditions for Effective Delegation

The preceding analysis of delegation presents a process that is relatively easy to understand and seemingly simple in nature; however, in actual practice a great deal of difficulty is experienced in achieving effective delegation. There is general agreement among students of management and management practitioners that three conditions must be met for the process of delegation to be most effective. These conditions are:

1. Parity of authority and responsibility
2. Absoluteness of accountability
3. Unity of command

Each condition is discussed briefly below.

Parity of Authority and Responsibility. For effective delegation, the authority granted to a subordinate must equal the assigned responsibility.

The concept of parity of authority and responsibility recognizes the need for delegated authority and emphasizes that delegated authority should be of sufficient scope so that the assigned responsibility may be accomplished. Too little authority usually manifests itself by managers having to consult their respective superiors before making relatively routine decisions. A manager of manufacturing, charged with the responsibility of producing the company's product within specified cost and quality limits, should be able to make decisions pertaining to purchasing raw materials, maintenance of equipment, selection and training of personnel, and the determination of the most efficient methods of manufacturing. In short, the authority granted should be of sufficient scope so that all related activities may be accomplished.

Although the granting of too little authority is a frequent reason for ineffective delegation, failure to fully understand and recognize the limitations normally inherent in managerial authority causes most of the difficulty in the application and interpretation of the principle of parity of authority and responsibility. One limitation, not always understood or appreciated, is that managerial authority seldom carries with it the power necessary for the literal achievement of the assigned responsibilities.

For example, a sales manager cannot force customers to buy, nor can a personnel director force a union to cooperate with management; yet, it is not uncommon to say that the sales manager is responsible for the sales in one territory and that the personnel director is responsible for establishing cooperative relations with the union. Another limitation on managerial authority results from restrictions imposed by the organization itself. Authority is not absolute; instead it is circumscribed by statements of company policy and procedure that have the effect of defining the limits of authority for each level of the organization. A regional sales manager may have a substantial advertising budget and the authority to select the media appropriate for a given geographic area, yet the total spent may not exceed the budgeted amount without prior approval from superior authority. Restrictions set by higher authority exist for every position within a company.

We have described three conditions that may result in an imbalance between authority and responsibility. First, there may be too little authority granted for the task at hand; second, there are situations in which a manager has little or no power to direct the actions of others; and third, organizational policies and procedures often limit the extent of a manager's authority. With such restrictions on authority, one might reasonably ask whether a concept of parity of authority and responsibility is practical. The answer is yes, because knowledge of the difficulties encountered in creating coextensive authority and responsibility should help in developing effective techniques of delegation and in realistically assessing the extent to which an executive should be held responsible for the accomplishment of assigned duties.

Absoluteness of Accountability. Although responsibility may be assigned to and authority may be delegated to subordinates, accountability to one's superior can neither be assigned nor delegated.

When the process of delegation is defined as the assignment of responsibilities, the delegation of authority, and the creation of accountability, it is evident that both responsibility and authority may be transferred. Indeed, the continuing redelegation of authority and reassignment of responsibility make organizations possible. Departmentation, the dividing of work into manageable units, is an example of the assignment of responsibility. When major departments are created, the chief executive is dividing responsibility—the work load—so that others may more effectively accomplish the tasks necessary for the achievement of organizational goals. At the same time that responsibilities are assigned, commensurate authority is also delegated so that managers of the newly created work units may effectively act or direct others to act. In turn, the major departmental units are further subdivided, with the managers of the subunits receiving assigned responsibilities and delegated authority. But accountability, the obligation to report to one's superior, cannot be delegated nor assigned. The president of a company, although assigning to a marketing vice-president the responsibility and delegating to that person the authority necessary to carry out the marketing function, remains accountable to superior authority, the board of directors, for the successful discharge of the marketing objectives. In turn, the marketing vice-president, though redelegating authority and reassigning responsibility to division marketing managers, remains accountable to superior authority, the president, for the successful discharge of the marketing function. In theory, the concept of accountability is absolute and cannot be transferred. However, in practice it is recognized that assigned responsibilities are performed by subordinates whose work may fall short of expected standards of performance. For example, the marketing vice-president considers the number of new and inexperienced sales representatives when evaluating the performance of a division marketing manager; and the president considers these facts when appraising the work of the vice-president.

Unity of Command. Each subordinate should be accountable to one, and only one, superior.[1]

The unity of command concept states something we all know—no person can serve two masters well. The expression, unity of command, stresses that the sources of command should be so unified that a subordinate receives assigned duties and delegated authority from one superior and is accountable only to that superior. The following four examples represent situations that result in a subordinate's having more than one master and serving none well.

Undifferentiated Organizations. Occasionally in small organizations there are work groups that are undifferentiated with respect to rank or job assignments.

---

[1] There is little empirical evidence to support the three classical principles relating to effective delegation. However, the following study supports the view that at least in a bureaucratic organization, a governmental agency, violation of the concept of unity of command results in dysfunctional consequences as evidenced by a change in attitudes of managers: Martin J. Gannon and Frank T. Paine, "Unity of Command and Job Attitudes of Managers in a Bureaucratic Organization," *Journal of Applied Psychology*, Vol. 59, No. 3 (June, 1974), p. 392.

Frequently the head of such a group characterizes the work force as one big happy family. An employee who is a member of an undifferentiated work group is not certain what is expected or sure of the relative powers of the several persons who offer direction. As a result, the subordinate is forced to select from several job assignments those believed to be most effective in placating the several supervisors. Even though an employee may succeed in keeping a job by "greasing the wheel that squeaks the loudest," it is doubtful that organizational objectives are being met effectively. Objectives may be attained much more efficiently when an organization structure is established so that each supervisor knows clearly the subordinates accountable to him or her and each subordinate knows to which supervisor to report.

Intentional Disregard of Unity of Command. Frequently organizations that have progressed beyond the undifferentiated work-group stage and have established well-defined superior-subordinate relationships intentionally assign one subordinate to two or more supervisors. Such assignments are justified on the grounds that the work load is light and that it is necessary for an employee to work in several departments in order to keep fully occupied. However, it must be recognized that disputes may arise when one supervisor demands more than the allotted share of time. These difficulties can be avoided or minimized by designating in advance a higher authority to determine which department has precedence.

Bypassing Intermediate Supervision. A third violation of the unity of command concept arises as the result of leapfrogging or bypassing one or more levels of intermediate supervision. For example, a plant manager who ignores the superintendent and directs a foreman to change a production schedule is bypassing an intermediate level of supervision. Such action is unfair to the foreman who is put into the position of serving two masters and carrying out two sets of conflicting directions. It is also unfair to the superintendent who remains accountable to the plant manager for the performance of subordinates even though effective control over their actions has been lost. The remedy for the difficulties and misunderstandings which appear as the result of bypassing is not found in recommending that each supervisor have contact only with one immediate superior and with immediate subordinates; rather, it is found in clearly defining the nature of these personal contacts. It is desirable and necessary for an executive to be aware, as the result of personal observation and contact, of the activities of all levels of the organization; however, the actual direction of subordinates should remain the specific responsibility of each subordinate's designated supervisor.

Staff Relationships. Figure 10–4 on page 210 illustrates the concept of functional staff authority and shows the relationship that may exist between two or more levels of staff personnel and between line-and-staff personnel at the plant level. The exercise of strong functional authority may result in circumstances that violate the unity of command concept.

Dual command arises when the supervisor of quality control at the plant level receives instructions establishing acceptable levels of quality from the division manager of quality control that conflict with those standards established by the plant manager, the direct line superior. In the same manner, a production foreman may be placed in the position of receiving orders from more than one source of authority when the plant quality control supervisor sets quality standards in conflict with those previously stated by the plant manager. The potential difficulties resulting from the dual authority sources of line and staff are minimized when the functional authority of staff is clearly defined and it is emphasized that, even though staff properly has authority within a given functional area, any direct orders are to be issued only by the immediate line superior.

Practical Suggestions for Successful Delegation

The conditions for effective delegation discussed above provide a basis for understanding more fully the process of delegation and recognizing the conditions that may result in ineffective delegation. Admittedly, a delegation of sorts can occur even though all three conditions are violated simultaneously, yet few deny that observance of the conditions of delegation results in more effective delegation. The following practical suggestions for successful delegation are offered as a means of putting into practice the conditions for effective delegation.[2]

1. Determine Objectives. Remember the principle of the objective: Before initiating any course of action, the objectives in view must be clearly determined, understood, and stated. The process of delegation affords an excellent opportunity for the application of the principle of the objective. As a first step, it is necessary to determine the goals expected as the result of a specific work assignment. A statement of goals is important to the process of delegation for two reasons. First, the duties and responsibilities of a job are derived from and directed toward the achievement of stated objectives. Second, persons who are assigned work are accountable to their respective superiors for the successful completion of those duties; consequently, unless work performed is pertinent to achieving stated goals, the concept of accountability becomes exceedingly vague.

2. Assign Duties and Delegate Commensurate Authority. Determine all the duties that must be performed to complete the task at hand; then assign the whole job—not just parts of it. There are too many instances where supervisors assign only the minor or routine details of a job and retain the key decision-making aspects of the job for themselves. Such assignments are not delegation in the true sense of the word since there is little need for the delegation of authority. Defining the whole job at the very start of a project brings into proper perspective the amount of authority needed to insure parity of responsibility and authority. Also, subordinates are more likely to be better motivated by assignments that encompass the whole job.

---

[2] Louis A. Allen, *Management and Organization* (New York City: McGraw-Hill, Inc., 1958), Chapter 7, "Better Methods of Delegation," p. 134. Chapter 7 presents an extensive discussion of specific methods that may be used for more effective delegation.

3. Select Subordinate. Select the candidate for the job in light of what is expected. Assigned responsibilities are in effect the duties of a job; and duties, if they are to be completed successfully, require certain skills and knowledge. In addition to possessing the necessary skills and knowledge, the best candidate for the job is the person who is willing to accept full responsibility for achieving stated objectives. Among the many reasons for a subordinate's unwillingness to accept responsibility are lack of understanding of what is expected, fear of failure or criticism, and insufficient motivation. Whatever the reason, if a choice must be made between two subordinates with one possessing the necessary skills and experience but unwilling to assume responsibility, and the other short on experience but willing to assume responsibility, it is probably better to choose the latter.

4. Establish Necessary Controls. The discussion of the second step of the process of delegation, the delegation of authority, states explicitly that delegation is not synonymous with abdication. Instead, the delegator retains the right to recall delegated authority and remains accountable for the responsibilities assigned to others. Thus it is necessary for the delegator to establish and exercise control over the actions of subordinates so that the delegator's obligations may be fulfilled. Essential to proper control is the maintenance of clear channels of communication between superior and subordinate so that a complete interchange of information is possible. Controls also imply that corrective action may be taken if needed to insure the fullfillment of stated objectives. Resentment of controls on the part of subordinates is minimal when the subordinate participates in establishing the controls to be used.

BEHAVIORAL ASPECTS OF DELEGATION

Thus far our discussion of delegation includes an analysis of the three steps in the process of delegation, a statement of three conditions that should be observed for most effective delegation, and specific practical suggestions for successful delegation. Yet if this were all of delegation, or even a major portion of the process of delegation, there would be little reason for discussing delegation so extensively in management literature. The real problems of delegation lie not in the observance of the conditions of delegation nor in following the practical suggestions for successful delegation. Instead they are found in the personality of the person doing the delegating.

The behavior of the superior who finds it difficult to delegate is characterized by an excessive attention to details, coupled with a marked distrust and questioning of the ability of subordinates. There are many reasons for these two characteristics, which for purposes of discussion may be grouped into four broad categories. First, there are those who seemingly have always been interested in activities and studies that require precision and exactness. These people often follow vocations requiring and emphasizing precise action. Second, there are those who immerse themselves in details as a means of avoiding the central problems of a situation. Third, there are those who refuse to relinquish any part of their job to others because of a deep-seated fear of failure. The fourth group who refuses to delegate and must retain all of a job for themselves are those who have a paranoid (fear of persecution) distrust of others. Let us examine each of these groups separately, realizing that there is considerable overlapping between each group and that most failures to delegate can be traced to one or more of the four categories.

Vocational Choice

Any discussion of personality factors and vocational choice may evolve into the proverbial question of which comes first, the chicken or the egg. In other words, does one enter a given vocation because of certain underlying personality traits or does the specific vocational training received mold the personality? Admittedly both processes operate simultaneously. There is much in our culture that emphasizes the importance of doing a job well and following it through to completion. Some people have been brought up with the admonition, If you want a job done well, do it yourself. Whatever the sources of desire for personal accomplishment, we are taught to respect those capable of hard and effective work.

There are specific forms of vocational training that tend to reinforce the normal inclinations of attending to detail. Accounting and engineering are good examples of such vocational training in that both courses of study require a meticulous attention to detail, a liking for exactness expressed in the form of numbers to the third decimal place, and considerable hard work and drudgery to complete the course. Upon graduation, the engineer may be doing exacting work on a drafting board and the accountant may be performing the work necessary for a detailed audit. It is the ability to do this first assignment—close attention to detail—and to do it well that results in promotion. Is it any wonder that a person with a normal liking for detail, reinforced by four years of college training in precise work and subsequently reinforced en route to success and promotions, should find it difficult to let go of the detail part of a job and turn it over to others?

Some of these highly trained people, and Thomas Dayton of Case Problem 11-A is one of them, are frequently very competent in their field of work, a competency often expressed by the comment, "I can do it better myself." Although they may not be able to do it better, they usually can perform the work as well. Another characteristic is the 12- to 16-hour day, which with few exceptions is the result of an inability to delegate rather than due to the press of important affairs. It is difficult to change people such as Thomas Dayton and make them successful delegators. Basic to the difficulty is their liking for work and their ability to do it well. Admonitions concerning health may fail to encourage them to delegate. Even after the occurrence of physical breakdown, some are still unable to slow down and delegate their work to others.

Avoidance of Major Issues

Attention to detail sometimes offers a security and comfort not possible when one's attention is directed toward the major problems at hand. In extreme cases the ability to attend to detail rather than to the central issue is important for life itself. On occasion facing the real problem may be so overwhelming that one is unable to carry on. An example of the extreme is illustrated in the following brief quotation describing the plight of a refugee:

> The refugee was a peasant woman from down San Carlos way. She was complaining of the haste with which she and her family had had to flee. The burden of her complaint was that her husband's new suit and his Sunday gloves had had to be left behind. I had heard exactly the same kind of protest years ago in China; I was to hear it later in Austria and Czechoslovakia. The mind of the refugee, dazed and uprooted, concentrates upon the small, specific losses that it can cling to with understanding. To be homeless and without food or shelter as a result of the "policy" of foreign dictators and prime ministers—that is a state so terrible that it cannot be taken in all at once. The new suit, the Sunday gloves, these are the losses one can still comprehend.[3]

Although managers may not be faced with problems of such personal magnitude as those confronting the war refugee, there are instances where some managers simply cannot cope with the central issues of their environment and as a result direct their attention to peripheral details that are related to, but are not the real problem. The marketing manager who personally reviews each sales representative's expense account and then tallies the amount spent on telephone calls may be avoiding the real problem of increasing the number of new customers. The president of a company who reviews every change in salary may hold down payroll costs and then complain that there is not enough time for the major task of coordinating the development of new products.

Fear of Failure

Feelings of personal insecurity with the attendant fear of failure may be the cause of inability to delegate. These are not the feelings of insecurity and unsureness associated with lack of knowledge and experience that are normal when one undertakes a new job; rather, it is the unsureness derived from a feeling of personal inadequacy. For some, fear of failure may be very real and imminent, for they may be on the brink of failure and realize that one more mistake can cost them their job or, at the very least, an opportunity for promotion. For others, failure may not be near, but there is the constant fear of what might happen if failure does occur. In either case, whether failure is imminent or imagined, the underlying thought processes are somewhat as follows: This is a very difficult job to be done. It is full of problems and pitfalls; it requires a great deal of attention, hard work, and skill. It is going to tax my

---

[3] Vincent Sheehan, *Not Peace but a Sword* (New York City: Doubleday & Co., Inc., 1939), p. 86. Reprinted by permission of Curtis Brown, Ltd.

abilities to the limit. Since it is such a hard job for me to do, how can anyone else possibly do this job?

Whatever the cause of personal inadequacy, the result tends to be the same—a refusal to delegate, with the firm belief that the job is so taxing that it is inconceivable that anyone else can possibly handle it. As expected, it is extremely difficult to persuade these individuals to let go, because the motivating force is a fear of personal failure. It is a fear that immobilizes action since there is a complete inability to take a risk.

Distrust of Others

A fourth reason for not assigning duties and delegating authority to subordinates may be the result of a paranoid distrust of the motives of others. The word paranoid is used to describe a person who has delusions or false beliefs of persecution. The term *paranoid distrust* as used here refers to a distrust of others based upon the false belief that a subordinate's drive for success is founded upon a desire to displace or discredit the boss. The supervisor who distrusts and fears subordinates may refuse to delegate authority to them as a means of countering their threat. Such refusal weakens organizational processes. There is also a long-range effect on the organization, for when a supervisor tormented by fears of distrust has the opportunity to select subordinates, there is understandably a strong tendency to select only those persons who are so submissive that they are incapable of threatening any superior's position.

To summarize, whatever the reasons for failure to delegate, whether it be a liking for detail work, a defense against having to face the central issues of a problem, the fear of failure, or the desire to maintain one's own security through weakening competition, the results are essentially the same. First, the refusal to delegate and let subordinates carry projects through to their normal completion results in the elimination of valuable training experiences. If the reason for reluctance to delegate lies in a well-founded belief that subordinates are not trained or capable, the sad fact remains that by not delegating, subordinates never become trained or capable since the opportunity to learn through experience is denied. Second, refusal to delegate has the effect of stifling initiative, with the result that suggestions and new ideas may cease entirely. The subordinate is wondering, Why should I say anything? I'm not allowed to do anything around here anyway. The third effect of refusing to delegate is that the better people, defining better people as those who need to develop and accept more responsibility, leave the company at the earliest opportunity. The industrial engineer of Case Problem 11-A is a case in point. The net result is not a pretty picture—a frustrated superior incapable of delegating and surrounded ultimately by subordinates incapable of accepting responsibility, even if it were offered.

DECENTRALIZATION OF AUTHORITY

Delegation of authority is described in the first part of this chapter as a process that transfers authority from superior to subordinate in an organization.

The extent to which authority is delegated to organizational units is a measure of the degree of decentralization of authority within that organization. The concept of decentralization of authority is relative; an organization is never completely centralized nor is it completely decentralized. Complete centralization of authority requires one person with no subordinates—hardly an organization—while complete decentralization implies that there is no longer a central authority, again a situation resulting in no organization.

In discussing decentralization of authority, it is necessary to define decentralization and to establish guides for determining the extent to which a company is decentralized. Next, the probable effects of the application of integrated-information decision-making systems upon the extent of decentralization within an organization are examined.

Definition of Decentralization

Before defining decentralization, it is well to differentiate between decentralization and two other processes often confused with it. These two processes are departmentation and geographic dispersion. In Chapter 9, *departmentation* is defined as the grouping of work and people into manageable units, and the bases most frequently used in the creation of departments are discussed. These bases are departmentation by function, product, customer, geography, process, and sequence. However, the mere creation of separate departmental units does not constitute decentralization. For example, the vice-president of marketing who appoints five marketing managers, each in charge of a different product, is further departmentalizing the marketing function along product lines but is not necessarily decentralizing the marketing function. The division of one large manufacturing plant into six widely separated smaller plants certainly results in *geographic dispersion*, but not necessarily in decentralization. The key to whether the appointment of product marketing managers or the building of geographically separate plants is decentralization or merely further departmentation is revealed by analyzing the effect of such changes on the decision-making process within the organization.

Decentralization is the delegation of authority to make decisions to the managers of lower echelon organizational units. The decentralization of the decision-making function is relative, and the degree of decentralization depends on the following three characteristics of the decisions made at lower levels of the organization: (1) frequency of the decisions, (2) breadth of the decisions, and (3) the extent of the controls exercised over lower level decisions. Let us examine briefly each characteristic.

Frequency of Decisions. The greater the frequency or number of decisions made at lower levels of an organization, the greater is the degree of decentralization in that organization.

Breadth of Decisions. The broader the scope of decisions made at lower levels of an organization, the greater is the degree of decentralization. The breadth of decision making is determined by the number of functions affected by the decisions. A plant whose manager is limited to making only those decisions directly affecting production is less decentralized than the plant whose manager's scope of decision making includes, in addition, the negotiation of labor agreements with a union.

Extent of Controls over Decisions. The extent of controls exercised over the decisions made at lower levels of an organization is an important measure of the degree of decentralization. Decisions are frequently classified in terms of the number of dollars involved, with dollar limitations placed on decisions that may be made without prior approval. Thus, an organization that permits a sales manager to approve customer credit up to $5,000 is more decentralized, other things being equal, than the organization that permits approval by the sales manager of only $1,000 credit. Timeliness of approval is also a factor. There is less decentralization when approval is required before the decision is made than when a superior is notified after the decision is made or when higher authority is not even informed. The number of approvals required prior to making a decision is also an index of the degree of decentralization. Generally the fewer the persons who must be contacted for approval, the greater is the degree of decentralization.[4]

Electronic Data Processing and Decentralization

The proper degree of decentralization is determined by carefully considering all factors in relation to the objectives of the organization. One factor that causes a great deal of interesting speculation is the effect of the introduction of high-speed electronic data processing equipment upon decentralization. For example, there are information systems capable of receiving an order for an electric motor from a customer, selecting the warehouse nearest the customer, and preparing in printed form the customer's name, address, and pertinent credit information. If the order reduces the inventory level below a predetermined point, the manufacturing plant is notified and that type motor is scheduled for production. It is also possible for large customers to place their orders directly from remote terminals in their own offices, thereby bypassing the local sales office.

When one considers that customers can order directly through an information processing system, it is easy to point to the sales office and conclude that the decision-making role of middle management is weakened with the introduction of electronic data processing. With the undermining of middle management's decision making and the centralization of information handling, one can develop the argument that modern information systems are more conducive to a centralized than to a decentralized form of organization. Whether or not this argument is valid depends on the definition of middle management decision making and

---

[4] For a discussion of the controls needed in order to have effective decentralization, see Charles Perrow, "The Bureaucratic Paradox: The Efficient Organization Centralizes in Order to Decentralize," *Organizational Dynamics*, Vol. 5, No. 4 (Spring, 1977), p. 3.

the company's basic philosophy regarding decentralization. If middle management's decisions are defined as the processing of orders, the checking of inventories, and the performance of other routine functions, then in all probability these functions are better handled by electronic equipment. Also, if the basic philosophy of the company is one of centralization—the desire to place as many decisions as possible in the hands of a few top executives—modern information-decision-making systems tend to strengthen that philosophy. But if the underlying philosophy of the company is one of decentralization, it is possible to direct the flow of information to subordinate managers so that they may make better decisions, thereby increasing their contribution to the organization and making their positions more secure. Companies which are centralized because needed information is complex and must be laboriously handled in a central location may find that modern data processing eases the burden of handling such information, thereby making it possible to decentralize. Thus, whether electronic data processing strengthens or weakens the trend toward decentralization depends on the definition of decision making on the part of middle managers and the company's basic philosophy regarding decentralization.[5]

A CONTINGENCY APPROACH TO ORGANIZING

Chapter 8 presents a contingency approach to organization theory (pages 165–169). The six situational factors of a contingency approach to organization are expressed in broad terms of organization structure and processes. In Chapter 9, the structural aspects of organization—departmentation, span of management, and committees—are discussed. Chapter 10 discusses the authority relationships between line and staff personnel. In this chapter we have analyzed the organizational processes of delegation and decentralization of authority. Now we reexamine each of the situational factors of a contingency approach—size of organization, degree of interaction, personality of members, congruence of goals, level of decision making, and state of the system—and show how each influences the organizing function. In the discussion that follows, the application of each of the parameters to departmentation, span of management, committees, line and staff relationships, delegation, and decentralization is summarized briefly.

Size of Organization

Perhaps the greatest effect of size of organization, defining size as number of people, is on the degree of formalization of both structure and processes. As size increases, the need for departmentation becomes evident. Whatever the basis selected for the creation of departments, whether it be function, geography, product, or any other unifying characteristic, an increase in the number

---

[5] William E. Reif, *Computer Technology and Management Organization* (Iowa City: Bureau of Business and Economic Research, The University of Iowa, 1968). In this empirical study, Mr. Reif analyzes the effects of the installation of electronic data processing systems upon a bank, a utility, and a manufacturing organization. The effect of computers on the degree of centralization is discussed in full in Chapter 7, p. 91.

of departments also results in an attendant increase in the span of management of the chief executive.[6] Committees are also characteristic of large organizations primarily because increased size requires a greater degree of coordination. Committees in large organizations, such as an executive committee, may also be charged with responsibility for decision making.

In large organizations there is a clearer delineation between line and staff functions than in small organizations. Specialized staff appears and is assigned responsibility for a given functional area throughout the entire organization. Delegation of authority with attendant responsibility for the completion of assigned duties becomes imperative in large organizations. The decentralization of authority to make decisions to the managers of lower level organizational units is another characteristic. In summary, the greatest effect of size of organization is the increased degree of formalization of both organizational structure and processes.

Degree of Interaction

An important guide in determining effective departmentation is the need for interaction between the members of an organization in order to achieve organizational goals.[7] Need for interaction arises when several persons find it necessary to communicate with each other in order to solve a common problem or when they are developing and using the same information. Occasionally the formation of committees satisfies the need for interaction.

The degree of interaction between persons supervised by one superior is often a factor in determining the upper limits of an effective span of management. The geometrically progressive increase in the number of relationships described by Graicunas is primarily a function of the cross relationships between those being supervised. It is a function recognized by Urwick in the qualifying phrase, "whose work interlocks."

There is need for interaction between line and staff personnel. Although the line organization is responsible for the achievement of organizational goals, it is necessary that there be free interaction between line and staff personnel in order that the services of staff may be utilized most effectively.

The need for interaction between superior and subordinate is obvious if there is to be an effective process of delegation. Similarly, the need for interaction often serves as a guide in determining whether the decentralization of decision-making authority to lower level echelons improves organizational effectiveness. The decentralization of authority that appears in many marketing departments is recognition of the need for close interaction between the customer, the salesperson, and the local marketing manager in reaching satisfactory solutions to com-

---

[6] For a complete review of the literature on span of management, see David D. Van Fleet and Arthur G. Bedian, "A History of the Span of Management," *Academy of Management Review*, Vol. 2, No. 3 (July, 1977), p. 356. The bibliography contains 255 items.

[7] For a discussion of the effects of interaction, read Jerome L. Franklin, "Down the Organization: Influence Processes Across Levels of Hierarchy," *Administrative Science Quarterly*, Vol. 20, No. 2 (June, 1975), p. 153.

mon problems. However, when decisions require close interaction between the members of several organizational units, it may be necessary to centralize the decision-making process at a higher organizational level rather than to move toward a greater degree of decentralization.

Personality of Members

The personality of the members of an organization (defining personality as the sum total of skills, abilities, expectations, interests, and personal characteristics) is an important consideration in determining departmental lines. Work is often departmentalized according to the skills utilized, an arrangement which encourages specialization and the maximum development of individual skills and abilities. Specialized knowledge concerning a specific product or function may well serve as the basis for defining a department. However, it is essential to maintain a balance between specialization, which often facilitates training and results in a high level of skill, and the enrichment of jobs so that there is a resultant maximum utilization of the capabilities of all personnel.

Personality is an important consideration in determining the upper limits of an effective span of management. First, consider the personality of the manager. It is axiomatic that there are variations in the capabilities of managers in respect to range of interests, breadth and depth of knowledge, and the amount of energy expended on the job. In addition to these readily recognized characteristics, there is that rare quality—the ability to inspire others. Managers who have the ability to inspire subordinates to "play over their heads" should have larger spans of management so that their dynamic qualities of leadership may influence as many subordinates as possible. The personality of subordinates is also a determinant of an effective span of management. If subordinates are well trained, interested in their jobs, and desirous of making their own decisions, less supervisory effort is required, thereby increasing the effective span of management. On the other hand, subordinates requiring close supervision decrease the effective span of management. Personality of members is also significant in the formation of committees. When problem solving is the goal it is often best to assign committee members who have a diversity of background, knowledge, and interests.

One of the basic problems existing between line and staff personnel arises from the manner in which the respective roles are perceived. Because of education staff managers have difficulty in accepting a secondary or supportive role. At the same time it is difficult for line managers to relinquish any authority believed necessary to accomplish line objectives. Policy statements setting forth well-defined relationships between line and staff personnel may reduce tensions between the two groups.

The personality of the chief executive is highly significant as a predictor of the extent and effectiveness of delegation and decentralization within an organization. If the chief executive is unable to delegate because of personality, the concept of decentralization of authority to lower level echelons is neither encouraged nor understood. However, if the chief executive is capable of delegating authority, the first step toward effective decentralization of authority is assured.

Congruence of Goals

When the immediate goals of several diverse activities are the same, such congruence may serve as a basis for establishing departments. Plant maintenance departments include personnel possessing the diverse skills of millwrights, electricians, plumbers, steamfitters, and machinists—a variety which seems to have little in common. Yet all are concerned with the immediate objective of keeping plant facilities in good repair. The placement of sales and service personnel under the direction of a sales manager is another example of combining personnel having a congruent goal—customer satisfaction. In the same fashion a committee composed of members having diverse backgrounds yet a common goal often increases the probability of developing creative solutions to a given problem.

When applied as a guide in determining an effective span of management, congruence of goals refers not only to the similarity of goals of each of the various work groups, but also includes the degree of congruence between the immediate goals of the individual and those of the organization. An argument often presented in support of incentive plans, relating pay to productivity, is that such plans are a means of making the goals of the individual congruent with those of the organization. In general, as the immediate goals of subordinates become congruent with the goals of the organization, the span of management may be increased.

When line and staff managers recognize that their respective goals contribute to the goals of the organization, misunderstandings and conflicts between line and staff personnel may be reduced. Also, when goals are congruent the delegation of authority from superior to subordinate is more likely to be successful. One method of increasing the probability of success of the process of delegation and increasing the effectiveness of decentralization of authority to lower level organizational units is to implement a management-by-objectives program.

Level of Decision Making

In some organizations the power to make important decisions is retained by the chief executive and senior vice-presidents. In others, decision making occurs at all levels of the organizational hierarchy. The hierarchical location of decision making is primarily a function of the technology of the organization. Some technologies result in an information flow where only the top level of the organization possesses sufficient information for sound decisions. Committees or departments may be created for the specific purpose of placing decision making at the level where it is most effective. The creation of decentralized divisions with decision-making powers is an example of the downward movement of decision making. The reasons most frequently advanced for such decentralization are the need for timeliness, better coordination, and the ability to meet and take full advantage of local factors such as the actions of competitors and the needs of customers.

The level of decision making in an organization has a direct bearing on the breadth of an executive's span of management. The executive who retains the responsibility for making decisions usually has a reduced span of management. If subordinates are permitted to make decisions, the span of management may be increased.

The relationship between line and staff personnel is also influenced by the level of decision making. In those organizations with highly centralized decision-making processes, it is not uncommon for staff personnel to exercise considerable authority in their functional speciality. If the organization is diversified and has many product lines, it may be better to place the decision-making function of both line and staff personnel at lower levels of the organization. When decision making is located at the top of the hierarchy, there may be a reluctance to delegate decision-making authority to lower level subordinates. Yet it is quite possible that a greater degree of delegation and decentralization might be more effective if the practical suggestions for effective delegation discussed on pages 221–225 were followed.

State of the System

The extent to which the organization is achieving its stated goals, the state of the system, is an important consideration in determining departmental units. Cost reduction, a continuing goal for most organizations, is frequently achieved by combining departmental units, thereby avoiding duplication of effort. At the same time, the needs of the organization may be such that it becomes necessary to emphasize a particular function by creating a separate department or committee reporting directly to the chief executive; for example, research and development. The desire to reduce costs or to emphasize a particular function are examples illustrating the elimination or creation of departments as the result of viewing the organization as a system and evaluating the extent to which that organization is meeting its stated goals.

The extent to which the goals of the organization are stabilized and the degree to which an organization is achieving these goals serve as guides in determining an effective span of management. When the organization is failing to meet its goals, the chief executive may decide to decrease the span of management as a means of structuring the organization so that it may be better controlled. One result is a more rapid adaptation to changing internal and external forces. However, if the organization is relatively stable and successfully fulfilling its goals, such conditions contribute to the effectiveness of an extended span of management.

The relationship between line and staff personnel is influenced by the extent to which an organization is meeting its goals. When line personnel fail to meet expected standards of performance it is likely that staff personnel will exercise more positive staff authority in order that such standards may be met. Similarly, when line personnel meet established standards and the organizational system is in a state of equilibrium, staff's role becomes less apparent and directive in nature.

The narrowing of the span of management in order to exercise a high degree of control during a crisis usually results in relatively limited delegation of authority. As the crisis is resolved it is probable that more subordinates will be assigned broader responsibilities and will be delegated the commensurate authority to fulfill those responsibilities. The state of the system is an important consideration in determining the optimum degree of decentralization. In addition to considering the extent to which organizational goals are being achieved during a crisis, consideration must also be given to the stage of organizational growth, the nature of the organization's purpose, and the availability of controls. As an organization succeeds in achieving stated objectives, it is possible to exercise a more permissive form of leadership and decision making. More permissive leadership and participation in decision making tend to further the process of decentralization.

The decentralization of authority to make decisions is not an either-or proposition as implied by the expression, centralization versus decentralization. Instead, the extent of decentralization is a point on a continuum with a high degree of centralization and a high degree of decentralization marking the limits of the continuum. Case Problem 11-B illustrates that the definition of the degree of decentralization depends on one's position in the organization. The chairman of Dynamic Industries honestly believes that the corporation is highly decentralized, but the president of a subsidiary company questions that view. The case also shows how a few well-chosen corporate controls—capital expenditures, budgets, and centralized industrial relations—effectively limit the degree of decentralization.

Case Problem 11-B

DECENTRALIZATION—FACT OR FICTION?

Dynamic industries, a diversified manufacturer of automotive replacement parts, is a company that is growing rapidly as the result of an aggressive policy of acquisition. Board chairman John Rafferty believes that the growth of his company is sound and that the main reason for the extremely rapid growth is due to the operation of the company on a highly decentralized basis. Since growth is the result of acquiring companies that are going concerns, Rafferty encourages the managements of the subsidiary companies to carry on as they had prior to joining Dynamic Industries. At present, discussions regarding merger are being held with Central Electronics, a company that manufactures a broad line of electronic components, many of which have applications in the defense and space industries. Central Electronics is interested in Dynamic Industries because Dynamic can supply the much needed capital to complete the final stages of the development of a high-performance transformer and the building of a plant in which to manufacture the new product. However, Rosa Vasquez, the founder and president of Central, realizes the potential dangers of merging with another company in that she might lose control of her own firm and be placed in the position of being an employee for a larger corporation.

But Rafferty continually assures Vasquez that Dynamic Industries operates on a highly decentralized basis and describes their concept of decentralization as follows:

"We expect you, as the president of a subsidiary company, to manage as you have in the past. You are successful with your own company and there is no reason why you shouldn't continue to be a success operating as a part of Dynamic. The major functions of sales, manufacturing, engineering, and product development are all yours to do with as you see fit. In a sense, we are sort of the banker; that is, we supply the money that you need for capital improvements and expansion. Even though the profits of each subsidiary company go into the corporate till, it is still like having your own company because your pay for the year is a combination of a guaranteed salary and a percentage of the net profits of your company."

Thus assured, Vasquez decided to merge with Dynamic Industries. During the first six months all went well, and Vasquez saw very little of anyone from corporate headquarters. At the beginning of the seventh month, the corporate controller paid Vasquez a visit and explained to her in detail the company's requirements for profit planning and requested that Vasquez develop a profit plan, a detailed forecast of Central's revenues and operating expenses, for the coming year. Though very pleasant, the controller made it quite plain that, should the performance of the company deviate significantly from the forecast, a team of cost analysts and industrial engineers would arrive from headquarters to determine the cause of the deviation and to recommend necessary changes.

Shortly after this experience with the controller, the industrial relations vice-president of Dynamic Industries called on Vasquez and informed her that a member of the corporate industrial relations staff would be on hand to conduct the coming negotiations with the union representing Central's employees. Vasquez protested, saying that she had been negotiating her own labor contracts for years; however, it was explained to her that because of company-wide employee benefit plans, such as pensions and insurance, and to prevent the unions from pitting one subsidiary company against another in the area of wages, centralized control over negotiations was very necessary. At the time of this visit, the provisions of the company's salary plan were outlined to Vasquez and arrangements were made for the installation of the corporate clerical and supervisory salary plans by a member of the headquarters industrial relations staff.

The following month Vasquez called Rafferty and asked what steps should be taken to secure capital for the new building intended for the manufacture of the high-performance transformer. Rafferty answered by saying, "I'll have someone from the treasurer's office call on you and show you how to fill out the forms used in requesting funds for capital expansion. It's quite a process, but remember you are only one of 15 subsidiaries and they all seem to want money at the same time. Whether or not you get it this year depends not only on your needs but also on the needs of the other 14 companies."

PROBLEMS

1. Has Dynamic Industries decentralized its operations as much as possible?
2. As Rosa Vasquez, president of Central Electronics, would you regard the management policies of the parent corporation as primarily centralized or primarily decentralized?
3. Is Dynamic Industries exerting too much control over Central Electronics? Why or why not?
4. Recommend the optimum degree of decentralization for the situation described in this case.

CHAPTER QUESTIONS FOR STUDY AND DISCUSSION

1. Why is it necessary to define the term *to delegate* precisely? How does such a definition contribute to an understanding of the control exercised by a person who does the delegating?

2. Why is it necessary to have three principles or conditions that must be met for the process of delegation to be most effective? Explain what would happen if accountability were not considered absolute.

3. Should the president of a company be held accountable for the following actions of subordinates?
   (a) Price fixing that is in violation of federal laws and stated company policies
   (b) Failure to meet stated company sales objectives
   (c) Loss of competitive position in development of new products

4. If one or more of the conditions of delegation is violated, is it possible for the process of delegation to work? Discuss.

5. How valid is the concept that an executive should be held accountable for the performance of a function even though there is no power to control the actions of others (for example, the sales manager who cannot force customers to buy)?

6. Give an example of each of the four situations that result in a violation of the condition of unity of command.

7. If delegation includes the granting of authority and empowers a subordinate to act, why is it necessary to establish controls to see that the subordinate performs as expected?

8. What is meant by the idea that the real problems of delegation are found in the personality of the person doing the delegating?

9. Differentiate between decentralization and geographic dispersion. Can geographic dispersion be transformed into decentralization of authority? Discuss.

10. Discuss the following statement: The development of electronic data processing systems tends to centralize authority and limit the decision-making powers of the middle manager.

11. Discuss each of the criteria which are used to determine the extent of decentralization.

12. How is the concept of decentralization of authority related to the concept of delegation? In what respects do these two concepts differ? In what respects are they the same?

Chapter 12

Organizational Change— Analysis and Development

Case Problem 12-A

CHARTING AN ORGANIZATION

Twenty-five years ago Stanley Johnson founded the Johnson Valve Company, which has grown and prospered over the years. Mr. Johnson, now 62 years old, realizes that he cannot continue as president indefinitely, but there are no well-formulated plans for management succession. The stock in the company is closely held by Mr. Johnson and members of his immediate family, with only 10 percent held by an outsider, the attorney who serves as the only outside member of the board and as general counsel for the corporation. The attorney has suggested that the position of executive vice-president be created and that a person be brought in from another company. This person will then be moved up to the presidency upon satisfactory performance and Mr. Johnson's expected retirement at age 65. Currently the organization is as follows.

Reporting directly to Mr. Johnson as an "assistant-to" is a man in his early thirties who has a master's degree in marketing. Although his title is assistant-to, his primary function is to conduct market research studies in the valve industry and to prepare detailed analyses of current sales. Johnson often refers to his assistant as "my forward-planning unit." Also reporting to the presi-

dent are the treasurer, the vice-president of sales, the purchasing director, the production vice-president, the chief engineer, and the plant manager. The plant manager, now nearing retirement, has been ill most of the past year, so in effect the plant superintendent reports directly to the president.

The treasurer, who for several years was the firm's only accountant, has been with the company since its founding. Reporting directly to the treasurer is the office manager who not only manages the office but also performs the personnel function for all salaried and clerical personnel. The controller, responsible for the cost accounting section, and the supervisor of general ledgers also report to the treasurer. The vice-president in charge of sales has been an officer of the company for the past five years; however, for many years she was in charge of the field sales force and the entire sales function with the title of sales manager. Although there is now a sales manager reporting to her, the vice-president actually directs the sales force and the sales manager spends most of the time in the office handling the paper work generated by the sales representatives. The supervisor of the sales order department also reports to the sales manager.

The purchasing director, with a staff of two buyers and a clerk, reports directly to the president as a result of Mr. Johnson's desire to control the cost of raw materials. Formerly, the director of purchases reported to the production manager, who is a vice-president and Mr. Johnson's sister-in-law, but the only person now reporting to the production manager is the head of the production scheduling department. The chief engineer, also an officer of the company, knows the product well and supervises the section chief of the drafting department, the chief metallurgist, and the director of the research laboratories.

Most of Johnson Valve Company's current problems center in the production area. The plant manager's staff consists of the maintenance foreman, the plant personnel and employment manager, and the foreman of the tool room; but for the past year, as the result of the plant manager's illness and absence, the plant staff has been reporting directly to the plant superintendent, who also reports on paper to the plant manager. Normally reporting to the plant superintendent are the shipping and receiving foreman, the machining foreman, the quality control manager, the factory stores supervisor, the assembly foreman, and the supervisor of the experimental shop, which is engaged primarily in carrying out projects assigned by the chief engineer.

PROBLEMS

1. Prepare an organization chart showing the present structure of Johnson Valve Company.
2. Prepare a plan for reorganization. Include a new organization chart and your justification for the changes suggested.

Organizations are not static structures; instead, organizations are made up of dynamic interrelationships existing between people performing those functions necessary for the achievement of organizational goals. As either goals or people change, the need for modification of organization structure and function arises. Symptoms calling for organizational change, such as those described below, reflect inadequacies or inefficiencies in any part of the organization.

1. *Faulty Decision Making.* Decision making may be too slow to gain full advantage of the situation, or erroneous decisions are being made. Perhaps the difficulty in decision making may be traced to the placement of the responsibility for decisions at a level of the organization not having access to necessary information.
2. *Failure in Functional Areas.* There may be failure or inefficiency in any one of the major functional areas. Production may not meet schedules or it may show excessive costs and quality defects. Marketing may show a steady loss of customers and failure to achieve expected market penetration, while finance may reveal an inability to provide for long-range corporate demands. In the area of personnel, the need for organizational change may arise as the result of personnel not meeting the requirements of changing positions, with poor performance as a result; or the need for change may be highlighted by excessive personality clashes between employees.
3. *Poor Communications.* It is possible that the failure in any one functional area, as described above, may be the result of poor communications between organizational subunits rather than the result of inefficiencies in the functional area. For example, failure to produce the proper quantity of products may be the result of poor communications between marketing and production scheduling rather than the result of inefficient production.

4. *Lack of Innovation.* There may be a dearth of new ideas, either in the form of new products or new and better ways of performing present functions. When innovation ceases, growth ceases also.

The presence of any of the above symptoms indicates the need for organizational change. Such change may occur within a relatively short period of time as a result of organizational analysis and an evaluation of organizational effectiveness—an approach that emphasizes change in structure. Or organizational change may occur as a result of implementing a long-range plan of organizational development that results in a changed organizational environment. Either approach, structural or environmental change, has its place. Discussed first is organizational analysis, including the procedures and techniques usually used in such studies, and a method of evaluating organizational effectiveness. Planned organizational development programs are discussed in the second part of the chapter.

ORGANIZATIONAL ANALYSIS

When conducting organizational analysis, one is planning for the future of the organization; therefore, it is helpful to follow a procedure based on an objective method.

Procedures for Organizational Analysis

The procedures for sound organizational analysis are an application of the scientific method. They are: (1) assign responsibility, (2) collect data, (3) prepare alternative plans of organization, and (4) install the best plan and follow up.[1]

Assign Responsibility. There are three questions to be answered in the assignment of responsibility for organizational analysis. The first of these questions is, who is to initiate the study? the second, who is to collect the necessary data and develop recommended changes? and third, who is to approve the recommended changes and place them in effect? An early study by K. K. White of 118 companies sheds some light on what is actually done by industrial firms in one phase of organizational analysis: preparing the organization chart.[2] White's study showed that the company president initiated the charting of the organization in 42 percent of the companies surveyed; a company vice-president in 22 percent of the companies; and the personnel executive in 12 percent of the companies. In most instances, i.e., 25 percent of the companies surveyed,

---

[1] A similar analysis of the steps necessary to establish a management development program is found in the following article: Jon English and Anthony R. Marchione, "Nine Steps in Management Development," *Business Horizons,* Vol. 20, No. 3 (June, 1977), p. 88.

[2] K. K. White, *Understanding the Company Organization Chart* (New York City: American Management Association, 1963), Research Study Number 56, pp. 16–17. A more recent study setting forth the role of the management consultant in organization analysis and change is Neil G. Davey, *The External Consultant's Role in Organizational Change* (East Lansing: Graduate School of Business Administration, Michigan State University, 1971).

the personnel executive compiled the necessary data and prepared the chart. The president of the company did the charting in 17 percent of the cases, a company vice-president in 14 percent, or an outside consultant in 13 percent of the companies. Final approval for any organizational change must come from top management itself. It goes without saying that the chief executive, usually the president, must approve any changes and, to insure maximum cooperation, approval of other members of top management is much desired.

Collect Data. Once the responsibility for analysis and preparation of proposed changes has been established, it is necessary to collect all pertinent information so that any proposed change is founded on fact rather than on supposition. The availability and type of information sought varies from one situation to another. Certain historical records are of interest, particularly those that show the growth of the company with respect to the number of people, their titles, their duties, and their personal backgrounds and qualifications. The pattern of growth of the company, as reflected by gross sales, is of value, especially when these figures can be correlated with the need for personnel. In this manner, definite trends may be established, and personnel needs for expected future levels of sales may be projected. The analysis of current reports and forms— for example, the monthly distribution of manufacturing costs—shows the flow of information within the company. Activity charts showing the distribution of an employee's time for each day or week may be prepared for key jobs or for all the jobs within a department. When interpreted in the light of information gained from an analysis of existing reports, the activity chart indicates whether the information is needed. Information gained from the organization questionnaire (discussed later) is of value in defining authority relationships, the nature of assigned responsibilities, and the extent of authority delegated to carry out these responsibilities. The gathering of data for an organizational analysis is often a long and tedious task, but it is an important step for it establishes the factual basis for any proposed change.[3]

Prepare Alternative Plans. Ultimately, any proposed change in organization must be sold to key personnel and alternative plans should be prepared as a form of insurance. Among these plans there should be an "ideal" structure that is theoretically desirable, but not necessarily attainable. Using the ideal as a starting point, modifications in the plan that consider the economic and competitive position of the company may be developed. If only a single plan is presented, it may be rejected by one displeased executive; an alternative plan is necessary since organizational change is a situation in which "half a loaf is better than none," and the adoption of the alternative plan is at least a step in the right direction.

---

[3] An evaluation of data obtained from the records of an organization compared with information obtained from questionnaires is presented in the following:

Vijay Sathe, "Institutional versus Questionnaire Measures of Organizational Structure," *Academy of Management Journal*, Vol. 21, No. 2 (June, 1978), p. 227.

Jeffrey D. Ford, "Institutional versus Questionnaire Measures of Organizational Structure: A Reexamination," *Academy of Management Journal*, Vol. 22, No. 3 (September, 1979), p. 601.

Install the Best Plan and Follow Up. When the plan is approved, it should be installed and there should be provisions for continuing study and analysis so that any necessary modifications can be made. This task is usually assigned to the group that proposes the initial change. Proper follow-up and modifications of the plan, when needed, emphasize the continuing nature of organizational change.

Tools of Organizational Analysis

There are many tools available for use in organizational analysis. Among those most commonly used are the organization questionnaire, the position description, the organization chart, and the organization manual. Each of these techniques used in studying organizations is discussed briefly.

The Organization Questionnaire. One of the first steps in describing the present organization is to determine the functions and positions of personnel. Organization questionnaires have been found useful in obtaining information from executives, supervisors, and department heads concerning their positions in the organization. The first portion of most questionnaires contains identification material, such as the name of the employee, the department, the major division, title of position held, and the location of the position. Also, the name and position title of the employee's immediate supervisor are requested. The employee is also asked to give the names and titles of subordinates along with the activities of subordinates and an indication of whether actions taken by subordinates are reported prior to action, reported after action has been taken, or not reported at all. The employee may also be asked to describe the responsibilities of the position held and close relationships with other personnel in the organization. The nature of authority is generally defined in terms of whether the employee may establish policy, incur expenses, make personnel changes, or establish procedures and methods. Membership on committees is also included and, if chairing the committee, the employee is asked to state the goals and accomplishments of the committee. The basic records that must be kept and regular or occasional reports that are required are also listed. Finally, the employee may be asked to make suggestions concerning changes that would improve the functioning of the organization.[4]

There are two methods of securing the information called for by the questionnaire. One method is to have the employee in the position fill out the questionnaire and return it to the person conducting the study; the other method is to secure the information through interview. While the latter method is more costly and time-consuming, it is generally agreed that the interview yields much more information and understanding of the organization as a result of side remarks and nuances of meaning implied in the way in which answers are given. Once

---

[4] Harry Levinson, Janice Molinari, and Andrew G. Spohn, *Organizational Diagnosis* (Cambridge: Harvard University Press, 1972). This work presents an in-depth study of the many techniques used in organizational diagnosis including the questionnaire. The use of the questionnaire and interviews are discussed thoroughly.

the questionnaires have been completed, they are usually reviewed with the next higher level of authority. It is at this stage that significant discrepancies in the opinions of superior and subordinate with respect to the nature of assigned duties, the nature and extent of delegated authority, and the lines of accountability may emerge.

The Position Description. The data obtained from the questionnaire is the primary source of information for preparing the *position description*, a written statement that describes a specific position in the organization. Whether a written position description merely sketches the major duties of the job or whether it goes into minute detail depends on its intended use. If the purpose is to define the major positions in the organization and show their relationships to each other, the description may be relatively brief; if, however, the primary purpose of the description is for training, the job duties may be so detailed that they approach the completeness of a procedural manual.

Most position descriptions include the following information. There is a section that *identifies* the job and may range from a statement of the title only to the inclusion of statements indicating the title of the immediate superior, the date of preparation of the description with dates of revision, and the number and types of employees supervised. Generally the name of the position holder is not included since a change in personnel would necessitate a revision of the description. Next, there is a statement of the major responsibility or *primary functions* of the job, a capsule description of the purpose of the position. A statement of *responsibilities* presents the major tasks that must be performed in order to fulfill the functions of the job. It is this portion of the description, when developed in great detail, that may serve as a useful training device; but, for the most part, executive and supervisory descriptions are limited to a statement of between six and ten major responsibilities. The *authority* delegated to the position in order to perform the required functions may appear as a separate section of the position description or it may be combined with the statement of primary responsibilities. The last section of most descriptions is a statement of *relationships*. The reason for stating relationships is twofold. First, it shows the position in its proper relationship to other positions within the company and relationships to people outside the company such as vendors, auditors, or public relations contacts. Second, a statement of relationships tends to answer the criticism often made of position descriptions that these descriptions force an employee into a narrow role, oblivious to other events and employees in the company.

As a general rule, position descriptions do not include a statement of the specifications and qualifications required of the position holder. If such specifications are prepared, they are on a separate sheet and include requirements regarding education, experience, and other personal characteristics. Specifications are of value as an aid in evaluating and selecting potential replacements.

The Organization Chart. An organization chart presents in graphic form the major functions and the lines of authority of an organization as of a given moment in time. Charts range in complexity from the simple chart shown in

ORGANIZATION CHART — XYZ CORPORATION

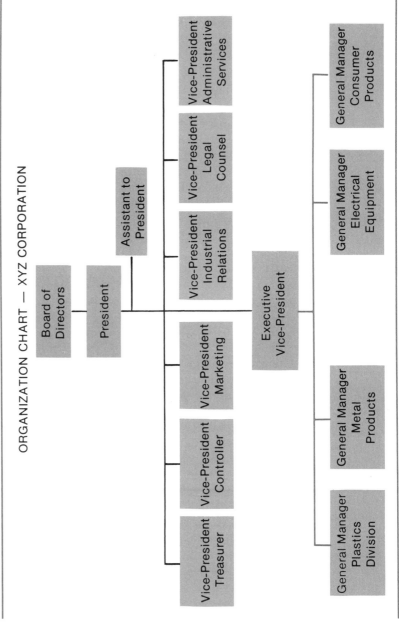

Figure 12–1
A VERTICAL ORGANIZATION CHART

Figure 12–1 to complex charts that use color and the photographs of the holders of key positions. However, for purposes of organizational analysis and reference, it is best to keep charts as simple as possible.

The mechanics of constructing an organization chart are not difficult. Table 12–1 presents ten suggestions for preparing organization charts. These are not hard-and-fast rules and they should be modified when the occasion demands.

Table 12–1 SUGGESTIONS FOR PREPARING AN ORGANIZATIONAL CHART

1. Identify the chart fully by showing the name of the company, date of preparation, and title of person or name of department responsible for preparation. If the chart is for one division of the company only, include such information as part of the title.
2. Use rectangular boxes to show either an organizational unit or a person. Plural executives and other committees occupy one box.
3. The vertical placement of the boxes shows relative positions in the organizational hierarchy; however, due to space limitations, line units are frequently shown one level below staff units. (See Figure 12–1.)
4. Any given horizontal row of boxes should be of the same size and should include only those positions having the same organizational rank.
5. Use vertical and horizontal solid lines to show the flow of line authority.
6. If necessary, use dotted or broken lines to show the flow of functional authority. (See Figure 10–4.)
7. Lines of authority enter at the top center of a box and leave at the bottom center; they do not run through the box. Exception: the line of authority to a staff assistant or an "assistant-to" may enter the side of the box. (See Figure 12–1.)
8. The title of each position should be placed in the box. The title should be descriptive and show function. For example, vice-president is not sufficient as it does not show function. The functional area, e.g., manufacturing, should be included even though it is not a part of the official title. Titles should be consistent; if necessary, revise titles so they are both consistent and descriptive.
9. Include the name of the person currently holding the position unless personnel turnover is so great that revision of the chart is burdensome.
10. Keep the chart as simple as possible; include a legend if necessary to explain any special notations. When preparing a separate chart for an organizational unit, include the superior to whom the unit reports.

By far the most common form of organizational charting is the *vertical* chart (Figure 12–1), which shows the organizational hierarchy ranked from top to bottom. A variation of the vertical chart is the *horizontal* chart, which is read from left to right rather than from top to bottom. A more complex form of charting is the *circular* organization chart, which places the chief executive in the center of the circle with the horizontal lines of the vertical chart forming a series of concentric circles around the chief executive. Proponents of the horizontal form of charting contend that we normally read from left to right and that a horizontal chart follows this natural tendency. Those who favor the circular chart claim that dynamic relationships are better portrayed through a series of concentric circles. However, precedent and ease of construction and interpretation favor the continued use of the vertical chart.

The Organization Manual. An *organization manual* is a compilation of descriptive statements usually bound in manual form concerning the organization of a specific company. The content of organization manuals varies widely; however, two of the tools of organizational analysis are included in almost all manuals—position descriptions and organization charts.[5] The combination of these two instruments shows the lines of authority and accountability, the major functions of each position, the responsibilities and authority for each position, and the primary interrelationships between key positions. In addition, organization manuals may include statements of company objectives and company policy. In large companies, it is not uncommon to find organization manuals consisting of several volumes, one for each of the major functional areas of the company. In such cases, each volume includes a statement of company objectives, policies, and the organization charts and position descriptions for that specific functional area.

Evaluation of Formal Organizational Analysis

Not all companies believe in using the formal tools of organizational analysis. The extent to which formal tools of analysis are used is related to the size of the company. The absence of charts, position descriptions, and organization manuals in small companies may be due to a belief that they are not needed, a lack of personnel to prepare such materials, or any of a number of similar reasons. However, large companies without charts have not prepared them because it is felt that the disadvantages of charting the organization outweigh the advantages. Let us examine the advantages and disadvantages usually attributed to the use of formal tools of organizational analysis.

Advantages of Formal Organizational Analysis. The advantage most frequently cited in support of preparing a formal analysis of an organization is that the process of analysis itself forces the key executives of the company into critical thinking directed toward organizational problems. The process of analysis leads to a reexamination of present structure and functions and makes possible the correction of organizational defects. Second, charts and manuals are of use in training replacements for present personnel. True, the person holding the position at present may not benefit greatly, but new people coming into the organization or a person moving into a new position find charts and manuals helpful during their period of orientation. The third reason advanced for formalizing the organization structure is that charts and position descriptions offer

---

[5] For a discussion of the use of organization charts as a means of planning for an organization's future the following is recommended: William L. Brockhaus, "Planning for Change with Organization Charts," *Business Horizons*, Vol. 17, No. 2 (April, 1974), p. 47.

an authoritative source which describes the major functions and responsibilities for each position and thus become a means of settling disputes that may arise concerning lines of authority and accountability.

Disadvantages of Formal Organizational Analysis. Those who prefer not to use formal analysis claim that the formalization of organization structure by charts and position descriptions leads to rigidity and inflexibility in organization structure and function. They point out that a new person coming into a position complete with chart and position description is bound by precedent and does not have the full opportunity for self-expression and for showing an ability to contribute to the organization. In a sense, these critics of charting are saying, "Put a person into a square and you have one." In addition to organizational inflexibility and the stultifying effects that charting may have on individuals, opponents of formal analysis state that formal charting completely ignores the informal organization—the many interpersonal relationships, lines of communications, and influence—which exists among people who work together every day and is often quite different from the formal relationships shown on the chart.

There is a need for balance. Charting is not intended to stultify or limit the achievement of individuals. It is intended to show in broad strokes major functions and relationships. Nor is charting intended to promote organizational inflexibility; on the other hand, an organization with relationships that change from day to day or with every crisis cannot properly be called an organization.

Evaluating Organizational Effectiveness

The application of the tools of organizational analysis—the organization questionnaire, the position description, and the charting of the present organization—is the second step in the process of organizational analysis. In order to complete the third step of analysis, to prepare alternative plans of organization, and move on to the fourth step of selecting the best plan for a given situation, it is necessary to establish a basis for evaluating present organizational effectiveness. Due to the dynamic nature of organizations resulting from patterns of leadership, the structure of the organization, the types of organizational authority, the efficiency of organizational processes such as delegation, and the utilization of groups to perform organizational functions, any concept of measuring effectiveness must recognize these variables and interpret them in terms of the needs of each specific organization. Table 12–2, Checklist of Organizational Effectiveness, is a systematic means of checking each major factor contributing to organizational effectiveness. Let us examine Table 12–2, remembering that the characteristics of organization are not absolutes; that is, they are neither black nor white.[6]

---

[6] Although there is not complete agreement concerning the criteria to be used in determining the degree of effectiveness of an organization, or any of its subunits, the following articles are illustrative of current approaches to the study of organizational effectiveness:

J. Barton Cunningham, "Approaches to the Evaluation of Organizational Effectiveness," *The Academy of Management Review*, Vol. 2, No. 3 (July, 1977), p. 463. (Footnote continued on page 251.)

1. OVERALL PLANNING
Written Statements of Company
 Objectives
Company Policies
 Marketing
 Finance
 Production
 Personnel
 Other

2. PATTERNS OF LEADERSHIP
Primarily
 Authoritative
 Participative
 Appropriate

3. ORGANIZATIONAL STRUCTURE
Departmentation
 Function
 Product
 Customer
 Geography
 Process
 Sequence
Span of Management
 One over One
 Two or Three
 Three to Seven
 Eight or More
Overall Impression
 Proper Balance
 Proper Emphasis

4. AUTHORITY RELATIONSHIPS
Factors Limiting Effectiveness of
 Authority
 Overlapping Authority
 Superior Authority
 Provisions for Subordinate
  Acceptance
Line and Staff Relationships
 Use of "Assistant-to:"

5. DELEGATION
Limits of Line Authority
Limits of Staff Authority
Task Force Organization
Parity of Authority and
 Responsibility
Absoluteness of Accountability
Unity of Command
Personality Factors

6. DECENTRALIZATION
Definition of Decentralized Unit
Scope, Type, and Frequency of
 Decisions
Availability of Controls
Statement of Goals for Unit
Degree of Decentralization
 Optimum
 Too Little
 Too Much

7. USE OF COMMITTEES
Committees
 Ad Hoc
 Advisory
 Management
 Composition
 Benefits
Board of Directors
 Outside Members
 Inside Members
 Contribution

8. PROVISIONS FOR CONTROL
Definitions of Standards
Units of Measurement
Reporting of Exceptions
Timeliness of Controls
Strategic Placement of Controls
Control Information for Line
 Managers

Table 12–2
CHECKLIST OF
ORGANIZATIONAL
EFFECTIVENESS

Overall Planning. The extent of overall planning lends direction and purpose to an organization and is basic to the effectiveness of any enterprise. In the collection of data for organizational analysis, the examination of company records may determine the extent of overall planning. Two questions are asked in this regard: Is there a written statement of company objectives? Is there a written statement of company policy? Objectives define the goals of the organization, while policy statements indicate the broad framework within which each of the functional areas of the firm should operate in achieving the objectives. As an absolute minimum, there should be policy guides for each of the major functional areas of finance, production, marketing, and personnel. Unless objectives and policies are clearly stated, there is very little hope for establishing effective organizational structure and processes.

Patterns of Leadership. Chapter 8 discusses Theory X, a work-centered approach to organizational leadership, and Theory Y, a people-centered or human relations approach to leadership. The contingency approach to organization theory holds that the most effective leadership pattern, whether it be predominantly authoritative or participative, is dependent on the characteristics of the organization and its members. As the organization grows in size, defining size as number of people, there is a tendency for leadership patterns to become more authoritative. The same tendency exists when there is little need for interaction between members, when members of the organization are submissive and dependent, when the goals of individuals and the organization are divergent, when decision making occurs at a high level of the organization, and when the organization is under pressure to survive and meet stated objectives. The converse of the above situation—a small organization or unit, need for interaction, independent members, congruent goals, decision making at all levels in an organization achieving its objectives—calls for a participative form of leadership. Although a judgment concerning the effectiveness of leadership is highly subjective in nature and its worth dependent on the skill of the person performing the organizational analysis, such a judgment should be made in evaluating an organization.

Organization Structure. When evaluating the structure of an organization, three structural characteristics are considered: departmentation, span of management, and an overall impression of balance and emphasis. The most frequently used bases for departmentation are function, product, customer, geography, process, sequence, and any combination of these. The basis chosen for forming a department varies from one level of the organization to another, and there may be variation in the bases for departmentation among units of the same level. The test of proper departmentation is whether or not the result is a grouping of activities that is capable of functioning effectively.

Michael A. Hitt and R. Dennis Middlemist, "A Methodology to Develop the Criteria and Criteria Weightings for Assessing Subunit Effectiveness in Organizations," *Academy of Management Journal*, Vol. 22, No. 2 (June, 1979), p. 356.

Raymond E. Miles *et al.*, "Organizational Strategy, Structure, and Process," *The Academy of Management Review*, Vol. 3, No. 3 (July, 1978), p. 546.

Andrew H. Van de Ven, "A Framework for Organization Assessment," *The Academy of Management Review*, Vol. 1, No. 1 (January, 1976), p. 64.

Span of management is the number of departments or functions under the direction of one manager. The checklist in Table 12–2 provides a basis for grouping the span of management into four broad categories. When a one-over-one arrangement is found, it deserves careful examination. A situation in which a one-over-one arrangement is probably effective and necessary is that of an executive vice-president as the sole person reporting to the president. In this instance, the president's other duties, such as relations with the board of directors and with groups outside the company, may make it mandatory that only one person report to the president. However, one-over-one relationships at lower levels of the organization should be regarded with suspicion. The designation of an assistant manager, a line relationship showing only one subordinate, may be justified if there is a clear understanding of those functions to be performed by the manager and those functions to be performed by the assistant manager.

An overall impression of the effectiveness of an organizational structure includes evaluating the structure; i.e., departmentation and span of management, with respect to the *balance* and *emphasis* accorded those functions and activities most closely related to the objectives of the organization. It is helpful to view the structure as components of a system, and the parameters of the contingency approach, as discussed in Chapter 8, are helpful as a basis for determining whether the departmentation, span of management, and the degree of balance and emphasis represent the optimum for organizational effectiveness.

Authority Relationships. In reviewing authority relationships, our concern is directed toward those factors that limit authority, the clarity of established line-and-staff relationships, and ultimately a consideration of the feasibility of a task force form of organization. When determining the effectiveness of lines of authority, it is necessary to determine the extent to which there is overlapping authority between managerial functions. The source of this information is the questionnaire and the position description. Occasionally authority may be ineffective because provisions for subordinate acceptance of authority are inadequate and may result in ineffective performance, lack of cooperation, and, on occasion, refusal to follow directions. The pattern of leadership is an important item to consider when assessing provisions for subordinate acceptance.

When checking line-and-staff relationships, review any position entitled "assistant-to" and question the practicality of designating a specific staff title more descriptive of the functions performed. In small organizations or in the case of new positions, descriptive titles may not be practical. When determining the authority relationships of established line-and-staff positions, attention is directed toward the degree to which authority relationships are defined—the stating of definite limits of authority for each, and the extent to which each authority understands the role of the other. In some organizations, characterized by changing projects, with well-defined objectives and limiting time tables, it is well to consider the possibility of using a task force organization designed for the specific task at hand. It is necessary that responsibility for the entire project be stated and that provisions be made for the reassignment of personnel upon the completion of the project.

Delegation. Violation of any of the three conditions for effective delegation may result in ineffective delegation. Admittedly these conditions are ignored on many occasions; but when ignored and when the resultant delegation seems effective, it is effective in spite of the fact that the conditions have been disregarded. Also, poor delegation may be due to personality characteristics of either the superior or the subordinate which make the process of delegation ineffective.

Decentralization. The measure of the effectiveness of decentralization of authority is whether it meets the needs of the organization. The parameters of the contingency approach form a useful set of guides concerning the appropriateness of the degree of decentralization. Additional questions may be raised concerning the definition of the decentralized unit, the scope and type of decisions made within the unit, provisions for adequate control, and the statement of goals for the unit. An overall determination of effective decentralization expresses the degree of decentralization as optimum, too little, or too much.

Use of Committees. When properly used, committees may perform quite effectively the managerial functions assigned to them. In rating the effectiveness of committees, it is necessary to determine the extent to which the duties assigned to the committee are in keeping with the functions normally assigned to a given type of committee. *Ad hoc* committees are temporary in nature and are formed to consider a specific question. They are disbanded upon the completion of their assignment. *Ad hoc* groups may appear at any level of the organization and the functions assigned may range from making recommendations to making decisions and taking action necessary for the completion of the assignment. Advisory committees are, as the name indicates, assigned advisory functions with the right to take action reserved for another, usually the person to whom the committee reports. The management committee, whose members are from the top level of the company, offers a means of coordinating the work of individual functional areas and may operate as a plural executive. Benefits derived from the proper use of committees are the value of pooled judgments coming from the diverse knowledge of the individual members, the creation of a favorable training situation, and improved cooperation on the part of individual members as the result of having participated in the work of the group.

In determining the contribution of a board of directors, review the backgrounds of individual members, not only regarding their status as employees of the corporation which determines whether they are inside or outside members, but also with respect to the amount of time each member is able to devote to the company. The contributions of a board depend on the manner in which they perform their directive functions of setting corporate objectives, selecting management, and subsequently reviewing and guiding management's efforts.

Provisions for Control. Though the control process is not discussed fully until Part 5 of this textbook, items concerning the control function are included in the checklist for organizational effectiveness for the sake of completeness. In evaluating control provisions, it is necessary to determine the extent to which standards of performance are clearly defined—particularly for the production and marketing functions. The units of measurement employed to measure performance against standard should be appropriate and as objective as possible. Consideration is also given to the degree to which controls report the exceptional deviation from standard, to their timeliness, and to their strategic placement. Since the last step of the control process may require corrective action, controls should provide necessary information for the responsible manager so that appropriate corrective action may be taken.

ORGANIZATION DEVELOPMENT

For many, organizational analysis and subsequent changes in structure are nothing more than tinkering with the organization. To these persons organizational analysis leads only to changes in organization structure and occasionally to changes in organizational processes. However, it does not result in meeting the real needs of organizational change that result in the development of the organization. *Organization development* (OD) is perceived as a social change in the organization. Organization development is also a change in the value system of the organization. OD has been referred to as a school, a program, a movement, a concept, and as a method of change. Whatever it is called, it is hoped that as a result of OD a change will occur in the internal environment, or culture, of the organization.

A Definition of Organization Development

Two major difficulties are encountered when discussing organization development. First, there is no agreed upon definition of what constitutes organization development. Second, the many definitions of organization development contain terminology that has meaning only as it relates to its use in organization development. In turn, consensus does not always exist regarding the meaning of this terminology. Despite the absence of agreed upon meanings of terms and a definition of OD, there are certain key words that appear in most definitions. Among them are *change, total organization, client system, change agent, intervention, behavioral science methods, strategies, individual versus organizational goals*, and *organizational effectiveness.*[7]

It is a truism that organizations must change if they are to survive. Structural change may occur in an organization as the result of the acquisition of another company. The personnel of an organization may change as the result of attrition; and the processes and functions of an organization may change as the result of governmental regulation. However, these are not the changes of organization

---

[7] The following two works are suggested as comprehensive statements of organization development goals and techniques:

Gerald Zaltman and Robert Duncan, *Strategies for Planned Change* (New York City: John Wiley & Sons, Inc., 1977). Zaltman and Duncan present material of value to those who wish to introduce an organization development program.

Glenn H. Varney, *Organization Development for Managers* (Reading, Mass.: Addison-Wesley Publishing Company, 1977). This book is written for the practicing manager and presents a broad overview of the field.

development. OD seeks to change the behavior, attitudes, and values of the members of an organization. Organization development is closely related to the human relations approach to management, and, as a result, the value system of organization development is people oriented. An organization with a successful OD program is best described as a Theory Y organization.

The key figure in an organization development program is the *change agent.* Change agents usually have training in the behavioral sciences—anthropology, psychology, or sociology. When they are employed by the organization they are referred to as *internal* change agents. A change agent may also be an independent consultant who offers services on a fee basis. As a consultant the change agent is referred to as an *external* change agent. The organization that engages an external change agent is known as the *client system* or the *target system.* Frequently both internal and external change agents work together in the establishment of an organization development program. Whether internal or external, the change agent functions as a catalyst in bringing about the desired social changes through the application of behavioral science methods. The hoped for end result of an OD program is an increase in *organizational effectiveness.* Organizational effectiveness may range from perceived changes in effectiveness, as viewed by the members of the organization, to measurable quantitative changes in such areas as profitability or sales volume.

Organization development is a planned change in the environment, or culture, of an organization as the result of changes in the attitudes, values, or behavior of its members. These changes are accomplished through the application of behavioral science methods in order to improve effectiveness in the attainment of organizational objectives.

OD Strategies

The application of organization development techniques is known as an *intervention.* Some of the techniques of OD serve several purposes. They may be used as an aid in diagnosing the needs of the organization, as a means of changing behavior and attitudes of the members of the organization, or as a means of evaluating other OD strategies.

Diagnostic Techniques. Interviews, frequently conducted by the change agent with individuals or with small homogeneous work groups, serve as a means of determining the needs of those being interviewed. These interviews, which may also be conducted by designated members of the organization, can be designed to explore the relationships that exist between organizational units having vertical relationships. Such interviews are referred to as *vertical sensing.* Interviews may also be designed for *horizontal sensing*—to determine the relationships between units that interact but are not in the same chain of command. Though the initial purpose of an interview technique may be to obtain information of a diagnostic nature, it may result in the establishment of a relatively permanent consulting team within the organization. For example, the division manager, the personnel director, and the change agent (either internal or external) may function as a consulting team for that division with the dual purpose of diagnosing the needs of the division and solving problems that arise within the division.

The organization questionnaire, discussed earlier in this chapter (pp. 244–245), is also used by organization development specialists. However, when used in connection with OD it is referred to as a *survey feedback* technique. In addition to the descriptive data sought for organizational analysis, a survey feedback seeks information on interpersonal relationships. Members of the organization are asked to report their perceptions of supervisors, subordinates, and peers with respect to such characteristics as cooperativeness, degree of innovation, and supportive behavior. The survey feedback may be used as a diagnostic tool prior to any intervention, or it may be used after the application of an OD strategy to determine the effectiveness of that intervention.[8]

Intervention Techniques. Virtually every means of changing either the structure or the processes of an organization or the attitudes, values, or behavior of its members have been claimed as an organization development intervention. The following are a few of the more commonly used intervention strategies.

Sensitivity Training. As the phrase suggests, the goal of sensitivity training is to heighten a person's awareness of himself or herself and to increase one's sensitivity to the feelings and attitudes of others. Sensitivity training is not the acquisition of more knowledge about human relations, nor is it directed primarily toward the improvement of skills in human relations. Instead, it is an emotionalized experience of interpersonal relationships. The result of the experience is often a change in attitudes and feelings toward oneself and toward others. Sensitivity training is conducted in groups of ten to twelve persons often referred to as *T-groups* (*T* meaning training). Although the members of a T-group may come from the same organization, usually they are from different organizations and have not met each other prior to the sensitivity training session. Since the sensitivity training program is conducted under somewhat controlled conditions, the method is also frequently referred to as *laboratory training*. There is no formal agenda. The group must decide the nature of its training activities. At the end of each training session each participant evaluates the other members of the group. The evaluation is in terms of how that person contributed to the activities of the group as perceived by the evaluator. In many instances the evaluations are highly critical and personal in nature. However, they are justified in that the participants are presumed to become more sensitive, as a result of the criticism, concerning the way in which they are perceived by others and at the same time more sensitive concerning the way in which they perceive the actions of others.

Team Building. Sensitivity training is directed toward the development of individuals; however, team building is directed toward the development of effective group activities. Team-building efforts are usually problem solving in nature

---

[8] Michael K. Lindell and John A. Drexler, Jr., "Issues in Using Survey Methods for Measuring Organizational Change," *Academy of Management Review*, Vol. 4, No. 1 (January, 1979), p. 13.

with the members of each team defining the problem, offering solutions as the result of group participation, and having the responsibility for executing the decisions made by the group. Team-building activities may be directed toward the creation of new teams that are required by a task force form of organization. Or the activities of team building may be directed toward improving the performance of existing groups. Existing teams may be re-formed because of changes in the organization as the result of acquisitions, mergers, or a change in organizational objectives. Team-building activities are recognition of the fact that groups, as well as individuals, must be trained to function effectively.

Intergroup Meetings. The emphasis of intergroup meetings is on solving problems that exist between organizational groups. For example, in a manufacturing firm a sales engineering department is often responsible for preparing a basic product design and cost estimate for a customer. There is also a manufacturing engineering department which is responsible for preparing specifications in such a way that the product can be manufactured efficiently. Intergroup meetings of these two departments should result in an improved degree of understanding of their respective problems and should assure better service to the customer and lower manufacturing costs. Also, tensions arising between line and staff personnel can be reduced by means of intergroup meetings. Perhaps the most difficult to arrange, yet offering a great deal of promise, are meetings between consumer advocates representing customers and the company providing the product or service in question.

Life and Career Planning. These sessions focus on the life and career plans of the individual members of the organization. Each member is encouraged to develop a career plan; hopefully that plan lies within the organization sponsoring the program. The participant is asked to relate the plan to activities occurring within the organization and within the community in which the individual works and lives. The objectives of such programs are to offer each individual the opportunity to reach a maximum degree of self-fulfillment.

Job Enrichment/Enlargement. The enrichment of jobs—i.e., making jobs more meaningful—is also considered an OD intervention strategy. Usually job enrichment means more than merely enlarging a job by assigning more tasks to be performed. Enrichment implies that the job is designed as a unified whole as opposed to the performance of a single task such as assembling one part of a product.

Behavior Modification. It may be argued that all the preceding intervention strategies are intended to modify behavior. However, as an OD technique behavior modification has a more specific meaning. It is a change in behavior brought about by means of *positive reinforcement*—giving a specific immediate reward for exhibiting the desired behavior. Behavior modification programs are based on the assumption that if a given form of behavior is rewarded (positive reinforcement), that behavior will be learned and repeated. An example of positive reinforcement is that of having employees set goals jointly with management with provision for immediate feedback showing the extent to which the goals are being met. Knowledge of results achieved can serve as positive reinforcement. Behavior modification has also been utilized as a means of improving attendance. A typical program is a drawing for a television set or some other major appliance, with only those employees having perfect attendance records for a specific period eligible for the drawing (Babb and Kopp).

Evaluation of Organization Development

There are undoubtedly many companies that are satisfied with the results of their organization development programs. However, evaluations of organization development as a method of achieving organizational change have not been favorable. Typical of such criticism is that of David G. Bowers, a recognized authority in the field of organization development.[9] Bowers presents three major criticisms of organization development—superficiality, commercialism, and problems attributable to the role of the change agent.

One aspect of the superficiality of organization development is revealed by the quality of the published studies which report the results of organization development programs. Very few of these studies present objective data showing the effectiveness of organization development. Very few studies present evidence that clearly shows that organizational changes, if any, are in fact the result of a specific organization development program. Bowers reviewed the literature reported during the 15-year period, 1960–1975, and found that of the thousands of studies published in that period of time only 18 studies presented what Bowers considered to be real evidence supporting the effectiveness of OD.

Organization development is also superficial in its approach to its objectives of changing the behavior and attitudes of members of an organization. It is generally recognized that changing the behavior of an adult is a process that takes continuous effort for relatively long periods of time. Yet the approach of organization development is confined to a relatively short period of time. Even though laboratory or T-group training can be a very intense experience for the one- or two-week training period required, it is a woefully inadequate amount of time to produce any lasting changes in behavior.

Finally, there is superficiality in the extent to which organization development programs are applied within a given organization. Despite the fact that these programs are referred to as *organization* development programs, there are few instances where such programs are utilized throughout the entire organization. For example, OD has not been applied to hourly rated employees to any great extent. Often the president of an organization is not a participant in the OD program. In addition, most OD programs are applied only to selected departments, not to the entire organization. In general, the literature indicates that organization development is not applied throughout the entire organization.

---

[9] David G. Bowers, "Organizational Development: Promises, Performances, Possibilities," *Organizational Dynamics*, Vol. 4, No. 4 (Spring, 1976), p. 50.

For an account of failures in organization development the following is recommended. Philip H. Mirvis, *Failures in Organization Development and Change: Cases and Essays for Learning* (New York City: John Wiley & Sons, Inc., 1977).

The criticisms of commercialism and problems relating to the role of the change agent are actually criticisms of the consultants who sell and administer OD programs. One aspect of commercialism is that the payoffs, or benefits, of OD are not known and are not easy to compute. Yet, despite the fact that a prospective client company does not know the benefits to be expected, that company is sold an OD program that is often presented as a panacea. Also, the outside consultant is probably competent in only a very few of the many OD strategies available—strategies that may or may not be the most appropriate means of modifying the organization of that particular company.

It was stated earlier that the consultant or change agent functions as a catalyst. Herein lies one of the major problems associated with the role of the consultant. As a catalyst the change agent is limited to the perceptions and proposed solutions of the members of the group where the change is to be applied. Somehow these ideas are to be transformed into the correct solution of the problem. Yet there are instances where a catalytic process is not appropriate. There may be a need for a completely new approach to the solution of the problem utilizing knowledge not available to the group. For example, the difficulties of a company with regard to its manufacturing processes may not be due to interpersonal problems between the production workers and their supervisors. The problems may be the result of a totally inadequate production control system. Similarly, the problems of a retail organization may be the result of an inadequate inventory control system rather than the result of interpersonal problems. Yet the typical consultant works as a catalyst seeking a change from within the organization rather than introducing a completely new solution such as a production or inventory control system not perceived or recommended by the group itself.

Performance Appraisals

The main purpose in evaluating an organization development program is to provide feedback so that the effectiveness of the program with respect to its contribution to the development of the entire organization may be determined. Evaluation of results is also necessary to revise personnel requirements and to update the information contained in the personnel inventory. Opinion and attitude surveys of those who have participated in the program are of value; however, there is evidence that the information elicited from such surveys may express at best only a general satisfaction with the "broadening effects" of organization development rather than provide the specific data necessary for the improvement of such programs.[10] The most common device used to evaluate the development

---

[10] Thomas Decotiis, Andre Petit, "The Performance Appraisal Process: A Model and Some Testable Propositions," *Academy of Management Review*, Vol. 3, No. 3 (July, 1978), p. 635.

Michael Keeley, "A Contingency Framework for Performance Evaluation," *Academy of Management Review*, Vol. 3, No. 3 (July, 1978), p. 428.

Ronald J. Grey and David Kipnis, "Untangling the Performance Appraisal Dilemma: The Influence of Perceived Organizational Context on Evaluative Processes," *Journal of Applied Psychology*, Vol. 61, No. 3 (June, 1976), p. 329.

of managers is the *performance appraisal.* Since the performance appraisal is used not only as a means of evaluating an organization development program but also as a means of supplying information for the management personnel inventory, there is considerable criticism concerning performance appraisals. Although a subordinate's performance is always appraised in some fashion by the superior, the introduction of formal performance appraisals into an organization is invariably met with resistance. Such resistance is usually evidenced by the inability to complete the required appraisals within the allotted time limits. Resistance is due in part to the lack of a clear statement of the purpose of appraisals, a definition of expected standards of performance, and an understanding of the objectives of the appraisal interview.

Purpose of Appraisals. There are two questions to be resolved in determining the purpose of performance appraisals. First, is the appraisal intended to measure current performance, or is it intended to measure the subordinate's potential for promotion? Second, is the appraisal to be used to determine advances in salary, or is it to be used as a basis for self-improvement?

It is difficult enough for a manager to appraise current performance without, as Douglas McGregor phrases it, "playing God" by being required to estimate a subordinate's potential capabilities in the organization.[11] Admittedly, a manager makes such estimates and an estimate of potential is reflected each time a subordinate is selected for promotion. But having to state potential capabilities in writing and perhaps having to reveal and defend the estimate to the subordinate during the interview is one of the major causes of resistance to formal appraisal systems. An appraisal is not only a statement of a subordinate's performance but also a mirror of the superior's personality and concept of adequate performance. If the superior lacks self-confidence and perhaps has lost hope of being promoted, these attitudes may be reflected in the appraisal of subordinates. Further, few managers have a sound basis for determining the ability required for any position other than their own. Indeed, the question of capabilities and manager performance has only begun to be answered. Thus, it seems wise to limit appraisals to an evaluation of current performance.

Having determined that the appraisal should be limited to an evaluation of current performance, the second question—whether the results of the appraisal should be used to determine salary or used as a basis for self-improvement— remains to be answered. When appraisals are used to determine whether a subordinate should receive an increase in salary, there is a tendency to distort the appraisal of current performance so that the decision in regard to salary may be justified. Performance is only one of several factors determining whether an increase in pay should be granted. Availability of funds, length of time on

---

[11] Douglas McGregor, "An Uneasy Look at Performance Appraisals," *Harvard Business Review,* Vol. 35, No. 3 (May–June, 1957), p. 89.

L. L. Cummings and Donald P. Schwab, *Performance in Organizations, Determinants and Appraisal* (Glenview: Scott, Foresman & Co., 1973). *Performance in Organizations* is one of the more recent comprehensive books on performance appraisal. Of significance is an annotated bibliography which makes up the final chapter.

the job, salary ranges, and the subordinate's position within the salary range are a few of the other factors that must be considered. Since the goal of an organization development program includes the development of individual managers, appraisals of performance should serve as a basis for improving that performance in the future. Objective discussions of current performance are possible only when salary considerations are set aside and attention is directed toward the improvement of performance and the development of the individual. Decisions concerning salary should be made at a separate time and should include all aspects of the company's salary policy.

Standards of Performance. Another problem encountered in the use of performance appraisals is that of developing criteria for measuring performance on the job. In many appraisal systems the manager is asked to rate subordinates on a five-point scale using a list of personality traits such as loyalty, promptness, and willingness to work. All too frequently this approach may again become a reflection of the rater's personality. Occasionally a superior is asked to rate the performance of each subordinate against that of each of the other subordinates. The shortcomings of this method are obvious, particularly when subordinates have different jobs requiring different abilities and levels of achievement. A third type of criteria is defined in terms of the goals of the job itself. However, for job goals to be effective standards of performance, they must be clearly stated, measurable, and within the control of the subordinate.

The Appraisal Interview. Most formal appraisal systems require an interview between subordinate and superior. The interview is supposed to offer an opportunity for the subordinate to discover where he or she stands, at which time the superior should outline steps to be taken for the improvement of job performance and self-development. An extensive study of the typical appraisal interview conducted at General Electric shows that praise has little effect, either positively or negatively, that criticism has a negative effect on future achievement, and that defensiveness results from criticism with no improvement of performance.[12] The same study indicates that discussions concerning salary should be held at a separate time and not as a part of a performance review. It is questionable whether the typical line manager has the necessary training or inclination to conduct a broad evaluative interview. As McGregor has noted, there is a reluctance to "play God," with the result that the typical interview is resisted by both superior and subordinate and usually becomes a mere formality, with little of the developmental benefits that should result from it.

Improving Performance Appraisals. The weaknesses of the typical performance appraisal are attributable to failure to define the purpose of the appraisal, the need for a well-defined set of criteria, and the inadequacy of the appraisal

---

[12] Herbert H. Meyer, Emanuel Kay, and John R. P. French, Jr., "Split Roles in Performance Appraisal," *Harvard Business Review,* Vol. 43, No. 1 (January–February, 1965), p. 123. The following article discusses performance appraisals in several other major United States corporations: Herbert E. Meyer, "The Science of Telling Executives How They're Doing," *Fortune,* Vol. 89, No. 1 (January, 1974), p. 102.

interview. Appraisals may be conducted to determine the potential of a member of management, to evaluate performance in his or her present job, or to develop a plan for self-improvement. Criteria may consist of a list of illusive personality traits, the performance of a subordinate's peers, or a statement of job goals. The inadequacy of the interview may result from the superior's having to evaluate performance and justify salary action at the same time, or from being required to assess personality and potential development—tasks the superior is not trained to do. The following five-step program eliminates the conflicting points of view in regard to purpose and criteria and, as a result, places the appraisal interview on much safer ground.

1. The individual discusses his job description with his superior and they agree on the content of his job and the relative importance of his major duties—the things he is paid to do and is accountable for.
2. The individual establishes performance targets for each of his responsibilities for the forthcoming period.
3. He meets with his superior to discuss his target program.
4. Checkpoints are established for the evaluation of his progress; ways of measuring progress are selected.
5. The superior and subordinate meet at the end of the period to discuss the results of the subordinate's efforts to meet the targets he had previously established.[13]

The five-step program suggested by Kindall and Gatza corrects the major weakness of the usual performance appraisal, since the purpose of the appraisal is clearly defined as the appraisal of current performance; the goals of the job are determined and agreed upon by both superior and subordinate; and the interview is confined to a discussion of performance with superior and subordinate equally interested in improving that performance. General Electric uses an appraisal system, called the Work Planning and Review program, that incorporates these five steps, and finds the program to be far more effective than the traditional approach to appraisals in improving job performance.[14]

Case Problem 12-B poses a series of questions encountered sooner or later by most companies and offers an opportunity to plan an organization development program. There is an obvious need for the development of a planned approach to the replacement of key executives of a company who are due to retire within the next few years under the provisions of the company's mandatory retirement plan. Contemplated expansion increases the need for a planned program of organization development since the requirements of an expanded organization must be met as well as the needs arising as the result of attrition in the present organization.

---

[13] Alva B. Kindall and James Gatza, "Positive Program for Performance Appraisal," *Harvard Business Review,* Vol. 41, No. 6 (November–December, 1963), p. 157. Copyright © 1963 by the President and Fellows of Harvard College; all rights reserved. This article presents a brief statement of the shortcomings of the typical appraisal program and then develops a plan for the installation of the five steps.

[14] Meyer, Kay, and French, *op. cit.,* p. 127.

Case Problem 12-B

ORGANIZATION PLANNING

Wanda Evans, president of Toolco, Inc., looked up as Robert Kessler, the director of industrial relations, entered her office. She asked, "What kind of progress are you making on the report I asked for last week?"

"Here are some notes I have prepared covering key executives in the company," Kessler answered as he handed Evans a copy of Exhibit I (pages 263 to 265). "It appears that the compulsory retirement plan that went into effect the first of this year is going to create a real need for replacements within the next five years."

"We not only have a replacement problem," Evans rejoined, "we also have some problems coming up as the result of our decision to move into the industrial products area and create a new industrial products division. As you know, our existing product line is purchased by individuals through department and hardware stores; however, the new division means not only manufacturing new products, it also means a new method of distribution."

"There is another factor other than replacement and expansion to be considered," Kessler stated.

"What is that?"

"The information I just handed you pertains only to replacements due to reaching the mandatory retirement age; thus far we have no information about the needs that could arise if we were to evaluate some of

these people in terms of the quality of their performance. We both know that some of our managers are not doing the job that we would like to see done."

"Are you suggesting that we get into the area of performance appraisals?" Evans asked.

"We're going to have to get into it sooner or later; otherwise, how are we going to know who is promotable to these key positions when they open up due to retirement?"

"Bob, as you know, we have an executive committee meeting at the end of next week. I wonder if you could show our needs in some graphic form that would impress everyone at the meeting. There are still some doubting Thomases who believe that the cream will rise to the top—personally I don't think it will, and even if it does I doubt that we have that much time. When we have this meeting, will you also recommend some definite name to designate this program we're going into? You and I have at various times called it executive development, management development, or organization development, and even organization planning. We ought to settle on a title that has meaning to everyone." Evans returned the notes Kessler had given her and closed with, "See me again a day or two before the committee meeting so that I can review the recommendations that you intend to present at the meeting."

Exhibit I

President—Age 62, founder of company and the driving force behind the institution of the company's compulsory retirement plan a year ago.

Reporting to the President:

Director of Marketing—Age 40, has been in position only a little over one year,

former director of economic research for an advertising agency. Performs economic research; has staff of two: a statistical typist and a statistician—both in early 30's. It was his recommendation that company enter industrial products field.

Legal Counsel—Age 45, functions primarily as liaison between engineering and outside firm of attorneys in patent matters. Occasionally handles real estate transactions; has one legal secretary.

Vice-President and Treasurer—Age 50, a CPA who has been with the company 20 years; formerly head of the cost accounting section. Has heads of cost and general accounting sections reporting to her; responsible for financial affairs of the company. As the company grew, it was her idea that position of controller be established as a separate function reporting to the president.

Controller—Age 45, has been with the company only three years; has a small clerical staff; is in the process of establishing and refining budgets in the manufacturing plants. Though the chief of the cost section reports to the treasurer, the controller maintains a close working relationship with him.

Director of Industrial Relations—Age 40, has been with the company five years; chief negotiator for the company; his staff consists of a secretary, a clerk, and a research assistant. Each plant has its own personnel director. Administers company-wide salary plan and employee benefits, including insurance and the new retirement plan. It will be his responsibility to administer any executive development program agreed upon.

Director of Purchasing—Age 60, formerly a purchasing agent in one of the plants. Serves in an advisory capacity to plant purchasing agents for the most part, although occasionally does purchase those items that can be used by all plants.

Executive Vice-President—Age 62, formerly vice-president in charge of manufacturing; over 20 years' service with the company; started as a plant manager in its Number 2 plant.

Reporting to the Executive Vice-President:

Vice-President, Manufacturing—Age 55, has been with the company five years; came to company as vice-president, manufacturing, when the post of executive vice-president was created. At that time it was believed that the plant manager of the Number 2 plant, then 55 years old, was capable of filling the vice-president position, but there was no suitable replacement for him in his plant. Since the Number 2 plant is the largest plant in dollar volume and profit, he was kept in that position. Reporting to the vice-president, manufacturing, in staff positions are the director of industrial engineering and the director of quality control. These positions were created shortly after his taking the job. Both are in their early 40's and well trained for their positions. Both have worked previously with the vice-president, manufacturing, in another company.

The managers of the five manufacturing plants report to the manufacturing vice-president. Each plant manager has managers of personnel, quality control, industrial engineering, purchasing, accounting, product engineering, and an assistant plant manager. Each staff department head has at least three exempt employees and several clerical employees. The assistant plant manager supervises directly the plant engineer (building maintenance), the master mechanic who is responsible for the tool room and the machine shop, and the general foremen in charge of the production departments. The following summary shows the ages of the plant managers, the number of hourly employees, and the number of general foremen and foremen for each plant.

Plant No.	Age of Plant Manager	Total Hourly Employees	General Foremen	Foremen
1 (outboard motors)	50	250	3	20
2 (engine plant)	60	700	4	32
3 (power hand tools)	45	400	3	18
4 (lawn mowers and edgers)	50	300	3	15
5 (power tools)	56	500	4	24

Vice-President, Engineering—Age 48, has been with the company 22 years. She has been in her present position five years. There are five supervising design engineers who report to her, one for each of the product lines. There is also a chief metallurgist who directs the metallurgical laboratory.

Vice-President, Sales—Age 61, has the advertising manager (age 50), the head of the sales order department (age 60), and the assistant general sales manager (age 58) reporting to him. Most of his efforts are devoted to the various advertising programs and promotional campaigns. The head of the sales order department acts as liaison between Plants 1 and 4 since these plants purchase 50 percent of the output of the engine plant. The assistant general sales manager directs four regional sales managers. Each regional manager has a clerical staff of two and approximately 15 sales representatives reporting to him. The manager of the Eastern region is 62 years old, the manager of the Central region is 58, the Southern regional manager is 50, and the manager of the Pacific region is 55.

PROBLEMS

1. Prepare an organization chart that shows clearly the replacement needs of Toolco for the next five years.
2. What title would you choose to designate the program being considered by Toolco?

Why would you choose this title?
3. How many people would you include initially as a part of any proposed development program?
4. Prepare a set of recommendations to be submitted to Evans prior to the committee meeting. Outline and justify each step in the proposed program.

CHAPTER QUESTIONS FOR STUDY AND DISCUSSION

1. What basic similarity exists between organizational analysis and planning for production and sales?
2. Discuss briefly the tools commonly employed in organizational analysis.
3. Rearrange Figure 12–1 so that it appears as a horizontal chart and as a circular chart. What are the advantages attributed to each form of charting—vertical, horizontal, and circular?
4. Discuss the strengths and weaknesses of formal organizational analysis. When would the disadvantages of formal analysis outweigh the advantages?
5. Why is it important to evaluate organizational effectiveness? Should this be done before introducing any organizational change or after the change has been introduced?
6. What is meant by the statement that most organizational studies are actually reorganizational studies?
7. What are the relative advantages and disadvantages of an internal change agent as distinguished from an external change agent?
8. What are the major criticisms of organization development? What major benefits may be gained from an organization development program?

9. In Chapter 8, "Organization and Management Theory," Case Problems 8-A and 8-B recount the experiences of Non-Linear Systems, Inc. Would you consider the changes made at Non-Linear Systems an organization development intervention? Why?

10. Discuss performance appraisals with respect to the following factors: purpose, strengths, weaknesses, and methods of improving performance appraisals.

11. Describe some of the symptoms that reflect inadequacies or inefficiencies in any part of the organization and that call for organizational change.

12. How does the five-step program, suggested by Kindall and Gatza, correct the major weakness of the usual performance appraisal?

Chapter 13

Personnel Management

Case Problem 13-A
THE *BAKKE* AND *WEBER* CASES

Allan Bakke, a blond, blue-eyed, 33-year-old male of Norwegian descent, had already earned a masters degree in engineering at Stanford University when he applied for admission to the University of California Medical School at Davis in the fall of 1972. Through his service as a Marine Corps anti-aircraft unit commander in Viet Nam and his work as an engineer in industry, he had demonstrated his maturity and sense of responsibility. His academic record was outstanding, and he scored in the 90th percentile on the medical school admission test. Yet Bakke was turned down by each of several medical schools to which he applied.

When told that he was almost accepted at Davis, Bakke reapplied. However, when rejected a second time, he sued, contending that his civil rights had been violated. Under the school's policy, 16 out of every 100 students admitted were from disadvantaged groups—blacks, Hispanics, and Asian-Americans. As a result Bakke was turned down while less-qualified applicants from these minority groups were accepted. In July, 1978, the United States Supreme Court upheld his right to admission—but the Court left many issues undecided. It ruled that rigid quotas, based solely on race or ethnic background, were illegal under Title VI of the Civil Rights

Act of 1964. The decision indicated, however, that race could legitimately be used as one standard for admission.

Justice Marshall argued that the decision would perpetuate the disadvantaged status of blacks. He supported the California regents in their belief that the school was only pursuing a goal of increased minority representation to offset chronic injustices of the past. However, the majority of the court held that quotas based strictly on race were illegal where no previous discrimination had been found. Justice Powell noted that the medical school was unable to explain why it had singled out for special treatment blacks, Mexican-Americans, and Asians when many other minority groups exist.

Far from providing a clear solution to the reverse discrimination problem, the Supreme Court in the *Bakke* case skillfully straddled the fence, taking a stand against a strict quota system without undermining the basis for affirmative action programs.[1] Thus, in one sense the *Bakke* decision was a delaying tactic which postponed a decision

---

[1] "Regents of the University of California, Petitioner, v. Allan Bakke," *United States Supreme Court Reports, Lawyer's Edition*, Vol. 57, No. 2 (August 18, 1978), p. 750.

on several legal issues until a more propitious time.

In a second reverse discrimination case, Brian Weber, a 31-year-old lab analyst with ten years of service in the Kaiser Aluminum and Chemical Corporation, filed suit against Kaiser and the United Steelworkers of America alleging job discrimination (November 17, 1977).[2] Weber's application for admission to a craft retraining program, through which he could eventually double his pay, was turned down because of a voluntary affirmative action program that was jointly agreed upon between Kaiser and the union. The program was an attempt to comply with presidential Executive Order 11246 and demands of the Office of Federal Contract Compliance. It removed a requirement of prior craft experience for on-the-job training and established a policy of admitting one minority to one white worker until the percentage of minority craft workers roughly approximated the percentage of minority workers in the geographical area of Gramercy, Louisiana, the city where Weber worked. Seniority was still the basis for selection, but the use of separate seniority lists prevented whites and blacks from competing with one another for openings.

Weber's claim that he was illegally discriminated against was upheld by the Fifth Circuit Court of Appeals. The decision focused on the fact that the training policy was not established because the company had been found to be illegally discriminating but was strictly a voluntary action to prevent possible charges of discrimination in the future. The Circuit Court's decision created a dilemma for other companies. They could shun affirmative action programs and get sued by a minority employee or take the initiative to establish a program and get sued for reverse discrimination. It is significant that in neither the *Bakke* nor the *Weber* case was there any official charge of past discrimination.

Prior to the Supreme Court decision on the *Weber* case, a government finding of past discrimination seemed to provide the only safe basis for an affirmative action program, a condition that changed dramatically on June 27, 1979. On that date the Supreme Court overturned the decision of the Circuit Court and officially approved Kaiser's affirmative action program.[3] Brian Weber clearly lost his case, and affirmative action programs, even programs that are not required by a government agency, were supported. The Court strongly emphasized that its decision was based on a narrow statutory question of whether Title VII forbids private employers and unions from voluntarily agreeing upon bona fide affirmative action plans. Chief Justice Berger, in a dissenting opinion, expressed a belief that the majority had effectively rewritten Title VII to achieve what it regarded as desirable results, since the law forbids all discrimination because of an individual's race, color, religion, sex, or national origin.

PROBLEMS

1. In what ways are the *Bakke* and *Weber* cases related to the work of the personnel manager?
2. How have discrimination problems affected the importance and status of personnel work?
3. Should the modern personnel manager be an attorney in order to formulate personnel policy effectively? Why or why not? If not, what kind of background is needed?

---

[2] *Reverse discrimination* is the practice of making personnel decisions (concerning selection, promotion, training, etc.) that favor members of disadvantaged groups in order to partially compensate for the effects of past discrimination. *Affirmative action programs,* sometimes viewed as a form of reverse discrimination, are company programs and policies structured specifically to offset the effects of past discrimination. More often than not, such programs have been encouraged by and involve an agreement with a government agency.

[3] "Decisions Announced June 27, 1979," *The United States Law Week,* Vol. 47, No. 50 (June 27, 1979), p. 4853.

> **4.** In view of the power of line managers, what can a personnel manager do to help the company avoid the kinds of problems exemplified by the latter cases?

The two legal cases presented in Case Problem 13-A represent one of the major problems currently facing management. The *Bakke* and *Weber* cases are concerned primarily with reverse discrimination. Reverse discrimination is an important problem in itself, but it is part of a much larger moral, legal, and economic problem. The larger problem is the elimination of bias and irrationality in all personnel decisions in order to achieve the dual objectives of respecting human rights and making optimal use of an organization's human resources. *Staffing*, the primary subject of this chapter, is the process of identifying, assessing, placing, evaluating, and developing individuals at work. It is the managerial function most directly concerned with the utilization of human resources.

Although much of the responsibility for staffing must be assumed by line managers, it is the personnel manager whose organizational duties center around the staffing process. This chapter is therefore concerned with personnel managers and their work; although the work of personnel managers is not limited to the few areas of responsibility discussed in this chapter. Other subjects for which personnel managers usually assume responsibility are the development and maintenance of the organizational manual and managing the performance appraisal system (discussed in Chapter 12). Personnel managers also become involved in developing and maintaining motivational and communications systems (discussed in Chapters 15 and 16).

THE CHANGING ROLE OF PERSONNEL MANAGERS

Human resources management is a new name that modern corporations are giving to the traditional *personnel management* position, and for good reason: the position is undergoing a dramatic change—becoming more respected, better paid, more powerful, and more a part of the top corporate decision-making group.

The Traditional Personnel Manager

The traditional image of the personnel manager was that of the *people person*—the caretaker of the employee records and benefit programs. The personnel manager was often viewed as a sort of sentimental employee advocate in a management structure dominated by hard-driving, production-minded managers whose attention was riveted on the primary goals of the organization. Although the traditional personnel manager was perceived as one who needed certain human relations skills, he or she was viewed essentially as a powerless advisor. Thus, director of personnel was a good job for loyal misfits and burned-out vice-presidents waiting for retirement. This stereotype is exaggerated, but in some companies it has been and still is an unfortunate reality.

The New Image

Several events have transpired in recent years to give the personnel manager a new image. The first of these occurred almost imperceptibly as departments of personnel gradually relieved line managers of such important functions as wage-and-salary administration, job analysis and design, job evaluation, and personnel selection. Line managers, preoccupied with routine operational problems, simply could not keep up with the increasingly sophisticated techniques used in performing these functions, even if time had not been a problem.

As long as personnel work was viewed primarily in terms of the technical and often tedious details of employee selection and other personnel functions, the prestige of personnel managers was relatively low. It is now obvious, however, that the matters with which personnel managers deal are directly related to the success of the organization. It is readily acknowledged that selection decisions, for example, affect productivity, employee turnover, union-management relations, and government-company relations. Therefore, by definition, personnel selection and personnel managers are important; and in progressive organizations, personnel managers have a new and exceptionally favorable image.

Labor Relations Experts. Since the National Labor Relations Act was passed in 1935, employees who become dissatisfied and attempt to unionize and bargain collectively with their employer are protected under the law. Since it is illegal for management to fire employees because of their union activity, and since the firm's experts in collective bargaining and labor relations are usually in the personnel department, personnel managers necessarily play an important role in management decision making.

Although line managers participate in negotiating union contracts, they depend heavily on the organization, research, knowledge, and bargaining expertise of labor relations specialists. After a contract has been negotiated, the role personnel managers play in advising line managers about how to live by the contract is invaluable. Personnel specialists can prevent grievances as well as negotiate with the union after a grievance occurs; and the actions of personnel specialists often determine whether a slowdown or a *wildcat strike* (an illegal strike under terms of the union contract) will be averted.

In nonunion companies, personnel managers are often responsible for creating and maintaining an organizational climate that will prevent employees from unionizing. They achieve this objective by carefully selecting employees, effectively training supervisors in human relations skills, maintaining equitable pay and employee benefits, and recommending management policies that produce employee satisfaction and personal commitment to the organization. Many companies that do not have and do not want unions are as preoccupied with employee relations as are the companies with unions, but the personnel actions of the former are more positive, less defensive, and involve less conflict. In either case, personnel managers may have a strong influence on major policy decisions as well as on routine operational decisions.

Personnel Problem Solvers. Herbert E. Meyer describes the new breed of personnel managers (or human resources managers) as hard-driving business managers who speak what they call "bottom-line language." They are as committed to the firm's profit goals as any other manager and view their positions as just one of many steps in a broader management career. Meyer gives several examples of such well-known companies as Delta Airlines, Eli Lilly & Co., IBM, and Dow Chemical Company in which personnel executives occupy powerful vice-presidencies and are not presumed to hold dead-end positions within the management hierarchy. Although the salaries of personnel executives have not been comparable to those of senior vice-presidents in finance and manufacturing, the salary gap is closing.[4]

Personnel managers who perceive themselves as general managers in personnel positions, rather than personnel managers in the traditional sense, approach their jobs in such a way that they are accepted into the top corporate decision-making group. Attuned to the central rather than peripheral corporate problems and objectives, such managers identify important problems and take the initiative to solve them.

Personnel managers who use this mainstream approach necessarily take high risks, as line managers typically do. Traditional personnel managers, in contrast, have a reputation as risk avoiders. Taking the risks involved in making innovative recommendations and, in effect, assuming the role of project manager to ensure the success of a recommended course of action are behaviors that win the respect of line managers. This holds true whether the personnel manager is a professional with no desire to move into line management or is basically a line manager functioning for a limited time in the personnel director position.

Personnel directors who perceive themselves as problem solvers have no difficulty finding opportunities to contribute directly to corporate profits. Meyer tells how IBM's Walter Burdick developed a policy by which IBM employees could indefinitely defer vacation time during years of peak corporate activity and take time off during years of recession.[5] Thus, helpful both in meeting peak production needs and in avoiding layoffs, the policy has benefited both the corporation and its employees. Other problems and opportunities that typically fall within the domain of personnel managers relate to employee turnover, job redesign, and evaluation and redesign of the firm's motivational systems. Because the training and management development function is located in the personnel department, personnel managers may also become involved in solving a variety of human relations problems involving conflicts among individuals as well as groups of managers.

---

[4] Herbert E. Meyer, "Personnel Directors Are the New Corporate Heroes," *Fortune*, Vol. 93, No. 2 (February, 1976), p. 84.

[5] *Ibid.*, p. 85.

When personnel managers are assertive in assuming responsibility for solving problems that are critical to their firm's success, they gradually begin to play a consulting role much as corporate attorneys do. Since most corporate decisions in some way involve people, personnel managers who prove to be competent assure themselves of an important place in corporate decision making.

The Future of Personnel Management

Such legislation as the Civil Rights Act of 1964, the Equal Pay Act of 1963, the Age Discrimination in Employment Act of 1967, and the Occupational Safety and Health Act of 1970 (OSHA) place heavy demands on companies in the selection and treatment of employees. The settlement of multimillion dollar antidiscrimination law suits, fines and law suits relating to employee safety, and government demands for affirmative action programs require serious attention. The result has been a requirement that personnel departments be staffed with management heavyweights. (Major legislation affecting the growth of the personnel function is shown in Table 13–1.)

Figures released by the Bureau of Labor Statistics in 1977 for publication in the 1978 *Occupational Outlook Handbook* estimated a 34.9 percent increase in personnel administrator jobs from 1976 to 1985 in contrast to a 19.2 percent general increase in jobs in the United States during that period.[6] Even if there were no other reasons to expect an increased need for personnel managers, it could be predicted because of the recent increase in government controls relating to safety and discrimination. Each regulation must be interpreted and translated into action. This requires the continual education of line managers and frequent consultations between line managers and personnel specialists about how specific matters should be handled. This educational and consultative role is highly compatible with the role personnel managers have long played in unionized companies to ensure management compliance with union contracts.

It is obvious that the major stimulus for the growth of the personnel function has been from outside the organization rather than from within. The passage of the Wagner Act (1935) created the field of labor relations, a major area of personnel work; and, although the Fair Labor Standards Act was passed three years later, its impact on the work of the personnel manager was minimal. Thus, from 1935 to 1964, a period of almost 30 years, there was little change in the personnel function other than the emergence of labor relations. The greatest change has come about since 1966 when litigation resulting from the Civil Rights Act began in ernest.

As large numbers of tasks previously performed by line managers have been taken over by technically educated staff personnel, there has been a tendency to play down the decision-making function of staff specialists. In recent years, however, it has become obvious that staff personnel play a major role in organiza-

---

[6] Jeremy Main, "Careers for the 1980s: Ten of the Best—and Ten of the Worst," *Money* (November, 1977), p. 62.

DATE	STATUTE	IMPLICATIONS FOR PERSONNEL MANAGEMENT
1935	NATIONAL LABOR RELATIONS ACT (WAGNER ACT)	Union growth encouraged. Management must avoid unfair labor practices and bargain collectively with a certified union.
1938	FAIR LABOR STANDARDS ACT	Minimum wages required. Amended in 1963 when the Equal Pay Act was passed (i.e., equal pay for men and women doing substantially the same work).
1947	LABOR-MANAGEMENT RELATIONS ACT (TAFT-HARTLEY ACT)	The strong pro-union bias of the Wagner Act was neutralized somewhat. Management was given more ability to resist unionization.
1964	CIVIL RIGHTS ACT OF 1964 (Title VII)	Outlaws all discrimination in employment which is based on race, color, religion, sex, or national origin.
1967	AGE DISCRIMINATION ACT	Outlaws all discrimination which is based on age of applicants or employees from ages 40 to 65.
1970	OCCUPATIONAL SAFETY AND HEALTH ACT	Subject to heavy fines, employers must provide a healthy and safe environment as judged by detailed Department of Labor standards.
1974	EMPLOYMENT RETIREMENT INCOME SECURITY ACT	Plans must meet specified minimum standards for employee participation, vesting rights, funding, and disclosure.
1978	AGE DISCRIMINATION ACT AMENDMENTS	With a few exceptions employers are prohibited from requiring an employee to retire before 70 solely because of age.

Table 13–1
LANDMARK
LEGISLATION
AFFECTING
PERSONNEL
MANAGEMENT

tional decision making. Specialists in such areas as law, engineering, accounting, and personnel make recommendations that often have the effect of decisions; generalist line managers who ignore the advice of specialists place their careers in jeopardy if such action diminishes the quality of their decisions. Some researchers are now suggesting that it may be time for personnel managers to gain the respect they deserve and need by ceasing to play games, masquerading as advisors, and admitting that they make independent decisions.[7]

---

[7] Harrison Trice and George Ritzer, "The Personnel Manager and His Self-Image," *Personnel Administrator*, Vol. 35, No. 1 (January, 1972), p. 46.

PERSONNEL SELECTION

Personnel selection has always been one of the main functions of a personnel department. Although the techniques employed and the financial investment made in selection vary greatly from one company to another, informed executives are in agreement that effective personnel selection is critical to organizational effectiveness. The companies that have been most effective in personnel selection have carefully planned for it.

Human Resources Planning

The larger the firm, the more complex and formal is the process of human resources planning. However, in each firm the essentials are the same: management must anticipate future needs and select personnel in such a way that those needs will be met.[8] Failure to have a cadre of broadly experienced managers prepared for promotion at the time of a major expansion can result in a serious setback for the firm, and the inability to employ skilled technicians in a tight labor market may be the deciding factor in whether the firm makes a profit. To cope with such problems, large organizations, in particular, attempt to recruit personnel with high potential for growth, to develop employee loyalty and commitment to a career path within the organization, and to provide continual education and work experience to meet both the employee's need for growth and the organization's need for competent personnel.

As indicated in Chapters 2 and 3, many complex, interacting factors must be considered in the planning process. In human resources planning the following activities are generally involved:

1. Analysis of present talent in light of present and future needs
2. Anticipating vacancies (short-term, intermediate, and long-term) because of promotions, transfers, dismissals, layoffs, resignations, deaths, and retirements; anticipating the effect that a given promotion will have on all lower positions within the career path; determining potential for promotion from within the organization and need for outside recruitment
3. Forecasting personnel needs because of normal growth, planned expansion, acquisitions, and other predictable changes
4. Planning for long-term succession into critical positions and for emergency replacement as needed
5. Forecasting business and economic trends and their effects on personnel needs

Human resources planning is anything but an exact science. When compared with an alternative hit-and-miss approach, however, it is efficient and effective.

The Selection Problem

Personnel selection is a four-dimensional problem-solving process. It involves (1) learning which human characteristics the job requires (mental abilities, val-

---

[8] For insights into various systems of human resources planning see D. R. Bryant, M. J. Maggard, and R. P. Taylor, "Manpower Planning Models and Techniques," *Business Horizons*, Vol. 16, No. 2 (February, 1973), p. 69.

ues, personality, education, skills, etc.); (2) locating potential candidates for the job; (3) determining the extent to which potential employees possess the qualities required; and (4) choosing from available candidates the one whose qualifications fit best. These are discussed here in terms of preparing job specifications, recruiting, and personnel selection.

Preparing Job Specifications. Job specifications, usually part of a written job description, are the personal characteristics required for a particular job (see Table 13–2). Specifications for a particular job may call for a college education, a 3.0/4.0 grade point average, high leadership potential, emotional stability, and high motivation. But how does one decide which qualifications are required? Often the matter is approached on a purely subjective basis and sometimes with little evidence that the desired qualities are related to performance. Ideally

---

JOB DESCRIPTION

INDUSTRIAL RELATIONS MANAGER

Department: Human Resources

Reports to: Human Resources Manager

Date of Last Revision: 3/9/81

Statement of Job: Works closely with the Executive Vice-President and Human Resources Manager; assumes responsibility for union-management relations, including contract negotiations and grievance settlement.

JOB DUTIES

1. Continually gathers data for contract negotiations.
2. Heads team of labor contract negotiators.
3. Advises managers on how to comply with labor contract.
4. Works with supervisors to settle formal grievance claims.
5. Anticipates and attempts to prevent labor problems.
6. Keeps abreast of relevant labor laws and decisions of the courts and the National Labor Relations Board. Educates other managers concerning relevant legislation and interpretations.
7. Maintains favorable corporation-government relations.

JOB SPECIFICATIONS

1. *Education:* Bachelors degree, preferably in management or economics, with labor relations concentration.
2. *Experience:* A minimum of three years of successful experience in contract negotiations.
3. *Knowledge, abilities, and skills:* Must have proven negotiating skills, high intelligence, high persuasiveness and perceptiveness, and a thorough knowledge of labor law. Must have outstanding oral and written communication skills. Must be able to fully support corporate labor policy and work with corporate management.

Table 13–2
EXAMPLE OF JOB
DESCRIPTION
WITH JOB
SPECIFICATIONS

job specifications are based on empirical studies which demonstrate that the presence of certain qualifications—a college education, superior communication skills, knowledge of shop arithmetic, above average hand-finger dexterity, etc.—increase the probability that an employee will succeed. In many cases the specifications are not expressed in writing, and when they are, they may be expressed in vague terms such as "high leadership potential." Across-the-board job specifications, such as the requirement that all employees be high school graduates, have recently come under close scrutiny because of their potential for discriminating against disadvantaged groups. Accordingly, organizations can no longer feel free to set arbitrary employment criteria.

At least one justification exists for not being too concise in developing job specifications. Since personnel are often selected in terms of their potential for several different jobs, employers are as concerned about applicants' adaptability, trainability, and overall growth potential as they are about their ability to function in the entry position. Thus, a college senior with only marginal ability to perform at the entry level may be employed because of his or her long-term potential.

The development of job specifications deserves more attention than it usually gets. Knowing specifically what to look for helps the manager decide how and where to recruit, which selection techniques to use, and how to decide among competing candidates. Job specifications increase objectivity in the selection decision; they reduce the likelihood that irrelevant criteria and personal bias will influence judgment.

Recruiting. Personnel managers realize that selecting the best available person depends heavily on *personnel recruiting*, the process through which potential employees are located and then encouraged to develop an interest in the organization. Effective recruiters also attempt to give prospective employees a clear picture of what to expect in the firm if they are hired.[9]

Most companies seek to improve their selection by developing a pool of applicants from which to choose. To achieve this, some of the more effective college recruiters visit campuses prior to their published recruiting days in order to talk with professors and administrators about students who may possibly meet the company's specifications. The recruiters then contact those recommended students rather than just hope that the students will request an interview. For other types of employees, recruiters may use newspaper or trade journal advertising in the hope of attracting a certain type of candidate. Executives are often located through professional recruiters or "headhunters" who receive a fee from the company for their services.[10] Effective recruiters learn to concentrate on the one or two means of recruitment that work best for a specific type of personnel.[11]

---

[9] J. P. Wanous, "A Job Preview Makes Recruiting More Effective," *Harvard Business Review*, Vol. 53, No. 5 (September–October, 1975), p. 16.

[10] Robert A. Simon, "What to Do if the Headhunter Calls," *MBA* (October–November, 1978), p. 20.

[11] Erwin S. Stanton, *Successful Personnel Recruiting* (New York City: AMACOM, 1977), p. 52.

Selection Techniques

There is no one best approach to personnel selection. Certainly one would not use the same techniques with construction laborers, salespersons, and corporate executives. In any event, selection may be thought of as a series of hurdles (Figure 13–1), any one of which may be sufficient to terminate the selection process. In each of the hurdles, the perceived qualifications of the individual are matched with the job specifications, and a decision is made as to whether to continue the selection process. As shown in Figure 13–1, the first hurdle involves a rough screening technique, most often a quick perusal of an application form. If large numbers of applicants are available, this relatively inexpensive and important step permits additional expenditures to be made only on applicants whose qualifications appear to match job requirements.

 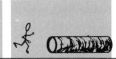

INITIAL SCREENING	PRELIMINARY INTERVIEW	TESTING PROGRAM	DEPTH INTERVIEW	REFERENCE CHECKS
Quick assessment, based on background information	Early impressions concerning critical characteristics	Measurement of skills, aptitudes, and abilities	Intensive check on critical qualifications	Telephone check on past performance

Figure 13–1 SELECTION PROCESS: INTRODUCING SUCCESSIVE HURDLES

Applicants who pass the first hurdle receive a preliminary interview—a short conversation that provides a quick impression about the candidate's interpersonal skills, motivation, attitudes, and other job-related qualities. Persons who pass this hurdle may progress to a testing hurdle, and in all but the lowest level positions they must later prove competitive in a more intensive interview. Depending on the job level, telephone reference checks precede the hiring decision, and many organizations require physical examinations.

The Selection Interview. A 1976 personnel survey conducted by the Bureau of National Affairs reported that 98 percent of the reporting companies used interviewing as a selection tool, 56 percent considered it their most important selection procedure, and 90 percent had more confidence in interview data than in data obtained from other sources.[12] How effective are interviews in discriminating among applicants with different qualification levels? A definitive answer is impossible because different interviewers use greatly varying techniques, and the interviews conducted by a given individual vary from person to person. However, we have identified some of the variables that affect interview performance, the most important of which is structure.

---

[12] Bureau of National Affairs, *Personnel Policies Forum*, Survey No. 114, September, 1976.

Structure is the degree to which interview questions and formats are formalized. In highly structured interviews, the questions are written out prior to the interview and are carefully followed. Some interviewers even use a standardized form in which space is provided after each question for writing in the interviewee's responses. When a standard form is used, some potential exists for tailoring questions to the individual by additions and omissions, but the technique is restrictive—best suited for use by relatively untrained interviewers.

Even the best trained interviewers find that some structure is beneficial in order to maximally use interview time. Thus, in addition to questions designed to answer specific questions about the applicant's background and qualifications, the interviewer may use a series of questions that have proved to be effective in eliciting certain types of valuable information. For example, some variation of the following instructions and questions are often used:

> Tell me about yourself—anything you think I may need to know about you. Just take your time, and go in whatever direction you prefer.
>
> What are your assets? your liabilities? your goals?
>
> If you could design a job that would in every way meet your needs and fit your abilities, what would it involve?

Skillful interviewers use such questions and instructions as points of departure. Then they follow up with *probes*—additional questions that are suggested by the interviewee's responses and therefore designed to ferret out specific information needed for the selection decision.

At the unstructured end of the continuum, the interview is simply an unplanned conversation. Although this approach is more natural and more comfortable than structured interviews, it is usually less effective. The interviewer tends to talk too much rather than ask questions and listen, and even when the interviewer has had years of experience, the reliability of the unstructured interview is likely to be poor.[13] Thus, structure is good, but interviews can easily become overstructured and rigid.

The interview continues to be extensively used and held in high esteem; thus, it undoubtedly has great value, especially when the alternatives are considered. Fortunately the interviewing effectiveness of a manager can ordinarily be improved through training, in which some of the potential weaknesses of interviewers (interviewer bias, failure to focus on relevant information, excessive interviewer talking) can be minimized.

Psychological Tests. Psychological testing for selection purposes has enjoyed varying degrees of success since World War I when tests were developed for armed forces selection and placement (for example, placing persons in work that best fits their abilities and interests). Wide varieties of tests are available to measure mental ability, manual dexterity, clerical or mechanical aptitude, leadership style, and personality characteristics. Some are crudely developed;

---

[13] R. C. Carson *et al.,* "Improvements in the Selection Interview," *Personnel Journal,* Vol. 50 (1975), p. 268; Benjamin Schneider, *Staffing Organizations* (Santa Monica, Calif.: Goodyear Publishing Co., Inc., 1975), p. 194.

others are scientifically designed and extensively evaluated for *reliability* (the consistency with which a test measures whatever it measures) and *validity* (the effectiveness of a test in measuring what it purports to measure or its effectiveness in predicting competency on the job).

Tests have recently come under attack by the Equal Employment Opportunity Commission and the Office of Federal Contract Compliance because they sometimes discriminate against minorities. Consequently, it has become necessary for companies to subject employment tests to extensive validation procedures to demonstrate that test scores significantly correlate with measures of job success. Because of the need for test validation, some companies have dropped their testing programs although the validation process is not highly complex nor prohibitively expensive. For purposes of meeting government requirements, there are two major validation techniques. The first develops a *predictive validity* coefficient; here test scores obtained but not used at the time of employment are correlated with subsequently obtained success measures such as performance ratings or rate of promotion. A *concurrent validity* coefficient is obtained by correlating test scores of present employees with measures of success (performance ratings, promotions, etc.) obtained at essentially the same time (i.e., concurrently). Where several tests are used as predictors, they are statistically combined in such a way that the validity of the *test battery* (a group of tests used together) is obtained.

Since 1966 the Equal Employment Opportunity Commission (EEOC) has published guidelines and revisions of those guidelines for test use; and contrary to the opinion of some, an organization can use tests with confidence.[14] Many organizations have continued to do so without government harrassment. Probably the most significant statement of the legal framework within which test users must operate was made by the United States Supreme Court in the *Griggs* v. *Duke Power Company* (1971). With reference to the Civil Rights Act of 1964, the Supreme Court unanimously held that:

> Nothing in the Act precludes the use of testing or measuring procedures; obviously they are useful. What Congress has forbidden is giving these devices and mechanisms controlling force unless they are demonstrably a reasonable measure of job performance. Congress has not commanded that the less qualified be preferred over the better qualified simply because of minority origins. Far from disparaging job qualifications as such, Congress has made such qualifications the controlling factor, so that race, religion, nationality, and sex becomes irrelevant. What Congress has commanded is that any tests used must measure the person for the job and not the person in the abstract.

A later court decision, *United States* v. *Georgia Power Co.*, United States Court of Appeals, February, 1973, emphasized that guidelines should not be "interpreted or applied so rigidly as to cease functioning as a guide and become an absolute mandate or proscription."

---

[14] Michael T. Matteson, "Employment Testing: Where Do We Stand?" *The Personnel Administrator*, Vol. 20, No. 3 (March, 1975), p. 27.

Most managers understand that a test or other selection devices should have validity. Actually a broader and more useful concept for evaluating a selection procedure is *utility*. The utility, or overall usefulness, of a test should include its validity plus (1) the extent to which a pool of applicants is available from which to choose, (2) the extent to which selection without the test is satisfactory, (3) the costs of testing, (4) whether an employee who does not succeed on the job can be economically trained or transferred, and (5) the extent to which the test improves the overall quality of the present work force. Varieties of statistical techniques are available for evaluating the utility of an organization's selection procedures.[15] In view of this fact, judgments about the usefulness of selection devices should be made on the basis of objective, quantitative methods rather than on strictly subjective bases.

Assessment Centers. As a means of solving the difficult problem of selecting espionage agents during World War II, the United States Office of Strategic Services expanded and popularized the *assessment center method*, a technique in which assessee performance in realistic problem-solving situations is rated by expert observers. The technique was later adapted by AT&T for the identification and selection of managerial personnel, and it has since become widely accepted as a valid means of personnel appraisal.

The *situational tests* used in assessment centers provide observers with a sample of behavior that approximates, as closely as possible, the work situations. The observers are sometimes psychologists but are more often operating managers. One example of a situational test is the *in-basket,* in which the assessee spends three to four hours answering a manager's correspondence and deciding how to handle specific problems. In another exercise, assessees analyze a practical financial problem, make an individual presentation of their results, and then participate in a one-hour leaderless group discussion that requires a written consensus solution. Numerous studies have demonstrated the validity of the assessment center method, the most notable of which was a long-term study at AT&T.[16]

The assessment center method typically involves two to three days of situational testing in a retreat environment that is free from the normal pressures of the workplace. The assessors spend long hours discussing their results and reaching a consensus decision on how assessees are to be rated (on a 1-5 scale) on a number of work-related variables such as persuasiveness, communication skills, decisiveness, and impact. One of the advantages claimed for assessment centers is that behavior is predicted from behavior, eliminating the error-prone

---

[15] Schneider, *op. cit.*, p. 206.

[16] D. W. Bray, R. J. Campbell, and D. L. Grant, *Formative Years in Business: A Long-Term AT&T Study of Managerial Lives* (New York City: John Wiley & Sons, Inc., 1974).

A. Howard, "An Assessment of Assessment Centers," *Academy of Management Journal*, Vol. 17, No. 1 (March, 1974), p. 115.

D. W. McKinnon, *An Overview of Assessment Centers* (Greensboro, N. C.: Center for Creative Leadership, 1975).

Joseph L. Moses, "The Development of an Assessment Center for the Early Identification of Supervisory Potential," *Personnel Psychology*, Vol. 26, No. 4 (Winter, 1973), p. 569.

leap of inference that exists when behavior is predicted from psychological characteristics measured by paper-and-pencil tests. A definite advantage is that the assessment center method has a much greater appearance of validity than traditional tests have and is, therefore, subject to less criticism.

MANAGEMENT DEVELOPMENT

One of the major personnel functions in most organizations relates to employee training and management development programs. In addition to the indoctrination programs most companies conduct for new employees, possibilities for course offerings for nonmanagerial personnel are limitless (shop arithmetic, blueprint reading, job skills training, and so forth). As a result, the training bulletins of some companies are comparable in size to college and university catalogs. The courses may be taught by line managers, personnel staff, or outside specialists. In addition to managing a curriculum of formal courses lasting from one hour to several hundred hours, the training specialist may also oversee apprentice training programs that require years of on-the-job experience and extensive testing over knowledge in the trade for which the employee is training (e.g., electrician, machinist, tool-and-die maker, or plumber).

Management development programs are more complex. They are less concerned with specific knowledge and typically involve leadership and decision skills that are difficult to teach. Management development programs attempt to involve the total person; they relate to the manager's need for planned growth experience over a number of years as he or she progresses through the management hierarchy.

Organizations invest heavily in management development. The most common justifications for such investments are:

1. To prevent management obsolescence and to develop managers who are capable of assuming higher levels of responsibility
2. To provide growth opportunities as a form of management compensation and thereby to avoid dissatisfaction and excessive management turnover
3. To promote an organizational climate that is conducive to continual adaptation to the demands of an ever-changing environment

Managerial obsolescence does not occur merely because one's formal education becomes dated, although that is a factor. The major cause of obsolescence—usually associated with personality rigidity, low self-esteem, and low motivation for growth—is the manager's failure to develop new capabilities.[17]

Development Methods

Small companies usually rely primarily on work experience for management development, augmented occasionally by outside management seminars. Unfor-

---

[17] Herbert Kaufman, *Obsolescence and Professional Career Development* (New York City: AMACOM, 1974); also Joseph Steger, "Manpower Obsolescence," *Academy of Management Journal,* Vol. 18, No. 2 (June, 1975), p. 263.

tunately the quality of the work experience may be poor, tending to limit learning opportunities and reinforcing ineffective managerial practices.[18] Progressive managers recognize that work experience should be tailored to the needs of the individual. It should be rationally planned to prepare the manager for increased responsibility and mobility. Otherwise the manager will not be highly motivated to learn.

Job Rotation and Transfers. Job rotation is a developmental technique in which managers are deliberately transferred into a variety of positions to maximize growth opportunities. It provides breadth of experience and capitalizes on the fact that learning is most rapid during the first few months on the job. Contrary to the old belief that the most qualified person for promotion is the one with the most seniority in a lower level position, job rotation provides managers an opportunity for *compressed experience*, that is, for gaining the maximum possible experience in the shortest period of time.[19]

In recent years some companies have reduced the number of management transfers that do not involve promotions.[20] The financial costs of transfers are high; lack of leadership continuity may lower managerial effectiveness; and too frequent transfers may disrupt a manager's family and social relations. Furthermore, now that a number of husbands and wives are both pursuing careers, the problems associated with frequent transfers are becoming increasingly serious.

Coaching and Counseling. To a limited degree, coaching takes place spontaneously in most superior-subordinate relationships. As a developmental technique, however, coaching is a deliberate process through which the superior (1) systematically provides subordinate managers with feedback on performance, (2) assists subordinates in diagnosing development needs, and (3) helps them plan programs for satisfying those needs. The coaching manager also develops subordinates by using routine, on-the-job problems as opportunities for teaching. This problem-directed coaching enables a manager to profit from mistakes and from the experience of his or her immediate superior.

Coaching does not occur to a satisfactory degree unless managers are taught how to do it well and are rewarded for their efforts. Harry Levinson makes the point that most managers, some of whom are in competition with their subordinates, give coaching too little time and are too intolerant of their subordi-

---

[18] Charles P. Bowen, Jr., chairman of Booz, Allen, & Hamilton, an international management consulting firm, makes a point for on-the-job experience in his insistence that no classroom training can ever be a substitute for making real decisions and thereby gaining the confidence to make even bigger decisions. See Charles P. Bowen, Jr., "Let's Put Realism into Management Development," *Harvard Business Review*, Vol. 51, No. 4 (July–August, 1973), p. 80.

[19] Eugene E. Jennings, *Routes to the Executive Suite* (New York City: McGraw-Hill, Inc., 1971), p. 55; also Robert Pitts, "Unshackle Your Comers," *Harvard Business Review*, Vol. 55, No. 3 (May–June, 1977), p. 127.

[20] "Taking the Jolts out of Moving," *Nation's Business* (November, 1975), p. 36; also "Moving on Loses Its Glamour for More Employees," *The Wall Street Journal* (August 3, 1976), p. 1.

nates' mistakes to maximize learning opportunities.[21] Because of these problems, coaching is often carried on by an outside consultant, in which case coaching is usually referred to as *management counseling.*[22]

Coaching and counseling programs may result in the use of a variety of experiences designed to develop general or specific qualities. The subordinate manager may, for example, be assigned committee responsibilities, special problem-solving projects, or specific readings. He or she may even be enrolled in formal university courses at company expense or may be temporarily assigned to work as an assistant to a person with the specific skills the manager needs to learn.[23]

Management Seminars. For many years the American Management Association has conducted seminars on a wide range of topics of interest to managers. Similar programs are offered by professional development centers of colleges and universities, and hundreds of seminars are offered annually by individuals and private seminar companies. These seminars usually last from one to three days and are tailored to a specific management group: new supervisors, purchasing agents, or presidents, for example. Seminars for new supervisors usually deal with a wide variety of topics; at higher levels the topics are more specific. Recent seminars in one company included effective recruiting, how to deal with union organizers, time management, assertiveness training, management by objectives, and elements of supervision.

The effectiveness of management seminars is seldom evaluated scientifically; nevertheless, seminars continue to be popular. The specific techniques employed vary greatly, the usual ones being lecture and discussion, case studies, and role playing. Sensitivity training groups (T-groups, or laboratory groups) are still used but have greatly declined in popularity since the 1960's as attention has shifted to attempts to modify behavior rather than personality.[24] For training in specific interpersonal skills, such as handling disciplinary problems or grievances, behavior modeling has proved effective. In behavior modeling, the manager (1) observes effective behaviors, often on film, (2) role plays the problem situation, (3) receives praise and support from program leaders and from other trainees, and (4) hopefully, transfers the new skills to real-life situations.[25]

---

[21] Harry Levinson, "A Psychologist Looks at Executive Development," originally published in Gene W. Dalton, Paul R. Lawrence, and Larry E. Greiner (eds.), *Organizational Change and Development* (Homewood, Ill.: Richard D. Irwin, Inc., and Dorsey Press, 1970), p. 259.

[22] Andrew J. DuBrin, *The Practice of Managerial Psychology* (Elmsford, N. Y.: Pergamon Press, Inc., 1972), p. 89.

[23] For additional information, read Roger O'Meara, "Off-the-Job Assignments for Key Employees," *Manpower Planning and Programming*, edited by Elmer Burack and James Walker (Boston: Allyn & Bacon, Inc., 1972), p. 339.

[24] William J. Kearney and Desmond D. Martin, "Sensitivity Training: An Established Management Development Tool?" *Academy of Management Journal*, Vol. 17, No. 4 (December, 1974), p. 755. Also George S. Odiorne, "The Hard Technologies of Training," *Training and Development Journal*, Vol. 29, No. 9 (October, 1975), p. 3.

[25] A. P. Goldstein and M. Sorcher, *Changing Supervisory Behavior* (New York City: Pergamon Press, Inc., 1974); also Joseph Moses and Richard Ritchie, "Supervisory Relationships Training: A Behavioral Evaluation of a Behavior Modeling Program," *Personnel Psychology*, Vol. 29, No. 3 (Autumn, 1976), p. 337.

MANAGEMENT COMPENSATION

One of the major functions of personnel managers is the administration of compensation systems. Because compensation is related to personnel motivation, satisfaction, and turnover, it is important to the organization. This section presents an overview of management compensation administration, but the motivational implications of various approaches to compensation are treated more thoroughly in Chapter 15.

Types of Management Compensation

Managers are compensated in many ways for their contributions. They, of course, receive salaries, but salary for a given manager may not be the major form of financial compensation. Thus, financial compensation may not be a manager's principal motivation for working or changing jobs. In 1977 Archie R. McCardell, president of International Harvester, received a salary of $76,666 but a bonus of $1,000,000. That same year Henry Ford II, chairman of Ford Motor Company, received $372,420 in salary and $620,000 as a bonus.[26] Many corporations allocate financial compensation in this way, thereby attempting to motivate managers to earn high profits and to keep management compensation relatively low in unprofitable years. Management bonuses, which are virtually always linked to company profits, may or may not accurately reflect the performance of an individual manager. In complex organizations it is often difficult to isolate and evaluate the performance of a single manager, and managers often try to avoid the problems involved in tailoring rewards to performance—such problems as how to justify paying one person more than another and how to control jealousy and conflict among competing managers.

Studies of why managers change jobs indicate that challenge and increasing responsibility are important forms of compensation,[27] as are opportunities for gaining experience and developing new skills. Other forms of compensation involve stock options and retirement programs, both of which offer tax advantages of great importance to well-paid managers. In recent years an increasing amount of attention has been focused on management *perquisites*, a term used to describe a variety of benefits that companies offer their managers. The following are the most common perquisites:

- Personal use of company automobiles or aircraft
- Unusually expensive travel allowances, including financial support of a spouse on business trips
- Club memberships and lump-sum entertainment allowances for which no documentation is required
- Medical examinations, comprehensive medical plans, and supplemental life insurance

---

[26] "The Kind of Pay Carter Wants to Restrain," *U. S. News & World Report* (June 12, 1978), p. 71.

[27] Gerald R. Roche, "Compensation and the Mobile Executive," *Harvard Business Review*, Vol. 53, No. 6 (November–December, 1975), p. 54.

- Legal or financial counseling
- Low-interest company loans or advantageous loans from a bank with which the company has influence
- Educational grants to a manager's children

Other less frequently provided perquisites include the use of company yachts or resort facilities, expensive vacations, and the services of chauffeurs or domestic staffs.[28] Perquisites sometimes enable a manager to enjoy a standard of living usually reserved for the very wealthy while keeping taxable income within modest limits.

Establishing Compensation Levels

The task of establishing equitable compensation levels is endless and frustrating. Companies attempt to establish equal pay scales for persons who do essentially the same level of work. At the same time, salaries must remain competitive locally and nationally, and the unique qualifications of individuals must be considered. In-company job evaluations provide a basis for pay categories, and surveys provide input about the external market; but establishing salaries remains difficult. Jobs constantly change, the performances of managers vary, managers receive different perquisites, and companies must bargain for the services of particular managers. All these factors complicate the problem of establishing equitable management pay scales. Therefore, because it is impossible to be completely fair, much less be perceived as being fair, most companies attempt to keep the compensation of individual managers a closely held secret.[29]

The salaries of officers in publicly held companies are a matter of public record, and most companies participate in wage-and-salary surveys that provide compensation bench marks. The United States Bureau of Labor Statistics conducts a national survey each year on the basis of which government service (GS) pay scales are set. Table 13–3 shows how jobs in the federal government are graded so that a person at a specific level can continue to receive raises without receiving a promotion in grade. For example, a GS-14 manager may earn from $32,442 to $42,171 plus a variety of side benefits. Government employees also receive across-the-board raises to offset the effects of inflation. Some variation of the government service compensation system is used in most medium- and large-size companies. (See page 286.)

Managers as a whole are highly paid, especially when bonuses, stock options, retirement plans, and perquisites are considered. Companies are often criticized by nonmanagement employees, union leaders, government officials, and shareholders for the generous way corporate managers are compensated. Nevertheless, companies hold steadfast to their compensation policies, perhaps because of the price managers usually pay in long hours of work, emotional stress, and

---

[28] "A Closer Look at Executive Perquisites," a booklet (prepared in 1977) by Arthur Young and Company to advise clients on disclosure requirements.

[29] Mary G. Miner, "Pay Policies: Secret or Open? And Why?" *Personnel Journal*, Vol. 53, No. 2 (February, 1974), p. 110.

GS	GENERAL SCHEDULE—5 U.S.C. 5332(a)										Amt. of Step Incr.
	1	2	3	4	5	6	7	8	9	10	
1	$6,561	$6,780	$6,999	$7,218	$7,437	$7,656	$7,875	$8,094	$8,313	$8,532	$219
2	7,422	7,669	7,916	8,163	8,410	8,657	8,904	9,151	9,398	9,645	247
3	8,366	8,645	8,924	9,203	9,482	9,761	10,040	10,319	10,598	10,877	279
4	9,391	9,704	10,017	10,330	10,643	10,956	11,269	11,582	11,895	12,208	313
5	10,507	10,857	11,207	11,557	11,907	12,257	12,607	12,957	13,307	13,657	350
6	11,712	12,102	12,492	12,882	13,272	13,662	14,052	14,442	14,832	15,222	390
7	13,014	13,448	13,882	14,316	14,750	15,184	15,618	16,052	16,486	16,920	434
8	14,414	14,894	15,374	15,854	16,334	16,814	17,294	17,774	18,254	18,734	480
9	15,920	16,451	16,982	17,513	18,044	18,575	19,106	19,637	20,168	20,699	531
10	17,532	18,116	18,700	19,284	19,868	20,452	21,036	21,620	22,204	22,788	584
11	19,263	19,905	20,547	21,189	21,831	22,473	23,115	23,757	24,399	25,041	642
12	23,087	23,857	24,627	25,397	26,167	26,937	27,707	28,477	29,247	30,017	770
13	27,453	28,368	29,283	30,198	31,113	32,028	32,943	33,858	34,773	35,688	915
14	32,442	33,523	34,604	35,685	36,766	37,847	38,928	40,009	41,090	42,171	1081
15	38,160	39,432	40,704	41,976	43,248	44,520	45,792	47,064	48,336*	49,608*	1272
16	44,756	46,248	47,740*	49,232*	50,724*	52,216*	53,708*	55,200*	56,692*		1492
17	52,429*	54,177*	55,925*	57,673*	59,421*	General Schedule Effective October 8, 1978 Office of Personnel—Veterans Administration					
18	61,449*										

Table 13–3
1978
GOVERNMENT
SERVICE PAY
SCHEDULE

* The rate of basic pay for employees at these rates is limited by 5 U.S.C. 5308 to the rate for level V of the Executive Schedule (as of the effective date of this schedule, $50,100); however, pursuant to the Legislative Branch Appropriation Act of 1979, the rate of basic pay *payable* may not exceed the rate for level V of the Executive Schedule as of September 30, 1978, $47,500.

sacrifice of family life. Whether managers are overpaid is to some degree a matter of opinion. John C. Baker, a leader in the field of management compensation, is convinced that boards of directors cannot exercise control over executive compensation, that compensation decisions are not based on hard facts, and that management compensation is too high.[30] Perhaps when compared with the wages of rank-and-file employees it is. However, it does not seem so high if the income of medical doctors, entertainers, and professional athletes is used as the standard of comparison.

The compensation of a few executives at the top of the organization lies beyond the influence of even the highest personnel executive. But below that point, personnel managers become deeply involved in wage-and-salary administration in which comparability with compensation in other organizations and perceived fairness within are critical factors. Here, as in their other responsibilities, personnel managers are called on to be both experts in organizational behavior and managers of complex systems.

Case Problem 13-B describes a typical managerial problem with which personnel specialists become involved. A line manager issues an order; a subordinate who refuses to obey justifies his action by the union-contract provisions. It is at this point that a personnel specialist in contract negotiation and interpretation

[30] John C. Baker, "Are Executives Overpaid? Readers Respond," *Harvard Business Review,* Vol. 56, No. 4 (July–August, 1978), p. 53.

is most likely to enter the scene to mediate the dispute. The skill with which specialists interpret such problems and subsequently recommend equitable solutions determines whether a problem will be settled immediately or result in serious union-management confrontation.

Case Problem 13-B
A DISPUTE IN THE MELTING DEPARTMENT

On the morning of September 12, 1978, Dennis Schilling, a third-shift Melting Department employee, ignored a request by Jack Dobbs, acting supervisor of the first shift, to perform a relief work assignment within Schilling's classification. This alleged act of insubordination resulted in disciplinary action which led to the grievance described here. Catherine Compere, assistant director of Industrial Relations, was assigned the task of compiling the facts and, if possible, resolving the dispute rather than permitting it to escalate into a serious union-management conflict and possibly being referred to a compulsory arbitrator.[31]

At the time the grievance occurred, the foundry was operating two ten-hour production shifts (6:00 a.m. to 4:00 p.m. and 4:00 p.m. to 2:00 a.m.). In contrast, the service departments worked regular eight-hour shifts. Schilling was working the third shift, from midnight to 8:00 a.m., on that day.

Jack Dobbs, a graduate metallurgist in charge of all Melting Department operations, was substituting for the vacationing supervisor of the 6:00 a.m. to 4:00 p.m. shift. In his role as acting shift supervisor, Dobbs, accompanied by a union steward, was contacting third-shift employees for the purpose of filling several vacancies on the first production shift which had occurred because of excused leaves and call-in absences. Two service employees contacted by Dobbs had already agreed to finish the last two hours of their shift doing production work. At 6:15

a.m. Dobbs approached Schilling as the latter was starting up the stairway to the lunchroom and asked him to take one of the first production shift assignments. Schilling ignored Dobbs' request, inaudibly mumbled something, and continued up the stairs. Following Schilling, Dobbs ordered him to take the assignment; otherwise, Dobbs stated, his time would be stopped for refusing a work assignment within his classification. (This was normally a legitimate request under the union contract which states that management has the right to assign duties and that workers will handle disputes through the grievance procedure rather than through strikes or slowdowns.) Since Schilling did not comply, Dobbs stopped Schilling's time at 6:18 a.m., penalizing him one hour and forty-two minutes and causing Schilling to file his grievance. Schilling's supervisor, David Hudson, was in another area of the plant at the time and was not aware of what had occurred.

Dobbs argued that, although he was not Schilling's supervisor, he was a recognized member of management and, therefore, had the right to make the work assignment. Thus, Dobbs believed that Schilling was obligated to comply as others had willingly done. Dobbs further contended that, if Schilling had a legitimate basis for refusing the assignment, he should have expressed it at the time or made an immediate protest through the union steward who was accompanying Dobbs. Instead Schilling was insubordinate and walked away, even after being warned.

Schilling perceived the situation differently and, therefore, stressed different facts: He had come to work at midnight but had

---

[31] This case was adapted from an arbitration award by Dr. A. Dale Allen, Jr., professor of Management and Labor Relations, Baylor University.

to wait until 1:35 a.m. to begin repairing Furnace A because it had been in use. Working continually, he cleaned, repaired the roof, and resanded the furnace in order to complete the job by 6:00 a.m., when the next production shift was scheduled to begin. Schilling insisted that he had complied with Hudson's request to put forth extra effort, despite the fact that the furnace was hot and the work was strenuous; from Schilling's perspective, he had thoroughly completed the night's work that Hudson had assigned.

By the time Dobbs contacted Schilling, the latter had been on duty approximately $4\frac{1}{2}$ hours without relief, even though the contract called for two 20-minute relief periods and a 20-minute lunch period during the shift. Dobbs contended that the waiting period from midnight to 1:35 a.m. more than offset the 60 minutes granted for relief and lunch. Work rules did not specify any particular time for the breaks; in critical situations it was common for maintenance employees to work long hours and take a relief break later when the situation permitted. Schilling argued that, since he was available to start work at midnight, it was irrelevant that he did not start until 1:35 a.m. As for Schilling's

behavior at the time Dobbs contacted him, Schilling was tired; he had earned a contractual break, and he was taking it. Had he gone with Dobbs, he would very likely have had to complete the entire shift without a break period. In contrast, all other persons who worked the third shift that night had taken a relief break. Schilling further argued that he had never been a problem employee—that he was and is considered a good performer by his supervisor and that he has 21 years seniority with an unblemished disciplinary record.

PROBLEMS

1. Did Dobbs handle the situation properly?
2. Was Schilling's behavior justified? Evaluate Schilling's perception of the situation.
3. What action should Compere take to resolve the dispute?
4. What is the effect of a formal grievance procedure on the decision-making authority of line supervisors where the judgment of the industrial relations expert is accepted as the company's official position? Do industrial relations specialists make supervisory decisions in such cases?

CHAPTER QUESTIONS FOR STUDY AND DISCUSSION

1. Why have high-level personnel positions been considered inferior to high-level finance and production positions? Why has a change occurred?
2. What differences between the laws passed prior to 1960 and those passed after 1960 caused management to take a new look at the personnel function?
3. What factors justify being nonspecific in developing job specifications?
4. Typical selection interviews are poor, so why do managers rely on them?
5. Managers often have strong biases for or against the use of tests in personnel selection. Should such biases determine whether tests are used?
6. What unique characteristics of the assessment center method give it an advantage over traditional testing programs?
7. What can an organization do to solve management obsolescence besides providing management development opportunities?
8. Why are managers most often ineffective in coaching their subordinates?
9. What are the advantages and disadvantages of (1) bonuses, (2) retirement plans, and (3) perquisites?
10. Why do most companies insist that management salaries be kept secret?

4

Leadership in Organizations

The quality of leadership exhibited by an organization's supervisors and high-level managers is a critical determinant of organizational success. Although leadership style and the more prominent theories of leadership are discussed in Chapter 17, we take the position that leadership effectiveness is contingent on a variety of factors other than the personal qualities and style of a particular leader. We therefore cluster five interrelated chapters under the title, "Leadership in Organizations." Leadership effectiveness depends on the total environment in which the leader functions—on such factors as organizational climate, the nature of an organization's communication systems, and organization-wide influences on employee motivation.

Chapter 14 begins with a discussion of how behavioral scientists conduct research and reach conclusions about human nature, on which leadership theory and recommendations for improving leadership behavior are based. Increasingly we tend to view armchair theorizing with suspicion and turn to empirical research as the basis for managerial theory and action. Chapter 14 also includes sections on two important contributors to individual differences in behavior—learning and perception—and it contains a section on the contribution of informal groups to organizational behavior. The final section discusses organizational climate, which influences leadership effectiveness and is in turn influenced by the individual, by informal groups, and by the structure and function of the formal organization.

Chapter 15, "Motivation in Organizations," provides the foundation needed to understand the leadership theories presented in Chapter 17 and required of anyone who proposes to acquire an in-depth understanding of organizations and people. Organizational behavior as a discipline proposes that effective leadership must be based on understanding rather than on techniques alone, on mature relationships of mutual trust rather than on manipulation, on depth of communication rather than on superficial verbal transactions that fail to transmit intended meanings, as pointed out in Chapter 16.

Chapter 18 focuses on the role of first-line supervisors. They are unique leaders because of their difficult role in mediating between the demands of the organization and the needs of individual employees who sometimes identify poorly with the goals of the organization. In addition to discussing the supervisory role, attention is given to various influences on supervisory performance and to the means of improving that performance.

Chapter 14

Personal and Social Dimensions of Organizational Behavior

MEASURING ORGANIZATIONAL CLIMATE

In this chapter *organizational climate* refers to those relatively permanent characteristics of an organization that influence the behavior of its members and serve to differentiate one organization from another. Since most readers of this text are students at a college or university, we limit this case problem of measuring organizational climate to educational institutions—specifically, the school that you attend. The concept of organizational climate presented in the chapter is, of course, much broader and is more concerned with business organizations than with educational institutions.

Different approaches may be used to measure the organizational climate of a college. In a highly objective fashion, institutions may be classified according to certain demographic characteristics such as size, source of revenue (private or public), location (rural or urban and section of the country), student/faculty ratio, number of courses and majors, and other similar data. This objective approach may also involve a study of the students: their socioeconomic backgrounds, scholastic aptitudes, academic performance, and career goals. Finally, the objective approach may involve direct observa-

tions of student behavior, dress, and participation in extracurricular activities.

An entirely different approach, often the most fruitful one and the one used here, employs a perceptual method—a more subjective approach than the one just described. It views the organization through the eyes of its members—as they describe it— rather than as it is described by objective facts. Granted that both approaches have merit and may even be used together, what advantage does the perceptual approach offer? This question is best answered by reference to the definition of organizational climate given earlier. It refers specifically to characteristics of an organization that influence the behavior of its members; and it is the perceived organizational characteristics rather than the objective real ones to which its members react. For example, its employees may react with anger and dissatisfaction because they believe they are poorly paid and overworked when in fact they are well paid and relatively unproductive. The perceptual report you are now asked to make on your school is in one sense a psychological profile of the institution: it is *your* description of the institution rather than *the* description of it.

PROBLEMS

1. Complete the College and University Organizational Climate Inventory presented in Appendix A. With which aspects of the institution are you most and least familiar? Which factors have the greatest influence on your behavior?

2. How would you expect a description of the institution made by your professor and/or dean to differ from your own? Which is most valid? Discuss.

The five chapters in this text that discuss the leadership function of managers cover subject matter included within the broad discipline of *organizational behavior* (OB)—the study of individual and group behavior within organizations and the application of the resulting knowledge.[1] Organizational behavior places more emphasis on research and theory than the related field of human relations and is more narrowly restricted to a study of people than is organizational theory. Organizational theory overlaps OB at several points because OB studies people in their organizational environments, while organizational theory studies the structure and process of those environments.

Organizational behavior relies heavily on empirical research and theory development as a basis for understanding human behavior in organizations. Increasingly the research has become identified with a contingency approach to management—an approach which rejects universal principles and emphasizes the uniqueness of each organization.[2] Because the contingency approach takes into consideration a large number of variables, it often requires the use of rather complex experimental designs. Accordingly, we begin this series of chapters with a brief look at some of the methods and terms used in organizational behavior research. The methodology section is followed by a discussion of two personal influences on organizational behavior—learning and perception. Our increasing knowledge of these important personal attributes has contributed significantly to our understanding of human behavior in organizations. The next section on informal groups introduces another stream of thought—a principal contribution of the human relations movement—that has helped to shape the development of organizational behavior as a discipline. We conclude the chapter with a discussion of organizational climate, a phenomenon that is influenced not only by personal qualities of learning and perception and the impact of informal groups on its members, but also by the qualities of the formal organization. Thus, we view organizational behavior as a discipline in terms of its methods and the three perspectives that span the breadth of its development.

---

[1] L. L. Cummings, "Toward Organizational Behavior," *Academy of Management Review*, Vol. 4, No. 1 (January, 1979), p. 92.

[2] Jay W. Lorsch, "Making Behavioral Science More Useful," *Harvard Business Review*, Vol. 57, No. 2 (March–April, 1979), p. 171.

RESEARCH METHODS IN THE BEHAVIORAL SCIENCES

The research methods used in organizational behavior are essentially the methods used in other behavioral sciences, such as psychology, sociology, and anthropology. In some instances, these research methods are little more than systematic observations with a concerted attempt to be objective; in others, they have a high degree of scientific rigor. This variation in methodology is evident in the following discussion of field and experimental studies.

Field Studies

As the term implies, *field studies* are conducted within the physical environment of the organization. At times the researcher simply observes what is occurring, trying not to influence that behavior by the observation process. The *survey study* is a field study technique in which data are collected from individuals by means of questionnaires or interviews. For example, mail surveys are used extensively to gain information about a wide variety of topics such as management practices, attitudes, and organizational structure. Although the mail survey has proved its worth, it sometimes suffers from *nonresponse bias*: distortion that occurs when those who respond are different in the variable studied from those who do not respond. Therefore, direct interviews are sometimes used to avoid this biasing factor and to reap the benefits of person-to-person communication.

Another field study method is the *case study,* the purpose of which is to provide a depth analysis of an industry, a company, or an organizational unit. Case study data may be gathered by a variety of methods such as observation, interviews, questionnaires, and objective indices of organizational performance such as costs, profits, and quantity and quality of production. Such documents as labor-management contracts, personnel records, job descriptions, and goal statements provide additional data.

Descriptive versus Predictive Studies. Field studies may be classified as either descriptive or predictive. As the term implies, a *descriptive* study is conducted for the purpose of describing a situation or condition, ordinarily to provide a basis for managerial action. Thus, the information obtained from a wage-and-salary survey describes current practices of paying workers and managers in a given locality and enables management to make better decisions about what wages and salaries in their company should be. In a similar way, the descriptive data from attitude surveys may help resolve interpersonal conflicts and improve an organization's psychological climate.

In contrast, *predictive* studies involve direct attempts to forecast future behavior and events from data gathered at a given point in time. For instance, a series of studies at AT&T demonstrated that success in management (as measured by promotions) could be predicted by performance ratings of management candidates. The ratings were obtained in an *assessment center*—a unique testing method in which the behavior of a small group of candidates is observed and evaluated while they collectively solve certain standardized but real-life problems.[3] By establishing with a large group of managers the relationship between assessment center performance and later measures of effectiveness, management was able to predict the likelihood of a candidate's success from the behavior samples obtained in the assessment center. In view of the many costs of selecting managers who fail, predictive studies of this sort contribute significantly to organizational effectiveness.

In other research, the prediction goal is implied but not explicitly stated. For example, studies performed by Fred Fiedler—studies that will be explained more fully in Chapter 17—show certain leadership styles to be more effective than others in certain work environments.[4] Although not specifically stated as a research objective, the knowledge obtained from such studies provides a basis for predicting managerial success in a given situation or for judging the likelihood that a situational change will improve managerial performance. As research studies reveal trends, theories are developed that integrate and explain research findings, thereby providing a basis for application and continued research.

Longitudinal Studies. In order to properly interpret and evaluate research studies, a distinction must be made between _cross-sectional studies, in which data are collected over a short period of time,_ and _longitudinal studies, in which data are collected over a long_ time span. Cross-sectional studies are an organizational snapshot; longitudinal studies consist of a series of snapshots.[5] This distinction is important because research findings under the two methods may differ considerably.

When does a study become longitudinal? The answer depends on the nature of the research. Ivancevich found, for example, that goals programs, which immediately improved productivity, suffered a decline after six to nine months.[6] Obviously the typical study of six weeks' duration would not have discovered that important fact. In one situation the benefits of a longitudinal study may be experienced in six months, while another may require six years. However, because of the difficulty in doing longitudinal studies, most published studies are cross sectional; therefore, their results cannot be accepted with complete confidence until repeated studies in different situations are conducted. To a lesser extent replications of longitudinal studies are also needed.

Sampling and Generalizing. Conclusions drawn from research studies are typically based on a _sample_ (a subset) of the _population_ (the whole set), about which conclusions or generalizations are to be drawn.[7] However, many problems

---

[3] Joseph L. Moses, "Assessment Center Performance and Management Programs," _Studies in Personnel Psychology_, Vol. 4, No. 1 (Spring, 1972), p. 4.

[4] Fred E. Fiedler, "Validation and Extension of the Contingency Model of Leadership Effectiveness: A Review of Empirical Findings," _Psychological Bulletin_, Vol. 76, No. 2 (1971), p. 129.

[5] John R. Kimberly, "Issues in the Design of Longitudinal Organizational Research," _Sociological Methods and Research_, Vol. 4, No. 3 (February, 1976), p. 321.

[6] John M. Ivancevich, "Different Goal-Setting Treatments and Their Effects on Performance and Job Satisfaction," _Academy of Management Journal_, Vol. 20, No. 3 (September, 1977), p. 406.

[7] An easily understood discussion of sampling is found in Eugene Stone, _Research Methods in Organizational Behavior_ (Santa Monica: Goodyear Publishing Co., Inc., 1978), p. 77.

occur in drawing conclusions because of biased, nonrepresentative sampling or because generalizations are made about individuals and groups that have little in common with the population studied (for example, generalizing to managers from a study of college students). Mention has already been made of the sampling problem created by nonresponse bias in mail surveys. Similar bias occurs when volunteers for a research study differ from persons in the population who do not volunteer,[8] when the most available or easiest-to-collect sample is used, or when a sample is simply too small to adequately represent the population from which it is drawn. Even when sampling is adequate, generalizations made by readers of published research are sometimes faulty because the research is old and no longer applicable. Because of the potential for such problems, extreme caution must be exercised in evaluating and applying research findings.

Experimental Studies

In theory the concept of the experiment is quite simple. By isolating and manipulating a single variable, while holding all other variables constant, the experimenter measures the effect that the manipulated variable (the *independent variable*) has on behavior (the *dependent variable*). Although simple in theory, in practice the design and execution of behavioral science experiments are quite difficult.

One of the most troublesome aspects of organizational experiments arises from the complexity of organizations—from the difficulty of holding constant all influential variables in order to ensure that the observed results are due solely to the independent variable. For example, study an experiment that tests the effect of work methods changes (the independent variable) on the productivity (dependent variable) of engine assemblers. In this job enrichment method— *job enrichment* referring to a practice of redesigning a job so that employees who perform it exercise more independence and assume more responsibility— three employees work as a team to produce an entire engine. To test the effect of the methods change, we isolate a small, representative group of employees, an *experimental group*, who are carefully taught to use the new method. Their performance is then compared with that of a *control group*, which continues to use traditional assembly-line methods. Supposedly any change in productivity will be due to the effects of job enrichment. The hypothesized change (increase) in motivation is called an *intervening variable*, an observable process or condition that helps explain linkages between the independent and dependent variables.

However, if productivity increases in this experiment, can we be certain that the increase is caused by increased motivation resulting from the new method? Can there be other causes of the production increase because of variables of which we are unaware? Perhaps the increased production has nothing to do with work methods as such. Perhaps it results solely from the fact that special attention is given to the experimental group. Good experimenters are

---

[8] Robert Rosenthal and Ralph L. Rosnow, *The Volunteer Subject* (New York City: John Wiley & Sons, Inc., 1975).

constantly alert for such possibilities and attempt to introduce experimental controls on as many variables as possible. (See Figure 14–1.)

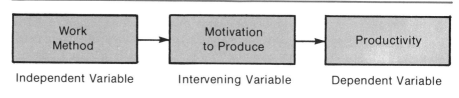

**Figure 14–1
A CAUSAL LINK
ASSUMPTION IN
EXPERIMENTAL
DESIGN**

Causation in research studies is always difficult to establish. Generally speaking, there is less problem in longitudinal than in cross-sectional studies,[9] but causation is typically inferred from the logic of the situation and should, therefore, be approached cautiously. It is especially important to note that simple correlation between two variables does not necessarily imply causation.

Another contributor to the outcome of an experiment is a *moderator variable*, a variable that exerts an influence on two or more other variables. As shown in the hypothetical experimental results in Figure 14–2, age moderates the relationship between job satisfaction and level of job enrichment. Notice that in Situation *A*, where all employees in the work group are considered, it appears that the degree of job enrichment has no effect on job satisfaction. Major changes in methods (high level of job enrichment) produce the same level of job satisfaction as do minor changes (low level of job enrichment). Note, however, that when the employees are divided into two groups—Situation *B*, those under age 25, and Situation *C*, those over age 25—the true relationship between job

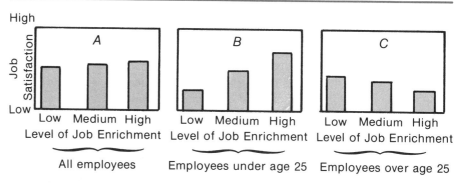

**Figure 14–2
THE EFFECT OF A
MODERATOR
VARIABLE: AGE**

[9] John R. Kimberly, *op. cit.*, p. 123. Further discussion of the causation problem is found in Barry M. Shaw, "Attribution of the 'Causes' of Performance: A General Alternative Interpretation of Cross-Sectional Research on Organizations," *Organizational Behavior and Human Performance*, Vol. 13, No. 1 (1975), p. 414.

enrichment and level of job satisfaction comes to light. In Situation *B*, the higher the degree of job enrichment, the greater the satisfaction of younger employees. With the older employees, the situation is just the opposite: satisfaction decreases as level of enrichment increases; perhaps because they have become more entrenched in their methods and dislike change. Such use of a moderator variable has created major improvements in research studies. As a result, research studies become more complex—but that is the only way they can effectively describe the real world.

Most experimental and field research attempts to quantify data and make statistical tests to determine whether differences and relationships are significant. When the results of a particular study occur by chance less than 5 times in 100, they are said to be *statistically significant.* As students of statistics and persons who are familiar with management journals know, this is a critical concept and research tool. However, it can be misleading, since statistically significant results do not always have *practical significance*; that is, they may or may not be relevant and useful. Because of the way statistics are computed, when large samples are employed very small differences prove to be statistically significant. For example, very small differences in the attitudes of male and female workers may be statistically significant where several hundred of each have been included in the sample. But deciding the practical significance of that fact, deciding which action should be taken on the basis of that knowledge, is quite another matter. In the final analysis, the practical significance, the meaning, and the value of behavioral science research are a matter of logical interpretation and common-sense judgment that should never be overshadowed by the sophisticated jargon and the impressive experimental designs of organizational behavior research.

In the section that follows we look briefly at two human qualities: learning and perception, which for many years have been emphasized in behavioral science research, especially in psychological research. Our growing understanding of these subjects has significantly increased the depth with which we understand organizational behavior.

PERSONAL INFLUENCES ON ORGANIZATIONAL BEHAVIOR

Organizational behavior differs from psychology in that the former seeks to understand, predict, and influence human behavior in a specific environment, the organization. However, in order to achieve that end—in order to achieve more than a surface understanding of such complex subjects as leadership, communication, and motivation in organizations—we need to know what psychology says about the individual. In previous chapters we used such concepts as McGregor's Theory X and Theory Y as a framework for understanding human nature and we discussed the personal dimensions of decision making. In preparation for future chapters we turn now to two additional contributors to individual differences in people: learning and perception.

The Learning Process

Students of human behavior must constantly cope with the fact that people are different. People think differently, act differently, and, given the same facts, reach different conclusions. Many of these differences can be attributed to *learning*, defined for our purposes as a relatively permanent change in behavior as a result of experience. Managers need a practical understanding of the learning process because of its value in understanding individual differences, in teaching others, and in allowing managers to optimally learn from their own experience.

Learning can legitimately be approached in many ways—by studying minute chemical and electrical changes in the nervous system, for example, or by learning how and why Pavlov used classical conditioning to teach dogs to salivate at the ringing of a bell. However, the aspect of learning that is of greatest value to managers is *reinforcement*, a process through which the consequences of a behavior increase the likelihood that the behavior will be repeated. This important concept is worthy of close examination.

Reinforcement. The concept of reinforcement is based on the *law of effect*, expounded by E. L. Thorndike in 1911. He stated that:

> . . . of several responses made to this same situation, those which are closely followed by satisfaction . . . will be more likely to recur; those which are accompanied or closely followed by discomfort . . . will be less likely to occur.[10]

Therefore, according to the law of effect, human behavior is learned because of the pleasant or unpleasant consequences that follow whatever a person does. For example, employees in one company learned to perform near the peak of their ability because such behavior tended to be followed by praise and other forms of reward. They learned the behavior because of *positive reinforcement*—the strengthening of a particular behavior because it is followed by a desirable consequence.

Behavior is also learned through *negative reinforcement*—the termination or withdrawal of an undesirable consequence. In one situation, managers learned to turn in certain monthly reports several days after their due date because by doing so they could reduce the likelihood that their superior would return these reports for reworking. Because their superior had a deadline for her own report, she was forced to use the late reports as they were originally presented. In another situation, aircraft support crews learned that by wearing noise suppressors they could avoid the discomfort of jet engine noise. Thus, through negative reinforcement, their new behavior was acquired because it terminated the undesirable consequence of an existing behavior.

As the terms are used in the behavioral sciences, negative reinforcement is not the same as punishment. Negative reinforcement strengthens and increases behavior (e.g., the wearing of noise suppressors) in order to terminate an undesirable consequence, while *punishment* introduces something undesirable (a "chew-

---

[10] Edward L. Thorndike, *Animal Intelligence* (New York City: Macmillan, Inc., 1911), p. 244.

ing-out," for example) in order to eliminate a certain behavior (say, failure to wear the noise suppressors in areas of exposure to dangerous noise levels). Both positive and negative reinforcements are generally preferable to punishment, which discourages undesirable behavior but does not actively encourage desirable behavior. Although punishment is sometimes necessary, attempts to teach by using punishment often have disadvantages. For instance, the development of hostility toward the punisher may offset the benefits of rewards that are presented by that same person at other times.

Experts in learning make the point that positive and negative reinforcements occur continually in the workplace, even when the persons involved are unaware of it. Thus, the supervisor who reinforced her subordinates' inclinations to turn their reports in late was not aware that she had actually taught the behavior she deplored. Since learning through reinforcement is continual, managers need to be aware of it and to make it work for, rather than against, them.

Behavior Modeling. Another aspect of learning that contributes directly to our understanding of organizational behavior is *modeling* or *imitation.* Humans learn by observing the behavior of others who serve as models. By observing in others the effectiveness of different behaviors, intelligent beings are able simultaneously to learn a response possibility and to anticipate its positive and negative consequences. Thus, a young manager observes the effectiveness with which a superior handles certain problems and, through modeling, learns to use the same methods. Some learning may occur even when the ideas do not result in overt behavioral change, but it is the behavioral implications of learning that interest most managers.

Behavior modeling is most likely to occur (1) when an individual has a deep need to learn a new response and (2) when the person serving as a model has high status or power. Accordingly, leaders are uniquely qualified to serve as models for their followers. It is significant that learning through both modeling and reinforcement occurs continually, whether it is planned or not. Therefore, the more aware managers are of this fact, the less likely they are to demonstrate unbecoming behavior patterns.

Perception

Perception is the process through which we select, interpret, and give meaning to the sensory data that we experience. Like learning, perception is a major contributor to individual differences. It is, therefore, necessary for persons who seek to understand organizational behavior to understand the perceptual process.

The person who is naive makes no distinction between reality and perception of reality or between sensation and perception. The more sophisticated person knows that seeing is not always believing—that there are many ways of viewing a situation, none of which may be totally realistic. Perception may first be understood by differentiating it from the more elementary process of sensation. *Sensation* occurs when physical stimuli affect one or more sensory receptors (e.g., touch, smell, taste, hearing, or seeing) and send an impulse to the brain.

It is there that those neural impulses are interpreted in the light of one's past experiences, including one's earlier perceptions. Thus, two persons who see the same situation identically, so far as sensory data are concerned, may perceive it in totally opposite ways.

The auditory sensation of a supervisor's voice attracts the attention of a subordinate despite many competing stimuli in the workplace. The subordinate's interpretation of that datum is that the supervisor desires increased productivity. At a higher, more abstract level of perception the subordinate perceives that the supervisor is irritated or angry. The high level of interpretation that is required in making assumptions about another person's emotional state or thought process creates a strong likelihood that reality and one's perception of reality will differ; yet we must constantly make these assumptions.

Selective Perception. Since it is impossible to give equal attention to all aspects of the world around us, we selectively pay attention to stimuli that are particularly strong or particularly relevant. If, at this moment, I allow my attention to wander, I will hear voices from the next office and noises from a busy street. I also hear the muffled sound of the air coming into my office and am aware that it is uncomfortably cold. Those sound and temperature stimuli are continual, though I am not continually aware of them.

Many factors determine which sensory stimuli are admitted into consciousness. Some are characteristics of the stimulus: a loud noise, a pungent odor, a flashing light, or a change in a speaker's voice. Stimuli are also filtered through the needs and concerns of the perceiver. We are more likely to selectively attend stimuli related to our active needs: the aroma of food when we are hungry, and the sounds in the hallway that suggest the class period should be over after a fatiguing or boring lecture. Interests also influence attention: marketing students are attracted to a firm's advertising practices, while computer science students particularly notice its information systems. Thus, selective perception alone is sufficient to ensure some degree of perceptual distortion.

Influences on Perception. Beyond the selection process, reality may be misperceived in numerous ways, the nature of the stimulus being an important determiner of the accuracy of what will be perceived. The more abstract and difficult a supervisor's instructions, for instance, the greater the probability that they will be misinterpreted. If the company is involved in labor-management contract negotiations and the employees are hostile and suspicious, a still further basis for misperception exists. Furthermore, the employee who is inclined to be neurotically defensive or paranoid may hear something quite different from what the supervisor intends to communicate.

Perception is also influenced by what a person believes to be true; and these beliefs are influenced by one's attitudes, values, education, and work background. Furthermore, all past perceptions have a potential influence on future perceptions. In view of these many contributors to differences in perception, it may appear that attempting to understand, predict, and influence human behavior is an exercise in futility; but the effort is saved by the fact that individuals are relatively consistent within themselves. Since the attitudes, values, and experiences that influence perception change slowly, their influence on perception is relatively stable; we can, therefore, predict with some accuracy how others will perceive what we say and do.

Prior to the 1930's, the popular authoritarian, task-oriented approach to management gave no thought to such a human characteristic as perception, perhaps because little was known about its effect on employee behavior. Even less was known about the impact of informal groups on the perceptions and behaviors of an organization's members; and what was known did not appear to be of importance to managers. With the emergence of the human relations movement, however, the field of management changed dramatically; and no influence contributed more to that change than three decades of research on informal groups.

INFORMAL GROUPS IN ORGANIZATIONS

Writers of the traditional management literature seemed unaware of the nature and power of informal groups, and practicing managers acted as though they were dealing only with individuals operating in relative isolation from one another. However, the massive research of the 1940's and 1950's, which indicated among other things that the power of management may be undermined by the influence of informal groups, demonstrated that organizational behavior cannot be understood apart from the behavior of informal groups. An *informal group* is a collection of interdependent individuals whose members influence one another's behavior and contribute to mutual need satisfaction; unlike formal relationships, however, the interpersonal relations among members of informal groups emerge spontaneously. They do not result from rational planning.

The Bases for Informal Groups

Informal groups spontaneously emerge from the interaction of people because groups meet individual needs that the formal organization does not or cannot meet. The most important of these needs are as follows:

1. *The Need to Belong.* Groups form because individuals need the sense of identity and self-esteem that comes from being accepted by other persons. People are especially attracted to others they perceive to be like themselves.[11]
2. *The Need to Achieve.* The ability of group members to help one another be effective in doing their work is a strong inducement for group membership. Stated negatively, persons without the support of informal groups may have difficulty succeeding on the job.
3. *The Need for Power.* Individuals often have difficulty standing up to management, but when a group speaks with a single voice, managers tend to listen. Individuals often feel isolated, uncertain, and insecure—feelings that are lessened by the

[11] Gerald H. Graham, "Interpersonal Attraction as a Basis of Informal Organization," *Academy of Management Journal*, Vol. 14, No. 4 (December, 1971), p. 483.

information and support that group members provide. Thus, groups fulfill a need for social power and the security it brings.

4. _The Need for Self-Esteem._ An individual's work may contribute little to his or her sense of self-worth, but the social relationships and power experienced in informal groups are often self-enhancing. They prevent excessive boredom and a feeling that life is being wasted.

The satisfaction of these needs provides ample motivation for the development of informal groups, although the individuals involved may not be consciously aware that groups are being formed. They may not even be fully aware of the existence of the one or more groups to which they belong and show allegiance.

Informal Group Structure

Informal groups vary greatly in degree of structure or organization. Some groups have vague, difficult-to-define boundaries and do not expect nor receive much allegiance from their members. Others are tightly structured; they have clearly defined member expectations and exert intense pressures on their members to conform. We look now at three aspects of informal group structure: role expectations, group norms, and group cohesiveness.

Role Expectations. One structural aspect of all groups is the development of _role expectations_—the behavior that group members have learned to expect of a particular individual because of that person's past performance in the group. Thus, one individual typically serves as group spokesperson in confrontations with management; another, because of a special communication source, keeps the group up to date on company politics; while yet another serves as the group comic or uses special powers of persuasion to ensure member compliance with group behavior standards. It is within the context of role formation that we understand how the leaders of informal groups emerge and how the follower status of nonleaders is established.

Group Norms. Another important dimension of group structure is concerned with the standards or _norms_ of group behavior. Unlike the rules or bylaws of a club, these norms are rarely formalized; nevertheless, they are well understood by insiders, and conformity to them is a requirement for membership.[12] In one group an important norm may be style and quality of clothes. In another, fashion does not matter, but withholding from management information about group activities and maintaining production within acceptable limits are considered vitally important. As shown in Figure 14–3, production norms may specify a range of acceptability, with extremely high or low production being prohibited. Obviously employees at the low extreme do not carry their part of the load, while employees at the high extreme make the group look inadequate and run the risk of causing management to raise production standards.

---

[12] P. C. Andre de la Porte, "Group Norms, Key to Building a Winning Team," _Personnel_, Vol. 51, No. 5 (September–October, 1974), p. 61.

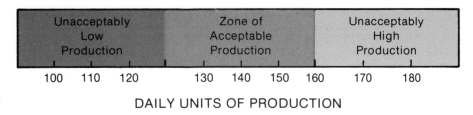

**Figure 14–3
GROUP NORMS
AS STANDARDS
OF
ACCEPTABILITY**

Most groups have *crucial norms*, those that are perceived as directly related to group survival, and *peripheral norms*, those that are desirable but not essential. Norms relating to production are usually crucial because they directly or indirectly affect how much employees will earn and how hard they will be expected to work, both of which are of primary importance in the workplace. How group members dress may be a peripheral norm, preferred, because it identifies the group or perhaps symbolizes its success, but not a membership requirement.

Informal groups use a variety of reward and punishment devices to control their membership and ensure conformity to norms. They can praise or verbally abuse, be supportive or withhold information needed to be effective at work, build self-esteem or make one a social outcast by creating false rumors. Because of the psychological and physical proximity of group members to one another, groups are uniquely successful in influencing member perception and attitudes and in controlling the flow of vital information to group members.[13]

In some situations individual employees appear to be totally dominated by the formal organization and the informal groups to which they belong. Nevertheless, research indicates that formal and informal controls allow employees considerable freedom to be themselves, and it is in the subcultures of informal groups that employees are most likely to drop their façades and be themselves. Within informal groups they can lower their inhibitions, use the language with which they are most comfortable, and enjoy prankish physical contact or other activities that would be unacceptable in the presence of their superiors.[14] Employees value an opportunity for such behavior because it releases some of the tension and boredom created by the constraints of the formal organization.

Group Cohesiveness. The amount of control a group has over its members is directly related to its *cohesiveness*: the group's unity of purpose and action, and the extent to which its members are able to function as a closely knit team.[15]

[13] J. Richard Hackman, "Group Influences on Individuals," *Handbook of Industrial and Organizational Psychology*, edited by Marvin D. Dunnette (Chicago: Rand McNally Company, 1976), p. 1456.

[14] Fred E. Katz, "Explaining Informal Work Groups in Complex Organizations: The Case for Autonomy in Structure," *Administrative Science Quarterly*, Vol. 10, No. 2 (September, 1965), p. 210.

[15] David A. Nadler, J. Richard Hackman, and Edward E. Lawler III, *Managing Organizational Behavior* (Boston: Little, Brown & Company, 1979), p. 128.

Several factors enhance group cohesiveness such as physical isolation from other groups, opportunity to communicate, and availability of effective leadership. It has been observed, for example, that members of a formal work unit who are physically located in an open work area with employees from other work units often fail to develop cohesiveness. The likelihood of cohesiveness is weakened by the identifications they form with employees outside their own group. Extremely noisy work areas, rules against carrying on conversations, and other barriers to communication also diminish cohesiveness—often significantly because informal communication is essential for the development of close personal relationships. Cohesiveness is greater when groups are stable (permitting deep friendships to develop), when they are relatively small (which discourages splintering into smaller groups), and when they have high status from which members may draw self-esteem. Cohesiveness is also enhanced when members have many characteristics, values, and needs in common (group homogeneity). Generally speaking, the more cohesive the group the more powerful it will be and the more effective it will be in achieving its objectives.

Informal Groups from Management's Perspective

Since informal groups may be committed to goals that clash with the goals of the firm (such as restricting production), they may appear undesirable. All things considered, however, their effect is distinctly positive. The contributions of informal groups to lateral communication, to coordinating the work flow, and to the sharing of technical knowledge are often required for efficient production. Similarly, the social rewards provided by groups—the warm, supportive relationships, the friendships, and the positive emotional bonds—are, in effect, a form of employee compensation that increases job satisfaction and reduces absenteeism and turnover. Formal motivation systems, however positive, are unable to satisfy all these needs.

The ability of managers to influence their subordinates is often reduced because of informal group activity, especially among employees who have no opportunity for promotion and do not depend upon the recommendations of supervisors for pay raises.[16] But the power of informal groups can just as easily be made to work for the organization. Some firms, for example, take full advantage of informal groups by using the work group rather than the individual as the basic unit for job design.[17] By grouping employees who perform interdependent tasks, informal groups are encouraged, particularly in situations where their potential contribution to the organization is high. Where such employees internalize their employer's values and objectives, the informal groups to which they belong become powerful, self-regulating forces in the interest of the firm.

---

[16] Noel Tiche, "An Analysis of Clique Formation and Structure in Organizations," *Administrative Science Quarterly*, Vol. 18, No. 2 (June, 1973), p. 204.

[17] Thomas G. Cummings, "Self-Regulating Work Groups: A Socio-Technical Synthesis," *Academy of Management Review*, Vol. 3, No. 3 (July, 1978), p. 625.

The formal structure of an organization, as reflected in its levels of management, spans of control, policies, and the like, has a major impact on the behavior of its members and on the likelihood that the firm will be successful. As we have seen, however, the impact of informal groups interacts with individual behavior and the effects of the formal organization to produce a highly complex, multifaceted work environment. Because these variables differ from one firm to another, each has its own unique organizational climate—the subject to which we now turn our attention.

ORGANIZATIONAL CLIMATE

Case Problem 14-A asks for a description of the organizational climate of your college or university—not a simple task since educational institutions are complex and the meaning of organizational climate is somewhat ambiguous. Since the concept has received wide attention as a means of describing organizations and is a valuable framework for understanding how organizational practices and procedures are reflected in human behavior,[18] we now investigate two views of organizational climate.

A Perceptual View

Following an early and often quoted definition, *organizational climate* may be viewed as "the set of characteristics that describe an organization and that (a) distinguish the organization from other organizations, (b) are relatively enduring over time, and (c) influence the behavior of people in the organization."[19] Although this definition serves as an introduction to the concept, it is not totally satisfactory. More concrete and understandable definitions emerge when we express the definition in *operational terms*; that is, when we set forth the operations by which organizational climate is measured.

Currently a trend is developing to measure organizational climate in terms of how it is perceived by its members. Hellriegel and Slocum developed the following definition as an adaptation of several earlier definitions:

> Organizational climate refers to a set of attributes which can be perceived about a particular organization and/or its subsystems, and that may be induced from the way that organization and/or its subsystems deal with their members and environment.[20]

This definition implies that climate refers to attributes of the organization rather than to attributes of the individuals who comprise the organization. How-

---

[18] Benjamin Schneider, "Organizational Climates: An Essay," *Personnel Psychology*, Vol. 28, No. 4 (Winter, 1975), p. 474.

[19] Garlie A. Forehand and B. von Haller Gilmer, "Environmental Variation in Studies of Organizational Behavior," *Psychological Bulletin*, Vol. 62, No. 6 (December, 1964), p. 361.

[20] Don Hellriegel and John W. Slocum, Jr., "Organizational Climate: Measures, Research and Contingencies," *Academy of Management Journal*, Vol. 17, No. 2 (June, 1974), p. 256.

ever, the attributes of the organization are measured by determining how its members perceive certain aspects of the organization, such as degree of formalization, nature and level of conflict, support and consideration given to the individual, standards and expectations, emphasis on production, the decision-making process, and risk to the individual.[21] In measuring such attributes it is important that the questions asked provoke descriptions (as perceived by organizational members) rather than attitudes that reflect evaluations of the attributes. The following examples of items used for this purpose are from the fifty-item *Litwin and Stringer Organization Climate Questionnaire*, an instrument used in several research studies.

> The jobs in this organization are clearly defined and logically structured.
>
> In this organization it is sometimes unclear who has the formal authority to make a decision.
>
> The best way to make a good impression around here is to steer clear of open arguments and disagreements.
>
> We are encouraged to speak our minds, even if it means disagreeing with our superiors.[22]

Items such as those listed here are not intended to measure attitudes. The last one, for example, does not ask respondents to express whether they like or dislike being encouraged to speak their minds. Nevertheless, such perceptual measures of organizational climate have often been criticized for reflecting attitudes and therefore describing attributes of individuals rather than organizations.[23] Even perceptions reflect characteristics of the individual as well as the organization.[24]

The definition given by Hellriegel and Slocum suggests that organizational climate may describe all or part of an organization. This is a meaningful point since the climates of major divisions or departments may vary greatly, and the more diversity there is in the way the subunits of the firm are managed, the greater the likelihood that the climates of subunits will differ.

An Objective View

Because the perceptual approach to measuring organizational climate is somewhat subjective, some researchers have proposed a more objective approach.[25] Instead of asking persons within the organization to describe it, an

---

[21] L. K. Waters, Darrell Roach, Nick Batlis, "Organization Climate Dimensions and Job-Related Attitudes," *Personnel Psychology*, Vol. 27, No. 3 (Autumn, 1974), p. 465.

[22] Paul M. Muchinsky, "An Assessment of the Litwin and Stringer Organization Climate Questionnaire: An Empirical and Theoretical Extension of the Sims and LaFollette Study," *Personnel Psychology*, Vol. 29, No. 3 (Autumn, 1976), p. 371.

[23] Russell E. Johannesson, "Some Problems in the Measurement of Organizational Climate," *Organizational Behavior and Human Performance*, Vol. 10, No. 1 (August, 1973), p. 118.

[24] Robert M. Guion, "A Note on Organizational Climate," *Organizational Behavior and Human Performance*, Vol. 9, No. 1 (February, 1973), p. 120.

[25] E.P. Prien and W.W. Ronan, "An Analysis of Organizational Characteristics," *Organizational Behavior and Human Performance*, Vol. 6, No. 2 (March, 1971), p. 215.

objective observer characterizes the organization in such terms as size, levels of authority, quantity and nature of formal rules and policies, goal structure, and ratio of administrative personnel to production personnel. Following this objective framework, an attempt is made to determine the impact of such organizational characteristics on the behavior of the individuals who comprise its membership. One may discover, for example, that in firms with many organizational levels, personnel near the bottom of the pyramid are especially inclined to believe that they have little control over their own destiny. Or the number of formal goals and policies of organizations may prove to be correlated with employees' feelings of security and confidence in their own work-related decisions. Such information describes potentially useful aspects of organizational climate.

Although the objective approach has merit, the following criticisms of it have been made: (1) the number of variables may be too numerous to be clearly interpreted, (2) studying organizational properties separately does not reflect their combined impact, and (3) perceptions are an important aspect of organizational climate and, therefore, should be considered in measuring climate.[26] The last point is especially noteworthy since the perceived characteristics of the organization rather than the objective characteristics influence member behavior. Whether or not these criticisms are totally valid, most researchers have accepted the perceptual approach. Thus, organizational climate from the perceptual view has become an important means of understanding how organizational practices and procedures are reflected in human behavior. We look now in more detail at one aspect of organizational climate: the management of conflict and stress.

The Management of Conflict and Stress

Employees at all organizational levels enter the firm with vast differences in experience, education, values, motives, and attitudes. These and other individual differences, combined with the frustrations arising from work-related problems and from the need to conform to numerous organizational demands, produce conflict among individuals and groups and stress within individuals. Since conflict is inevitable, it is a significant dimension of organizational climate that influences both the effectiveness and satisfaction of organizational members. It is important to note that even if it were possible to eliminate conflict, such action would be inadvisable; conflict makes positive contributions to organizations when managed appropriately.

The Nature of Organizational Conflict. As used here, *conflict* is the process which begins when one party perceives that one or more of its concerns have been or are about to be frustrated (blocked) by another party.[27] A moderate

---

[26] William R. LaFollette, "How Is the Climate in Your Organization?" *Personnel Journal*, Vol. 54, No. 7 (July, 1975), p. 376.

[27] Kenneth Thomas, "Conflict and Conflict Management," *Handbook of Industrial and Organizational Psychology*, edited by Marvin D. Dunnette (Chicago: Rand McNally & Company, 1976), p. 891.

degree of conflict may increase motivation, stimulate creativity, and require that fuzzy ideas be clarified. Excessively low conflict may produce what Irving Janis called *groupthink*, in which decision makers engage in self-censorship, collectively rationalize what they want to believe, and put pressure on dissenters to conform.[28]

Nevertheless, conflict between individuals and groups may result in decreased organizational effectiveness and excessive pressure on the individuals involved. There is evidence that bitter, unresolved conflict is widespread and increasing, possibly because of an increased emphasis on human values and rights.[29] A survey conducted by the American Management Association indicated that chief operating officers perceive that conflict management, especially as it relates to personality clashes, requires a significant amount of their time (about 20 percent) and is growing in importance.[30]

Deliberate attempts to minimize organizational conflict have taken a variety of forms. Organizational Development (OD) change agents use *confrontation meetings* to bring conflicting groups together to resolve their differences,[31] and similar approaches are used by management counselors to resolve conflicts between individuals. Several studies indicate that conflict between groups can be reduced if the parties are helped to cooperate in achieving common goals—called *superordinating goals* [32]—although this technique, according to its critics, may simply avoid and, therefore, perpetuate the major source of conflict. Alonzo McDonald, the managing director of a major international consulting firm, believes that the destructiveness of organizational conflict in the executive suite is related to managerial ethics and can be dealt with best by carefully selecting and promoting managers who have proved themselves to be ethically sensitive.[33]

Stress: Causes and Cures. *Stress* refers to the psychological and physiological changes that occur within an individual when the demands of the environment threaten to exceed that person's capabilities. Under such conditions (when, for example, employees with limited freedom to alter their situation perceive their employer's expectations to be excessive) a wide range of physiological changes occur to help the individual cope with the situation.[34] These changes are designed to prepare a person for *fight* or *flight*, for aggressive action or retreat, and include a slowing down of the digestive processes, an increase in blood sugar, increased heartbeat, perspiration, and other bodily activities with which we are all familiar from personal experience.

---

[28] Irving L. Janis, *Victims of Groupthink* (Boston: Houghton Mifflin Company, 1972), p. 9.

[29] Rensis Likert and Jane Gibson Likert, *New Ways of Managing Conflict* (New York City: McGraw-Hill, Inc., 1976), p. 1.

[30] Kenneth W. Thomas and Warren H. Schmidt, "A Survey of Managerial Interests with Respect to Conflict," *Academy of Management Journal*, Vol. 19, No. 2 (June, 1976), p. 315.

[31] Organizational Development is discussed in Chapter 13 of this text.

[32] J. David Hunger and Louis Stern, "An Assessment of the Functionality of the Superordinating Goal in Reducing Conflict," *Academy of Management Journal*, Vol. 19, No. 4 (December, 1976), p. 591.

[33] Alonzo McDonald, "Conflict at the Summit, a Deadly Game," *Harvard Business Review*, Vol. 50, No. 2 (March–April, 1972), p. 59.

[34] For a detailed explanation of the nature of stress, read Hans Selye, *Stress without Distress* (New York City: J. B. Lippincott Company, 1974).

When the *stressor* (the stress-provoking stimulus) is removed—when the problem is solved or a stress-provoking deadline has been passed—the bodily functions return to normal and the adaptive functions of the body work effectively. However, when the stressor persists and the individual cannot psychologically adjust in such a way that the perceived threat is reduced, the body's preparation for emergency action may cause serious bodily harm such as damage to the digestive system, high blood pressure, severe headaches, or heart trouble. When continual job-related tensions are combined with perceived failure and feelings of inadequacy, some persons even become depressed and suicidal.[35] In recent years medical researchers have increasingly attributed physiological disorders and failure to respond to treatment to the effects of stress.

Typical Causes. Stress has many causes, not the least of which are inadequate coping techniques. What some persons accept as a challenge, others perceive as a threat; and, because the primary source of the problem is embedded in their own personalities, modifying the work environment provides little help. Ultimately such persons may cope with their stress by alienating themselves from the organization and detaching themselves from their work, regardless of how favorable the work environment may be. In such situations, productivity usually declines.

Where stress is high among large numbers of employees and managers in a particular organization, it is reasonable to assume that some of the causes are due to the organizational climate—for example, ambiguity of a superior's evaluations, fear of being arbitrarily discharged, inadequate authority, excessive workload, or having to engage in tasks that violate one's ethical standards. Several studies have shown that poorly defined roles in the workplace increase stress [36] as does a Machiavellian style of management (manipulative, distrustful, autocratic).[37] Other studies have demonstrated that managers who perceive themselves to be in control of their own destiny are less likely to experience stress than are managers who perceive themselves to be closely controlled by others.[38] Environmental stressors can theoretically be dealt with in a straightforward way; in practice, however, the needed changes are often difficult to make. Even under ideal environmental conditions, individual perception of external threat cannot be eliminated because perception is influenced by emotional as well as logical considerations.

Possible Cures. Managers tend to prefer certain techniques for handling stress. For example, 300 managers from 12 companies in Ontario, Canada,

[35] Harry Levinson, "On Executive Suicide," *Harvard Business Review*, Vol. 53, No. 4 (July–August, 1975), p. 118.

[36] Robert Miles and M. M. Petty, "Relationship between Role Clarity, Need for Clarity, and Job Tension and Satisfaction for Supervisory and Nonsupervisory Roles," *Academy of Management Journal*, Vol. 18, No. 4 (December, 1975), p. 877.

[37] Gary R. Gemmill and W. J. Heisler, "Machiavellianism as a Factor in Managerial Job Strain, Job Satisfaction, and Upward Mobility," *Academy of Management Journal*, Vol. 15, No. 1 (March, 1972), p. 51.

[38] Carl R. Anderson, Don Hellriegel, and John W. Slocum, Jr., "Managerial Response to Environmentally Induced Stress," *Academy of Management Journal*, Vol. 20, No. 2 (June, 1977), p. 260.

view the following five techniques as the best means for coping with job-related stress:

1. Build resistance by regular sleep, exercise, and good health habits.
2. Compartmentalize work and nonwork life.
3. Engage in physical exercise.
4. Talk through problems with peers on the job.
5. Withdraw physically from the situation.

That same group of managers views the following as the five worst coping techniques:

1. Change to a different work activity.
2. Change strategy of attack on work.
3. Work harder.
4. Talk through problems with spouse.
5. Change to a nonwork activity.[39]

In recent years an increasing number of managers have resorted to tranquilizers and alcohol as coping devices—at best, stop-gap methods. Some use *biofeedback*, a process through which body tension is magnified electronically and fed back through an auditory stimulus that helps the individual learn to relax. Electrodes attached to an individual's forehead are transmitted to an instrument that registers skin tension and thereby measures the extent to which the individual is tense or relaxed. Excessive effort to relax usually increases rather than decreases tension, a condition of which the person becomes immediately aware through the increased frequency of an electronic beep. On the other hand, any physical or mental change that produces relaxation (and, consequently, a reduced frequency of the beep) is also noted. Thus, one learns to behave in ways that produce relaxation and avoid tension. After the learning has occurred, the electronic support is no longer necessary.

Finally, *transcendental meditation* techniques, originally associated with Oriental religions, have been modified so that persons in stress-producing jobs can periodically use them as an aid to relaxation. Herbert Benson, a Harvard University professor of medicine, recommends to executives a "relaxation response," which is a combination of mental conditioning, muscle relaxation, and deep-breathing exercises that enables a person to modify the physical symptoms associated with stress.[40] Although stress is an inevitable part of organizational life, most managers learn to cope with it and function effectively; relaxation techniques such as biofeedback and Benson's relaxation response show promise as coping devices. However, the latter has the advantage of not requiring electronic hardware and, therefore, of placing the manager in total control of his or her destiny.

---

[39] John H. Howard, Peter A. Rechnitzer, and D. A. Cunningham, "Coping with Job Tension—Effective and Ineffective Methods," *Public Personnel Journal*, Vol. 4 (May, 1975), p. 317.

[40] Ruanne K. Peters and Herbert Benson, "Time Out from Tension," *Harvard Business Review*, Vol. 56, No. 1 (January–February, 1978), p. 120.

Case Problem 14-B, What Killed Bob Lyons?, is a descriptive statement of the interaction of one man and his environment. Although the dynamics underlying Bob Lyons' decision to commit suicide are not discussed in the text, they are readily available elsewhere.[41]

Case Problem 14-B

WHAT KILLED BOB LYONS?

Those who knew Bob Lyons thought extremely well of him. He was a highly successful executive who had an important position in a large company. As his superiors saw him, he was aggressive, with a knack for getting things done through other people. He worked hard and set a vigorous pace. He drove himself relentlessly. In less than ten years with his company, he had moved through several positions of responsibility.

Lyons had always been a good athlete. He was proud of his skills in swimming, hunting, golf, and tennis. In his college days he had lettered in football and baseball. On weekends he preferred to undertake rebuilding and repairing projects around the house, or to hunt, interspersing other sports for a change of pace. He was usually engaged, it seemed, in hard physical work.

His life was not all work, however. He was active in his church and in the Boy Scouts. His wife delighted in entertaining and in being with other people; so their social life was a round of many parties and social activities. They shared much of their life with their three children.

Early in the spring of his ninth year with the company, Bob Lyons spoke with the vice-president to whom he reported. "Things are a little quiet around here," he said. "Most of the big projects are over. The new building is finished, and we have a lot of things on the ball which four years ago were all fouled up. I don't like the idea of just riding a desk and looking out the window. I like action."

About a month later, Lyons was assigned additional responsibilities. He rushed into them with his usual vigor. Once again he seemed to be buoyant and cheerful. After six months on the assignment, Lyons had the project rolling smoothly. Again he spoke to his vice-president, reporting that he was out of projects. The vice-president, pleased with Lyons' performance, told him that he had earned the right to do a little dreaming and planning; and, furthermore, dreaming and planning were a necessary part of the position he now held, toward which he had aspired for so long. Bob Lyons listened as his boss spoke, but it was plain to the vice-president that the answer did not satisfy him.

About three months after this meeting, the vice-president began to notice that replies to his memos and inquiries were not coming back from Lyons with their usual rapidity. He noticed also that Lyons was developing a tendency to put things off, a most unusual behavior pattern for him. He observed that Lyons became easily angered and disturbed over minor difficulties which previously had not irritated him at all.

Bob Lyons then became involved in a conflict with two other executives over a policy issue. Such conflicts were not unusual

[41] Harry Levinson, "What Killed Bob Lyons?" *Harvard Business Review*, Vol. 41, No. 1 (January–February, 1963), p. 127. © 1963 by the President and Fellows of Harvard College; all rights reserved. The introductory material of this article appears as Case Problem 14-B. Dr. Levinson's statement of the reasons why Bob Lyons' reaction to his environment resulted in suicide and some practical conclusions to be drawn from this study are presented in the *Student Enrichment Activities*.

in the organization since, inevitably, there were varying points of view on many issues. The conflict was not a personal one, but it did require intervention from higher management before a solution could be reached. In the process of resolving the conflict, Lyons' point of view prevailed on some questions, but not on others.

A few weeks after this conflict had been resolved, Lyons went to the vice-president's office. He wanted to have a long private talk, he said. His first words were, "I'm losing my grip. The old steam is gone. I've had diarrhea for four weeks and several times in the past three weeks I've lost my breakfast. I'm worried and yet I don't know what about. I feel that some people have lost confidence in me."

He talked with his boss for an hour and a half. The vice-president recounted his achievements in the company to reassure him. He then asked if Lyons thought he should see a doctor. Lyons agreed that he should and, in the presence of the vice-president, called his family doctor for an appointment. By this time the vice-president was very much concerned. He called Mrs. Lyons and arranged to meet her for lunch the next day. She reported that, in addition to his other symptoms, her husband had difficulty sleeping. She was relieved that the vice-president had called her because she was beginning to become worried and had herself planned to call the vice-president. Both were now alarmed. They decided that they should get Lyons into a hospital rather than wait for the doctor's appointment which was still a week off.

The next day Lyons was taken to the hospital. Meanwhile, with Mrs. Lyons' permission, the vice-president reported to the family doctor Lyons' recent job behavior and the nature of their conversations. When the vice-president finished, the doctor concluded, "All he needs is a good rest. We don't want to tell him that it may be mental or nervous." The vice-president replied that he

didn't know what the cause was, but he knew Bob Lyons needed help quickly.

During five days in the hospital, Lyons was subject to extensive laboratory tests. The vice-president visited him daily. He seemed to welcome the rest and the sedation at night. He said he was eating and sleeping much better. He talked about company problems, though he did not speak spontaneously without encouragement. While Lyons was out of the room, another executive who shared his hospital room confided to the vice-president that he was worried about Lyons. "He seems to be so morose and depressed that I'm afraid he's losing his mind," the executive said.

By this time the president of the company, who had been kept informed, was also becoming concerned. He had talked to a psychiatrist and planned to talk to Lyons about psychiatric treatment if his doctor did not suggest it. Meanwhile, Lyons was discharged from the hospital as being without physical illness, and his doctor recommended a vacation. Lyons then remained at home for several days where he was again visited by the vice-president. He and his wife took a trip to visit friends. He was then ready to come back to work, but the president suggested that he take another week off. The president also suggested that they visit together when Lyons returned.

A few days later, the president telephoned Lyons' home. Mrs. Lyons could not find him to answer the telephone. After 15 minutes she still had not found him and called the vice-president about her concern. By the time the vice-president arrived at the Lyons home, the police were already there. Bob Lyons had committed suicide.

PROBLEMS

1. Describe in your own words the reasons for Bob Lyons' suicide.
2. Was Lyons' reaction attributable primarily to his work situation, to his personality,

or to an interaction between his personality and his work environment? Explain.

3. How much of Lyons' problem is attributable to this particular work situation? Describe a situation that would minimize stress for him.

4. Describe one or more constructive courses of action that Lyons could have taken to cope with his stress.

CHAPTER QUESTIONS FOR STUDY AND DISCUSSION

1. Both survey studies and case studies sometimes use questionnaires and interviews for the purpose of gathering data. How do the two research methods differ?
2. Why are longitudinal studies generally superior to cross-sectional studies?
3. In experimental studies, why are control groups necessary? What, if any, value is there in having more than one control group?
4. In what way does positive reinforcement differ from reward?
5. In what sense are leaders uniquely qualified to serve as models for their followers?
6. What are the major contributors to biased perception? Can anyone avoid perceptual bias?
7. If a manager is foolish enough to try to prevent the formation of informal groups among his or her subordinates, that action will probably cause an increase in such groups. Why?
8. How do you account for the high degree of control an informal group often has over its members?
9. Why is the perceptual view of organizational climate more useful than the objective view?
10. What are the benefits of conflict in organizations?
11. What is misleading about describing situations as being stressful?
12. What advantages can Benson's relaxation response have over biofeedback as a means of helping managers relax?

Chapter 15

Motivation in Organizations

PART I: AN EMPLOYEE BENEFIT PROGRAM

Acme Manufacturing Company, located in an eastern metropolitan area, produces a complete line of small household electrical appliances such as toasters, blenders, coffee percolators, and electric can openers. The products are of good quality and are distributed through department stores and mail-order houses under private labels. The small fractional horsepower motors and heating elements used in the products are purchased; however, the company does its own stamping, machining, plating, painting, and assembly. Two hundred hourly paid workers perform these operations.

The personnel policies of Acme Manufacturing are not stated in writing, nor is there an employee handbook. The company conducts an annual wage survey and maintains its wage level at the average of the area for similar jobs. There has not been the same effort to maintain fringe benefits at a competitive level. Surveys concerning employee benefits are not conducted on a regular basis; the last survey was completed about five years ago. The company has never conducted an attitude or morale survey.

John Rider, the general manager, is somewhat puzzled by one aspect of the monthly personnel department activity report. For the second successive month there are ten production jobs to be filled. To the best of his knowledge there have been no changes in production schedules, nor has he authorized any additional factory personnel. Consequently, Rider wonders why the ten openings exist. He has called the personnel manager to determine the reasons for the vacancies.

As Margaret Marlow, the personnel manager, entered his office, Mr. Rider said, "Margaret, I notice that for the second straight month we have ten vacancies in our plant labor force. If this rate of turnover continues, we will be replacing over half our labor force within a year. What is the reason for our hiring so many new employees?"

"Part of the reason is that we still have four vacancies to be filled from the preceding month, and the other six are vacancies that were created by employees with less than six months' service who quit last month," Marlow answered.

"About the four jobs remaining from last month, why haven't we filled them?"

"Well, these are all skilled jobs. Even so, we managed to hire two people, but they didn't report for work. Both called and said they had taken better jobs somewhere else."

"Do you know where they went to work?" Rider asked.

"Yes, and neither company has a higher wage rate than we have." Anticipating the next question, Marlow continued, "The only reason that they go to these companies is that they are offered better employee benefits than ours; and in a tight labor market such as we have now, that difference is significant.

"I also notice from your report that our absentee rate is running about 8 to 10 percent a day—about twice what it was this time last year. Is that a part of the same pattern?"

"I believe it is," Marlow answered.

"In that case I suggest that we take a good look at our fringe benefits. After you have determined what is happening in the area, summarize the results and recommend the level that we should adopt for our company. I know that we have more or less paid the average in wages, but in view of our increasing quality problems and our productiv-ity rate per employee-hour, I'm willing to pay more for fringe benefits if that will help quality and production."

PROBLEMS

1. What effect would an expanded employee benefit program have on employee turnover, absenteeism, productivity, and product quality? Explain.
2. Compared with other companies in the area, what level of employee benefit program do you recommend for Acme (below average, average, upper 25 percent, upper 10 percent)?
3. Is there justification for the common practice of referring to employee benefits as fringe benefits?
4. What factors are most likely to determine whether employee morale and general satisfaction with the employment situation will influence productivity?

Few subjects have received as much attention in recent years as employee motivation. As it has become obvious that authoritarian leadership is inadequate, as employees have become more independent and demanding, and as our understanding of human motivation has expanded, motivation has been increasingly accepted as a basic subject for a study of management. It is a particularly important prerequisite for understanding managerial leadership.

Definitions of motivation vary greatly, partly because authors tend to formulate definitions in terms of specific theories and partly because motivation is extremely complex. The term *motivation* is derived from the Latin word *movere*, meaning *to move*. Thus, motives are movers, energizers, or goads to action. *Human motivation* is the process by which behavior is mobilized and sustained in the interest of meeting individual needs and achieving organizational objectives. Although motivation can be defined and understood from many perspectives, our primary concern is motivation in the workplace.

EMPLOYEE NEEDS AND GOALS

The most persistent theme in motivation theory is that the purpose of behavior is to satisfy needs—physiological needs for food and water, for example, and psychological needs for belonging, love, and self-acceptance. As we shall see, not all motivational theories are explicitly based on the concept of need gratification, but that concept is a logical place to begin a study of motivation.

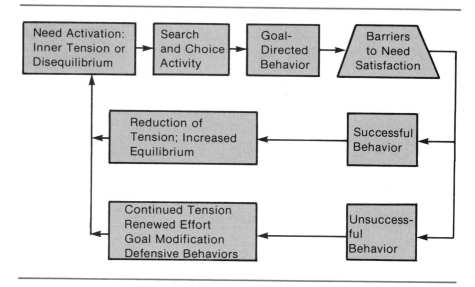

Figure 15–1
A GENERAL
MOTIVATIONAL
MODEL

As shown in Figure 15–1, the presence of an active need (say, a need for recognition) is expressed as an inner state of disequilibrium or tension from which the individual seeks relief. In order to satisfy this need, the individual engages in search activity that terminates in a choice of means. The need for recognition, for example, may be satisfied, in part, by achieving a promotion. This goal, in turn, may lead the individual to take night-school courses, work longer hours, and engage in other goal-directed activities to overcome the obstacles to need satisfaction. These barriers may be *internal*, such as an inadequate education; *external*, in the form of high performance by competitors; or they may be *conflict* barriers, which exist when an individual has difficulty satisfying one need without increasing another. For example, the long hours of work and study expected to result in a promotion may clash with a manager's family life and thereby diminish overall need satisfaction. If, however, one's behavior successfully overcomes the barriers, tension is reduced and an inner state of satisfaction or equilibrium is achieved. If not, Figure 15–1 shows that tension continues and motivation to discover another means of restoring the equilibrium persists. The manager who fails to receive the promotion may continue his or her efforts to reach that goal while simultaneously seeking to satisfy the same need by running for membership on the City Council. Or, as an alternative, he or she may rationalize the failure with "I didn't want the promotion anyway."

Although the general model shown in Figure 15–1 is accurate, as far as it goes, it is grossly oversimplified. For example, it says nothing about the conditions under which a promotion or other potential incentives will be motivational or why one person will exert additional effort to get a promotion while another person will not. This general motivational model leaves us with little or no basis for predicting the motivational effects of managerial actions, such as improving employee benefits (Case Problem 15-A), enriching jobs, or paying employees on the basis of individual productivity. The motivational theories and research discussed in this chapter are reasonably effective in helping us to understand such issues.

Maslow's Concept of Need Hierarchy

In 1943 Abraham Maslow published a theory of motivation based on clinical observation and logic (in contrast to empirical research). It received wide acceptance among managers and scholars and played a major role in further theory development.[1] Although Maslow's views on motivation continue to evolve,[2] they are essentially condensed to the following:

1. Need Classes. Human needs fall into five clusters or classes:
   a. *Physiological needs*—the needs for air, food, water, rest, avoidance of bodily injury, etc. These needs are concerned with the preservation of the physiological organism.
   b. *Safety needs*—security; freedom from environmental threat.
   c. *Social needs*—love, friendship, belonging or acceptance.
   d. *Esteem needs*—self-respect that is soundly based on real capacity, achievement, and respect from others; also prestige, recognition, and appreciation.[3]
   e. *Self-actualization needs*—self-fulfillment; doing that for which one is best suited; achieving one's highest potential.
2. Need Hierarchy. The five need classes for the hierarchy are shown in Figure 15–2. This hierarchy is based on potency and probability of occurrence, the

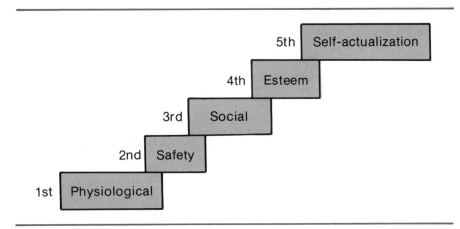

Figure 15–2 MASLOW'S HIERARCHY OF NEEDS

[1] A. H. Maslow, "A Theory of Human Motivation," *Psychological Review*, Vol. 50, No. 4 (July, 1943), p. 370.

[2] This evolution can most easily be traced from the 1943 article just listed through two editions of Maslow's book on motivation. See A. H. Maslow, *Motivation and Personality* (2d ed.; New York City: Harper & Row, Publishers, Inc., 1970).

[3] Maslow, *op. cit.*, p. 381.

physiological needs being the most powerful and having the highest probability of occurrence. These need classes and the hierarchy, unlike superficial desires, have a cross-cultural, universal quality;[4] that is, Maslow's theory assumes that this hierarchy applies to everybody.

3. Deprivation-Domination. The greater the deprivation of a need (i.e., the less it has been fulfilled), the higher its importance and strength. The lowest level of unfulfilled needs dominates all others; thus, if the physiological needs are not met, all the person's resources will be mobilized to satisfy them, even if higher level needs must be neglected.

4. Gratification-Activation. Beginning with the physiological needs, as needs on a given level are gratified they lose their strength and the next level of needs is activated. In other words, it is only after the needs on a given level have been reasonably well satisfied that the higher levels, in sequence, emerge or come into existence as motivational forces.

Motivational Implications. If Maslow's theory is valid, it has many implications for human motivation. For example, since a satisfied need is not a motivator (i.e., the need loses its potency when satisfied), managers should seek to discover their subordinates' emerging, active, unsatisfied needs when making motivational appeals. The employee whose physiological needs are well satisfied can be expected to become more concerned about safety or security provisions, such as seniority rules and other forms of protection against arbitrary management decisions. We may also expect the sometimes powerful needs for belonging and acceptance to become relatively poor motivators once they have been reasonably satisfied and once esteem needs have begun to emerge. Finally, when the low-level needs have been satisfied we should expect to find a strong emergence of the self-actualization needs—a strong desire, for example, for interesting, self-fulfilling work. Unlike low-level needs, satisfaction at the self-fulfillment level does not reduce the potency of that need. It is reasonable to expect, therefore, that a person's needs can never be completely satisfied and that there is always a basis for motivation.

Evaluation. For several reasons, Maslow's theory is difficult to test empirically: his terms are poorly defined, the theory has loosely evolved over many years, and, despite Maslow's sweeping claims that the theory applies universally (cross-culturally), he has proposed many exceptions and modifications. These factors make the theory difficult to pin down and seem to contradict the idea that it applies universally. In the latest revision of his book, Maslow suggested that the hierarchy might unfold or emerge over a lifetime so that the levels relate more to age and career levels than to the satisfaction of lower needs.[5] Nevertheless, a large number of studies have been conducted to test various aspects of his theory, most of which have not been very supportive.[6]

---

[4] Maslow, *op. cit.*, 1970, p. 54.

[5] *Ibid.*, p. 20.

[6] M. A. Wahba and Lawrence G. Bridwell, "Maslow Reconsidered: A Review of Research on the Need Hierarchy Theory," *Organizational Behavior and Human Performance*, Vol. 15, No. 2 (April, 1976), p. 212.

Although imperfections in the research make it risky to say that Maslow's theory has been totally disproved, specific aspects of it are extremely weak. The need categories are vague and clearly overlap one another, and the lock-step hierarchy is simply not a universal characteristic. There is, however, some evidence—not yet fully convincing—of the existence of a dual-level hierarchy consisting of the *maintenance* needs (physiological and safety) and *growth* needs (the remaining high-level needs).[7] As for a satisfied need decreasing in strength, in some cases the theory holds; but there is evidence that the opposite is sometimes true—that a need for which deep satisfaction on the job is experienced is judged to have great importance.[8] For example, it may be true that the more status and power a person acquires, the stronger the needs for status and power become.

Thus, Maslow's theory is intuitively attractive and has been a point of departure for numerous research studies with broad implications, but the theory itself has become increasingly suspect. It is convenient, for example, to refer to self-actualization as a high-level need and safety as a relatively low-level need. Serious questions begin to surface, however, when we examine Maslow's ideas about how the hierarchy developed, the specific nature of the hierarchy, how it affects motivation, and the consistency of the hierarchy from one person to another.

Alternative Need Theories

Because Maslow's theory was developed early, endorsed liberally, and for many years was tested sparingly, it became for many practicing managers almost synonymous with motivation theory. But other need theories were developed, too, most of which borrowed from Maslow and either dropped some of his questionable concepts, such as the lock-step hierarchy, or combined need theory with parts of other theories (to be discussed later in this chapter).[9] Although no other motivation theory has received the attention given to the need hierarchy theory, each provides insights that go beyond Maslow's contributions to need theory.

One extensively researched need theory, developed by McClelland, Atkinson, and their associates, is the *theory of need achievement*.[10] It is based on the idea that motivation to strive for a particular goal results from the strength of the basic need the goal is intended to satisfy and two environmentally influenced factors: (1) the expectation that the goal will be achieved and (2) the

---

[7] *Ibid.*, p. 236.

[8] H. P. Dachler and C. L. Hulin, "A Reconsideration of the Relationship between Satisfaction and Judged Importance of Environmental and Job Characteristics," *Organizational Behavior and Human Performance*, Vol. 4, No. 4 (March, 1969), p. 252.

[9] Clayton W. Alderfer, "An Empirical Test of a New Theory of Human Needs," *Organizational Behavior and Human Performance*, Vol. 4, No. 2 (May, 1969), p. 142; Martin G. Wolf, "Need Satisfaction Theory: A Theoretical Reformulation of Job Satisfaction/Dissatisfaction and Job Motivation," *Journal of Applied Psychology*, Vol. 54, No. 1 (January, 1970), p. 87.

[10] J. W. Atkinson, *Introduction to Motivation* (Princeton: D. Van Nostrand Co., 1964); D. C. McClelland *et al.*, *The Achievement Motive* (New York City: Appleton-Century-Crofts, 1953).

perceived value of the goal.[11] McClelland's research, in particular, shows that by identifying certain payoffs (e.g., recognition, promotion, status) and strengthening expectations that payoffs will follow improved performance, the need to achieve and consequently the motivation to produce can be increased.[12]

In the theory of need achievement, *motives* are viewed as relatively stable, learned tendencies or sources of potential energy that remain dormant until aroused by the presence of one or more incentives or situational cues.[13] McClelland and Atkinson place their primary emphasis on the needs for achievement, power, and affiliation, needs that are described here because of their prominence in motivational literature and their practical implications for management.

The Need for Achievement. According to McClelland and Atkinson, the *need for achievement* is defined by the extent to which a person's time is spent thinking about how to do a better job, how to accomplish something unusual or important, or how to progress in his or her career. Persons with a high need for achievement (often written *n Ach*) are interested in monetary rewards primarily as feedback about how well they are achieving. Thus, money is sought as a measure of success rather than for its exchange value only.[14] Persons with a high *n Ach* seek responsibility, set moderate (achievable) goals, take calculated risks, and desire feedback on their performance.

The Need for Power. The *need for power* is defined in terms of the degree to which a person spends time thinking about influencing and controlling others or about gaining a position of authority and status. Power-motivated individuals who have little need for warm, personal relationships and have high authoritarian values often become autocratic leaders. On the other hand, power-motivated persons who have deep respect for the rights and needs of others may behave quite differently in a leadership situation. In his early writing, McClelland emphasized the importance of *n Ach* in managerial motivation; his later research indicated that the need for power is the primary motivator of successful managers.[15]

The Need for Affiliation. Persons who spend much time thinking about warm, friendly relationships have a strong *need for affiliation*. They are deeply concerned about restoring disrupted relationships, soothing hurt feelings, and engaging in work that permits close companionships on a continuing basis. Therefore, persons with an excessively high need for affiliation may be motivated to avoid managerial work, since hostility from subordinates is virtually inevitable;

---

[11] This is a form of *expectancy theory*, a subject discussed later in this chapter.

[12] David C. McClelland and David G. Winter, *Motivating Economic Achievement* (New York City: The Free Press, 1969).

[13] John P. Campbell and Robert D. Pritchard, "Motivation Theory in Industrial and Organizational Psychology," *Handbook of Industrial and Organizational Psychology*, edited by Marvin D. Dunnette (Chicago: Rand McNally & Company, 1976), p. 112.

[14] David C. McClelland, "Achievement Motivation Can Be Developed," *Harvard Business Review*, Vol. 43, No. 6 (November–December, 1965), p. 6.

[15] David C. McClelland and David H. Burnham, "Power Is the Great Motivator," *Harvard Business Review*, Vol. 54, No. 2 (March–April, 1976), p. 100.

yet managers with an extremely low need for affiliation may not show adequate concern for the needs of others.

The Need for Autonomy. Although the need for autonomy has not been emphasized by McClelland, it has recently begun to receive attention as a major need with broad implications in the work environment.[16] Persons with a strong need for autonomy place high value on freedom, independence, and control over their own destiny.[17] Accordingly, they may prefer employment as professors, physicians, or entrepreneurs as opposed to corporate manager positions. Autonomy can often be gained through power; on the other hand, power-seeking managers must often sacrifice autonomy—a price paid for organizational power. Even an autonomy-seeking entrepreneur involved in entrepreneurial activities may not find satisfaction of the autonomy need that initially motivated those activities. As one supposedly independent business person remarked, "Now that I'm my own boss, I'm free to get to work any time before seven o'clock in the morning and leave any time after seven at night." [18]

Although many other needs are important in vocational selection and as motivators for work, these four needs—achievement, power, affiliation, and autonomy—occupy a special position of prominence. As defined here, they were obviously not considered of great importance to Maslow, but they do overlap the needs he described. For example, affiliation and Maslow's social needs seem to be synonymous; and Maslow's esteem needs are said to be based, in part, on achievement. Nevertheless, both classification schemes are valuable as a basis for understanding motivation and neither conflicts with the other unless one insists on the idea of a rigid need hierarchy.

Motivational Aspects of Goals

Closely associated with the concept of need, goal setting is recognized, implicitly or explicitly, by all major theories of work motivation.[19] The closeness of association is seen in the fact that subjectively we make little or no distinction between needs and goals. The executive with a strong need for power and status and a deep commitment to the goal of receiving steady promotions tends to relate to that goal (the means for satisfying the status and power needs) as if it were the needs themselves. Thus, goals and needs blend imperceptibly into one another. Generally we tend to think of *goals* as ends to which an individual is committed in order to satisfy needs; in reality, deeply internalized goals function as learned or secondary needs.

---

[16] L. B. Barnes, "Douglas McGregor's Theory of Motivation," *Organizational Behavior and Administration*, edited by P. R. Lawrence *et al.* (3d ed.; Homewood, Ill.: Richard D. Irwin, Inc., 1976), p. 114.

[17] Thomas Harrell and Bernard Alpert, "The Need for Autonomy among Managers," *Academy of Management Review*, Vol. 4, No. 2 (April, 1979), p. 259.

[18] *Ibid.*, p. 261.

[19] Edwin A. Locke, "The Ubiquity of the Technique of Goal Setting in Theories of and Approaches to Employee Motivation," *Academy of Management Review*, Vol. 3, No. 3 (July, 1978), p. 594.

Locke's Theory of Goal Setting. Most of the research on the motivational aspects of goals has resulted from a theory of goal setting proposed by Locke and based on the premise that a person's conscious intentions regulate his or her actions;[20] that is, an individual who is consciously committed to a goal will behave in such a way that the goal will be reached, if possible. The goal not only will affect the effort a person will exert and his or her level of performance, it will also influence choice of behaviors, such as how time will be used and which work methods will be employed.

Going beyond his initial premise, Locke's theory states that (1) difficult goals result in higher performance than do easy goals, (2) specific goals get better results than do generalized do-your-best goals, and (3) feedback on performance, monetary incentives, participation in decision making, and competition, affect performance only insofar as they are related to a person's goals. Furthermore, goals that are assigned by a supervisor will affect a subordinate's performance only to the extent that they are consciously accepted by that subordinate.[21] We look now at results of the research that directly or indirectly relates to these propositions.

Research Findings on Goal Setting. Although the research studies completed to date are not conclusive, they provide "strong support for Locke's propositions that specific goals increase performance and that difficult goals, if accepted, result in better performance than do easy goals."[22] There is less support for the idea that goals affect the value of incentives and feedback on performance.

A number of factors affect the acceptance of a goal. Although research results are mixed, they tend to support the idea that employee participation in goal setting (in preference to having goals assigned by a superior) contributes positively to goal acceptance.[23] To some degree acceptance of goals is also related to previous experience with goal setting—related, that is, to whether previous goals have been reached and consequently have increased self-esteem.[24] A number of other factors such as the perceived difficulty of the task and the perception of the effort required also influence whether an individual will genuinely internalize a goal rather than reject it outright or perhaps pretend to accept it.[25]

---

[20] E. A. Locke, "Toward a Theory of Task Motivation and Incentives," *Organizational Behavior and Human Performance*, Vol. 3, No. 2 (April, 1968), p. 157.

[21] *Ibid.*, p. 174.

[22] Gary P. Latham and Gary A. Yukl, "A Review of Research in the Application of Goal Setting in Organizations," *Academy of Management Journal*, Vol. 18, No. 4 (December, 1975), p. 824.

[23] Gary P. Latham and Lise M. Saari, "The Effects of Holding Goal Difficulty Constant on Assigned and Participative Set Goals," *Academy of Management Journal*, Vol. 22, No. 1 (March, 1979), p. 163. Gary P. Latham and Gary A. Yukl, "Effects of Assigned and Participative Goal Setting on Performance and Job Satisfaction," *Journal of Applied Psychology*, Vol. 61, No. 2 (April, 1976), p. 167.

[24] Douglas T. Hall and Lawrence W. Foster, "A Psychological Success Cycle and Goal Setting: Goals, Performance, and Attitudes," *Academy of Management Journal*, Vol. 20, No. 2 (June, 1977), p. 282.

[25] Richard M. Steers and Lyman W. Porter, "The Role of Task-Goal Attributes in Employee Performance," *Psychological Bulletin*, Vol. 81, No. 7 (July, 1974), p. 434; J. C. Wofford, "A Goal-Energy-Effort Requirement Model of Work Motivation," *Academy of Management Review*, Vol. 4, No. 2 (April, 1979), p. 191.

Much remains to be discovered about the conditions under which goal setting will be motivational. Although there is convincing evidence concerning the importance of goal acceptance, it is becoming obvious that this factor interacts with others to determine whether goal setting will motivate a particular individual. Differences in personality and in the nature of the task goal, the nature of the rewards that follow goal achievement, and other as yet unidentified factors interact with acceptance to determine its impact.[26] An additional complicating factor arises from the fact that the motivational effect of goals may not be sustained indefinitely. Some studies have shown that the initial gains from goal setting dissipated after nine to twelve months.[27]

INTRINSIC VERSUS EXTRINSIC MOTIVATION

The intrinsic-extrinsic distinction has in recent years become a popular means for describing employee motivation. Although the terms have not been consistently defined, motivation is usually considered to be *intrinsic* when persons perceive themselves to have control over both environmental events and their own behavior.[28] If these conditions are absent, motivation is considered to be *extrinsic.* Thus, research scientists or electronics technicians are more likely to be motivated by the intrinsic qualities of their work (say, the intriguing possibility of making a discovery or the satisfaction of solving a problem) than are assembly-line employees. The latter are more likely to be motivated by the extrinsic factors of their work, such as pay and job security. For the beginnings of the intrinsic-extrinsic classification, we consider the research and concepts of Frederick Herzberg's two-factor motivation theory.

The Motivation-Hygiene Theory

On the basis of published literature and a series of interviews with 200 engineers and accountants, Herzberg developed his *two-factor theory* of motivation.[29] The idea of the two factors evolves out of Herzberg's belief that the work factors, which we normally classify as potential motivators (money, promotions, status, etc.), should actually be divided into two groups: (1) *motivational factors,* which he called *satisfiers,* and (2) *maintenance factors* or *dissatisfiers.*

[26] Steers and Porter, *op. cit.,* 1979.

[27] John M. Ivancevich, "Effects of Goal Setting on Performance and Job Satisfaction," *Journal of Applied Psychology,* Vol. 61, No. 5 (October, 1976), p. 605; John M. Ivancevich, "Different Goal Setting Treatments and Their Effects on Performance and Job Satisfaction," *Academy of Management Journal,* Vol. 20, No. 3 (September, 1977), p. 406.

[28] Laurie A. Broedling, "The Uses of the Intrinsic-Extrinsic Distinction in Explaining Motivation and Organizational Behavior," *Academy of Management Review,* Vol. 2, No. 2 (April, 1977), p. 274.

[29] Frederick Herzberg, B. Mausmer, and B. Snyderman, *The Motivation to Work* (2d ed.; New York City: John Wiley & Sons, Inc., 1959); Edward E. Lawler III, *Pay and Organizational Effectiveness: A Psychological View* (New York City: McGraw-Hill, Inc., 1971), p. 28; F. Herzberg, *Work and the Nature of Men* (Cleveland: World Publishing Company, 1966).

The motivational factors are the intrinsic or *job content* factors that make a job rewarding in itself. Examples of intrinsic factors are achievement, recognition, advancement, responsibility, the work itself, and growth possibilities. Examples of extrinsic or *job context* factors are pay, status, job security, working conditions, company policy, peer relations, and supervision. The extrinsic factors are hygienic: they are health-producing and desirable, but are not motivational. Only the presence of intrinsic factors is considered motivational. Although the presence of extrinsic factors is not motivational, their absence causes dissatisfaction. For example, interesting work will motivate one to exert increased effort; but the possibility of pay raises or increases in status will not motivate one to exert increased effort. Their absence, however, may cause dissatisfaction. Thus, one set of job factors leads to satisfaction at work (the motivation factors) and an independent set leads to dissatisfaction (the hygiene factors).

Although research using Herzberg's methods has often supported the two-factor theory, it has also been subjected to a high degree of criticism.[30] One of the most serious criticisms concerns the interview method used by Herzberg, since researchers using other methods tend to get different results. Also, there are both research and logical grounds for rejecting the notion that job factors should always be placed in one category or another—that money and status, for example, are never motivators, or that responsibility and growth possibilities are necessarily motivators.

Herzberg's theory is in many ways a gross oversimplification, as various aspects of other motivational theories clearly show, but it has made a major contribution in focusing attention on job redesign for the purpose of making the work more intrinsically satisfying.

Motivation and Job Satisfaction

For the most part research has been consistent in indicating that there is less absenteeism and lower turnover among satisfied employees; feelings of job satisfaction motivate employees to go to work and to remain with the organization. It is also clear that satisfaction is very much influenced by the rewards employees receive in exchange for their contributions to the organization.[31] The relationship, however, between job satisfaction and performance on the job is less clear.

The published literature of the human relations era implies that a happy worker is a productive worker—a belief that has proved to be unfounded. Employees may, in fact, enjoy their employment situation specifically because the country club atmosphere provides good times and few of the pressures involved in high productivity requirements. This does not mean, however, that job satisfac-

---

[30] For a summary evaluation of this research, most of which was done in the 1960's, read John P. Campbell *et al., Managerial Behavior, Performance, and Effectiveness* (New York City: McGraw-Hill, Inc., 1970), p. 381.

[31] Edward E. Lawler III, *Motivation in Work Organizations* (Monterey, Calif.: Brooks/Cole Publishing Co., 1973), p. 71.

tion bears no relationship to productivity. Certainly productivity is affected by absenteeism and employee turnover, two factors that are influenced by satisfaction. We know, too, that dissatisfaction may result in work slowdowns, uncooperativeness, and a reluctance to contribute suggestions that will lead to the solution of problems. Thus, a satisfied employee is not necessarily a productive employee, but a dissatisfied employee may negatively affect production.

On the positive side, a renewed interest in job design—designing jobs that are intrinsically satisfying and motivating—offers some promise of increasing productivity.[32] Scientific management emphasized *job dilution*—breaking jobs into small components for purposes of productive efficiency, with no thought as to whether the work was boring and dissatisfying. Partly as a result of Herzberg's ideas, many companies are attempting to reverse this process through *job enlargement*, in which employees perform a number of small operations, or *job enrichment*, in which more job content factors (e.g., responsibility and autonomy) are added.

It has become obvious that not all jobs can be made more intrinsically satisfying without destroying the satisfaction that results from high productivity and the enjoyment of the extrinsic rewards of that productivity. Nevertheless, most experts agree that efforts should be made to make jobs intrinsically satisfying where possible.[33] Although some employees resist job enrichment or job enlargement, preferring instead the routine that enables them to daydream and/or socialize with co-workers, others respond favorably to opportunities that enable them to become more involved in their work. Persons whose higher order needs have been strongly developed, who are older, who prefer self-control to external control, and who believe in the Protestant Work Ethic [34] are more likely to make their work a central life interest and become involved in it than are those who lack such qualities.[35] Since potential for work involvement depends on a number of work, environmental, and personal factors, it is unwise to assume that all jobs can or should be enriched or enlarged.[36] Design changes do not always result in increased satisfaction; and there is little reason to believe that we should always expect a positive relationship between job satisfaction and productivity.[37]

---

[32] Richard M. Steers and Richard T. Mowday, "The Motivational Properties of Tasks," *Academy of Management Review*, Vol. 2, No. 4 (October, 1977), p. 645.

[33] J. Richard Hackman, "Is Job Enrichment Just a Fad?" *Harvard Business Review*, Vol. 53, No. 5 (September–October, 1975), p. 129; Charles N. Greene, "The Satisfaction-Performance Controversy: New Developments and Their Implications," *Business Horizons*, Vol. 15, No. 5 (October, 1972), p. 31.

[34] Persons who are committed to the Protestant Work Ethic believe that it is morally correct to work hard, to use one's God-given talents to the fullest, to be responsible, and to be thrifty.

[35] Samuel Rabinowitz and Douglas T. Hall, "Organizational Research on Job Involvement," *Psychological Bulletin*, Vol. 84, No. 2 (March, 1977), p. 265; Greg Oldham, J. R. Hackman, and J. L. Pearce, "Conditions under Which Employees Respond Positively to Enriched Work," *Journal of Applied Psychology*, Vol. 61, No. 4 (August, 1976), p. 395.

[36] David A. Whitsett, "Where Are Your Enriched Jobs?" *Harvard Business Review*, Vol. 53, No. 1 (January–February, 1975), p. 74.

[37] William E. Gallagher, Jr., and H. J. Einhorn, "Motivation Theory and Job Design," *Journal of Business*, Vol. 49, No. 3 (July, 1976), p. 125.

Intrinsic-Extrinsic Additivity

In 1968 DeCharms raised an interesting question about employee motivation with his argument that people have a high need for mastery and that

> . . . whenever a person experiences himself to be the locus of causality for his own behavior (to be an origin), he will consider himself to be intrinsically motivated. Conversely, when a person perceives the locus of causality for his behavior to be external to himself (that he is a pawn), he will consider himself to be extrinsically motivated.[38]

This proposition has stimulated a number of research studies concerning the *locus of control*; that is, concerning whether persons believe that they control their own destiny, as they are presumed to do when motivated by job content factors, or whether they are externally controlled, as they are presumed to be when motivated by external rewards such as pay. The importance of this concept stems from a further contention of DeCharms: that intrinsic and extrinsic rewards are not additive as most motivation theories assume—that extrinsic rewards may, in fact, subtract from intrinsic motivation if they are perceived as forms of external control. A parent-child example will clarify this concept. Do you think that an adolescent girl who runs several miles a day because she loves the sport will be more highly motivated if her parents decide to pay her for every mile she runs? According to the locus of control theory, the pay will suggest to her that she is being externally controlled and will, therefore, decrease her motivation. If this theory is valid, then employees on enriched jobs should not be paid on the basis of productivity (piece-rate pay or merit-pay increases) because that can shift the perceived locus of control and offset the benefits of the intrinsic motivators.

Several studies have been conducted to test DeCharms' propositions, most of them centering around research by Deci who translated DeCharms' ideas into testable hypotheses.[39] Agreeing with DeCharms, Deci concluded that in order to avoid decreasing intrinsic motivation, employee pay should not be based on productivity. Job redesign and participative management should be used to increase intrinsic motivation and satisfy higher order needs; the noncontingent system of compensation satisfies employees' lower needs and thereby ensures that higher order needs will remain active.[40]

A few studies have supported Deci's conclusions and prescriptions, lending credence to the idea that contingent financial rewards can reduce intrinsic

---

[38] R. DeCharms, *Personal Causation: The Internal Affective Determinants of Behavior* (New York City: Academic Press, Inc., 1968), p. 328.

[39] E. L. Deci, "The Effects of Externally Mediated Rewards on Intrinsic Motivation," *Journal of Personality and Social Psychology*, Vol. 1, No. 1 (January, 1971), p. 105; E. L. Deci, "Notes on the Theory and Metatheory of Intrinsic Motivation," *Organizational Behavior and Human Performance*, Vol. 15, No. 1 (February, 1976), p. 130.

[40] E. L. Deci, "The Effects of Contingent and Non-Contingent Rewards and Controls on Intrinsic Motivation," *Organizational Behavior and Human Performance*, Vol. 8, No. 2 (October, 1972), p. 227.

motivation.[41] Nevertheless, many scholars and managers remain unconvinced because of the contrary results that tests of other theories have produced, and because the research in support of Deci's position was conducted under unrealistic laboratory settings rather than under real-world conditions. On the basis of research with 81 store managers, Dermer found that the higher the store managers' intrinsic motivation, the greater their motivation for recognition, increased responsibility, advancement, and increased pay. "Thus, it appears that those higher in intrinsic motivation are also significantly higher in their motivation for performance-contingent extrinsic rewards."[42] This study raises a serious question about whether Deci's findings apply to employee motivation, and it supports the traditional belief that intrinsic and extrinsic motivations are additive.

EXPECTANCY THEORIES OF MOTIVATION

Expectancy theory represents what Nadler and Lawler describe as "the most comprehensive, valid, and useful approach to understanding motivation."[43] This does not imply that it is a fully developed or tested theory; it is not. It is, in fact, rapidly evolving; but fortunately it is flexible enough to take into consideration a great many variables and to evolve indefinitely.

Although the basic concepts on which expectancy theory is based can be traced back much further, the beginnings of expectancy theory are usually attributed to a 1964 publication by V. H. Vroom, the first person to express expectancy concepts in the form of a practical theory of motivation in organizations.[44] While not specifically denying the possibility of unconscious motivation or motivation through positive reinforcement, *expectancy theory* is based on the idea that work motivation results from a deliberate, conscious choice to engage in certain activities for the purpose of achieving predetermined outcomes. In its simplest form, it states that motivational force is equal to the product of valence times expectancy: $MF = V \times E$. We look first at the meaning of valence.

Valence

In expectancy theory, *valence* refers to the value a person places on a particular *outcome* (reward or punishment: the consequence of an action). If, for example, a manager is obsessed with a desire to become the company president, then the goal, outcome, or consequences of certain actions would for that individual have a high valence (value) and, depending on some other variables we

[41] Robert D. Pritchard, K. M. Campbell, and D. J. Campbell, "Effects of Extrinsic Financial Rewards on Intrinsic Motivation," *Journal of Applied Psychology*, Vol. 62, No. 1 (February, 1977), p. 9.

[42] Jerry Dermer, "The Interrelationship of Intrinsic and Extrinsic Motivation," *Academy of Management Journal*, Vol. 18, No. 1 (March, 1975), p. 127.

[43] David Nadler and Edward E. Lawler III, "Motivation: A Diagnostic Approach," originally in J. Richard Hackman, E. E. Lawler III, and L. W. Porter, *Perspectives on Behavior in Organizations* (New York City: McGraw-Hill, Inc., 1977), p. 26.

[44] V. H. Vroom, *Work and Motivation* (New York City: John Wiley & Sons, Inc., 1964).

will discuss, that high valence would contribute to high motivation. Motivation could be just as high to avoid an outcome: say, to avoid being fired. Maximally positive valences are given a value of +1.00, maximally negative valences a −1.00, and outcomes that are neutral carry a valence of zero. Actually these numerical values are unknown in real-life situations, but the concept helps us to understand expectancy theory.

Expectancy

Valence alone does not motivate. Most of us would very much like to win a $1,000,000 sweepstakes, but many of us would not pay for the chance to win it in a nationwide contest. Why? Because we do not expect to win. *Expectancy* refers to the subjective probability a person perceives to exist—which may or may not be realistic—that a given outcome will occur. The executive who strongly desires to be president (Valence = .95) will be motivated to exert extra effort to achieve that objective only if there appears to be a high probability that the extra effort will get results. Like any probability, expectancy ranges from zero (no perceived chance of the outcome occurring) to 1.00 (subjective certainty that the outcome will occur).

Motivational Force

The potential of an expected outcome to increase goal-directed effort and change behavior (its *motivational force*) can be high only if both its valence and expectancy are high; and, since anything multiplied by zero is zero, the absence of either factor will prevent a motivational appeal from being effective. However, as indicated by the bottom box in Figure 15–3, the simple $MF = V \times E$ formula does not tell the whole story, since a given behavior may be expected to produce more than one outcome. The production worker may value highly the increased income resulting from high productivity (say, $MF = .90 \times 1.00$ or .90). At the same time, that employee is certain ($E = 1.00$) that a highly undesirable outcome will occur if productivity is increased (punishment by peers for being a rate-buster, for which $V = -.95$). Thus, a strong conflicting motivational force ($MF = -.95$) more than offsets the desired financial payoff. Let us expand this scenario by introducing still other positive outcomes: the increased production is perceived as likely ($E = .75$) to lead shortly to a desired promotion involving higher status ($V = .60$) and to highly interesting work ($V = .99$). Assuming additivity of motivational appeals, the employee may, under these circumstances, be motivated to tolerate the peer pressure and to increase productivity. Obviously the manager who hopes to motivate subordinates must be keenly aware of the way they think; that awareness will make it clear that there are great individual differences in the value placed on different outcomes and in the expectations of their occurrence.

In a notable addition to earlier concepts of expectancy theory, Campbell *et al.* developed a *hybrid expectancy model* that introduces other important

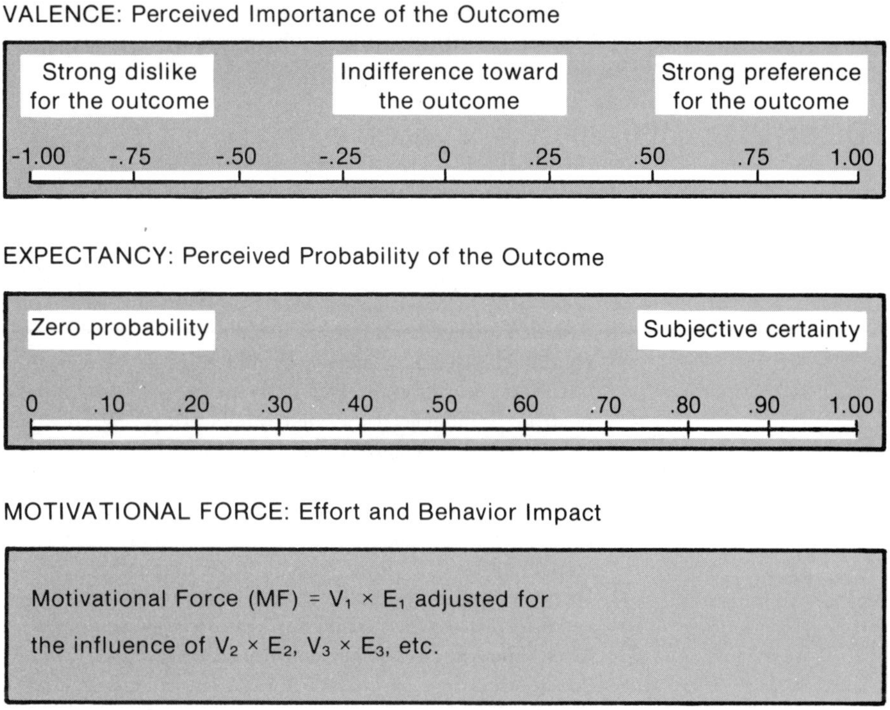

VALENCE: Perceived Importance of the Outcome

Strong dislike for the outcome	Indifference toward the outcome	Strong preference for the outcome

-1.00   -.75   -.50   -.25   0   .25   .50   .75   1.00

EXPECTANCY: Perceived Probability of the Outcome

Zero probability	Subjective certainty

0   .10   .20   .30   .40   .50   .60   .70   .80   .90   1.00

MOTIVATIONAL FORCE: Effort and Behavior Impact

Motivational Force (MF) = $V_1 \times E_1$ adjusted for

the influence of $V_2 \times E_2$, $V_3 \times E_3$, etc.

**Figure 15–3
EXPECTANCY
THEORY OF
MOTIVATION**

variables into the expectancy formula.[45] They point out that an important expectancy in the formula must be based on an individual's perception of the task relative to the perception of his or her own ability to perform it. The woman who very much wants to become a high-level executive (high valence for the outcome) and fully expects that she will get the promotion if she manages satisfactorily (a high expectancy) will not be motivated by that outcome and expectancy unless she has a high expectation that she can perform. That subjective probability is based on her self-concept, her previous experience, and her perception of the nature and difficulty of the task. In addition, Campbell *et al.* correctly noted that the valence of what they call *first-level outcomes* (the executive position in our example) is affected by its perceived relationship to a *second-level outcome*, which is the satisfaction, or lack of it, of the inner needs toward which the first-level outcomes are purportedly directed. Like human motivation itself, this model just continues to become more complex; but perhaps this is a good place to stop adding variables to our example.

In practical situations, expectancy theory provides a valuable framework for sorting out the possible causes of motivational problems. Although empirical tests of the theory have produced mixed results, a great many respected scholars

[45] Campbell *et al.*, *Managerial Behavior Performance and Effectiveness* (New York City: McGraw-Hill, Inc., 1970), p. 345.

are optimistic about its future.[46] Its increasing complexity poses a growing problem for persons who are applying and testing expectancy theory, but its capacity to deal logically with complexity is one of its virtues.

THE EQUITY MODEL

Equity theory (also called *exchange theory, social comparison theory,* and *distributive justice theory*) states that the primary source of work motivation is the amount of equity or fairness the employee perceives to exist in the workplace.[47] The following are major propositions of the theory:

1. Whether or not an employee perceives that his or her pay (any kind of pay) is equitable, depends primarily on the ratio of his or her perceived contribution to the compensation received from the organization (inputs/outcomes). This ratio is strongly influenced by what others are perceived to receive for their inputs.

   Inputs may include quantity and quality of production, experience, education, special skills, seniority, loyalty—any contribution or attribute that is valued by the organization. Outcomes include pay, security, status symbols, recognition, praise, status, perquisites, effective supervision, and need-fulfilling work—valued contributions of the organization to its employees.

2. Inequity in either direction creates tension; the employee is consequently motivated to remove the tension and restore inner equilibrium. Equity is experienced when inputs and outcomes lie within a *zone of acceptability* (or a *zone of tolerable dissonance*).

3. Perceived underpayment motivates a variety of behaviors designed to restore equilibrium. Just which action is taken depends on the extent of the perceived inequity and individual differences that influence perception and response. This may be understood in terms of *level of involvement.*

   There is a lower level of involvement within which the organization will not retain the employee and the employee will not remain with the organization.[48] Thus, one employee reaction is to seek other employment. This is most likely to occur at the level of *alienative involvement,* in which the employee's work is viewed as meaningless and his or her situation is viewed as powerless.

   At a higher level of *calculative involvement,* where employees believe that they can influence their situation, they may react to inequity by such behaviors as asking for a raise, filing a grievance, reducing productivity, being absent from work, and breaking organizational rules. At this level inputs and outcomes are "free to fluctuate and find an equilibrium." [49]

---

[46] Terrence R. Mitchell, "Expectancy Models of Job Satisfaction, Occupational Preference, and Effort: A Theoretical, Methodological, and Empirical Appraisal," *Psychological Bulletin,* Vol. 81, No. 12 (December, 1974), p. 1053; Nadler and Lawler, *op. cit.*

[47] There have been many contributors to this theory, but their contributions are not considered separately. The theory is most closely associated with Adams and Hohman. See J. Stacy Adams, "Inequity in Social Exchange," *Advances in Experimental Social Psychology,* Vol. 2, edited by L. Berkowitz (New York City: Academic Press, 1965); also George C. Hohman, "Social Behavior Exchange," *American Journal of Sociology,* Vol. 63, No. 6 (May, 1958), p. 597. In addition, a review of literature may be found in Richard M. Steers and Lyman Porter, *Motivation and Work Behavior* (New York City: McGraw-Hill, Inc., 1975), p. 135.

[48] Sam Gould, "An Equity Exchange Model of Organizational Involvement," *Academy of Management Review,* Vol. 4, No. 1 (February, 1979), p. 53.

[49] *Ibid.,* p. 54.

At a higher level of *moral involvement*, the organization's standards and values have been so thoroughly internalized that much compensation is intrinsic. At this level external inducements such as pay or supervision must get far out of line to be motivational. Presumably, if they are perceived as extremely inadequate, the employee will regress and begin to operate at the calculative level.

4. Perceived inequity is greater when persons are underpaid than when they are overpaid.

5. One way of removing inequity that differs in kind from those already mentioned is a change in perception. This may occur when an individual has a strong need to avoid conflict or when external solutions are extremely difficult to find.

6. Persons seek to maximize positive outcomes (to receive as much as possible) and to minimize effort (to put out no more than what is perceived as fair in exchange for what is received); that is, employees attempt to maintain a favorable position in relation to their employer.

It is difficult at this point to evaluate equity theory. Although not all its propositions have been fully tested, in general the theory has received support.[50] Steers and Porter emphasize its usefulness in helping us to understand a wide variety of social relationships in the workplace.[51] We know, for example, that employees are often quite satisfied with their pay until they discover that specific others are receiving more. Certainly equity theory should be considered in establishing pay systems and in dealing with the difficult question of whether to have an open policy about employee wages and salaries. Nonetheless, much research needs to be done on equity theory. For example, we know that employees can adjust to across-the-board raises that do not take individual contributions into account.[52] Thus, concepts of parity or equality must somehow be more thoroughly integrated with equity theory. There is some evidence that very high producers prefer equity or fairness while average and low producers prefer that everyone be compensated equally without reference to productivity.

MOTIVATION AS REINFORCEMENT

Modern behaviorists, like those who began the behaviorist school of psychology early in this century, seek to avoid the subjectivity involved in discussions of such unobservable inner states and processes as needs, satisfactions, expectancies, and valences. Instead, doctrinaire behaviorists base their motivational schemes on the simple idea that behavior followed by positive consequences tends to be repeated, and behavior followed by negative consequences tends not to be repeated. These concepts were introduced in Chapter 14 under "The Learning Process" (pages 298–299). Since any reference to a motive implies

---

[50] R. Dennis Middlemist and R. B. Peterson, "Test of Equity Theory by Controlling for Comparison Co-Workers' Efforts," *Organizational Behavior and Human Performance*, Vol. 15, No. 2 (April, 1976), p. 335.

[51] *Ibid.*, p. 143.

[52] Laurie Larwood, M. Kavanagh, and R. Levine, "Perceptions of Fairness with Three Alternative Economic Exchanges," *Academy of Management Journal*, Vol. 21, No. 1 (March, 1978), p. 69.

assumptions about inner processes or needs, behaviorists prefer to use the language of reinforcement and therefore make no reference to motives.

The current literature on reinforcement theory (also referred to as operant conditioning) is often found under a *behavior modification* title, a term that refers to the manipulation of reward structures in order to engineer, shape, or alter behavior. Thus, within the framework of reinforcement theory, managers are not concerned with motivating employees; at least they do not use that term. Instead, they seek to modify their employees' behavior—to shape their employees' behavior in ways that support the organization. We turn now to some of the applications, methods, and implications of the behavioral approach.

The Inevitability of Reinforcing Behavior

One of the important insights that reinforcement theory has contributed to management is that reinforcement is an ongoing process, whether or not it is planned. Employees have a concept of what their supervisors and employers reward and punish, and to some degree thay shape their behavior accordingly. Reinforcement may be expressed in terms of praise, criticism, promotions, special consideration, a smile, a frown, or just total indifference. Few consequences of behavior are stronger negative reinforcers than outstanding performances followed by nothing. If behavioral consequences shape behavior, the latter consequence says to the subordinate, "It really doesn't matter what you do; the consequences are the same either way."

Steven Kerr provides a number of examples of unplanned and undesirable reinforcement in society at large.[53] Politicians, for example, are often rewarded (by being elected) for engaging in double-talk rather than communicating clearly about where they stand on critical issues. Universities hope that their professors will be effective teachers, but they reward them for publishing in prestigious journals. Similarly, coaches preach teamwork but reward individual performance.

In business, management-by-objectives (MBO) programs reward managers for reaching specific goals, sometimes with little regard for other important but nonquantifiable goals and for overall effectiveness. Individual supervisors often reward employees who complain and make trouble just by giving them attention and by occasionally giving them what they ask for. Thus, say behavior theorists: since (1) reinforcement is inevitable and (2) managers often reinforce the wrong behaviors, it is critically important (1) that managers continually evaluate the nature of reinforcement within their organizations and (2) that they consciously establish schedules for reinforcing on a rational basis.

Positive Reinforcement Applications

Numerous applications have supported the use of positive reinforcement principles, the most publicized of which occurred at Emery Air Freight. In

---

[53] Stephen Kerr, "On the Folly of Rewarding *A*, While Hoping for *B*," *Academy of Management Journal*, Vol.18, No. 6 (December, 1975), p. 769.

one example, by encouraging employees to increase their use of containers, combining small shipments to the same destination, Emery realized an annual saving of $650,000.[54] By using positive reinforcement Emery was also able to reduce tardiness from its 1 percent average to a target goal of ¼ of 1 percent. The Emery study called attention to the importance of setting measurable behavior standards and then following up to determine discrepancies between what employees should have been doing and what they thought they were doing.

Most companies generously reward their employees with sick pay, paid holidays, coffee breaks, and comfortable lounges for either absenteeism or for not working. To reverse this process, a large hardware store with six outlets applied reinforcement principles that achieved impressive results. The program involved monthly drawings for prizes by employees who had perfect records of attendance and punctuality (one prize for every 25 employees). As an extension of this incentive, every six months a drawing was held for a major prize—a color television. The results were impressive: sick-leave payments decreased 62 percent, and absenteeism and tardiness decreased 75 percent during the first 16 months of the program.[55]

Employers who install behavior modification programs show a high degree of ingenuity in defining areas for application and in establishing reward systems. Behavior modification can be applied to a wide variety of areas, including human resources management, management by objectives, personnel development, compensation, and facilitating change by positively reinforcing behavior rather than attitudes.[56]

Guidelines for Modifying Behavior

There is no one way to establish a behavior modification program. There are, however, some rules or guidelines that research and experience have shown to be helpful. The following are among the most important:

1. Positive reinforcement is more effective than negative reinforcement. Punishment is sometimes necessary, but it produces side effects that work against goal-directed behavioral change.
2. Rewards should follow as soon as possible after the desirable behavior has been performed.
3. Employees should know which behaviors will be rewarded. Persons who are clearly aware of what is expected of them and of the standards by which their performance is evaluated have built-in feedback systems; they are, therefore, able to make continual judgments about their own work and enjoy maximum autonomy.[57]

[54] "At Emery Air Freight: Positive Reinforcement Boosts Performance," *Organizational Dynamics*, Vol. 1, No. 3 (Winter, 1973), p. 41.

[55] W. R. Nord, "Improving Attendance through Rewards," *Personnel Administration,* Vol. 33, No. 6 (June, 1970), p. 37.

[56] Harold W. Babb and D. G. Kopp, "Applications of Behavior Modification in Organizations: A Review and Critique," *Academy of Management Review,* Vol. 3, No. 2 (April, 1978), p. 281.

[57] W. Clay Hammer and Ellen P. Hammer, "Behavior Modification on the Bottom Line," *Organizational Dynamics,* Vol. 4, No. 4 (Spring, 1976), p. 3.

4. Behavioral objectives should be stated in clear and measurable terms.
5. Feedback on performance is vital. Employees should know what they are doing wrong as well as what they are doing right, although criticism should be given privately in order to minimize negative side effects.
6. A need for reinforcement should not be confused with a need for training. Some employees need knowledge rather than reinforcement (i.e., rather than motivation).
7. Rewards should be given for movement toward a goal rather than for only the achievement of the ultimate behavioral goal. By rewarding so-called *successive approximations,* individuals can be moved in the right direction from their starting point (*baseline behavior*) to their ultimate destination (*target behavior*).

Reinforcement Theory: A Critique

Whatever opinion one may hold about behaviorism—and there are strong reasons why many have difficulty identifying with it as a philosophical-psychological school of thought—the applications of reinforcement theory cannot help but be impressive. There is no denying that under certain circumstances behavior can be modified by reinforcement methods. Nevertheless, the critics of behavior modification techniques are many.

One of the major criticisms of behavior modification centers around the idea that it is manipulative and dehumanizing—that behavior modification promotes dependence rather than self-determination and maturity.[58] Reinforcement can be interpreted as a form of bribery in which an appeal is made for performance solely to acquire external rewards rather than to make a contribution and otherwise satisfy one's higher order needs. Reinforcement theory makes no appeal to one's sense of dignity and self-worth, nor does it contribute to the development of these qualities. Behavior theorists respond with the argument that making explicit the consequences of behavior gives the individual a clear choice and is, therefore, not at all manipulative.

More pragmatic criticisms can also be made of reinforcement theory in that it is simplistic and does not take into consideration some important variables such as valence and expectancy. Individual differences, which are largely ignored by behavior theory, may greatly improve our ability to change behavior.

All things considered, it appears that reinforcement theory makes a valuable contribution to our ability to change behavior—to motivate. However, most theorists and practicing managers are less than enthusiastic about accepting a doctrinaire behaviorist position that denies the valuable contributions of other points of view. Since management is by definition a practical art and science, we would do well to heed Perry London's admonition to separate entirely the applied technology of behavior modification from its philosophical moorings in behaviorism.[59]

---

[58] Chris Argyris, "Beyond Freedom and Dignity by B. F. Skinner, A Review Essay," *Harvard Business Review,* Vol. 4, No. 4 (August, 1971), p. 550.
[59] Perry London, "The End of Idology in Behavior Modification," *American Psychologist,* Vol. 27 (1972), p. 913.

The differences among the various approaches to understanding motivation are enormous, and in a few instances parts of theories are mutually exclusive: if one is valid the other is not. But it is unnecessary to reject totally any of the major theoretical positions discussed in this chapter. Each makes a contribution to our understanding of motivation in organizations, and as our understanding deepens we gain new insights into how the divergent viewpoints can be integrated. Some of the individual theories are complex—collectively they are extremely complex—but that should be expected. Such is the nature of human motivation.

Case Problem 15-B describes the results experienced by Acme Manufacturing Company after having raised the level of its employee benefit program and poses another question to be resolved by the same management group: Should the company install a monetary incentive plan or should it embark upon a program of job enrichment?

Case Problem 15-B

PART II: INCENTIVES OR JOB DESIGN?

It is approximately 18 months after the meeting described in Case Problem 15-A. Margaret Marlow, the personnel manager, and Alice Conrad, the manager of industrial engineering, are in the general manager's office discussing ways of improving productivity and product quality. Following the survey of fringe benefits, Acme changed its practices with regard to holidays, vacations, life insurance, hospitalization insurance, and sick leave. The company now ranks in the upper 25 percent of companies in the area with respect to these particular benefits. The company decided not to initiate employee services such as legal aid, counseling, a credit union, and a recreation program because very few companies in the area offered these benefits. No change was made in the policy of setting wage levels equal to the average of the area.

After increasing the level of its fringe benefits, the company was able to hire replacements without undue delay; turnover, which had been most noticeable among employees with less than six months' service,

declined to its previous level; and the rate of absenteeism was reduced. However, there was no change in productivity per employee hour, nor was there any improvement in product quality. An analysis by the quality control department showed that about 80 percent of the quality problems were due to errors in assembly.

Because of the persistent quality problem and the lack of improvement in productivity, Mr. Rider, the general manager, requested two feasibility studies. One of these, prepared by industrial engineering, discussed the feasibility of an incentive plan for hourly employees; the other was a report by the personnel department concerning job enlargement. After reading these reports, Rider asked for a conference with the heads of the industrial engineering and the personnel departments.

Rider turned to Ms. Conrad and said, "Apparently your department questions the value of incentives as a means of increasing productivity. Would you summarize your position for Margaret's benefit?"

"As you know," Ms. Conrad began, "we now have a measured day work plan; that is, we have time standards in most departments, but we do not have an incentive pay plan. The plant average is about 90 percent of standard for those departments that have standards. The press room, where we form the metal parts of our appliances, and the machining department average about 93 percent; the plating and painting departments run about 95 percent; the assembly department, about 85 percent; and in shipping and receiving the packers are the only ones on standards and they average about 85 percent also."

At this point Marlow commented, "It seems that assembly and the packers are the ones pulling the plant average down."

"That is right," Conrad continued. "Even so, a plant average near 90 percent is not too bad. Frankly I question how much we would gain with an incentive. In the press room and the assembly departments, the big factor in determining the output is the engineering design of the equipment and the manner in which it is maintained. Also, chrome plating requires a specified length of time for a given thickness of plate, and the capacity of the drying ovens is the limiting factor in our paint department. Improvement in production in these departments would be relatively small and the net gain in terms of earnings may be even smaller."

"Why is that?" Rider asked.

"To maintain standards for an incentive pay plan, I would have to double the size of my department. We would have to set additional standards for jobs that are run only infrequently. Complaints about standards would have to be answered promptly. All this takes more people—I estimate at least an additional $50,000 a year in salaries alone. Sooner or later we would be forced into the position of paying the plant average to all workers—maintenance workers, janitors, shipping and receiving—because they will contend that they are having to do more work since more units are being produced;

yet, actually, their workload would change very little."

Looking at Margaret Marlow, Mr. Rider said, "It seems to me that it is questionable whether we would actually gain very much from an incentive pay plan in view of what Conrad has said. What about your recommendation of job enlargement?"

"Since most of our difficulty is in the assembly department, I would suggest that we start there by eliminating the assembly lines and having each person assemble the entire product and then pack it. There have been several instances where this approach has worked. If we had each person assemble the entire unit, inspect that unit, then insert an inspection slip into the box after packing the unit, we would have a much better control over quality."

"But assembly accounts for only one department," Ms. Conrad said. "What about the other departments?"

"In the press room and the machining departments we could have the operators learn how to make their own setups and make minor repairs instead of having the tool room make the setups and the maintenance department making all repairs, even the minor ones."

"You do that and we will have to pay all the machine operators a much higher rate since they will be classed as skilled rather than semiskilled," Conrad interrupted. "Also, we would be undertaking a tremendous training program, and at present we don't have that kind of staff."

Rider realized that he was no nearer a solution after talking to Conrad and Marlow than he had been before the conference. He decided to meet with them again in a week.

PROBLEMS

1. As the general manager of Acme, would you accept the recommendations of the personnel department? Why?
2. What additional information would you need to make a decision?

3. Is the industrial engineering department correct in not recommending an incentive plan? Discuss.

4. To what aspects of specific motivation theories are the different parts of this case related?

CHAPTER QUESTIONS FOR STUDY AND DISCUSSION

1. Following Maslow's theory, we may expect that social needs, for example, will not serve as motivators once they are reasonably well satisfied. What does being satisfied mean in this context? Are any of a person's needs—one's safety or social needs, for example—ever satisfied? Discuss.

2. Contrary to Maslow's theory, research conducted by Dachler and Hulin suggests that deep satisfaction of a need may increase rather than decrease its motivational potential. Develop a line of thought to explain why this may occur in some instances.

3. How does McClelland increase the need to achieve in the persons with whom he works? With what motivation theory is his approach most closely associated?

4. Does the high need for power that McClelland found to exist in most successful managers necessarily indicate that most successful managers will be authoritarians in their approach to leadership? Explain.

5. Name three vocations in which persons are likely to find satisfaction for each of the following needs: achievement, affiliation, power, and autonomy.

6. Why do you think goals are motivational? Why do you think the motivational aspect of goals sometimes diminishes after a few months?

7. Evaluate Herzberg's practice of placing motivational factors (pay, recognition, supervision, etc.) in one of two categories.

8. How does job satisfaction influence productivity?

9. What are the different forms of expectancy that may affect work motivation?

10. Why do some workers prefer parity to equity pay systems?

11. What practical lessons about motivation can managers learn from reinforcement theory?

Chapter 16

The Communication Process

A MESSAGE FOR MANAGEMENT

Regina Osterman, president of Federated Manufacturing Company, recognizes the importance of keeping employees informed about the economic problems of the company. She realizes that her company is entering a difficult competitive period resulting from a steady decline in prices. Osterman knows that she must lower prices in order to retain her share of the market.

She believes that her monthly letter, entitled *From The President's Desk*, which is sent to all employees, is adequate as a means of transmitting information. However, when a major crisis arises, she summons all department heads to the austere oak-paneled board room, an action which, in her opinion, assures them that they are a part of management and are participating in major decisions. The established protocol for these meetings requires that all attending personnel be seated prior to the scheduled time and that they arise when Mrs. Osterman enters the room and remain standing until asked to be seated again. Regina Osterman has made her entrance and has indicated by a curt nod of her head that all may be seated.

"I have called you together to explain our dire economic situation. We are face to face with competitive wolves who are snapping at our heels. They are making us sell at prices that are too low and with delivery schedules that are utterly impossible to meet. If this great company of ours—one of the bulwarks of free enterprise—is to survive, we must all pitch in and pull together. Let me tell you what I mean."

Following her opening remarks, Regina Osterman glared at everyone in the room as though she were daring them to speak. No one spoke, since all knew that any expression of opinion would be classified as negative thinking by Mrs. Osterman.

"First, what we need here is imagineering. We need positive thinkers and everyone has to play on the same team. We have to optimize production, and nothing can be left out of account when we are considering cost reduction. To implement this crash program of cost reduction, I have gone outside the company and hired a top-drawer production manager.

"The second thing we have to do is maximize quality. Quality means everything in this business. Every machine has to be inspected on a regular schedule by the supervisor of the department and when that machine starts up in production, it means that the supervisor has given it the stamp of approval. Nothing is too small to overlook when we are thinking of quality.

"Third on my list of items deserving serious consideration is beefing up our sales force. Customers are the lifeblood of this business, and even though they are not always right, they still must be handled with kid gloves. Our sales representatives have to learn how to put themselves across and make every call count. Our method of compensating sales representatives is eminently fair, but even so, we're going to try to sweeten the pot by upping the commission rates on slow-moving items. We would do it across the board, but we have to hold the line on costs.

"The last thing on my list is teamwork. This we need more than anything else. Unless we all pull together, we can't make it. Leadership is teamwork, and teamwork is striving and straining for the same goal. You are the representatives of management, you are the leaders, and you know what our goals are. Now let's all put our shoulders to the wheel and wrap up the whole ball of wax immediately. Remember, we're one big happy family."

As Regina Osterman concluded, all arose and stood by their chairs while she gathered her papers and left the board room through the connecting door to her office.

PROBLEMS

1. What was the purpose of this meeting?
2. What is Regina Osterman trying to say? Rewrite her remarks in simple, direct language. Do you think that her analysis was correct?
3. What factors besides language cause a communication barrier in this case problem?
4. How would you arrange the above meeting to assure two-way communication?

The word *communication* as it is used in management literature has two distinct, yet compatible, meanings. One of these meanings emphasizes the dissemination of information and is commonly referred to as *formal communication*. The other meaning of the term refers to interpersonal communications between two or more people. *Interpersonal communications* transmit much more than information since psychological needs, motives, and feelings are often revealed that may be in conflict with the expressed verbal message.

Since formal communication is based on the science of semantics, we examine some of the fundamental concepts of semantics. Next, formal communications are considered, then problems inherent in interpersonal communications are examined, and lastly, the means of improving both formal and interpersonal communications are discussed.

THE MEANING OF MEANING

Communication is defined in its broadest sense as the transmission of meaning to others. However, the definition as it now stands does not mean or signify much, since two words used in the definition—*transmission* and *meaning*—need further elaboration. The word *transmission* as used in the definition is broad and does not limit the methods of communication to the use of language in either spoken or written form. The word *meaning* is also broad. It includes information consisting not only of facts and descriptive statements of objects and other people but also attitudes and feelings that may be conveyed to others. For purposeful communications, such as those in a formal organization, it is necessary to restrict our definition further by stating that communication is the transmission of *intended* meaning to others. The above restriction implies that the sender of the communication has a clear concept of the meaning to be conveyed; and, in order for the communication to be purposeful, the receiver must interpret the message in such a manner that the intended meaning is received.

The scientific study of meaning is known as *semantics*, a word derived from the Greek term, *semantikos*, which means significant. Semantics is concerned with the relationship between (1) objects and/or events, (2) the thought processes involved in interpreting these objects and/or events, and (3) the signs and/or symbols used to express a given thought or to describe a specific object or event. First, let us discuss these three aspects of semantics and then apply the lessons learned in analyzing Case Problem 16-A.

The Triangle of Meaning

The relationship between objects and events, their interpretation, and the development of signs and symbols are shown in Figure 16-1, The Triangle of Meaning.[1] Objects and events are known as the *referent*; thoughts, interpretations, and emotions are called the *reference*; and devices used to express the reference are called *signs* or *symbols*.

The following example shows the relationship between a referent, a reference, and the way in which meaning is attached to a sign or a symbol. The object in question is taken from the ocean; it is elliptical in shape, three inches long, an inch and one half in width, an inch thick. The surface is a rough, brown, shell-like substance. Three persons are observing (thinking about) this object. One of them, a scientist, recognizes the object immediately and labels it a bivalve mollusk of the genus *Ostrea*. The second observer sees a dozen such objects

---

[1] C. K. Ogden and I. A. Richards, *The Meaning of Meaning* (8h ed.; New York City: Harcourt, Brace & Co., 1956). *The Meaning of Meaning*, first published in 1923, still stands as one of the basic works in the field of semantics. Figure 16–1 is adapted from a figure on page 11 entitled Thoughts, Words, and Things. *The Meaning of Meaning* is a good reference for the serious study of semantics.

The following references are also suggested:

Alfred Korzybski, *Science and Sanity, An Introduction to Non-Aristotelian Systems and General Semantics* (4h ed.; Lancaster: Science Press Printing Co., Distributors for the International Non-Aristotelian Library Publishing Co., 1958). Count Korzybski, a mathematician, applies general semantics to all fields of science as they existed in 1933. *Science and Sanity* is recommended only for the advanced student.

Samuel I. Hayakawa, *Language in Thought and Action* (2d ed.; New York City: Harcourt, Brace & World, 1964).

William V. Haney, *Communication and Organizational Behavior: Text and Cases* (3d ed.; Homewood, Ill.: Richard D. Irwin, Inc., 1973).

Robert M. Carter, *Communication in Organizations, A Guide to Information Sources* (Detroit: Gale Research Company, 1972).

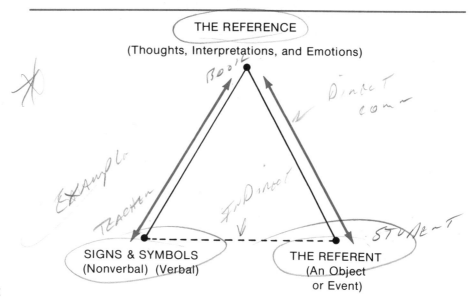

Figure 16–1
THE TRIANGLE
OF MEANING

on the half shell ringing a platter full of ice; to this person it is an object to be eaten, an oyster. The third person takes one look, grimaces, turns pale, and leaves the room. All have seen the same object, yet three distinct meanings are reflected in their labeling of the object. The scientist uses the symbol, bivalve mollusk of the genus *Ostrea*, to label the object; to that individual it is one more form of marine life to be classified in relation to other forms of life. To the person who calls it an oyster, the object is food and a source of delight. However, the third person does not use a symbol (word) to label the object. Instead, there is an eloquent expression of the interpretation of the meaning of the object by the signs of grimacing, becoming pale, and leaving the room— the object is a source of disgust.

Let us examine each element of the triangle in greater detail.

Signs and Symbols. Signs and symbols, the left-hand base of the triangle (Figure 16–1), are the labels used to initiate a particular thought, or reference, with regard to a specific referent. The two terms, signs (nonverbal) and symbols (verbal), are used to emphasize that communication is not dependent on language. There is no intrinsic meaning in the color red, yet a red light as part of a traffic signal means that one must stop; but when used as a running light on a boat, red indicates the port side. Likewise, silence on the part of a supervisor may express disapproval as effectively as a dozen words. Status in an organization is conveyed almost entirely by signs; for example, a carpeted office, special parking privileges, punching a time clock, and the hour at which one reports for work all designate status.

Note that the base of the triangle is a dotted line and that the two sides of the triangle are solid. There is a direct relationship between the referent that calls up a certain thought and between the thought and the symbol used in its expression. Similarly, there is a direct relationship between symbol and thought and between thought and referent. There is, however, no such direct relationship between the label (symbol) and the object itself. The label, either a sign or a word, is *not* the object; it is used only to identify a specific object. Labels are arbitrary, and to be meaningful they must establish the same reference (thought) in both the sender and the receiver of a communication. Yet one of the most common causes of misunderstanding results from filling in the base of the triangle and assuming that the label is the referent. Loyalty oaths are a good example of filling in the base of the triangle. The act of signing an oath does not make one loyal; yet the assumption underlying such oaths is an identity between loyalty and the act of signing an oath.

Verbal symbols vary considerably with respect to their value as tools for communication. All words are abstractions; they are not the object or event itself. As words become more abstract—i.e., further removed from the specific object or event—their meanings become more difficult to transmit and their value as instruments for communication decreases. Words as names of things may be classified as follows:

1. *Names for objects* are a table, a chair, a milling machine, a lathe, an automobile, a truck, a machinist, and a clerk. When naming an object, we are at a relatively low level of abstraction, and there should not be too much misunderstanding since the referent may be seen and touched, and its characteristics may be detailed with a high degree of accuracy.
2. *Events* are more complex in their nature since action and time, in addition to an object, are implied. A table turning over, a milling machine cutting metal, a moving automobile, and a machinist reporting late for work are all statements of events—something happening to a specific object at a specified time.
3. Labels may be used to designate *clusters*, *groups*, or *collections of objects or events* which are composed of elements that have varying degrees of similarity. We refer to furniture, machine tools, motor vehicles, and employees.
4. At the highest level of abstraction, the referent may not be an object or event at all; instead, the referent is an *essence* or *value judgment* of an object or event. The furniture is described as beautiful, machine tools are valuable, motor vehicles are either necessities or luxuries, and the employee is lazy (the machinist reported late for work). Also in this category of high order abstractions are such labels as democracy, free enterprise, truth, and honesty.

Reference and Referent. There are at least two persons involved in communication—a sender and a receiver. Symbols should create within the receiver a thought process (call it a mental image, if you wish) that leads the receiver down the right-hand side of the triangle to the desired referent. Conversation has been described as the art of saying something when there is nothing to be said. In contrast, communication is saying something when there is something to be said and saying it clearly. The purpose of communication is to influence the behavior of another person. Behavioral changes may consist of additional knowledge, a change in attitude, or action on the part of the receiver. Conversation takes place almost entirely on the left side of the triangle, from symbol to thought and back to another symbol again. There is no need for a common meaning between sender and receiver because the purpose of conversation is merely to occupy time. In communication, however, there is a purpose; and in order for the intended meaning to reach the receiver both sender and receiver must travel the same route around the triangle from symbol, to reference, to referent.

A Semantic Analysis

A great deal can be told about how much meaning is transmitted through a given communication by answering these questions:

1. What is the purpose of the communication?
2. Do the symbols used by the sender have a precise meaning understandable to the receiver?

Let us ask these two questions in our semantic analysis of Case Problem 16-A, A Message for Management. At the same time we must keep in mind the triangle of meaning—symbol, reference, and referent.

What Is the Purpose of the Communication? Before there can be any communication, the sender must determine the purpose of the communication. Why has Regina Osterman called her department heads together? In the first paragraph of her talk, she states that she has called them together to explain "our dire economic situation." She closes her opening remarks with the statement that she is going to explain what she means. Apparently Osterman is trying to state four things that the company needs in order to survive the dire economic situation. These needs are imagineering, which she does not define; instead, she talks about cost reduction. The second need is quality, the third is beefing up the sales force, and the last is teamwork. The conclusion is inescapable: Osterman is not sure of what she wants to say or why she wants to explain an economic condition to her department heads.

The purpose of the meeting is not to explain; instead, it is to influence or modify the behavior of the department heads—to change their actions so that the company may make a profit and at the same time lower the prices of its product to the level established by competition. Information concerning the actions of competitors and the development of attitudes resulting in teamwork and effective leadership are necessary if management is to do its job well. The purpose of the meeting is to change behavior.

Do the Symbols Have a Precise Meaning for the Receiver? Look at the first paragraph of Osterman's speech again. It is filled with abstractions having no precise meaning. She starts with a high order abstraction, "dire economic situation," and does not bother to define what she means. Somehow she manages to drag into her remarks "the bulwarks of free enterprise," again without definition. Further, her use of metaphors indicates that she is not thinking clearly. How can she be "face to face with wolves snapping at her heels"? Prices are too low, but what does too low mean? If the delivery schedules are utterly impossible, how does the company manage to stay in business? The remainder of her talk is nothing but a collection of worn-out, meaningless words and phrases. What is "imagineering"? What is "positive thinking"? Are they going to play on the same team or are they working for the same company? What does she mean by "beefing up" the sales force? Does she want the sales representatives to gain weight? Is leadership teamwork? If so, leadership is striving and straining for the same goals. How does one simultaneously "put our shoulders to the wheel" and "wrap up the ball of wax"?

Regina Osterman is having a wonderful time running up and down the left-hand side of the triangle—from symbol to reference and back to symbol without once attempting to go down the right-hand side of the triangle to a common referent. To some of you, Osterman's message for management may seem overdrawn and exaggerated. It is not. It is hoped that you will not have to sit through many such meetings as a member of management and that you *never* conduct a meeting as Regina Osterman did. Remember this case as an example of how *not* to communicate.

The above analysis of A Message for Management answers two questions. When the questions are recast as statements, they form a guide for effective communication.

For effective communication the sender must determine the purpose of the communication and use symbols having the same meaning for sender and receiver.

The following guidelines are presented to aid in developing effective communication:

1. Determine and state the purpose of the communication.
2. Develop a plan of presentation. Consider the information to be transmitted and the interests and abilities of the receiver.
3. Eliminate unnecessary words.
4. Use words known to the receiver. Establish the meaning of abstractions by referring to objects and events within the experience range of the receiver.[2]

---

[2] It is beyond the scope of this book to develop a manual of style. The following references are presented for students who want additional help in improving their ability to express their thoughts clearly:

George Orwell, "Politics and English Language," *Shooting an Elephant and Other Essays* (New York City: Harcourt Brace and World, 1950). Reprinted in Norman R. F. Maier *et al.*, *Superior-Subordinate Communication in Management* (New York City: American Management Association, 1961), AMA Research Study 52, p. 78. Orwell's essay is one of six presented in the AMA research study. Orwell presents six rules for clarity of expression; and, although his essay is concerned primarily with the language of politics, it is applicable to all subject matter. The annotations of George H. Hass provide many examples of hackneyed expressions used in business communications.

William Strunk, Jr., and E. B. White, *The Elements of Style* (3d ed.; New York City: Macmillan, Inc., 1978). *The Elements of Style* deals with English usage and style. Professor Strunk had the book privately printed and for many years used it in his English classes at Cornell University. The 1978 edition, revised by E. B. White, includes a chapter on how to write. *The Elements of Style*, dubbed "the little book" by Professor Strunk, reduces English rhetoric to 18 rules with examples of correct and incorrect usage to illustrate each rule.

FORMAL COMMUNICATIONS

Although the transmission of intended meaning is the central problem in formal communications, there are areas other than the lack of agreement on intended meaning that contribute to communication problems. One such difficulty in formal communication is that all too often managers are not aware of the media available for communication; hence, a brief analysis of commonly used media is presented.[3]

Communication Media

Communication media within a company may be classified either with respect to the method used to transmit information or according to the directional flow of the communication. Using the means of transmission as a basis for classifying media, communications are either *written* or *oral.* When directional flow is the basis for classification—defining direction in terms of the organizational hierarchy—communications flow *downward, upward, horizontally,* and *diagonally.* Examples of written and oral communications are discussed briefly below.

Written Communications. Letters, memos, and reports are examples of written communications used to transmit information either downward, upward, or horizontally within an organization. Formal statements of policies, procedures, and methods are designed primarily for downward communications. Bulletin boards, house organs, annual reports, and handbooks are also directed downward. Written grievances, suggestion systems, and union publications serve as a means of upward communication. The information gained from attitude and morale surveys provides another means of directing information to higher levels of the organization. Letters and memos between department heads are examples of the horizontal or diagonal flow of communications. The distribution of carbon copies of written materials to all interested parties may be used as a means of directing information in several directions at one time.

Oral Communications. Even though a business may consume tons of paper during the course of a year in written communications, by far the greater percentage of information is transmitted by informal oral communications, either face to face or by telephone. Oral communications may involve as few as two people or as many as hundreds attending a training session or conference. All oral communication offers the potential of two-way information flow; and, depending on the relative organizational positions of the participants, the communication may be directed either vertically or horizontally. Most members of an organization prefer oral to written communications because they seem quicker and offer an immediate feedback in the form of questions and expressions of approval

---

[3] For a discussion of new approaches to the study of communication, both formal and interpersonal, the following is recommended: Richard V. Farace and Donald MacDonald, "New Directions in the Study of Organizational Communication," *Personnel Psychology,* Vol. 27, No. 1 (Spring, 1974), p. 1.

or disapproval. The advantages of speed and feedback may be more imagined than real, since oral messages are notoriously subject to misinterpretation and to the effects of barriers arising from interpersonal relationships.

INTERPERSONAL COMMUNICATIONS

Thus far the discussion has been directed to one of the meanings of communication, the dissemination of information, with the emphasis on the type of information needed. Interpersonal communications permit not only the transfer of information but also the expression of psychological needs and motives. Superior-subordinate communications are considered first with an assessment of the degree of understanding and the common barriers to effective communications that exist between superior and subordinate. Next, some of the problems encountered in horizontal communications are reviewed; and, finally, the ubiquitous grapevine and its role are examined.

Superior-Subordinate Communication

It is generally assumed that superior-subordinate communication operates as a two-way information system permitting a free flow of information upward as well as downward. Yet there are barriers in the superior-subordinate relationship that markedly interfere with free two-way flow of information. Before discussing these barriers, it is well to determine the effectiveness of superior-subordinate communication in a relatively objective and limited area—in relation to a subordinate's job.

Superior-Subordinate Understanding. In an early study the American Management Association conducted a statistical research project to determine the extent of agreement between superior and subordinate concerning the subordinate's specific job duties.[4] Fifty-eight superior-subordinate combinations from the upper management levels of five different companies were selected for this study, and the information from both members of each pair was obtained by patterned depth interviews. The following specific areas of the subordinate's job were discussed:

1. Job duties—a descriptive statement of what the subordinate does in the performance of his job
2. Job requirements—a statement of the skills, background, experience, formal training, and personal characteristics needed for the job

---

[4] Norman R. F. Maier *et al.*, *Superior-Subordinate Communication in Management* (New York City: American Management Association, 1961), AMA Research Study 52. In addition to the presentation and interpretation of the statistical results of the study, there are six interpretative comments on the project and its findings in Part 2 of the report.

Another study designed specifically to complement the American Management Association study and one which yields the same basic results is the following: Bradford B. Boyd and J. Michael Jensen, "Perceptions of the First-Line Supervisor's Authority: A Study in Superior-Subordinate Communication," *Academy of Management Journal*, Vol. 15, No. 3 (September, 1972), p. 331. Boyd and Jensen note that the American Management Association study is the only published work prior to their study dealing with communications within management itself.

3. Future changes in job duties—anticipated changes in either job duties or requirements that might be anticipated in the next several years
4. Obstacles in the performance of the job—problems that interfere with getting the job done, as seen by the subordinate and as viewed by the superior

The results of the study are presented in Table 16–1. An analysis of Table 16–1 shows that 85 percent of the pairs interviewed agree on one half or more of the subordinate's job duties (Columns 2, 3, 4), but the extent of the agreement with respect to subordinate qualifications drops to 63.7 percent. Only 53.3 percent of superiors and subordinates agree upon anticipated changes in the subordinate's job within the next few years. In interpreting the obstacles in the way of subordinate success, 68.2 percent showed either no agreement or agreement on less than half of the obstacles. The following is a narrative summary of the study by the authors:

> If a single answer can be drawn from this detailed research study into superior-subordinate communication on the managerial level in business, it is this: If one is speaking of the subordinate's specific job—his duties, the requirements he must fulfill in order to do his work well, his intelligent anticipation of future changes in his work, and the obstacles which prevent him from doing as good a job as is possible—the answer is that he and his boss do not agree, or differ more than they agree, in almost every area. Also, superior and subordinate very often disagree about priorities—they simply don't see eye to eye on which are the most important and the least important tasks for the subordinate.[5]

	0 Almost No Agreement on Topics	1 Agreement on Less Than Half the Topics	2 Agreement on About Half the Topics	3 Agreement on More Than Half the Topics	4 Agreement on All or Almost All Topics
Job Duties	3.4%	11.6%	39.1%	37.8%	8.1%
Job Requirement (Subordinate's Qualifications)	7.0%	29.3%	40.9%	20.5%	2.3%
Future Changes in Subordinate's Job	35.4%	14.3%	18.3%	16.3%	18.7%
Obstacles in the Way of Subordinate's Performance	38.4%	29.8%	23.6%	6.4%	1.7%

Table 16–1
COMPARATIVE AGREEMENT BETWEEN SUPERIOR-SUBORDINATE PAIRS ON BASIC AREAS OF THE SUBORDINATE'S JOB

SOURCE: Norman R. F. Maier *et al., Superior-Subordinate Communication in Management* (New York City: American Management Association, 1961), AMA Research Study 52, p. 10.

Barriers to Communication. The effect of communication barriers, whether they arise from semantic problems or from one of the specific superior-subordinate relationships discussed now, results in either a distortion of meaning because

---

[5] Maier *et al., op. cit.,* p. 9.

of embellishment or a filtering of information by suppression or withholding. Semantic barriers usually result in a distortion of meaning. Distortion also occurs as the result of introducing errors into a message. Filtering information results in only a part of the message getting through. Filtering of communications by either the sender or the receiver of the message may be intentional or unintentional. The following barriers are frequently found in superior-subordinate communications; nonetheless, remember that these same barriers may occur in any two-way personal communication.

Semantic Problems. One barrier to communication, not limited to superior-subordinate relationships, is a semantic problem—determining a common referent and meaning for the symbols used in communication. In the research study described above, descriptions of the subordinate's job, of necessity, require the use of high order abstractions. These are middle management jobs and, unlike operative jobs, they cannot be described as movements to be completed in a given sequence. Judgment, the interpretation of data, anticipation of future events, and skill in interpersonal relations are the important requisites for managerial jobs, and all these characteristics are abstractions. Rudolf Flesch, in his comment on the study, believes that the problem of superior-subordinate communication as presented in Table 16–1 presents a somewhat exaggerated view of the inability of superior and subordinate to communicate effectively.[6] According to Flesch, who interpreted the same data, the lack of agreement is no greater than what might be expected when the subject is abstract and viewed from two entirely different positions; i.e., superior and subordinate. In brief, Flesch is saying that to some extent the results of the study are due to the methodology used in the study.

Status. Another barrier arises from the relative positions of the superior and subordinate in the organization. There is a strong tendency in formal organizations to express hierarchical rank through the use of signs known as status symbols. Status symbols within an organization, such as a better type of office furniture, may be deliberate as an attempt to reinforce the superior's position of authority. However, too much emphasis on status may increase a subordinate's perception of organizational distance and consequently widen the communication gap between subordinate and superior.

Pressure of Time. In business organizations the pressure of time plays an important role as a communication barrier. The busy superior with many subordinates simply does not have the time to see all of them as frequently or to talk with them as fully as might be desired. Also, busy subordinates do not have the time nor the inclination to report every detail of every problem to their superiors. Supporting the subordinate's position is the concept of delegation. Responsibilities have been assigned, and the authority to fulfill these responsibilities has been delegated. In addition, accountability to one's superior has been

---

[6] *Ibid.,* "Is the Problem Exaggerated?" p. 60. Flesch discusses the results of the study as a semantic problem.

established. It might be argued quite properly that, as the effectiveness of the process of delegation increases, the need for detailed communication between superior and subordinate decreases. The pressure of time and the presence of an effective delegation process may decrease the amount and frequency of superior-subordinate communication; but, even so, communication may be more than adequate because information necessary for the operation of the business is being transmitted.

Value Judgments. Making value judgments of a message prior to receiving the entire communication interferes with receiving the intended meaning of the message. A value judgment is the assignment of overall worth to a message and may be based upon its origin, its reliability, or its anticipated meaning. When value judgments are made too hastily, the receiver hears only that part of the message that he or she wishes to hear. Closely related to hearing only selected parts of a message is the lack of sensitivity to the emotional content of the communication, which is often reflected by the mannerisms and tone of voice of the sender. In many instances the real message is conveyed not by the words of the sender, but by the emotions and feelings accompanying the expression of the message.

Subordinate's Mobility. A specific characteristic of the superior-subordinate communications is the dependency relationship of subordinates upon their superiors for advancement within the organization—either more pay for the present position or attaining a higher position. Several studies support the hypothesis that the more a subordinate desires to advance in an organization, the greater the tendency to filter information sent upward to one's superior. If the subordinate desires to advance, only good news and the positive aspects of achievement are sent upward. Problem-oriented aspects of the subordinate's work are suppressed or filtered. It has also been reported that the amount and nature of the information transmitted upward, even by the subordinate strongly desiring advancement, is influenced greatly by the degree of trust subordinates have toward their superiors and the extent of perceived influence of superiors. As trust in the judgment and understanding of one's superior increases, and as the perceived influence of that superior on the subordinate becomes greater, the amount of problem-oriented information communicated upward increases.[7]

Horizontal Communication

Traditional organization theory with its concepts of line authority and the chain of command emphasizes vertical lines of communication between superior

---

[7] The following two studies discuss the needs of subordinates in organizations and their effect upon superior-subordinate communication.

John C. Athanassiades, "The Distortion of Upward Communication in Hierarchical Organizations," *Academy of Management Journal*, Vol. 16, No. 2 (June, 1973), p. 207.

Karlene H. Roberts and Charles A. O'Reilly III, "Failures in Upward Communication in Organizations: Three Possible Culprits," *Academy of Management Journal*, Vol. 17, No. 2 (June, 1974), p. 205.

and subordinate. Figure 16–2 shows in schematic form the transmission of a message from D_1, supervisor of production department 1, to D_2, supervisor of production department 2, using the chain of command as a channel of communication. The advantage claimed for this formalized line of communication is that A, who is responsible for both production departments, is better able to coordinate the functioning of the two departments when fully informed of the activities of each department. The obvious disadvantages of following these formal lines of communication are the amount of time taken to transmit a message, the increased risk of error and distortion, and the loss of flexibility necessary to meet emergencies. The extent to which an organization insists that its lines of communication conform to the organizational lines of authority depends to a large extent on the technology of that organization. Failure to recognize communication needs arising from and depending on technology often results in poor communications.

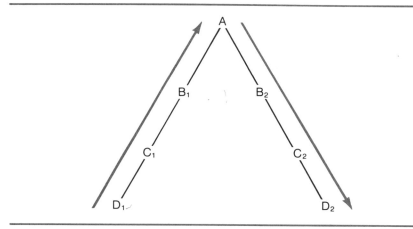

**Figure 16–2
TRADITIONAL
VERTICAL COM-
MUNICATION**

There are several empirical studies that show the need for horizontal and diagonal communications between first-line supervisors as a function of the technology, or method, of production. In one of the earliest studies of an automobile assembly line, Blau found that the role of the foreman is one of problem solving and expediting material flow. The line itself determines the pace of production, and the jobs on the line are well defined. Under these circumstances there is relatively little need for the traditional vertical communications of giving orders to subordinates and there are not many orders received from one's superior. The result is that the bulk of the foreman's communications is with other foremen on the assembly line and with other departments such as material handling and maintenance.[8] All of these relationships are either horizontal or diagonal. However, Faunce, in a study of a highly automated automobile factory, finds, in an apparent contradiction, that there is a marked need for vertical communica-

---

[8] Peter M. Blau, "Formal Organization: Dimension of Analysis," *American Journal of Sociology,* Vol. 62 (July, 1957), p. 58.

tions through the traditional chain of command.[9] Simpson, in a study of the spinning department of a textile mill, obtains results similar to those of Blau; namely, a decrease in the need for vertical communications between superior and subordinate and an increase in the need for communications between supervisors on the same level.[10] In Simpson's study, the primary direct communication between the general foreman of the department and subordinate foremen consists of a written message stating the type and amount of material to be produced on each machine for each shift.

Simpson also resolves the apparent discrepancy between his findings, similar to those of Blau, and the findings of Faunce. He describes three broad types of technology used in production and suggests that the relative need for vertical or horizontal communication is determined by the technology. First, in unmechanized operations there is a relatively greater need for vertical communications than there is for horizontal communications. In this situation the various production departments are relatively independent, and the amount of work produced is determined by the effectiveness of the supervisor of the department. The manager responsible for coordinating the work of all departments needs detailed information from each supervisor. Second, when technology is characterized by mechanization, such as a textile mill or an automobile assembly line, separate departments are bound together by that technology. The success of the foreman of an assembly line depends on the right part arriving at a certain place in the line at a scheduled time and on the reliable functioning of the tools used in production. Providing the necessary parts for assembly is the function of the production control and material handling departments, and the proper operation of the tools for production is the function of the maintenance department. Rate of output is determined by the speed of the assembly line or other automatic equipment. Under these circumstances the need for horizontal communications among the foremen of the various departments increases. Third, in highly automated plants where the breakdown of a single machine may result in the shutdown of all production facilities, the need for control becomes greater and the need for vertical communications also increases.

In summary, no mechanization or a low degree of mechanization emphasizes vertical communications; moderate mechanization (such as the assembly line) requires a great emphasis on horizontal communications; and highly automated production facilities reestablish the need for vertical communications.

The Grapevine

Our discussion of the problems of communication has been directed toward formal channels and methods of communication. It is necessary for management to recognize that there are also informal methods of communication that may

---

[9] William A. Faunce, "Automation in the Automobile Industry," *American Sociological Review*, Vol. 23 (August, 1958), p. 401.

[10] Richard L. Simpson, "Vertical and Horizontal Communication in Formal Organizations," *Administrative Science Quarterly*, Vol. 4 (December, 1959), p. 188.

be far more effective in some respects than the formal means of transmitting information. An informal system of communication is generally referred to as the *grapevine*. As the name suggests, the grapevine is entwined throughout the entire organization with branches going in all directions, thereby short-circuiting formal vertical and horizontal channels.

Two characteristics of communications via the grapevine are noted by those who have studied it. First, the grapevine is often an exceedingly rapid form of communication; and, second, the information transmitted is frequently subjected to a great deal of distortion. Formal channels of communication, particularly those following the vertical chain of command, usually pass information from one person to another—a time-consuming process. In contrast, the grapevine transmits information along a pathway described as a *cluster chain*.[11] Instead of passing information from one person to another, as in superior-subordinate communication, information is passed to a group of three or four persons, and, from this initial link in the cluster chain, one or two individuals inform other groups. Thus, there is an ever-increasing rate in the flow of information. In part this is due to the makeup of the grapevine; people who work near each other or whose work regularly brings them in contact with others are frequently on the same grapevine. The grapevine that includes the mail clerk, the switchboard operator, or any other person whose work requires contact with several groups transmits information much more quickly than formal channels of communication. Another factor encouraging rapid communication is that the information carried by the grapevine reflects the interests and personal concerns of its members; for example, news of an impending layoff, an increase in pay, or news about other people.

The grapevine is notorious for distorting information, so much so that information received from this source is often referred to as rumor. In the discussion of superior-subordinate communications, the filtering of information—passing on only certain parts of a message—is mentioned as one of the causes of distortion. The grapevine information as its source is often fragmentary and incomplete, with the result that there is a strong tendency to fill in the missing parts. Since the grapevine is informal, there are no formal lines of accountability. Consequently, members of the grapevine do not have to answer to their superiors for any misstatement of facts. Further, the elaboration of a fragment of news into a full-blown story offers to some people an opportunity to express feelings of self-importance and to compensate for feelings of insecurity.

The characteristics of the grapevine are summarized by Keith Davis as follows:

---

[11] Keith Davis, "Communication within Management," *Personnel* (New York City: American Management Association, 1954). In this article Professor Davis discusses a method of communication analysis and applies the method to the communications of one company. He also discusses the grapevine in management communications.

The following article presents another method of analyzing informal communication known as the semantic differential: William E. Reif, Robert M. Monczka, and John W. Newstrom, "Perceptions of the Formal and the Informal Organizations: Objective Measurement Through the Semantic Differential Technique," *Academy of Management Journal*, Vol. 16, No. 3 (September, 1973), p. 389.

1. People talk most when the news is recent.
2. People talk about things that affect their work.
3. People talk about people they know.
4. People working near each other are likely to be on the same grapevine.
5. People who contact each other in the chain of procedure tend to be on the same grapevine.[12]

IMPROVING COMMUNICATIONS

Two approaches are available for the improvement of communications. The first of these approaches is from the point of view of the sender of the message. Recognize the purpose of the communication, the significance of the symbols used, the organizational lines through which the communication travels, and its possible effect on the receiver. These and other ways of improving one's ability to communicate clearly as a sender of messages are discussed below as ten general rules for improving communications. The last of these rules states that in order to achieve effective communication it is necessary to learn how to listen. It is a listening to the feelings and emotional content of messages expressed by others as well as being able to understand the factual information that is being presented. The process of learning how to detect the emotional content of communications is discussed under the heading, "Empathetic Listening."

Rules for Improving Communications

The American Management Association refers to the following rules as the Ten Commandments of Good Communication:

1. *Seek to clarify your ideas before communicating.* The more systematically we analyze the problem or idea to be communicated, the clearer it becomes that this is the first step toward effective communication. Many communications fail because of inadequate planning. Good planning must consider the goals and attitudes of those who will receive the communications and those who will be affected by it.
2. *Examine the true purpose of each communication.* Before you communicate, ask yourself what you really want to accomplish with your message—obtain information, initiate action, change another person's attitude? Identify your most important goal and then adapt your language, tone, and total approach to serve that specific objective. Don't try to accomplish too much with each communication. The sharper the focus of your message the greater its chances of success.
3. *Consider the total physical and human setting whenever you communicate.* Meaning and intent are conveyed by more than words alone. Many other factors influence the overall impact of a communication, and the manager must be sensitive to the total setting in which he communicates. Consider, for example, your sense of timing—i.e., the circumstances under which you make an announcement or render a decision; the physical setting—whether you communi-

---

[12] Davis, *op. cit.*, p. 212.

cate in private, for example, or otherwise; the social climate that pervades work relationships within the company or a department and sets the tone of its communications; custom and past practice—the degree to which your communication conforms to, or departs from, the expectations of your audience. Be constantly aware of the total setting in which you communicate. Like all living things, communication must be capable of adapting to its environment.

4. *Consult with others, where appropriate, in planning communications.* Frequently it is desirable or necessary to seek the participation of others in planning a communication or developing the facts on which to base it. Such consultation often helps to lend additional insight and objectivity to your message. Moreover, those who have helped you plan your communication will give it their support.

5. *Be mindful, while you communicate, of the overtones as well as the basic content of your message.* Your tone of voice, your expression, your apparent receptiveness to the responses of others—all have tremendous impact on those you wish to reach. Frequently overlooked, these subtleties of communication often affect a listener's reaction to a message even more than its basic content. Similarly, your choice of language—particularly your awareness of the fine shades of meaning and emotion in the words you use—predetermines in large part the reactions of your listeners.

6. *Take the opportunity, when it arises, to convey something of help or value to the receiver.* Consideration of the other person's interests and needs—the habit of trying to look at things from his point of view—will frequently point up opportunities to convey something of immediate benefit or long-range value to him. People on the job are most responsive to the manager whose messages take their own interests into account.

7. *Follow up your communication.* Our best efforts at communication may be wasted, and we may never know whether we have succeeded in expressing our true meaning and intent, if we do not follow up to see how well we have put our message across. This you can do by asking questions, by encouraging the receiver to express his reactions, by follow-up contacts, by subsequent review of performance. Make certain that every important communication has a feedback so that complete understanding and appropriate action result.

8. *Communicate for tomorrow as well as today.* While communications may be aimed primarily at meeting the demands of an immediate situation, they must be planned with the past in mind if they are to maintain consistency in the receiver's view; but, most important of all, they must be consistent with long-range interests and goals. For example, it is not easy to communicate frankly on such matters as poor performance or the shortcomings of a loyal subordinate—but postponing disagreeable communications makes them more difficult in the long run and is actually unfair to your subordinates and your company.

9. *Be sure your actions support your communications.* In the final analysis, the most persuasive kind of communication is not what you say but what you do. When a man's actions or attitudes contradict his words, we tend to discount what he has said. For every manager this means that good supervisory practices—such as clear assignment of responsibility and authority, fair rewards for effort, and sound policy enforcement—serve to communicate more than all the gifts of oratory.

10. *Last, but by no means least: Seek not only to be understood but to understand—be a good listener.* When we start talking we often cease to listen—in that larger sense of being attuned to the other person's unspoken reactions and atti-

tudes. Even more serious is the fact that we are all guilty, at times, of inattentiveness when others are attempting to communicate to us. Listening is one of the most important, most difficult—and most neglected—skills in communication. It demands that we concentrate not only on the explicit meanings another person is expressing, but on the implicit meanings, unspoken words, and undertones that may be far more significant. Thus we must learn to listen with the inner ear if we are to know the inner man.[13]

Empathetic Listening

The tenth rule admonishes us to listen to others—listen to the explicit meaning and also the implicit meaning. Explicit meaning is conveyed by the meaning of the words used by the sender, and in order to understand it is necessary that we pay careful attention to what is being said. However, we must also listen with the "inner ear" if we are to hear the "inner person." Hearing the inner person, the implicit meanings of the message, calls for *empathy*—the ability to put oneself in the other person's place, to assume that person's role, viewpoint, and emotions. *Empathetic listening* is hearing and understanding the emotional content, the feelings, and the mood of the other person. Empathetic listening requires a special technique of listening.

Case Problem 16-B, A Case of Misunderstanding, should be read now, for it is the basis of our discussion of empathetic listening. As stated in the third paragraph of the case, we do not know exactly what Hart, the supervisor, said to Bing, the worker. We do know what each said to the personnel representative. With this information, let us reconstruct the conversation between Hart and Bing.

Hart: Bing, I want to talk to you.

Bing: Yeah?

Hart: Listen, why don't you try to get along here like other people do for a change?

Bing: How?

Hart: Well, for one thing, stop deliberately upsetting this department by going to lunch early and asking others to go with you.

Bing: I haven't been to lunch early for a week.

Hart: You have, too. And another thing, I want you to stop carrying three panels at one time over to your bench for inspection—you know the rules on that.

Bing: That's what I want to talk to you about. I've got an idea . . .

Hart: Never mind your ideas, just follow the rules and you'll get along better.

Bing: I want a transfer.

Hart: We'll see about that. In the meantime, stop singing around here. What do you think this is, a nightclub, and you're Frank Sinatra?

The above conversation and the comments made by Hart and Bing to the personnel representative show quite clearly that Hart is not listening to Bing. It appears that Hart is more interested in telling Bing off than in trying to

---

[13] "Ten Commandments of Good Communication," (New York City: American Management Association, Copyright, 1955).

determine the reasons for Bing's behavior. Hart is *not* using the techniques of empathetic listening. Without empathetic listening there cannot be two-way communication.

Listen with Understanding. Empathetic listening as a part of two-way personal communications is a concept borrowed from the methods of nondirective psychotherapy that have been highly developed by Dr. Carl Rogers.[14] In this form of psychotherapy the role of the therapist is one of encouraging not only good communications between the therapist and the patient, but also good communications within the patient. The patient must learn how to express himself or herself and have the opportunity for that expression. Although a supervisor and other members of management are not therapists, if they are to have successful two-way communications with others, the others must have the opportunities to express themselves. In order to encourage such expression, nondirective techniques are employed. The one conducting the interview encourages the expression of the feelings, emotions, and desires behind the words of the other persons. In order to do this the interviewer listens instead of talking. In the previous conversation, Hart does most of the talking, not Bing. If Hart were listening with understanding, his comments would have been designed to encourage Bing to talk and the following conversation might have occurred:

Hart: Bing, I want to talk to you.
Bing: Yeah?
Hart: I've noticed that you have been carrying three panels over to your bench for inspection. Do you have a new idea for a methods change?
Bing: Well, maybe.
Hart: Um-hum.
Bing: Well, maybe it won't work all the time, but with these smaller panels there is no reason why three of them can't be carried at once.

With this approach to communication, Hart is encouraging Bing to talk, not to defend himself. The problems caused by Bing's leaving for lunch early and his singing may be explored in the same easy manner.

Guides for Listening. The following guides for empathetic listening have been found to be as effective in industrial settings as in their original clinical setting.

1. *Avoid making value judgments.* Value judgments are global in nature and made from the point of view of the listener, not from the frame of reference of the

---

[14] Carl R. Rogers and F. J. Roethlisberger, "Barrier and Gateways to Communications," *Harvard Business Review*, Vol. 30 (July–August, 1952), p. 46. The first part of the article is written by Dr. Rogers, who suggests that the major barrier to communication is the tendency to evaluate and that the main gateway to communication is listening with understanding. In the second part of the article, Dr. Roethlisberger analyzes a communications situation and suggests positive steps that may be taken to improve communications.

For a full discussion of Dr. Rogers' views on therapy, see Carl R. Rogers, *Client-Centered Therapy* (Boston: Houghton Mifflin Company, 1953).

The following brief article, autobiographical in nature, summarizes Rogers' perception of his own work: Carl R. Rogers, "In Retrospect: Forty-Six Years," *American Psychologist*, Vol. 29, No. 2 (February, 1974), p. 115.

person doing the talking. Such judgments place a single value—good or bad, desirable or undesirable, true or false—on a series of complex statements, each of which varies considerably with respect to any given characteristic. In addition, the origin of value judgments is often derived from an earlier judgment of the source of the statement. How can Bing say anything worthwhile to Hart when he is prejudged by Hart as being mentally deficient and a sow's ear? Once the value judgment is made, the mind is closed and it becomes impossible to understand the other's point of view.

2. *Listen to the full story.* In the first interview, Bing started to say that he has an idea, but is stopped abruptly by Hart. In order to understand, listen to the whole story. Time is a critical factor in empathetic listening, and arrangements must be made for adequate time and a place where there will be no interruptions. Ask the other person to be seated; if he or she smokes, offer a cigarette. Do everything you can to put the other person at ease.

3. *Recognize feelings and emotions.* Remember, empathetic listening is putting yourself in the position of the other person. Try to pinpoint the meaning of the feelings and emotions behind the statements being made, rather than the meaning of the words being said. Look for signs of eagerness, hesitancy, hostility, anxiety, or depression. At the same time watch for evasions, the things left unsaid, or areas of discussion consistently avoided.

4. *Restate the other's position.* As a test of your understanding, restate the other person's statement from his or her point of view, not yours. For example, Hart might say, "You believe that I'm watching you like a hawk, treating you like a naughty kid, and as a result you feel like a marked man." Imagine the change in Hart's behavior if he can make the statement above with the same feeling that Bing would put into it.

5. *Question with care.* The simplest way to keep the conversation going is to use the noncommittal "um-hum." If this is insufficient, questions such as "and then what happened?" or "what did you do?" may start the story again. Occasionally restatements such as the one mentioned in (4) may be rephrased as questions. Avoid argumentative statements such as "that isn't true" or "I don't believe you." These statements not only cause you to lose your objectivity and become emotionally involved, but also put the other person on the defensive, thus making it impossible for the individual to express his or her true feelings.

The guides for empathetic listening are relatively easy to remember; however, their application requires a skill that may take years to develop. As a manager you will have to develop these skills to achieve two-way communication. Solving the problems for Case Problem 16-B is the first step in learning the techniques of empathetic listening and effective communicating.[15]

---

[15] F. J. Roethlisberger, "The Administrator's Skill: Communication," *Harvard Business Review,* Vol. 31 (November–December, 1953), p. 55. Copyright © 1953 by the President and Fellows of Harvard College; all rights reserved. This case (names and places disguised) is adapted from a case in the files of the Harvard Graduate School of Business Administration.

A CASE OF MISUNDERSTANDING

In a department of a large industrial organization, there were seven workers (four men and three women) engaged in testing and inspecting panels of electronic equipment. In this department one of the workers, Bing, was having trouble with his immediate superior, Hart, who had formerly been a worker in the department.

Had we been observers in this department we would have seen Bing carrying two or three panels at a time from the racks where they were stored to the bench where he inspected them together. For this activity we would have seen him charging double or triple setup time. We would have heard him occasionally singing at work. Also, we would have seen him usually leaving his work position a few minutes early to go to lunch, and noticed that other employees sometimes accompanied him. And had we been present at one specific occasion, we would have heard Hart telling Bing that he disapproved of these activities and that he wanted Bing to stop doing them.

However, not being present to hear the actual verbal exchange that took place in this interaction, let us note what Bing and Hart said to a personnel representative.

What Bing Said

In talking about his practice of charging double or triple setup time for panels which he inspected all at one time, Bing said:

"This is a perfectly legal thing to do. We've always been doing it. Mr. Hart, the supervisor, has other ideas about it, though; he claims it's cheating the company. He came over to the bench a day or two ago and let me know just how he felt about the matter. Boy, did we go at it! It wasn't so much the fact that he called me down on it, but more the way in which he did it. . . . I've never seen anyone like him. He's not content just to say what's on his mind, he prefers to say things in a way that makes you want to crawl inside a crack on the floor. What a guy! I don't mind being called down by a supervisor, but I like to be treated like an adult, and not humiliated like a schoolteacher does a naughty kid. He's been pulling this stuff ever since he's been . . . promoted; he's lost his friendly way and seems to be having some difficulty in knowing how to manage us employees. He's a changed man over what he used to be like when he was a worker on the bench with us several years ago.

"When he pulled this kind of stuff on me the other day, I got so damn mad I called in the union representative. I know that the thing I was doing was permitted by the contract, but I was intent on making some trouble for Mr. Hart, just because he persists in this sarcastic way of handling me. I am about fed up with the whole damn situation. I'm trying every means I can to get myself transferred out of his group. . . . He's not going to pull this kind of kid stuff any longer on me. When the union representative questioned him on the case, he finally had to back down, because according to the contract an employee can use any time-saving method or device in order to speed up the process as long as the quality standards of the job are met.

"You see, he knows that I do professional singing on the outside. He hears me singing here on the job, and he hears the people talking about my career in music. I guess he figures I can be so cocky because I have another means of earning some money. Actually the employees here enjoy having me sing while we work, but he thinks I'm disturbing them and causing them to goof off from their work. Occasionally I leave the job a few minutes early and go down to the washroom to wash before lunch.

Sometimes several others in the group will accompany me, and so Mr. Hart automatically thinks I'm the leader and usually bawls me out for the whole thing.

"So, you can see, I'm a marked man around here. He keeps watching me like a hawk. Naturally this makes me very uncomfortable. That's why I'm sure a transfer would be the best thing. I've asked him for it, but he didn't give me any satisfaction at the time. While I remain here, I'm going to keep my nose clean; but whenever I get the chance, I'm going to slip it to him, but good."

What Hart Said

Here, on the other hand, is what Hart told the personnel representative:

"Say, I think you should be in on this. My dear little friend, Bing, is heading himself into a showdown with me. Recently it was brought to my attention that Bing has been taking double and triple setup time for panels which he is actually inspecting at one time. In effect, that's cheating, and I've called him down on it several times before. A few days ago it was brought to my attention again, and so this time I really let him have it in no uncertain terms. He's been getting away with this for too long and I'm going to put an end to it once and for all. I know he didn't like my calling him on it because a few hours later he had the union representative breathing down my back. Well, anyway, I let them both know I'll not tolerate the practice any longer, and I let Bing know that if he continues to do this kind of thing, I'm going to take official action with my boss to have the guy fired or penalized somehow. This kind of thing has to be curbed. Actually I'm inclined to think the guy's mentally deficient, because talking to him has actually no meaning to him whatsoever. I've tried just about every approach to jar some sense into that guy's head, and I've just about given it up as a bad deal.

"I don't know what it is about the guy, but I think he's harboring some deep feelings against me. For what, I don't know, because I've tried to handle that bird with kid gloves. But his whole attitude around here on the job is one of indifference, and he certainly isn't a good influence on the rest of my group. Frankly, I think he purposely tries to agitate them against me at times, too. It seems to me he may be suffering from illusions of grandeur, because all he does all day long is sit over there and croon his fool head off. Thinks he's a Frank Sinatra! No kidding! I understand he takes singing lessons and he's working with some of the local bands in the city. All of which is OK by me; but when his outside interests start interfering with his efficiency on the job, then I've got to start paying closer attention to the situation. For this reason I've been keeping my eye on that bird and if he steps out of line any more, he and I are going to part.

"You know there's an old saying, 'You can't make a purse out of a sow's ear.' The guy is simply unscrupulous. He feels no obligation to do a real day's work. Yet I know the guy can do a good job, because for a long time he did. But in recent months he's slipped, for some reason, and his whole attitude on the job has changed. Why, it's even getting to the point now where I think he's inducing other employees to goof off a few minutes before the lunch whistle and go down to the washroom and clean up on company time. I've called him on it several times, but words just don't seem to make any lasting impression on him. Well, if he keeps it up much longer, he's going to find himself on the way out. He's asked me for a transfer, so I know he wants to go. But I didn't give him an answer when he asked me, because I was steaming mad at the time, and I may have told him to go somewhere else."

PROBLEMS

1. Based on Hart's (and Bing's) report to the personnel supervisor, what are the factors that would make empathetic listening difficult for Hart to achieve?

2. Reconstruct in full the conversation as it probably occurred.

3. Reconstruct in full an interview between Bing and Hart utilizing the techniques of empathetic listening, as described in this chapter.

4. Discuss Bing's responsibility to listen empathetically to Hart.

CHAPTER QUESTIONS FOR STUDY AND DISCUSSION

1. Explain in your own words the triangle of meaning. Why is it important that the triangle have a dotted line for its base?

2. What are some of the things transmitted by an oral face-to-face message other than facts descriptive of a situation? Can these other things be transmitted as effectively in written form? Discuss.

3. Does highly effective and efficient communication between people eliminate conflict between them? If not, why not?

4. Why is conversation not necessarily communication?

5. Why are superior-subordinate communications more susceptible to certain types of communication problems than communication between two persons on the same organizational level?

6. Differentiate between embellishment and filtering. Are communications directed downward in an organization likely to be filtered or embellished? Explain.

7. Develop an argument that supports the thesis that sound processes of delegation minimize the need for face-to-face communication between superior and subordinate.

8. Develop several examples showing how the technology of the organization influences the need for and the type of formal communications.

9. How can the grapevine be used effectively as a communications device?

10. Since communication is primarily the sending of a message, why is it necessary to be able to listen empathetically?

11. What is meant by a value judgment? Why are value judgments often barriers to effective communication?

Chapter 17

Leadership Patterns

Case Problem 17-A

THE RELUCTANT FOLLOWER

The Jefferson Apparel Corporation, a producer of men's sportswear with headquarters in St. Louis, operated 18 plants in seven states from North Carolina to Oregon. In addition to doing contract work for a large brand-name manufacturer, Jefferson sold directly to 11 large retailers. Although its sales had gradually expanded to about $200 million annually, Jefferson had established no brand name of its own and was, therefore, highly dependent upon its relationships with a few large customers. The Jefferson family, the founders of the company, had sold most of its shares in 1953—when the company went public—and the stock was widely dispersed. Few shareholders took interest in the firm or believed that they could exert any influence over its management.

In September of 1974 James Cahill acquired 53 percent of Jefferson Apparel stock through a tender offer that was bitterly opposed by the firm's management. Cahill, who had spent most of his 63 years as an apparel manufacturer, had acquired great wealth in the industry; and, because he was a past president of the American Apparel Manufacturers Association, he had many friends among industry leaders. The firm's president, Edward Sullivan, led the opposition against Cahill's takeover, but once the ownership issue was settled, Cahill became chairman of the board, and Sullivan continued as president. After discovering that Cahill had other business interests and lived in Florida, Sullivan concluded that the change of ownership would make little difference in his own power and control.

Sullivan, a persuasive and charismatic individual, had a background in marketing and paid little attention to the production end of the business. Furthermore, the production vice-president handled production with great efficiency and neither needed, nor wanted, nor received direction from anyone. Sullivan maintained close personal relationships with the managers of client companies, spending much time traveling and lavishly entertaining on an unlimited expense allowance. Since business had been good for several years, there were relatively few pressures within the management group, freeing Sullivan for the customer relations work and the life-style he enjoyed.

Most financial affairs were handled by the controller, Frank Carr, an honest, tense, introverted man of 60, who could remember individual transactions for years and had an outstanding mind for accounting. However, he had failed to modernize the firm's management information system and, generally speaking, he was opposed to change. He, like most other home-office managers and employees, was well paid and content.

Most of the home-office personnel, however, became justifiably apprehensive about the change of ownership. Cahill took an intense interest in his new company. He soon began talking about acquiring new plants, developing a nationally advertised brand name, and broadening the firm's customer base, all of which were openly resisted by Sullivan. Further blocking Cahill's initiatives was Carr's sole control of the financial records, which made it difficult for Cahill to get the information needed in order to know the condition of the business and whether current operating decisions were sound. Because of these information problems, Cahill could not be certain that his ideas about expansion were supportable. Also, he was hesitant to override Sullivan on major issues for fear that Sullivan would go to a competitor and take some major customers with him. Sullivan's position was further strengthened by his strong personal ties within the Jefferson management, and he had a contract that would reward him handsomely if he were to be fired for any cause.

Determined to gain control of the firm, Cahill rented an apartment in St. Louis and set up an office next door to Sullivan, giving the impression that the move was only temporary. He personally employed a well-known auditing firm to establish a management information system and, supposedly at the insistence of a partner in that firm, hired an internal auditor (a highly competent Certified Public Accountant who had no previous contact with Jefferson Apparel). As Sullivan became apprehensive about Cahill's involve-

ment, he began to spend more time in the home office. Meanwhile Cahill increased his contact with customers and suppliers. On several occasions Cahill hired outside consultants for studies and opinions, thus reinforcing confidence in his own appraisal of the situation. These activities continued for about eight months. Finally, after a long and frustrating planning session, during which Sullivan remained unconvinced that Cahill's desires for expansion and establishing a brand name were feasible, Cahill took the big step that he would rather not have taken.

On Friday at 6:00 p.m., quitting time, Cahill asked for Sullivan's keys and company credit cards and told him to come back on Monday for his personal belongings. On Saturday afternoon Sullivan went to the office building only to discover that his extra front-door key no longer fit the lock. On Monday morning Cahill temporarily assumed the position of president.

PROBLEMS

1. Compare the leadership styles of Cahill and Sullivan. What factor do you think contributed most to the difference in the type of leadership each provided the company?

2. How did the environment into which Cahill came prevent his exercising effective leadership?

3. What does this case suggest about the relationship between power and a manager's ability to lead? What were the primary sources of power exercised by Sullivan and Cahill?

4. What factors will probably be most instrumental in determining Cahill's future leadership success in the Jefferson Company?

The case of The Reluctant Follower illustrates the complexity of managerial leadership. Cahill's ability to lead in this situation—a situation in which he had a legitimate right to lead—was influenced by a number of interacting factors. Among the most important were his own skills, motivation, goals, values, and the personal characteristics of the individuals and groups who logically were expected to follow his leadership. Our growing awareness of the complexity of leadership has greatly increased our understanding of the subject, but that awareness has also complicated our ability to define it.[1]

Fiedler and Chemers note that two common threads run through the most used definitions of leadership: first, leadership is a relationship between people in which there is a legitimate difference between the power and influence of leaders and followers; second, there are no leaders without followers.[2] Another generally accepted aspect of leadership is that an individual may be able to lead quite effectively in one situation and fail miserably in another. This is because the kind of behavior that effectively influences a certain individual or group under a given set of circumstances may be inappropriate when conditions or objectives are different. With these variables in mind, we define *leadership* as behavior through which an individual influences others to achieve specific objectives in specific situations. Thus, leadership refers to something a person does rather than something one is; it implies a sense of direction or goal orientation; and the effectiveness of one's attempts to influence is contingent upon unique situational factors. The implications of this definition will unfold throughout the following discussion.

STYLES OF LEADERSHIP

Managers and other leaders are relatively consistent in the way they attempt to influence the behavior of others. The manager who dominates subordinates in one situation is not likely to use a high degree of consideration and participation in another. The more-or-less consistent pattern or constellation of behaviors that characterize a leader is called *leadership style*. Although the behavior of most managers is too complex to be described by a single style, and some managers exhibit considerable flexibility of style, the concept provides a useful way of understanding leadership.

Autocratic Style

The *autocratic style*, identified earlier with McGregor's Theory X view of human nature, is closely associated with the classical approach to management. The *pure autocrat*, an increasingly ineffective leader in democratic societies, is a dictator. Such a leader confidently decides without consultation, then gives orders and expects them to be obeyed.

Since the autocrat does not seek the opinions of subordinates, both conflict and creativity among subordinates are held to a minimum. The autocrat usually

[1] Discussions of the problem of defining leadership are found in the following articles: Jeffrey Pfeffer, "The Ambiguity of Leadership," *Academy of Management Review*, Vol. 2, No. 1 (January–February, 1977), p. 104, and Barbara Karmel, "Leadership: A Challenge to Traditional Research Methods and Assumptions," *Academy of Management Review*, Vol. 3, No. 3 (July, 1978), p. 475.

[2] Fred E. Fiedler and Martin M. Chemers, *Leadership and Effective Management* (Glenview, Ill.: Scott, Foresman & Co., 1974), p. 4.

supervises closely and motivates through incentives and fear; subordinates generally react by doing only what is expected and by suppressing their frustrations. Sometimes they react aggressively through verbal abuse of their supervisor and at times through work stoppage and even sabotage.

To the autocrat, the basis for legitimate leadership is formal authority. Thus, the development of close interpersonal relationships with subordinates is superfluous. The autocrat is task oriented and places little intrinsic value on showing consideration to subordinates as a leadership technique. Nevertheless, as autocrats learn that their tactics can interfere with achievement, they often modify them to a degree. In some cases, they become *benevolent autocrats*, making decisions and hard selling them to subordinates rather than giving orders. They, therefore, get a small degree of subordinate participation as a manipulative technique. However, benevolent autocrats usually become pure autocrats when their benevolence does not achieve the results they seek. Thus, autocracy is the *fall-back style* of a benevolent autocrat.

Some benevolent autocrats may be described as *paternalistic*, implying that such persons play the role of a kind father caring for his children, showering them with gifts (employee benefits), and disciplining them when they get out of line. However, when this occurs the leader does not really respect subordinates and consequently does not treat them as mature, responsible adults. And, since adults dislike being treated as children and need to believe that they earn and therefore deserve their compensation, paternalism is seldom successful. It is particularly unsuccessful in the United States; its greatest success appears to have occurred in Japan.

Participative Style

A *participative style* of leadership is one in which managers involve their subordinates in organizational decision making. It does not imply democratic governance or majority rule, nor does it necessarily indicate that the leader is merely a *group facilitator* whose task is to help a group reach a consensus. While the latter, labeled *democratic leadership*, was not broadly accepted by management, it was highly touted in the literature of the human relations movement and was the focus of extensive research during the 1940's and 1950's.

Although some authors reserve the term *participation* for situations in which the decisions reached affect a group rather than an individual,[3] the style employed by a manager may permit a high degree of subordinate participation in the decision-making process, as the superior seeks opinions of individual subordinates and requires that they make recommendations about how problems are to be solved. Some managers who have a high regard for participation are often uncomfortable with assigning problems to groups; instead, they prefer a *consultative* form of participation in which continual input from subordinates is conscientiously sought while managers at all levels reserve the right to the last word.

---

[3] Arlyn J. Melcher, "Participation: A Critical Review of Research Findings," *Human Resource Management*, Vol. 15, No. 2 (Summer, 1976), p. 12.

Thus, consultative participation may make use of committees and other groups, but with the understanding that these groups recommend rather than decide. As discussed in Chapter 9, the advantages of participative decision making tend to outweigh the disadvantages; and consultation reaps these advantages without sacrificing individual accountability.

Sometimes management writers become enthusiastic about methods that are ignored by practicing managers, but participative leadership does not fall into that category. A 1973 study indicated that, generally speaking, managers are in agreement about what participation means and that most accept the idea that the use of participative methods, combined with the directive actions required to keep performance high, have practical value. The following are the three characteristics of participation that were most often selected by this group of 318 executives:

1. Gives subordinates a share in decision making
2. Keeps subordinates informed of the true situation, good or bad, under all circumstances
3. Stays aware of the state of the organization's morale and does everything possible to make it high [4]

A later study of the views of 49 chief executives (a sample taken from *Fortune's* top 500 companies) suggested that, although top executives are favorably disposed toward participative management, they are less inclined to practice it than their rhetoric implies.[5] The main problem with participative leadership in the form of group decision making is accountability. Some companies report success in holding each group member accountable for a group decision, as though each had made the decision alone, but that is almost impossible to do.

One final point about participative and autocratic styles needs to be emphasized: in the real world, all possible combinations of the two styles are practiced (Figure 17–1, page 366). The two discrete categories are valuable as reference points, but we may expect to find few, if any, managers whose leadership practices are not at some time drawn from both styles. The following discussions will indicate that this is probably a fortunate circumstance.

Laissez-Faire Style

Managers who use the *laissez-faire*, or *free-rein*, leadership style do as little supervising as possible. Given a situation in which the work to be done by each subordinate is clearly defined—from routine machine tending to the tasks of a research scientist—such leaders maintain a hands-off policy. They make few attempts to increase productivity, to develop their subordinates, or to meet their subordinates' psychological needs.

The *laissez-faire* style may be that of a deserter, a person who hangs on to a leadership position because it is profitable, but who has no identification

[4] Larry E. Greiner, "What Managers Think of Participative Leadership," *Harvard Business Review*, Vol. 51, No. 2 (March–April, 1973), p. 111.

[5] Donald P. Crane, "The Case for Participative Management," *Business Horizons*, Vol. 19, No. 2 (April, 1976), p. 15.

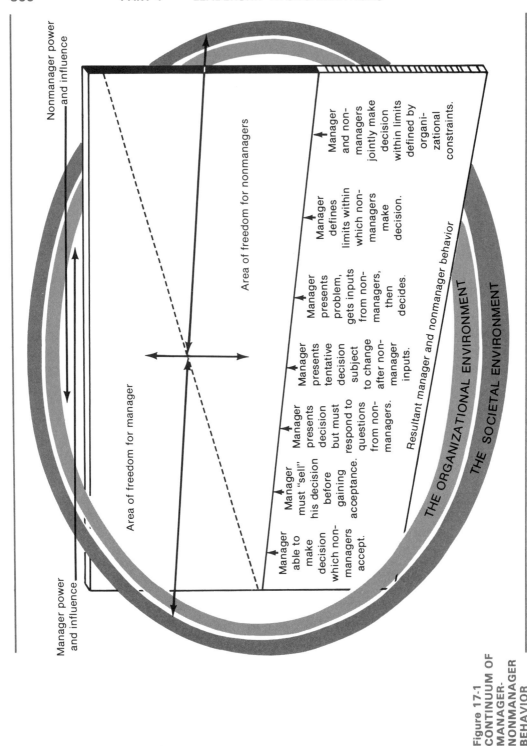

Nonmanager power and influence

Manager power and influence

Area of freedom for manager

Area of freedom for nonmanagers

Manager able to make decision which nonmanagers accept.

Manager must "sell" his decision before gaining acceptance.

Manager presents decision but must respond to questions from nonmanagers.

Manager presents tentative decision subject to change after nonmanager inputs.

Manager presents problem, gets inputs from nonmanagers, then decides.

Manager defines limits within which nonmanagers make decision.

Manager and nonmanagers jointly make decision within limits defined by organizational constraints.

Resultant manager and nonmanager behavior

THE ORGANIZATIONAL ENVIRONMENT

THE SOCIETAL ENVIRONMENT

Figure 17-1
CONTINUUM OF
MANAGER-
NONMANAGER
BEHAVIOR

SOURCE: Robert Tannenbaum and Warren H. Schmidt, "How to Choose a Leadership Pattern," *Harvard Business Review,* Vol. 51, No. 3 (May–June, 1973), p. 167. Copyright © 1973 by the President and Fellows of Harvard College: all rights reserved.

with organizational objectives and no concern for other people. On the other hand, in a few situations the *laissez-faire* style may be appropriate: when managing a group of highly motivated professionals such as scientists, university professors, or medical doctors. In situations of this kind, the routine behavior of the free-rein leader may be quite similar to that of a manager who places heavy emphasis on goal setting and becomes personally involved in supervising subordinates only when problems occur. However, such a general (versus close) leadership style, called *management by exception*, is not an abdication or desertion of the leadership role; it involves a strong emphasis on productivity and on the controls needed to make sure that production goals are met.

The Managerial Grid®

The most thoroughly conceptualized approach to understanding leadership style, the *Managerial Grid*, was developed by Robert Blake and Jane Mouton. The Managerial Grid describes a manager's leadership style along two dimensions: concern for production and concern for people. As shown in Figure 17–2, each of these concerns exists in varying degrees along a continuum from Level 1 (low) to Level 9 (high). These concerns for production and people are not merely additive; they interact with one another to produce a variety of leadership styles. In order to understand the nature of the interactions between the two primary dimensions, it must be understood that the two scales are attitudinal in nature rather than behavioral;[6] that is, the styles refer to modes of thinking—to what leaders perceive to have value or to be important—rather than to what leaders actually do. It is this particular mix of concern for people and concern for production that determines behavior. To understand fully this concept we must first examine the styles themselves.

Grid Styles. According to Blake and Mouton the following five styles, briefly described here and shown in Figure 17–2, represent the more important style differences among managers:[7]

9,1. Maximum concern for production (Level 9) is combined with minimum concern for people (Level 1) to produce a leader who attempts to maximize production by using authority and power to achieve control over subordinates. Managers with the 9,1 combination of concerns see no reason to involve their subordinates in planning. Likewise, they predictably view their organizing and directing responsibilities from an authoritative stance. They decide on work assignments, provide subordinates with detailed instructions, and supervise closely to make sure their directives are properly carried out.

1,9. Managers who employ this style have a minimum concern for production coupled with a maximum concern for people. Since 1,9 managers believe that attitudes and feelings are of utmost importance, their emphasis is on promoting good feelings. Such managers have an unhealthy need to be accepted; they

[6] Robert R. Blake and Jane S. Mouton, *The New Managerial Grid* (Houston: Gulf Publishing Company, 1978), p. 9.
[7] *Ibid.*, p. 12.

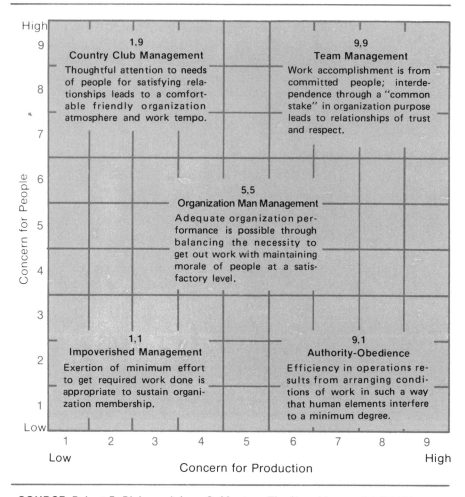

**Figure 17–2
THE
MANAGERIAL
GRID®**

SOURCE: Robert R. Blake and Jane S. Mouton, *The New Managerial Grid* (Houston: Gulf Publishing Company, 1978), p.11.

even need the approval of persons for whom they have no personal feelings of warmth. They constantly live in fear of disapproval. The 1,9 manager may be highly motivated to work hard, but that motivation is based on a need for approval and acceptance rather than a commitment to the production goals of the organization.

1,1. The 1,1 orientation expresses minimum concern for both production and people. Managers with 1,1 concerns are essentially indifferent to the needs of subordinates and the goals of the organization. They do only what is required to hold their jobs. They are uninvolved and indifferent as long as their own position is not jeopardized. They can ordinarily find ways to save face, despite their low productivity and lack of involvement, by rationalizing or placing blame on others. Causes for such attitudes may relate to the deeply embedded personality characteristics of the individual, to conditions existing in the work environment, or to an interaction of the two.

5,5. The 5,5 orientation represents a middle-of-the-road philosophy, a compromise position that seeks neither to do everything possible to meet the needs of people nor to achieve the highest production attainable. Because 5,5 managers are highly motivated to look good and to succeed, they may use participative leadership and engage in a variety of enlightened leadership practices. However, their motivation arises more from a need to be a part of the group and to be successful than from a commitment to such practices. Because 5,5 managers do not have a high commitment to either people or productivity, they sometimes behave as crafty organizational politicians, often taking action that will be acceptable and profitable in the short run with little concern for its long-range implications.

9,9. The 9,9 style is a goal-oriented team approach that seeks to achieve a high level of productivity through involvement and redirection of conflict that can potentially reduce productivity and interfere with employee satisfaction. Managers with 9,9 styles believe that organizational goals can best be met as individuals become committed to the values and goals of their employer and, consequently, satisfy their own needs through productivity and cooperative work involvement. The achievement motivation of the 9,9 manager "comes from developing the competence required to make a positive contribution and, therefore, to search for and pursue goals and objectives that are simultaneously personal and corporate." [8]

Style Interactions. In a sense, each of the five styles just described represent a set of assumptions for using power to link people to production. Thus, each manager who desires to achieve objectives through people has a choice of alternative means, and the means selected depend on the assumptions made—upon the manager's concerns for people and productivity.

As mentioned earlier, concerns for productivity and people must be understood as interactive rather than additive. Consider, for example, the 9,9 leadership pattern. If we think solely in terms of behaviors that are often associated with high concern for production, a high concern for production may suggest strong controls, jobs designed solely to achieve maximum production, and minimum opportunity for choice behavior and its potential for human error. To this can be added a high concern for keeping happy employees who are subjected to that high degree of control and high demands for productivity. This particular 9,9 mix may result in a form of paternalism. Note, however, that such a combination is not at all what Blake and Mouton mean by the 9,9 style. Within the Grid framework the concerns for production and for people are qualitatively different under different assumptions—for example, under the 1,9 and 9,9 assumptions. In the 1,9 style, the high concern for people is that they be happy; but, in the 9,9 style, in which high concern for people interacts with a high concern for production, the high concern for people is that they grow, become involved in their work, exercise maximum autonomy, and find satisfaction through cooperative achievement. These differences in concerns or attitudes toward people necessarily result in different methods for achieving high productivity.

---

[8] *Ibid.*, p. 95.

One Best Style. Within the context of the Grid philosophy, the 9,9 style is always best. Since sound human relationships are based on behavioral science principles that are not contingent on situations, managers need not be concerned about when it is appropriate to apply those principles. The manager who endorses this value orientation believes, for example, that a superior-subordinate relationship that permits free and open communication is always better than a boss-dominated relationship, a relationship that can tolerate candor is always better than one that is deceptive and guarded, a relationship in which people help one another by providing feedback is always better than one in which feedback is neglected, and a relationship in which conflict is confronted and resolved is always better than one in which it is suppressed or compromised.

Commitment to these basic principles does not, however, mean that leadership behavior should not be conditioned in part by the situation.[9] The basic 9,9 managerial strategy should not shift to a 5,5 or a 9,1, for example, merely because situations differ. On the other hand, the tactics one uses within the context of a 9,9 set of concerns may vary greatly. For example, managers who are strongly committed to cooperative decision making will not use the same approach with inexperienced assembly-line workers as they will with a group of experienced, well-informed supervisors or research scientists. Similarly, involvement of subordinates in goal setting will be handled differently with these groups of personnel, but these tactical differences do not necessitate rejection of the basic principles. A pure contingency approach to management suggests a *flexibility* that permits the substitution of one style for another (say, a fallback to a 9,1 style when the 9,9 does not get immediate results); the Grid approach prefers a *versatility* in which the strategy remains the same—leadership behavior is governed by principle—but tactics, consistent with that strategy, vary with the situation.[10]

Evaluation. Since there is presently a wide diversity of views on leadership, it can be expected that each viewpoint has its critics. Grid theory is no exception. Certainly persons who advocate a contingency approach do not accept the idea that there is one best way to lead. Furthermore, Grid theory and other two-dimensional theories with which Grid theory has rightly or wrongly been identified [11] have been criticized because of their assumptions about how the people and production dimensions interact. Some researchers have concluded that the interaction factor unnecessarily complicates our understanding of leadership styles.[12] If such a conclusion should ever prove to be totally applicable to Grid management, the model will be hard to support.

---

[9] *Ibid.*, p.128.

[10] *Ibid.*, p.130.

[11] Stephen Kerr and Chester Schriesheim, "Consideration, Initiating Structure, and Organizational Criteria—An Update of Korman's 1966 Review," *Personnel Psychology*, Vol. 27, No. 4 (Winter, 1974), p. 555; Edwin Fleishman, Edwin F. Harris, and R. D. Burtt, *Leadership and Supervision in Industry* (Columbus: Ohio State University Press, 1955); Edwin A. Fleishman and Edwin F. Harris, "Patterns of Leadership Behavior Related to Employee Grievances and Turnover," *Personnel Psychology*, Vol. 15, No. 1 (Spring, 1962), p. 43.

[12] L. L. Larson, J. G. Hunt, and R. N. Osborn, "The Great Hi-Hi Leader Behavior Myth: A Lesson from Occam's Razor," *Academy of Management Journal*, Vol. 19, No. 4 (December, 1976), p. 628.

In defense of Grid theory, it provides an evolving rather than a static model. For example, in Mouton and Blake's 1978 book on Grid Management, they have more fully conceptualized a third leadership dimension: personal motivation.[13] In addition, their concept of versatility within the 9,9 style allows for a considerable amount of adaptability to the situation, to some degree making Grid theory compatible with the best of contingency management without asking that a leader abdicate a consistent commitment to values. In view of the great number of possible combinations, the problem of understanding how the two main dimensions interact is a complex one; it is essentially the same problem that contingency theory faces with its endless number of variables to be studied. Nevertheless, Grid Management has proved to have practical value, and its theoretical base continues to develop.

Although the Grid model for understanding leadership style has been the object of more intense research and development than other models, it is by no means the only model available.[14] Some researchers and writers in the leadership field believe that the identification of a small number of leadership styles—whatever those styles may be—places an unnecessary limitation on our ability to understand and describe leadership behavior;[15] that is, not everyone is convinced that the basic concept of leadership style contributes greatly to our understanding of leadership. It is, however, highly regarded by others and is enjoying considerable acceptance by many practicing managers.

PERSONAL ASPECTS OF LEADERSHIP EFFECTIVENESS

In discussing leadership style, we have dealt with leader behaviors that tend to cluster—behaviors that are so often observed together that patterns can be identified. What we have for the most part avoided, in the interest of maintaining a behavioral approach, is linking those behaviors with personality characteristics. However, it is not altogether illogical to do so. It is relevant, for example, that the reason some leaders adopt an autocratic style is that they have authoritarian personalities, that persons with a high need for approval may develop a country club style, that a desire to avoid responsibility may motivate the compromiser to use participative methods, or that leaders' attitudes and values influence which style they are most likely to select. So, looking back on leadership style, we can see that personality factors are important, and the literature on leadership style recognizes that fact.

In the forthcoming discussion of contingency theories it will again be apparent that the characteristics of individuals are important variables, even though

---

[13] Mouton and Blake, *op. cit.,* p. 233.

[14] W. J. Redden, *Managerial Effectiveness* (New York City: McGraw-Hill, Inc., 1970); Pradip M. Khandwalla, "Some Top Management Styles, Their Context and Performance," *Organization & Administrative Sciences,* Vol. 7, No. 4 (Winter, 1976/1977), p. 21.

[15] Louis R. Pondy, "Leadership Is a Language Game," *Leadership: Where Else Can We Go?* edited by Morgan W. McCall, Jr., and Michael M. Lombardo (Durham, N. C.: Duke University Press, 1974), p. 90, and Jim R. David and Fred Luthans, "Leadership Reexamined: A Behavioral Approach," *Academy of Management Review,* Vol. 4, No. 2 (April, 1979), p. 237.

personality may not be the point of emphasis. We will discuss, for example, such factors as preferences for co-workers; the needs, goals, and perceptions of leaders; and the expectations of subordinates that high performance will be rewarded. Thus, wherever we turn in leadership theory, personality variables are involved, but we attempt to keep them in perspective along with characteristics of followers and the environment.

Lacking this perspective, some of our earliest leadership studies focused exclusively on personality. It seemed only logical that to understand the nature of effective leadership, we should have studied the lives of persons who had proved themselves in leadership roles: Alexander the Great, Churchill, Ghandi, Roosevelt, Eisenhower, and, of course, successful business executives. The idea that leader success results exclusively or even primarily from the leader's personality traits became known as the *great man theory* of leadership. It is also called the *trait approach* because of its extensive use of research that is based on the measurement of personality traits.

The Trait Approach

A major impetus was given to the trait approach during World War I when a high demand for military and industrial leaders produced a pressing need for effective leadership selection. Since that time most of the leader trait research has focused on manager selection and early identification of managerial potential.

As large numbers of personality tests were developed from the 1920's through the 1950's, literally hundreds of studies were done in an attempt to isolate personality traits associated with leadership—extroversion, initiative, decisiveness, social ascendancy, etc. Unfortunately most of the traits were poorly defined and poorly measured, resulting in endless lists of overlapping traits that supposedly characterized effective leaders but which also characterized many persons who exhibited very little leadership behavior. Because of the simplistic nature of the research and the conclusions that were drawn from it, the so-called great man theory of leadership fell into disrepute. Furthermore, as researchers became increasingly aware of the importance of situational factors in leadership effectiveness, their writings often seemed to imply that the personal characteristics of leaders bear no relationship to leadership effectiveness.[16] This was an unfortunate pendulum swing, a reaction caused in part by an implicit assumption that acknowledging the influence of personality differences on leadership performance was synonymous with accepting the great man theory.

---

[16] It was the research of the human relations movement, with its emphasis on informal groups and emergent leaders, that led to the deemphasis of leadership characteristics. Nevertheless, in the heyday of the human relations movement some research supported the great man theory. See Edgar F. Borgatta, Arthur S. Couch, and Robert F. Bales, "Some Findings Relevant to the Great Man Theory of Leadership," *American Sociological Review*, Vol. 19, No. 6 (December, 1954), p. 755.

The failure of the trait approach was due to several factors, the most important of which are the following:

1. Trait naming does not indicate how much of the trait is needed.
2. Traits are usually poorly defined and overlapping.
3. The personality tests used to measure traits are often unreliable and of questionable validity.
4. Trait psychology contains inherent flaws since personality functions as a whole with all traits interacting, thereby producing unique and sometimes unpredictable behavior. Accordingly, two persons who are identical in one trait (say, assertiveness) may behave differently because of the presence of other personal characteristics (such as values and sense of responsibility). Finally, there is no general agreement about what a trait is; apparently any personality-related characteristic is a trait, but that definition needs some explaining.
5. The trait approach fails to recognize that leadership requirements vary from one situation to another.
6. The trait approach fails to distinguish between traits that are necessary for success in a certain situation and traits that are merely desirable (for example, the necessity for decisiveness in some supervisory jobs). Similarly, it fails to show how persons who lack a certain highly desirable trait, such as skill in interpersonal relations (if, indeed, that is a trait), may succeed because of a compensating quality such as superior decision-making skills relating to technical or financial matters.

Research on Leadership Characteristics

As research methodologies and theory development have improved, so has our ability to identify individual differences that contribute to leader effectiveness while avoiding some of the pitfalls of the trait approach.[17] Although massive literature surveys by Ralph Stogdill indicate that certain characteristics of leaders have been identified,[18] most researchers prefer to move in the direction of a contingency approach, studying only a specific type of leader—the manager— or better still, studying a particular type and level of manager in a particular organization. Fiedler and Chemers conclude that:

> On the basis of the evidence which we have presented so far, it would certainly not seem very fruitful to predict leadership status or leadership effectiveness from personality traits. At the same time, a number of studies indicate fairly conclusively that we can predict to some extent the effectiveness of *managers* from personality tests and inventories.[19]

A survey of the research literature by Campbell and others led them to conclude that "from 30 to 50 percent of the variance in estimates of overall

---

[17] It is noteworthy that we can deal with personal characteristics without accepting trait theory as such. For example, a leader's decisiveness or assertiveness may be operationally defined in terms of certain behavior. As long as consistent definitions are employed, good research can be conducted.

[18] Ralph M. Stogdill, *Handbook of Leadership: A Survey of Theory and Research* (New York City: The Free Press, 1974), p. 81.

[19] Fiedler and Chemers, *op. cit.*, p. 31.

general managerial effectiveness can be expressed in terms of personal qualities claimed by managers taking part in investigations." [20] Many aspects of the published research studies prevent our knowing the extent to which personal characteristics influence leader effectiveness, and the 30 to 50 percent estimate may be too high or too low depending on the situation. It is obvious, however, that even though personal characteristics do not deserve the place of importance given them by the great man theory, they are important. Some studies indicate that first-line supervisors—especially those who work in highly structured, machine-paced environments with a strong union influence—often exert very little influence on production or even on employee satisfaction. In contrast, the personal qualities of some entrepreneurial owner-managers are expressed in virtually every aspect of the organizations they control. Their personal leadership directly accounts for or influences the existence of the organization, the typical leadership style of its managers, its policies and procedures, its ability to survive in times of crisis, and its overall level of success.

The most common form of research on the characteristics of managerial leadership was used in a Standard Oil of New Jersey (SONJ) study in an effort to identify managerial potential among current managers. The *subjects* (i.e., the persons studied) were 443 SONJ managers who performed a variety of functions such as marketing, research, production, and accounting. The *criterion* measure (the measure of effectiveness) was a composite score based on the position level to which the manager had advanced, salary history, and rankings on overall managerial effectiveness. Personal characteristics were measured by a lengthy battery of tests, a background study, education, and experience, a composite of which yielded a correlation of .70 with the success criterion. Such a correlation means that about 49 percent of the variance in effectiveness measures was accounted for by personal characteristics.[21] Thus, for SONJ managers a significant relationship existed between success and personal attributes, even though many different types of managers were grouped together in the study.

Although it is reasonable to expect that the personal characteristics that differentiate successful from unsuccessful managers vary somewhat among organizations, studies of different business firms produce moderately consistent results. This is not surprising in view of the ease with which managers in one company are able to adapt immediately to similar management positions in another—particularly within the same industry. Thus, we should expect that in a variety of business situations, managers who have a high degree of decisiveness, self-objectivity, resistance to stress, assertiveness, and motivation to succeed may have an edge over persons who have fewer of these qualities.[22]

---

[20] John P. Campbell *et al.*, *Managerial Behavior, Performance and Effectiveness* (New York City: McGraw-Hill, Inc., 1970), p. 197.

[21] *Ibid.*, p. 165.

[22] To understand the basis for such comparisons, see D. W. Bray and D. L. Grant, "The Assessment Center Measurement of Potential for Business Management," *Psychological Monograph*, Vol. 80, No. 17 (Entire No. 625); Glen Grimsley and Hilton Jarrett, "The Relation of Past Managerial Achievement to Test Measures Obtained in the Employment Situation: Methodology and Results," *Personnel Psychology*, Vol. 26, No. 1 (Spring, 1973), p. 31; Thomas Harrell and Margaret Harrell, "The Personality of MBAs Who Reach General Management Early," *Personnel Psychology*, Vol. 26, No. 1 (Spring, 1973), p. 127; Campbell *et al.*, p. 165.

CONTINGENCY LEADERSHIP THEORIES

From our previous discussions of contingency theory, it should easily be inferred that contingency leadership theory is based on the idea that the best style of leadership depends on a variety of factors relating to the individuals involved and to the environment in which leadership occurs. Furthermore, contingency theory seeks to make scientifically validated statements concerning the conditions under which any given leadership style is most likely to be effective. We now look briefly at the main features of two recognized contingency approaches to the study of leadership.

Fiedler's Contingency Model

Fiedler's model, the most thoroughly researched of the contingency theories, attempts to specify the conditions under which leaders should use task-oriented and relationship-oriented styles. Rather than recommend one best style, Fiedler acknowledges that the situation should influence the leader's choice of style; accordingly, he begins by isolating some situational categories for study.

Situational Favorableness. Fiedler defines *situational favorableness* as "the degree to which the leader has control and influence and, therefore, feels that he can determine the outcomes of the group action." [23] To be more concrete, Fiedler's measurements of situational favorableness are based on the following factors:

1. *Position Power*—the extent to which the organization provides the leader with the means of rewarding and punishing subordinates
2. *Task Structure*—the extent to which the leader knows exactly what to do; the extent to which the tasks to be completed are defined in detail
3. *Leader-Member Relations*—the extent to which subordinates accept and support their leader

To visualize the effect of these situational variables on leader effectiveness, think of yourself in a line supervisor's job in which (1) your superior fails to delegate the authority you need in order to do your job, (2) you cannot determine what is expected in terms of productivity and the means of achieving it, and (3) you have inherited years of bad labor-management relations from your predecessors. This is a very unfavorable situation, and it is easy to imagine how difficult it would be for personal leadership qualities to overcome its negative impact on leader effectiveness. On the other hand, if each of these variables were highly favorable, only mediocre talent and effort would be required to achieve high group productivity.

Leadership Style. Fiedler evaluates the leader's style, the second major influence on effectiveness, by means of the *least preferred co-worker* instrument

[23] Fred E. Fiedler, "The Leadership Game: Matching the Man to the Situation," *Organizational Dynamics*, Vol. 5, No. 2 (Fall, 1976), p. 10. The most complete statement of Fiedler's model is found in Fred E. Fiedler, *A Theory of Leadership Effectiveness* (New York City: McGraw-Hill, Inc., 1967).

shown in Case Problem 17-B. Whether the leader is primarily task or relationship oriented is measured by how favorably the leader describes his or her *least preferred co-worker* (LPC)—the person from among all past co-workers with whom he or she would least like to work. The logic of the LPC scale lies in the assumption that persons who describe their least preferred co-worker in relatively positive terms perceive that co-worker not just as a co-worker but as a person of intrinsic worth. The leader with a high LPC score sees favorable interpersonal relations as a requirement for effectiveness and sees people as they are described by McGregor's Theory Y.

Fiedler strongly emphasizes that LPC score differences refer to differences in goals, not to differences in leader behavior. Thus, "the accomplishment of the task might well call for very considerate and pleasant interpersonal behaviors, while the maintenance of close interpersonal relations might be possible only by driving the group to success." [24] Style, therefore, refers to the consistency of the leader's goals, needs, or motives over different situations and may result in a great variety of behaviors.[25] We look now at some different situations which influence the effectiveness of task-motivated and relationship-motivated styles.

Effectiveness. Fiedler and many others have performed numerous studies to determine the relationships between leadership style, situational favorableness, and leadership effectiveness. The major results of this research (Figure 17–3) indicate that in very unfavorable or very favorable situations the task-motivated style is most effective, but in situations of intermediate favorableness the relationship-motivated style is better. Taking into account all the possible variables

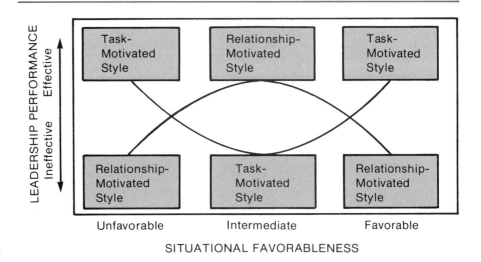

Figure 17–3 FIEDLER'S THEORY OF LEADERSHIP EFFECTIVENESS

[24] Fiedler, *op. cit.*, 1976, p.10.
[25] Fiedler, *op. cit.*, 1967, p. 36.

that can be considered, these are rather sweeping generalizations, although they are based on a great deal of research and have achieved a considerable amount of acceptance. This fact does not, of course, mean that Fiedler's theories have achieved general acceptance by scholars; and there is little evidence that practicing managers have been greatly influenced by the research findings expressed in Figure 17–3.

From our previous discussion, it should be obvious that Fiedler's approach to understanding leadership is unacceptable to persons who believe there is one best theory, since it proposes no consistent commitment to a way of viewing people. Others criticize Fiedler's theory because of weaknesses in the use of the LPC concept as a basis for classifying leadership styles.[26] Finally, a general criticism, applied to all leadership theories based on the concept of style, is applicable: we may unnecessarily constrict our understanding of leadership by restricting our research to a few variables, as if these were the only variables or even the most important variables involved in leadership.

Path-Goal Theory

The path-goal theory, originally formulated by Robert J. House, is so named because its primary focus is on how a leader influences subordinate behavior and perceptions of their work, their goals, and their satisfactions.[27] The theory, like some others, employs the concepts of consideration (people orientation) and initiating structure (establishing controls and other means of achieving production); however, it is unique in its application of expectancy motivation theory to these concepts. To be specific, the role of the leader is to provide subordinates with "coaching, guidance, support and rewards necessary for effective and satisfying performance that would otherwise be lacking in the environment.[28]

Path-goal theory is currently subject to intensive testing and is increasingly being identified with several researchers. It is an evolving theory, which makes it difficult to state exactly what the theory presently includes. Nevertheless, the basic theory contains the following propositions:

1. The leader can increase employee motivation and satisfaction by helping subordinates see that improved performance leads to desirable rewards. In expectancy theory terms, the leader is in a position to increase the expectancy of a payoff or a potential reward. The *valence* of work goals may also be increased as employees see the clear relationship between their achievements and valued payoffs such as raises, promotion, and recognition. (You will recall from Chapter 15 that within expectancy theory Motivational Force = Valence × Expectancy.) Thus,

---

[26] Chester A. Schriescheim, Brandan D. Bannister, and William H. Money, "Psychometric Properties of the LPC Scale: An Extension of Rice's Review," *Academy of Management Review*, Vol. 4, No. 2 (April, 1979), p. 278.

[27] Robert J. House, "A Path-Goal Theory of Leader Effectiveness," *Administrative Science Quarterly*, Vol. 16, No. 3 (September, 1971), p. 321.

[28] R. J. House and G. Dressler, "The Path-Goal Theory of Leadership: Some *Post Hoc* and *A Priori* Tests," *Contingency Approaches to Leadership*, edited by J. G. Hunt and L. L. Larson (Carbondale, Ill.: Southern Illinois University Press, 1974), p. 29.

a strategic leadership function is "recognizing and/or arousing subordinates' needs for outcomes over which the leader has some control." [29]

2. In situations where goals are ambiguous and tasks are poorly defined, the leader can increase motivation by providing structure (clarifying goals, policies, and work methods; providing training and supportive supervision, etc.). This structure clarifies the path to the goal and thus increases expectations of success.

3. Situations that are already highly structured, where adding more structure would probably lead to dissatisfaction, call for increased consideration. The leader may influence both satisfaction and motivation by providing praise, understanding, and related forms of support in such a way that desirable performances are reinforced (see Chapter 15 for references to reinforcement-motivation theory).

The leader has a unique opportunity to know personally and to relate to subordinates as individuals: for example, by recognizing and satisfying the strong needs of a given employee for affiliation, security, or status. By clarifying the path to goal achievement, by providing support, by rewarding high performance, etc., on an individual basis, the supervisor can motivate and increase job satisfaction in ways that extend beyond the effects of the organization's incentive systems, employee benefit programs, and other impersonal aspects of the environment.

The research on the path-goal theory is currently inconclusive, although there is considerable evidence to support it.[30] Research results are often mixed, as was the case in a study of military officers and Civil Service personnel in which the theory was supported with respect to consideration but not regarding initiating structure.[31] Another study, involving research and development personnel of an airframe manufacturer and an electronics firm, raised a question about the validity of some of the causal relationships presumed to exist by previous path-goal researchers.[32] Nevertheless, the path-goal theory shows promise, especially since it is sufficiently flexible to permit a wide variety of variables to be studied.

The techniques for measuring leadership style necessarily differ, depending on the leadership theory employed. Case Problem 17-B, based on Fiedler's contingency theory, employs the least preferred co-worker (LPC) method to determine whether a leader is likely to use a task-motivated or a relationship-motivated style. By working through Fiedler's LPC scale, you will gain insight into his methodology and into your own leadership style.

---

[29] Robert J. House and Terrence R. Mitchell, "Path-Goal Theory of Leadership," *Journal of Contemporary Business*, Vol. 3, No. 4 (Fall, 1974), p. 81.

[30] House and Dressler, *op. cit.*; A. D. Szilagyi and H. P. Sims, Jr., "Leader Structure and Subordinate Satisfaction for Two Hospital Administrative Levels: A Path Analysis Approach," *Journal of Applied Psychology*, Vol. 60, No. 2 (April, 1975), p. 194.

[31] John E. Stinson and Thomas W. Johnson, "The Path-Goal Theory of Leadership: A Partial Test and Suggested Refinement," *Academy of Management Journal*, Vol. 18, No. 2 (June, 1975), p. 242.

[32] Charles N. Greene, "Questions of Causation in the Path-Goal Theory of Leadership," *Academy of Management Journal*, Vol. 22, No. 1 (March, 1979), p. 22.

Case Problem 17-B

MEASURING LEADERSHIP STYLE

Instructions

Before completing the least preferred co-worker scale, give some thought to what you perceive your leadership style to be. When playing a leadership role, are you primarily motivated to maintain good interpersonal relationships or to complete the assigned task even if it disrupts those relationships? Think about this question and write out an explanation of your response before completing the LPC scale.

The LPC exercise on page 380 consists of pairs of words that are opposite in meaning, such as *Very neat* and *Not neat*. You are asked to describe the one person with whom you have worked and with whom you would least prefer to work again. The individual need not be someone you like least, but should be the person with whom you had the most difficulty in getting a job done.

PROBLEMS

1. To compute your LPC score, add your scores on the 16 traits and divide by 16. A high LPC score ranges from 4.1 to 5.7 and a low LPC score ranges from 1.2 to 2.2.
2. Does your LPC score support your own evaluation of your leadership style? Discuss.

Place an *X* in one of the eight spaces between the two words that best describes your least preferred co-worker. Each space refers to how well the adjective fits the person you are describing.

FOR EXAMPLE: If you describe the person with whom you least prefer to work as being quite neat, orderly, or tidy, place an *X* in the space over the words, Quite neat, as shown below:

Very neat :_____: X :_____:_____ |_____:_____:_____:_____: Not neat

8	7	6	5	4	3	2	1
Very neat	Quite neat	Some-what neat	Slightly neat	Slightly untidy	Some-what untidy	Quite untidy	Very untidy

If you ordinarily think of the person with whom you can work least well as being only slightly neat, mark your *X* as follows:

Very neat :_____:_____:_____: X |_____:_____:_____:_____: Not neat

8	7	6	5	4	3	2	1
Very neat	Quite neat	Some-what neat	Slightly neat	Slightly untidy	Some-what untidy	Quite untidy	Very untidy

If you think of that person as being very untidy use the space above those words as follows:

Very neat :_____:_____:_____:_____ |_____:_____:_____: X : Not neat

8	7	6	5	4	3	2	1
Very neat	Quite neat	Some-what neat	Slightly neat	Slightly untidy	Some-what untidy	Quite untidy	Very untidy

Exhibit I
A MEASURE OF LEADERSHIP STYLE

LPC SCALE

Follow directions carefully. Work rapidly. Do not omit any items, and mark each item only once.

Pleasant	:___:___:___:___|___:___:___:___	: Unpleasant
	8 7 6 5 | 4 3 2 1	
Friendly	:___:___:___:___|___:___:___:___	: Unfriendly
	8 7 6 5 | 4 3 2 1	
Rejecting	:___:___:___:___|___:___:___:___	: Accepting
	1 2 3 4 | 5 6 7 8	
Helpful	:___:___:___:___|___:___:___:___	: Frustrating
	8 7 6 5 | 4 3 2 1	
Unenthusiastic	:___:___:___:___|___:___:___:___	: Enthusiastic
	1 2 3 4 | 5 6 7 8	
Tense	:___:___:___:___|___:___:___:___	: Relaxed
	1 2 3 4 | 5 6 7 8	
Distant	:___:___:___:___|___:___:___:___	: Close
	1 2 3 4 | 5 6 7 8	
Cold	:___:___:___:___|___:___:___:___	: Warm
	1 2 3 4 | 5 6 7 8	
Cooperative	:___:___:___:___|___:___:___:___	: Uncooperative
	8 7 6 5 | 4 3 2 1	
Supportive	:___:___:___:___|___:___:___:___	: Hostile
	8 7 6 5 | 4 3 2 1	
Boring	:___:___:___:___|___:___:___:___	: Interesting
	1 2 3 4 | 5 6 7 8	
Quarrelsome	:___:___:___:___|___:___:___:___	: Harmonious
	1 2 3 4 | 5 6 7 8	
Self-assured	:___:___:___:___|___:___:___:___	: Hesitant
	8 7 6 5 | 4 3 2 1	
Efficient	:___:___:___:___|___:___:___:___	: Inefficient
	8 7 6 5 | 4 3 2 1	
Gloomy	:___:___:___:___|___:___:___:___	: Cheerful
	1 2 3 4 | 5 6 7 8	
Open	:___:___:___:___|___:___:___:___	: Guarded
	8 7 6 5 | 4 3 2 1	

Exhibit I
(continued)

SOURCE: Fred E. Fiedler, *A Theory of Leadership Effectiveness* (New York City: McGraw-Hill, Inc., 1967), Table 3–1, p. 40.

CHAPTER QUESTIONS FOR STUDY AND DISCUSSION

1. What negative effects typically result from an autocratic leadership style? In view of these effects how can one ever justify the use of autocratic leadership behaviors?

2. What does the term *participative leadership* imply? How does that differ from *democratic leadership*? Of what practical value is this distinction?

3. If it is true that the styles of practicing managers vary along a continuum between the extremes of autocracy and participation, what value is there in describing only two of these styles?

4. Of what significance to Grid theory is the idea that the style descriptions relate to concerns rather than behaviors?

5. What are the pros and cons of the belief that there is one best leadership style?

6. In Grid theory a high concern for people (a 9-level concern) is qualitatively different in the 1,9 and 9,9 styles. What is the difference? What rationale can you give for the difference?

7. In everyday conversation, when we observe someone who is extroverted, persuasive, and makes a good impression, we are likely to refer to that person as a leader. What is technically incorrect or misleading about such a statement?

8. List some leadership behaviors that appear to support the position that personal characteristics are important contributors to leadership effectiveness. Why have such characteristics been deemphasized in recent years?

9. In what kind of environment would you expect studies most likely to show little relationship between personal characteristics of first-line supervisors and subordinate productivity and satisfaction?

10. What is Fiedler's logic in using high scores on the least preferred co-worker scale as a measure of people orientation?

Chapter 18

The Role of the Supervisor

Case Problem 18-A

NO SMOKING

The managers of Apex Manufacturing, a company with approximately 750 employees, pride themselves in running what the company calls a tight ship. They are satisfied with the results of a recent attitude survey which shows that most employees believe that supervision is strict, but fair. Like most of the other members of management, John Sweeney has come up through the ranks and is currently assigned to Department 40, the lacquer department, where he supervises 35 hourly employees. He has been with the company for 20 years, and for the last 10 years he has been a foreman. John tries to be fair to those working for him. At the same time, he tries to administer company policies in accordance with the wishes of the general superintendent who is very strict in the interpretation of company rules and regulations. John is waiting in his office for the arrival of Vera Huber, the union steward for Department 40.

"John, I'd like to talk to you about Jim Wilson, the worker you discharged yesterday afternoon."

"Not much to talk about, Vera. John replied, "You know he was smoking in a restricted area."

"That's just the point, John. The rules don't say that you have to discharge him.

All they say is that anyone who violates any of the Group One rules is *subject* to immediate discharge. That's a long way from saying that you *have* to discharge him."

"Look, Vera, I know that you have your job to do with the union and that you have a perfect right to question any action that I may take. But look at this case: Jim has been with the company for over 12 years; certainly in that length of time he should know what the company rules mean. They are there for a reason. You know that this whole plant could blow up if there was a fire in here, what with this lacquer the department has to work with. There are *No Smoking* signs all over the place, and the workers in the spray booths even wear rubber soles so there is no chance for sparks. Sorry, nothing I can do about it; one mistake here can blow us all to hell and back."

"You say that Jim has been with us 12 years. That's true, but he's only been in your department for three months. He just forgot, maybe worried or something."

"I can't help that. Maybe it was some guy down the street last month who was just worried, or new, or something, and you know what happened there. That fire took the lives of three employees in that plant and cost millions of dollars; none of them are back to work yet. We don't want that happening here, and it won't if I have anything to do about it."

"John, you aren't leaving me much choice. I'm going to file a grievance, and I promise you this one will go all the way to arbitration. Twelve years of service without a single reprimand ought to mean something." With that remark, Vera Huber, the steward, left the foreman's office.

PROBLEMS

1. Do you agree with the action taken by John Sweeney, the foreman? Explain.

2. Has the steward presented her case well? Is she quibbling when she says that the words "subject to" do not mean that the foreman must discharge an employee?

3. The next step of the grievance procedure in Apex Manufacturing calls for a decision by the general superintendent. If the superintendent reverses Sweeney's stand, what effect will this have on Sweeney's relations with his workers?

4. Of what significance are the "fire down the street" and the "12 years of service without a reprimand"?

Many statements have been made concerning the importance of first-line supervisors because of their role in the attainment of production goals of the organization and because their position in the managerial hierarchy results in their being the only members of management who direct the work of nonmanagerial employees. Numerous studies show that there is no consistent relationship between productivity and job satisfaction or morale. However, these studies do reveal a predictable relationship between supervisory practice and productivity; hence, the importance of the supervisor in the achievement of the production goals of the organization.

This chapter is intended to provide an insight into the problems encountered by a supervisor. Many of the examples of supervisory practices refer to the manufacturing supervisor; however, it should be recognized that the supervisor of an accounting section or an order processing group has essentially the same problems. In order to provide insight into supervisory practices the following topics are discussed: (1) The Supervisor's Job, (2) Training of Supervisors, and (3) Improving Supervisory Performance.

THE SUPERVISOR'S JOB

The terms *supervisor* and *foreman* are frequently used interchangeably; however, in this chapter the term *supervisor* is used since it is somewhat broader in its application and also implies one of the major functions of supervision—to supervise. The term *foreman* is usually limited to supervisors in manufacturing organizations or to those supervising semiskilled or unskilled workers. The title supervisor is applicable to those who direct the work of others in laboratories, offices, retail establishments, and sales organizations as well as to those directing the work of hourly paid employees in manufacturing concerns. By definition, a supervisor is a part of management. The supervisor's position in management is unique—it is the only level of management charged with the responsibility of directing the work of nonmanagerial employees. Members of middle and top management perform various administrative tasks, and if they do direct the work of others it is the work of other managers.[1] The supervisor's position, between the upper levels of management and the hourly nonmanagerial employees has been described rather caustically, if not disparagingly, as the "man in the middle"[2] and the "marginal man of industry."[3] The supervisor has also been referred to as both "master and victim of double talk" as well as being "victim, not monarch, of all he surveys."[4] It is important to recognize that the supervisor is in the middle and because of that sometimes ambiguous position we have the key to the primary function of the job—"the linking-pin function."[5] Before developing the concept of the linking-pin function, let us review the legal definition of the supervisor's job.

Legal Definition

As defined by federal legislation, a supervisor is:

. . . any individual having authority, in the interest of the employer, to hire, transfer, suspend, lay off, recall, promote, discharge, assign, reward, or discipline other employees, or responsibility to direct them, or to adjust their grievances, or effectively to recommend such action, if in connection with the foregoing the exercise of such authority is not of a merely routine or clerical nature, but requires the use of independent judgment.[6]

Another federal law, the Fair Labor Standards Act of 1938 (as amended), is often called the minimum wage law. One of its tests in determining whether or not a person is a supervisor is the amount of time spent performing work that is the same as that performed by the people under the supervisor's direction. Supervisors are expected to spend no more than 20 percent of their time doing the same kind of work that is performed by employees whom they are directing. In effect, the National Labor-Management Relations Act determines who is eligible to join an employees' union, and the Fair Labor Standards Act determines whether or not an employee is to be paid on an hourly basis (usually with overtime for hours in excess of a specified number) or whether the supervisor is to be paid a salary with no compensation required for overtime. Supervisors

---

[1] It is recognized that many members of middle and top management may have secretarial employees reporting to them, but the direction of these employees is incidental to the primary function which is usually administrative or the performance of a staff duty.

[2] B. B. Gardner and W. F. Whyte, "The Man in the Middle: Positions and Problems of the Foreman," *Applied Anthropology*, Vol. 4 (Winter, 1945), p. 1.

[3] D. E. Wray, "Marginal Man of Industry: The Foreman," *American Journal of Sociology*, Vol. 54 (January, 1949), p. 298.

[4] F. J. Roethlisberger, "The Foreman: Master and Victim of Double Talk," *Harvard Business Review*, Vol. 23 (September, 1945), p. 283.

[5] Rensis Likert, *New Patterns of Management* (New York City: McGraw-Hill Book Co., 1961), p. 113. Chapter 8, "An Integrating Principle and an Overview," p. 163, presents a detailed discussion of the linking-pin function of supervision.

[6] National Labor-Management Relations Act (Taft-Hartley), 1947 (as amended), Section 101, Subsection 2 (11).

cannot join a union of production or clerical employees; however, they can form a union composed entirely of supervisors. Supervisors are paid a salary and are exempt from the provisions of the law requiring compensation for overtime. Hence, supervisors are commonly called *exempt employees*.

The net result of these two pieces of legislation is that supervisors are by definition a part of management, but supervisors do not always view themselves as being the same as the other members of management.

The Self-Perception of Supervisors

We have mentioned that the supervisor's position is unique in that it requires interaction with nonmanagerial employees as well as with management. There is also a personal history characteristic that tends to set the supervisor apart from other members of management. Typically the first-line supervisor is promoted from the hourly ranks, and it is not at all unusual for the person to then supervise employees who have been known for years as friends and coworkers. Other levels of management usually start their careers as managers and are not in the position of having to change their attitudes as they advance in the organization. With this difference in background it is worthwhile to ask if the supervisor's self-perception is the same as other members of management.

Lyman W. Porter administered a self-description inventory consisting of 64 pairs of adjectives to 172 first-level supervisors, 291 upper level management personnel, and 320 hourly production employees.[7] Each person was required to check one adjective of each pair that in his or her opinion offered the best self-description. The results of this study show that supervisors most frequently see themselves as deliberate, calm, fair-minded, steady, responsible, civilized, self-controlled, logical, judicial, and honest. Upper level management personnel, a group including department heads, staff personnel, and vice-presidents, see themselves as resourceful, sharp witted, sincere, thoughtful, sociable, reliable, dignified, imaginative, adaptable, sympathetic, and generous. Hourly workers believe themselves to be ambitious, industrious, sharp witted, efficient, thoughtful, sociable, pleasant, reliable, and adaptable.

Note that there is a clear differentiation between each of the three groups. The supervisors see themselves as moderate, if not conservative, individuals who act as a stabilizing influence—an image not at all unsuited for "the man in the middle." The upper levels of management picture themselves as successful entrepreneurs who are imaginative, resourceful, and sharp witted; yet thoughtful, sympathetic, and dignified. The hourly worker is clearly on the way up. There does not seem to be any trend in self-image from the hourly ranks, through the supervisory group, to the upper levels of management. The supervisor's self-image does not retain the elements of the hourly image, nor has it acquired the outgoing self-confident characteristic of the higher levels of management.

---

[7] Lyman W. Porter, "Self-Perception of First-Level Supervisors Compared with Upper-Management Personnel and with Operative Line Workers," *Journal of Applied Psychology*, Vol. 44 (June, 1959), p. 183.

Another study in a nonmanufacturing situation compared the attitudes of supervisors and managers toward their respective jobs. The sample consisted of 404 supervisors and 317 managers of the General Services Administration, a government administrative agency providing supply, maintenance, and protection services. Both supervisors and managers completed a 50-item questionnaire. Eight job attitudes were measured for each group. They are (1) equity of rewards, (2) adequacy of the work force, (3) goal quality, (4) commitment or initiative in the organization, (5) adequacy of performance appraisal, (6) adequacy of authority and freedom, or autonomy, (7) planning and coordination of work, and (8) skill utilization in the organization. Supervisors expressed more negative attitudes than managers with respect to the factors of equity of rewards, adequacy of the work force, and the degree to which their skills were utilized. The supervisors' attitudes toward the equity of rewards may be due to the fact that typically there is not too great a differential in pay between that of a supervisor and the hourly worker being supervised, especially when one considers overtime earned by hourly workers. The second factor, adequacy of the work force, is the result of the supervisor's unique position. The supervisor is in direct contact with the work force while managers do not have such direct contact. The third factor in which supervisors differed, utilization of skill in the organization, shows that they perceive themselves as being capable of performing more responsible tasks.[8]

Dimensions of Supervisory Performance

The preceding discussion provides some insight concerning the way supervisors view themselves in comparison with other managers and in relation to hourly workers. It tells us little about the broad aspects of supervision or those factors that determine effective supervisory performance. The Sandia Corporation, in Albuquerque, New Mexico, wanted to know the independent dimensions or factors of administrative and general supervisory positions. Four hundred and fourteen supervisors were asked to write an essay describing the performance of the best supervisor that they knew at Sandia Corporation. The descriptive statements were tabulated and a questionnaire containing 303 items describing supervisory performance was constructed. Three hundred and seventy-two supervisors then applied this questionnaire as a checklist to develop a descriptive rating of the best and the worst supervisor they knew. These ratings were analyzed by means of multiple factor analysis, and six independent dimensions of supervisory performance were obtained:

1. Establishment of work climate
2. Management ethics
3. Self-development and subordinate development
4. Personal maturity and sensitivity

---

[8] Frank T. Paine and Martin J. Gannon, "Job Attitudes of Supervisors and Managers," *Personnel Psychology*, Vol. 26, No. 4 (Winter, 1973), p. 521.

5. Knowledge and execution of corporate policies
6. Technical job knowledge [9]

Establishment of Work Climate. Descriptive statements characteristic of this factor are: expects a day's work, disciplines when necessary, and expects only the best. Supervisors rating high in this respect establish and maintain high performance standards. They are goal oriented and, if necessary, place the attainment of stated objectives above the likes and dislikes of subordinates.

Management Ethics. The essence of this dimension is ethical behavior on the part of a supervisor in interacting with other supervisors and members of top management. The same ethical behavior is also shown in those relationships with subordinates. Statements characterizing this trait are: gives credit where due, honest in discussing development of subordinates, no under-the-table deals, and doesn't promise anything that cannot be done.

Self-Development and Subordinate Development. Effective supervisors are interested in personnel development—the growth of subordinates as well as their own. They attempt to make assignments interesting and challenging and try to know their subordinates better so that they may direct their growth. They encourage outside study and pursue such activity themselves. They try to keep up with the professional aspects of management through reading and participation in outside groups.

Personal Maturity and Sensitivity. Two elements are closely related in this factor; one is personal maturity and emotional stability, and the other is empathy—a sensitivity to the feelings of others. Supervisors strong in this dimension maintain an open door policy, they have a knack of saying the right thing at the right time, do not lose control under pressure, and seem to lighten serious situations with a sense of humor.

Knowledge and Execution of Corporate Policies. Note that knowledge of policy is not sufficient; there must also be execution of policy. Strong supervisors keep up with changes in policy and procedures and keep their subordinates informed of such changes. Those strong in this characteristic are orderly and tend to follow the letter of the law. The result of this trait is that it gives a supervisor's behavior consistency and predictability.

Technical Job Knowledge. This dimension of supervision suggests not only technical knowledge but also the drive and willingness to get the job done. Supervisors usually have sufficient background and information to understand a new problem quickly. They are generally technically competent and do more than that expected of them.

---

[9] Sherwood H. Peres, "Performance Dimensions of Supervisory Positions," *Personnel Psychology*, Vol. 15 (Winter, 1962), p. 405. Seven factors were isolated; however, the seventh factor is a bias factor resulting from the halo effect present in rating scales. It is not a true factor of supervisory performance.

The "Linking-Pin" Function

The legal definition of a supervisor cited at the beginning of this chapter details only the relationships between supervisor and subordinates. If questioned, many managers would also answer that a supervisor's job is to direct the work of subordinates. The preceding discussion of the dimensions of supervisory performance shows the narrowness and inadequacy of a definition that stresses the direction of subordinates. The analysis of supervisory positions at Sandia Corporation reveals that successful performance requires a person capable of much more than directing the efforts of others. Successful performance requires a structuring of the work situation; ethical behavior in personal relationships with superiors, peers, and subordinates; and effective execution of company policy.

The key to the primary function of supervision is the supervisor's singular position in the organization—the only member of management in direct contact with nonmanagerial personnel. As a result, the supervisor is the one member of management capable of linking management to operative personnel. For this reason the supervisor's major function is best described as a *linking-pin* function.[10]

Current Problems in Supervision

Though the Civil Rights Act of 1964, as amended, was passed more than a decade ago, its effect on organizations in both the public and private sectors has been relatively recent. Section 703 (1) of the Act makes it unlawful to discriminate on the basis of "race, color, religion, sex, or national origin." Though much has been written about the Act there have been relatively few research studies showing its effect on the supervisory process. One such study conducted in the private sector shows the effect of a minority hiring program on the first-line supervisor. Another study compares the leadership behavior of male and female supervisors.

Supervisor Role Conflict. In an effort to combat hard-core unemployment, a company employed 49 black males who met the following criteria: [11] they were between the ages of 21 and 50 years, residents of the inner city for a period of more than one year, and during the past two years had been employed for a period of less than six months. In addition, when last employed the employment had to be for a period of less than three consecutive months with the same employer. Prior to their actually going to work the supervisors to whom they would be assigned attended a special 12-hour training program divided into six equal sections of two hours each. During these training sessions anticipated problems and tentative solutions were discussed. Despite the preparation

---

[10] Rensis Likert, *New Patterns of Management* (New York City: McGraw-Hill, Inc., 1961), p. 113.

[11] This discussion is based on a study which was conducted in a large midwestern city: R. A. Hudson Rosen, "Foreman Role Conflict: An Expression of Contradictions in Organizational Goals," *Industrial and Labor Relations Review*, Vol. 23, No. 4 (July, 1970), pp. 541–552.

for the problems to be encountered, the employment of the hard-core unemployed created problems for the supervisors best expressed as *role ambiguity*—an inability to determine the proper supervisory role because of the conflicting messages being received.

The supervisors complained that they did not have adequate information on the newly hired employees. In part the complaint was true, because staff personnel had deliberately withheld some information concerning the background of individual workers since such information could bias the supervisors against the employees. The supervisors also complained that it was extremely difficult to communicate with the new employees. Perhaps the most serious complaint of all was that as supervisors they were forced to work with dual standards. For example, the management of the company indicated that the supervisors must accommodate the special group, but there was no change in expected production despite an excessively high absentee rate. Those employees who had been in the department prior to the special employment program complained that the new hires were being given preferential treatment, especially with regard to discipline and absenteeism.

There were many special problems to be solved by the supervisors. Much of the absenteeism was caused by inadequate transportation; so the supervisors had to advise these new employees concerning the bus routes and the establishment of car pools. There were also requests for advances in pay to tide them over until the first pay period. In addition, there were problems relating to poor health that resulted in taking an entire day off to go to a clinic rather than going to the company physician. All these problems took additional time, yet there seemed to be a lack of recognition on the part of higher supervision that the work load had increased. The supervisors were unable to get support and direction from top management stating what was expected of them. Thus, with the complaints of subordinates who resented the dual standards and the pressures from superiors who demanded the same level of performance, yet failed to recognize changed conditions, the supervisor's role became intolerably ambiguous.

A Comparison of Male and Female Supervisors. In addition to providing equal employment opportunities for minorities, the Civil Rights Act has been interpreted as protecting the rights of women. Again, much has been said about the utilization of women in supervisory and managerial roles. Yet there are relatively few studies that compare the performance of male and female supervisors in similar positions. Traditionally private industry has not employed women as supervisors to any great degree. However, the federal government has made efforts to promote women to supervisory positions. The following study compares the leader behavior of male and female supervisors.[12]

Day and Stogdill report the leader behavior of 37 male supervisors and 36 female supervisors who were civilian employees of the United States Air

[12] David R. Day and Ralph M. Stogdill, "Leader Behavior of Male and Female Supervisors: A Comparative Study," *Personnel Psychology*, Vol. 25, No. 2 (Summer, 1972), p. 353. This discussion is based on the study by Day and Stogdill.

Force Logistics Command in the continental United States. The leadership behavior of each group was analyzed with respect to leadership effectiveness, the relationship between leadership behavior and effectiveness, and the relationship between behavior, effectiveness, and biographical information for both male and female supervisors. In each instance, subordinates described the leader behavior and the effectiveness of their supervisors. The supervisory positions were comparable in nature.

The results of the study show that when rated by their immediate subordinates male and female supervisors occupying similar positions and performing similar functions show the same patterns of leadership behavior and effectiveness. Second, despite the description of leader behavior and effectiveness as being similar, such behavior and effectiveness are not related in the same manner for both groups with regard to advancement. For the male supervisors those rated as more effective advance more rapidly; whereas, the advancement of female supervisors is not related to effectiveness. Thus it seems that, though males and females as reported in this study exhibit the same behavior and the same degree of effectiveness, there is a difference in the rate of advancement. Despite the fact that the study was performed in the public sector, the federal government, there is no reason to assume that the behavior and effectiveness of female supervisors in the private sector would be any different than in the public sector.

TRAINING OF SUPERVISORS

"You could dispose of almost all the leadership training courses for supervision in American industry today without anyone knowing the difference." [13]

The above statement, made many years ago by Robert H. Guest, is not intended as a criticism of the content or methods of leadership training programs for supervisors. Instead, it is intended to emphasize that the demands of the supervisor's job, such as those described in the hard-core employment program, are often such that it is difficult, if not impossible, to exercise the type of leadership expected. Despite the very real limitations on supervisory leadership imposed by the structure of the job, much effort and money are spent on supervisory training. In addition to training in leadership, programs are designed to improve other skills necessary for effective supervision.

The content of supervisory training programs is geared to the needs of the supervisor. Thus, there is considerable variation in content and method from one organization to another, and within the same organization from one level of supervision to another. Figure 18–1 shows a useful classification proposed by Georgopoulos and Mann of the skills needed for supervision.[14] Note that

---

[13] Robert H. Guest, "Of Time and the Foreman," *Personnel* (New York City: American Management Association, 1956), p. 478.

[14] Basil S. Georgopoulos and Floyd C. Mann, *The Community General Hospital* (New York City: Macmillan Co., 1962), Chapter 9. Reprinted in Robert A. Sutermeister (ed.), *People and Productivity* (New York City: McGraw-Hill Book Co., 1963), p. 381.

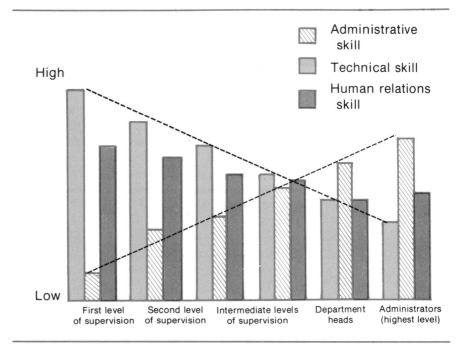

High

Administrative skill

Technical skill

Human relations skill

Low

First level of supervision   Second level of supervision   Intermediate levels of supervision   Department heads   Administrators (highest level)

Figure 18–1
RELATIVE
IMPORTANCE
OF
DIFFERENT
SUPERVISORY
SKILLS

Source: Basil S. Georgopoulos and Floyd C. Mann, *The Community General Hospital* (New York City: Macmillan Co., 1962), p. 431.

the range of supervisory positions included in Figure 18–1 is from the first level of supervision through department heads, and includes the highest level of administrators. With each step upward in the organizational hierarchy, the mix of supervisory skills changes. Technical skills are the skills and knowledge necessary for the performance of a given supervisory position in a specific industry. For the first-line supervisor, technical skills include the knowledge and skill required to perform jobs at the operational level. The technology of the industry must be known by the supervisors so that immediate subordinates can be trained. Administrative skills require a concept of the entire organizational system and the coordination of the component parts of the system. Planning, organizing, assigning work, and the establishment and exercise of necessary controls are administrative skills. For the first-line supervisor these skills are relatively less important than the technical and human relations skills. Human relations skills require a knowledge of the principles of behavior and an ability to work with subordinates, peers, and superiors. Let us examine briefly some of the content and methods of technical and administrative training.

Technical and Administrative Skills

Technical training has as its goal the understanding of the technical aspects of a supervisory position. The supervisor in manufacturing must understand the design, operating principles, and maintenance of production equipment; the specifications of raw materials and component parts; and the quality standards of the finished product. The technical phases of a data processing supervisor's position include a working knowledge of the principles used in the design of electronic equipment, an understanding of the binary number system, and the ability to prepare computer programs. Training in the administrative area acquaints the supervisor with company policies and procedures as they apply to a specific department. The supervisor must know purchasing procedures, production scheduling methods, and the company's cost accounting system. Knowledge of the application and interpretation of company personnel policies is also required. If there is a labor union, one should be familiar with the provisions of the labor agreement.

The content of training programs in the technical and administrative areas is dependent upon the technology and administrative procedures of each individual company. As a result, most training programs are designed and conducted internally. The methods used are traditional in nature and rely heavily on written materials such as technical manuals and statements of company policy and procedure. Formal classes are held at periodic intervals and may be supplemented by departmental meetings. In many large companies supervisors are furnished bound volumes of company policies and operating procedures to serve as a basis for technical and administrative decisions.

Training in Human Relations

Training in human relations poses problems not present in the development of skills in the technical and administrative fields. First, there is no concise definition of subject matter to be mastered. Second, there is typically a marked disparity between responses given in answer to written questions and the ability to transfer knowledge into effective supervisory patterns. Third, training in human relations requires the use of teaching methods quite different from those employed in the technical and administrative areas. Training programs in human relations stress (1) communications, with particular emphasis on empathetic listening—the perception of the meaning and feeling of communications from subordinates; (2) the making of decisions involving people based on the perceptions gained from empathetic listening; and (3) overcoming resistance to change, usually through the use of a participative leadership style.

In this section we present a brief overview of the methods used in human relations training and review experimental studies illustrative of specific problems in human relations encountered by all supervisors. The methods used in developing skills in human relations include the *case method*, the *incident process*, and *role playing*. Each of these methods is discussed briefly below.

Case Method. The case method of leadership training utilizes case problems much like those contained in this book. The case problem usually sets forth a sequence of events in such a manner that a question calling for a solution is posed. Or, as in Case Problem 18-A, No Smoking, the solution is provided as part of the case and the learner is asked to evaluate the given solution. In order to solve a case problem it is necessary to acquaint the participant with the principles or procedures to be applied, a task usually accomplished by lectures or assigned readings. Case problems should describe a situation that is part of the learner's background or a situation that is understandable to all learners. The case method arouses greater interest than that created by answering questions not related to a specific situation. Also, a case problem offers a chance to apply the principles and methods to be learned. Thus, the case problem offers an opportunity to increase interest, to participate in discussion, and to illustrate the application of principles, policies, or methods to simulated or real situations.

Incident Process Method. The incident process method, a variation of the case method, is used in small discussion groups. If Case Problem 18-A were rewritten as an incident, the incident described could be the fact that the supervisor discharged a worker for violating the no smoking regulations of the company. A bare statement of the fact—discharge for violation of a no smoking rule—cannot be evaluated without additional information. In the incident method, participants draw from the discussion leader all the information necessary to make a sound evaluation of the action taken and to recommend alternative courses that may have been available. Skill in questioning is developed by the incident method and experience is gained in gathering information needed in order to make sound decisions in the area of human relations.

Role Playing. The role-playing method offers the advantages of the case method and, in addition, provides training in the perception of the attitudes and feelings of other persons. As the name suggests, role playing is the assignment of a definite role to each member of a training group. There is usually a brief explanation and discussion of the supervisory problem under study prior to the assignment of roles.

Case Problem 18-A may be adapted for role playing in the following manner. The supervisors of the plant in which the smoking incident occurred might attend a company training session concerned with the enforcement of company rules. The rules may be explained, the need for their enforcement stated, and the duties of the union steward described. Following this general session for all supervisors, groups of three or four meet separately and each member of the small group is assigned a specific role. One is selected to be the supervisor, another the steward, and the remaining members assume the role of the employee in question who, in this instance, acts as an observer and evaluates the effectiveness of the steward in representing the case and the equity of the supervisor's decision. Each member is given a written statement describing the role to be assumed and is not aware of the details of the roles of the others in the group. The supervisor's statement may indicate that the employee *must* be discharged and cite as a reason the fire in a neighboring plant and the need to enforce company rules. The supervisor's role may or may not specify the employee's long service record. The steward's role emphasizes that one who violates the rule is only subject to discharge, and the long, faithful record of the employee may be outlined for the steward. Remaining members of the small group—no more than one or two—are asked to evaluate the behavior of the supervisor and the steward from the standpoint of an employee with long seniority who has admittedly violated a rule.[15] Roles may be rotated either within the same group or by forming new groups. Either way, each participant has the opportunity to assume the role of the supervisor and the steward and to evaluate the incident as the employee. Role playing is particularly effective in developing empathy—the understanding of the other person's feelings and attitudes.[16]

Specific Problems in Leadership Training

Let us study in detail two specific problems in the area of leadership training. The first is concerned with discipline; the second, with the effectiveness of training in group decision making.

Discipline. Maintaining discipline is one of the perennial problems of supervision. In general, there are two approaches to disciplinary problems: (1) a *judicial* approach—determining the rightness or wrongness of an act as defined by a specific rule and applying the penalty prescribed and (2) a *human relations* approach—an emphasis on problem solving with an ultimate goal of improving the employee's behavior.[17] A judicial approach may be forced on a supervisor by his or her superior as intimated in Case Problem 18-A. Some supervisors, by reason of personality, may be rigid, insecure, and incapable of flexibility. These persons find in the rule and its prescribed penalty a ready-made justification for their own rigidity. Still others would prefer the human relations approach but are fearful of where it may lead—they envision an ultimate state of complete anarchy. The studies described below show how supervisors tend to enforce company rules and point up the need for training in human relations.

The subjects of the study were approximately 500 supervisors from a variety of industries attending the Foremen's Conferences held at the University of Michigan.[18] Following a lecture on attitudes and how to understand them, the supervisors were divided into workshop groups to study a "No Smoking" case using the role-playing method. Each of the 172 role-playing units consisted of three persons: the supervisor, the steward, and the employee. The case was much like Case Problem 18-A, with one important exception—the penalty for violating the rule was a three-day layoff rather than a discharge. The roles assigned made it clear that a violation of the rule had occurred, and that the

---

[15] The following article discusses the factors influencing decisions concerning disciplinary actions: Benton Rosen and Thomas H. Jerdee, "Factors Influencing Disciplinary Judgments," *Journal of Applied Psychology*, Vol. 59, No. 3 (June, 1974), p. 327.

[16] Norman R. F. Maier and Lester F. Zerfoss, "MRP: A Technique for Training Large Groups of Supervisors and Its Potential Use in Social Research," *Human Relations*, Vol. 5 (May, 1952), p. 177. This article is a relatively brief statement of the multiple role-playing technique. For a more detailed treatment of role playing, see Norman R. F. Maier, Allen R. Solem, and Ayesha A. Maier, *Supervisory and Executive Development*, A Manual for Role Playing (New York City: John Wiley & Sons, 1957).

[17] Norman R. F. Maier and Lee E. Danielson, "An Evaluation of Two Approaches to Discipline in Industry," *Journal of Applied Psychology*, Vol. 40 (October, 1956), p. 319.

[18] *Ibid.*

worker knew the rule had been violated and knew the penalty involved. The worker acted as an observer in the role-playing situation, with the interaction occurring between the supervisor and the steward who was instructed to press the worker's case. A 20-minute time limit was placed on the discussion between the supervisor and the steward.

Maier and Danielson found that slightly over half the supervisors (52 percent) used the human relations approach and resolved the problem with an adjusted solution that did not call for the three-day layoff penalty. Adjusted solutions ranged from no penalty, a warning or reprimand, or a one- or two-day layoff. Thirty-five percent of the supervisors followed the judicial approach and found the worker guilty, invoked the penalty, and refused to change their positions. The problem was not settled in the alloted time by 13 percent of the supervisors. The human relations approach resulted in greater satisfaction as judged by all three participants with a problem-solving type interview rather than argumentative, and the worker seemed more satisfied with the actions of the steward and less inclined to restrict future production. In another study the same authors found that only 7 percent of the supervisors in a similar role-playing situation laid off a worker who violated a safety rule.[19] In the safety case the situation was ambiguous; i.e., the supervisor was not sure that the employee, a lineman for a utility company, was wearing his safety belt and the penalty was much more severe—a three-week layoff. Despite the fact that 45 percent of the participants who played the role of the lineman admitted violating the safety rule, only 7 percent were laid off in accordance with the prescribed penalty.

These two studies indicate that supervisors are inclined to use the human relations approach to discipline. Further, the formulation of strict rules with no latitude in their interpretation poses a dilemma for the supervisor. However, if the supervisor uses judgment and modifies the penalty, the wishes of the higher echelon are not being followed. Yet, by enforcing the letter of the law, the supervisor is demonstrating a lack of understanding and harshness toward subordinates.

Training for Decision Making. In another study Maier investigated the effect of training in group decision making.[20] Forty-four role-playing groups of supervisors were given an eight-hour presentation of the methods of group decision making. These experimental groups also participated in four hours of discussion that permitted them to ask questions and to express their attitudes toward the role-playing problem which was introduced as part of the training. The 36 control groups were given no training in group decision methods, but were given one half hour of instruction explaining the role-playing situation. The problem is a proposed change in method—a change sure to arouse resistance—for a group of three workers who normally rotate three production jobs

---

[19] Lee E. Danielson and Norman R. F. Maier, "Supervisory Problems in Decision Making," *Journal of Applied Psychology*, Vol. 40 (October, 1956), p. 319.

[20] Norman R. F. Maier, "An Experimental Test of the Effect of Training on Discussion Leadership," *Human Relations Journal*, Vol. 6 (May, 1953), p. 161.

among themselves at the end of each hour during an eight-hour day. There is a variation in the length of time it takes each worker to perform the duties of each position as shown in Table 18–1, Time Per Operation. A methods engineer has suggested that the work be assigned on a permanent basis as follows: Jack to the first position, Steve to the second position, and Walt to the third position.

Table 18–1 TIME PER OPERATION

	Position 1	Position 2	Position 3	Total
Jack	3 min.	4 min.	4½ min.	11½ min.
Walt	3½ min.	3½ min.	3 min.	10 min.
Steve	5 min.	3½ min.	4½ min.	13 min.
				34½ min.

SOURCE: Norman R. F. Maier, "An Experimental Test of the Effect of Training on Discussion Leadership," *Human Relations Journal*, Vol. 6 (May, 1953), p. 164. This table was originally published by John Wiley & Sons in Norman R. F. Maier's *Principles of Human Relations*, Applications to Management, 1952.

The reduction in time would amount to 2¼ minutes per cycle, a savings of 17 percent or 80 minutes per eight-hour day. In other words, compared to the optimum solution, the men are now loafing 80 minutes a day.

In the role-playing situation, the supervisor desires to install the solution recommended by the methods engineer and is met with varying degrees of resistance on the part of each of the three workers. The result of the role-playing situations for trained and untrained supervisors, Table 18–2—Percentage of Successes, Failures, and Compromises of Trained and Untrained Groups—

Table 18–2 PERCENTAGE OF SUCCESSES, FAILURES, AND COMPROMISES OF TRAINED AND UNTRAINED GROUPS

	Failures	Compromises	Successes
Trained leader	4.5	36.4	59.1
Untrained leader	50.0	0	50.0

SOURCE: Norman R. F. Maier, "An Experimental Test of the Effect of Training on Discussion Leadership," *Human Relations Journal*, Vol. 6 (May, 1953), p. 168. This table was originally published by John Wiley & Sons in Norman R. F. Maier's *Principles of Human Relations*, Applications to Management, 1952.

shows clearly the effect of training. Only 4½ percent of the trained supervisors experience failure—with failure being defined as no solution, no change, or open rebellion against the supervisor's imposed solution. On the other hand, 50 percent of the untrained leaders experienced failure. However, the striking result is that the untrained leader did not produce a single compromise. It must be pointed out that many compromise solutions might in practice be the optimum, or best solution, since the compromises contained varying plans for rotation of jobs to minimize the effects of monotony and boredom on production.[21]

IMPROVING SUPERVISORY PERFORMANCE

In Chapter 15, "Motivation in Organizations," it is stated that no consistent relationship is found between measures of employee morale and productivity. Fortunately there is a distinct positive relationship between supervisory practices and productivity. There are many characteristics of effective supervisory action; however, four stand out above all others. The first factor determining effective supervision, *organizational climate*, is largely beyond the control of supervisors and determines how effectively they may exercise the other three characteristics of sound supervision. Good practices in *delegation*, the second factor, are necessary for effective supervision. The third requisite for effective supervision is an orientation toward the job, best described as a *situational* approach, with a balanced emphasis on the task and the maintenance of good relations with subordinates. The fourth requirement is an ability to use *employee participation* skillfully to introduce change.

Organizational Climate

The quotation from Guest's "Of Time and the Foreman," appearing at the beginning of the preceding section on training, dramatizes the limiting effects of organizational climate on the efficacy of training. Fleishman also emphasizes the limitations of training unless the "leadership climate" is such that supervisors can readily put to use their newly found skills.[22] Organizational or leadership climate is made up of the attitudes and practices of top management and is reflected by the extent that management practices delegation, the degree that it recognizes the organization as a system, and its use of participation as a method of introducing change. Yet the chief advantage gained by a supervisor from the organizational climate created by higher management is increased *influence* or power in relation to immediate subordinates.

Pelz and others of the University of Michigan's Survey Research Center show that a supervisor's influence or power has a great deal to do with productivity and employee satisfaction.[23] In work groups having high production records,

---

[21] The following book is of interest in the training of supervisors: Arnold P. Goldstein and Melvin Sorcher, *Changing Supervisor Behavior* (Elmsford, New York: Pergamon Press, 1974).

[22] Edwin A. Fleishman, Edwin F. Harris, and Harold E. Burtt, "Leadership and Supervision in Industry." Reprinted in Robert A. Sutermeister (ed.), *People and Productivity* (New York City: McGraw-Hill Book Co., 1963), p. 410. This reading is a re-edited and up-to-date version of Chapter 9 of *Leadership and Supervision in Industry* (Columbus, Ohio: Bureau of Educational Research, Ohio State University, 1955) by the same three authors.

[23] Donald C. Pelz, "Influence: A Key to Effective Leadership in the First-Line Supervisor," *Personnel*, Vol. 39 (November, 1952), p. 209.

A more recent study by Ronan indicates that direct supervision is significant as a determinant of positive relationships between job satisfaction and behavior on the job. W. W. Ronan, "Individual and Situational Variables Relating to Job Satisfaction," *Journal of Applied Psychology Monograph*, Vol. 54, No. 1 (February, 1970), p. 1.

promotions recommended by supervisors were generally approved by higher management; or no recommendations were made at all. On the other hand, the supervisors of low-producing groups frequently made recommendations for promotions that were not approved by higher authority. Three factors seem to contribute most to a supervisor's influence: (1) the supervisor's contribution to decisions made by superiors, (2) the freedom and autonomy exercised in the operation of one's own department, and (3) salary, interpreting salary as a measure of responsibility and status within the organization. Note that these conditions determining the amount of supervisory influence are not the direct result of a supervisor's actions within his or her own department or something that may be asked for and received; these traits are a reflection of the supervisor's position and status in the organization—the result of organizational climate.

Improved Delegation

One of the keys to effective supervision, as measured by productivity and employee satisfaction, is the ability to delegate responsibility to subordinates and to allow as much leeway in the performance of assigned duties as the situation permits. Improvement in delegation requires that the supervisor have a clear perception of the leader's role and that a careful study be made to determine how closely the work of subordinates should be followed. Let us discuss, first, the differentiation of the supervisor's role.

Differentiating the Supervisor's Role. Dr. Robert L. Kahn and Dr. Daniel Katz, in a summary of much of the work of the Survey Research Center of the University of Michigan, report that supervisors of groups with high production records assume a role that is more differentiated from the work of those supervised than the role assumed by the supervisors of low-producing work groups.[24] High-producing supervisors perform those tasks traditionally associated with the managerial functions of planning, organizing, directing, and controlling. The differentiation between the task of the worker and the supervisor begins with the supervisor's self-perception as a member of management and an understanding of the functions of management. At the same time, subordinates have an unusually acute perception of what their supervisor is doing in comparison with what should be done. The supervisory task perceived most readily by subordinates is that of planning the work to be done. Members of high-producing railroad section gangs and departments in a tractor manufacturing company rate their supervisors as superior in planning work, providing materials, and watching or supervising the performance of the work. Supervisors with better-than-average production records also spend more time than their low-producing counterparts in solving the interpersonal problems arising in the work group. Low-producing supervisors are prone to get lost in paper work and

---

[24] Robert L. Kahn and Daniel Katz, "Leadership Practices in Relation to Productivity and Morale," from Dorwin Cartwright and Alvin Zander (eds.), *Group Dynamics*, Research and Theory (2d ed.; Evanston, Ill.: Row, Peterson & Co., 1961), p. 554.

spend too much of their time doing the same type of work performed by subordinates. Supervisory tasks include not only the planning function but also directing on-the-job training.

Closeness of Supervision. The supervisor who spends a large percentage of time performing those tasks normally associated with supervision is delegating authority and assigning responsibility. The supervision of hourly workers is primarily the assignment of responsibility to perform work. However, the delegator still remains accountable for the performance of assigned duties. Close supervision is associated with excessively detailed instructions, constant checking on progress, and insistence that all decisions be approved before being put into effect. However, a careful engineering of the work to be performed and the establishment and exercise of necessary controls to assure proper progress are not considered excessively close supervision; instead, they are part of the normal supervisory function. Closeness of supervision refers primarily to the personal conduct of the supervisor, and when supervision becomes too close, it is a reflection of the supervisor's own insecurity and inability to delegate.

In studies of clerical workers in an insurance company and production workers manufacturing tractors, it is found that there is an inverse relationship between closeness of supervision and productivity; i.e., the closer the supervision, the lower the productivity. Also, the closeness of supervision has a great deal to do with the three dimensions of employee morale. Employees not closely supervised are more likely to have a high degree of satisfaction with their jobs, their supervisors, and the company, than those who are closely supervised. However, there is evidence that closeness of supervision is in many instances a reflection of the type of supervision received by the supervisor. If a superior fully delegates authority, the supervisor is likely to do the same. But when the supervisor is closely supervised, it is difficult for the process of delegation to occur.

A Situational Approach

Much has been written about supervisors being either *production centered* or *employee centered* with respect to attitudes concerning the work of their departments and their subordinates. Early research in the area of job satisfaction and morale implicitly assumed that the orientation of the supervisor is best described in terms of a continuum with production-centered concepts at one pole and employee-centered concepts at the other extreme. However, later studies, particularly those conducted at the tractor company, cast doubt upon the usefulness of a continuum as a model for describing supervisory orientation. High-producing workers at the tractor company reported, as might be expected, that their supervisor took an interest in them, that they got along well with him, and that he was easy to talk to. Yet, they also stated that production was important to their supervisor and that he supervised them in such a manner that production standards were met—a situation quite impossible to describe on a continuum model.[25]

Dr. Robert L. Kahn suggests that we use a four-celled table to describe the orientation of the supervisor.[26] In one cell are those supervisors who are high in their interest in production and at the same time have a high interest in the welfare of their employees. Another cell would best describe those with a high orientation toward production but low in employee-centered attitudes. The third square would fit those low in production but high in employee-centered interests. The fourth possibility consists of those supervisors with low interests in both production and employees. In effect, the four-celled table represents a systems orientation, with the most effective supervisor recognizing simultaneously the goals and needs of the organization and its members.

At first glance it may seem quite impossible to be production centered and employee centered at one and the same time. Such is not the case provided the supervisor meets the following three requirements. First, the supervisor must make clear that high but realistic and attainable standards of performance are expected. In so doing the tenor of the operation is established. Second, the supervisor must have the power to deliver appropriate rewards or punishment if the stated goals are to mean anything. Third, the supervisor must demonstrate to the satisfaction of subordinates that supervisory power is used effectively. One of the best ways of demonstrating a wise use of power and influence is a willingness to go to bat for subordinates when the need arises. But the supervisor does not stand alone in meeting these three conditions. The management that the supervisor represents must create the climate to make possible the exercise of an effective emphasis on production and at the same time a concern for subordinates.

Participation and Change

Overcoming resistance to change is a problem confronting all levels of supervision. The proposed change in method or content may have little direct effect on the worker's ability to perform his or her job, or the change may be of such a nature that the learning of new skills or the transfer of existing skills to a new work situation is required. Regardless of the amount or type of change, there are varying degrees of resistance that are manifested by an extremely long period of time to learn the new job, open expressions of hostility toward management, or an increase in the number of voluntary terminations of employment. One explanation that has been offered for resistance to change is that the rate of learning for the new job is inhibited because of its similarity to

---

[25] The following two review articles are recommended as summaries of the literature concerning supervisory style:

Stephen M. Sales, "Supervisory Style and Productivity: Review and Theory," *Personnel Psychology*, Vol. 19, No. 3 (Autumn, 1966), p. 275.

Abraham K. Korman, " 'Consideration,' 'Initiating Structure,' and Organizational Criteria—Review," *Personnel Psychology*, Vol. 19, No. 4 (Winter, 1966), p. 349.

[26] Robert L. Kahn, "Productivity and Job Satisfaction," *Personnel Psychology*, Vol. 13 (Autumn, 1960), p. 275.

the old job. For example, an expert typist may experience greater difficulty initially in learning the finger movements required in playing a piano than one with no skill in typing. However, research indicates that resistance is caused by psychological factors and may be controlled by using participation when introducing change.

The Coch and French experiments concerning resistance to change were conducted in the plant of the Harwood Manufacturing Company, a garment manufacturer in Marion, Virginia. Harwood's employees are paid on a piece-rate incentive system, with 60 units representing the standard production for one hour. Further, the company normally tries to cushion the effects of change by conducting orientation programs and by paying a special bonus to those affected by change. Despite these efforts, any change in production methods usually results in failure to meet production standards in the same length of time required by a new employee to learn the job, an increase in the number of resignations, and expressions of hostility toward the management of the company.

In the experiments, four groups of employees were studied. Group One, the control group, had the change introduced in the usual fashion, with no participation on the part of employees in the change. However, the reasons for the change were presented to them in a meeting. Group Two elected representatives who participated in developing the change and were trained as special operators to work out the details of the change prior to its being adopted by the entire group. In Groups Three and Four, the total participation groups, all employees participated from the very beginning in developing the need for the change and working out the details of how the changed jobs should be performed. Though the changes made in the jobs varied for each group, they were comparable and minor in nature. Group One, pajama pressers, formerly stacked their finished work in lots of one-half dozen on pieces of cardboard. The change required them to stack their finished work in one-half dozen lots in boxes. Group Two had to alter their method of folding pajama coats, while Groups Three and Four, inspectors, were required only to cut certain threads from the garment and inspect all seams instead of cutting all loose threads and inspecting all seams.

Resistance developed in the control group immediately. There was conflict with the methods engineer, grievances were filed, and 17 percent of the group quit during the first 40 days after the change. As a group they did not reach the standard of 60 units an hour. Group Two, the one with elected representation, produced 61 units per hour at the end of 14 days; also, there was only one act of aggression against a supervisor and no layoffs during the first 40 days after the change. The two total participation groups recovered faster than Group Two. There was a slight drop in production the first day of change, but it immediately rose to 14 percent above prechange levels. There were no acts of aggression, nor any quits during the first 40 days. Later the remaining members of the control group were reassembled as a unit and a change was introduced in their work; but this time they participated in the change. As expected, they performed in the same way as the total participation group had.

The results of these experiments are clear—participation reduces resistance to change. Yet two limitations must be presented. Participation in the introduction of change is not decided by the supervisor; it is an expression of organizational climate. Second, at the present time there is no record of a company that has used total participation to introduce change over an extended period of time. Thus, the question arises as to how effective participation would be in overcoming resistance to change if it were a normal operating procedure.[27]

Case Problem 18-B, The New Truck Problem, is different from the other cases you have analyzed in that its solution calls for role playing.[28] You may be asked to assume the role of the foreman or one of the repairmen. If you are not a participant, you will be asked to observe and evaluate the decision made by the foreman.

Case Problem 18-B

THE NEW TRUCK PROBLEM

"General Instructions for Crew.

"You are repairmen for a large company and drive to various locations in the city to do your work. Each of you drives a small truck and you take pride in keeping it looking good. You have a possessive feeling about your trucks and like to keep them in good running order. Naturally you like to have new trucks, too, because a new truck gives you a feeling of pride.

"Here are some of the facts about the trucks and the men in the crews who report to Walt Marshall, the supervisor of repairs.

"George—17 years with the company, has a 2-year-old Ford truck.

"Bill—11 years with the company, has a 5-year-old Dodge truck.

"John—10 years with the company, has a 4-year-old Ford truck.

"Charlie—5 years with the company, has a 3-year-old Ford truck.

"Hank—3 years with the company, has a 5-year-old Chevrolet truck.

"Most of you do all your driving in the city, but John and Charlie cover the suburbs.

"In acting your part, accept the facts as given as well as assume the attitudes supplied in your specific role. From this point on let your feelings develop in accordance with the events that transpire in the role-playing process. When facts or events arise which are not covered by the roles, make up things which are consistent with the way it might be in a real-life situation."

---

[27] For an interesting account of how an organizational climate conducive to change was established for two companies brought together as a result of a merger the following is recommended: Alfred J. Marrow, David G. Bowers, and Stanley E. Seashore, *Management by Participation*, Creating a Climate for Personal and Organizational Development (New York City: Harper & Row, Publishers, 1967).

[28] Norman R. F. Maier and Lester F. Zerfoss, "MRP: A Technique for Training Large Groups of Supervisors and Its Potential Use in Social Research," *Human Relations*, Vol. 5 (May, 1952), p. 180.

Note to Instructor: Since role playing requires that participants be unaware of hidden motivations of others in the role-playing situation, the roles of the crew are not included in the case. They are in the instructor's manual and should be reproduced on separate sheets of paper and distributed prior to the role playing.

Since this problem differs from previous problems in the text—in that role playing is involved—you may wish to consider the following questions in making your decision(s).

PROBLEMS

1. What is your reaction to the role you played?
2. Do you agree with the decision made by the foreman as to who should receive the new truck?
3. Which of the repairmen do you think should receive the new truck?
4. Do you think seniority should be given primary consideration in solving this problem? Or should the condition of the repairman's truck and his area of driving be emphasized?
5. How does role playing serve as an effective means for training supervisors?

CHAPTER QUESTIONS FOR STUDY AND DISCUSSION

1. The supervisor has been described as being "the man in the middle." Is this characterization borne out by the two legal definitions of the supervisor? How?

2. What inferences could you make concerning the organizational climate of a company whose supervisors petitioned for a union of their own? As a member of middle or top management, what action would you recommend upon receiving notification of such a petition?

3. Recognizing that most supervisors are promoted from the hourly ranks, why is there such a cleavage between the hourly worker's self-description and the self-perception of the supervisor?

4. Discuss and give an example showing the significance of each of the dimensions of supervisory performance as described by Peres.

5. What is meant by the "linking-pin" function? How is this function related to the supervisor's position in the organization? Is it of significance in the motivation of employees? How?

6. The Day and Stogdill study reports that male supervisors advance more rapidly than female supervisors even when both have the same degree of leadership effectiveness. Why? Discuss.

7. Comment on the following statement: You could dispose of almost all of

the leadership training courses for supervision in American industry today without anyone knowing the difference.

8. Describe and give an example illustrating the methods commonly used for training in human relations.

9. Define in your own terms the meaning of organizational climate.

10. Evaluate each of the factors that contributes to a supervisor's influence. Which do you believe to be the most important? Relate the concept of influence and the performance of college graduates in training positions.

11. What major factor limits the applicability of participation as a means of introducing change? What is the next step if employees fail to see the need for change?

5 Managerial Control

The three chapters of this section discuss the control function of management—a three-step process of setting standards, measuring current performance against standards, and taking corrective action when necessary to bring performance in line with standards. The characteristics of good control are summarized. Commonly used nonbudgetary controls, ranging from personal observation and reports to the more complex break-even and time-event-network techniques, are examined. Internal audit programs, with emphasis on the relatively new human resource accounting procedures and ratio analysis, are also among the nonbudgetary controls examined in Chapter 20. A discussion of budgetary controls follows. Types of budgets are discussed and the methods of securing flexibility with budgets are described. The concept of zero-base budgeting is introduced.

The third step in the control process, the taking of corrective action, touches on the lives of people. Attitudes held toward control are as important as techniques of control in determining the success of managerial control. The last part of Chapter 21 discusses behavioral reactions to all controls, nonbudgetary as well as budgetary. The typical control procedure, a seemingly endless cycle of control, resistance, and more control, is analyzed in terms of its effect on people. The reasons for resistance to controls and the unfavorable responses to controls are presented in detail. The chapter closes with recommendations for the effective use of controls.

Chapter 19

The Basis of Control

Case Problem 19-A

A NEED FOR CONTROL

Standard Building Service Company of St. Louis is a 15-year old company that provides janitorial services for office buildings and industrial plants. Standard was purchased five years ago by Leslie Waller and, at the time of the purchase, annual sales were approximately $500,000. In three years she was able to double the sales volume to the present level of $1,000,000, but for the past two years sales volume has remained relatively constant. Waller attributes the lack of growth for the past two years to her being unable to call on new accounts because the business has grown to such an extent that her full energies and time are required in solving the myriad of problems that arise each day. She recognizes that the few new accounts she does obtain do no more than offset the normal turnover of accounts lost each month.

Janitorial services are usually performed after the tenants have left the building for the day; consequently, very few of Standard's employees start work before 6 p.m. Waller has found from experience that in order to keep employees, she must offer them at least 20 hours of work a week. On the other hand, very few people seem willing to work more than 25 hours a week. As a result,

the work force of approximately 275 men and women are part-time employees. Waller also found that by hiring persons presently employed she is assured of stable, motivated employees. However, since her employees are working full time elsewhere, there is considerable resistance when supervisors expect an above average amount of work from them.

A recent analysis of the 121 accounts serviced by the company shows that 40 customers require the services of only one person working a maximum of 25 hours a week. Thirty-five accounts require two people with total worker-hours ranging from 35 to 50 hours a week. Fifteen accounts require an average of 100 worker-hours a week, thus utilizing the services of up to four employees. There is one large industrial plant that requires 500 hours of service each week and approximately 20 workers. The remaining 30 accounts range between 100 and 400 worker-hours each week, and require between four and sixteen employees.

Waller is not sure which size job yields the most profit. Jobs are priced on a rule-of-thumb basis and depend upon the type of floor surfaces, the amount of building traffic, number and types of offices, and other similar factors. Waller and one of her two full-time supervisors estimate the number of workers needed for each new job. An analysis of company records shows that for the past five years variable costs—direct labor and materials (waxes, detergents, etc.)—average about 80 to 85 percent of total revenue.

The full-time organization consists of Waller, two supervisors, a secretary, an accountant, and a supply person who also maintains some of the large pieces of cleaning equipment such as the floor polishers. In addition, there are five part-time supervisors, each of whom supervises 40 to 50 workers in a given geographic area of the city. Most of their time and energy is spent in delivering supplies and materials to the various buildings within a given geographic area of the city. They also reassign personnel as the need arises and collect the weekly time cards. The two full-time supervisors have no specific duties assigned to them nor is either one responsible for the work of any particular part-time supervisor.

At the present time Waller has only two sources of information to guide her in the operation of her business. One of these is customer complaints, which serve as a check on the quality of work. The other is the weekly payroll, which is prepared by a local bank. Each week time cards are submitted to the bank and from these records payroll checks are prepared. The bank also maintains the necessary social security and income tax records. In addition, a summary is prepared showing the total worker-hours per week for each job. At present, no consistent use is made of this information. However, on the occasions when she has examined these weekly reports, Waller has found that the total hours per week run as much as 400 hours in excess of the number of hours used in computing the price of the services. There is no record of the use of supplies for each job.

PROBLEMS

1. Is there a need for control in this company?
2. If controls are needed, what areas of the business are most in need of control?
3. What type of standards are now being used? What kind would you recommend?
4. How can the organization be modified to improve the control function?

The control function is one of the four major functions of the process of management. The usual sequence assigned to these functions places planning first, next is organizing, the third is the human relations function—frequently called leading—and the last function is control. The word *control* and its position in the management process sequence are indicative of the nature of the control function. In this chapter we will first examine the nature of the control function, and, second, we will study in detail the steps of the control process. The characteristics of effective controls are then discussed and from this discussion several principles of control are developed.

THE NATURE OF CONTROL

If plans were never in need of revision and were executed flawlessly by a perfectly balanced organization under the direction of an omnipotent leader, there would be no need for control. However, as Robert Burns observed years ago, "The best laid schemes o' mice an' men gang aft agley." [1] In addition, organizations do not always work smoothly and need revision to meet changing conditions. Also, the effectiveness of leadership is often open to question. It is the purpose of the control function to take the corrective action necessary to assure the fulfillment of organizational objectives. Although control denotes corrective action that may be objective in all respects, the reactions of those subjected to controls may be highly emotionalized and tinged with resentment. The reason for this reaction is that control always touches the people who make up organizations, for they are charged with responsibilities and are accountable to their superiors for the performance of these duties. When determining whether goals are being met, it is the performance of the people of the organization that is actually being reviewed. One way of developing an understanding of the nature of control is to place the control function in perspective within the framework of a systems concept.

Cybernetics and Control

The study of how dynamic systems maintain a state of equilibrium, or steady state, though subject to changing environmental conditions is called *cybernetics*.[2] Examples of cybernetic systems are numerous and familiar. The thermostat maintains the temperature of a room at a predetermined level by making or breaking an electrical circuit that starts or stops the furnace. The rotating arms of a steam engine governor rise or fall with changes in centrifugal force, thereby controlling the input of steam into the cylinders of the engine with the result that a constant speed is maintained under varying load conditions. Another example is a photoelectric cell placed in a circuit to turn on lights in the evening when daylight illumination decreases to a predetermined level and to turn off the artificial lighting the next morning when natural illumination is sufficient.

The above examples of cybernetic systems illustrate the major characteristics of such systems. First, there is a predetermined steady state or equilibrium to be maintained. In the first example, a constant temperature is the state of equilibrium to be maintained; the second illustration focuses upon speed as the steady state, and the third example uses a predetermined intensity of light as the state of equilibrium. Second, in all the above instances there is constant change in the environment within which the system operates, thus forcing adjustments

---

[1] The closing stanza of Robert Burns "To A Mouse" is a statement that could be made by many of today's executives:

Still thou art blest, compared wi' me!
The present only toucheth thee.
But och! I backward cast my e'e
     On prospects drear!
And forward though I cannot see,
     I guess an' fear!

[2] For a discussion of the comparative values of the homeostatic and the cybernetic paradigms for control, the following is recommended: Geert Hofstede, "The Poverty of Management Control Philosophy," *The Academy of Management Review*, Vol. 3, No. 3 (July, 1978), p. 450.

within the system in order to maintain an equilibrium; hence, the term *dynamic system*. Third, there is a transfer of information from the external environment to within the system. The "information" that activates the thermostat is a change in temperature; centrifugal force is the information transmitted by the steam engine governor, and the intensity of light is the information received by the photoelectric cell. Fourth, there is a mechanical device so designed that corrective action is taken, with the result that the equilibrium of the system is maintained. The bimetal of the thermostat makes or breaks the electrical circuit, the moving arms of the governor open and close a valve regulating the flow of steam, and the photoelectric cell responds to the intensity of light by opening or closing the circuit. In each of these instances the control device is engineered to perform the specific function necessary to maintain the system's equilibrium.[3]

All living organisms are by definition cybernetic systems, for they must maintain equilibrium in order to survive. It is useful to apply the concept of cybernetics—the maintenance of a steady state through the interpretation of information and subsequent corrective action—to organizations. The concept of cybernetic systems is not being introduced for the first time in this chapter. The systems concept is first discussed in Chapter 2. In Chapter 5, Figure 5–1 (reproduced here as Figure 19–1) shows how the major business functions of finance, production, marketing, and personnel form a self-correcting system with a feedback loop to the external environment between the marketing department and the external environment, the customer. Feedback loops with outside forces could also be shown between finance and sources of capital, between production and vendors, and between personnel and the labor supply. There is also a continual exchange of information internally between the major functions of an organization.

Steps in the Control Process

There is agreement among students of management concerning the three steps of the control process:

1. Establishing standards of performance
2. Measuring current performance in relation to established standards
3. Taking corrective action

Let us now interpret these three steps of the control process in the light of what we know about cybernetic systems. The establishment of standards defines the desired state of equilibrium. Standards are definitions of the objectives of an organization, but it must be remembered that objectives can and do change. The second step, measurement of current performance, requires that information be processed and interpreted by someone so that a conclusion can be drawn concerning present position, or performance, relative to the desired position

---

[3] Robert Chin, "The Utility of System Models and Developmental Models for Practitioners," from W. G. Bennis, K. D. Benne, and Robert Chin (eds.), *The Planning of Change*, Readings in the Applied Behavioral Sciences (New York City: Holt, Rinehart & Winston, 1961). This article discusses several types of models and their application to business situations.

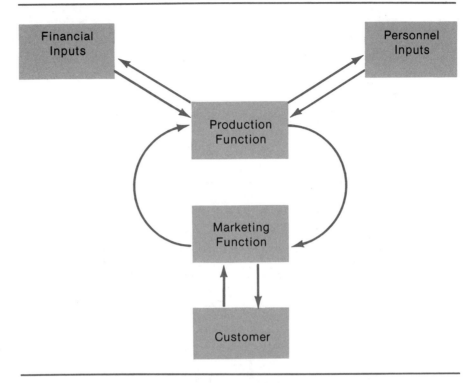

**Figure 19–1
MAJOR
BUSINESS
FUNCTIONS AS
A CYBERNETIC
SYSTEM**

as defined by the standards. The information used in measurement is not limited to financial data reflecting the economic condition of the company; it also includes reports on the quality of the product, the amount of inventory, the morale of personnel, or even the intuitive judgment of a manager that all is not going well. Taking corrective action intended to bring performance in line with predetermined standards requires executive decision making and a realignment of company resources. The person who makes the decision corresponds to the control device of the mechanical cybernetic system.[4]

The next major section of this chapter discusses in greater detail each of the three steps of the control process; first, however, there is one more question to answer for a more complete understanding of the nature of control. Who does the controlling?

Who Controls?

Many students, particularly those majoring in accounting, consider as a personal career objective the position of controller of a business organization. Table 19–1 presents two typical position descriptions—one, the controller of a

---

[4] For a comprehensive review of the literature concerning control theory from 1900 to 1972, the following provides a summary of the knowledge available to the executive in performing the control function: Giovanni B. Giglioni and Arthur G. Bedeian, "A Conspectus of Management Control Theory: 1900–1972," *Academy of Management Journal*, Vol. 17, No. 2 (June, 1972), p. 292.

FUNCTIONS OF THE CONTROLLER IN THE LARGE COMPANY

Objectives

The controller (or Comptroller) of Accounts is responsible for the effective financial and cost controls of the company's activities.

Functions

1. Prescription of principles and methods to govern accounting controls throughout the enterprise
2. Provision of adequate protection against loss of the company's money and property
3. Prescription of principles of accounting determining cost of product and normal volume of production in order to compute costs and install appropriate systems
4. Verification of the propriety of expenditures
5. Providing comparison of capital expenditures and appropriations
6. Preparation of the accounts of the corporation
7. Determination of income and expenditure allocation among plants and departments
8. Proposals regarding the nature of the corporation's financial statements
9. Preparation of the financial statements
10. Preparation of analyses assisting others to improve the earnings of the enterprise
11. Observation of the manner of performing accounting responsibilities

Relationships

The Controller of Accounts reports to the Vice-President for Finance.

FUNCTIONS OF THE TREASURER AND CONTROLLER IN THE MEDIUM-SIZE COMPANY

1. Accountability for the safekeeping and custody of corporate funds, securities owned by the company, and the corporate seal
2. Establishment of a General Accounting Department with the following duties:
   a. Post-audit of plant transactions
   b. Installation and maintenance of primary books of accounts
   c. Setting the policies, procedures, and standards of accounting and cost records and reports
   d. Setting up methods of cash disbursement, accounts receivable, plant and equipment records
   e. Cash management
   f. Preparation of financial statements and reports
   g. Credit approval
3. Establishment of a cost accounting department with a view to
   a. Prescribing and administering factory timekeeping and payroll procedures
   b. Maintaining inventory controls
   c. Supervising of timekeeping methods
   d. Setting up a cost system in each plant
4. Establishing a budget department to present standards of performance to management with a view to
   a. Showing the results of operations
   b. Estabishing standards of performance
   c. Proposing a budget forecast
   d. Informing executives of variations from the budget
   e. Continuous revision of the budget

SOURCE: Ernest Dale, *Planning and Developing the Company Organization Structure* (New York City: American Management Association, Research Report No. 20, 1952), p. 200.

Table 19–1 FUNCTIONS OF THE CONTROLLER

large company, and the other the combined position of treasurer and controller in a medium-size company. In general the controller is closely associated with the finance function of the company, but may or may not report to the vice-president for finance. If not reporting to the financial officer, the controller reports to the president or chief executive officer of the company. Controllers are usually responsible for designing the systems and procedures necessary for management control; thus, in companies having integrated data processing systems the controller may be responsible for the design and maintenance of such systems. Traditionally the controller's function is concerned with those aspects of the business that can be reduced to dollars and cents; for this reason the controller is usually concerned with the efficiency of production and the cost of sales. Few companies require that the controller secure information concerning morale of employees, the status of innovations in the organization, or the quality of management; yet these factors are legitimate areas of control.[5]

We still have not answered the question, Who controls? Note in Table 19–1 there is no statement saying that it is the duty of the controller to control by taking corrective action. Control, the act of taking corrective action, is a function of the line manager. The controller, a member of the staff organization, may design the information system, secure and interpret data concerning performance, and even make recommendations as to what might constitute the most appropriate corrective action. However, the final decision and the request for corrective action are the responsibility of the line manager. Nor is control by the line organization limited to any level of management; indeed, for effective control all levels of management must exercise control over those functions assigned to them. There is much that first-line supervisors can control in their departments that cannot be controlled directly by anyone else in the organization.

THE CONTROL PROCESS

We have described the control process as consisting of the following steps: (1) establishing standards of performance, (2) measuring current performance in relation to the established standards, and (3) taking corrective action. Standards are the basis of the control process, for without adequate standards the subsequent steps of measurement and corrective action are meaningless. Let us examine, first, the nature of standards; then, problems encountered in the measurement of performance; and last, the kind of corrective action that should be taken.

---

[5] The expanding horizons of the controller's job are discussed in the following: Robert J. Mockler, "The Corporate Control Job: Breaking the Mold," *Business Horizons*, Vol. 13, No. 6 (December, 1970), p. 73.

As the result of disclosures of illegal payoffs, especially to foreign governments, the interesting question arises concerning the control of controllers. Vijay Sathe, "Who Should Control Division Controllers?" *Harvard Business Review*, Vol. 56, No. 5 (September–October, 1978), p. 99.

Establishing Standards

The dictionary definition of standards includes two concepts. First, a standard is a rule (unit) for measuring. It is intended to serve as a model or criterion. Second, a standard is established by authority. *Thus, a standard may be defined as a unit of measurement established to serve as a model or criterion.* The 72-stroke par for an 18-hole golf course is an excellent example of a standard. Par is a recognized level of performance or achievement established by authority (custom and the various golfing associations). Second, par demonstrates clearly that a standard is not perfection—many professional golfers consistently exceed, or break, par. Nor is par the average of the level of performance for all golfers; indeed, the average would be considerably higher than 72. Thus, par is a difficult, but attainable, level of performance. It serves as a criterion for comparing the proficiency of one golfer against that of another in terms of an objective unit of measurement—the number of strokes required to complete the course. Par is analogous to the work standards established by a company for its employees.

Scope of Business Standards. Standards in business organizations are not limited to establishing levels of performance for individual workers; instead, they are applicable to all phases of the operation. Ralph C. Davis suggests that standards be set for all activities that contribute to the primary service objectives of the organization. He recommends establishing standards of service, including the development of criteria for the particular good or service being offered by the organization. Standards of policy and function include an evaluation of the organization structure and its method of operation. Standards should also be determined for the evaluation of the physical facilities of the organization, for determining the characteristics of the kind of personnel required, and for determining the level of performance of personnel.[6]

Another approach to describing the scope of standards is to set standards for each of several key result areas. General Electric uses this approach and establishes standards for each of the following eight key result areas:

1. Profitability
2. Market position
3. Productivity
4. Product leadership
5. Personnel development
6. Employee attitudes
7. Public responsibility
8. Balance between short-range and long-range goals.[7]

Some of the major considerations necessary to establish standards for each of the key result areas are discussed now.

---

[6] Ralph C. Davis, *The Fundamentals of Top Management* (New York City: Harper & Brothers, 1951), p. 28. Chapter 2, "Standards and Standardization," p. 21, presents a complete discussion of standards in business organizations.

[7] Robert W. Lewis, "Management, Reporting, and Appraising Results of Operations with Reference to Goals, Plans, and Budgets," from the report, *Planning, Managing, and Measuring the Business*: A Case Study of Management Planning and Control at General Electric Company (New York City: Controllership Foundation, 1955), p. 29. Lewis discusses the problems inherent in the measurement of performance in each of the eight key result areas. (Footnote continued on page 415.)

Profitability. The standard for profitability may be expressed by means of the widely used rate-of-return ratio, percentage of profit to sales, or total dollar volume.[8] The expression of profit as a ratio between profits earned and capital employed is useful in comparing the contribution of each of several decentralized units with respect to current performance and is also of value in determining which of several alternatives to select for future operations. Deviations from expected profit expressed as a percentage of sales may indicate variations in cost or the need for changing the price of the product or service. However, profit expressed as a ratio—either return on investment or percentage of sales—is not necessarily a valid measure of the contribution of personnel to the profitability of a given operation. For example, the profit of a retail store expressed as a percentage of sales may be a function primarily of the cost of goods sold and the cost of renting physical facilities, factors that may be beyond the control of the manager. The expression of profits in terms of total dollars earned is a measure of the effectiveness of sales effort on the part of store personnel over a period of time. Standards of profitability should reflect the contribution of personnel in controlling costs and expanding volume as well as the utilization of physical and financial resources.

Market Position. The position of a company in a chosen market is a measure of the extent to which its product or service is accepted by the customer and an indication of the effectiveness of its sales-promotion techniques. Standards intended to measure a company's market position must be expressed in terms of the total market. A company may, for example, increase its sales at the rate of 2 percent a year and be the largest in its field; yet, if the total market for the good or service offered is increasing at the rate of 4 percent a year, that company's market position is deteriorating.[9]

Productivity. Measures of productivity are immediately associated with the production function, but standards of productivity should be set for administrative and sales functions as well as for production. Typically productivity is expressed as the relationship between total output, measured with respect to dollar volume or units produced, and units of input—for example, the number of worker-hours required for a stated level of output. Standards of productivity should be determined for other units of input as well as for worker-hours.

The student should also review the eight major objectives of an organization described by Peter Drucker and note the similarity between Drucker's objectives and the key result areas of Lewis. Drucker suggests objectives for each of the following eight areas: market standing, innovation, productivity, physical and financial resources, profitability, manager performance and development, worker performance and attitude, and public responsibility. See Chapter 3, "Ethical and Social Responsibilities of Management," and the following:

Peter F. Drucker, "The Objectives of a Business," from *The Practice of Management* (New York City: Harper & Brothers, 1954).

[8] The following article discusses return on investment in relation to planning and control: J. Fred Weston, "ROI Planning and Control," *Business Horizons*, Vol. 15, No. 4 (August, 1972), p. 35.

[9] The following article discusses the effects of competition on the structure of control. Pradip N. Khandwalla, "Effect of Competition on the Structure of Top Management Control," *Academy of Management Journal*, Vol. 16, No. 2 (June, 1973), p. 285.

Efficiency of production may be expressed in relation to the number of machine hours, and a retail establishment is interested in the dollar volume produced per square foot of floor space. The use of total payroll dollars as an index of input indicates whether the rate of productivity is keeping pace with the increasing cost of labor—sometimes a more significant measure than the number of worker-hours employed.

Product Leadership. Standards for profitability, market position, and productivity are not too difficult to express in relatively objective, quantitative units of measurement, but corporate achievement must be measured in areas where the criteria are qualitative in nature rather than quantitative. A company's position with respect to product leadership is difficult to express quantitatively; yet an estimate of position is necessary if it is a company objective to become or remain a leader in its field. A simple count of new products or services introduced is not sufficient. The significance of the new contribution should also be weighed. Standards of quality and performance for current products should be compared with those of competitors. Determination of the significance of research in the development of new products and an evaluation of research effort offer a means of estimating potential leadership capabilities. Customer surveys indicate the degree of product acceptability and may furnish suggestions for product improvement. Finally, a value judgment must be made as to whether the company is meeting its goals of product leadership.

Personnel Development. Standards for measuring the effectiveness of management development programs are also qualitative in nature. Since management development is usually the result of long-range planning and intended to meet future needs, it is difficult to assess the success of any such program on a year-to-year basis. However, an annual reporting of developmental activities establishes a trend in this area, and, when compared with projected managerial needs resulting from expected growth, an estimate may be made concerning the need for expanding the management development program. The number of people participating in formal developmental programs, the success of those who have received training compared with those who have not been trained, and the number of managers hired from outside the company should be included in annual reports of personnel development. A current inventory of personnel skills when compared with forecasts for immediate personnel needs may indicate the short-range effectiveness of a management development program.

Employee Attitudes. Although there is some question regarding the existence of a positive relationship between employee attitude and short-range production goals (Chapter 15), there is no doubt that employee attitudes have their effect on the success of an organization over a long period of time. Attitudes may be measured operationally by an analysis of labor turnover, absenteeism, grievances, and safety records. Measurement of these factors can be accomplished in an objective, quantitative manner; the difficulty lies in establishing the standard, or criterion, of what is acceptable or desirable. Year-to-year figures and comparisons between different units in the same organization or with industry experience may be used as a guide to determine expected results. Product quality, if within the control of employees, and the number of suggestions for improvements in operating methods may be used as measures of employee attitudes. Attitude surveys conducted at periodic intervals indicate the degree of progress being made in the improvement of employee attitudes. The determination of employee attitudes is significant for the company desirous of maintaining a position of respect and leadership in its community.

Public Responsibility. The fulfillment of goals in the area of public responsibility is highly intangible and difficult to measure. Included are contributions to the life of the community in the form of stable employment, participation in community affairs, and the leadership supplied for community activities. Standards of performance are not readily expressed in quantitative terms; consequently, the results obtained in the area of public responsibility are appraised in terms of their broad contribution to the public.

Balance Between Short-Range and Long-Range Goals. Again, the measure of success is subjective in nature. Implied in this measurement is the existence of long-range goals, say 15 or 20 years from now; and the existence of intermediate and short-range plans to achieve the objectives of those long-range goals. The inclusion of a measurement of the balance between short-range and long-range goals forces a company to review its entire planning process and emphasizes that future success is dependent upon the execution of carefully developed plans.

Methods of Establishing Standards. It is apparent from the number and kinds of the areas for which standards may be established that one method of establishing standards cannot be applied to all areas. There are three methods used to determine the level of expected performance. One is to develop statistical, or normative, data from sources internal and external to the company; another is to appraise results in the light of experience and judgment; and the third method is to develop engineered standards.

Statistical Standards. Statistical standards, sometimes called historical standards, are standards based upon an analysis of past experience. The data used may be drawn from the company's own records or may be a reflection of the experience of several companies. The particular statistic selected for the criterion may be the average or it may be a stated point above or below the midpoint, for example, the upper quartile. While an analysis of past experience may be helpful in setting standards of performance in some areas, the statistical approach has many pitfalls in setting production standards. The following example illustrates the weakness of a historical analysis.

> The accounting department of a rebuilder of automobile parts kept a careful, complete record of the number of labor hours, broken down into direct and indirect labor hours, required to rebuild each of several parts. At the end of each fiscal year, the average number of hours required to rebuild each part was determined. Thus, the average for the past year became the standard for the current year and deviations from the average were reported as above or below standard. Despite the fact that this company was producing parts well within the limits set by its

own standards, its labor costs were considerably in excess of those of its competitors. A consultant called in to review the situation discovered that there were many bottlenecks in the production control department and that the output per worker-hour was only 70 percent of what could reasonably be expected based upon sound time study standards.

The lesson is clear: meeting standards of past performance is not sufficient, particularly when past performance is only a fraction of potential performance.

Yet, if used as an adjunct to other sources of information, statistical data is not only helpful but sometimes the only guide available. Indexes of profitability vary widely from one industry to another, and an analysis of industry data may prove helpful in setting criteria of profitability. Analysis of the experience of competing firms and one's own historical records of growth aid in setting realistic goals relative to market position. Companies choosing to set standards in the area of employee attitudes may find it useful to analyze the results obtained by other firms using the same attitude or opinion survey. The average contribution to charities and educational institutions may be significant in setting goals of public responsibility. In all these instances, before a final criterion can be set, the information gained from statistical sources is combined with another factor—judgment.

Standards Set by Appraisal. Standards do not have to be expressed in units of measurement accurate to the third decimal place. Some areas of corporate performance are, in the last analysis, appraised primarily in terms of a manager's past experience and judgment. As indicated in our discussion of statistical standards, normative data is a useful adjunct in setting standards of performance with regard to profitability, market position, employee attitudes, and to some extent in the area of public responsibility. However, the final determination of what constitutes a satisfactory level of performance is a judgment based on management's past experience. Standards set by appraisal are essentially *value* judgments and can be as realistic and attainable as statistical or engineered standards. In the absence of standards determined by formal study and analysis, all managers are expected to appraise the output of their subordinates in terms of what they, as managers, believe to be a satisfactory day's work. In so doing, standards are being set by appraisal.

Engineered Standards. Engineered standards, so called because they are based on an objective, quantitative analysis of a specific work situation, may be developed for the measurement of machine output and for measuring the output of individual workers. Machine output standards express the production capabilities of a given piece of equipment and are determined by mechanical design factors. Machine capacity figures are developed by the designers of the equipment and represent the optimum output of the equipment in normal production use. Machine capacities are significant in determining output standards in industries using automatic equipment; for example, the metal and glass container industry.

Engineered standards developed to measure the output of individual workers, or groups of workers, are called either *time standards* or *time study* standards.

The reason is that time is the element of measurement and is almost always measured by means of a stopwatch.[10] The first time studies in this country were completed by Frederick W. Taylor in 1881 at the Midvale Steel Company. His studies were directed toward an analysis of the productivity of hourly workers in a steel mill. Since then, time study techniques have been applied to all types of production jobs—including material handling and maintenance—clerical positions, and even sales jobs.

In setting time standards the actual time taken to perform a given job is determined. This value is termed the *actual* time. The standard time is the time that should be required to perform the job under certain specified conditions. These conditions are usually defined as an average worker, trained in the skills of the job, working at normal pace (rate of speed), and following the prescribed methods for the job. Determining effort, or pace, is a matter of judgment and is related to the effort expended—and the speed required—to walk three miles an hour on level ground. Standard times are usually developed for a normal eight-hour workday and include allowances for fatigue, unavoidable delays, personal time, and other interruptions of work that occur at predictable intervals. Workers who perform their work according to the standards set for the job are said to be working at 100 percent of standard. The use of the expression, 100 percent of standard, causes much of the initial misunderstandings of time study. The term *100 percent* normally conveys the idea of perfection, of maximum effort and maximum output. A more acceptable expression would be to use the term *par*.

Time study standards are essential if incentive plans are to be installed, but it does not follow that incentives are necessary to make effective use of time study. On the contrary, time standards can be used quite effectively as a means of increasing production without the introduction of incentives. The presence of time standards alone tends to increase production. Time standards also form the basis of standard costs. Standard costs are composed of the cost of labor performing at standard plus standard allowances for materials and allocated overhead.

The need for establishing standards varies widely from one company to another, but any company that has labor costs greater than 30 percent of its total product or service cost should investigate the possibility of establishing time standards to serve as the basis for control when measuring human output.

Measuring Current Performance

There is an intermediate step in the control process between the first step of the process, establishing standards, and the final phase of the process, the

---

[10] The student is referred to the following reference for a more complete discussion of time study methods:

Marvin E. Mundel, *Motion and Time Study*, Principles and Practice (4h ed.; Englewood Cliffs, N. J.: Prentice-Hall, Inc., 1970).

For a point of view that is highly critical of time study methods, the following book is suggested:

William Gomberg, *A Trade Union Analysis of Time Study* (2d ed.; Englewood Cliffs, N. J.: Prentice-Hall, Inc., 1955).

taking of corrective action. The middle step is that of measuring current performance. To a degree, the problems of measurements are defined, and sometimes partially solved, by the manner in which standards are defined. Standards of profitability, for example, imply that the measuring unit be one of dollars; but the statement of criteria in the areas of product leadership and public responsibility requires ingenuity in developing satisfactory methods of measurement. The variety and the number of performance factors for which standards may be set make it virtually impossible to discuss problems of measurement by describing units of measurement applicable to all business situations. Nonetheless, there are certain characteristics of effective control measurements to be examined. In addition, further elaboration of the significance of the measurement of current progress to the entire control process is helpful in assessing the worth of measuring devices.[11]

Fundamental to sound control measures is recognition that management control systems are cybernetic systems, defining cybernetics as the processing and the interpretation of information. Thus, control systems are best regarded as information systems. The appropriateness of corrective action, the end point of the control process, is dependent almost entirely on the kind of information received. Information intended to measure and describe current performance can be evaluated by seeking answers to the following five questions:

1. Is the information timely?
2. Are the units of measurement appropriate?
3. How reliable is the information received?
4. Is the information valid?
5. Is information being channeled to the proper authority?

Let us discuss each of these questions so that the problems of measuring performance are better understood.

Timeliness of Information. Control information, to be of greatest use, must reflect present position. Typically managers rely too much on data supplied by the accounting department and as a result fail to develop other sources of information. Accounting statements are prepared at the end of a given time period, for example a calendar month, and, even with efficient procedures, seven to ten working days are required to prepare statements of the preceding month's operations. Though this information may have historical significance and be of value in the preparation of annual reports, it is of little or no value to the manager responsible for the efficiency of day-to-day operations. Ideally managers of each operating unit should have information presented to them during the course of each working day so that they have an adequate basis for corrective action. Is such timeliness possible? The following example suggests that it is.

The manager of a plant producing stamped automobile parts devised the following method of securing information concerning the quantity produced by each of

---

[11] For a discussion of the measurement of output and personal surveillance, the following is suggested: William G. Ouchi and Mary Ann Maguire, "Organizational Control: Two Functions," *Administrative Science Quarterly,* Vol. 20, No. 4 (December, 1975), p. 559.

several production departments on an hourly basis. Departments were designated by the operations performed and included the following: shearing, stamping, chrome plating, and buffing and polishing. The manager placed in his office a large blackboard ruled into vertical columns for each production department. Horizontal lines were drawn for each hour of the day. A production clerk checked with the foreman of each production department at the end of each hour, received the quantity produced by each department, and posted the information on the board in the manager's office. In this way the manager became immediately aware of trouble spots and could anticipate future difficulties likely to arise resulting from a shortage of parts or from a breakdown in earlier operations in the production sequence.

Another result of the control procedure described in the above incident is that the foremen of the various departments confer more frequently with each other and with the plant manager to minimize delays in production. Timely control information can be obtained through telephone calls, daily reports, or personal observation without having to wait for information prepared and distributed by formal reporting systems.

Appropriate Units of Measurement. One of the most difficult tasks in measuring current performance is the selection of an appropriate unit of measurement. Occasionally the use of several different units offers a partial solution to this problem. For example, profit is expressed as a percentage of sales, as the percentage return on capital invested, and as total dollars. Similarly, production may be measured and described as a ratio of output to input or as total units produced. Market position is also measured by several different methods. The use of multiple measures to describe performance is sound because each measure serves as a cross check on the information provided by the other measures and at the same time emphasizes one particular aspect of the performance under review.

The measurement of performance against standard for profits, productivity, and sales utilizes quantitative units of measurement. However, much of the evaluation of a company's progress depends on qualitative, rather than quantitative, units of measurement. In the absence of quantitative measures, managers drawing on past experience and their own sets of values must judge for themselves whether standards are being met. Such judgments must be made in the areas of personnel development, public responsibility, and determining the balance between long-range and short-range goals. Attempting to express achievement in these areas by relying solely on quantitative units can be misleading. For example, measuring personnel development by a head count of the number of persons who have completed a given training program does not answer the question of the effectiveness of the program in improving performance on the job. Even though qualitative measures are difficult to apply and generally unreliable when compared with quantitative units, it is a mistake not to set standards in those areas where measurement must be made in qualitative terms.

Reliability of Information. Reliability of information pertains to its degree of accuracy. It is assumed that the data is free from clerical errors. Thus, the accuracy referred to by the term *reliability* is with respect to the consistency of data and the extent to which all aspects of the problem are measured. Almost always a compromise must be made between reliability and timeliness. Usually the reliability of information is positively related to its completeness. Computer predictions of election returns illustrate the increasing accuracy of predictions as more and more data is reported and interpreted. However, most managerial interpretations of operations—and the subsequent corrective action—are based on incomplete information. Sales managers having reports for only the first two weeks of a calendar month may be required to take corrective action even though data is not fully reliable because it is not a complete description of the month's activities. Even so, partial information on recurring time cycles, such as monthly sales and production reports, can be analyzed and related to the entire cycle and provide a relatively accurate basis for analysis and action.

In addition to decreased reliability of information when using data for only a part of the reporting period, there is a marked decrease in the reliability of data covering initial phases of an operation. The reason for this type of loss in reliability is best explained by the adage, practice makes perfect. At the start of a new operation quality and quantity of performance are at their lowest point; but, with time, there is improved individual performance and better methods are usually developed. Graphic representations of improved performance are called *learning curves*. The aircraft industry, constantly faced with changing products, short runs, and the threat of contract cancellation, has developed techniques to predict with considerable accuracy the average level of performance by projecting an improvement or learning curve. Data from the beginning of an operation is not characteristic of the entire operation or its latter phases and is a highly unreliable source of information unless interpreted as part of a learning curve. Though the use of learning curves is most highly developed in the aircraft industry, the same techniques are applicable to the prediction of final performance in maintenance operations, in building heavy equipment, in construction, and in the performance of salespeople introducing a new product. The danger lies not in using the initial data of a new operation but in failing to recognize that there is a predictable improvement factor.[12]

Validity of Information. It is possible for information to be highly reliable, yet not valid. Likewise, the appropriate unit of measurement, either quantitative or qualitative, can be established, and yet the information received may not be valid. The validity of a measurement refers to the degree to which a measurement actually reflects the phenomenon that it is intended to measure. An example of a highly reliable, quantitative measure with virtually no validity is the experience of a printing company in trying to determine the quantity of daily production. The figure used was the total number of pounds of finished materials shipped each day. There are several reasons why the total number of pounds shipped is not a valid measure of the company's productivity. First, the total number of pounds bore no consistent relationship to dollar volume of sales,

---

[12] Winifred R. Hirschmann, "Profit from the Learning Curve," *Harvard Business Review*, Vol. 42 (January–February, 1964), p. 125. Hirschmann's article discusses the characteristics of the learning curve and the reasons why it has not been accepted widely, and suggests some practical applications of the concept.

profitability, or worker-hours required for production because of the diversity of product line, which included cellophane and Pliofilm packaging materials, lithographed products, foil wrappings, and fiberboard cartons. Second, the pounds shipped bore only an indirect relation to production for any given day, since up to 40 percent of the orders shipped on any given day came out of a warehouse and not directly from that day's production. Thus, the number of pounds shipped did not measure what it was intended to measure—the amount of goods produced in a given day.

Another example of a measurement that may or may not be valid is the use of gross sales as an index of profitability. Whenever the performance being reviewed is complex and composed of many different elements, it is extremely difficult to develop one single unit of measurement that adequately portrays what it is intended to portray. In these situations it is best to measure each segment of performance separately rather than use a single indicator that may not be valid.

Channeling Information to Proper Authority. The timeliness of information, the appropriateness of the unit of measurement, and the reliability and validity of control data are directed toward having the right information at the right time. A fifth requirement must be met, the channeling of information to the proper authority. Only then do we have all ingredients of a good information system for control—the right information at the right time and at the right place. What constitutes the proper channel for information flow varies with each company organization structure, the kind of information to be interpreted, and the kind of corrective action required to attain expected standards. Even so, the following generalization can be made: control information should be directed toward the individual assigned responsibility for the operation and at the same time having authority to take corrective action.

There is much discussion concerning the effect of integrated data processing systems upon the flow of information. Some argue that integrated systems encourage centralized control, with the result that the control of an organization ultimately rests in the hands of a few at the top of the organization. Others point out that the speed with which information can be handled and the variety of information processed make it possible to supply control information to first-line supervisors and middle management never available to them before. Although there seems to be a trend toward centralized control, the trend is not necessarily a function of integrated data processing systems. Rather, it may be an expression of a desire to place control information in the hands of those possessing the authority to take action.[13]

In summary, the measurement of organizational performance with respect to stated standards is not precise; yet measure we must if we are to improve

---

[13] The following articles discuss problems inherent in the establishment and measurement of control structures. J. Timothy McMahon and G. W. Perritt, "The Control Structure of Organizations: An Empirical Examination," *Academy of Management Journal*, Vol. 14, No. 3 (September, 1971), p. 327. J. Timothy McMahon and G. W. Perritt, "Toward a Contingency Theory of Organizational Control," *Academy of Management Journal*, Vol. 16, No. 4 (December, 1973), p. 624.

the quality of corrective action. An awareness of the difficulties inherent in measuring current positions eventually leads to the development of meaningful control information.

Taking Corrective Action

The third and last step of the control process, taking corrective action, epitomizes the busy, efficient executive. Here is a person making things happen and getting things done. Without action there is no control. The actions taken are the result of executive decisions and as such reflect the personality of the person taking the action as well as being determined by situational, or environmental, factors. Thus, the personality of the person in control has much to do with the kind of control. Before discussing the range of action available to the controlling executive, it is well to examine more closely the influence of personality upon corrective action, to determine who should take corrective action, and to make sure that causes—not symptoms—are being corrected.

Personality and Control. Personality factors, rather than the demands of the situation, are the cause of the extremes in control. One extreme is typified by the Captain Queeg approach to management—too much control. The other extreme might be called the Will Rogers approach to management—too little control. Captain Queeg, as described by Herman Wouk in *The Caine Mutiny*, hewed to the letter of the law and insisted that his men do the same. He had to know every detail of what every man aboard his ship did and rationalized such excessive control as a means of assuring himself, and the Navy, that all regulations were being carried out. The same approach in an industrial organization results in a mass of paperwork, so much so that the real work of the organization is neglected.

What motivates a Captain Queeg to check on every last detail? The answer is simple: The same personality that makes it impossible to delegate effectively. When effective delegation is practiced, there is little need for tight control. In Chapter 11, four personality characteristics that interfere with effective delegation are discussed. They are worth recounting at this point. First, there are those who by vocational choice—notably engineers and accountants—are trained to attend to details and as a result find it difficult to delegate effectively when placed in a supervisory position. Next there are those managers who want to avoid the major issues and occupy themselves by attention to petty detail. Third, there are those who, for either real or imagined reasons, fear failure; and, last, there are those who have a mistrust of others. These are the traits that prevent effective delegation and at the same time result in excessive control over the relatively unimportant. The effect on an organization is stultifying. Initiative, innovation, and creativity on the part of subordinates are stifled.[14]

---

[14] For discussions of the relationship between the types of control and certain measures of satisfaction in a manufacturing organization and in two state agencies, the following articles are recommended: J. Timothy McMahon and John M. Ivancevich, "A Study of Control in a Manufacturing Organization: Managers and Nonmanagers," *Administrative Science Quarterly*, Vol. 21, No. 1 (March, 1976), p. 66. William E. Turcotte, "Control Systems, Performance, and Satisfaction in Two State Agencies," *Administrative Science Quarterly*, Vol. 19, No. 1 (March, 1974), p. 60.

The other pole in control, the Will Rogers approach, is equally ineffective in achieving organizational goals. Here everything is assumed to be going along just fine, there is no need to check because these are wonderful people in the organization, and things are bound to work out just right in the long run. Also, there is a hesitancy about offending people by questioning them about their performance. The Will Rogers type is a defender of the Theory Y approach to organization. Eventually, however, the manager wants to know more about the operation than the mere fact that there is a certain amount of money in the bank at the end of each month. With no clearly defined organization, the inevitable happens—an "assistant-to" is created to perform the controlling for the manager. It is quite possible that the assistant-to might become another Captain Queeg. But more importantly, the creation of an assistant-to leads us once again to the question, Who controls?

Who Controls? The payoff of the control process is not the setting of standards, nor is it the measurement of performance against standards. It is taking the corrective action necessary to bring performance in line with the standards. The logical person to take this action is the manager who has been assigned the responsibility of managing a particular aspect of the business and who has been delegated the authority necessary to fulfill the assigned responsibilities. Thus, effective control is the result of sound organizational structure and the practice of an important organizational process—delegation. Taking corrective action is executive action and as such is in the hands of the line manager. The controller's office may be involved in the setting of standards and almost always participates in the measurement of current position against standard, but the taking of corrective action belongs to the manager of an organizational unit.

Symptoms or Causes? Prior to taking corrective action it is necessary to differentiate between symptoms and causes. Most of us have had the experience of taking an antihistamine drug at the first sign of a cold, and after a day or so we stop taking the medicine. Sometimes, much to our disgust, the sniffling and sneezing return and we discover that we have done an excellent job of treating symptoms but not getting at the cause of the cold. A manager must learn to recognize a symptom for what it is and to devote attention to the cause of the problem. Cost control, or the control of expenses, often falls into the category of treating symptoms rather than causes.

Excessive costs are an indication that something has gone wrong; they are the result of someone's performance, and if costs are to be brought in line it is the performance that must be corrected. First, it is wise to examine the standard to determine whether or not the costs in question are in fact excessive. Next, try to determine the contribution of each factor that makes up the total cost. How much of total cost is attributable to direct labor, to materials, and to overhead? Finally, examine each of these factors separately and determine how performance can be improved in each area. The same analytical procedure can be applied to the marketing function. The answer to a declining sales volume is not necessarily more salespeople or better performance on the part of the present sales force; instead, the decline in sales may be the result of a poorly designed product or the failure to meet the challenge of competitors.

The Management Process Cycle. After determining the cause for poor performance, corrective action is in order. It is impossible to formulate a list of actions available to the manager; each situation is unique and calls for its own solution. There is, however, a frame of reference of value to the manager in evaluating a proposed action. That framework is the management process cycle—replanning, reorganizing, redirecting, and continuing control since in a going organization all these functions have been performed in one way or another. Failure to meet expected levels of performance is sometimes unavoidable and calls for the development of new plans with the possibility of revised standards of performance. Though there is merit in the adage, "the difficult we do immediately; the impossible we do tomorrow," there are times when one must recognize that the impossible cannot be accomplished in accordance with present plans. Delays in a construction schedule resulting from inclement weather necessitate a revision of plans. Failure to meet a marketing objective may mean allocating more money for advertising or a restatement of expected results.

The present organization may need revising. Is the organization structured in such a manner that there is clear-cut responsibility for each organizational unit, or is there need for the creation of a new unit? What about the people in the organization? Are they performing their assigned duties satisfactorily? A change in either organizational structure or personnel may be necessary to correct the causes of poor performance. Or the difficulty may lie in leadership. Sometimes a restatement of what is expected brings the desired results. Finally, there is the control process itself—it must be exercised continually. The management cycle is not composed of the four discrete steps of planning, organizing, leading, and controlling; instead, it is a continuous process, with control functioning as a catalyst to produce an integrated continuous process.

CHARACTERISTICS OF GOOD CONTROL

In the preceding discussion of the steps of the control process, many of the characteristics of an effective control system are implied and touched upon briefly. Control is an extremely critical factor in the achievement of organizational objectives, with the effectiveness of the control function dependent on the information received. Control systems, to be of greatest use, must possess certain characteristics. Again, we are unable to describe all control systems since each control situation is unique. Despite this difficulty, there is general agreement that good control has the following characteristics: timeliness, follows organizational lines, strategic, economical, shows both trends and status, and stresses the exception.[15] Each of these characteristics is discussed separately.

---

[15] For a discussion of the relationship between strategy and structure that contributes to an effective management control system, the following is recommended: John Todd, "Management Control Systems: A Key Link Between Strategy, Structure, and Employee Performance," *Organizational Dynamics*, Vol. 5, No. 4 (Spring, 1977), p. 65.

Timeliness

Accounting records are relatively precise, detailed statements of a company's activity for a stated period and are historical in nature, since they are prepared after the period has closed. Frequently these reports are of great value to the planning process, but they are often inadequate as control reports because they are not timely. Ideally the optimum form of control information should forecast deviations from standard prior to their occurrence. In practice such forecasting is seldom achieved, but every effort should be made to report deviations from standard while the event in question is still in process. We mentioned the control device developed by the plant manager of an automobile parts manufacturer that enabled the plant manager to keep abreast of the output of each production department at hourly intervals. Supervisors of production departments frequently find it necessary to develop control information during the course of the day. One supervisor in a large printing company placed a small blackboard at the end of each press, with the cumulative standard production posted for each hour. This supervisor requested the presspeople to post actual production for each hour alongside the posted standard. One immediate result of this procedure was that the presspeople called the supervisor when trouble began to develop, thereby permitting the rescheduling of work to other presses.

Another means of focusing upon timely information is to require unit managers, such as plant managers and sales managers, to prepare monthly forecasts and to submit revisions of these forecasts on either a weekly or a biweekly basis. While it is true that the information used in these forecasts may not be accurate when compared with the accounting records prepared at the close of the period, the process of forecasting and revising forces the manager to develop and rely upon timely information. If a choice must be made between timeliness and accuracy of control information, timeliness should be emphasized for the control of current operations.

Follows Organizational Lines

The excessive control of a Captain Queeg and the hands-off attitude of a Will Rogers, with the eventual inevitability of an assistant-to, reflect the same organizational shortcoming—a failure to delegate. Responsibility is not assigned nor is authority delegated, with the result that clear-cut accountability to superiors in the organization is not established. The control function can in no way substitute for poor organizational practices and structure. Good controls are closely related to organizational structure and reflect organizational structure and processes in their design and function.

Accumulated total product costs are of great significance to the sales department in the pricing of a given product, yet such figures may not be meaningful to manufacturing personnel charged with the responsibility of controlling costs. To be meaningful to manufacturing departments, cost data must reflect the portion of total cost added to the product by each department. Only then is the manager aware of the chargeable departmental costs and in a position to control those costs. Defects in quality should be traced to component parts and reported to the operating department responsible for the production of the defective part. Wage and salary plans can be utilized for control by reporting the average rate paid for each job classification and each salary grade. The information should be prepared for each organizational unit as well as for the entire company. Directing information to the responsible manager is an effective way of making it possible to exercise control at the lowest possible echelon of the organization.[16]

Strategic Placement

It is impossible to establish controls for every aspect of even a small to medium-size business because of its complexity. Thus, it becomes necessary to establish controls at certain points of the operation selected because of their strategic value. A company whose primary contact with customers is through letters written by the correspondents in the sales order department may experience difficulty in maintaining good customer relations as the result of inconsistencies from the many sources of contact with customers. A strategic control of correspondence is the requirement that all letters be prepared for the signature of the sales manager, a step that permits the manager to sample all outgoing correspondence. Most governmental agencies require the signature of the chief administrator on all outgoing mail.

Quality control programs rely heavily on the selection of strategic points where inspection approaches the 100 percent level as a means of meeting quality standards. A major appliance, such as a refrigerator, is checked after final assembly by connecting it to a test circuit to see if it cools properly. Also, the components of the compressor are subjected to complete dimensional checks prior to assembly to insure proper fit. Establishing key control points prior to the assembly of a critical component and after final assembly minimizes the likelihood of expensive rework and the possibility of defective products reaching the customer.

A few well-chosen measures of performance are often sufficient for the overall control of medium-size business operations. The owner-manager of a firm manufacturing trays for use in cafeterias and drive-in restaurants received weekly reports containing the following information: the backlog of orders, finished goods inventory, number of units shipped, and total hours of factory labor. A change in the order backlog with the other measures remaining relatively constant indicated the effectiveness of sales effort, and the number of units shipped was closely related to gross sales for the month. Total labor hours when balanced with inventory and units shipped let the manager know something about manufacturing efficiency, and a rising inventory indicated the need for either increasing sales effort or decreasing direct labor hours. To this manager, changes in the interrelationships of these four measures revealed potential trouble spots and enabled immediate corrective action.

---

[16] William G. Ouchi, "The Transmission of Control through Organizational Hierarchy," *Academy of Management Journal*, Vol. 21, No. 2 (June, 1978), p. 173.

Economical Administration

In addition to its stifling effects on human effort, the excessive control of a Captain Queeg can be expensive. The story is often told of a consultant encountering strategic controls similar to those used by the manager of the tray manufacturing company. The consultant suggested that in addition to these overall controls there was a need to control overhead costs. The recommended controls were put into effect. At the end of several months a marked decline in profits was noticed, and the amount of the decline corresponded to the additional costs of administering the new controls.

There is an old saying that you can inspect yourself out of business. Yet failure to detect defective products results in a loss of customers. One method of balancing the cost of quality control against the cost of not taking action is the use of sampling techniques where every 10th or 100th item is checked thoroughly. Another area deserving careful attention is the use of incentives as a means of reducing unit labor costs. Although incentives may reduce the cost of direct labor, the indirect costs of maintaining up-to-date time studies by the industrial engineering department may more than counterbalance any savings in direct labor. Some companies have found measured day work—the use of time standards to determine a fair day's work—to be satisfactory since the standards do not have to be maintained with the same degree of accuracy as required when standards are used as the basis for incentive pay. Accuracy of measurement is an important factor in determining the cost of a given set of controls. Sometimes the presence of a deviation from standard and its direction, rather than the precise amount of the deviation, is sufficient for control purposes.

Reveals Trends As Well As Status

Controls that show the current status of a specific phase of an operation are relatively easy to prepare since all that is needed are periodic statements of the particular activity in question. Although such measures show present status, they do not necessarily reveal the trend of performance; i.e., monthly production reports do not show whether production is increasing or decreasing. This limitation of periodic reporting is overcome by using a graphic method of presentation that shows successive measures, thus forming a trend line, or by presenting the data in tabular form and including year-to-date or month-to-date figures. However, establishing and showing the trends of specific business functions do not always provide sufficient control information. It is necessary to include supporting information that is closely related to the primary function under observation. In the case of production, concentration on the number of units produced without the inclusion of a measure of units of input gives no indication of the cost or efficiency of production—an aspect of production that may be more important for control purposes than the total produced.

Interpreting trends in the light of related happenings is of special significance in the development of control information for the measurement of market position. There is the well-known example of a soap manufacturer who recorded continuous gains in the sales of soap, but neglected to focus attention on the increasing share of the home laundry market claimed by detergents, with the result that the company discovered too late that it was last in the newer and larger market. One of the largest and oldest manufacturers of men's suits measured market position not only with respect to the market for suits but also with respect to the total amount spent for men's outer wear. As a result, the company discovered that an increasing share of the money spent for outer wear was spent on sports clothes and thus established plants for the manufacture of men's sportswear. Control data showing market position should show position in relation to competitive items as well as the position relative to that of competitors.

Stresses the Exception

In Chapter 2, Jethro's recommendations to Moses are presented. The three recommendations are: teach "ordinances and laws" to the people; select leaders and assign them "to be rulers of thousands, and rulers of hundreds, and rulers of fifties, and rulers of ten"; and those rulers should administer all routine matters and bring to Moses only the important questions. The third suggestion is often referred to as the *principle of the exception.* There are two reasons why effective systems of controls stress the exception. First, the amount of information generated in even small organizations is so great that it becomes difficult, if not impossible, to determine the significance of all information. To review every action of subordinates or to consult with them prior to taking action consumes too much of the time and energy of the manager. Second, when information stressing the exception is presented to the manager, attention is directed toward those items that require corrective action.

Examples of control that point up the exception are numerous in all functions of management. The sales data presented to a national sales manager should specify those districts that deviate from predicted standards of performance beyond a predetermined range; for example, those districts that vary more than plus or minus 5 percent. The exceptions must include those areas that exceed expected performance as well as those that fail to meet the standards. It is quite possible that the reasons for successful performance can be applied to those districts where performance is below par. The reporting of the exception is of value in the control of quality, cost, production, or any other measure of performance for which standards have been set. Usually acceptable performance is defined as performance within the limits of a predetermined range, with the breadth of the range varying for each performance factor, rather than satisfactory performance as a point value with no tolerance allowed.

Control by exception is closely related to the process of delegation and is not necessarily the exercise of corrective action after the function in question has been performed. Instead effective control is exercised by either approving or disapproving the exceptional action prior to its occurrence. When responsibilities are assigned, authority within prescribed limits is delegated in order that these responsibilities may be fulfilled. Occasionally a manager requires greater authority in order to fulfill assigned responsibilities. When need arises, managers may request their respective superiors to recognize the exception and grant additional authority. For instance, the supervisor of a manufacturing department may have the authority to spend $100 for the repair of any one piece of equipment and $1,000 per month for total repairs in the department. Deviations beyond these maintenance cost standards require prior approval from the plant manager. The plant manager, in turn, may be permitted to spend $1,000 on any single item of general plant maintenance and $5,000 in any month. For the expenditure of sums exceeding these limits, the plant manager must secure prior approval from the manufacturing vice-president. Clearly defined limits of authority and the requirement of prior approval to exceed these limitations permit the control of the exception prior to its happening. Thus, the concept of control by exception is used to control deviations from standard before the exception occurs as well as to emphasize those areas in need of corrective action.

Each of the six preceding characteristics of an effective control system—timeliness, following organizational lines, strategic placement, economical administration, showing both trends and status, and stressing the exception—is important to the control of operations. These characteristics are descriptive of two different aspects of the control process and as such can be condensed and stated as two principles of control. The establishment of controls that present information while it is still timely, that reveal information that is of strategic value in the control of operations, and that follow established organizational lines is descriptive of the purposes and structures of the control system. The characteristics of economy of administration and the reporting of trends as well as current status are also a function of the purpose and structure of the control system. The last of the six characteristics, stressing and reporting the exception, leads directly to the essence of control—corrective action. Thus, logically there are two fundamental principles of control. The *principle of control design* emphasizes the nature and design of the control system and states:

> Effective control systems are designed to be economical in their administration and to reflect organizational structure. Such systems should provide management with information that is timely, of strategic value, and descriptive of the trends of operations as well as current status.

The *principle of the exception* emphasizes the essence of the control process—taking corrective action:

> The most efficient use of managerial time and energy is possible when control information stresses the exception and focuses attention upon those functions that need corrective action.

Case Problem 19-B describes two widely divergent degrees of control within the same organization and offers an opportunity to determine the proper degree of control that is needed and the methods to be utilized in establishing such control.

Case Problem 19-B

CONTROLLING SALES EXPENSE

Frank Montano, a district manager for Paper Products Company, has been in charge of the Chicago district sales office for two months. Prior to his transfer to Chicago to replace Tom Aderly, who had been in Chicago for 30 years, the last 20 as sales manager, Montano had been assistant manager of the New York sales district. When reviewing his new assignment with the vice-president in charge of sales, Montano was told that the Chicago sales expenses were 50 percent higher than those for New York and that sales volume had not kept pace with the rate of increase shown by other large offices. He was advised that he should first reduce the cost of operating the Chicago office and that as soon as costs were under control he should take steps to increase sales volume.

Montano arrived in Chicago a month prior to Aderly's retirement and had occasion to review with him the operations of the office. Aderly recognized that the Chicago expenses were higher than those for New York but attributed this difference to the size of the district, which covered many more square miles than New York. When Montano asked to see the records of daily calls made by each sales representative, a list of potential customers, and the names of the new customers for each month, Tom Aderly answered as follows:

"Frank, I don't bother much with things like that. Every morning I visit with each of my eight reps when they come into the office. I've known every one of them since the first day they started to work here. I know that they have the best interests of the company at heart, and I'm sure that they're all doing their very best. I help them when they ask for it, but otherwise I let them follow their own leads. Makes for a nice friendly atmosphere."

After Aderly formally retired, Montano had the opportunity to examine more closely the representatives' expense accounts. He found that the average expense advance was $250 instead of the $100 maximum allowed by company policy, and that one sales representative had drawn a $500 expense advance. Montano realized that, in order to bring expenses and sales volume into line with those of other districts in the company, a radical change in the method of managing the Chicago office was needed. He decided to present these changes in memo form and to discuss the changes in the first of the newly instituted weekly meetings scheduled for Friday afternoons. The following is a copy of the memorandum.

To: Sales Representatives, Chicago District, Paper Products Company.

Re: Expense Control.

You are all aware that the expenses of the Chicago District sales office are much higher than those of offices in other large cities. For example, our expenses are 25 percent higher than those of Los Angeles, a district of comparable size. It is necessary that we get our expenses in line with those of similar offices in the company. The following procedures are effective beginning next Monday.

1. Expense advance will be limited to the $100 per week as outlined in the company sales policy manual. Those of you who have outstanding balances of more than $100 will not be permitted to draw additional advances; further, the amount in excess of $100 must be paid by the end of this month. If not paid by that time, authorization will be requested to deduct the balance in excess of $100 in three equal monthly installments from your salary.

2. Sales representatives will no longer report to the office each morning; instead, each of you is expected to telephone the office between 9 and 9:30 each morning

and give my secretary a schedule of the calls you intend to make that day. You are also asked to call between 1 and 1:30 p.m. so that we may relay messages from customers that have been received during the morning.

3. Each representative is expected to report to this office in person between 4 and 5 p.m. every day to review with me the calls made during the day and arrange appointments for calls on large accounts so that I can make the calls on these customers with you.

4. Daily expense records will be kept and are to be completed each afternoon when you are in the office.

5. Prior approval must be obtained for any entertainment expense exceeding $25.

6. Monthly time and expense reports must be summarized by the 25th of each month, showing total number of sales calls made, total expense, and total dollar volume of orders received. These summaries will then be forwarded to New York. No salary checks will be issued to any representative until monthly time and expense reports have been received by the New York office.

PROBLEMS

1. How would you characterize Mr. Aderly and Mr. Montano with respect to their methods of exercising control?

2. Is there need for stricter controls in the Chicago office? Why?

3. Do you agree that there is need for the controls set forth in Montano's memo? Do you approve of the method he is using in establishing these controls?

4. How would you have handled this situation? Explain.

CHAPTER QUESTIONS FOR STUDY AND DISCUSSION

1. Define in your own terms the meaning of the word *cybernetics*. Give an example of a cybernetic system and explain why it is so classified.

2. Comment on the following statement: All dynamic systems involve the transmission of information.

3. Relate the three steps of the control process to the concept of a cybernetic system.

4. What are the major functions of a person holding the title of controller in an organization? In an organization, whose responsibility is it to take the corrective action?

5. Describe the relationship between the controller and the manager of an organizational unit.

6. What are the characteristics of a standard? Does the concept of par, borrowed from the game of golf, provide a good analogy for the understanding of the concept of standard? Why?

7. How are standards and objectives related? Illustrate by example.

8. Evaluate the three methods of establishing standards by indicating which methods are most likely to be appropriate in establishing standards for each of the eight key result areas.

9. Discuss each of the major problems encountered in the measurement of performance.

10. What relationship, if any, exists between the process of delegation and the control process? Explain fully.

11. As a manager, what steps should you take to assure yourself that you are able to distinguish symptoms from causes?

12. If it is true that each control system is unique, how is it possible to develop the characteristics of a good control system? State briefly why each of these characteristics is necessary.

13. How are the principle of control design and the principle of the exception related to the characteristics of a good control system? What are the likely results when these principles are violated?

Chapter 20

Nonbudgetary Control

IMPROVING OPERATING RATIOS

Margaret von Rolf, long a manager for a Chicago-based national moving and storage company, has recently been assigned the position of manager of a newly acquired company, Sunshine Moving and Storage Company. Sunshine's annual sales are approximately $850,000. Though the company is not as profitable as similar companies in the national system, Sunshine was considered a good buy because it is well located in a West Coast city of one million people, the rolling equipment is relatively new, and the two warehouses are modern and well kept. The parent corporation believes that increased sales efforts should produce an annual sales volume of at least $950,000 and a net profit before taxes of 6 percent of annual sales.

After studying the operating statement for the previous year, shown in Exhibit I, von Rolf prepared a summary of the major operating ratios used as guides by the parent company in evaluating the performance of company-owned moving and storage facilities and in advising those privately owned companies that operate under a franchise system. Regarding revenue sources, it is recommended that companies located on the West Coast derive no more than 25 percent of their revenue from long-distance moving, with at least 27 percent of their revenue coming from local moving. It is important to control the ratio between long-distance and local-moving revenues because the direct operating expenses incurred by long-distance moving approximate 80 percent of long-distance revenue, while local-moving operating expenses are about 77 percent of local-moving revenue. It is also recommended that storage and warehousing revenue account for at least 18 percent of total revenue, with 20 percent of total revenue from this source being entirely possible. Similarly, packing and crating revenues should range between 14 and 16 percent of the total, and commissions earned from business booked for vans from other terminals should account for at least 10 percent of total revenue. Commissions are regarded as a particularly valuable source of revenue because little capital equipment is utilized and there is usually additional income resulting from required packing and crating.

Recommended ratios for major expense items are summarized in the figures shown on page 437.

SUNSHINE MOVING & STORAGE COMPANY

Revenue Sources:

1. Long distance	$301,750
2. Local moving	204,850
3. Commissions	85,000
4. Storage and warehousing	128,350
5. Packing and crating	130,050
Total revenue	$850,000

Expense Items:

6. Traffic and sales

Supervision, sales, and clerical salaries	$ 34,000
Advertising	12,750
Other expenses	12,750
Total traffic and sales	$ 59,500

7. Administrative and general expense

Salaries (officers and managers)	$ 42,500
Other administrative salaries	45,900
Other general administrative expense	90,950
Total administrative and general expense	$179,350

8. Trucking expense (includes long distance and local moving)

Equipment maintenance	$ 39,515
Insurance and safety	19,757
Depreciation	20,264
Taxes and licenses	15,705
Transportation—supervisor, wages, fuel oil	351,316
Total trucking expense	$426,557

9. Storage and warehousing expense

Supervision and clerical employees	$ 5,519
Building expense	34,783
Insurance, taxes, maintenance and supplies	11,423
Wages	25,625
Total storage and warehousing expense	$ 77,350

10. Packing and crating expense

Supervision and office employees	$ 2,601
Depreciation, insurance, taxes	11,835
Materials and supplies	22,499
Wages	41,265
Total packing and crating expense	$ 78,200

Profit or loss:

11. Profit	$ 29,043

Exhibit I
ANNUAL
OPERATING
STATEMENT

DEPARTMENT	PERCENTAGE OF TOTAL REVENUE
Traffic and Sales:	
Supervision, sales, and clerical personnel	5.7%
Advertising	3.0
Other expenses	.9
	9.6%
Administrative and General:	
Salaries (officers and managers)	4.5%
Other salaries....................................	5.5
Other general expenses	10.5
	20.5%

	PERCENTAGE OF DEPARTMENTAL REVENUE
Trucking Department:	
Equipment and maintenance	6.0%
Insurance and safety	3.5
Depreciation.....................................	3.5
Taxes and licenses...............................	2.5
Transportation (including fuel, wages, and	
subsistence)	62.0
	77.5%
Storage and Warehousing:	
Supervisory and office personnel	4.5%
Building expense	28.0
Depreciation, insurance, and taxes	9.5
Wages	20.0
	62.0%
Packing and Crating:	
Supervison and office personnel....................	3.1%
Depreciation, insurance, and taxes	9.5
Materials and supplies	15.0
Wages	29.0
	56.6%

Exhibit II
RATIOS FOR
MAJOR
EXPENSE
ITEMS

PROBLEMS

1. Are company expectations for sales and profits reasonable? What action would you take to increase sales?

2. Analyze each of the operating departments—trucking, storage and warehousing, and packing and crating—with respect to company recommendations for such operations and indicate the steps you would take as manager of Sunshine Moving and Storage Company in order to bring performance in line with expected results.

3. How profitable is each of the four sources of revenue—commissions, trucking, storage and warehousing, and packing and crating—when traffic and sales expense and administrative and general expense are apportioned to each in the same percentage amount that the source is of total sales?

In Chapter 19, it is stated that standards may be set for each of the following key result areas: (1) profitability, (2) market position, (3) productivity, (4) product leadership, (5) personnel development, (6) employee attitudes, (7) public responsibility, and (8) balance between short-range and long-range goals. Since the nature of the goals and the kind of performance required to meet stated objectives in each of these areas are different, it seems highly unlikely that a single control device can be used with equal effectiveness in all areas. Such is the case. Budgets, discussed in Chapter 21, are a very effective means of controlling expense and revenue items; thus, they are particularly useful in controlling performance in the areas of profitability and productivity. However, there are other means of control, conveniently referred to as *nonbudgetary*, that are necessary to establish an effective and complete system of control. These techniques of nonbudgetary control, arranged in order from the simple to the more complex, are as follows: personal observation, reports, audit programs, ratio analysis, break-even analysis, and time-event-network analysis.

PERSONAL OBSERVATION

Personal observation is a means of securing control information applicable to all key result areas and is used by all levels of management. The supervisor in charge of a manufacturing department or a clerical section relies to a great extent upon impressions gained as the result of personal contact with subordinates. Output is judged by observing the pace of subordinates; quality can be evaluated by personally inspecting the work in progress; and an estimate of morale and attitudes results from seeing employees, listening to their spontaneous remarks, and obtaining responses to questions. The plant manager who makes a daily tour of the plant is able to obtain firsthand information concerning conditions in the plant that are not revealed by formal reports. Similarly, many presidents and chief executive officers visit all company installations at least once each year so that the personal impressions thus gained may become a part of the basis for their decisions.

Personal observation as a means of gaining information is time consuming and is often criticized for this reason. Also, there is the possibility that subordinates may misinterpret a superior's visit and consider such action as meddling or failure to delegate. Finally, the value of firsthand information obtained from personal contact is limited by the perceptual skills and interpretative ability of the observer. Even so, personal observations are often the only means of substantiating impressions gained from other sources, and personal contacts almost always have a salutary effect upon subordinates since the presence of one's superior reveals an interest in the operation.

REPORTS

In designing or evaluating control reports, two closely related questions arise: (1) What is the purpose of the report? and (2) Who should receive the report?

Purpose of Control Reports

The primary purpose of control reports is to supply information intended to serve as the basis for corrective action if needed. At the same time, the significance of control reports must be kept in proper perspective. Control reports are only a part of the planning-control-planning information cycle that is necessary for a complete management information system. Control information includes nonfinancial as well as financial data, it measures performance, and it isolates variances from standard. Control information also provides feedback so that planning information may be updated and corrected.

An example of a set of relatively simple control reports that contribute to the control process as well as provide a basis for updating the planning process is presented in Chapter 19, page 428. In this illustration the owner of a company manufacturing trays for cafeterias and drive-in restaurants receives reports containing information that shows the current backlog of orders, finished goods inventory, number of units shipped, and total hours of factory labor. A decline in the backlog of current orders, with the other three measures remaining relatively constant, indicates the need for corrective action resulting in increased sales. In this instance, the information provided serves primarily the control function. However, an increase in the order backlog, again with all other measures remaining constant, signals the need for additional planning so that production may be increased to meet the increased demand. Whenever possible, control reports should be designed so that they provide feedback for the planning process as well as provide information of immediate value to the control process.

Distribution of Control Reports

Since the culmination of the control process is the taking of necessary corrective action to bring performance in line with standards, it follows that control information must be directed to the person who is organizationally responsible for taking the required action. Usually the same information, though in a somewhat abbreviated form, is given to the responsible manager's superior. The supervisor of a manufacturing department requires detailed information that describes the performance of equipment and personnel of the department. The plant manager may receive condensed summary statements showing performance in relation to standard, expressed as a percentage, for each of several operating departments. A district sales manager needs a complete daily record of the performance of each salesperson; yet the report forwarded to the regional sales manager summarizes only the performance of each sales district in the region. In preparing reports for higher echelons of management, summary statements and recommendations for action should appear on the first page; substantiating data, usually the information presented to the person directly responsible for the operation, may be included if needed.

Characteristics of Good Reports

Since control reports are an integral part of a control system, they should incorporate the characteristics of an effective control system as described in

Chapter 19, pages 426 to 431. They should be timely, particularly those prepared for a unit supervisor. When reports provide information intended primarily for the purpose of control, they should follow organizational lines. It must be remembered that for the same information to become effective as a basis for additional planning, it is necessary to cross organizational lines. Reports should be prepared to reveal activity in the more sensitive or strategic areas of the business. In organizations where progress depends on new products, frequent periodic reporting of research and development activities may be required. A firm whose chief concern is manufacturing efficiency may emphasize a detailed reporting of the production process. Reports should be economical, and their costs should be measured in terms of the extent to which they actually contribute to the control process. In preparing reports, sufficient data should be included so that trends as well as current status are reflected. Finally, reports should be prepared so that the exception is emphasized. Summary statements should stress performance that deviates from standard and should show clearly both the direction and magnitude of the deviation.

AUDIT PROGRAMS

Traditionally, auditing, an independent appraisal of a company's financial records, seeks to test the reliability and validity of financial records by determining the degree of accuracy and the extent to which financial statements reflect what they purport to represent. As a result, audit programs are often regarded as a means of encouraging honesty on the part of employees and safeguarding the company's financial resources. This concept of auditing, the verification of company financial records, is limited in scope and is associated with *external audits* conducted by outside agencies such as bank examiners or a firm of public accountants. When conducted by a specialized staff made up of company personnel, auditing can be an effective means of control as well as a means of verifying financial records, and is known as the *internal audit.* It is possible also to apply the techniques of auditing as a means of assessing the overall effectiveness of management, an application often referred to as the *management audit.* In addition, *human resource accounting* can be used by companies whose production depends primarily on the creativity of its personnel. Each of these forms of auditing, the external audit, the internal audit, the management audit, and human resource accounting is discussed in turn.

External Auditing

The external audit is usually conducted by a firm of public accountants. Its primary purpose is to determine whether or not company records of financial transactions present a true statement of the company's financial condition. It is essentially a verification of the accuracy of the records and a determination of the consistency of application of accepted accounting procedures. In order to make a summary statement of the financial condition of a company, it is necessary for the auditors to spot check all types of basic financial transactions to determine their accuracy. It is the checking phase of the auditing process that causes many to regard external auditing as a means of encouraging honesty on the part of employees. For example, a review of inventory records, a part of the process of verifying assets, may reveal shortages that may be the result of dishonesty.

The contribution of the external audit to the control process is indirect and limited in its nature. For instance, a company might wish to allocate certain capital expenditures as expense items, but independent auditors will not certify such allocations unless they are consistent with previously established accounting procedures. The same indirect form of control may be exerted if a company attempts to modify its statement of assets by altering established practices of evaluating finished goods or raw material inventories. The value of the external audit as a means of assessing financial position is limited by the appropriateness, or validity, of existing accounting procedures. When the summary information of the audit—usually a verification of the balance sheet items of assets, liabilities, and net worth—is used as a basis for formulating the corrective action of the control process, its worth is no greater than the validity of the accounting techniques used to record the financial condition of the company.

Internal Auditing

As the name implies, the internal audit is conducted by a specialized staff made up of company personnel. Like the external audit conducted by an outside source, the internal audit verifies the accuracy of company records and determines whether or not such records are what they purport to be. However, the purpose of the internal audit is to provide a means of internal control. It seeks to determine the effectiveness of other controls; consequently, the internal audit may be regarded as a master control over all other forms of control.

The potential benefits of an effective internal auditing program are many; however, there are three contributions that stand out above all others. First, internal auditing provides a way of determining whether established procedures and methods are effective in meeting stated company objectives and insuring compliance with stated policies. If, for example, it is the objective of a company to build a product having the highest possible quality, procedures are established to insure that component parts of the product are the best available. In reviewing purchase requisitions, the internal audit team goes beyond the accuracy of the records of the purchasing department and seeks to determine whether or not, in fact, components are of the highest available quality. The determination of the extent to which company policies are observed leads directly to the second major contribution of internal auditing—formulating recommendations for the improvement of policies, procedures, and methods so that they are more effective in the attainment of stated objectives. It may be necessary to modify existing controls, establish new controls, or change present procedures or methods. Deviations from established procedures may arise because someone has discovered a supposed short cut, or there may have been an honest misunderstanding of the procedure due to its complexity. Whatever the reason, it is the task of the internal auditor to recommend those changes necessary to insure compliance, including the recommendation for additional or improved controls.

The third benefit of an internal auditing program may seem paradoxical at first glance. Internal auditing is a means of providing a greater degree of delegation of authority and, if desirable, a means of facilitating the decentralization of operations. Delegation of authority and its broader organizational counterpart, the decentralization of authority to operating units, do not imply an absence of centralized control. On the contrary, the extent of delegation and decentralization is dependent to a large measure upon the effectiveness of central control. Internal auditing offers a means of continually checking the effectiveness of established controls and recommending needed improvements.

The use of the internal audit as a means of control has been increasing, particularly in large companies. Even though many small and medium-size companies do not have internal auditing departments, the function of internal auditing can still be accomplished to a degree by emphasizing that one of the functions of control is to determine the extent to which procedures and methods are being observed and to recommend improvements.

The success of internal auditing is dependent not only upon the attitude of top management but also upon the degree of acceptance accorded the audit team by lower and middle echelons of management. Acceptance by other members of management is more readily attained when internal auditors perform the functions of consultants and act as special staff advisors concerned with the improvement of all operations rather than appearing as custodians of company resources.[1]

The Management Audit

The external audit is concerned chiefly with verifying the reliability and validity of financial records. Internal auditing goes a step further and determines the degree of compliance with company policies, procedures, and methods, and, if necessary, makes recommendations to insure the observance of established company practices. An even broader form of auditing is the *management audit,* a systematic approach to the appraisal of the overall performance of management.

One of the better known methods of appraising managerial performance is the management audit developed by Jackson Martindell of the American Institute of Management (AIM).[2] The AIM management audit evaluates the performance of a company in relation to the performance of other companies

---

[1] The following article suggests that participation is a means of making an audit committee more effective. Michael L. Lovdal, "Making the Audit Committee Work," *Harvard Business Review,* Vol. 55, No. 2 (March–April, 1977), p. 108.

[2] Jackson Martindell, *The Appraisal of Management for Executives and Investors* (New York City: Harper & Row, Publishers, 1962). This book is a revised statement of Martindell's original program that was first published under the same title and by the same publisher in 1950.

Jackson Martindell, "Management Audits Simplified," *The Corporate Director,* Special Issue, No. 15 (December, 1951), p. 1.

in the same industry and in relation to the performance of outstanding companies in other industries. Some of the information needed for the management audit is a matter of public record, but much of it comes from the answers to a 300-item questionnaire. Point values for the answers given to each question are assigned, with the maximum number of points being 10,000. Managerial performance in each of the following 10 categories is evaluated: [3]

1. Economic Function
2. Corporate Structure
3. Health of Earnings
4. Service to Stockholders
5. Research and Development
6. Directorate Analysis
7. Fiscal Policies
8. Production Efficiency
9. Sales Vigor
10. Executive Evaluation

There has been much criticism of the AIM audit. For many, it is oriented too much toward the investment concept of business management. Of the 10,000 total points, only 500 are allowed for corporate structure, 2,200 for executive evaluation, and 800 for directorate analysis—making a maximum of 3,500 points for these categories. Production efficiency and sales vigor comprise a maximum of 2,000 points; the remaining 4,500 are distributed among the categories of economic function, health of earnings, service to stockholders, research and development, and fiscal policies. Another criticism is that the audit rates past performance too heavily and does not attempt to evaluate future performance.[4] In support of these criticisms, instances are cited of companies with ratings of "excellent" that experienced severe financial difficulties. For example, Douglas Aircraft Company received the rating of "excellently managed" for 1957, 1958, and 1959, and then suffered severe financial reverses during the latter part of 1959 and 1960. In 1957 Allis Chalmers Manufacturing Company and Olin Mathesen Chemical Company received "excellently managed" ratings that were soon followed by marked financial problems [5]

Despite the shortcomings of the management audit, the audit program developed by the American Institute of Management establishes firmly the concept that the performance of management can and should be subject to evaluation as a part of an overall control program. The management audit focuses attention upon many aspects of managerial performance rather than upon one or two easily measured performance areas. Second, the audit emphasizes the measure-

---

[3] Jackson Martindell, "The Management Audit," *The Corporate Director*, Vol. 9 (December, 1962), p. 1. This is a paper presented to the Academy of Management at the annual meeting held in Pittsburgh in December, 1962.

[4] Robert B. Buchele, "How to Evaluate a Firm," *California Management Review*, Vol. 5 (Fall, 1962), p. 5. Buchele presents a method for evaluating a firm that attempts to weight the future more than the past.

[5] The ratings are presented in *Manual of Excellent Managements* (New York City: American Institute of Management, 1957).

ment of the results of managerial performance rather than appraising the purpose of managerial performance. Third, individual companies that work seriously with the concept of auditing management's performance may develop as the result of experience within their own organization a means of assigning weight to the various performance categories that will prove a valid predictor of future performance.[6]

Human Resource Accounting

An approach that offsets some of the major shortcomings of the AIM management audit, particularly its inability to predict future performance, is human resource accounting. Fundamental to the concept of human resource accounting is the positive relationship that exists between the performance of an organization and the quality and quantity of its human resource capability. The quality of human resources is highly significant for those companies whose product or service relies upon knowledge, research, and creativity. Traditionally the expenditure of funds for recruitment, training and development, and other items associated with the acquisition and upgrading of personnel are treated as expense items. Human resource accounting regards these expenditures as an investment in assets. Conventional accounting practices do not offer a true picture of an organization's effectiveness or potential. For the firm that is building human resources faster than they are being consumed, conventional accounting understates net income; conversely, the firm that is consuming its human resources faster than the replacement rate has an overstatement of its profits. Also, in the budgeting process expenditures for physical facilities are regarded as capital expenditures and are not necessarily justified in terms of revenue for the current year. Yet the manager who wishes to invest in human resources is forced to justify expenditures in this area in terms of additional revenue for the current year since costs associated with people are considered an expense. Human resource accounting seeks to treat expenditures in human resources as an investment in assets thereby enabling one to predict future performance as the rate of consumption of human resources relative to the rate of replacement of human resources becomes known.[7]

The R. G. Barry Corporation, a leisure footwear manufacturer headquartered in Columbus, Ohio, instituted a plan to develop human resource accounting in conjunction with William C. Pyle, Director of Human Resource Accounting Research of the University of Michigan. As noted by Robert J. Woodruff, Jr., vice-president—human resources of R. G. Barry Corporation, the company has a technology comparable to the apparel industry with one of the lowest ratios of capital investment per employee of any industry and with labor repre-

[6] The following reference may be of interest to small businesses: *Management Audit for Small Retailers* (Washington: Small Business Administration, 1972).

[7] C. Ray Gullett and Robert W. Peddy, "Human Resource Accounting: Can It Be Implemented Now?" *Personnel Administrator*, Vol. 23, No. 6 (June, 1978), p. 60.

Philip H. Mirvis and Barry A. Mach, "Human Resource Accounting: A Measurement Perspective," *The Academy of Management Review*, Vol. 1, No. 2 (April, 1976), p. 74.

senting a significant portion of total product costs. Further, the R. G. Barry Corporation has long had a strong philosophical commitment to the recognition of the importance of people to its operations. The seven functional accounts developed by the R. G. Barry Corporation for use in its human resource accounting are:

1. *Recruiting outlay costs*—costs associated with locating and selecting new (management) personnel. This category includes search fees; advertising; interviewer or interviewee travel expenses; allocations of personnel; and acquiring department time for internal screening, interviewing, testing, and evaluation expenses. Outlay costs for unsuccessful candidates are allocated to the cost of obtaining the candidate hired.

2. *Acquisition costs*—costs incurred in bringing a new employee "on board." This category includes placement fees, moving costs, physical examination, allocation of personnel, and acquiring department time in placing an employee on the payroll and situating him or her with the necessary equipment to perform the job.

3. *Formal training and familiarization costs*—costs normally incurred immediately after hire or possible transfer from one location to another. These refer to formal orientation programs, vestibule training, etc.

4. *Informal training costs*—costs associated with the process of teaching a new person to adapt his or her existing skills to the specific job requirements of the new job. The costs related to this process are normally salary allocations only and vary with each position depending upon the level of the job in the organization, number of subordinates, interaction patterns outside the department, etc.

5. *Familiarization costs*—costs associated with the very complex process of integrating a new manager into the organization to the point where he or she can be a fully effective member. Such costs include learning the company's philosophy, history, policies, objectives, communications patterns, past practices, precedents, understanding of the people with whom the new position-holder will regularly interact. These costs, which can be sizable, depending upon the level and scope of the position, include salary allocations.

6. *Investment building experience costs*—costs associated with investments in on-the-job training which occur after the initial familiarization period and which are expected to have value to the company beyond the current accounting period. Investment building experience is the development of a capability which would not reasonably be expected as a normal part of the person's job.

7. *Development costs*—costs associated with investments in increasing a manager's capabilities in areas beyond the specific technical skills required by the position. In this category are management seminars, university programs or courses, etc. Costs are collected by means of a "Training & Development Requisition," and are modified by the participant's evaluation of the pertinency of the study.[8]

The R. G. Barry Corporation later developed a pro forma balance sheet, an income statement that shows the effect of human resource accounting concepts upon the conventional accounting statement.[9] In effect, human resource accounting provides internal control over the long-term management of human resources.

---

[8] R. L. Woodruff, Jr., "Human Resource Accounting," *Canadian Chartered Accountant*, Vol. 97, No. 3 (September, 1970), p. 156. The functional accounts are stated on pp. 157–158.

[9] *Annual Report 1968* (Columbus, Ohio: R. G. Barry Corporation).

RATIO ANALYSIS

A *ratio* is a way of expressing the proportional relationship that exists between two measures. Ratios may be expressed as:

1. A proportion, by using a colon to separate two measures—1:2.
2. A fraction—½.
3. A percentage—½ × 100 = 50%.

Whatever the method of expression—proportion, fraction, or percentage—a ratio shows the magnitude of the relationship between two measures. The analysis of ratios existing between various measures of organizational performance is a very useful and necessary control technique.

Single measures of organizational performance seldom have much meaning. For example, the statement that a company earned $100,000, after taxes, during the past fiscal year expresses only the dollar volume of earnings. For a statement of earnings to have more meaning, it is necessary to compare and describe the earnings of a competitor. In a like manner, the fact that a salesperson sold $5,000 worth of goods last month or that a production worker produced 50 units yesterday conveys little information. We have to know the performance standards for salespeople and production workers before drawing conclusions concerning the adequacy of their performance.

Ratio analysis is not new, and much has been written about it as a control technique. It is beyond the scope of this chapter to survey all or even a majority of the ratios used in analyzing and controlling business operations since there are many of them and the usefulness of a given set of ratios varies considerably from one industry to another. However, a few of the most frequently used ratios are presented and discussed briefly. For convenience, the ratios discussed are classified as *financial ratios*—contributing primarily to a greater understanding of the financial condition of a company—and *operating ratios*—providing greater understanding of the operational aspects of a company. Some of the difficulties in interpreting ratios are also presented.

Financial Ratios

Admittedly, financial ratios tell us something about the manner in which a company is operated as well as reveal financial condition. Yet these ratios may be regarded as primarily financial in nature since much of the basic data is derived from the balance sheet and the information provided by these ratios is descriptive of a company's financial condition. The first and second ratios discussed below are statements of profitability; the last two ratios are statements of liquidity and are of particular significance to creditors.

Profit as a Percentage of Capital Invested. Many consider the relationship between profit (after taxes) and invested capital to be the most important single ratio. In the use of this ratio, profit is expressed as a percentage of invested capital, and when computed annually, a trend line is established. Profit as a percentage of invested capital reveals how well the capital resources are being utilized. Comparisons may be made with other companies in the same industry, but the value of such comparisons is limited because the method used in evaluating invested capital varies from one company to another. Although there is no means of determining the optimum level of profitability, a realistic minimum level can be defined. The return on invested capital, after taxes, should be greater than the return guaranteed by other forms of investment—for example, tax-exempt municipal bonds. In addition to the basic rate of return offered by securities, there should be some compensation for risk and managerial effort.

Profit as a Percentage of Sales. Again, it is necessary to compute profitability from year to year so that a trend may be established. Also, comparisons with other companies in the same industry are valuable. Expressing profit as a percentage of sales volume is particularly helpful when analyzing the possible contribution of new product lines or when considering the deletion of current products. The profit-to-sales ratio is of value in measuring managerial effectiveness in the control of variable or controllable costs. For instance, within a retail chain, units of similar sales volume and fixed costs can be compared and differences in profitability may be attributed to the control of variable costs.

Current Ratio. The *current ratio* is of particular significance to creditors because it is an indication of a company's ability to pay its bills promptly. Current ratio is determined by dividing current assets by current liabilities as stated on the balance sheet. Unlike the measures of profit, which are usually expressed as a percentage, current ratio is expressed as a proportion; i.e., 2:1 or 2.5:1. Although there seems to be general agreement that a company should have a current ratio of assets to liabilities of at least 2:1 to insure ability to pay current obligations, the determination of what constitutes a satisfactory ratio is much more complex than it appears to be. Some of the problems encountered in interpreting the current ratio are discussed later under the heading, "Interpreting Ratios."

Quick Ratio. The *quick ratio,* sometimes called the *acid test ratio,* is found by dividing the company's quick assets, usually cash and negotiable securities, by current liabilities. Accounts receivable and inventory, generally a part of current assets and used in computing the current ratio, are excluded since there may be considerable time required to convert these items into cash. A minimum quick ratio of 1:1 indicates that there is sufficient cash to meet maturing obligations.

Operating Ratios

There are several ratios that contribute more to an understanding of the operations of a company than they do to an appreciation of the financial structure of a company; thus, they are referred to as operating ratios. Three of these ratios contribute to our knowledge of the sales function of a company. The fourth ratio is a generalized concept of input-output functions.

Net Sales to Average Inventory. Dividing net sales by average inventory value yields a measure of inventory turnover. For instance, net sales of $600,000 with an average inventory evaluation of $200,000 indicates that the inventory turnover rate is three times a year. If desired, the average number of days required for a complete inventory turnover can be computed as follows: $\frac{\text{Average Inventory} \times 365}{\text{Net Sales}}$. In the example above, the average number of days is 121. The net sales to average inventory ratio is an indication of how well the working capital invested in inventory is being utilized; consequently, the ratio should be interpreted in conjunction with profitability expressed as a percentage of sales. A profit of 2 percent on net sales, typical of many retail food operations, does not seem very great; but with an average inventory of $100,000 and an annual inventory turnover rate of 35, the absolute dollar volume of profit is considerable in relation to the amount of capital invested in inventory. The sales to inventory ratio provides the control information that is needed to insure maximum inventory turnover.

Net Sales to Total Market. Expressing net sales as a percentage of the total market—defined either geographically or by product line—indicates whether or not a company is maintaining its share of an ever-changing market potential. Dollar volume of sales does not provide such information since it is quite possible for a company's sales to show an annual increase, yet the rate of increase may be less than the market's rate of growth. Thus, a firm with an annual sales increase of four percent in a market that is expanding at a rate of six percent shows an increasing sales volume and a decreasing share of the potential market.

Selling Expense to Net Sales. Expressing selling expense as a percentage of net sales offers a means of determining the efficiency of the selling function. Selling expense may be broken down into greater detail by specifying the costs of maintaining a sales force, of advertising, or of administrative costs.

Input-Output Ratios. The number and the kind of input-output ratios used as control measures vary a great deal from one company to another. Such ratios are almost always expressed as percentages and are measures of efficiency in the utilization of inputs. Some of the more common measures of inputs and outputs are as follows:

Inputs	*Outputs*
Payroll dollars	Net sales
Employee-hours worked	Units produced
Square feet of floor space	Units sold
Advertising costs	

Each input can be paired with any one of the outputs.

Interpreting Ratios

Although ratios are widely used, there are three difficulties encountered in their interpretation that limit their value as a means of providing precise control information. First, a ratio is a quotient obtained by the arithmetic process of dividing a numerator by a denominator. A change in the value of a quotient may result from a change in the value of either the numerator or the denominator. There is no way of determining which member of the fraction changed in value by noting the change in the quotient. An analysis of the current ratio illustrates this point. Assume that a company has current assets of $60,000 and current liabilities of $30,000, thereby producing a comfortable current ratio of 2:1. Do we know what has happened if we read that the company now has a current ratio of 3:1? Fixed assets may have been sold in the amount of $30,000 and added to current assets to yield the 3:1 ratio. Or the amount realized from the sale of assets may have been $10,000 and applied to the reduction of current liabilities, again creating a 3:1 ratio. When changes occur in a ratio, it is necessary to inspect the original data used in arriving at the numeric values of the numerator and the denominator in order to have a sound basis for determining the significance of the change that has occurred.

Second, it must be realized that there is no precise means of determining what constitutes a good or a satisfactory ratio. Ratios should be used over a period of time so that trends may be established. Only then can a determination be made as to which ratios offer significant information for the control process. Occasionally it is helpful to compare ratios with those of similar companies in the same industry. Even so, there must be some assurance that the accounting systems used by the several companies are comparable.

The third danger inherent in the use of ratios is that of inferring causal relationships that are not warranted. A marketing manager may conclude that an increase in selling expense as a percentage of sales indicates a decrease in the number of units sold by the sales force, but the real reason could be due to a decrease in unit price. Most faulty inferences result from a failure to examine closely the direction and magnitude of change in both the numerator and denominator and failure to evaluate the validity and reliability of the data used in computing the ratio.

Despite the difficulties encountered in interpreting ratios, they remain a useful control device when there is a thorough understanding of the manner in which they are developed and when there are several related ratios presented so that the significance of any one ratio may be checked by comparing it with another.

BREAK-EVEN ANALYSIS

Break-even analysis utilizes the same concepts employed in the construction of variable budgets (Chapter 21, pages 466 to 469). There are striking similarities between the break-even chart (Figure 20–1) and the graphic representation of a variable expense budget shown in Figure 21–1, page 467. However, there are two important differences: First, the vertical axis of the break-even chart is designated as a revenue-expense axis rather than an expense axis; and second, the sales revenue line of the break-even chart shows the expected revenue for

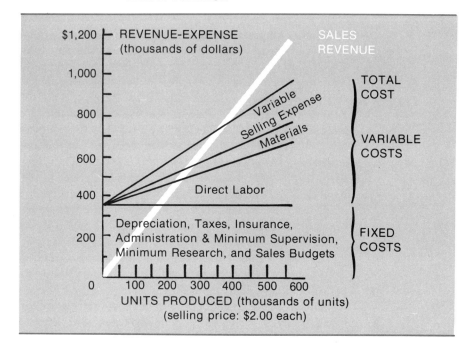

**Figure 20–1
BREAK-EVEN
CHART**

each level of sales volume. The point where the revenue line intersects the total cost line is the break-even point.

An understanding of the dynamic relationships existing between the factors included in the break-even chart enables one to forecast and plan for profit. The break-even point and consequently the amount of profit vary with changes in any one of four factors: unit volume, fixed cost, variable cost, and unit selling price. Further, the precise effect upon the break-even point resulting from a change in one or any combination of these variables can be determined by means of the following formula:

$$\text{Break-Even Point} = \frac{\text{Fixed Expense}}{P/V\,\text{ratio}}$$
$$\text{when } P/V = \frac{\text{Sales } - \text{Variable Costs}}{\text{Sales}}$$

The ability to predict changes in profits under various operating conditions has obvious applications to the process of planning. A knowledge of the relationship of the factors that influence profit is equally applicable to the control process, a re-emphasis of the continuous nature of the planning-control-planning cycle. Specifically, break-even analysis provides information that aids in the control of costs and underscores the importance of sales volume.[10]

---

[10] For a discussion of the application of break-even analysis to small businesses, the following is recommended: Peter G. Goulet, "Attacking Business Decision Problems with Break-Even Analysis," *Management Aids* (for Small Manufacturers) (U. S. Small Business Administration), No. 234, March, 1978.

Cost Control

Break-even charts can be prepared so that they contribute to overall control by showing both fixed and variable costs for the entire company. They can also be prepared for smaller operating units such as manufacturing departments or sales districts. In either case, fixed costs are segregated from variable costs. Fixed costs move slowly and show little variation as the result of changes in sales volume. Variable costs, on the other hand, vary directly as a function of volume. By their very nature, variable costs are subject to some degree of control. By clearly separating these variable costs, attention is directed toward those areas where corrective action is possible. When presented in the graphic form of a break-even chart, deviations from budgeted expenses are readily recognized.

Sales Volume

An analysis of the break-even formula above shows clearly the effect of sales beyond the break-even point on profit. The P/V ratio, the denominator of the fraction on the right side of the equation, expresses the profitability of an operation after the break-even point has been reached. Too many small and medium-size firms tend to express profitability as a percentage of total sales rather than as a percentage of sales beyond the break-even point. The following operating statement indicates a net profit of 10 percent of total sales:

Revenue from sales		$1,000,000
Variable costs	$500,000	
Fixed costs	400,000	
Total costs		900,000
Net profit		$ 100,000

However, the P/V ratio $\dfrac{\$1,000,000 - \$500,000}{\$1,000,000}$ indicates that the profitability of each unit sold beyond the break-even point is 50 percent. By emphasizing the contribution to profit of additional sales beyond the break-even point, there is greater incentive to stimulate and control sales effort.

TIME-EVENT-NETWORK ANALYSIS

To meet the requirements of what has been called "an age of massive engineering"—in contrast to repetitive production—a number of fairly sophisticated techniques for the analysis of networks have been developed.[11] Two time-event-network analysis techniques were developed separately and published in 1959. The Program Evaluation Review Technique (PERT) was developed by the Special Projects Office of the U. S. Navy Bureau of Ordinance, with the assistance of staff members of the management consulting firm of Booz, Allen, and Hamil-

---

[11] See "Thinking Ahead: The Age of Massive Engineering," *Harvard Business Review*, Vol. 39 (January–February, 1961), p. 138.

ton. It was first used in the development of the Polaris Fleet Ballistic Missile.[12] The Critical Path Method (CPM) of network analysis was developed by DuPont to reduce downtime for periodic maintenance.[13] PERT is credited with saving two years in the development of the Polaris missile, while the CPM cut DuPont's downtime for maintenance in the Louisville plant from 125 to 93 hours.[14] Before discussing the relative merits and applications of PERT and CPM, let us review some of the fundamentals of network analysis.[15]

Fundamentals of Network Analysis

In order to use network analysis for purposes of planning and control, several conditions must be met:

1. *A clearly recognizable end point or objective.* One-of-a-kind projects, such as developing and building the first prototype of the Polaris missile or the construction of a shopping center, meet this requirement. The installation of a data processing system, the construction of a highway interchange, or the building of a piece of special machinery all have clearly definable and recognizable end points. In contrast, the 100,000th car from an assembly line is difficult to distinguish from its immediate predecessor or successor.

2. *A series of events.* There should be a series of clearly defined, separate, but interrelated, events leading up to the completion of the final project. In constructing a highway interchange, temporary routes must be built, bridges constructed, drainage facilities installed, service roads prepared, and many other distinct subprojects completed before the interchange is ready for use.

3. *Time for each activity.* The time required for the completion of the work or activity preceding each event must be calculated. Herein lies one of the major differences between PERT and CPM. PERT employs a method of estimating probable time, even though there has been no prior experience to serve as a basis for estimating time. CPM implies some prior experience or knowledge of the time estimated for the completion of activities leading to each event.

4. *A starting point.* There must be a recognizable starting point—the issuance of a sales order for a piece of special machinery, notification from the government to begin the development of a weapons system, or the date of a scheduled plant shutdown as the beginning of an annual maintenance program.

Figure 20–2 is a schematic diagram of a network analysis. Each square in the diagram represents an event. The number that appears in each square except the first is a statement of the amount of work, expressed in days, that must

---

[12] Donald G. Malcolm *et al.*, "Applications of a Technique for Research and Development Program Evaluation," *Operations Research*, Vol. 7 (September–October, 1959), p. 646.

[13] James E. Kelley, Jr., and Morgan R. Walker, "Critical Path Planning and Scheduling," *Proceedings of the Eastern Joint Computer Conference* (December, 1959).

[14] F. K. Levy, G. L. Thompson, and J. D. Wiest, "The ABCs of the Critical Path Method," *Harvard Business Review*, Vol. 41 (September–October, 1963), p. 100. On pp. 102–103 there is a discussion of how to determine the critical path through the use of a relatively simple algorithm.

[15] The term *review* is used advisedly since network analysis required by PERT and CPM is similar to the analysis of information systems required in the design of an integrated data processing system.

be completed so that the event in question can occur. Events, as such, require no time; they merely serve as milestones. The letter in each square designates the event and in an actual chart would be explained in a legend. The arrows indicate the sequence of events. The length of each arrow has no particular significance. The color arrows represent the *critical path*, the longest route in time from start to finish. If the duration of the project is to be shortened, it must be shortened by reducing the time intervals necessary for the completion of each event along this pathway. To reduce the work time along another path would not reduce the total time required for the project; instead, it would merely create more "slack"—excess time in the other pathways.

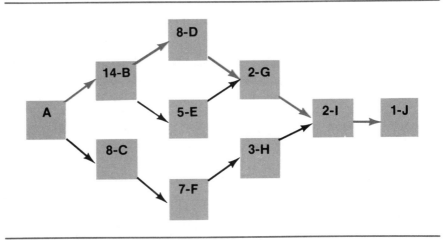

**Figure 20–2
SCHEMATIC
NETWORK
ANALYSIS**

Let us assume that the project represented by the network in Figure 20–2 is a piece of special purpose machinery including both electrical and mechanical components. In charting a network, the analysis of the project commences with the end result, the finished machine, and then works backwards, step by step, until the origin of the project is reached, the issuance of a sales order. The machine is ready for shipment when it has passed final inspection (J), a process that takes one day after the completion of final assembly (I). Thus, the number 1 and the letter J are entered in the square designating the completion of the project. Final assembly takes two days to complete but cannot be started until the subassembly of all electrical components (H) and all mechanical components (G) is finished. To perform the mechanical subassembly, components must be released by the milling department (D) and the lathe department (E). The largest single requirement for time in this network is the 14 days needed to procure mechanical components (B). The project starts with the issuance of the sales order (A). The same procedure is followed in analyzing the sequence of operations in the production of the electrical components of the manufacturing process.

Two major advantages result from the use of time-event-network analysis techniques. In the first place, breaking a project down into its component events, specifying the time required for the completion of each activity, and designating the sequence of events force a degree of planning that improves any production process. Presenting this information pictorially as a network offers the second advantage—a clear understanding of the interdependence and relationships that exist between the various events. We know that the critical path, by definition, is the longest route in time. In the example discussed, and shown in Figure 20–2, the critical path is 27 days. If the duration of the project is to be shortened, attention and control effort must be directed toward the critical path.

With this introduction to network analysis, let us examine PERT in more detail.

PERT

PERT in its original form stresses the time required to perform the activities necessary for a given event to occur. The unique contribution of PERT as a form of network analysis is that it provides a means of obtaining a probability estimate of the expected time to complete activities that have not been performed previously and, therefore, have not been measured. The building of the Polaris missile, the first application of PERT, is a case in point. None of the activities leading up to the specified events had been performed before; consequently, there were no historical records or time study standards to serve as a basis for estimating expected times.

To determine the probable expected time for activities leading to an event, PERT requires three time estimates. First is the most optimistic time—the time that is required if everything goes right. The probability of a most optimistic set of circumstances occurring is about 1 out of 100. Second, the most likely time is estimated—the time required in the normal course of events. The third time estimate is most pessimistic—the time required if everything that could go wrong does go wrong. Again, the probability for the most pessimistic set of circumstances occurring is 1 out of 100; however, catastrophies such as floods, fires, and strikes are excluded. Designating the most optimistic time as a, the most likely time as m, and the most pessimistic time as b, the expected time, T_e, is found by substituting estimated times in the following formula:

$$T_e = \frac{a + 4m + b}{6}$$

There is also a formula to determine the standard deviation of the expected time, thus making it possible to state a statistical probability that the expected time will fall within a stated range.[16]

---

[16] There has been much discussion concerning the mathematics of the PERT time estimate. The following report discusses the Beta distribution, a fundamental assumption of the estimated time computation: *PERT Summary Report, Phase I* (Washington: Special Projects Office, Department of the Navy, July, 1958).

A brief description of the mathematics of PERT, along with a discussion of its application, is presented in the following article: Robert W. Miller, "How to Plan and Control with PERT," *Harvard Business Review*, Vol. 40 (March–April, 1962), p. 93.

CPM

The difference between PERT and CPM (Critical Path Method) is one of degree rather than kind. PERT emphasizes time and provides a way of computing the most probable time; however, CPM emphasizes cost as well as time.[17] CPM differs from PERT in three respects. First, only one time estimate is given for each set of activities leading up to a given event, instead of the three time estimates required by PERT. Second, with CPM, a cost estimate is included along with each estimated time for both normal and crash operating conditions. *Normal* operating conditions are usually defined as the least-cost method for the performance of an activity; *crash* conditions represent the time and cost incurred in the performance of activities in less than the normal time. For example, under normal operating conditions two persons assigned to the day shift take three days to complete a job. The time can be shortened under crash conditions by assigning two persons to each of three consecutive shifts—a reduction in elapsed time but with a resultant increase in cost because the workers on the second and third shifts will receive premium pay. Third, CPM assumes some previous experience with the work necessary for the completion of each event; otherwise, it would be impracticable to state a single time and cost estimate.

These differences explain to a large degree why PERT is used primarily for one-of-a-kind projects involving an extensive amount of research and development prior to the building of a prototype and for similar projects where time is of greater importance than cost. CPM, on the other hand, is widely used in complex construction and maintenance projects where cost is a significant factor and prior experience offers a basis for making a reliable estimate of both time and cost.

Evaluation of PERT and CPM

There are three major benefits to be derived from the use of either PERT or CPM in the planning and control of certain production functions. First, the application of network analysis techniques forces a high degree of planning and results in plans that are objective, structured, and flexible.[18] In so doing, either PERT or CPM approaches the optimum condition summarized in Chapter 4, page 78. The second advantage of network analysis is that the establishment of a network system makes it possible to determine the critical path. The significance of the critical path to the control process is that knowledge of the key elements in a complex production system makes possible the design and administration of a set of forward-looking controls so that corrective action may be taken before serious deviation from schedule occurs. Third, network analysis

---

[17] Levy, Thompson, and Wiest, *op. cit.*, p. 98.

For another discussion of the critical path method, see Walter Cosinuke, "The Critical Path Method," in Stilian *et al.*, *op. cit.*, p. 147.

[18] The following article emphasizes the importance of PERT/CPM to the planning process: Richard J. Schonberger, "Custom-Tailored PERT/CPM Systems," *Business Horizons*, Vol. 15, No. 6 (December, 1972), p. 64.

shows clearly the interrelationships between the various organizational components of a complex production system, thereby making it possible to improve both communications and organizational structure.

Nonetheless, there are two limiting conditions that must be fulfilled before the advantages described above can be realized. First, network analysis is most effective when applied to one-of-a-kind projects that include several subprojects. Further, both the main project and the various subprojects must be fairly well defined and recognizable. They cannot be too nebulous. Examples of activities amenable to network analysis are construction projects, research and development programs, the installation of an integrated data processing system, the design and construction of a weapons system, and the design and manufacture of special machinery or equipment. The second factor that limits the effectiveness of network analysis is organizational structure. Experience has shown that a task force or project form of organization is necessary to obtain maximum benefits from either PERT or CPM (see Chapter 10, page 214). Task force organization requires organizational flexibility and highly trained personnel. In summary, both the project and the organization must be appropriate if full benefit is to be realized from the application of either PERT or CPM as a means for planning and control.[19]

Case Problem 20-B offers an opportunity to determine how the critical path in building a house can be shortened. Though a contractor might include more separate events than shown in the case problem, there are sufficient events presented to enable you to see for yourself how CPM points up the interrelationships of the various phases of a complex process.

Case Problem 20-B

SHORTENING THE CRITICAL PATH

Ralph Billings, an independent building contractor, has completed building the fifth house of a projected development of 25 homes in the $70,000 price range. Recently he read of an application of the Critical Path Method to the building of a shopping center and became interested in applying the method to his own business. Currently he employs four carpenters and two laborers. Much of his work, such as excavating, plumbing, grading, cement work, bricklaying, and electrical work, is performed by subcontractors who base their charges on a combination of materials and worker-hours required

---

[19] There have been relatively few reports in the literature concerning the limitations of network techniques and difficulties encountered in their application. The following two studies indicate some of the limitations.

Lawrence S. Hill, "Perspective: Some Possible Pitfalls in the Design and Use of PERT Networking," *Academy of Management Journal,* Vol. 8, No. 2 (June, 1965), p. 139.

Peter P. Schoderbek, "A Study of the Applications of PERT," *Academy of Management Journal,* Vol. 8, No. 3 (September, 1965), p. 199.

for each job. Billings hopes that the application of CPM to his operation will result in a reduction of the total number of days required to build a house and in better utilization of the labor he now has.

As a first step in applying the Critical Path Method to his own building efforts, Billings determined the average time required for each phase of the building of the first five houses. These values, along with the sequence of each building operation, are shown in Exhibit I.

PROBLEMS

1. Using the information presented in Exhibit I, construct a schematic network analysis similar to Figure 20–2 and determine the critical path.
2. What recommendations would you make to shorten the critical path?

Job No.	Description	Immediate Predecessors	Normal Time (Days)
a	Start		0
b	Excavate and Pour Footers	a	4
c	Pour Concrete Foundation	b	2
d	Erect Wooden Frame Including Rough Roof	c	4
e	Lay Brickwork	d	6
f	Install Basement Drains and Plumbing	c	1
g	Pour Basement Floor	f	2
h	Install Rough Plumbing	f	3
i	Install Rough Wiring	d	2
j	Install Heating and Ventilating	d, g	4
k	Fasten Plaster Board and Plaster (including drying)	i, j, h	10
l	Lay Finish Flooring	k	3
m	Install Kitchen Fixtures	l	1
n	Install Finish Plumbing	l	2
o	Finish Carpentry	l	3
p	Finish Roofing and Flashing	e	2
q	Fasten Gutters and Downspouts	p	1
r	Lay Storm Drains for Rain Water	c	1
s	Sand and Varnish Flooring	o, t	2
t	Paint	m, n	3
u	Finish Electrical Work	t	1
v	Finish Grading	q, r	2
w	Pour Walks and Complete Landscaping	v	5
x	Finish	s, u, w	0

Exhibit I
SEQUENCE AND TIME REQUIREMENTS OF JOBS

SOURCE: F. K. Levy, G. L. Thompson, and J. D. Wiest, "The ABC's of the Critical Path Method," *Harvard Business Review*, Vol. 41 (September–October, 1963), p. 100. Copyright © 1963 by the President and Fellows of Harvard College; all rights reserved.

CHAPTER QUESTIONS FOR
STUDY AND DISCUSSION

1. What factors in the situation and what factors in the manager would tend to either increase or decrease the value of personal observations as a means of securing control information?

2. What points should be considered when designing or using control reports? Develop examples to illustrate both effective and ineffective control reports.

3. Comment on the following statement: Control reports are primarily a part of an information system rather than a control system.

4. Differentiate between internal and external auditing and show by example the strengths and weaknesses of each type of audit.

5. State in your own words the basic assumptions underlying the concept of human resource accounting. Is there a relationship between the technology used by a firm and the potential value that might result from the use of human resource accounting? If so, state the relationship.

6. Give an example of each of the more common forms of operating ratios and financial ratios.

7. How can the difficulties in interpreting ratios be minimized?

8. How do the techniques of break-even analysis contribute to the effectiveness of the control process?

9. In your opinion, do break-even analysis and P/V analysis have greater impact in the area of manufacturing through cost control than in the area of sales planning? Why?

10. Under what conditions would you recommend the use of PERT as opposed to CPM?

Chapter 21

Budgetary Control

Case Problem 21-A

DEVELOPING A REVENUE AND EXPENSE BUDGET

Adele Barr suddenly found herself in the retail business as a result of the unexpected death of her father, James O'Leary, who owned and managed The Avenue, a men's clothing and furnishings store. Ms. Barr was appointed acting manager by the executor of her father's estate and served in that capacity during the peak sales period that normally occurs during the last three months of the calendar year. When the estate was settled in mid-December, Ms. Barr and her husband, who had recently retired from the Air Force, decided to continue managing the store rather than sell it. The records kept by O'Leary were rather sketchy and incomplete, but they did indicate that net sales had been $200,000 a year for the past three years and that net profit before taxes had varied between 4 and 5½ percent of net sales for the same period.

Mr. Barr had worked with budgets as an officer in the management control section of the Air Force and decided that the development of a revenue and expense budget would serve as a useful guide during the coming year. After studying the information made available to them by the Small Business Administration and the publications of the National Association of Retail Clothiers

and Furnishers, the Barrs decided to use the percentages for revenue and expense items as shown in Exhibit I. They considered dividing the total for each of these accounts by 12 to develop a budget for each month, but later decided that the variation in sales volume and advertising costs from month to month was great enough to require that these items be computed on the basis of the variations shown in Exhibit II. Both Exhibit I and Exhibit II are based on an annual net sales volume of $200,000.

PROBLEMS

1. Develop monthly revenue and expense budgets for a year for the store owned and operated by the Barrs.
2. What additional information would you need to prepare a cash budget? a balance sheet budget?
3. What kind of standards have the Barrs used in determining budgeted performance?
4. Would flexible budgets be of any value in allocating monthly sales volume and advertising expenses?
5. Of what value will this budget be in succeeding years?

ACCOUNT	PERCENTAGE OF NET SALES
Sales	
1. Gross sales	102.6
2. Customer returns and allowances	2.6
3. Net sales	100.0
Cost of goods sold	
4. Beginning inventory	30.9
5. Net purchases plus transportation charges paid	66.1
6. Total cost of merchandise handled	97.0
7. Ending inventory	32.3
8. Net cost of merchandise sold	64.7
9. Net busheling (alterations) cost	2.1
10. Total cost of merchandise sold	66.8
11. Gross margin	33.2
Operating expenses	
12. Payroll	
A. Salaries of owners	7.3
B. Salaries and wages of employees	9.0
Total payroll	16.3
13. Rent expense	2.9
14. Taxes and license fees (omit real estate, federal income and sales taxes)	1.1
15. Insurance	.6
16. Depreciation and amortization	.8
17. Repairs	.2
18. Supplies (omit repair materials)	1.0
19. Services purchased	.9
20. Traveling (business trips)	.3
21. Communication (include parcel post)	.4
22. Advertising and publicity	2.8
23. Professional services (outside professional agencies)	.2
24. Unclassified (all expenses not under headings):	
A. Losses from bad debts	.3
B. Other unclassified expenses	.5
Total unclassified expenses	.8
25. Total expenses	28.3
26. Net profit (or loss) before federal income taxes	4.9

**Exhibit I
BUDGETED
OPERATING
REVENUE AND
EXPENSES FOR
ANNUAL NET
SALES OF
$200,000**

MONTH	PERCENTAGE OF ANNUAL NET SALES	PERCENTAGE OF ANNUAL ADVERTISING COSTS
January	8	9
February	5	7
March	6	6
April	6	7
May	8	7
June	9	8
July	7	7
August	7	8
September	7	9
October	9	8
November	10	10
December	18	14

Exhibit II
BUDGETED NET
SALES AND
ADVERTISING
COSTS FOR
EACH
MONTH

The budget is without doubt the most widely used control device in both business and government; indeed, it is used so extensively that for many people the word *budget* is synonymous with control. Yet the preparation of budgets originates as part of the planning process, and the budget itself is the end point of the planning process—the statement of a plan. Some companies, in order to avoid the negative reactions often associated with the concept of control, refer to their budgetary controls as either *profit plans* or *profit paths.*

In our discussion of budgetary controls we shall first examine the nature of budgets and review the types of budgets used most frequently. The success or failure of either budgetary or nonbudgetary controls (discussed in the previous chapter) depends on their acceptance by the people in an organization; consequently, consideration is given to behavioral reactions to control.

THE NATURE OF BUDGETS

A *budget* may be defined as a plan expressed in quantitative terms. However, this overly simplified definition of a budget does not tell us much about the nature of budgets or of budgetary control. The process of preparing a budget is planning in every sense of the word, and the budget itself is the resultant plan. As such, the budget, like any other plan, should possess the characteristics of objectivity, structuralization, and flexibility. The extent to which a budget reflects these characteristics is a measure of its probable success.[1]

Even so, there are certain aspects of budgets that differentiate them from other plans. First, the reason for preparing a budget is to provide a means for controlling operations. Second, as a means of controlling operations effectively, a separate budget is usually prepared for each organizational unit, and individual

---

[1] See Chapter 4.

budgets may be prepared for each of the several functions within an organizational unit. Third, a budget is designed to cover a specific period of time. The fiscal year is the unit of time used most frequently, but this unit may be subdivided into semiannual, quarterly, or monthly periods. Also, budgets may be prepared for periods of time greater than one year; for example, capital expenditure budgets. Finally, budgets are expressed in financial terms since dollars serve well as a common denominator and thereby permit the comparison and coordination of all phases of a company's operations.

Though planning is an essential ingredient in the process of preparing budgets, the preparation of budgets is more closely related to the control process than it is to the planning process. The budget itself is the stated standard of performance. Thus, preparing budgets is, in effect, setting standards—the first step of the control process. The measurement of current performance against standards, the second step in the process of control, is facilitated because the budget expresses standards of performance in quantitative terms—dollars. Deviations from budgeted or expected results are readily identified and show the need for corrective action, the last step in the process of control. Undoubtedly the preparation of budgets refines the planning process necessary for the establishment of standards, or goals; however, the greater value of budgeting lies in its contribution to improved coordination and control. When budgets are prepared for all organizational units and the various functions performed by these units, a basis is provided for the coordination of the efforts of the organization. At the same time budgets establish a basis for the corrective action of control since deviations from expected results are more readily identified and measured. Thus, the preparation of budgets may be expected to result in better planning and improved coordination, and to provide a basis for control—the primary purpose for establishing budgets.

Types of Budgets

Virtually every aspect of the operations of an organization can be budgeted. A business firm may prepare budgets for sales, inventory, shipments, production, maintenance, direct labor, and indirect labor. Budgets may also be used to forecast the operations of the industrial relations department, the cost of industrial engineering, and the needs for research and development. The list of organizational units and functions susceptible to budgetary control is almost endless. Fortunately there is a logical framework that provides an easily remembered classification of budgets. This classification follows roughly a time sequence in the operation of a business and results in the following four types of budgets:

1. Revenue and expense budget
2. Cash budget
3. Capital expenditure budget
4. Balance sheet budget

As we shall see, each of these major types of budgets may be further subdivided so that the individual needs of each company may be fully met.

Revenue and Expense Budget. If one were starting a new business or beginning to prepare the initial set of budgets for a going concern, the first need would be a summary statement of the company's operations. The *revenue and expense budget,* sometimes called an *operating budget,* provides a bird's eye view of operations. Since revenue from the sale of products or services is the main source of income, the revenue budget is often referred to as the *sales budget.* All other budgets must be coordinated with the sales forecast since revenue from sales defines the upper limits of expenses and profits.

Sales Budget. In preparing a sales forecast, careful consideration must be given to external environmental factors as well as to conditions within the company itself. General economic conditions, the availability of credit, and the action of competitors are illustrative of the external factors that influence a company's level of sales. Accurate sales forecasts are difficult to achieve, at best, but the experience gained from the preparation of successive annual sales budgets gradually narrows the gap between budgeted and actual sales.

The content and the format of the sales budget vary with each company; however, certain generalizations are possible. For companies with multiple products or services the expected revenue from each product or service should be stated separately. For large companies a breakdown of expected sales by territory is essential. Sometimes the forecast should reflect expected sales for each class of customer. Since sales are seldom the same for each month of the year, the expected revenue for each calendar month should be stated to show clearly the seasonal variations. A forecast of revenue by month is necessary for the preparation of cash budgets.

Expense Budget. The second part of the revenue and expense budget is a statement of expected expenses. Two considerations guide the preparation of expense budgets. First is a determination of the classification of items to be included in expense budgets and, second, the allocation of expense items according to organizational unit. Expense budgets may be prepared for every item listed in the expense division of the company's chart of accounts. In manufacturing firms a manufacturing budget is prepared to show the expenses anticipated in the manufacture of the company's products. Included are the cost of material, the cost of inventory, direct and indirect labor charges, factory overhead including the cost of supervision, and the cost of maintaining equipment and other manufacturing facilities. General administrative costs and the cost of sales are shown separately.

If the budget is to be an effective tool in the control of expenses, a budget must be prepared for each organizational unit and placed in the hands of the managers of those units. Manufacturing budgets are prepared for operating departments and become a statement of expense responsibilities for the manager of each department. Managers of territorial or product divisions of the sales department are charged with the responsibility of keeping the cost of sales within budgeted limits. Difficulties encountered in controlling expenses are often a result of ill-defined organizational structure rather than an unwillingness on the part of departmental managers to cooperate in reducing expenses.

Cash Budget. The *cash budget*, derived from the basic data included in the revenue and expense budget, shows the cash requirements of the business during the budget period. The need for a specific budget detailing cash requirements arises from the fact that rarely does the flow of cash into the firm from sales coincide with the amount and frequency of disbursements necessary to pay expenses. For example, if too little cash is on hand to purchase materials in order to increase inventory levels to meet seasonal sales requirements, it may be necessary to borrow and thereby incur the added cost of interest. Also, having sufficient cash on hand makes it possible to take advantage of cash discounts offered by suppliers. Excess cash may be used for short-term investments, or it may make possible an earlier than expected fulfillment of capital expenditure plans. When the amount of cash falls below budgeted expectations, it may be an early warning that accounts receivable are running too high. Budgeting cash requirements may not alter significantly the amount of profit earned by a firm, but it does help to assure a liquid position and is considered one of the hallmarks of prudent management.

Capital Expenditure Budget. If the planning and control of the revenue and expense budget are successfully managed, revenue should exceed expenses. A part of this balance is reinvested in the company to insure the continued existence and growth of the firm. Since these expenditures produce revenue, they are classed as capital expenditures and are included in the *capital expenditure budget.* Typically one finds in the capital expenditure budget allotments for the replacement of present facilities, including plant and equipment, and funds for the expansion of facilities for increased production of the present product line or the development and manufacture of a new product.

However, there are expenses other than those for physical facilities and equipment that require the appropriation of fairly large sums of money and the passage of a relatively long period of time before the anticipated results become apparent. Executive development programs, including the recruitment of college graduates, require support on a continuing basis; and it may take many years before the results of such personnel programs can be assessed. The decision to spend a greater than usual amount on advertising in order to develop new markets is another long-range investment of company funds. Research and development plans for new and improved products require continued appropriations for their completion. Institutional advertising intended to establish a desired public image also requires special budgetary appropriations. Consequently, some companies develop a single *appropriation budget* to reflect intended expenditures for capital equipment, personnel development, the development of new markets, research and development programs, and institutional advertising.

Budgeting capital or appropriation expenditures poses some rather difficult problems not directly related to the control of expenses. Since emergency needs in the five areas mentioned above arise infrequently, the control of expenses is relatively easy to achieve—one simply does not spend more than the budgetary allowance. Instead the difficulty in preparing budgets for special appropriations arises from the long-term nature of these investments and the limited amount of money available for such expenditures. Because these projects are long term, their true worth cannot be computed until completed or until their useful life, in the case of capital equipment, is exhausted. Even then one is not sure that the course selected is of more value than some of the rejected alternative courses of action. But alternative courses must be weighed and choices made since the funds available to a company are never unlimited. Difficult as the appraisal of the results of capital expenditure budgeting may be, there are, nonetheless, several important benefits to be gained from this class of budget. First, capital or appropriation expenditures should be controlled and can be controlled relatively easily once they are budgeted. Second, budgeting the major appropriations forces an improvement of the planning process in each of the functional areas so that a careful weighing of alternative forms of investment may be accomplished. Third, capital expenditures require cash and as a result must be budgeted if the cash budget is to be of maximum value as a control device. Fourth, special appropriations must be included so that the greatest degree of coordination of the company's resources, especially financial, is achieved.

Balance Sheet Budget. The *balance sheet budget* is a forecast of expected financial status as of the last day of the budget period, usually the close of the fiscal year. The balance sheet forecast, a statement of the relationships between assets and liabilities, does not require the preparation of any additional budgets; rather, it is a consolidation of all preceding budgets. Preparing a balance sheet forecast shows what might be expected if performance meets the standards defined in the other budgets. By preparing a forecast of anticipated financial position, management may discover that the other budgets when consolidated do not result in an entirely favorable financial condition as revealed by certain key ratios. For example, the ratio between current assets and current liabilities or expected earnings and current market price per share may be such that the value of the company's stock would be adversely affected. When this happens, the other budgets have to be recast. The balance sheet showing the actual financial position at the close of the budget period serves as a useful check on the accuracy of preparation and the degree to which all other budgets have been met. Also, deviations between the actual and the forecast balance sheets may show the need for preparation of special budgets to improve control over performance in certain areas; for instance, accounts receivable, accounts payable, or finished goods inventory.

Securing Flexibility with Budgets

Several disadvantages may arise as the result of an overzealous application of budgetary controls. In the administration of budgetary controls, it is all too easy to emphasize conformance to the budgetary goals of the organization. For example, a regional sales manager who is experiencing difficulty in meeting sales objectives may have every reason to believe that a market research study would be of help in solving the problem; yet it may be impossible to conduct such a study because there is no provision for it in the budget. Another criticism arising from the use of budgets is that the statement of objectives in numeric terms lends a degree of precision and exactness that is seldom warranted. After all, goals stated numerically are no more reliable than the original estimates from which they are drawn. However, the greatest potential danger of budgetary control is that it may lead to inflexibility. Budgets are statements of plans and, like any other plan, if they are to be successful, they must be flexible as well as possess the characteristics of objectivity and structuralization. Flexibility in budgetary control may be achieved by either one of two methods: *periodic budgetary reviews* and *flexible budgets.*

Periodic Budgetary Review. Normally budgets are prepared in advance for a 12-month period. However, changes in operating conditions may occur that make the attainment of stated budgetary goals a virtual impossibility. Some of the factors frequently subject to change during the course of the budget period are labor costs, selling price, and the predicted volume of business. Periodic budgetary reviews are intended to incorporate and reflect changes in any of the first two factors, while flexible budgets are designed specifically to reflect changes in the anticipated volume of business.

Periodic budgetary reviews may be prepared on a monthly basis, prior to the beginning of the new month. Then, during the third month of the budgetary period, a revised quarterly estimate is prepared. For example, a company whose fiscal year is the same as the calendar year would prepare revised estimates of the budget for the months of January, February, and March prior to the beginning of each of these months. During the month of March, a revised quarterly budget for the second quarter might be prepared in addition to the revised estimate for April. Also, revised quarterly budgets may be prepared for the third and fourth quarters prior to their beginning, along with the usual monthly revisions.

However, there is a danger inherent in the use of periodic budgetary reviews as a means of recognizing changing conditions. If changes are made too frequently and if the magnitude of these changes is too great, it is quite possible for the original budget to become meaningless. Also, the other extreme is possible; that is, periodic reviews of the budget, backed by ample evidence, may show the need for a restatement of budgeted goals but may not be permitted because the original budget is considered inviolate. One way of minimizing the variation between the annual budget and the revised budget resulting from periodic reviews is to anticipate in the preparation of the annual budgets the changes that might reasonably be expected in labor rates, raw materials, and selling prices. Past experience is a good guide in these areas. Changes suggested as the result of periodic reviews must not only be substantiated, but reasons must also be given showing why it was impossible to anticipate these changes in the preparation of the original budget. In this manner the accuracy of the original budget is improved over a period of years.

Flexible Budgets. Periodic budget reviews allow management to compensate for changes in labor costs, selling price, the cost of raw materials, a change in technology, or the method of operation. In many respects the amount of change resulting from these factors is unpredictable, with the result that the extent of their effect on the budget can be determined only after the change has begun. However, the effect of changes in the volume of business of a company upon the revenue and expense budgets can in many instances be predicted in advance. When budgets are prepared for the coming fiscal year, they are prepared on the basis of an assumed or predicted level of revenue or volume—a statement of expected expenses for an expected amount of revenue. Flexible or variable budgets show the effect of changes in the volume of business upon certain expense items in the revenue and expense budget (Figure 21–1).

From our study of break-even analysis (Chapter 20), we know that some costs regarded as fixed or standby do not vary proportionately with the volume of business and that other costs vary proportionately with changes in volume. Good examples of fixed and variable costs are the costs incurred in operating an automobile. The costs of depreciation, insurance, and garaging the automobile are not a function of the number of miles driven (volume). Rather, these costs are incurred at the time the car is purchased and do not change appreciably as a result of the number of miles driven. For this reason these costs are termed fixed, or standby, costs. On the other hand, the costs of tires, oil, gasoline, and repairs vary directly with the number of miles driven; hence, these costs are called variable costs. Similarly, a company's costs for depreciation, insurance, and administration remain relatively unchanged within wide ranges of volume and are termed fixed costs. Labor costs, the cost of materials, and variable selling expenses such as commissions are representative of those costs that vary directly with changes in volume and are called variable costs.

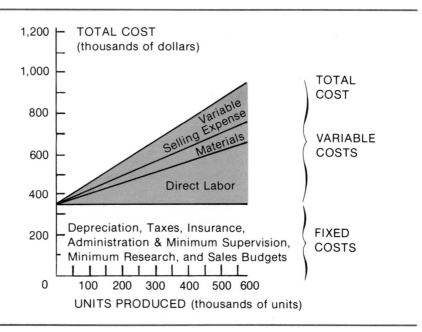

Figure 21–1 GRAPHIC REPRESENTATION OF A VARIABLE EXPENSE BUDGET

Figure 21–1 shows in graphic form the relationship between the fixed and the variable expenses of a flexible budget. Determination of the nature of the relationship between variable costs and volume level may be accomplished by (1) a historical analysis of costs incurred at varying levels of volume and (2) the development of standard costs.

Historical Analysis of Costs. The historical approach is an effective tool for determining the relationship between variable costs and volume when the company's product line is limited to a few products and when each product contributes a relatively constant percentage to total sales volume. In its simplest form, historical analysis may consist of determining actual costs incurred in producing the company's historical maximum volume and the costs incurred for the lowest point of the sales record. These two points, the high and the low, may be plotted on a graph and a straight line drawn to connect them; thus, by interpolation, a prediction may be made concerning expected costs for each level of volume between the historical high and low points. More sophisticated techniques include plotting sales and cost data for each year and determining by the method of least squares the line of best fit. For those companies with diverse product lines, it becomes necessary to analyze the variable costs for each product.

Standard Costs. Standard costs for each product may be developed and may show the predicted cost for labor, materials, and supplies that might be expected for each unit produced. The predicted standard costs become the budgeted amount of variable costs, and the total cost for varying levels of volume can be readily computed.

Evaluation of Flexible Budgets. Variable budgets, particularly those utilizing standard costs, are often criticized as being too costly from the standpoint of both time and money in their preparation. Another criticism of variable budgets is that in practice they are extremely difficult to apply in a manner that results in savings in variable expenses. Part of the difficulty arises from an inability to predict short-term variations in volume. Even when this can be done, it is sometimes impracticable to take advantage of this information. For example, a department supervisor may normally supervise a work force of 15 machinists. A decline in volume for a period of two months does not necessarily result in a reduction in force since it may be more economical in the long run to retain highly skilled employees instead of running the risk of losing their services as a result of a layoff. Also, a sudden upturn in business may be handled more efficiently by assigning overtime work rather than incurring expenses resulting from training new employees. An advantage of variable budgets is that there is a budgeted goal for varying levels of volume without having to rework the entire budget each time a significant change in activity occurs. However, a greater advantage comes not from the variable goals feature of the flexible budget but from the study and analysis necessary for the preparation of a flexible budget. In addition to focusing attention on the variable costs that contribute to the total cost of each unit, the preparation of flexible budgets requires a closer analysis of all costs in separating fixed and variable costs.[2]

Zero-Base Budgeting

The application of flexible budgets is primarily limited to manufacturing operations and at best offers a means of controlling variable manufacturing and sales costs. The question arises, How does one control the costs of supportive or staff functions? Some states have passed sunset laws to control the proliferation of regulatory agencies. These laws provide that a given agency is established for a specified period of years, and then is automatically eliminated at the end of the stated time period. In order to be reestablished the agency must justify its existence to the legislature by showing the benefits received in relation to the costs expended for its services. Business firms and other formal organizations can create their own sunset laws by requiring support functions to start their budgeting process at ground zero at the beginning of each budget period.

Zero-base budgeting is quite simple in concept. First, it is necessary to describe each support activity as a "decision" package. Second, each of the discrete decision packages, or activities, is evaluated and ranked by means of cost-benefit analysis (see Chapter 4, pages 81–82). Third, the resources of the organization are allocated on the basis of the results of the second step and in accordance with the contribution of each function to the attainment of the goals of the organization.

In the normal budgeting process it is tacitly assumed that the current budget for service functions is necessary. Thus, the question is whether to increase the present budget or to continue it at its present level. Zero-base budgeting requires that one must consider what would happen if the function were eliminated. For example, the zero-base budget of a quality control department or a production control department would be the elimination of both departments entirely. The functions of quality control and production planning could be assigned to the first-line manufacturing supervisor, thereby saving the total cost of the operation of both departments. However, such an operation would place undue burdens on manufacturing supervisors and would undoubtedly create many problems and inefficiencies due to poor quality and late deliveries that could offset the savings gained by eliminating the departments. Consequently, the proposed budget should contain an alternate form of operation funded at a level below the current level with a statement of the attendant costs and benefits to be derived. The present funding is justified in a similar manner. Perhaps it might be wise to increase the funding if it can be shown that the benefits gained outweigh the costs incurred. Finally, it may be possible to combine similar functions. For example, if sales engineering and manufacturing are both operating

---

[2] Adolph Matz and Milton F. Usry, *Cost Accounting,* Planning and Control (7h ed.; Cincinnati: South-Western Publishing Co., 1980), p. 444. The three chapters on budgets, Chapters 16, 17, and 18, provide a discussion of the nature of budgets and offer many problems and examples of budgetary controls.

a quality assurance program, the activities may be combined and thereby save the cost of at least one departmental manager. Ultimately each support area must be ranked and evaluated by top management at each proposed level of funding so that the final allocation of funds represents the greatest benefits for the organization in relation to the costs incurred.

Admittedly such decisions are difficult to quantify and many times are based on judgment. Decisions are especially difficult in such areas as personnel. A zero-base budgeting process applied to a personnel department would probably include interviewers and personnel clerks at the lowest level of funding. The presence or absence of a labor union determines whether or not a separate labor relations function is established in the personnel department. In addition, increasing regulation of the personnel function by outside agencies such as the Equal Employment Opportunity Commission may create the need for increased funding. A personnel department may request increased funds for the employment of an equal employment opportunity specialist. The costs are the additional salaries and expenses. The benefit that may be expected is the avoidance of monetary penalties that might be assessed as the result of an infraction of the EEOC regulations.

Though difficult to apply, zero-base budgeting affords a means of determining periodically whether the costs of given support or staff functions can be justified in terms of the benefits received. Also, analyzing each separate support function offers the possibility of combining some functions thereby offering a means of controlling the ever-increasing cost of support activities.[3]

Advantages of Effective Budgetary Control

Although budgets are one of the most widely used control techniques, it must be remembered that they are but one of several control devices. There are potential dangers as well as distinct advantages resulting from the use of budgets. Oddly enough, one of the strengths of budgets—the conversion of all aspects of organizational performance into a single comparable unit of measurement, dollars—can become its greatest weakness because it may result in measuring only those things that are easy to measure; i.e., those aspects of organizational performance readily converted into dollars. Equally important factors, such as manager performance and plans for organizational development, may be ignored because achievement in these areas is not readily convertible into dollar units. Second, there is a danger of identifying symptoms as causes. A decline in revenue from sales does not necessarily call for greater sales effort; instead, the real cause may be a poor product, the action of competitors, or general economic conditions. And finally, there is a danger of autocratic control by the staff organization. The function of the controller or the budget director is to coordinate

---

[3] The following article discusses the application of zero-base budgeting to both the private sector and to the public sector. Mark W. Dirsmith and Stephen F. Jablonsky, "Zero-Base Budgeting as a Management Technique and Political Strategy," *Academy of Management Review*, Vol. 4, No. 4 (October, 1979), p. 555.

and guide the development of budgets, but the actual control of performance must remain in the hands of the line managers.

The obvious advantage of budgetary control is that a comparable statement of goals is provided for all organizational units; and since the budget serves as a standard of performance, deviations from this standard are readily measurable and provide the basis for necessary corrective action. However, there are indirect advantages resulting from the proper use of budgets. The consistent and uniform application of budgets results in a more clearly defined organizational structure since budgets measure the performance of organizational units. Second, more meaningful accounting systems and terminology are developed. Traditionally, accounting has a deep preoccupation with the preparation of historical and tax records rather than focusing on the reporting of current operations and the forecasting of future performance. Third, better planning of all phases of the company's operations results from the use of budgets. Budgets are carefully structured plans and serve to emphasize the continuous nature of the planning-control-planning cycle. Lastly, a clearer statement and understanding of organizational goals comes from the use of budgets because managers are forced to develop and state attainable goals for organizational units. Thus, wishful thinking with respect to organizational objectives is minimized.[4]

BEHAVIORAL REACTIONS TO CONTROL

The application of any control device, whether it is one of the nonbudgetary controls (discussed in the preceding chapter) or a budget, bears directly on the people of an organization. The success or failure of a control program depends to a greater degree on the attitudes of those subjected to control—members of middle management as well as hourly employees—than it does on the accuracy and kind of technique used in its preparation. Attitudes and overt responses to controls vary from open hostility and resentment, through indifference and tolerance, to complete understanding and appreciation of the need for controls. Before discussing the commonly observed reasons for resistance to controls and the usual reactions to controls, let us examine a procedure that is usually followed in the establishment and administration of controls.

Typical Control Procedure

All too often the establishment and the administration of controls seemingly follow an endless cycle destined to have little chance of success. Top management

---

[4] For a discussion of the relationship between information utilized in accounting systems and its effect on organizational members, the following is of interest. Klaus Macharzina, "On the Integration of Behavioral Science into Accounting Theory," *Management International Review*, Vol. 13, No. 2–3 (1973), p. 3.

Larry L. Cummings, Bernard L. Hinton, and Bruce C. Gobdel, "Creative Behavior as a Function of Task Environment: Impact of Objectives, Procedures, and Controls," *Academy of Management Journal*, Vol. 18, No. 3 (September, 1975), p. 489.

determines objectives and sets the standards of performance required to meet these objectives; however, middle management and hourly employees react with attitudes and responses of hostility and resentment or indifference and bare tolerance. Such reactions are interpreted by top management as evidence of the need for additional and firmer controls. Robert Katz describes this cycle of control, resistance, and more control as follows:

1. The predetermined program is implemented. It is characterized by general, non-personal rules, division of labor, specialized competencies, and continuous checking to assure compliance.

2. Here the program immediately encounters unsought-for behavior as employees and subordinate managers seek to maintain their feelings of self-worth, their potential for self-determination, and their needs to have others acknowledge these capabilities.

3. Employees' reaction—Management's unilateral imposition of rules and detailed programming of behavior conflicts with employees' needs for self-determination and self-respect.

   Employees feel misunderstood, unappreciated, manipulated. They develop behavior patterns which enable them to resist rigid task pressures and permit some degree of self-regulation through informal social relationships.

   Performance stabilizes at the minimum level tolerated by management. Employees tend to produce well below their capacities, have low involvement in their tasks, show little initiative, do only what they are directed to do.

4. Subordinate manager's reaction—Expected by top management to obtain the employees' compliance in the program without deviation, subordinate managers are likely to feel helpless, asked to do the impossible, and misunderstood. They try to escape their feelings of inadequacy by blaming "unreasonable and uncontrollable" employees or "unreasonable and unsympathetic" superiors.

   Depending on their temperament, individual managers will tend either to (a) insist on more precise performance of the program, instituting closer controls, closer supervision, more rigorous use of rewards and punishments, or (b) abdicate, contacting subordinates as little as possible, giving instructions, and then busying themselves elsewhere.

5. In either case, whether the subordinate manager cracks down or withdraws, his employees tend to react to his response by developing new behavior patterns. These patterns tend to stabilize at a new level of minimal performance and minimal satisfaction so that all of the old problems remain while new anxieties are created.

6. At this point, top management becomes apprehensive and convinced that things are "out of control." Seeing widespread deviation from its predetermined program, top management is likely to respond to its anxieties by replacing the subordinate manager, applying more pressure for compliance, establishing more elaborate controls, or trying to train the subordinate manager in "how to get people to do what he wants them to."

7. Top management's action only serves to heighten the subordinate manager's anxieties and feelings of inadequacy. The proverbial "man in the middle," he finds his superiors expecting that he *should* be able to get his employees to perform strictly according to plan, and his subordinates expecting that he should attend to *their* needs which underlie their deviation.

8. No matter what the subordinate manager does, the likely outcome is that employees will feel more unappreciated and misunderstood than before, the subordinate

manager more helpless and insecure, and top management more anxious about its lack of control.

9. Top management responds by devising new predetermined programs, installing new controls, shuffling personnel, but *not* by questioning any of its original assumptions. Thus, the cycle of unanticipated consequences starts all over again.[5]

Obviously something is wrong. The cycle of control, resistance, and more control cannot go on endlessly. Usually a compromise, or more accurately, a stalemate, is reached. Top management settles for standards of performance that fall short of budgeted expectations; and subordinates, including middle management, tacitly recognize but do not wholly accept or understand the need for control. An understanding of the reasons for resistance to controls enables us to prepare and install them in such a manner that the cycle of control, resistance, and more control never begins.

Why Resistance Develops

Seemingly, most of us have a built-in resistance to any form of control; perhaps such reactions are necessary for the preservation of one's own individuality. Nonetheless, as managers, we must learn not only to cope with our own reactions to control but also to meet and minimize the resistance of subordinates to control. The three steps of the control process—setting standards, measuring performance, and taking corrective action—provide a logical outline for our discussion of resistance to controls.

Standards Too Tight. A frequent initial reaction to budgets and other forms of control is the complaint that the standard of performance is unreasonable or too tight. There are several reasons why people respond in this manner. There may be no understanding of or desire to meet organizational objectives expressed by the standard. Such reactions occur when standards are imposed without any explanation concerning their need. Unless the reasons for standards can be presented in such a way that they become personal objectives for persons who are expected to meet such standards, complaints that the goals are unreasonable are sure to arise.

Another reason for objecting to standards is that historically they have a way of moving in only one direction—up. Consequently, is it any wonder that the initial reaction to them is the belief that they are unreasonable or too tight? A sales budget may show that a higher dollar volume is expected from each sales representative for the current year; however, the increased volume may be the result of higher prices rather than the result of an increase in the number of units sold. In a like manner, an increase in the number of units expected from a production worker is often the result of improved methods or more efficient production equipment that actually call for less effort on the worker's part. Since budgets are prepared annually and usually show a steady increase

[5] Robert L. Katz, "Toward a More Effective Enterprise," *Harvard Business Review*, Vol. 38, No. 5 (September–October, 1960), p. 86. Copyright © 1960 by the President and Fellows of Harvard College; all rights reserved.

in expected performance, it is necessary that those affected by standards understand not only the reasons for the changing objectives but also how the new standards can be met.

The third reason for resistance to standards lies in the way in which they are administered on a day-to-day basis. Regardless of how carefully standards may have been developed, unexpected conditions arise that make their attainment impossible. Materials that fail to meet stated specifications or machine breakdowns lower the output of the production worker. Unexpected product developments by competitors or even unseasonable variations in the weather can affect the performance of a sales representative. In such cases the wise administrator notes the reasons for variances from standards and does not place undue pressure upon subordinates.

Measurements Not Accurate. Many times standards of performance are accepted, but the methods used in measuring performance are considered inaccurate. When control measures are criticized as not being accurate, more often than not factors other than accuracy are involved. The real complaint on the part of a supervisor operating under budgetary controls may be that the information provided is not timely enough to be of use in the operation of the department. Also, a supervisor's superior may criticize control measurements because they are not timely enough to aid in the coordination of the activities of several departments.

The comment is often heard that the measures used are satisfactory as far as they go, but they do not begin to measure all that is being done. The implication is that the measurements being used are not measuring those things that are important. The production foreman may agree that the unit count is an accurate statement of what is produced but reveals nothing about the decline in the number of units rejected by final inspection and the consequent decrease in the cost of rework. A salesperson may readily admit that the dollar volume statement of sales is correct and at the same time complain that the information used to measure sales performance is unfair because it does not reflect the number of new accounts or the miles and travel time required in order to call on customers. Before corrective action is taken, it is well to make sure that all the significant aspects of performance are being measured.

However, the bitterest complaint of all concerning measurements used in the control process is that they do not measure effort. Students may receive a grade of C on an assignment that in their opinion was worth at least a B in terms of the amount of effort expended. Unfortunately for those whose work is subject to measurement and comparison to standard, the information required for control purposes is an accurate statement of the amount of variance from standard. A good supervisor will note the effort spent in doing a job and should commend a subordinate for such effort. By so doing, one may be able to minimize the normal resistance of subordinates to having their work measured—particularly when performance does not meet expected goals.

Dislike of Corrective Action. In the first paragraph of this section on behavioral reactions to control, it is stated that the administration of controls bears directly on the people of an organization. Specifically, it is the corrective action taken as the result of failure to meet standards that is disliked and sometimes even feared. Somehow there is the belief that where there are no controls there is always the possibility that poor performance will not be noticed and, if detected, plausible excuses can be offered and will be accepted.

One reason for disliking corrective action, even a mild form of admonition, is that it is a form of criticism directed toward an individual. Criticism of a person can never be completely impersonal even though such criticism might be based on an objective analysis of all the facts. Consequently, we all have a tendency to reject at least a part of any criticism and to interpret what is said with some degree of animosity.

Another reason for disliking corrective action is that it exposes a person's shortcomings to one's peers and sometimes to subordinates and superiors in the organization as well. Such exposure is practically unavoidable when demotion or discharge is the corrective action taken. It is the dislike and the fear of potential corrective action more than resistance to standards and criticisms of the methods of measurement that lead to most of the undesirable reactions to controls.

Unfavorable Responses to Controls

Our analysis of resistance to controls shows that any of the three steps of the control process may serve as a focal point for resistance. To some observers, resistance is regarded as a reaction to the pressures created by application of controls. Before studying the specific form of resistance demonstrated by either an individual or a group, let us find out why controls are commonly regarded as pressure devices.

Controls as Pressure Devices. There are two major reasons why controls, especially budgets, are commonly regarded as pressure devices. First, controls are standards of performance. Standards, like the 72-stroke par of golf, should be difficult but attainable. It is expected that the amount of effort expended by an individual in attaining a standard is somewhat greater than the amount expended if there were no stated standard. Thus, a certain degree of pressure is inherent and intended in any statement of standards. The second source of pressure arises from the procedures frequently followed in the installation and administration of controls. More often than not, controls are developed solely by top management and imposed upon the middle and the lower echelons of the organization. Supervisors and hourly employees alike cannot help but believe that top management is not entirely satisfied with the usual level of performance. Many times top management affirms their subordinates' view of controls as a means of pressure by pointing to the increases in productivity that occur after the installation of controls. Often the reaction to control imposed from above results in the control, inadequate response, more control cycle described earlier.

Improperly conceived and administered controls can result in serious human relations problems. One writer has summarized what may happen when budgets are improperly applied.

1. Budget pressure tends to unite the employees against management, and tends to place the factory supervisor under tension. This tension may lead to inefficiency, aggression, and perhaps a complete breakdown on the part of the supervisor.
2. The finance staff can obtain feelings of success only by finding fault with factory people. These findings of failure among factory supervisors lead to many human relations problems.
3. The use of budgets as "needlers" by top management tends to make each factory supervisor see only the problem of his own department.
4. Supervisors use budgets as a way of expressing their own patterns of leadership. When this results in people getting hurt, the budget, in itself a neutral thing, often gets blamed.[6]

Note that the pressure of budgets can affect both individuals and groups in an organization.[7]

Effects on Individuals. Unfavorable individual responses to budgets or other controls on the part of supervisors are essentially reactions resulting from their failure either to understand or to meet stated budgetary goals. Occasionally the tensions and pressures created by budgets may result in a supervisor suffering a complete breakdown. Apathy, loss of interest in the job, and compliance to the letter of the law are forms of behavior that reflect a withdrawal from an unpleasant situation. Some supervisors respond with overt aggressiveness that is intended to shift the responsibility for failure to meet standards from themselves and their department to other departmental managers or to members of the staff organization.

Budgetary controls always contain the potential threat of disrupting cooperative relationships between members of the line and staff organizations. When imposed from above, the budget is developed and administered by a specialized staff group—usually a part of the controller's office. The measure of success of the budget staff is the extent to which the line managers meet the budgeted goals. Failure to meet these goals is interpreted as failure on the part of the line organization rather than the result of poorly stated or unattainable goals by the budget group. When budgets are fulfilled, ensuing budgets can be tightened so that they are more difficult to attain; thus, the line manager is once again faced with the threat of failure. Under these conditions, it is understandable

---

[6] Chris Argyris, "Human Problems with Budgets," *Harvard Business Review,* Vol. 31 (January–February, 1953), p. 108. Copyright © 1976 by the President and Fellows of Harvard College; all rights reserved. Argyris's article is a report of a research study undertaken for the Controllership Foundation to determine the effects of budgets on human relationships in an organization and the extent to which budgets accomplish their purpose. Suggestions are given to improve the effectiveness of budgets.

[7] The following articles describe the effects of control on individuals and groups:

Chris Argyris, "Personality vs. Organization," *Organizational Dynamics,* Vol. 3, No. 2 (Autumn, 1974), p. 3.

M. Edgar Barrett and LeRoy B. Fraser III, "Conflicting Roles in Budgeting for Operations," *Harvard Business Review,* Vol. 55, No. 4 (July–August, 1977), p. 137.

William G. Ouchi and Jerry B. Johnson, "Types of Organizational Control and Their Relationship to Emotional Well-Being," *Administrative Science Quarterly,* Vol. 23, No. 2 (June, 1978), p. 293.

why the relationships between the line manager and the controller's staff are in a state of perpetual conflict.

The departmental supervisor may generalize the conflict with the controller's staff and attempt to broaden the blame for difficulties arising from controls to other staff groups. The personnel department may be criticized for failure to enforce disciplinary action and for not supplying qualified and sufficient personnel. Quality control may be accused of setting quality specifications that make it impossible to meet budgeted cost and production standards. The production control staff comes under attack for failure to schedule long production runs and for scheduling unreasonable sequences in the production of different products. Plant maintenance departments receive their share of criticism for not maintaining production equipment and other facilities at peak levels of efficiency.

The reactions discussed so far are descriptive of how the individual supervisor might react when controls are interpreted as a means of exerting pressure. The supervisor may withdraw from the situation through sickness or apathy or by becoming aggressive and striking out in any and all directions. There may be an attempt to shift the blame to other operating departments, to the controller's staff, or to other staff groups. Unfavorable reactions to controls do not remain individual reactions indefinitely; instead, individuals form cohesive groups and the strength of the group is utilized to combat the pressures of control.

Group Reaction to Pressure. Organized group resistance to any kind of external control pressure does not develop immediately, nor is it planned. However, the formation of group resistance is inevitable and follows a consistent evolutionary pattern. Argyris describes this process well:

1. First, the individuals sense an increase in pressure.
2. Then they begin to see definite evidences of the pressure. They not only feel it, they can point to it.
3. Since they feel this pressure is on them personally, they begin to experience tension and general uneasiness.
4. Next, they usually "feel out" their fellow workers to see if they too sense the pressure.
5. Finding out that others have noted the pressure, they begin to feel more at ease. It helps to be able to say, "I'm not the only one."
6. Finally, they realize that they can acquire emotional support from each other by becoming a group. Furthermore, they can "blow their top" about this pressure in front of their group.[8]

When leadership crystallizes and emerges, the group is ready to act in unison. Let us see what happens: first, on the hourly level; then, within the ranks of management.

The Hourly Level. Assume that the production of a manufacturing department, or the output of a clerical section, is stabilized at a rate that time study

---

[8] Chris Argyris, "Human Problems with Budgets," *Harvard Business Review* (January–February, 1953), p. 100. Copyright © 1960 by the President and Fellows of Harvard College; all rights reserved.

shows to be 65 percent of standard. Certain conditions or forces are holding production at this level. Perhaps supervision is satisfied, and an output of 65 percent of standard may be the most comfortable pace considering the methods used in performing the work. The individual worker has no reason for deviating from this pattern since conformance assures continued membership in the group and enables one to assume the protective coloring of the group. Now incorporate the time study data into standards and express these standards as part of a budget—unannounced and imposed from above. Pressure is felt first by the supervisors, who, in turn, attempt to enforce the newly stated standards by requiring an increased level of production. The development of group cohesiveness as described by Argyris begins. Eventually a static state of balance between the pressures of the budget and the pressures of the group may be reached; a level higher than the original 65 percent but still short of the budgeted 100 percent. These are the *frozen* groups of Zaleznik or the *sick* groups described by Gellerman.[9] When the informal group achieves cohesiveness and adopts the leadership and resources of a formal organization—the union—the groundwork is laid for labor-management strife.

Groups within Management. The formation of groups whose primary purpose is to combat the pressures exerted by top management is not limited to groups composed of hourly or clerical employees. Informal groups may develop within the ranks of management as well. The first-line supervisors of a plant may feel themselves caught between the pressure of the budget from above and the resistance of their subordinates from below. They are literally caught in the middle and seek the support offered by others who are in the same position. When talking with subordinates, the supervisor blames the "budget people" for the pressures of production. When reporting to a superior, the incompetence and the uncooperativeness of subordinates are offered as the causes for failure to meet budgeted expectations. There are instances of supervisory groups having become so firmly solidified that they eventually became formal unions of supervisors. Many supervisory or management clubs have been formed to nullify the cohesiveness of informal groups of supervisors and forestall their becoming formal union organizations. The labor unions of engineers and scientists, though not directly the result of budgetary controls, are another example of resistance to top management that has led to the formation of groups so that group pressure may be applied in opposition to the pressure exerted by management.

Informal groups may develop within either the line or the staff organization and make it almost impossible to achieve the benefits that might be realized from the application of budgets or other forms of control. When line management unites as a group and opposes the recommendations of the staff organization, one can be sure that the staff, as a group, will oppose any suggested modifications of their programs that come from members of the line organization.

---

[9] See Chapter 15, "Motivation in Organizations."

Effective Use of Controls

Our review of those aspects of the control process that cause resistance, the concept of pressure associated with the administration of budgets, and the responses of individuals and groups to pressure does not seem to offer much encouragement for the successful application of controls. Fortunately there are ways to minimize resistance to controls. The following suggestions have been found helpful in making the application of controls more effective.

Establish Proper Attitudes. The attitudes of the members of an organization toward controls depend on the underlying motivation of top management. Controls can be established as a device to goad managers into better performance, or they can be used by the managers themselves as an instrument for measuring and guiding performance. These two divergent uses of controls are analogous to the uses that may be found for two long pieces of wood. At the end of one piece of wood there is a sharp point. This piece of wood is used as a prod to keep managers in line and moving in the right direction. Another piece of wood—the same length—is divided into 36 equal segments and becomes the familiar yardstick, a tool that can be used to measure progress. For controls to be most effective, they must be regarded as yardsticks developed to measure performance rather than prods intended to keep people in line. The development of proper attitudes towards the goals established by control is most likely to occur when there is participation in the goal-setting process.[10]

Place Controls in the Hands of Managers. One of the best ways top management has of expressing its understanding of controls is by placing the responsibility for their preparation and administration in the hands of departmental managers. True, a well-trained controller's staff is valuable in company-wide consolidation and coordination, but the preparation and administration of controls at the operating level are best accomplished by the responsible manager. In preparing controls, managers should make the first draft; then, if revisions are needed, cooperative effort between the controller's office and line management is required to reach a final statement of goals. In order to administer controls properly, managers must have adequate standards of performance, timely information concerning their performance, and freedom to manage. Standards serve as a measure of performance and form the backbone of any control. In manufacturing departments, standards should be developed for labor, materials, supplies, and the maintenance of equipment. Standards of performance and cost can also be determined for administrative and sales units. The controller should provide departmental managers with timely information so that necessary corrections may be made and so that performance conforms to budgeted expectations.

---

[10] See the discussion in Chapter 4 of management by objectives, p. 72.

Also the following two papers support the need for participation in setting budgetary and other control goals. Roger L. M. Dunbar, "Budgeting for Control," *Administrative Science Quarterly*, Vol. 16, No. 1 (March, 1971), p. 88, and D. Gerald Searfoss and Robert M. Monczka, "Perceived Participation in the Budget Process and Motivation to Achieve the Budget," *Academy of Management Journal*, Vol. 16, No. 4 (December, 1973), p. 541.

Controls are not intended to restrict the activities of managers; they must have freedom to manage. So that freedom in operations may be increased, some companies state only the total of the expense items and leave to the discretion of the manager the allocation of the amount to be spent for each item. Finally, procedures must be clearly stated to set forth steps to be followed in securing revisions, and practice must show that such revisions are possible.

Follow Organizational Lines. Fundamental to effective budgetary control is a clear concept of organization structure. Managers of departments must know their immediate superiors and also their immediate subordinates. In addition, the relationships with other departments must be clearly defined. When organizational lines are clearly stated, the budgets become the yardstick capable of measuring performance; however, when organizational lines are fuzzy and ill defined, there is a tendency to use the budget as a prod since there is no means of defining duties and assigning responsibilities. The clarity of organizational definition marks the upper limit of the effectiveness of controls as a determinant of organizational performance.

Case Problem 21-B is a continuation of Case Problem 21-A. All did not go as planned, and now there is need for corrective action. Two points are illustrated in this closing case. First, even though performance did not measure up to expectations, the presence of a budget pinpoints the areas requiring corrective action. Second, each variation from a budget may be small, but the aggregate can sometimes be alarming.

Case Problem 21-B

A NEED FOR CORRECTIVE ACTION

It was the latter part of January before the Barrs completed the proposed revenue and expense budget described in Case Problem 21-A. Only then did they know they would not make a profit during the first quarter of the year and that the best they could expect would be to break even by the end of June. In an attempt to offset the normally slow months of February, March, and April, they decided to increase advertising outlays and to gain a competitive advantage by lowering prices slightly. During the year they hired additional sales personnel to offset their own lack of sales experience and knowledge of the men's clothing business. Also, the lease expired during the year, and a new one was negotiated at a somewhat higher figure. The results of the Barrs' first full year of managing the store are shown in Exhibit III, page 481.

PROBLEMS

1. Are the results shown in Exhibit III attributable to poor budgeting techniques or to poor management? Explain.
2. What corrective action would you take as manager of this store?

THE AVENUE MEN'S STORE

Account	Budgeted % of Net Sales ($200,000)	Actual Dollar Rev./Exp.	Actual Percentage of Budgeted Net Sales ($200,000)
Sales			
1. Gross sales	102.6	$206,000	103.0
2. Customer ret. & allow.	2.6	5,000	2.5
3. Net sales	100.0	201,000	101.0
Cost of goods sold			
4. Beginning inventory	30.9	61,800	30.9
5. Net purchases plus transportation charges paid	66.1	137,000	68.5
6. Total cost of merchandise handled	97.0	198,000	99.4
7. Ending inventory	32.3	66,800	33.4
8. Net cost of mdse. sold	64.7	132,000	66.0
9. Net busheling (alterations) cost	2.1	6,000	3.0
10. Total cost of mdse. sold	66.8	138,000	69.0
11. Gross margin	33.2	62,000	31.0
Operating expenses			
12. Payroll:			
A. Salaries of owners	7.3	14,600	7.3
B. Salaries and wages of employees	9.0	21,000	10.5
Total payroll	16.3	35,600	17.8
13. Rent expense	2.9	6,000	3.0
14. Taxes and license fees (omit real estate, federal income and sales taxes)	1.1	2,200	1.1
15. Insurance	.6	1,200	.6
16. Depreciation & amort.	.8	1,600	.8
17. Repairs	.2	200	.1
18. Supplies (omit rep. mat'ls.)	1.0	2,400	1.2
19. Services purchased	.9	1,400	.7
20. Traveling (business trips)	.3	400	.2
21. Communications (include parcel post)	.4	1,200	.6
22. Advertising and publicity	2.8	6,400	3.2
23. Professional services (outside professional agencies)	.2	200	.1
24. Unclassified:			
A. Losses from bad debts	.3	800	.4
B. Other unclassified	.5	1,200	.6
Total unclassified expenses	.8	2,000	1.0
25. Total expenses	28.3	60,800	30.4
26. Net profit (before federal income taxes)	4.9	1,200	.6

**Exhibit III
BUDGETED AND
ACTUAL
PERFORMANCE**

CHAPTER QUESTIONS FOR
STUDY AND DISCUSSION

1. How are budgets different from other kinds of business plans? Show why each of these differences is necessary.

2. Are the terms *budget* and *standard* synonymous? If so, what type of standards are utilized in the development of the four major types of budgets?

3. Discuss the following statement: Flexible budgets make periodic budgetary reviews unnecessary.

4. What is the purpose of zero-base budgeting? What benefits may be derived from the utilization of the zero-base budgeting concept?

5. Should expense budgets be stated at a lower figure than that actually computed in order that final expenses will not exceed the budgeted amount? Support your answer.

6. Why are budgets or other controls many times regarded as pressure devices?

7. Of what worth would a control be if it did not create pressure? Discuss.

8. What are the attitudes essential for the effective use of controls?

9. Describe the steps you would take to offset the usual resistance that develops when controls are installed.

10. Describe the steps you would take in establishing an effective sales budget.

Cues II—
College and University
Environment Scales

DIRECTIONS: Colleges and universities differ from one another in many ways. Some things that are generally true or characteristic of one school may not be characteristic of another. The purpose of the College & University Environment Scales (CUES II) [1] is to help describe the general atmosphere of different colleges. The atmosphere of a campus is a mixture of various features, facilities, rules and procedures, faculty characteristics, courses of study, classroom activities, students' interests, extracurricular programs, informal activities, and other conditions and events.

You are asked to be a reporter about your school. You have lived in its environment, seen its features, participated in its activities, and sensed its attitudes. What kind of a place is it?

There are 160 statements in this scale. You are to answer them *True* or *False*, using the answer sheet given you for this purpose.[2]

As you read the statements you will find that many cannot be answered True or False in a literal sense. The statements contain qualifying words or phrases, such as *almost always, frequently, generally,* and *rarely,* and are intended to draw out your impression of whether the situation described applies or does not apply to your campus as you know it.

As a reporter about your college you are to indicate whether you think each statement is *generally characteristic,* a condition that exists, an event that occurs or might occur, the way people generally act or feel—in short, whether the statement is more nearly True than False; or conversely, whether you think it is *not generally characteristic,* does not exist or occur, is more nearly False than True.

The CUES II is not a test in which there are right or wrong answers; it is more like an opinion poll—a way to find out how much agreement or disagreement there is about the characteristics of a campus environment.

---

[1] C. Robert Pace, *College & University Environment Scales: Technical Manual* (2d ed.; Princeton, N. J.: Educational Testing Service, 1969). Directions and CUES II are copyrighted by C. Robert Pace and are published and distributed by ETS, Princeton, N. J. These materials are reproduced with the permission of the author and publishers. They should not be used in any manner other than as a part of Case Problem 14-A. Colleges and universities desiring to conduct a formal evaluation using CUES II as the measuring instrument should write directly to Institutional Research Program for Higher Education, Educational Testing Service, Princeton, N. J.

[2] Answer sheets for CUES II, Form x-2s, are in the *Student Enrichment Activities.*

1. Students almost always wait to be called on before speaking in class.
2. The big college events draw a lot of student enthusiasm and support.
3. There is a recognized group of student leaders on this campus.
4. Frequent tests are given in most courses.
5. Students take a great deal of pride in their personal appearance.
6. Education here tends to make students more practical and realistic.
7. The professors regularly check up on the students to make sure that assignments are being carried out properly and on time.
8. It's important socially here to be in the right club or group.
9. Student pep rallies, parades, dances, carnivals, or demonstrations occur very rarely.
10. Anyone who knows the right people in the faculty or administration can get a better break here.
11. The professors really push the students' capacities to the limit.
12. Most of the professors are dedicated scholars in their fields.
13. Most courses require intensive study and preparation out of class.
14. Students set high standards of achievement for themselves.
15. Class discussions are typically vigorous and intense.
16. A lecture by an outstanding scientist would be poorly attended.
17. Careful reasoning and clear logic are valued most highly in grading student papers, reports, or discussions.
18. It is fairly easy to pass most courses without working very hard.
19. The school is outstanding for the emphasis and support it gives to pure scholarship and basic research.
20. Standards set by the professors are not particularly hard to achieve.
21. It is easy to take clear notes in most courses.
22. The school helps everyone get acquainted.
23. Students often run errands or do other personal services for the faculty.
24. The history and traditions of the college are strongly emphasized.
25. The professors go out of their way to help you.
26. There is a great deal of borrowing and sharing among the students.
27. When students run a project or put on a show everybody knows about it.
28. Many upperclass students play an active role in helping new students adjust to campus life.
29. Students exert considerable pressure on one another to live up to the expected codes of conduct.
30. Graduation is a pretty matter-of-fact, unemotional event.
31. Channels for expressing students' complaints are readily accessible.
32. Students are encouraged to take an active part in social reforms or political programs.
33. Students are actively concerned about national and international affairs.
34. There are a good many colorful and controversial figures on the faculty.
35. There is considerable interest in the analysis of value systems, and the relativity of societies and ethics.
36. Public debates are held frequently.
37. A controversial speaker always stirs up a lot of student discussion.
38. There are many facilities and opportunities for individual creative activity.
39. There is a lot of interest here in poetry, music, painting, sculpture, architecture, etc.
40. Concerts and art exhibits always draw big crowds of students.

41. Students ask permission before deviating from common policies or practices.
42. Most student rooms are pretty messy.
43. People here are always trying to win an argument.
44. Drinking and late parties are generally tolerated, despite regulations.
45. Students occasionally plot some sort of escapade or rebellion.
46. Many students drive sports cars.
47. Students frequently do things on the spur of the moment.
48. Student publications never lampoon dignified people or institutions.
49. The person who is always trying to "help out" is likely to be regarded as a nuisance.
50. Students are conscientious about taking good care of school property.
51. The important people at this school expect others to show proper respect for them.
52. Student elections generate a lot of intense campaigning and strong feeling.
53. Everyone has a lot of fun at this school.
54. In many classes students have an assigned seat.
55. Student organizations are closely supervised to guard against mistakes.
56. Many students try to pattern themselves after people they admire.
57. New fads and phrases are continually springing up among the students.
58. Students must have a written excuse for absence from class.
59. The college offers many really practical courses such as typing, report writing, etc.
60. Student rooms are more likely to be decorated with pennants and pin-ups than with paintings, carvings, mobiles, fabrics, etc.
61. Most of the professors are very thorough teachers and really probe into the fundamentals of their subjects.
62. Most courses are a real intellectual challenge.
63. Students put a lot of energy into everything they do in class and out.
64. Course offerings and faculty in the natural sciences are outstanding.
65. Courses, examinations, and readings are frequently revised.
66. Personality, pull, and bluff get students through many courses.
67. There is very little studying here over the weekends.
68. There is a lot of interest in the philosophy and methods of science.
69. People around here seem to thrive on difficulty—the tougher things get, the harder they work.
70. Students are very serious and purposeful about their work.
71. This school has a reputation for being very friendly.
72. All undergraduates must live in university approved housing.
73. Instructors clearly explain the goals and purposes of their courses.
74. Students have many opportunities to develop skill in organizing and directing the work of others.
75. Most of the faculty are not interested in students' personal problems.
76. Students quickly learn what is done and not done on this campus.
77. It's easy to get a group together for card games, singing, going to the movies, etc.
78. Students commonly share their problems.
79. Faculty members rarely or never call students by their first names.
80. There is a lot of group spirit.
81. Students are encouraged to criticize administrative policies and teaching practices.

82. The expression of strong personal belief or conviction is pretty rare around here.
83. Many students here develop a strong sense of responsibility about their role in contemporary social and political life.
84. There are a number of prominent faculty members who play a significant role in national or local politics.
85. There would be a capacity audience for a lecture by an outstanding philosopher or theologian.
86. Course offerings and faculty in the social sciences are outstanding.
87. Many famous people are brought to the campus for lectures, concerts, student discussions, etc.
88. The school offers many opportunities for students to understand and criticize important works of art, music, and drama.
89. Special museums or collections are important possessions of the college.
90. Modern art and music get little attention here.
91. Students are expected to report any violation of rules and regulations.
92. Student parties are colorful and lively.
93. There always seem to be a lot of little quarrels going on.
94. Students rarely get drunk and disorderly.
95. Most students show a good deal of caution and self-control in their behavior.
96. Bermuda shorts, pin-up pictures, etc., are common on this campus.
97. Students pay little attention to rules and regulations.
98. Dormitory raids, water fights, and other student pranks would be unthinkable.
99. Many students seem to expect other people to adapt to them rather than trying to adapt themselves to others.
100. Rough games and contact sports are an important part of intramural athletics.
101. The vocational value of many courses is emphasized.
102. Most people are aware of the financial status of students' families.
103. Student organizations are required to have a faculty adviser.
104. There are good facilities for learning vocationally useful skills and techniques.
105. Most faculty members really know the regulations and requirements that apply to student programs.
106. There is a well-organized and effective job placement office for the graduating students.
107. Many faculty members are involved in services or consulting activities for outside groups—business, adult education, etc.
108. Professors will sometimes increase a student's grade if they think he or she has worked especially hard and conscientiously.
109. Most students want to get a degree because of its economic value.
110. Vocational guidance is a main activity of the counseling office.
111. New ideas and theories are encouraged and vigorously debated.
112. Students who don't make passing grades are quickly dropped from school.
113. Students are allowed to help themselves to books in the library stacks.
114. Excellence in scholarship is the dominant feature of this institution.
115. There are lots of quiet and comfortable places for students to study.
116. Even in social groups students are more likely to talk about their studies than about other things.
117. There are many excellent facilities for research on this campus.
118. The main emphasis in most departmental clubs is to promote interest and scholarship in the field.

119. Most students are pretty dissatisfied if they make less than a *B* grade.
120. The library is one of the outstanding facilities on the campus.
121. The campus design, architecture, and landscaping suggest a friendly atmosphere.
122. Student groups often meet in faculty members' homes.
123. Counseling and guidance services are really personal, patient, and helpful.
124. There are courses which involve students in activities with groups or agencies in the local community.
125. Most of the students here are pretty happy.
126. There are courses or voluntary seminars that deal with problems of marriage and the family.
127. In most classes the atmosphere is very friendly.
128. Groups of students from the college often get together for parties or visits during holidays.
129. Most students seem to have a genuine affection for this school.
130. There are courses or voluntary seminars that deal with problems of social adjustment.
131. There is a regular place on the campus where students can make speeches about controversial issues.
132. Students are free to cut classes at their own discretion.
133. Many faculty members have worked overseas or frequently traveled to other countries.
134. There is a lot of variety and innovation in the way many courses are taught.
135. Many professors permit, and sometimes welcome, class discussion of materials that are outside their field of specialization.
136. Many students are interested in joining the Peace Corps or are planning, somehow, to spend time in another part of the world.
137. Many student groups invite faculty members to lead special discussions.
138. Groups of students sometimes spend all evening listening to classical records.
139. Student chorus, orchestra, and theater groups are really excellent.
140. Students like to browse in book stores.
141. Many professors require students to submit an outline before writing a term paper or report.
142. The Dean of Students office is mainly concerned with disciplinary matters.
143. Faculty members always wear coats and ties on the campus.
144. A major aim of this institution is to produce cultivated men and women.
145. In literature, drama, and music the main emphasis is on the classics.
146. Nearby churches have an active interest in counseling and youth programs.
147. Proper standards and ideals are emphasized in many courses.
148. Most professors think of themselves as no different from other adults in the community.
149. Faculty members are always polite and proper in their relations with students.
150. In most exams the emphasis is on knowing the correct answers rather than on being able to defend a point of view.
151. There are students on many academic and administrative committees.
152. Students have real authority to determine some campus policies and procedures.
153. Some faculty members are active in experimenting with new methods of teaching, new courses, and other innovations.
154. There is much student interest and activity about social issues—such as civil rights, justice, peace.

155. The administration is receptive and active in responding to student proposals for change.
156. There is an "experimental" college or program where a variety of new courses are offered (whether for credit or not).
157. Massive disruption, force, or violence by students would be unthinkable on this campus.
158. The attitude of most college officials about drugs is generally patient, flexible, and tolerant.
159. The response of most college officials toward sit-ins or other 'confrontations' is (or would be) firm, forceful, and unsympathetic.
160. Due process considerations are expected by students who are accused of violating laws or college rules.

Comprehensive Case –
Buying and Operating
a Motel

The accommodations industry with annual sales in excess of $10 billion provides the industrial setting for this comprehensive case study.[1] There are several reasons for selecting a 95-unit motel as the specific setting of the case. First, almost every student has been a guest in a motel; consequently there is some knowledge of the characteristics and services provided. Second, motels and motor hotels are the growth segment of the accommodation industry. Further, the modern motel is a complex operation and offers a career opportunity for the professionally trained manager.

The format of the case parallels the major parts of the text. The first part of the case presents a discussion of the nature of the industry and offers an opportunity to formulate specific internal and external business objectives. The second part examines the planning required to determine whether or not the purchase of the property in question is a sound decision. Next, you are asked to determine the optimum organization necessary for the efficient, long-term operation of the motel. Questions concerning the most effective type of leadership and means of motivating employees are considered. Finally, the controls normally used in the operation of a motel are developed. Each major part of the case may be considered as an integrating case to be studied in conjunction with the corresponding part of the text, or the case may be regarded as a comprehensive case drawing upon all the functions of the management process. However the case is used, it is suggested that you read the entire case before analyzing each of the five parts. Also, the information presented and the experience gained in analyzing the case should enable you to evaluate a motel in your area as either an investment opportunity or for employment as a manager.

The author wishes to thank the following persons of the Ramada Inn organization who gave generously of their time in supplying information for the preparation of this case: Prentiss R. Moore, Regional Manager; James Daniels, Manager of the Arlington, Texas, Inn; and Charles Steadman, Assistant Director of Training, Management Development Center, Phoenix, Arizona.

[1] *Trends in the Hotel/Motel Business*: *Thirty-fifth Annual Review* (New York City: Harris, Kerr, Forester & Company, 1971). Much of the information concerning the operation of the hotel-motel industry was drawn from this report which was provided by Eric Green, partner, Harris, Kerr, Forester & Company, Certified Public Accountants.

THE NATURE OF THE MOTEL BUSINESS

It is axiomatic that if one is to fulfill the accommodation needs of the traveler such facilities must be located so that they are readily accessible. The earliest accommodation facilities established in this country were for those who traveled on foot or horseback and are typified by the colonial inns of New England.[2] As stagecoach routes developed so did the way station and the coffee house. In the mid-nineteenth century the railroad system of this country began its development, and in time the inn, the way station, and the coffee house diminished in importance and were replaced by the downtown hotel. But few major hotels in large cities are still located near rail terminals. With the advent of the automobile and interstate highways, the mode and pattern of transportation shifted again. Tourist cabins appeared along the highways to accommodate motorists.

The development of the tourist cabin, soon followed by the tourist court and the motel, marks the completion of a full circle that began with the New England inn to accommodate the individual traveler, followed by the downtown hotel for those using the mass transportation of the railroads, and back to roadside facilities for the individual traveling by automobile. However, change in the mode and pattern of transportation still continues. The large jet airport, the result of mass air transportation, is located away from the central city and has created the need for a new type of lodging facility readily accessible to the airport.

Types of Facilities

For many years the mainstay of the accommodations industry has been the transient hotel. Although most of these hotels were built prior to 1930, new transient hotels have been built in recent years. These are full service hotels which provide all the services that a traveler needs, whether traveling for business or pleasure, or attending a convention. There are resort hotels which are located in resort areas and characterized by marked seasonal fluctuations in business. In addition, some hotels are classed as residential since the majority of their guests are permanent residents rather than transients.

The modern motel had its beginnings in the tourist cabin and the tourist court. In the 1920's, mainly in the South, Southwest, and California, roadside tourist cabins made their appearance to serve those who were traveling by automobile. These early facilities were in rural areas and offered minimal services. Private baths, telephone service, food, and linen service were unknown. Tourist cabins soon developed into the tourist court and many services associated with hotels were added. Sometime during the 1930's the descriptive term *motel* made its appearance and was readily accepted. The motel of this period was a relatively

[2] George O. Podd and John D. Lesure, *Planning and Operating Motels and Motor Hotels* (New York City: Ahrens Publishing Co., 1964). Much of the background information of the industry was obtained from this source, which is a comprehensive treatment and analysis of the problems encountered in operating a motel or motor hotel.

modest establishment and did not pose a serious threat to the well-established hotel industry. For the most part there was individual ownership, often husband and wife, who performed all the work necessary for its operation. The capital investment was small, $2,000 to $3,000 per unit with an average of ten units, and units could be added as desired. Managing a motel became a way of life for many retired persons.

With the development of the interstate highway system and the construction of new airports the characteristics of the motel industry, again adapting to the mode and pattern of transportation, changed significantly. The number of guest rooms increased sharply with the result that motels with 300 units were not unusual. Also, full hotel services, including public meeting rooms and facilities for conventions, made their appearance. One is tempted to describe the modern motel as a horizontal hotel, but that description is not accurate since many so-called motels are multistory buildings, and some are even located in the central city. If one must distinguish between the full service motel and the traditional hotel, it is in the availability and accessibility of parking facilities. Usually the motel has a parking lot or parking garage which is adjacent to and an integral part of the building complex.

The Tradition of Innkeeping

Since the primary function of the accommodations industry is to provide a service, it may be considered a part of that broad segment of industry known as the service industry. It is also a part of the retail industry since services are sold to the customer who is also the consumer. However, the accommodations industry differs from other service and retail establishments in that there is a distinguishing relationship between the customer and the seller. It is a relationship that is best described by the terms *guest* and *host*. Guests are more than travelers away from home; they are there by invitation. Managers or owners do more than merely provide services; they must, in the tradition of innkeeping, provide the personal attention, warmth, and courtesy that make travelers truly welcomed guests. It is not an easy task. The guest-host relationship is not easily attainable with corporate ownership and professional management, yet the traditional innkeeping relationship of guest and host should be one of the major objectives of any motel.

The Business Aspects

In addition to formulating service objectives within the tradition of innkeeping, there are significant financial considerations in the operation of a motel. A motel is a long-term investment in real estate. The initial land investment is improved with the construction of a special purpose building. If the real estate improvement does not succeed as a motel, the only value that normally remains is the value of the land. Further, the capital investment per room is significant. Construction costs of $15,000 per guest unit are not uncommon. Though the rewards are great, the risk is high. The construction of a new highway, a new airport, the closing of a major industry in the area, or the building of additional rooms by competitors can all spell disaster. Thus, the need arises to determine a reasonable rate of return on equity capital invested in an enterprise having a substantial degree of risk which is often due to factors beyond the control of the investor. Return on other investments having a lower degree of risk, such as corporate and tax free municipal bonds, must be examined. For these reasons a rate of return on equity capital of 10 to 12 percent a year is considered minimal.

PLANNING TO BUY

The Apex Motel, which is readily accessible and visible from the interstate highway, is located 40 miles from a major city with a population of 850,000. The motel property is within the city limits of a town that has a population of 50,000. The metropolitan area is one of the ten largest in the United States and ranks sixth with respect to expected population growth. The motel was built eight years ago and opened with 98 guest rooms, an apartment for the manager, a lobby newsstand and sundries shop, and a large swimming pool. At the present time there are 95 rooms available to guests since one of the intended guest rooms is used as an employee's lounge, one for storage, and another is equipped as a maintenance shop. Shortly after opening, a separate restaurant with three public meeting rooms was built adjacent to the motel. The present owner intends to retain and operate this property; however, the purchase agreement includes an option to buy the restaurant in three years. There are adequate parking facilities for both motel and restaurant guests, and the courtyard and pool area are attractively landscaped. The rooms are comfortably furnished and most of the carpeting has been replaced, but there is need for a planned refurnishing of all guest rooms. The present owner is asking $1,330,000 and is willing to finance 50 percent of this amount for 15 years at an annual rate of 10 percent.

How does one determine a fair price for an existing motel? When building a new motel, the first step is a feasibility study to show immediate and expected market potential, the cost of land and construction, and projected operating revenues and expenses. However, when purchasing an existing property, current operating statements (see Exhibit I for operating statement of Apex Motel) are of primary significance; yet the feasibility study must be updated to obtain a reliable forecast of the future.

Current Operations

The primary source of income for motels without restaurants is almost entirely room sales revenue which should range between 92 and 95 percent of total income.[3] Telephone service (usually operated at a loss) should provide 2

---

[3] The classification of accounts used in this discussion and presented in Exhibit I, Table 1, and Exhibit II are based on the following industry sources. (Footnote continued on page 494.)

		Percentage of Total Income
TOTAL SALES & INCOME		
Rooms	$606,812.00	95.0
Telephone	25,549.00	4.0
Other	6,388.00	1.0
Total	$638,749.00	100.0
DEPARTMENTAL EXPENSES		
Rooms Department		
Salaries & Wages	$136,032.00	21.3
Payroll Taxes & Employee Benefits	10,882.00	1.7
Laundry	31,300.00	4.9
Other—China, Glass, Cleaning Supplies	30,660.00	4.8
	$208,874.00	32.7
Telephone	31,950.00	5.0
Total	240,824.00	37.7
GROSS OPERATING INCOME	$397,925.00	62.3
DEDUCTIONS FROM INCOME		
Administrative & General Expenses		
Salaries & Wages	$ 61,320.00	9.6
Payroll Taxes & Employee Benefits	6,400.00	1.0
Other A & G Expenses	24,272.00	3.8
	$ 91,992.00	14.4
Advertising & Sales Promotion	17,250.00	2.7
Heat, Light & Power	47,900.00	7.5
Repairs & Maintenance	44,700.00	7.0
Total	201,842.00	31.6
GROSS OPERATING PROFIT	$196,083.00	30.7
Fire Insurance & Franchise Taxes	7,026.00	1.1
PROFIT BEFORE REAL ESTATE TAXES & OTHER CAPITAL EXPENSES	$189,057.00	29.6
Real Estate Taxes	41,519.00	6.5
PROFIT AFTER REAL ESTATE TAXES BUT BEFORE OTHER CAPITAL EXPENSES	$147,538.00	23.1

Exhibit I
APEX MOTEL
CURRENT
OPERATING
REPORT FOR
YEAR ENDING
DECEMBER 31,
19—

to 5 percent of gross sales, and miscellaneous income derived from vending machines and space rentals such as a lobby sundries shop and newsstand usually contributes between 1 and 2 percent. The direct costs of operating the rooms—wages for the rooms department employees, linens, cleaning supplies, glassware, and other supplies—and the cost of providing telephone service are deducted from total sales. The result is defined as gross operating income, which should be between 67 and 75 percent of total income. Administrative and general expenses, including the manager's salary and the cost of front office personnel; advertising; heat, light, and power; and the cost of repairs and maintenance are subtracted from gross operating income to determine gross operating profit, an amount that should range between 40 and 50 percent of total income. Fire insurance, approximately 1 percent of total income, and real estate taxes—from 4 to 9 percent of total income—are deducted from gross operating profit to determine operating profit before other capital expenses. Profit after real estate taxes usually ranges between 35 and 45 percent of total income. The most recent operating statement of Apex Motel is shown in Exhibit I.

An examination of the operating statement shows an operating profit, after real estate taxes but before other capital expenditures, of 23.1 percent of total revenue. Though many buyers assume that they have the management skill to improve operating ratios, the prudent buyer makes no such assumption and forecasts net profit based on current operations and projected capital expenses. Counsel advises that the proposed selling price of $1,330,000.00 may be distributed on the following basis expressed as cost per guest room:

Land	$ 1,400.00
Buildings	10,600.00
Pool	300.00
Furnishings	1,700.00
Total	$14,000.00

Counsel indicates that the buildings may be depreciated on a 20-year basis and that the pool and furnishings may be depreciated on an 8-year basis. Both depreciation schedules are computed by the straight-line method. The 10 percent, 15-year mortgage with fixed monthly payments, including payments on principal, results in an interest charge of $60,681.00 and payments on principal of $20,895.00 for the first year. Total debt service is $81,576.00 per year. Proposed capital expenses are shown in Table 1.

When interest on mortgage and depreciation charges, i.e., 9.5 percent and 11.6 percent of total income respectively, are deducted from profit after real estate taxes, profit before federal and state income tax is 2.0 percent, also a return of 1.9 percent on the equity capital of $665,000.00. It is difficult to

---

Edward F. Chirhart, Kemper W. Merriam, and Robert W. McIntosh, *Uniform Classification of Accounts for Motels, Motor Hotels, or Highway Lodges* (Temple, Texas: Tourist Court Journal, 1962).

Uniform System of Accounts and Expenses Dictionary for Motels, Motor Hotels, and Small Hotels (New York City: American Hotel and Motel Association, 1962). This publication was prepared under the direction of Co-Chairmen Thomas J. Hogan, C.P.A., and John D. Lesure, C.P.A., and is approved by the American Hotel and Motel Association.

Table 1
APEX MOTEL
PROPOSED
CAPITAL
EXPENSES

		Percentage of Total Income
Interest on Mortgage	$60,681.00	9.5
Depreciation on Buildings and Furnishings	74,099.00	11.6
Profit Before Income Taxes	$12,758.00	2.0

project income taxes since each buyer's situation differs; however, assume that Apex is being bought by a newly formed corporation and that there are no other properties. The federal tax of 17 percent on the first $25,000.00 of corporate earnings amounts to $2,169.00 which must be paid out of the $12,758.00 profit.[4] From the balance, $10,589.00, repayment of principal, $20,895.00, is deducted and results in a net loss of $10,306.00. Any state income tax creates a greater loss.

An obvious first step in determining the reasonableness of a proposed selling price for real estate is to request a professional appraisal. Such an appraisal has been made of the Apex Motel, and the report indicates that the asking price is equitable; that is, the appreciation sought by the original owner is in line with similar properties in the area. Further, with proper maintenance, the building is expected to have a useful life of 20 years with minimal risk of obsolescence. Nonetheless, there is a question concerning the true worth of the room furnishings, and the appraiser's report strongly recommends that all room furnishings be replaced within three years. It is estimated that the cost of refurnishing will average $1,500.00 per room.

A motel is more than bricks and mortar on a parcel of land; it is an ongoing business. Rules of thumb have developed and serve as guides in evaluating the worth of a given property. The gross income multiplier is obtained by dividing the selling price by gross income. The normal range of gross income multipliers is three to seven, with four being the average. The net operating profit multiplier is another index. Net operating profit is defined on a cash flow basis and shows the amount of money available from net profit and depreciation after debt service which includes payments on principal and interest. This value is also termed net spendable and when divided into the equity investment the result is the pay out period for the recovery of equity capital. It is estimated that a buyer should recover equity capital in four to five years.

The Feasibility Study

A remark attributed to Mr. E. M. Statler, founder of the Statler Hotels, states that there are three factors that determine the success of a hotel: location, location, and location. The original feasibility study indicated that the site selected for Apex Motel was the last available motel site within the city limits and that there were no planned changes in either the state highway system or

---

[4] The 1978 Internal Revenue Service Code provides for a 17 percent tax on the first $25,000.00.

the interstate system. At the request of the present owner of Apex the consultants who did the original feasibility study have recently brought the earlier study up to date. The favorable economic forecast for the entire metropolitan area remains the same. The university in the town where Apex is located has grown and now has an enrollment of 15,000 students. In addition, there are plans for a community college scheduled to open within a year. Four additional manufacturing plants have located within five miles of Apex during the past five years. The nearby major city has built a convention center and now has a National Football League team and a National League baseball team. There are also professional basketball, hockey, and soccer teams. Several seasonal amusement parks, similar to Disneyland, have been established in the last eight years.

The current survey of the occupancy rates of the five motels (there are no hotels) competing directly with Apex is presented by month in Table 2. The current annual occupancy rate for the area is 70 percent, the same occupancy rate that Apex experienced during the last full year of operation. The consultants believe that Apex could increase its occupancy rate by replacing room furnishings. They also recommend an evaluation of the current rate structure so that the average revenue per room may be increased from the present $25.00 to $27.00 per room, an amount that would put Apex in line with the immediate area. No decrease in occupancy rate is foreseen, provided the rooms are well maintained.

MONTH	OCCUPANCY RATE	MONTH	OCCUPANCY RATE
January	55%	July	82%
February	60	August	85
March	70	September	68
April	79	October	76
May	78	November	58
June	80	December	49
Annual Occupancy Rate—70%			

**Table 2
AREA
OCCUPANCY
RATES**

THE ORGANIZATION

The organizing function for small service organizations is primarily a staffing problem rather than one of creating a managerial hierarchy. Apex Motel is large enough to warrant the services of a full-time manager who lives on the premises and is classified as an exempt employee. All others are nonexempt and their base pay is computed on a 40-hour week. Determining an optimum organization is complicated by the need for maintaining a 24-hour day, 7-day week operation, and by daily and seasonal fluctuations in the occupancy rate.

It is difficult to set precise staffing standards because of variations in physical layout, service objectives, and the availability and quality of labor. Even so, normative data indicate that total payroll costs, excluding payroll taxes, for motels without restaurants range between 22 and 28 percent of total sales and income. The average is 26 percent and results in an annual cost of $924.00 for each available room and $1,273.00 for each occupied room. Payroll costs (excluding the cost of payroll taxes) for the rooms department should be between 14 and 18 percent of room sales. A labor cost of 16 percent is acceptable. The total cost of operating the rooms department, including payroll taxes and the cost of supplies, should be about 25 percent of room sales.

The present staffing of the rooms department is considerably above the recommended average and is the result of the present owner's method of allocating motel labor costs. An analysis of the payroll costs, excluding payroll taxes and other benefits, charged to the rooms department shows a total of $136,032.00, or 21.3 percent of room sales. These costs are distributed as follows:

12 Housecleaners	$ 81,120.00
1 Housekeeper (supervisor)	7,280.00
1 Houseman	7,072.00
6 Porters	40,560.00
Total	$136,032.00

It is difficult to determine how many housecleaners are required to service a motel effectively. Under normal conditions a housecleaner is expected to clean a room in approximately 30 minutes, and during the course of an eight-hour day he or she can be expected to clean 14 rooms. In addition to the seasonal variations in occupancy, shown in Table 2, there are variations in the daily occupancy rate with Friday, Saturday, Sunday, and Monday showing a lower rate than the days in the middle of the week. Also, there are the factors of absenteeism and the need to maintain a seven-day week operation. Proposed staffing, allowing for these factors, results in a monthly average of eight housecleaners. If labor costs remain constant, $3.25 per hour, total annual projected payroll costs for housecleaning service is $54,080.00. The supervising housekeeper, who schedules the housecleaners and is responsible for maintaining the cleaning supplies inventory, is expected to be retained at the present rate of $3.50 per hour. The houseman picks up the clean linen and delivers the soiled linen to the local linen service, cleans the hallways, and performs other services as required. The houseman's annual pay, at $3.40 an hour, is $7,072.00. Three porters, with an hourly rate of $3.25, earn a total of $20,280.00. The total annual cost of the proposed staffing for the rooms department is $88,172.00, excluding payroll taxes.

There are relatively few persons allocated to the administrative and general payroll account. There are four desk clerks, one of whom works as relief and on weekends. Payroll cost for each person is $665.00 per month and the annual cost for desk clerks is $31,920.00. All the clerks know how to operate the switchboard and can perform the duties of cashier when assigned that duty. The layout of the front office is such that a full-time telephone switchboard operator is not needed. The night auditor, who works from 11:00 p.m. to 7:00 a.m., has agreed to remain at the present monthly salary of $945.00. The manager also indicates that he will continue at his present salary of $18,060.00 per year. It is highly doubtful that any significant changes can be made in the operations of the front office; thus, projected payroll costs shown in Exhibit II, page 499, for A & G personnel are the same as in Exhibit I.

The total payroll costs for maintenance personnel are $21,288.00. The maintenance engineer is a good mechanic and is capable of handling all minor repairs and painting. The groundskeeper fills in occasionally as a porter and also helps the maintenance engineer. On a monthly basis the payroll cost (including payroll taxes) for the maintenance engineer is $1,178.00, and for the groundskeeper the amount is $596.00. Considering the age of the motel and the need for refurnishing all rooms, it seems wise to retain both these employees. If the number of persons assigned to maintenance and administrative and general expenses remains constant, and if the proposed staffing for the rooms department is achieved, total payroll costs at present hourly rates are $180,448.00, including all payroll taxes.

THE PROBLEM OF LEADERSHIP

In Chapter 14 a distinction is made between leadership style and leadership behavior. Leadership style pertains to the interpersonal relationships that exist between a leader and the members of the group. Leadership behavior encompasses all those actions normally associated with the management process and includes formal and informal communications, methods of motivating and compensating employees, and supervisory practices. In addition to those characteristics necessary for effective interpersonal relationships, the manager of a motel must have the ability to establish the guest-host relationship discussed earlier. The purpose of this section of the case is to offer you an opportunity to crystallize your thinking with regard to the leadership function in a motel. The recommendations that you make to the manager of Apex Motel and the standards used to judge his performance as a leader may or may not apply to other forms of business organizations.

Leadership Style

Whether an authoritarian personality, one who is highly directive in his or her relationship with subordinates, can establish and maintain an optimum guest-host relationship is open to question. If one assumes that it is possible for the authoritarian manager to maintain an effective guest-host relationship, the effect of such a personality on subordinates must be considered. How effective will their performance be, what attitudes will they demonstrate toward guests, and how will they react to control?

As one moves away from the authoritarian pattern of leadership, there are varying degrees of participative leadership. What is the optimum degree

			Percentage of Total Income
TOTAL SALES & INCOME			
Rooms	$606,812.00		95.0
Telephone	25,549.00		4.0
Other	6,388.00		1.0
Total		$638,749.00	100.0
DEPARTMENTAL EXPENSES			
Rooms	$157,769.00		24.7
Telephone	31,950.00		5.0
Total		189,719.00	29.7
GROSS OPERATING INCOME		$449,030.00	70.3
DEDUCTIONS FROM INCOME			
Administrative & General Expenses	$ 91,992.00		14.4
Advertising & Sales Promotion	17,250.00		2.7
Heat, Light & Power	47,900.00		7.5
Repairs & Maintenance	44,700.00		7.0
Total		201,842.00	31.6
GROSS OPERATING PROFIT		$247,188.00	38.7
Fire Insurance & Franchise Tax		7,026.00	1.1
PROFIT BEFORE REAL ESTATE TAXES & OTHER CAPITAL EXPENSES		$240,162.00	37.6
Real Estate Taxes		41,519.00	6.5
PROFIT AFTER REAL ESTATE TAXES BUT BEFORE OTHER CAPITAL EXPENSES		$198,643.00	31.1
Interest on Mortgage	$ 60,681.00		9.5
Depreciation on Building & Furnishings	74,099.00		11.6
		134,780.00	21.1
PROFIT BEFORE FEDERAL INCOME TAX		$ 63,863.00	10.0

Exhibit II
PROPOSED
BUDGET
(ASSUMING NO
CHANGE IN
OCCUPANCY
RATE OR
AVERAGE RATE
PER ROOM)

of participation? In discussing the organization structure of a motel it is noted that problems arise in staffing a 24-hour day, 7-day week operation with a fluctuating work load. Should work schedules be fixed or should they be rotated? More important, who should make the determination, the manager or the employees? Also, how much should employees participate in setting the standards used for control? Your answers to these and similar questions are indicative of your own leadership style and influence your judgment of the effectiveness of managerial performance.

Leadership Behavior

Now let us consider the formal actions of the manager in determining and administering personnel policies. As noted in Chapter 15, there is marked interest in the measurement of job satisfaction. Although many studies show a consistent, but low, correlation between job satisfaction and performance, a conclusion that there is a causal relationship between job satisfaction and performance is not warranted. Considering these findings and also considering the nature of the motel business, what steps would you take as a manager to determine the level of job satisfaction of your employees?

The present owner of Apex Motel has not formulated any clear statement of personnel policy; however, during preliminary discussions he stated that he believed that the large motel chains with formal policies and retirement plans were able to attract a better quality employee than he did. Thus, the question arises concerning the advisability and nature of a formal statement of personnel policy for an independent operation such as Apex Motel.

ESTABLISHING CONTROLS

Exhibit II presents the optimum operating ratios that the group considering the purchase of Apex Motel has developed as a basis for establishing a budget. The group believes that these ratios are attainable, since they are virtually the same as those presented in Exhibit I. The major difference between Exhibit I and Exhibit II is that the latter reflects a reduced staffing in the rooms department.

The proposed budget must be evaluated with respect to the extent to which it fulfills the financial objectives of the purchasers and the probability that it can be attained. If the financial objectives of those desiring to purchase Apex Motel are not fulfilled by the budget proposed in Exhibit II, there are additional steps that may be taken before making a decision to withdraw and invest their capital elsewhere.

Author Index

Subject Index

A

Absoluteness of authority, 222–223

Acceptability, zone of, 330

Accountability: absoluteness of, 222–223; in committees, 191; creation of, 221; defined, 220–221; difference between responsibility and, 221

Accountability view of social responsibility, 44–45

Accounting, human resource, 440, 444–445

Achievement, need for, 301; according to McClelland and Atkinson, 320; theory of need for, 319–321

Acid test ratio, 447

Action plans, 72

Activation-gratification, 318

Actual time, 419

Additional product. *See* Marginal product

Ad hoc committees, defined, 188, 253

Administration: defined, 23; Fayol's principles of, 21, 23–25; human relations approach to, 22; management, a principle of, 22; production efficiency, a factor in, 23

Administrative decisions, 107

Advertising, 95

Advisory authority, 208

Affiliation, need for: according to McClelland and Atkinson, 320

Affirmative action programs, defined, 268n

Affluence power, defined, 203

Alienative involvement, 330

Allocation problems, the use of linear programming and, 45

Appraisal interview, 261

Appropriation budget, 464

Assembly-line technology, defined, 139–140. *See* Mass production; Detroit automation

Assessment center, 280–281; defined, 293

Assets, fixed, 90

Assistant manager, defined, 206–207

Assistant-to a manager, defined, 206–207

Attitudes, defined, 51, 114; employee, 416–417; for establishing controls, 479

Audit: external, 440–441; internal, 440, 441–442; management, 440, 442–444

Audit programs, 440–446

Authoritarian organizations, defined, 155. *See* Theory X organization

Authoritative committees, defined, 188

Authority: to act, a characteristic of, 197; advisory, 208; affluence power and, 203; Barnard's definition of, 199; charismatic power and, 203; decentralization of, 218–239; defined, 24, 197, 201; delegation of, 218–239; effectiveness of, 199–201; expertise power and, 202; expert power and, 203; functional, 208; illustration of the exercise of functional, 210; institutional source of, 198; legal powers and, 203; legitimate power and, 202; line of, 24, 197, 204; managerial, 197; meanings of, 197–198;

overlapping, 200; parity of responsibility and, 221–222; of personality, 160; position power and, 202; power and, 201–203; power, a characteristic of, 197; power relationships and, 195–217; process of decentralization of, 220; referent power and, 203; relationships of, 252; reward power and, 202; as a right, 197; service, 208; sources of, 197, 198–199; staff, 197, 204, 205, 206–209; of the state, 197; subordinate-acceptance concept of, 198–199, 201; subordinate power and, 203; superior, 200; within the context of a Theory X organization, 155; within the context of a Theory Y organization, 155

Authorization routine, defined, 112

Autocratic style of leadership, 363–364.

Automation, 140–142; capital-intensive, defined, 135; closed-loop systems and, 141; continuous-process, defined, 141n, 140–142; John Diebold's description of, 140; mechanization and, 140; open-loop systems and, 141

Autonomy, need for, 321

Average inventory, ratio of net sales to, 448

B

Balance, defined, 34

Balance sheet budget, 465

P